studies in jazz

Institute of Jazz Studies, Rutgers University
General Editors: *William M. Weinberg & Dan Morgenstern*

Metuchen, N.J., London, 1985 Studies in Jazz No. 3

The Scarecrow Press and the Institute

Erroll Garner

The Most Happy Piano

JAMES M. DORAN

of Jazz Studies, Rutgers University

Library of Congress Cataloging in Publication Data

Doran, James M., 1946-
Erroll Garner, the most happy piano.

(Studies in jazz ; no. 3)
Bibliography: p.
Discography: p.
Filmography: p.
1. Garner, Erroll. 2. Pianists—United States—
Biography. 3. Jazz musicians—United States—
Biography. I. Title. II. Series.
ML417.G33 1985   786.1'092'4 [B]   84-17886
ISBN 0-8108-1745-4

For my uncle and friend
Joseph E. Doran
(1922–1980)

CONTENTS

III. His Recorded Music   157

FOREWORD

Erroll Garner was a phenomenon. His style, already formed when he emerged on the jazz scene in his early twenties, was uniquely personal and beyond categorization, and it continued to develop independently, uninfluenced by trends and fashions in jazz. The appeal of his music also transcended fashions and fads, just as it reached far beyond the confines of the jazz audience. As his career progressed from relative obscurity to international fame, he remained himself and retained his joy in creating music.

It was this joy that communicated itself to audiences throughout the globe, directly and spontaneously. Garner didn't sing, dance or tell jokes—in fact, he never spoke to his listeners. Yet he riveted their attention from first note to last—and he was a performer of tremendous energy and endurance whose concerts were never padded with "added attractions" or featured sidemen—purely on the strength of his music and the pleasure he so obviously derived from making it.

This pleasure was so great that he might well have spent his life bestowing his gifts to the world without reaping the tangible rewards they deserved. Fortunately, his career was taken in hand by dedicated and responsible management, and from the 1950s on it blossomed. Garner became the most successful and acclaimed jazz artist of his generation, appearing in the most prestigious venues. Eventually, the man who could not read music was accompanied by famous symphony orchestras and became the first jazz artist to be booked by the great impresario Sol Hurok.

Fame and publicity notwithstanding, Garner remained a private man. Though friendly and charming to his fans and a willing signer of autographs, he was a man of few words and kept his own counsel. That is why this book, which presents many hitherto unknown facts about Garner's life, career, and recordings, is such an important contribution to the literature of jazz.

It is the result of many years of hard and dedicated work by James M. Doran, who became fascinated with Garner's music while still in his teens, amassed a huge collection of his records, traveled far and wide to see him perform, and eventually decided to gather and organize as much information as was humanly possible about him, spending most of his free time in doing so. Doran thus represents the tradition of jazz scholarship and research, which, in spite of the new-found acceptance of this great music as a subject fit for academic study, by and large remains the province of selfless, dedicated amateur scholars. (I use the word amateur in its primary sense of one motivated not by gain or glory but by love.)

In compiling the mass of information contained in this book—much of it new; most of it hitherto scattered in myriad and often obscure sources; some of it clarifying long-disputed points of fact—Doran interviewed scores of persons associated with Garner over the entire span of his life, spent long hours poring over archival materials in the United States and Europe, and organized this wealth of documentation into a clear and accessible format. This book will serve scholars and fans for years to come, not to mention future biographers.

The discography alone is a great accomplishment, presenting invaluable information about not only Garner's issued recordings but also the large body of unissued materials. The career chronology and family history break new ground, as do the interviews, which—in the nature of oral history—express the views of the speakers, not the author. Doran also obtained many interesting photographs never published before.

The Institute of Jazz Studies is pleased to have played a part in bringing Jim Doran's achievement to fruition. We also note with pride that the discography employs the methodology introduced by Arnold Laubich and Ray Spencer in *Art Tatum: A Guide to His Recorded Music,* a previous publication in this series. None of this, of course, would have been possible without the sympathy, patience and expertise of the staff of Scarecrow Press.

DAN MORGENSTERN

Director
Institute of Jazz Studies
Rutgers University

Erroll Garner with Jim Doran, Brandi's Wharf, Philadelphia, March 17, 1972. (J. Doran Collection)

INTRODUCTION AND ACKNOWLEDGMENTS

This book is my dream come true. It all began on March 7, 1963, in Evergreen Park, Illinois. I was sixteen. Nat Pierce, then with Woody Herman's band, introduced me to the music of Erroll Garner through his haunting arrangement of Garner's "Misty." That moment was so captivating to me that I wanted to see and hear the man who composed the melody.

Two years later, in September 1965, I saw Garner in person at Chicago's London House. From that evening on, my greatest desire was to own every record that Garner ever produced. As yet, this has not happened, but this book has.

For the years that followed I would go out of my way to see Garner perform anytime he was within a several hundred mile radius of where I lived. Sometimes my excursions took me across the country. I became obsessed with collecting every record I could find. I spent many weekends in dusty, old record shops searching out anything I didn't already have.

Except for a brief handshake at the London House, the first time I met Garner was a few hours prior to his Carnegie Hall appearance on February 18, 1967. While in college I cashed in an old insurance policy, which was supposed to be used for college expenses, and flew from Oklahoma City to New York to see the concert. A few hours before the concert I noticed five well-dressed men. I recall seeing this little fellow trailing along with them. It was Erroll! I said, "Erroll, Erroll! I came all the way from Oklahoma City to see you tonight." He looked at me as though I were crazy. Out of a brown paper bag I pulled three of his albums, all collector's items, which I had hunted for that day, and asked him to sign one of the album jackets. By then he believed my story. Erroll always recalled that incident whenever he saw me.

Shortly after college I joined the Air Force. I often spent half of my 30-day furlough going to Garner concerts. In October 1972, after a tour in Southeast Asia, I returned home. I called Martha Glaser, Erroll's personal manager, from Goldsboro, North Carolina, to say I was on furlough, and wherever Erroll would be, I would be there that night. That evening I was three tables deep, sipping scotch in the Congo Room at the Sahara Hotel in Las Vegas.

Over the years I saw more than 70 of his club and concert appearances. To meet him, to hear him, and to collect his records had been more than I ever expected. One day to write a book about him would be extraordinary.

In June 1977, several months after Garner's death, Martin Rand suggested I write a discography on Garner. His Garner discography and endless leads gave me a strong base on which to build. With Rand's encouragement and the help of Garner's sister Ruth, I expanded this work to include an oral history and a chronology.

This book is not a complete biography but a straightforward account of the man and his works told by those individuals who in some way were able to reconstruct their part in Erroll Garner's life. I chose to do an oral history because I believe it is the most effective way for the people close to Garner to re-create his story. No attempt has been made to paraphrase or standardize dialectal expressions or regional idioms. I made every attempt to maintain the authentic voices of the narrators. In many instances I have asked the narrators to recall fifty or more years. Generally the facts are consistent, but opinions will vary. The voices, however, remain authentic.

I have attempted to place the interviews in chronological order. Occasionally, however, the events discussed in one interview overlap with those events discussed in others. Some interviews span the entire life of Erroll Garner, and some span only a month or two. Therefore, it was difficult to put each interview under a particular chapter title.

Time and space limitations made it impossible to include interviews of every person who was ever associated with Erroll Garner. Noticeably absent is Garner's personal manager for 27 years, Martha Glaser. She declined to be interviewed or to provide discographical information. Although she receives a few barbs in some interviews, her reputation as a personal manager is unparalleled. I feel that no other artist in jazz has been so well represented as Erroll Garner. Martha Glaser's tenacious style and her sincere loyalty to Garner and his artistic talents helped to make him an international celebrity. Undoubtedly, Erroll Garner's talents would have been discovered anyway, but his wide international recognition and financial success can be attributed primarily to Glaser's managerial capabilities. Wherever his name appeared, it was always with distinction, due in no small way to his distinguished manager.

Several familiar descriptions of Garner have evolved from the countless articles and biographical notes written over the years. Among them are that Garner composed "Misty," could not read music, grunted while he played, and sat on a Manhattan telephone directory. Beyond these "facts" very little biographical information exists, probably because Garner was an intensely private man. Offstage he was shy and usually provided "pat" answers for the questions that frequently were asked. Therefore, it has been difficult to identify the man behind the word.

The most debated issue concerning Garner's biography is the year of his birth. Erroll Garner was born on Wednesday, June 15, 1921 (not 1923), at 8:25 a.m. I was able to document this fact only after obtaining a valid birth certificate, two separate school records, and verbal confirmation from family members.

Another inconsistency that surfaced in the early articles was the spelling of his name, both as *Earl* and as *Errol.* Garner's original birth certificate did, in fact, have his name as *Earl;* but his sister Martha Murray confirmed that his name at birth was *Erroll.* He was named after a family physician, Doctor Erroll Brown. The birth certificate was simply a mistake and later was legally changed.

Similarly, I was interested in learning more about Garner's involvement with the Kan-D-Kids. According to published reports, the Kan-D-Kids were a group of black children who played on KDKA radio, but there is more to the story. The Kan-D-Kids were actually on KQV radio in Pittsburgh, and they were founded by Lee Matthews and his wife, Dorothy. Mrs. Matthews died several years ago, but her husband is still living in Pittsburgh and is over 80 years old. His interview proved to be a very informative and warm account of this group of black children, the first such to perform on radio.

The brief reports about Garner's Asbury Park appearances were never specific. When I visited Martha Murray, Erroll's oldest sister, she let me go through an old trunk. We found a photograph of Erroll at the piano and a friend at the organ. When I turned the photograph over it said, "Bob Brittingham and Erroll, Asbury Park 1941 or '42." I phoned Mrs. Brittingham in Asbury Park and she said her husband had died in 1964. However, she was able to give me the name of Jewel Walters who was the manager of Paul's "Edgewaters" in the early 1940s until she retired in 1970. A search of advertisements on microfilm in the *Asbury Park Press* revealed that Garner performed at Paul's "Edgewaters" in Asbury Park during the summers of 1942 and 1944.

With few exceptions, the photographs used in this book have never been published. Although many publicity photos are available, it would seem pointless to try to include every known photo of Garner. Some pictures could not be published because the proper release from the photographer or the owner was denied or could not be obtained. Fortunately, Martha Murray found some rare photos of Erroll as a child. I am pleased that these photos are appearing in this book for the first time.

Throughout the seven years I spent in writing this book some wonderful things have happened to me. People and events have come along at precisely the right time to help move this book from infancy to its final completion. My labor of love would have been a lonely experience had it not been for the spirit of camaraderie I enjoyed with some wonderful people from around the world. The Garner family—Martha Murray, Linton, Ruth Moore, Berniece Franklin and Erroll's twin brother, Ernest—provided me with ongoing support that was of immeasurable help. The family shared many documents, rare photographs and personal memories that enhanced this book far beyond what it would otherwise have been. They also introduced me to friends of Erroll's who were able to broaden my perspective.

I owe a special thank you to Martin G. Rand, who suggested I write this book. His assistance, guidance and patience on the discography portion of this volume were truly generous.

Douglas Dunbar, founder of the Erroll Garner Club (Erskine House, Aberlady, East Lothian, Scotland), introduced me to members throughout the world and assisted me in discovering some rare European issues for my discography. I am very grateful to Douglas and his family for their warm hospitality during my 1982 visit to Aberlady.

Maurice Rolfe (England) and Thomas Schleuszner (West Germany) individually provided me with a "book" of corrections and updates to my discography. Their scrutiny of my numerous discographical drafts allowed me to feel confident when the work was finally submitted to the publisher.

During my week-long visit to the Danish Jazz Center, Rønnede, Denmark, Arnvid Meyer and his wife, Karen, allowed me to research the Timme Rosenkrantz archives, which were essential to Garner's discography from October to December 1944. Their generous assistance helped to make this short but crucial period in Garner's discography more accurate.

Also deserving a special mention is Art Zimmerman who constantly came up with leads to enhance my research until the deadline arrived. His high-spirited attitude has allowed others besides myself to uncover much "missing" information.

I would like to thank Dan Morgenstern and his staff at the Institute of Jazz Studies, Rutgers—The State University of New Jersey, for accepting this book for their "Studies in Jazz" series. Ed Berger, curator of the Institute, provided many helpful comments and made many significant editorial decisions. Also, my thanks to Marie Griffin and Vincent Pelote, who were on the lookout for new Garner issues for my discography.

My special thanks go also to all those whom I interviewed, especially Leroy Brown, who showed me through Pittsburgh's "Hill District" and took me to the sites of many of the clubs in which Garner played prior to his move to New York City.

For their enormous time and significant contributions toward this endeavor I would like to thank the following: John F. Alblas (England), Dick and Patti Gaudy, Claire P. Kayser, Ray Knight, Wayne Knight, Vicki Lyons, Bill Miner, Arthur Newman, Anis Khan Satti (Pakistan), Suzanne Scherer, Annette Schneider, Hank Simon and Peter Wainwright (England).

I would like to thank these contributors for their valuable assistance: Tony Adkins (Wales), Paul Allen, Steve Allen, David Allyn, Bob Altschuler, Carl Arter, Nat Atkins, Jeff Atterton, Ray Avery, Anthony Barnett (England), George Boyle, Katherine Brittingham, Eric Brown (Australia), Ray Bryant, Madeline Burrell, Kathryn Bushman, Jaki Byard, Dick Campbell, David Chertok, John Clement, Ron Clough (England), Fred Cohen, Ronnie Cole, Chester Commodore, Gerhard Conrad (West Germany), Reg Cooper (England), Stanley Dance, Manek Daver (Japan), Nathan Davis, Vic Dickenson, Peter Dimperio, Doug Dobell (England),

Jerry Doran, Frank Driggs, George Duvivier, Ed Eberstadt, Lynn Farrell, Ellis Feibush, Harry and Rita Fein, Jerry Fox, Sheldon Frommer, Terry Gahman, Olive Gambrell, Helen Gottesman, Frances Garner, Leslie Garner, Al Grey, Johnny Guarnieri, Ben Hafey (Canada), Carolyn Hager, Walt Harper, Johan Helø (Norway), Jim Heymann, Ron Holder, Swanson Hudson, Guy Hunter, Cathy Kroepil, Arnold Laubich, Cliff Leeman, Claude Lefèvre (France), John Levy, Lenny Litman, Nick Lomakin, Rainer Lotz (West Germany), Jim Lowe (England), Alf Lumby (England), Martine McCarthy, Jack McKinney, Arnold Maran (Scotland), Lemon Moses, Sr., Ulrich Neuert (West Germany), Gil Noble, Gene Norman, Wally Osborne, Bennett Owens, Remo Palmier, Robin Platt, Bob Porter, Francis Poudras (France), Bobby Pratt, Buddy and Alice Price, Erik Raben (Denmark), David Redfern (England), Wally Richardson, Michel Ruppli (France), Brian Rust (England), Zina Satti (Pakistan), Morton Savada, Phil Schaap, Joan Schockey, Dick Sears, Yasuo Segami (Japan), Jim Seidelle, Sue Simmons, Don Sollash (England), Pauline Stone, Klaus Stratemann (West Germany), Deborah Tawsley, Caroline Thistlethwaite (England), Ernest Tucker, David Tuff (Canada), James Turner, Dorothy Updyke, Jerry Valburn, Piet van Engelen (The Netherlands), Bob Waits, Charles Walters, Thaylor Whitely III, Erik Wiedemann (Denmark) and Shirley Wood.

Finally, I would like to thank my sister Virginia Lazzara for coming halfway across the country to get me out of a typing jam and help sort out thousands of index cards. Thanks also to my mother, Virginia Doran, for her support and assistance when I needed another typist.

Most of all, I would like to thank my father, Richard J. Doran. It was he who taught me to appreciate good music. I will be grateful to him forever for his encouragement and understanding of my musical needs as a child. Had it not been for him, this dream never would have come true.

JAMES M. DORAN

... of an Erroll Garner concert ...

A pyrotechnic display of unparalleled virtuosity, ebullience and sheer incandescent joy!—A seduction of the senses into a world of indescribable climactic beauty!—A dazzling, audacious, high-flying acrobatic trapeze act executed without benefit of a net or truss!—A journey into time differentials of space and form!—An in-depth creation and exploration of extemporised, harmonic and melodic thematic content!—A titillation and assuagement of aesthetic sensitivities and emotive appetites!—An extravaganza of legerdemain!

JOHN F. ALBLAS

I. His Story

The Garner twins, Ernest (left) and Erroll at the age of three, on the steps of their home at 212 North St. Clair Street, Pittsburgh, summer 1924. This picture was supposed to be taken with the twins on a pony. Afraid of the pony, they thought the steps would be the safer choice. (Martha Murray)

Reverend Allen, who was the minister for the Presbyterian Church, was very appreciative of Erroll's talent . . . . Erroll was the only kid who could get away with playing jazz in the church.

RUTH GARNER MOORE

The Garner Family

MARTHA

Martha Garner Murray was born in Pittsburgh on January 2, 1914. She is the eldest of the Garner children. Her remarkable memory, timing, and sense of humor made it a pleasure to interview her. In this interview she discusses the family, Erroll's birth, and early childhood.

Erroll had that ear. He was born with a gifted ear because whatever he heard he could play. I always tell people, I said, "Well Lord, when our music teacher came and she would be teaching us, and if she had a new piece that she was going to teach us, she'd start us out and give us just a portion of it to learn. By the time she came for the next weeks lesson, we'd have it in pretty good shape." She would always take that particular number and play it clear through so we would know how it sounded when it was a finished product. Well, Erroll would sit down and play behind Miss Bowman just like she played it. He's done that all his life. And that was classical stuff! I don't play jazz because I don't have the gift to play it like Erroll or Linton . . . you give it to me to read and I know where I'm going, but he could take that classical stuff and go to town with it. He could do as well with Bach and Brahms because he had that kind of ear . . . he had true pitch.

Erroll started taking lessons, like we did, from Miss Madge Bowman. Miss Bowman was a graduate of the Pennsylvania College for Women, which is now called Chatham College. She'd lose a whole half-hour or more trying to find Erroll when she arrived for his lesson. At that time we all took piano lessons from Miss Bowman. When we got to Erroll, piano lessons didn't cost but a dollar per week.

One day she took Erroll to Carnegie Tech, which is now called Carnegie-Mellon, for the professors to hear him. We knew it was a gift, and she knew it was a gift, and that's why she took him because she wanted to know for herself. After the professors heard him and saw what he could do, they told her that it was a God-given gift that nobody could take from him and noboby could do it like him.

Father had given Mother a gift. It was a beautiful mahogany Victrola, which was very prominent in homes in those days. It was the kind you wound up, and at night Mother would play records for us. One musician we would listen to was Zez Confrey. She'd get so many records out and play them, and we'd sit up in our beds and listen. That was quite a treat for us because all of us went to school, and we had to be in bed at a certain time. In the morning Erroll would come down, sometimes before Mother could even put his clothes on . . . . He'd be in his little pajamas, and he'd crawl up on the stool, and he'd start playing. He remembered what he heard the night before.

We never thought of Erroll in terms of being a genius. We were family, and we knew he played and everybody in the neighborhood knew he played. We had an upright piano with one of those stools that you had to wind. Mother had to wind the stool up as high as she could so he could reach the keyboard 'cause he was that small . . . . His feet couldn't touch the floor. When he began to wear shoes, his feet still weren't long enough to reach the floor, so he kept time by kicking the panel of the upright, which he completely wore out. Somebody said to me, "When did he start, about four or five?" I said, "Oh no, Erroll started playing when he was two years old." I know that to be a fact. He never started to play the piano like a child . . . da da dum . . . not with one finger. He didn't! He put both hands on the piano and began to play. And this is what we've known all our life, so we never thought there was anything outstanding or phenomenal about it. We just took it in stride.

At that time people had a lot of socials; they'd get him to play for so long, and then they'd return him home 'cause they knew he had to go to bed because he had to go to school the next morning. This is why everybody at some time or another from various clubs would give affairs, and if they needed music, they figured they could get Erroll to do the playing. Well, they would borrow him for that particular evening, and he played well enough and hard enough that you didn't need to have a horn or anything along with him because he naturally made the piano sound like he had a full-size orchestra. Even as a child he could always do that!

Erroll enjoyed doing things that the average kid did: baseball, roller skating, and things of this sort. He wasn't the type that was in the house playing the piano all the time. He got out and played with the other children because Mother saw to that. He played all the kid games that all the rest of us played when he was young. That's what I mean when I say his childhood was normal. Sometimes you find children that are in the genius realm, and they don't bother with things like that. But life for

him was just like the others. He went to school, he played, he had things
to do when he got home, but still he got out there and played with the
neighborhood kids. At that time we lived in an area where there was quite
a few children and everybody played with each other. I heard him laugh
one time when he mentioned they had made, out of boards and roller
skates, a scooter type of a thing. He did all those kinds of things. He
enjoyed himself in that respect.

Dick Powell came to our house and wanted my father to let him go
to Hollywood. My father put his foot down and said, "No way." Erroll
was a very small boy at the time. We had a big theater in East Liberty
called the Enright Theater, and Dick Powell was the emcee then, and it
was here that Dick Powell got his break from there to go to Hollywood.
Well, Erroll and Ernest were allowed to go to the shows . . . . They carried
what they called kiddie shows on Saturday mornings where the youngsters
would go and perform, and they would have shows for them and this type
of thing.

Dick Powell heard about Erroll's playing and tried his best to talk my
father into letting Erroll go to California. He tried to show him that he
would get his education and be at school, and what he could do for him.
Father refused, and I never will forget his saying, "I'm not going to be
the cause of Erroll going to the devil." As far as older folks were concerned,
if children became involved in that sort of thing, they were headed for
no good. Father wasn't a mean person, but his belief was that Erroll was
too young to be taken away from home.

Nothing was done without the permission of my parents by any of us.
My Dad was a stickler about that. That was one thing about our family . . . you didn't do anything without permission. If they said, "No," you
could just throw it out of your mind 'cause they wouldn't hear of it. If
they said, "Yes," you could do it. Whoever was taking Erroll out, my
father was going to go along to see that things go as they ought to go,
and whoever was taking Erroll would be sure that they brought him back
just like they took him.

We had a wonderful neighborhood on North St. Clair Street. Everybody
knew everybody, and everyone was friendly. It was a neighborhood where
everybody enjoyed life. There was no porches . . . . There were like three
steps that led from the street up to the house. The neighbors would sit
out there and chat with one another on the steps.

Our property belonged to the church. There were three houses in a brick
row, and we lived in the middle house on the second floor. Mrs. Sheraw
lived on the first floor. Later, when Mrs. Sheraw's husband died, she
moved 'cause by then we had a big family. Fortunately, where we lived
there was a big yard that was fenced in on the side of the houses. All
of us played until it was time to come in and get ready for bed. That was
when my mother said it was her time to rest.

Mother came from Staunton, Virginia, to a place called Connellsville,
Pennsylvania, where she stayed with a lady by the name of Mrs. Lina

Strothers until she finished her high school education. She then came to
Pittsburgh to go to Avery College. This college was for all young ladies;
they also taught them sort of like a trade. That's where Mother received
her certificate in dressmaking and millinery. Mother could make anything;
she made all our clothes. I never had a dress that Mother didn't make
until I was twelve years old. And that was because she was ill at Easter,
and I had to have a white dress, so my godmother, Mrs. Susan Sheffey,
took me to the store to buy it. Mother also was a good cook and hair-
dresser. She went along life's ways and did what she had to do. She had
a truly good education.

Mrs. Strothers and Grandmother were very close friends, and from the
way they talked, I think she was a distant relative. My mother's father
[Charles Darcus] was a lay minister. Grandmother used to travel with him
on the weekends to the little churches around the area.

Now how exactly she met my father I don't know. I do know they both
belonged to the same church, the very church that I go to now, St. James
A.M.E. [African Methodist Episcopal]. That's where Erroll's funeral was.
At that time my father sang in the choir as a tenor, and my mother was
a contralto. Both of them had very beautiful voices, and at that time neither
one of them was married. I think when my father died, mother had been
married to my father for almost sixty years. They were married in my
godmother's home, the same house that I was born in.

Father was born in Randolph County, Thomasville, North Carolina.
He came to Pittsburgh at an early age, from what I heard him say. He
had one brother [Dolphus] who has been dead for many years. Now I
kind of feel that he came up here because this brother was in this area.
I don't know what age he was or what year he came to Pittsburgh.

Father worked at Westinghouse for quite a number of years, and at one
time he used to cook for a club called the East Liberty Hunting and Fishing
Club. Both were full-time jobs. I believe in the beginning he was in the
Maintenance Department at Westinghouse, if I'm correct. Then during the
war he left and then came back again. Fortunately, by going back with
his years of service, that's how he was able to retire from Westinghouse.
He also worked as custodian of the Calvary Episcopal Church. This was
during the tenure of Dr. Harvey Gaul. He was the choirmaster at the
Church. My father always wanted to do concert work, but he suffered
from asthma. He suffered from asthma like Erroll did. Dr. Gaul told him
that his condition would be a great hindrance to him. By the time you
travel from place to place, you get into these areas where the weather is
inclement and what have you, and it naturally affects the voice of any
singer. So Father just stuck to working with the quartet here in the city,
and he did solo work at the various churches. He was a good tenor.

Father played a little bit of piano by ear, and he also played the
mandolin and saxophone. He had an orchestra at one time. They traveled
around to the nearby little towns and played for dances. It was sort of
a dance orchestra. He played saxophone when he had the orchestra. Most

of the time there was a man that used to direct this orchestra, a man who was very, very capable, by the name of Mr. McDew. At one time Father used to run a dance hall called the Baby Grand. Mr. McDew was the head of this orchestra, and he was a great musician. They played all different kinds of music.

My father had five cars. In fact, the last car that Father had was a Marmon; it was a big, light blue touring car. I never will forget it. It was on Easter Sunday he told Mother, "Look what I bought for you." She made a big fuss over that car. When it came time to go to church, we all got to ride in the car. We just knew we were the talk of the church by that time. By buying a large car, he and Mr. McDew could transport the band back and forth to various engagements.

Fortunately for us, we had a father who was very gracious. Father was the kind of person years ago when it came to Easter Sunday he would wear morning trousers and a frock tail coat. Talk about an Easter parade! Honey, when you went to church, you were well dressed. Father was also a person who was very active in the churches in the city, and he was in these weddings, which were called "million dollar" weddings. He had these type of clothes—that's the reason that when all of us got married he didn't have to rent anything. He had the bosom shirt with the tux and the pleats, the patent leather slippers, he had the trousers. For years, people didn't know who my mother was because they'd say, "I've known your father for years. I saw him with Miss so-and-so, and she was the bride in this "million dollar" wedding, and I saw your Poppa struttin' down the aisle." Now, when I got married everybody said to me, "We're definitely going to be at the wedding because we want to see your father struttin'." Poppa could! Honey, when he brought me down the aisle, he reared back like he was carrying Princess Grace of Monaco. I wanted to go to the front to see how he looked coming down.

Mother was a very quiet, soft-spoken person, a very highly refined lady, and she had compassion for everybody. She wasn't a person to downgrade anybody; she wasn't like that, and she always saw good in everybody. Mother was a pretty woman, with a nice, round face. She was very stylish, had a pretty complexion, always pleasant and had a pleasant smile. She saw something good in all of us. She was a sweet person. Everybody loved Mother, as I said, no one could speak differently about her, 'cause even through all of her illness people always said, "Lord, I hope I can be like your mother, 'cause all that she has gone through she never complained." She always would lend a hand, and if she couldn't go out, I was sent to go. I was the one to do the going and doing for her because she would tell me very quickly, "Now such and such a thing had happened to Mrs. so-and-so, and you'd better go and let her know that I'm thinking about her." I didn't exchange any words. I just said, "Yes ma'am," and went on.

My father was a person that was full of life and always had a joke to tell. Mother had a very wonderful sense of humor, but she would do it in such a subtle way you'd have to laugh. But Dad would always have you uproariously howling with laughter about the jokes that he could tell you and the things that had happened. He was a person that practically everyone in the city knew, and he was that type of person: outgoing, full of life, fun, and laughter. For both of them the family came first. Neither of them did for one that they didn't do for the other, so we were all treated alike, and we were all given the very best that they could give us. We didn't have a lot of money, but we had a good time; one thing I can say, Mother always managed to feed all our crew and half of the neighborhood. Many times we had 12 to 15 folks drop in unexpectedly on Sunday, and she always had enough food to feed them. We didn't know they were coming, but they were friends of hers from church, and sometimes (reason I can remember so well is because Linton and I had to wash dishes afterwards!) when dinner time came, they didn't ask you, "Will you have some dinner?" We were just told to set the table for the family and to put on the extra plates for whoever was there. It was never any problem for her because she loved to cook, and she always had plenty to eat. We were never denied anything. If we wanted seconds on desserts, we were given it, but we had to be sure that the dinner plate had been cleared of everything.

Even through her sickness I did as much entertaining with Mother as I did when she was well because she liked people. After she passed away, it seemed so funny that Sunday would come, and there wasn't a visitor; that just wasn't our household. Always somebody visiting, and even when she was sick, people steadily came, and we had things for her, and we had a good time with her. I remember when her birthday came, I gave her a surprise party, and I think I had 30 some people there that day. Everyone had a good time. She kept up with her club, and they would come when it was time for her to hold the meeting and make a big fuss over it. I would get her downstairs, and we had a nice, good old-fashioned time with lots of fun and food to eat. The ladies would come and stay late into the evening. They always said when they left they felt like they hadn't been anywhere to visit the sick; they just had a good time because she was as gay as everyone else was.

Mother had sugar diabetes, and the first unfortunate thing we had to get adjusted to was the fact that she lost her sight. Later in life she had to have the amputation of the leg, which we had not expected. It was one of those things we just couldn't do anything about. Before she died, she lost both legs. She lost her sight between 1958 and '60 because of the diabetes.

Mother got along beautifully. I took Mother to church, shopping, and we went everywhere and did all kinds of things. In fact, with her sight gone we took her to Connecticut and then New Jersey, and we carried her all around. It didn't bother her, and she never complained about it. She got along very, very well. The ironic part of it was she outlived the sugar. Before Mother died, they had taken her off of insulin because she didn't need it. The doctor always said he wished all his patients had been like Mother because she did not fret, and she didn't complain about anything. This is the reason that she got along so beautifully as she did.

One of the hardest things for Erroll to get adjusted to was Mother losing her sight. They did everything they could possibly do to save her eyes. He was always very, very fond of her. She always made the biggest fuss when Erroll or Linton, my oldest brother, visited. Linton was big and tall. She would always say, "Oh, Mother's big boy," and I said, "I'm going up to New Kensington [Pennsylvania] and come back and see if she'll greet me like that." And she'd laugh. He was so big we all used to get such a big kick out of it. She always made such a great to-do over her boys. All of us were crazy about Mother because she always had such a way. When you asked a question, she could always give you a definitive answer; the answer would always be a constructive answer.

Mother had excellent judgment, a very brilliant woman. She was marvelous with figures. That's why she was always able to help us so much in our schoolwork because she knew it. Telephone numbers, Lord have mercy, she couldn't even see, and I'd holler to her, "What's Mrs. so-and-so's number?" and she'd rattle it right off as if she was reading it . . . and I'd laugh. Even with her handicap, as long as that phone was near the bed so she could reach it and answer it. People would say, "How are you?" and she'd say, "Very well, thank you." I don't think I ever heard her tell anyone (when they called) that she didn't feel well.

Her sense of hearing was extremely keen. She knew all of us by our footsteps. And my father would be sitting at the table, and we would be coming around the side of the house, and she would tell him, "Go to the door because so-and-so is coming." He would say, "I don't hear nobody," and she said, "Go to the door! So-and-so is coming." Well, by the time he got to the door, the bell rang! I said to him, "I think after fifty-some years of being married you'd pay attention to what she tells you." And he'd get a big laugh out of it. She couldn't see, but she knew exactly who was coming in that house. She knew all of our footsteps, and she would name us. Sure enough, it would be just who she said.

Erroll would come home, and she would always cook something he preferred. He might not have gotten home until 4 o'clock in the morning, but Mother would set up a table, and Erroll would rear back just like it was 2 o'clock in the afternoon. He didn't get home very often, and if he would come to this area to perform at one of the clubs, he would always manage to go out there to see Mother and Father. Sometimes he would get there between the last of the midnight hour and the beginning of the morning hour, but Mother would always feed him something. He'd come, and she'd tell me to get a napkin for my brother. I was busy setting up the table, and I just laid a paper napkin down and she heard the napkin rustle, and she said, "Get a good napkin, a linen napkin for your brother." I said, "Now, how did you know I put a paper napkin down," and she said, "I heard it."

Dr. Erroll Brown was the physician that delivered me. That's who little

Erroll was named after 'cause I always heard Mother say that. Now if you wanted to upset Mother you just call him *Earl* and his name was *Erroll*, and she would take precise care to pronounce it correctly, and she spelled it for you. He was just a fine, outstanding doctor.

Dr. S. O. Cherry delivered the rest of our family. Dr. Cherry was a handsome man. Now, he was very tall, very aristocratic, and very elegant!—his style, his carriage and all. He was so fair complexioned that most white people thought he was white.

None of us were born in a hospital but were born at home. Erroll was born at 212 North St. Clair Street on the second floor in Mother's bedroom. I can remember that incident because I was going to school, and my godmother, Mrs. Susan Sheffey, lived next door to us at that time. When I came home from school at lunch time, she told me that we had twin brothers. In those days older people didn't tell you much about children being born. You didn't have the knowledge that young people have nowadays, so we never thought anything about it. We went to school, and when we came home, Aunt Sue gave us our lunch and afterwards told us we had two brothers. We went up to the bedroom, and I can remember Mother had these two babies, and I picked up Ernest and Linton picked up Erroll. As they grew older and Mother thought we could handle them, it was our job to see, when we came from school at noon time, whether they were wet or dry, and we were trained to change their diapers while she tended to getting the lunch ready.

Mother realized Ernest was retarded, but she never said too much about it. There were two teachers: one is dead now and I'm not sure about the other one. Erroll and Ernest were put in a school called Larimer School. Ernest was put there because he was what they called a slow learner. One of the teachers came to the house one day and said to Mother, "Mrs. Garner, have you heard about Polk [Pennsylvania] School?" It was just one of those things that happen, and you just don't broadcast it all over the world. All of us around the area knew about the school, but outsiders didn't. It was no disgrace or anything. She went on to tell us that it was hard to get in there because someone had to die up at the school before a spot would open up. She talked to Mother about it and told her to think it over as it was a difficult decision. Mother never really said much, but she finally gave in for his safety, so that no harm could come to him.

Finally, a spot became available and he was admitted. Ernest stayed at home all his life; he went to school, and you see, he was a big boy when he went to Polk. He wasn't put there as a small child. In those days no one bothered you. By the time he had gotten older, there were too many things going on. The teacher said he could be innocent, but he would be accused of something he didn't even know about. This is what the teacher was trying to get across to Mother; it would be a better place for him where his life wouldn't be in danger.

Erroll spent a lot of time with Ernest. They went to the movies together. Mother sent them together; they went to Sunday school together and everything. That was the stipulation in our household. It meant to go together and to come together. Mother didn't want to hear anything different. All of us were brought up like that. It's amazing because when we all started out for Sunday school, everybody left the house together, and she knew when we were coming back. Ernest was the type that if he was walking with you and if you stopped to tie your shoe lace, he didn't stand and wait for you to get it tied. He kept walking. Mother used to laugh years later and said that he was the only child that she could ever send to the store, and he would come directly back. The rest of us had to stop and chat with somebody along the way.

What Ernest knew, he knew well and he didn't forget. He was terrific at dusting. We would just dust the top of the things or just the surface. He would do the bottoms of chairs and things that we always missed. We were always told to do our dusting over, but he got everything right the first time. Ernest was the kind of child that spoke to everyone. He thought everybody meant well. He didn't know the difference between right and wrong. I know it was quite a problem for Mother to have to live through (to give up her child) 'cause I remember hearing her tell my godmother that. She really took it like a good soldier and with good grace. The basic foundation of it is just plain slow learning. I do recall Mother telling someone once that the doctor said that Erroll got it all, and Ernest didn't get everything he was supposed to. Now, he does pretty well.

After he went to Polk, they put him in school, and now they tell me he's able to sign his checks and things, and they taught him how to go to the bank. Somebody goes with him, of course. The clerks in the banks know him and help him since he's not good at counting money. He's able to do other things. As far as his clothing and his personal appearance are concerned, he likes his clothes, and he like his clothes clean.

I would never live off Erroll's laurels. He was making a living for himself doing what he knew to do, and I'm here making a living for myself doing what I know to do. We were all taught when we came along. "You do the best that you can and whatever you feel that you are best trained for." Mother used to always say, "Every tub has to stand on its own bottom." That was an old way of putting it. So you knew when you came along, and you got up into the world, and you went to work. You took care of yourself, and you didn't expect your brother or sister to take care of you 'cause that was not their duty. If they choose to do something for you, fine. As Mother used to tell us when we were little when it came to eating, we had to learn to eat everything because she used to always say, "I have no guarantee that I will live to do by you all, all of my life." But God was good and God was gracious. He let her raise all six of us. Ironic as it stood, and in a way it was a blessing, I was sorry to lose Erroll, but I was glad that it happened when it did, after Mother had gone on, because it might not have gone too well with her in her condition. All of them (Father, Mother and Erroll) died three years apart.

Erroll's earliest musical influence had to be our neighbor's son, Mr.

William Duckett. He was one of the old ragtime jazz players. His parents lived around the corner from us on the next street, and he would come down from Boston during the summer to visit them. They were members of our church, and Mr. Duckett would always play a number or two on the piano for us children. In fact, Mother said, "Sometimes I think you all just worshipped him." Funny thing he didn't mind it. We'd say, "Mr. Duckett, ya gonna play for us?" and he'd say, "Yeah, I'll be back after awhile."

He always wore a black derby that was cocked off to the side of his head, and he chewed a cigar that he kept in the corner of his mouth. He'd push that cigar aside and boy, he'd sit down and give us some old ragtime music. We were just delighted! Little things like that . . . people never refused us. Mother would remember all these things, and she'd laugh about it later as we grew older, and we'd get a big kick out of it.

Our family was great for mimicking people, just we kids having fun. We'd say, "You know, Miss so-and-so used to play like this." And everybody would get up and demonstrate what went on, how they sounded on the piano, patted their feet, and so on. We had a household that had a lot of activity. We kids always enjoyed it. It was a house where everybody could have a good time.

LINTON

Linton Garner has had a long and distinguished career as a pianist and arranger. Born March 25, 1915, Garner started piano lessons at the age of eight, but by the time he was ten, he fell in love with the cornet. He played all through school and played first-chair trumpet in the senior high school band. Problems with his teeth, at an early age, forced him to go back to the piano. Garner joined the Jimmy Murray Band at Van Buren Point, a summer resort outside of Buffalo, New York. (Jimmy Murray was Martha Garner Murray's late husband.) In 1941, Fletcher Henderson fired his entire band and picked up Murray's band. Henderson didn't need another pianist, but the group refused to join unless Linton was allowed to stay as the band pianist. Garner stayed with the Henderson Band until he was drafted into the Army in 1943. After almost three years in the Army, he came out in March, 1946, and played with Leroy Brown's group in Pittsburgh for three months. In June, 1946, he joined Billy Eckstine's Big Band in Chicago and was with Eckstine until the band broke up in 1947. Today Linton Garner is the pianist in residence at the Four Seasons Hotel in Vancouver, British Columbia, where he has been a regular for almost eight years. He is also host of the Linton Garner Show on CHQM Radio in Vancouver.

I knew Martha Glaser before Erroll. I met Martha, I believe, in Detroit at the Paradise Theater while I was working with Timmie Rogers. I'm not certain how Erroll and Martha got together, but once she heard him play, she was hooked. She recognized immediately that he was a great talent, and she felt she wanted to be a part in shaping his career. As we know, she subsequently made a tremendous contribution to his career. I don't know anyone else that could have done a better job. She did everything she could to defend him at any cost, and she would literally defend him physically if she had to. I know there were times when agents and so forth would be abusive, and she would crawl right up their backs. She's a fighter! She was very protective and didn't pull any punches either. She would tell Erroll what his shortcomings were too.

We lived in a joined row of brick houses, which were owned by the church. Our home was in the middle of the row, and we occupied two floors since our family was so large. On either side of us there were families occupying each floor. We had three rooms downstairs (a kitchen, living room, and dining room) and three bedrooms upstairs. We had a wood and coal-burning stove and an open-hearth grate in the living room, and we kept the coal in the cellar. We had gaslights in our home, which were made of a very fine woven asbestos, which would last about four to six weeks. We had no bathroom, but we had our own individual toilets, which were in the cellar, and we also had our own individual lockers. We had the large galvanized tub in the kitchen where we would bathe. We just took our turn. This wasn't unusual to have this setup back then unless a family was affluent.

Across the street was an old butcher shop where we used to get our meats. Mr. George Kirk owned the shop. My dad had an account there, and he'd usually pay the bill on Saturday night. We would go with him, and Mr. Kirk would give us each a slice of bologna and let us stick our hands in the cookie barrel and get a couple of cookies. They gave that stuff away then; they don't do that now.

In those days Mr. Ellis would come by in his vegetable wagon. He was one of the main hucksters, as we used to call them. He'd come by on Wednesday then again on Saturday, so we were fixed up for Sunday's dinner.

We were about a block from the Church [St. James A.M.E.] which was on the corner of Euclid Avenue and Harvard Street. We lived on North St. Clair and Harvard Streets, and the neighborhood was completely integrated although blacks couldn't eat in the five-and-ten and we had to sit in the balcony of the theater. It was routine in those days.

My father played guitar, and he had a small concertina and a mandolin. My mother could play a few hymns, but that's about all, and she would rarely do that, but my dad—he could tinker around. He also played what we called "in the crack" piano. My father was not really a great instrumentalist, but he was a fine singer. He sang very well, and he sang with some very fine quartets. One time he sang in a church choir. He wanted to be a concert singer, but being a chronic asthma case, they advised him against it.

I have never known anyone to call him anything other than Ernest. Jimmy Pupa called him "Poppa Deke." I don't know exactly where he got that name. It might have been an expression that he used. My dad was very colorful and very demonstrative. He managed a pool room and was a very good pool player. He also used a lot of expressions of the day but was not a vulgar man by any means. I never heard him swear. He had many expressions that he would use. They were just little things that I guess mainly black people would use.

The pool hall that he had was on Frankstown Avenue. He was at Westinghouse, and then he worked at the Hunting and Fishing Club. He was at Westinghouse twice. He was there in his early years, and then he left and he was away for 15 or 16 years. Then he went back. The pool hall was around 1934–1936 for about three years. He was always into something. He was quite enterprising. He had a dance hall in his early years, and he used to have an orchestra, and he learned how to play the saxophone. He also had a little sandwich shop. They were not ongoing businesses, only for short periods of time.

Only in a general sense would I have any recollection of when Erroll first started to play. It seems like I can always remember him playing, but I can't pinpoint the first time. He used to imitate those piano rolls. We just enjoyed him. He'd play every second of the day if you would let him. It was no big thing to him because he just enjoyed it. He was always happy-go-lucky and a very strong personality. He was a hard head as far as discipline was concerned. He could only challenge my mother so far. She would tell him he couldn't go out, and he would put his coat on and go to the door and look at her and never set a foot out of that door. He would wind up sitting on a little stool beside the door and finally fall asleep there with his hat and coat still on. There was also a fairly wide gap in our ages, and that might be the reason I don't remember more about his activites. Being a little kid brother, you're not quite in the scene with his other little friends.

As a pianist, Erroll's hands had complete independence. It was almost like being able to split your thinking in half, the right and left side of the brain. Drummers do that a lot because they have four to five different rhythms going on at the same time. I think it's unusual for a pianist to do it. It was unbelievable! There are many fine pianists who have great independence in their playing, but he was unusual in that respect.

Erroll was just a super little guy. I'd like to add that I'm now working on a tribute to Erroll. I'll have that finished soon, and Sarah Vaughan expressed an interest in possibly doing it. I wrote the lyrics and the music. It's about how I feel about my brother, Erroll.

RUTH

*A constant source of information and encouragement throughout this project,
Ruth Garner Moore's dedication has been extraordinary. Ruth was born
December 26, 1917, in Pittsburgh and offers some candid comments about
her brother Erroll and the Garner Family.*

I was always the religious fanatic in the family, and because of my religious
activities, the Missionary Society from Wilkensburg Presbyterian Church
offered me a scholarship to Barber-Scotia Jr. College in Concord, North
Carolina, which was a mission school. I didn't want to go there. I had
my heart set on Boston University or the University of Chicago, but I
didn't have the money for either, so I ended up going where the scholarship
sent me.

I remember Mrs. Brown. I can see her now; she took Berniece and I
by the hand upstairs to see our new baby brothers. My father used to
pay Annie Brown to help my mother with the laundry on Mondays since
she lived right next door to us. They were laying in this small crib, and
I clearly remember the two of them just laying there. One of the neighbors
was there to help take care of my mother. I can't remember who it was,
but my guess is that it would have been Mrs. Susan Sheffey, who was
Martha's godmother, and Lucy Sheffey's mother. She remarried and her
name became Susan Doyle. It was in her home that my mother and father
were married. Her daughter Lucy would often baby-sit when my mother
and father would go to movies or elsewhere in the evening.

Mother and Father were married in Susan Sheffey's house. She wasn't
a relative just a good friend, and she became Martha's godmother. Aunt
Mary Mills was the godmother for all the rest of the children. Aunt Mary
was a cousin on my mother's side. We always felt closer to her than we
did to any other relative because she was the only one we really ever saw.
Her husband's name was Ambrose, and we called him "Uncle Arms." I
never heard of a godfather in those days. I don't say they didn't have them,
but we didn't have one.

St. James A.M.E. was our church. When we moved from St. Clair Street
to Rowan Avenue, we were closer to the Bethesda Presbyterian Church.
It was the only church that had Vacation Bible School in the summer and
also had weekday religious activities during the school year. The older
children—Martha, Linton, and I—went to weekday activities every day
after school at the Presbyterian church. Erroll and Ernest didn't go because
they were too young, but they did go to Vacation Bible School during
the summer.

Reverend Allen, who was the minister for the Presbyterian Church, was
very appreciative of Erroll's talent, and each day during Vacation Bible
School he would have Erroll give a little concert during assembly when

all the classes came together. Erroll was the only kid who could get away with playing jazz in the church. It was always such a contrast from everything we had just been learning.

My mother felt that because the Presbyterian church was offering us a service that we couldn't get at our own church, we should show our appreciation by attending some of their Sunday services. Therefore, on Sunday she made us go to the Presbyterian church for Sunday school, since they had Sunday school in the morning, and our Methodist church had Sunday school in the afternoon. That was her way of saying thanks to the Presbyterian church for providing weekday activities for her children. She felt we should support the church in that way. All of us, including Erroll and Ernest, went to the Presbyterian Sunday school at 9 o'clock, and then we walked to the Methodist church for service, which started at 11 o'clock, and then Sunday school was in the afternoon. We went back to the Methodist church for "Christian Endeavor" which was at 6 P.M. on Sunday. Erroll and Ernest were included in that as well until the time Erroll left home.

It was on Rowan Avenue that Erroll began taking music lessons from Miss Madge Bowman. We were in that house on Rowan Avenue for maybe five or six years. My father was sick for almost a whole year, and we lost that home because of it. Erroll only had one piano lesson because my dad got sick, and we weren't able to pay for it, so Martha, Linton, and I continued taking the lessons. We just dropped Erroll. Erroll was about six years old then because we all started taking lessons at the age of six. He played well the first time he ever played. The first time anybody heard him play he was playing good. He knew all of our music; he knew it better than we did.

Erroll and Ernest started at the Lincoln School, and then they transferred to the Larimer School in second or third grade. They were transferred to Larimer School as part of the program for children with learning disabilities. Those types of programs were just beginning to get started at that time. It was nothing to be ashamed of. They discovered after they got into this program that Erroll didn't have a learning disability. Ernest, however, remained at Larimer until he was eighteen years of age. Erroll didn't have any problems learning. It was just that he was always playing the piano and wasn't in the classes long enough to learn anything.

In my opinion I didn't see how anyone could tell whether Erroll was a slow or fast learner since he was spending so much time playing the piano during class time. They always had him playing concerts in both Larimer and Lincoln most of the day, especially during the recesses and lunch periods. The piano was in the main foyer, and music was always played during recess. The children always marched to music while changing classes.

I remember at the Lincoln School it was always the music teacher who was supposed to play. I can see her now, Miss Lind, who was a fair-looking person with brown hair, straight, and fixed in a bun in the back, very neat-looking in appearance, with rimless glasses, and blue eyes. She often turned over her seat to Erroll. Everybody was so excited over Erroll they almost always had him play for the recesses. The other lady who sometimes played was Miss McSweeney, who was the physical education teacher. She played beautiful piano. She was very petite, with short, curly, light hair. She was a different type of a pianist. We loved her music, as she would play all Sousa band music. Miss Lind played more classical music, and she had a very light touch. Miss McSweeney, however, tiny as she was, had a heavy touch so that it made you want to march. You couldn't march to Miss Lind's music, but you just wanted to stop and listen to her.

Erroll imitated Miss McSweeney, and whenever visitors came to school, they would pull Erroll out of class and have him play for the visitors. The two teachers would alternate days at the piano. The recesses were in the middle of the morning and afternoon. Lunch hour had music too because you marched to go home for lunch. Three times a day there was music. After Erroll had gone to Westinghouse, Ernest remained in Larimer School in that special education class.

Erroll and I had very similar personalities. I think of all the members of our family he and I were more alike. And this is why I saw and felt him suffering while always trying to please the public because it would be the same way with me if I had to do it. I don't see Martha or Berniece suffering through trying to please the public. Both were never shy, but Erroll and I were always rather shy. I was, perhaps, worse than him, but then I wasn't exposed as he was. Linton is not necessarily shy, but he is just very reserved, and that's just his makeup. He has always been calm. Nothing ever disturbs him, and if it did, one would never know it. I remember my mother saying he was that way when he was a baby. Erroll was more hyper, always nervous and high strung, and went to pieces if he couldn't have his own way. When he was scolded, he would sit on a favorite old stool and pout and almost always finally fall asleep. He would put his cap and coat on and say he was going out of the house, even if told not to do so. But he never had the courage to disobey parental orders, and he would eventually fall asleep with his cap and coat on.

He always had lots of friends, but he rarely ever played with children, except at school. Everybody would ask him to play the piano and, if he ever played any games, it was in school. I don't think Erroll was ever out in the street playing as other children did. At Westinghouse High, Mr. Carl McVicker said he attempted to play almost every instrument in the orchestra and band at Westinghouse Junior and Senior High.

My dad and a group of his friends had an orchestra that used to rehearse at our home. Erroll would have gone to bed before they even came, and we thought he was asleep, but the next morning I remember my mother saying, at 6 o'clock in the morning, that they heard him downstairs playing the piano. He had climbed out of his crib and was playing everything that the orchestra had been practicing the night before. This became a regular thing. The neighbors began to hear him, and they would be standing around our house as early as 7 or 8 o'clock in the morning listening to the concert.

Dad was very proud of Erroll. Anytime Erroll played in Pittsburgh, he was there. One time I was in Pittsburgh when Erroll was playing at a nightclub in East Liberty, which was walking distance from our home. I never in my life have been in a nightclub, and nobody thought it odd that I didn't go. I was terribly religious at that time. I remember my father saying, "Baby, this is one time Daddy is going to want everybody in the family to go and see your brother, and God is not going to hold this against you." So we all went.

Dad had a stroke, and he entered a nursing home a few days before Erroll was scheduled to be at Carnegie Hall in Pittsburgh [April 12, 1970]. Dad, of course, was unable to come. The day of the concert he had lost his ability to speak completely, and we weren't too sure he could hear us. But anyhow we went to the concert, and I taped it and brought it back to the nursing home the next morning and played it for him. I knew he could hear it because he was smiling, and when the audience applauded, he gave a great big smile. He was hearing, but he couldn't say a word. Erroll came over to the nursing home that morning, and that was the last time he saw Dad. He died about a month later on May 14, 1970.

Erroll and Berniece always used to clown around together. Once they were dancing some kind of crazy dance, and he slipped and fell on the kitchen floor and broke his leg. Mother and Dad said that this would be something to keep him home for awhile, but it didn't! The boys in the neighborhood would come and sneak him out through the window and carry him to wherever they could find a piano. We were still looking for him even during those weeks that he had a broken leg. Even during normal times it was the same thing. We'd come home from school and couldn't find Erroll. Then Martha, Berniece, and I always had to go hunting for him. All three of us would go in a different direction and listening for a piano being played. Sometimes he was too far from the neighborhood, but his friends would always bring him back. Most of the neighborhoods we lived in were basically white neighborhoods. As a rule, it was always some of the white boys that had Erroll.

Linton used to shine shoes after school because my father was ill and was unable to work. He was supporting the family, after he was in junior high, by playing at night. Erroll was playing for parties and various affairs, and although he wasn't drawing any salary, his tips were enough to help support the family. He would have been twelve or thirteen by that time. I remember hearing him talk about the riverboats, but I don't know anything else about it.

Linton and I were in the same grade after he got to high school. Because he had spent so much time working he must have failed a semester, and that's how I caught up with him. Otherwise he would have been ahead of me, but now we were to graduate at the same time. My mother didn't know how she was going to buy his suit and my dress for graduation, so he decided to drop out of school a few months before graduation so that I would get my dress, and they would not have to buy him a suit too. That was a big sacrifice in 1935.

It was on a Sunday afternoon that Erroll was to play for a Jewish wedding reception in Squirrel Hill, which in those days was a wealthy section of Pittsburgh. When the people came to pick up Erroll, we couldn't find him. He was actually playing somewhere else. So the people were just frantic because it was time for their affair. Berniece said she would go and take his place. My mother nearly had a fit since she thought it was ridiculous for Berniece to even think that she could play well enough to take Erroll's place. These people said if she substituted for him they would be glad to pay her. Berniece was tickled. They persuaded my mother to let Berniece do it, but she was very reluctant to let her go. We never did find Erroll, so she played for the reception the entire time, and they were just delighted. They brought her back home and said she filled the bill, and she got the pay. That was always a big laugh for the family. I can't remember what Erroll's alibi was, but it encouraged Berniece to practice harder in anticipation of getting more jobs. That was the first time we realized how much alike she and Erroll were in playing the piano. She could not play fast, but it was the chords she imitated so well. She said she stayed up many a night working on those chords.

On January 2, 1977, Linton's wife, Frances, and two sons, who lived in Quebec, Canada, were visiting me here in Pasadena, California. They had come to California for New Year's, and it was also Martha's birthday. It was just about noon hour, and because we had been up late, we were about to have brunch. Frances and I were cooking. I said, "Before we eat, let's call Martha and say happy birthday to her." It so happened that I have two phones in the house. I was dialing the one phone to call Pittsburgh, but before I finished dialing, the other phone rang. I hung up and answered the other phone. When I answered someone said, "This is the L.A. Police Department, Sergeant somebody. Are you Ruth Moore?" I said, "Yes." He said, "Are you the sister of Erroll Garner?" I said, "Yes." "Well, since you are the closest next of kin to Mr. Erroll Garner, who has just passed away in the elevator of his apartment building, could you get here as soon as possible?" It was between noon and 1 o'clock. A friend of ours had come over to take Frances for a drive around the city, but instead, he immediately drove us to Erroll's apartment in Beverly Hills. When I arrived, the body had already been removed, which shocked me because I thought it wasn't to go until I got there. Rosalyn Noisette, the lady he was seeing, was sitting there crying. She was terribly upset. It was quite a trauma for her. She had wanted to get an ambulance. She had been in San Francisco when Erroll called her to come home. Martha Glaser called me from New York while I was there at the apartment. She said that Erroll had been calling her all morning telling her he was having trouble waking up. My guess is that this was the diabetes, which might have caused him to go into little comas. She had called his doctor and requested that he get him into the hospital. It must have been around noon. It all happened so quickly, because it was after 12 o'clock when the police called us. Martha called me and told me not to worry because Linton was going to take care of all the necessary arrangements. Martha Glaser bought Rosalyn and me airplane tickets to go to Pittsburgh for the funeral.

My sister-in-law told me that Martha Glaser didn't like anybody for Erroll. She didn't want anybody to be interested in Erroll. So Martha Glaser's attitude toward Rosalyn was not different than it had been towards any other girl that might have been interested in Erroll. Rosalyn has a beautiful personality; she was a very nice-looking woman. She has the type of personality that attracts men to her. So Rosalyn was hurt, and I guess she figured she would get back at them and thus flew to Cleveland and filed suit when his body wasn't even cold yet. She was really a decent person as far as I was concerned. Her aunt didn't like Erroll, but I think she's the only one who didn't.

As far back as I can remember, there were only four other jazz pianists that came anywhere close to Erroll's ability to completely satisfy my personal listening ear. They were Earl "Fatha" Hines, Teddy Wilson, Art Tatum, and Peter Nero. I would rate the last named as being second to Erroll.

The quality of Erroll's music always appealed to me more than that of any other musician that I heard. His style of playing any piece of music always seemed to be the most satisfying. I was quite reluctant to make known my feelings to others because they might think I was partial simply because he was my brother. Had we not been related, I would have felt the same way.

The thing I admired most about Erroll was the fact that he was so completely absorbed in his playing that he seemed never in need of an audience. His facial and bodily expressions indicated how very much he enjoyed and appreciated his creative ability. His happiest moments in life, as far back as I can remember, were the moments he spent "tickling the ivories."

Although I always thoroughly enjoyed Erroll's piano playing, I regret that I did not make known to him my innermost feelings regarding his music. Because of my religious beliefs, I silently disapproved of his playing in nightclubs. Now I realize that my uneducated and narrow thinking was detrimental to him. It caused him to shy away from me because he felt uneasy being in my presence. Unknowingly and unwillingly I must have displayed the "holier than thou" attitude. I will never forget the extreme expression of disbelief when I told him about the birth of my child, Ralph, out of wedlock. It seemed impossible that I, who was so devout, could possibly have committed such a sin. Nevertheless, during his lifetime he expressed only love and forgiveness toward me and accepted Ralph as though he were a child of his own.

Yes, Erroll was a loner, so to speak, completely absorbed in his musical creativity. Even during his last days of physical weakness, he failed to admit to his loved ones his needs. My greatest regret is that I did not force myself into his privacy and lend him a helping hand when he needed it most.

BERNIECE

Berniece Garner Franklin was, according to family members, the only Garner who could imitate Erroll and take his place at house socials. Born July 14, 1919, in Pittsburgh, Berniece discusses Erroll and his twin brother, Ernest.

When it came time for Erroll's music lesson, he would always run. He'd run out into the streets with his friends because he didn't want to take his lesson. When we caught up with him and sat him down, he knew it. Miss Bowman would go over it with him, play it for him, and then he'd go right behind her and play it. Just like her! Nothing to it! He wouldn't be reading the notes, but he knew it.

Speaking of myself, I played by ear but not like my brother! Oh, never could I, no way! As a matter of fact, none of us had the touch that Erroll had. But my brother Linton plays beautifully. The first time he was here at my house he played my piano so pretty. Oh, I could hear his music in my ears for a long time after he left. His touch is beautiful. And Erroll's was beautiful, too. But they're two different sounds. Two different styles. Ruthy also plays beautiful piano and organ. She played at my wedding.

Erroll loved Ernest very much. When Ernest comes to my home, I always put that record (*One World Concert*) on of Erroll's, and he'll sit and listen very, very quietly. I remember the last time I played it for him. Whereas he cannot explain things, I know he loves his brother's music. I'll bring him home all the time and I'll say, "You want to hear Erroll?" and he says, "Yes Berniece," and I put the record on, and when it comes to "Misty," his face is so pretty; it looks like it brought tears to his eyes. And he'll just sit there. He can't express himself, you know. I'll say, "You like that? Now, what's the name of that song?" and he says "Misty." He always calls his full name—"That's Erroll Garner's 'Misty'!" But he takes it all in, every bit. He's very, very sensitive. He can sort his feelings out when he hears his brother Erroll.

Ernest is working now at the V.R.C. [Vocational Rehabilitation Center]. He goes to work every day. It's a wonderful organization for retarded adults. They have little boxes of things they assemble or pack. They may pack nails or hardware items. Sometimes they will put different little things together. It's a beautiful place on Forbes Avenue, just opposite Duquesne University here in Pittsburgh.

Ernest lives in a supervised apartment. There are two persons to a room, and it is simply beautiful. They have wonderful supervision. Ernest's manners are perfect, and he responds to everyone. It's just his makeup. He has a wonderful memory for remembering dates and things. He'll say, "Oh, Memorial Day will soon be here." He knows that. He knows people's birthdays. People that we've known for years, I have to stop and rack my brain to remember their birthday.

Erroll played what they call "house socials" years ago. People would crowd into neighbor's houses on a Friday night after school. They'd charge you ten cents to come in, and Erroll would be there playing the piano, and there'd be other people around him listening and having a great time.

We were living over on Deary Street when poor little Erroll broke his leg. They wanted him to play for a social and he still went. He was wearing his little cast. He and I were dancing in the kitchen, and he fell down and broke his leg. He was in the cast for about six months or so 'til it healed, but he kept going. Crutches and all, people just loved to hear him play.

We called Erroll, "Aggie," because he loved to play marbles. He was a terrific marble shooter with his left hand.

ALLEN "LICORICE" CARTER

The Kan-D-Kids

LEE MATTHEWS

Lee A. Matthews was born on May 16, 1902, in St. Louis, Missouri. He was raised and educated in Cleveland and came to Pittsburgh in 1917, where he studied at the George Hyde Radio and Technical Training School. Matthews is the founder of the Kan-D-Kids and along with his first wife, Dorothy (now deceased), holds the honor of organizing the first group of black children to appear over the radio. Today Lee Matthews, in his eighties, is active in numerous civic and fraternal organizations. He is an ordained deacon of the Central Baptist Church in Pittsburgh, teaches Sunday school, sings in the choir and serves as spiritual counselor and advisor to many young men and women in the Pittsburgh community.

My wife and I belonged to community clubs, and we worked together doing community work. Her mother used to get after me for keeping her out late at night, so she told us that we'd better get married. It was a real love affair. She was a wonderful pianist, and that's why I let them use the title "Dorothy Matthews and the Kan-D-Kids." I was the real founder of the Kan-D-Kids, but I let her use it on the air because she was doing the playing.

Louis Abel was "Uncle Henry," and he had a group of white children called the "Radio Rascals" on KQV Radio. I wanted some black kids on the air, so I had the kids come over and rehearse at my house on Monroe Street. I had a hundred or more kids on my list, and I would pick them out and separate them in sections and then grade them. My wife at times played the piano, and we would teach them tap dance and song. I would teach them how to stand before the microphone, so when

I thought I had them ready, which was about a year, I went down and talked to Mr. Abel about getting the kids a spot on the air. After the audition, which was successful, we got a spot on KQV on Saturday morning. [First broadcast was December 12, 1931.]

The name Kan-D-Kids came about because every week at rehearsal I had a big box of candy. I would give them as much candy as they could eat; I just bought plenty of it. One of the kids in the group said to me, "Mr. Matthews, why don't you name us the Candy Kids since we eat so much candy?" I said, "Gee, that's a good idea, but we'll spell it a little different. We'll spell it Kan-D-Kids, which we'll use on the air."

The first place they played was the Roosevelt Theater, in front of an audience. We had to put on three shows; they were so good. Right after that is when they went on the air.

We started to make appearances in local theaters, and back in those days we had quite a few community theaters all around town. I organized a little ten-piece band of the Kan-D-Kids and made appearances in all these little theaters until I had a little trouble with the law about keeping them out late at night. I used to get notes about them from everywhere.

Erroll Garner was one of my little stars. The way I used to teach him is that I would play a record, and his little feet were so short, I had to get him elevated. When we started making these big theater appearances, I had to get one of those small pianos, which was an octave shorter than the regular piano, so that he could play on it. The very first number that Erroll learned how to play was the "Mule Face Blues." He played that whenever we'd make a theater appearance, and oh, he'd bring the house down with the applause.

I later made the change from KQV to WWSW at the Schenley Hotel on Forbes Avenue because I wasn't getting any recognition, and I was doing all the work for them. Also Louis Abel, who was the announcer, made an announcement that I didn't like. He said, "Ladies and gentlemen, we have something new for you this morning. We have a group of pickaninnies." I did not care for that type of name, and I told him off. That's what happened. You should have seen all the letters and how people rallied for the kids. That's when we went to the Schenley Hotel and broadcast over station WWSW.

Lemon Moses, Sr., the father of the "Fudge" and "Taffy" dance team, was lots of inspiration in giving his thoughts and suggestions for keeping the group together. He brought the Moses kids over to my house. They were the beginning. Erroll was one or two kids after the Moses kids.

I was the manager of the Savoy Ballroom, and Harry Hendel was the owner. Hendel also owned the Roosevelt and the Granada. When he got the Savoy Ballroom, we were getting different groups, so we picked up Vern Stern's band, who we used as the house band at the Savoy. We used Vern when we were making a real play. They would back up the Kan-D-Kids.

My wife, Dorothy, accompanied the group only during rehearsal, but when they were on, they were on their own. They were good too. She taught Erroll little riffs on the piano and how to chord a little bit because he didn't know anything about reading. He just went from there and did real good. He could play all the popular songs that were out at that time. I would get a recorder and play the recording at rehearsal with him and let him listen to it. Then my wife would get on the piano and show him how to play it. That little kid would pick up on it right away.

Olive "Tootsie Roll" Douglas was a blues singer, and she, at a real young age, had a heavy voice, but she was very good. Her brother Billy "Carmel" Douglas [Bill Richardson] sang. "Fudge" [Lemon Moses] and "Taffy" [Rudy Moses] were good at tapping. They would get on that tap board on the radio, and everyone was crazy about them. Vern Stern's Band, I remember, used to play "Sweet Sue–Just You" for the Moses Brothers to tap by. Allen "Licorice" Carter was a very good singer. He was one of the stars of the show.

I tried to bring them out with the songs of the day. Although we used to have them do older songs like "St. Louis Blues," too. Neil "Peppermint" Johnson would tap dance and sing. He was a single and would sing and dance at the same time, where "Fudge" and "Taffy" were tap dancers. William "Marshmallow" Bush was a singer. Florence "Bon Bon" Wright was also one of the beginners of the Kan-D-Kids. She passed away. I took her around with me to different places, and she did solo work. I called her my daughter, but we weren't related. When I gave up the Kan-D-Kids, her mother tried to get a bunch of them together. They never got anywhere with it. She called them the "Rhythm Kids."

I always loved children; in fact, I'm still quite a church worker and deacon of my church. I've always been like that, and I wanted to see something like the Kan-D-Kids happen, and it did happen.

BILL "CARMEL" RICHARDSON

Bill "Carmel" Richardson was born in Coraopolis, Pennsylvania, on April 9, 1919. He and his sister, Olive "Tootsie Roll" Douglas, began their singing career in their church. In the early 1930s when the family moved to the East Liberty section of Pittsburgh, they started with the Kan-D-Kids.

My sister and I were the two first originals. Neil "Peppermint" Johnson was the next to join the group. He was the tap dancer. Several other kids joined; then Erroll came in. I don't remember exactly how he got into the group, although I believe it was through Neil Johnson since the

Johnson family lived several doors up the street from Erroll in East
Liberty. Erroll came in as "Gumdrop."

After about six or seven weeks, the group became very, very big. Maybe
we had ten people in it. Erroll was in the original ten. If I'm not mistaken,
Erroll was about the fifth person to join. Mrs. Dorothy Matthews played
the piano; she played our accompaniment. We used to have a half-hour
program every Saturday morning.

We never got any money. We would have rehearsal maybe once or twice
a week and the best thing that I can remember about Erroll is that the
band would be rehearsing a new song, and they would be having one hell
of a time with it, so they would take a break. Then Erroll would sit down
at the piano and just play the thing straight through, no problem. And
these fellows being a lot older than we were, they used to get as mad as
wet hens.

I remember Mrs. [Jane] Alexander was our music and voice teacher at
Westinghouse. I believe Erroll was in the seventh grade. Mrs. Alexander
was very knowledgeable as far as music and voice training were concerned.
Erroll naturally would sing in his growling voice, which she accepted, but
she marveled at his great gift of being able to play anything that he heard.
Later Erroll dropped out of the singing classes and went into the band.
Mr. McVicker, the band leader, told Erroll he would teach him how to
play the tuba. He gave Erroll the tuba and gave him music and tried to
teach him how to read. When Mrs. Alexander heard about this, she really
dressed Mr. McVicker down. "Don't ever try to teach this boy to read
music. He has a gift from God, and by teaching him to read music, you're
going to ruin him."

After the Kan-D-Kids broke up, Erroll continued to play around at
different clubs. Several of the musicians out of Vern Stern's band used
to take him down to the Musician's Club and several other after-hours
places in Pittsburgh, and he would play the piano hour upon hour, never
getting a penny for it. He played at the Berryman and West Club. He
also played at Gus Greenlee's Crawford Grill. Greenlee was the owner
of the Baseball Crawfords, the black team in Pittsburgh. Anyhow, Erroll
played at his place once in a while. He played with several bands for a
while, one was Tommy Enoch, and they played the Savoy Ballroom which
Harry Hendel owned on Centre Avenue.

I got married in 1940, and we were still at the time going to the
Musician's Club, which was the gathering place of most musicians that
came to town. Whoever was at the Savoy would work their way down
to the Musician's Club: Duke Ellington, Cab Calloway, Woody Herman,
you name them.

The Musician's Club was a gathering place for supposedly poor musicians. They had associate members because there weren't enough musicians to keep the place alive. So for a two-dollar card you could became
an associate member. Erroll used to play there quite often. This happened
even when we were in the Kan-D-Kids. We would go to parties, and it

was definite that Erroll would have to play the piano. Everybody imposed on him and he never said no. He loved it!

On the Kan-D-Kids program Erroll was a soloist. He did not accompany us on any of our routines. Once in a while he would accompany Neil [Johnson] because he could play jazz a bit better than Mrs. Matthews. All he had to do was hear it once, and he used to keep the guys in the orchestra boiling mad all the time. He could hear it once, and that was it; he could improvise and blow them out. This really rattled their cages. They'd say, "This young punk thinks he's smart. He can do this real quick, and here we are struggling beating our butts trying to get this out."

LEMON "FUDGE" MOSES

"With a name like Lemon as the first name, then Moses which is Jewish, and being a Catholic and a black in the South, I've gotta know what I'm doing." Lemon "Fudge" Moses was born June 4, 1920, in Savannah, Georgia, and left for Pittsburgh with his father and older sister when he was two years old. As a Kan-D-Kid, under the direction of Lee and Dorothy Matthews, Moses was an emcee and also part of a tap dancing team with his brother Rudy "Taffy" Moses. To complete the family affair, Lena "Lollipop" Moses, their younger sister, participated as a singer and also recited the poem "Colored Lady on the Telephone" by Paul Laurence Dunbar.

When the Kan-D-Kids came on radio station KQV, everyone was quite proud of us. We worked around the neighborhood theaters, concert halls and school auditoriums. We didn't do too much traveling other than around the Pittsburgh area.

Florence Wright was referred to as "Bon Bon." She was a very pretty girl and, of course, the love of all our lives. Erroll was very fond of her in his own way. Neil "Peppermint" Johnson was a tap dancer and Allen Carter was called "Licorice." Cornell Cooper, who never had a candy name was a special singer they used when they wanted to expand the show at the Roosevelt Theater, which was our base theater when we weren't at KQV.

The show would start, "Ladies and gentlemen, the Roosevelt Theater presents . . . The Kan-D-Kids!" The band would start "Happy Days Are Here Again," and we'd all start singing in a choral group, real loud. Then I'd come out in the spotlight, as the emcee, and tell them all about the show. A big buildup, you know. A lot of times I imitated Ted Lewis and all the big emcees. Dick Powell was also one of our local emcees at the

Stanley Theater before he went to Hollywood. Every week Dick Powell had a new show under him. He was the steady emcee at the Warner Brothers Stanley Theater downtown.

The famous Edgar Jefferson was a Kan-D-Kid. We called him "Jelly Bean." He was recently shot on the street, coming out of a night club in Detroit. Edgar developed a style of scat singing, which was out of this world. Edgar got that motivation from watching us on our Kan-D-Kids show. We were the stars compared to him in those days. So he later came on to be a star in his own right. We didn't think Edgar Jefferson had any talent, so we thought. So we'd use him because he was very funny. He had very big teeth, and when he opened his mouth and rolled his eyes and laughed, that would be funny enough. He just had that kind of face. But he eventually became a very suave, sophisticated guy with his scat singing and, of course, became very successful.

In those days when you were a Kan-D-Kid, you were *somebody* in my neighborhood. And any kid who just rubbed shoulders with you, lived in the shadow of that glow. We'd go to school on Monday and the school teacher would say, "Lemon, I heard your show on Saturday," and they'd be very proud of that. That's probably why I was just a dumb student. I was very bright; I knew all the answers. But I was so busy being a funny guy, the teachers got a little tired of my shenanigans.

ALLEN "LICORICE" CARTER

Allen "Licorice" Carter was a close childhood friend of Erroll Garner's and a singer with the Kan-D-Kids. Carter was born September 16, 1921, in Pittsburgh and lived just a couple of doors away from the Garners on Pittsburgh's Fifth Avenue.

As I look back on it, Erroll was a special kind of child, and sometimes that robs you of a normal kind of childhood. It was recognized very early in Erroll's life that he was a genius, and that genius that he had in him naturally took over his young life because he was constantly playing the piano. He didn't have much opportunity to play ball or to go skating or to stand on the street corner. The times that he did, he enjoyed very much. His whole young life was spent demonstrating this ability to people. Everybody wanted to hear him play.

In those years we played a game called mushball. In later years it became softball. We used to play at the Lincoln School playground quite a lot, and Erroll was a left-hander all the way. We called Erroll "Aggie" because he loved to play marbles. The playing marble was called an aggie. He was a terrific marble shooter with his left hand.

During the time we were in Westinghouse, they had a class for non-achievers. Each class had a homeroom where you would report to and then disperse to another classroom. Erroll's homeroom was right next to mine in the music room. This particular day we heard a big commotion, so our room went next door to the non-achievers' home room, and there was Erroll playing all the instruments that were in the band room. He picked up the trumpet and played it; he picked up the tuba and played it; he played the drums, he played the saxophone. We were amazed! Here was a boy that was supposed to be a non-achiever, and yet he was a genius. The interesting thing that came out of that was that they didn't have a piano for him to play, so they let him play tuba in the band. And at all the football games there was more attention on Erroll playing tuba then there was on the football field! He just had a knack. That's when his young boyhood started shifting. Everyone found out that the boy was a tremendous piano player, and from then on his childhood changed because he was in pursuit of making a living. He just started playing in all the clubs.

At that time in Pittsburgh we had what we call "after-hours" clubs, clubs that weren't licensed by the city or the state and didn't have a liquor license, but everybody went to them. Erroll played at all of the after-hours clubs there. We would always meet after he got through playing at the Original Hotdog Stand on Station Street. Folks came from all over the world to eat "Original" hotdogs. We were thirteen or fourteen at the time. If you understand that the authorities were lax and they let these clubs stay open, then you understand that open admission policy was there. No one checked on ages at that time, and when you're bringing in five or ten dollars to help the family, there was usually no problem with that.

Fate Marable was, at that time, one of the leading musicians that came out of St. Louis on the riverboats. We weren't allowed on the riverboats, but when Fate came to town, by that time Erroll had built up quite a following, and it was the thing to do to put out a sign saying that Erroll Garner would be playing the piano. Marable was assured of huge crowds.

In Pittsburgh everybody knew him. Pittsburgh is a small town, not like New York or Baltimore, and everybody knew everybody. Westinghouse was the leading athletic school in the city. Everybody knew about Westinghouse, but Erroll brought more attention to Westinghouse than the football team. When Erroll started swinging, that was it.

Mrs. Lyons was principal at Westinghouse at the time. She was a very heavy, big woman. We always thought she was very mean. She was in charge of this non-achievers' class which they called the "Lyons' Den." She later became an Erroll Garner convert, too.

Erroll didn't have a temper, and he wasn't a good fighter either. I guess that's why he and I got into fights. It was more envy of his ability and my not getting the attention that he was getting. I would just try to dominate him. I was a singer, and he and I used to do a lot of shows together, apart from our involvement in the Kan-D-Kids. We did a show at the Triangle Theater on Frankstown Avenue and at the Elks Club on Lincoln Avenue. Lee Matthews would make the arrangements and chaperone. We weren't paid but we made a lot of money strictly in tips. When you said, "Erroll Garner is going to play here," you could be sure of a full house.

I got into the Kan-D-Kids through Erroll's parents. I was about seven or eight years old when I auditioned for Dorothy Matthews. That was a tremendous experience. It was a very talented group. We really enjoyed the half hour of performing, but as a result of that, we did those other shows.

"King Aggie" [Erroll] made it all worthwhile. We knew we weren't going to have a bad show with him on it. We could experiment with the second-team quarterbacks because when we wanted a show stopper, we always had Erroll. He would always try to make everyone think that he knew keys. He would always say, "What key do you want it in?" We knew that he didn't know keys, so we started humming, and that's where it was.

Musically, little giant, you had no peer.
And it's our loss, that you're leaving us here.
For where you're going is going to be more fun,
As you and the rest of the giants can play Sun to Sun.

LEROY BROWN

The Pittsburghers

CARL McVICKER

Carl McVicker, a native of Pittsburgh, was born on June 25, 1904. As the band director and music teacher at Westinghouse High School, he coached Erroll Garner on the tuba in the high school band. McVicker's list of distinguished graduates is impressive. They include Ahmad Jamal, Billy Strayhorn, Al Aarons, and Grover Mitchell.

It was 1935 or '36 when I had Erroll. He and I were very close, and my wife knew him, and we both treated him like a son. Even after he became well-known, his manager called one day to invite us to one of his club appearances as his guest. We were included when he played at Carnegie Hall [Pittsburgh]. That night I took his mother, who was almost blind, and helped her up the steps to his dressing room. He was always very accessible.

To put it mildly, I was very upset about that article in the *New Yorker* [February 2, 1982] because this fellow who wrote the article called me and quoted me out of context about Erroll being made out to be stupid.

It really disturbed me while I was at Westinghouse that the teachers put anyone down that was a good musician. Some of them did poorly in class because they didn't concentrate on their academic work like they did their music. Erroll didn't do well in his academic work because of his IQ. My point was this: An IQ does not determine or show musical talent like Erroll had. It was very misrepresentative of him because he was able to memorize thousands of tunes, thousands of rhythms and was able to play them perfectly. So that disturbed me that an IQ would make him out like a fool instead of the genius that he was. What I tried to convey in that article was that while he didn't make a big name for himself academically, he was a star musically. He was a star in his field, and while his star didn't twinkle very high in math, he could have cared less.

One particular spring I was rehearsing a group in my band room for what they called the Variety Show. I had my best players from the bands and orchestras in there. It was a select group. My pianist was one that had classical training. We were playing a standard, what they called a commercial arrangement of a pop tune, and the second ending goes into a special chorus, and it was rather intricate; it changed key, modulated, and everything. Every time we came to that place, the pianist would fumble for the notes and lose the beat. He didn't keep the solid 4/4 going. This was going on and on, and we were getting nowhere. Finally, one of the boys said, "Mr. McVicker, let Erroll Garner try it." Erroll was sitting back there just listening. He wasn't in the group because he couldn't read music. I said, "What's the use? He can't read music." The boy said, "Oh, let him try it anyway." I guess the feeling was he couldn't do any worse. I said, "OK, Erroll come on." He jumped right down and sat at the piano. We started at the top, and he came to that place and put a part in there that fitted harmonically and rhythmically with what they were doing, without missing one beat. He had no musical training at all; all he had was God's gift of a tremendous talent. I said, "Erroll, I don't care whether you read or not. You're in my band from now on."

Erroll came to me and said there were people who told him that because of his ability, he should take piano lessons. I said, "Erroll, don't do that. You have God's gift, and if you had to be tied down by reading the notes, that would completely foil what He has given you. Just keep the natural way and develop what you have." I was a confidant of his; he and I were very close.

My band room had three rows of risers which were permanent chairs. I had them taken out later because it just screwed up my seating arrangement. They finally gave up on Erroll in the regular classes because the little son-of-a-gun would cut classes. He would slip into my band room and hide behind that doggone row of seats. Halfway through the class I'd see this little head sticking up. Finally the principal, Clark Kistler, said, "Mr. McVicker, how would you like to have Erroll Garner for half a day at a time? He's not doing anything else, but he loves your subject." So I said, "Sure, it won't bother me." He just wanted to be in music. You almost had to lasso him to get him off the piano stool.

My classes were all elective, and you don't elect something you hate. I had the right to drop anybody that didn't cooperate. You can't do that in English class because that's mandated. But in music class, if a kid didn't show up for a concert or parade, I'd say, "Bring your uniform in on Monday. You're through."

Erroll had a wonderful personality. That's the thing I liked about the kids I had in those days. They were all one to me, not one black and one white. That's the kind of rapport we had. Very friendly, outgoing, and he loved to play. You just couldn't help but like the guy. He had a wonderful devotion to me because I represented to him a whole new outlook on life. He did try to learn to read music when I had him in the beginning band on tuba. He had no problems with beginners' music, the standard "Twinkle, Twinkle, Little Star," and "America." He did "Yankee Doodle" on tuba, but he played piano in the top group and tuba in the band. I didn't go in too deeply because he just laid out on the parts where he had to read the music. I couldn't have him wandering around like a lost sheep, so I had him in beginning band. Later, I put him in the senior band with a marching part.

My experience at Westinghouse was just one long history of satisfaction and pleasure. The kids were wonderful, and having worked with them over the years was a real thrill. I go to these class reunions and they say, "Mr. McVicker we remember what you would say at the beginning of the school year." I would say when I got up to the podium, "I don't care what religion you are, what sex or what race; it's how you blow the horn that counts with me."

BASS McMAHON

William "Bass" McMahon has been part of the Pittsburgh jazz scene for over 50 years. McMahon was born on May 13, 1918, in Birmingham, Alabama, and started playing the cello as a child with the Kan-D-Kidders as part of the children's backup orchestra for the Kan-D-Kids. As a bassist, his earlier associations have been with Tiny Bradshaw and Jimmy Murray. He joined Fletcher Henderson in March, 1942, for two years and in 1945–46 was with Billy Eckstine's short-lived big band. In our interview McMahon discusses the jazz clubs in Pittsburgh's Hill District and his early association with Erroll Garner.

Before the days of the Musician's Club around 1933 or '34, if you went down on the corner of Fullerton and Wylie on a Wednesday or Thursday, different proprietors would come up, and if they saw a musician they knew, they'd ask him if they could get him for a certain club for a certain number of nights. A lot of times the guys would stand there on the corner with a horn under their arm hoping someone would come up and say, "Hey, buddy! Can you play? Can you play that horn?" He might get a job, and it would last for a week or maybe a month.

When they tore up Fullerton and Wylie, that was my main corner. We used to go to Godfrey's Restaurant, which was one of those little eating places along Wylie Avenue. It was popular as far as the musicians were concerned, because they could get a nice meal for a reasonable price. I used to go down to Godfrey's and get a nickel bowl of chili, and that was my meal! We used to take ketchup and hot sauce and fill up the bowl of chili to stretch it. You laugh, but that was serious back then.

The Crawford Grill No. 1 was real popular. All the boxers and baseball players used to come there because the owner, Gus Greenlee, built a field up there on the hill called Greenlee Field. Down off Wylie Avenue across the alley from the Crawford Grill was the Berryman and West. That was like an after-hours club. Erroll would finish an early gig and then go up there and have another gig playing there.

The Musician's Club was on the same side of the street as the Crawford Grill, but it was farther down. It was below Logan Street, and it was a building that was actually owned by Gus Greenlee. Prior to it becoming the Musician's Club, he rented it out to different night club owners, and they called it the Paramount Inn. It had black shows, bands, vocalists and dancers, the whole complement. The union [Local 471] had offices in the Musician's Club. It was actually separate; they just rented space from the Musician's Club.

The Musician's Club was where all the musicians met. You got a chance to see your fellow musicians, and you might get a job because a lot of jobs came in there. It was a place where you could play all night. The band would actually play from 11 o'clock to 3 or 4 o'clock in the morning, and after that anyone who wanted to sit in and play could do so. Most of the big bands that came through Pittsburgh would come down there because they could see musicians they knew or some of their fans that they hadn't seen in a while.

There was a time that if you didn't have a job by Wednesday or Thursday, it was going to be a bad weekend for you. Just by circulating around the Musician's Club and meeting guys, you usually got two or three nights of work. I used to start out on Wednesday night because that was Celebrity Night, and you would have guys like Billy Daniels, who used to be the star at Mercur's Music Bar, and he would bring a certain element of the white people from downtown, and so there was a cross-mixture where you could mix freely.

The territory in Pittsburgh was fragmented. The black union was Musician's Protective Union, Local 471, and the white union was Pittsburgh Musical Society, Local 60. Local 60 had all the choice territories. The black local's territory was very limited. At that time it was limited to the Hill District and part of East Liberty. Even though our territory was restricted, there were white club owners who were forever coming to the "Hill" to different clubs asking for bands and picking out guys. We ended up playing different territories, and it wasn't our territory anyway.

I went over to Cleveland in 1947 to the Tijuana Club with Erroll and his cousin, Monte Hicks, who played drums, and we had Verna White singing. We practiced every day religiously, and we really had it down. The train was late getting into Cleveland, so we rushed to get to the club.

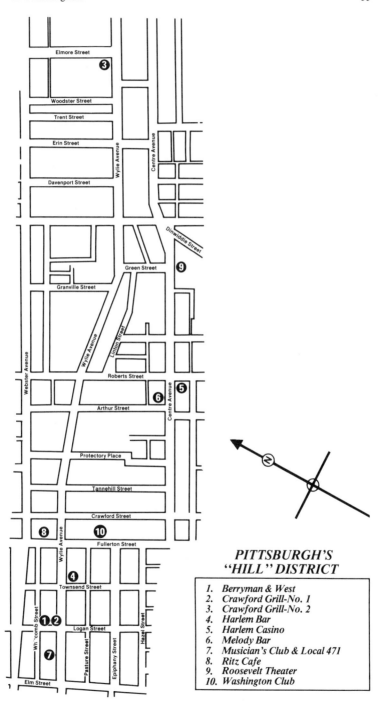

PITTSBURGH'S
"HILL" DISTRICT

1. *Berryman & West*
2. *Crawford Grill-No. 1*
3. *Crawford Grill-No. 2*
4. *Harlem Bar*
5. *Harlem Casino*
6. *Melody Bar*
7. *Musician's Club & Local 471*
8. *Ritz Cafe*
9. *Roosevelt Theater*
10. *Washington Club*

The house band had played a little extra until we got ourselves together. We got up on the bandstand, and everything was fine. Verna didn't sing right away. We played a couple of tunes, so when Verna got up there, we were on a revolving stage so Verna had to step on that. She called the song she wanted to sing, and Erroll started out the introduction just like we rehearsed, but one thing was wrong—he was in a different key! She started into him and was cussing over the microphone. The place was packed. She really cut loose, but the people laughed so that cooled things down a little so we could regroup. We finally got Erroll in the right key, and the audience just applauded. After that, we could do no wrong.

It was also about that time that Erroll got a gig at the Original Hot Dog House in East Liberty. He hired Ben Webster, who was playing for Leroy Brown and his band down at the Hollywood Show Bar. So it was Erroll, Ben Webster, Monte Hicks on drums, and me. It was a Sunday afternoon thing, 4 [o'clock] to 8 [o'clock], something like that, but we got there and Webster didn't show up. We just went on and played. People were kind of disappointed that one of Duke Ellington's famous sidemen didn't show up. He finally came in about two hours late and he played like nothing had happened. You know what? Maybe that was his way of making his entrance. He blowed like hell when he got there!

ART BLAKEY

The time is 1934, the scene is the Ritz Club in Pittsburgh, Blakey's birthplace. "It was run by gangsters," he said jovially. "I had a 16-piece band in there and I played piano—couldn't read a note! Played in about two keys," he laughed. Keys or not, he was able to pull musicians together and get them to do things, as he's been doing ever since.

"Then this big show came in from New York—Tondelayo and Lopez. They had special music written by Raymond Scott. It was called *Powerhouse*. Really impressive stuff—bamp, bomp, be-doodle-lee-doo-doo-de-lee. All written out. Looked like fly shit on those sheets. It scared the hell out of me.

"I'd come in late, you know. The star. Wearing a sweater, big towel around my neck. 'All right brass,' I says, 'run that down.' Now these guys' chops are getting tired. And they got to play that night. But I had to keep stalling so I wouldn't have to play my part. 'All right reeds, play your part.' Finally, Tondelayo comes over and says to me: 'Mr. Blakey, we'd like to hear the piano part.'

" 'That's all right, take your time. You'll hear it, you'll hear it.' Soon she played the business on a record machine. Now I tried to listen to it, to pick it up—but they were playing too damn fast. And it wasn't in my key! All the while, this kid has been sitting in the corner wiping his nose on his sleeve, listening.

"Anyway, I kept fooling around," he went on, "instead of being honest. Brother, that was my first lesson in honesty. I stood in front of the band and told them to go through it one more time, and it was so way out I didn't know what to do, so I hollered: 'You know damn well I can't read!' Finally this little cat in the corner came over and said, 'Mr. Blakey, can I try it?'"

" 'Sure kid. Go ahead,' I told him. So while the kid is mounting up at the piano, I go over and start showing the drummer how to do it. I knew something about the drums, and I wanted to make *somebody* think I knew what the hell I was doing. Well, that piano part came around and the cat not only played it but he added his own dressings. Fantastic. And that kid's name was Erroll Garner.

"Through all this, the owner of the club was sitting in the back with his big .38. Finally, he calls me over and says, 'Look kid, I think you better let that other feller play the piano and you play the drums.' I didn't like the idea too much, but he says to me, 'You want to work here?' 'Sure,' I says, 'I been working here a year and a half. I got a contract with you, ain't I?'

"This gangster looks me in the eye and says, 'You ain't got a contract if you're playing piano.' " That's how Art Blakey came to play the drums full time, and he's been wailing ever since.

Thomas Tolnay, "Art Blakey's Jazz Message," *down beat,* March 18, 1971, p. 15. Reprinted by permission of *down beat* magazine.

RAY BROWN

Ray Brown noted in our interview that his switching from piano to bass was very simple: "In junior high school they had two bass players and three basses, so there was an extra bass to be had. They had 26 piano players and 1 piano." Brown was born in Pittsburgh on October 13, 1926. He has worked with Dizzy Gillespie, Oscar Peterson, Bud Powell, Ben Webster, and countless other jazz greats. Brown is currently managing the Modern Jazz Quartet.

I was working with Henry Foster's five-piece band in Pittsburgh when I was in high school. Foster was an alto saxophone player, who had a day job and used to play gigs on the weekends. He thought that if we joined the Elks, we would all have an inside track to play at all the Elks' lodges. We always had a job on the weekends doing these gigs. Even after Erroll was working downtown at Mercur's Music Bar, he'd come out and jam with us. It was nice. He would stop by the Elks on Lincoln Avenue out by his house and come in and sit in with us. Walt Harper [Pittsburgh pianist and band leader] first introduced me to Erroll. We played hookey one day, and we went over to Erroll's house to jam, which I didn't do very often. I was afraid to, but I got away with it a few times.

The Musician's Club in Pittsburgh was a very famous place. In those days whenever there was a visiting band in town at night, they would come up and jam. The local musicians would try to put themselves against the visiting musicians. We always would stick Erroll Garner with somebody. "Honey Boy" Minor wasn't that great a drummer, but he could do more tricks than anybody else thought. He could throw his sticks in a corner and catch them and throw them, build a pyramid with 25 sticks, he could do all kinds of stuff. He wasn't a great musician, but he was a great entertainer. "Honey Boy" worked at the Celebrity Club on Centre Avenue and Elmore Street. Erroll would go to the Celebrity Club mostly to see "Honey Boy" do his show. He was known all over the country. We're not talking about tricks with Erroll. He was just a good piano player, a natural piano player.

Guys with Erroll Garner's talent don't have any fear of keys because they don't relate to keys; they relate to sounds. You don't know how difficult that is until you study music, and the more you study the more difficult F sharp gets.

The first thing you have to say is that Erroll Garner played with such feeling that you feel like paying him to play with him. This guy plays in such a groove that it's a pleasure to play with him; there was nothing difficult about it. He was difficult to follow because he wouldn't do the same thing twice, but it didn't matter because the groove was good. I don't think of difficulties when I think of Erroll Garner, just one happy time.

Erroll's music is something that cannot be explained. It is something that belongs to the ear. You're dealing with the grain of the heart. This doesn't take anything away from Peterson or Powell. Milt Jackson calls Erroll the "fun man." Somebody else gave him the name, but I first heard it from him. They called him the "fun master." That's the answer!

BILLY ECKSTINE

Billy Eckstine was born in Pittsburgh on July 8, 1914. He started his big band in 1944, with Erroll's brother Linton joining him a few years later as the featured pianist. Although he is best known as a vocalist, Eckstine is also a trombonist. In this interview he recalls the little kid in the neighborhood who played boogie-woogie piano.

The Garner family was right in the same neighborhood. We all grew up in East Liberty. Linton and I were of the same age, and we were in a band in Pittsburgh called Laird Payne and his Pied Pipers. Linton, at that time, was playing trumpet; later he switched to piano.

Erroll used to play boogie-woogie piano when he was a kid—a little baby, you know. He'd sit up and he'd play boogie-woogie. The rest of the Garner family were all very accomplished, learned musicians, and Erroll came along and never could read anything, and he made all the bread in the family. Linton is a fine arranger and a great pianist. When I started my band, my big band, Linton played piano. He also played with Timmie Rogers.

I jammed with Erroll many times 'cause see there used to be a place called Kay's Community House in the neighborhood, and we used to go down there, and different kids used to rehearse dancing and things like that. And they'd get Erroll to play for them.

He was playing in Pittsburgh later at a place called Mercur's Music Bar. Well, he was playing in there and the thing about Erroll—like we'd work in certain little clubs around there and somebody would ask you to sing, and you'd get up, and if Erroll hadn't heard the song, he'd just say to you, "Start singin'" and he'd play it right behind because, by not knowing how to read, he depended on his ear. For whatever the song was, he could follow you, whatever the key, anything. Keys didn't mean anything because he couldn't read.

Then he came to 52nd Street, and from then on it was just an association back and forth. We'd always be around each other because a lot of the Pittsburgh guys would gravitate towards each other. Roy Eldridge and others were from Pittsburgh, and we'd all had our little "smoketown twists" there.

All along, Erroll was original. He never sounded like anybody. And in those times, the great pianists like Art Tatum, Earl "Fatha" Hines, with whom I played, and Fats Waller . . . Erroll could play like any of them. Tatum, oh, oh, he loved him! Art Tatum loved Erroll! But see Erroll could play like anybody. He depended on his ears, so whatever that sound was, he could do it.

Art Tatum was the most appreciative person you ever met in your life as far as piano players were concerned . . . . You'd see Art and there would be nine piano players behind him following him around wherever he went. You know, he loved 'em. He'd sit up all night and play for you. I guess that's why he was a genius. Earl Hines was the same way. That's the way they learned. That's the way you learned your instrument, by constantly playing it, you know. Erroll would just sit and hum and play.

Erroll grunted when he was in Pittsburgh. Erroll's grunting was a rhythmic thing. It wasn't a case of his humming what he was playing, like Slam Stewart hums what he's playing. See Erroll would go de-da-do-dum—you know. It was a rhythmic grunt that he did.

JIMMY PUPA

Jimmy Pupa was born in Beaver Falls, Pennsylvania, on December 5, 1917. Pupa lived a few houses away from Erroll on Pittsburgh's Deary Street and attended Westinghouse High School. Although he was a few years older than Garner they played together in the Westinghouse "Bulldogs" Marching Band, under the direction of Carl McVicker. Jimmy Pupa later went on to play trumpet with Paul Whiteman, Benny Goodman, Tommy Dorsey, Charlie Barnett, and Red Nichols.

We were called the Barrel House Four. We got barrels and cut them in half to make music stands out of them. Erroll was the piano player, I was the trumpet player, Nick DeLuca was the tenor sax player, and Benny Nozilo was the drummer. We played all over Pittsburgh for several years.

We went out to a place they called the Blue Moon in Pittsburgh. We really had a hell of a band. We auditioned and asked for only $3 a night. That would be only $12 a night for all four of us. The couple that owned the place said it was too much money. Look at all the talent they let go down the drain.

We played the Flower Garden which was a little road-house tavern. We also played the Hazelwood Literary Club. This was a place in the old days where they'd open a little peep hole in the door and ask, "Who is it?" You'd say, "Pete," and they'd say, "Okay, come on in." We played up there at least four nights a week for all the Pittsburgh elite. Each one of us got $15 week in those days. They really didn't know at the time what potential was up on that bandstand. Since Erroll couldn't read music, we used to teach him his keys. He was a genius! He memorized the whole show.

We used to play dances for churches and schools from 9 P.M. to 1 A.M. Even though the neighborhood was tough, we had no problems. You see, we were three Italian boys and like the Irish, they kick ass. Nick DeLuca, who later became my brother-in-law, was a big fellow about 5'11" and 225 pounds. Benny Nozilo was tall and thin and I'm short, about 5'4". Nick took care of all of the heavy work.

The neighborhood was pretty well integrated. We had Blacks, Jews, Italians, and Irish. Wylie Avenue, which they call the Hill District, was all Black. A white fellow, in those days, could walk through, and no one would bother him. Today it's a different story.

The last time I saw Erroll was back in 1968, out in California. He went out of his mind when he saw me. He stopped playing and jumped right off the piano bench. He knew my wife well, too. Back in Pittsburgh he used to come over to my wife's house and play the piano. During the depression days, he would just sit there and play, and everyone would listen. You just can't predict your future. Ben Nozilo went into the plumbing business, and the other three of us stayed in the music business. That's the story of the Barrel House Four.

BEN NOZILO

Ben Nozilo was born in Pittsburgh on November 12, 1917. As the drummer for the Barrel House Four, he recalls his fond memories and good times with Erroll Garner.

Erroll got me to start playing drums. He used to come over to my house and play piano. The guys in the neighborhood were starting a little orchestra and Erroll said, "Why don't you play drums?" He was going to borrow a set of drums from a friend of his; they were homemade things. He got the set of drums, and right away I caught on, and liked it, so I went on to study the drums. Nick DeLuca, Erroll, Jimmy Pupa, and myself played a long time together, Jimmy Pupa on trumpet and Nick DeLuca on tenor sax. We played the many clubs of Pittsburgh. It was around 1935, and we played for four or five years.

We played Charlie Ray's, a club in East Liberty, the Flower Garden Club on Babcock Boulevard. In fact, they fired us because we played too much. We had an upright piano there, and at that time Billy May was playing with Barron Elliott [1937-38]. Billy May played beautiful trumpet. He played Westview Park, and our place was on the way to Westview Park. He was union and we were non-union. He'd get in back of the piano so nobody could see him, and he'd blow his horn with Erroll. We'd start playing and we'd never stop. The proprietor said, "People aren't sitting down to drink. You guys play too much."

Erroll learned from us, and we learned a hell of a lot from him. We got the beat from him. He always kept that left hand going. We used to go into piano stores in town, and we'd have Erroll sit down and play. The guy would always chase us out, but we'd go back in. He said, "You guys can't play around here," but once he stopped getting mad at us and listened, he just went crazy. He said, "I never heard anything like that in my life."

The Andrews Sisters were in town about 1936 or '37 at the Stanley Theater, downtown. I think Gene Krupa was in the band. We snuck Erroll up backstage after the show and had him play a rehearsal piano. The Andrews Sisters just came off the stage. When they heard Erroll they called the other guys in the band to listen. Their mouths were hanging open. They said they never heard anything like that in their life.

We played with Art Farrar's big band in Charleston, West Virginia. He had an eighteen-piece band, a good band. They wouldn't let Erroll in the restaurant. He had to stay outside. I remember we had to bring him sandwiches because he had to sit in the car. Everyone else was white, and he was the only black boy, and they didn't go for that too much down there. In fact, when he walked in the restaurant, the restaurant owner said, "Who's that nigger belong to?" The leader just said he belongs to me, and he's staying. It looked pretty tense, so they asked him to sit out in the car. Erroll was a young kid at the time. It didn't really bother him.

I got interested in music through Erroll. Jimmy Pupa's brother is a fine drummer and a teacher. Right away I went to him, and I studied about three or four years with him. That's all I wanted to do; I would practice 'til my mother kicked me out of the house.

We were playing Charlie Ray's Club on the second floor. The owner was something. He'd ask, "How do you like the band?" If you said you didn't, the band went down the steps. We were his boys up on the balcony. Another drummer had the job before me, and he hired Nick, Erroll and Jimmy. After the first night they fired the drummer; they said he couldn't play. They got rid of him and they called me. We played there a heck of a long time. Then one night I got up to come to work, and Erroll wasn't there. Billy Strayhorn came in, another fine piano player. Billy had taken Erroll's place because Erroll went to New York.

I remember Benny Goodman came to town in 1936 or '37. The band had white suits on. The next day we went out and bought white suits, which back then were $5 or $6. I made music stands out of barrels; we cut them in half. We used those as music stands, and we were trying to imitate Benny Goodman. We bought these suits at Kay's Clothing Store, "Home of Snappy Clothes." Benny Goodman played at the Stanley Theater. We were playing the Flower Garden at the time.

By now we are playing pretty good, so Erroll said, "I got us a spot on KQV radio." So we carry our instruments up to the studio, and the guy comes up to us and says, "Are you Erroll Garner?" He says, "Yeah." The guy turns to us and says, "I want to see all you amateurs over here." I said, "Erroll, what is this?" Erroll said to the guy, "What do you mean amateurs?" He said, "Yeah, this is amateur hour; that's what I was going to put you on." Erroll said, "Man, we're big time; we ain't no amateurs." We walked out. We really raised hell with Erroll.

The four of us were on a street corner on New Year's Eve because we couldn't get a job. We wanted too much money. Here we were standing on the corner, sucking our thumbs, and other guys that didn't play as well as us had jobs. That's the way it was in Pittsburgh. I called them "corn-cobs." Erroll said, "There's something wrong when we're not working New Year's Eve." I always said if Erroll had stayed in Pittsburgh, he never would have been recognized. A lot of good musicians came out of Pittsburgh. They are taken for granted.

He sure had some gift; I don't know when I'm ever going to hear another

piano player like him. They're not around anymore. I was just driving
to a job the other day and thinking, while I heard one of his records, and
thought, "Why did he have to go?"

LEROY BROWN

*Leroy Brown was born in Waycross, Georgia, December 16, 1910. At the
age of thirteen, with no previous musical training, Brown picked up the E
flat clarinet. Later he went on to the alto and soprano saxophone. Leroy
explained, "It was a gift from God! I played by ear and made good money."
At the age of seventeen, he took lessons for three or four years from Mr.
Maurice in Pittsburgh. This was enough to give him the fundamentals. In
1937 he formed his first combo with young Erroll Garner as his featured
pianist. In 1962 Brown had throat surgery which ended his horn blowing.
A few years later he took off again on the electric bass. Based in Pittsburgh
for over two decades, the Leroy Brown Orchestra is still considered to be
one of the best in the history of Pittsburgh's big bands.*

My first major job was with the Leroy Bradley Orchestra in 1932. We
were playing primarily at the Club Mirador through 1932 and 1933. I
worked with Bradley for five years and spent six months in 1934 at the
Cotton Club in Cincinnati, Ohio. When the orchestra came back to
Pittsburgh, we went to the Harlem Casino. In 1935 we went back to the
Cotton Club and stayed there for three months.

Summertime, 1937, came and the Harlem Casino closed. All of us
disbanded, and a few of us started our own group called "Honeyboy and
the Buzzin' Bees." James "Honey Boy" Minor was on drums, I was on
alto sax, Ellsworth Liggett on bass, and Herman Aimery on piano. We
played together at the Harlem Bar on Wylie Avenue the entire summer
of 1937. We were doing so well that when the Harlem Casino re-opened
in the fall of 1937, we decided not to rejoin the Bradley Band. We stayed
together for about a year until the summer of 1938. "Honey Boy" Minor
started his second group called the "Buzzin' Bees," and I started my own
little group called The Leroy Brown Combo.

I first knew of Erroll Garner from his participation with the Kan-D-
Kids. Having kept abreast of his activities, I went to his home in East
Liberty to ask him if he would like to join the group I was forming. Having
heard about me and after discussing it with his parents, he decided to join.
He was about sixteen at that time. The combo consisted of myself on
alto sax and clarinet, Erroll on the piano, Dave Page on trumpet and Leroy
Jones on drums. Jones also did the vocals.

Co 1689
Horace

NOV., 25, 1941.

Musicians' Protective Union
Local 471, A. F. of M.

H. J. Jackson, Pres.   S. S. Melendez, Sec.
11 Federal St., Pgh., Pa.   7408 Susquehanna St. Pgh
Tel. FA 6323   Tel. C H 6696

At 7800

Ext 23

Musicians Roster,

Including all names of active and inactive
for the information of members.
To ascertain the status of any musician
consult the secretary.

Name	Address	Tel.	Inst.
Abbua Betute	2937 Wylie Ave. Pgh.		Singer, Piano
Alexander Gerald			
Luzern Berman	2525 Elba St. Pgh., Pa.		Piano
Anderson John H.	6 Granville St. "		Trpt.
Anderson Edward			
Angel La George	6632 Deary St. "		Drms.
Angel Theodore			Violin
Austin Benjamin	4562 Sylvan Ave."		Vibraharp-Piano
Austin Gordon			Tuba-Trb.
Austin Theodore			Drms.
Aubuern O.			
Avery Fred	2269 Bedford Ave. Pgh.		Alto Sax
Banks Raley			Trb.
Banks William	125 Clarissa St. "		Piano
Banks Davis	2020 Preble Ave "		Vibres; Drms.
Barth Arthur			
Baker Theodore			Trpt.
Baldwin James	7455 1/2 Fletcher St. Pgh		Drms.
Bates Orville			
Beatty James	1927 Wylie Ave. Pgh, Pa.		Trpt.
Bell William	415 Michigan St. "	Ev. 5047	Sax, Cler.
Bell Wilson			Trpt.
Biggs William	32 Elmore St. "	Co. 4723	Sax.
Blakey Arthur	639 Junilla St. "		Piano, Drms.
Blakely George			Trb.
Brown Carl	2939 Webster Ave."		Piano
Brown Bernard	c/o Cotton Club, Cinn., O.		Alto-Sax.
Brown Fred	317 Dinwiddie St.		Tenor Sax, Clar.
Brown Leroy	2209 Center Ave. Pgh Pa.	Co 3444	Sax.
Brown William			
Brown Matthew			
Bradley Leroy	186 Devilliers St. "		Piano
Brooks Alice	1842 Rose St. "		Piano
Buchanan Walter	7324 Monticello St."		Viol
Burford William	5640 Eva St. "	Mo. 3835	Drms.
Burley Stafford	241 6th Ave. Homes'td., Pa.		Piano
Burch Thedrus	2338 Wylie Ave., Pgh., Pa.		
Brassfield Dr. P. C.			Trpt.
Catlin Mrs. Charlotte E.			Piano
Carton James A.	1535 Garfield Ave. "		Drms.
Clyde Carter			Violin
Charles Jr., Howard	547 Heisel St. Homs'td, Pa.		Trpt.
Clinton William	1306 W. Hills boro St. Pgh.	Wa. 1014	Sax, Clar.
Clifort Henry	3432 Webster Ave. "	Ma. 4096	Drms.

Page 2
Musicians Roster Cont.

November 25, 1941.

Name	Address	Tel.	Inst.
Cooper Larry			Piano
Covington Frank			Drms.
Crosby Don			
Crawford Holland (Raymond)	c/o Cotton Club, Cinn. O.		Sax, Clar
Davis Eugene	1520 Clark St., Pgh. Pa.		Drms.
Dixon Council	4500 Sylvah Ave. "		Trpt.
Drake Thomas			
Dunn Nathaniel	2418 Wylie Ave. "		Viol
Enoch Thomas			Trpt.
Ferrell Oliver			
Fitch Floyd E.	2813 White St. "	MA 7180	Trpt.
Fisher Claude E	2823 Webster Ave. "	MA 6134	Sax
Floyd George			Vocalist
Gambrell Seth	5817 1/2 Broad St. Pgh.		Piano
*Garner Earl			Piano
Garner Linton	c/o Cotton Club Cinn. O.		Guitar
Garrison Byron	2518 Upton St. Pgh., Pa.	Banjo,Sax, Clar.
Gibson Harry			Piano
Gibson Purnell	6907 Mt. Vernon St., Pgh. Pa.		Sax, Clar.
Gloster Stoney	804 Shawnee St. "		Trpt.
Gould Frederick C.	200 Frederick Ave. Sewickley, Pa.		Drms.
Goore Hamlet E.			Sax, Clar
Greene George			
Greene Elmer	820 Adelaide St., Pgh., Pa. Sch. 0204	Sax, Clar.
Greene Willa	7245 Campania St. "		Piano
Gray Richard (Mickey)	14 Chestnut St. "		Piano
Gross Lee			Alto Sax.
Harris Eddie	2179 Bloomer Way "	Trpt.	
Harris Cozy	1300 Hazel St. "		Accordion
Harris Walter	2323 Wylie Ave..c/o Cotton Club Cinn O	Trb.
Harper Ernest	713 Clarissa St. Pgh., Pa.		Piano
Hampton R. C.	c/o Cotton Club, Cinn, O.		Sax.
Hammond William			Trpt.
Hazel Maron	2012 Webster Ave. Pgh., Pa.		
Hawkins Rod			Trpt.
Hall Maylon			Sax. Clar
Heard Archie			Drms.
Hitchcock William			Trb, Tuba, Bar.
Hill Herman	2437 Webster Ave. "		Bar. Trb.
Hodges William			Sax
Howell George	2617 Webster Ave. "		Viol
Hunt Elmer	1212 Filson St. "		Drms.
Hunter Guy	3071 Center Ave. "		Alto Sax.
Hudson James	12 Miller St. Rankin, Pa.		Trpt.
Humphreis Frank	232 Carrington St. Pgh., Pa. Ce. 3156	Trpt.
Humphreis Hildred	232 Carrington St. " Ce. 3156	Sax.
Ingram Coldon			Guitar
Jackson Henry J.	11 Federal St. " FA 6323	Tuba
Jenkins Eugene			Alto Sax.
Jordan James	248 Alpine Ave. "		Sax.
Johnson Albert	2521 Center Ave. "		Viol
Johnson Samuel	1314 Clark St. "		Piano
Jones Margarett Ann	1105 Warlo St. "		Piano
Jones Leroy	2933 Wylie Ave. " Sch. 1724	Drms.
Lavotty James			Drms,Trpt.

I had signed a contract for a lengthy engagement at the Melody Bar on Centre Avenue and Arthur Street in the summer of 1938 to go into effect in two weeks, which meant that we had to start rehearsing and get measured up for suits. This, by the way, was Erroll's first suit, and was he proud! The suits were double-breasted blue shadow stripes with white shirts, maroon neckties, and maroon handkerchiefs for the coat pocket.

On opening night we were received very warmly as a group, and each member of the group got a chance to do his own thing. This little group, The Leroy Brown Combo, turned out to be one of the greatest in Pittsburgh and could have held its own anywhere.

The Melody Bar was a small place, but many big names like Charlie Shavers, Count Basie, and Lionel Hampton would stop in to hear Erroll play. No pianist would dare sit in with us while Erroll was there. He just played so much piano they might be embarrassed.

We were at the Melody Bar about twelve months until the summer of 1939. In between we played many single engagements until we started at the Harlem Casino in early 1940. On the single engagements we augmented the band to include Joe Westray on guitar, George Howell on bass, and Joe Porter on trombone. We played all the big hotels in Pittsburgh, like the William Penn and the Fort Pitt.

When we started at the Harlem Casino, we had to augment the band to eleven pieces. We added Guy Hunter on alto sax, Byron Garrison, tenor sax, Andrew Penn, trombone, William Mosby, trumpet. At the Harlem Casino, James "Honey Boy" Minor replaced Leroy Jones on drums. We played six nights a week at the Harlem Casino, and our shows were broadcast over radio station KDKA, and the broadcasts could be heard all over the country.

After our show all of us would go down to the Musician's Club. We used to jam until the early hours of the morning. Often the bandstand got crowded. I remember Erroll would be at the piano, and one of the older guys would whisper to Erroll to go to E natural and A natural. The guys who couldn't play in those tougher keys would have to get off the bandstand.

In April, 1940, our band closed the Harlem Casino. The owner, Gus Greenlee, had financial problems and couldn't keep up his payments. The last night at the Casino all the guys in the band bought whiskey and food and charged it because we knew we wouldn't get all our money. We stuck with Gus because he was a great guy, and he was always good to us.

In June of 1940 we added Henry "Henpie" Gerald on tenor sax, so we were up to twelve pieces. "Honey Boy" Minor left shortly thereafter to form another version of the "Buzzin' Bees." William "Diz" Smalls replaced "Honey Boy," and Maron "Boonie" Hazel replaced William Mosby on trumpet. The singers in the band were Joe Westray, George Howell, and Joe Porter. Billy Eckstine even sang with us at one time. He was in charge of the show at the Harlem Bar.

Every once in awhile we would have "The Battle of the Swing Bands."

One night we had the battle with Tommy Enoch's and Vern Stern's bands at the Savoy Ballroom. We killed them! When it was all over, everyone would vote, and we always came out on top. The musicians in my orchestra were the best in Pittsburgh.

Erroll left our band and went to New York in late 1941. He really didn't want to go, but we made him go because this would be a great opportunity for him. He went as an accompanist to a woman singer. Erroll became the show! He played so much piano that she got rid of him. After a while he came back to Pittsburgh and played as a single at the Red Door and Mercur's Music Bar. Then he went to New York in 1944 and shortly thereafter joined Slam Stewart.

The scales for the white and colored unions were different. However, if our orchestra played the same place a white band would play, we would get the same price they would get. Otherwise our scales were less because we were playing the colored places. They couldn't afford to pay more. In those days our pay was $25 to $30 per man per week or whatever the scale was. There were three scales A, B. and C. A scale paid about $85 per week for a sideman and $150 for the leader.

There have been articles that said Erroll was refused membership in the union. This was not true because I have the Musician's Roster for the Local 471 American Federation of Musicians, dated November 25, 1941. I was a board member. We made exceptions. The average person had to take a test because if he wasn't up to a standard, it would be a bad reflection on the union. In Erroll's case we made allowances. A man with that much talent, it didn't matter if he could read because he could play anything.

Three things about Erroll: He was great, he always smoked, and he was always late.

ALYCE BROOKS

Mercur's Music Bar and Paul's "Edgewaters"

1942–1944

ANNE BAKER

Anne Baker was born in Homestead, Pennsylvania, and grew up just outside of Pittsburgh in Washington, Pennsylvania. She started her singing career as a child in local plays for school and church. When she was a singer at Mercur's Music Bar, Erroll Garner provided the accompaniment. She later toured with the Louis Armstrong Orchestra.

Erroll was playing solo for a few months at a little place called the Red Door, next to Mercur's Music Bar, in downtown Pittsburgh. The owner of the Red Door was very fond of Erroll. He didn't care if anyone came in there or not. He just wanted him in there for his own pleasure.

I had never heard of Erroll and people kept telling me that I should go next door to hear this fellow play the piano. One night I decided to check him out. I went out the back door of Mercur's Music Bar into the front door of this little place called the Red Door. This owner had the piano painted white with glitter on it. It was a little, dark, dimly lit place. As I walked in, Erroll Garner was playing "Stormy Weather." My God, I never heard it played like that before or since. I enjoyed him so much. I was almost late to make my own appearance at Mercur's—I had never heard anything like it!

I had a three-week contract with an option, so I told them I would take the option if they got Erroll to come over and play piano for me. Lew and Al Mercur agreed. So with Erroll on the piano, I sang the blues 'til the early morning hours. We were just marvelous together. No rehearsals, no nothing, I just started to sing, and he just played. He was just wonderful. Lew Mercur used to be with Alice Gerber. His brother, Al, used to be with me. They kind of sponsored us since everyone had their favorites. The Mercur Brothers were just marvelous. I used to sing rhythm and blues ballads, just everything with Erroll. He was just that type of person. I sang some of everything with Erroll because when we were on, we could do what we wanted to do. We had 20 minutes on and half an hour off. Erroll would have about 10 minutes of solo, and then Dale Harkness and Alice Gerber played. The better class of Pittsburgh came to Mercur's. There was no room for dancing, just seating along the wall and little tables for two. It was an intimate place with the stage located in the back of the bar.

REID JAYNES

Musically self taught, Reid Jaynes played duo piano with Erroll Garner at Mercur's Music Bar in the spring of 1944. Born October 15, 1918, in Pittsburgh, Jaynes is still a well-known Pittsburgh attraction.

I had just left a group at the William Penn Hotel in the spring of 1944. I had been approached several times by the people at Mercur's Music Bar because it was strictly a music bar. They had twin pianos behind the bar. Erroll and another man by the name of Dale Harkness, who had some health problems, worked there. Lew and Al Mercur, the owners of Mercur's Music Bar, finally decided to switch to a two-piano format and keep it like a continuous thing. The schedules ran so that each one of us had a solo stint, and then our schedules blended so that we had a duo for about 20 or 25 minutes. It was really much fun because Erroll was a great stylist, and we both had perfect pitch, so there wasn't any problem with calling out keys. When I'd hear a tune, I could tell what key it was in. We'd bounce things back and forth; one guy would call the tune, the other could call the key. People thought we had these big productions worked out, but they were strictly off the top of our heads. He was a very flexible man to work with. He had a habit of laying back with his right hand, playing behind the beat, and if you listen to his right hand, it could get confusing like he was dragging the time, but he never did. We had much fun. We worked together about five months, and then he scratched up some money and went to 52nd Street in New York.

I first met Erroll on a Monday night at Mercur's Music Bar. I saw him the Saturday before. He was working some spots on "The Hill," and he wasn't making very much money at the time. Finally, he came downtown to Mercur's. Mercur's was a classy place, and it was jammed all the time. It was like the place I play now, the Grand Concourse, down on Station Square. He was at Mercur's for about four out of the seven months that I was there. We would go a half an hour on and an hour off, and our schedules overlapped, so we had two pianos going. It was continuous music, so they hired a third pianist by the name of "Teeney" Trent [Sylvester Trent]. He wasn't, to be kind, a swift player, but the way the schedules ran, we each had to have a two-piano stint with him. The way the schedule worked, I was first. So I asked Teeney, "What do you want to play?" and Teeney said, "Anything, man, anything." I picked "Night and Day." You can't get more plain vanilla than "Night and Day." He hit that first chord and my ears folded. Erroll was sitting at the bar laughing, and so I said, "Don't worry, buddy, it's your turn next!" The beautiful thing about Erroll was that he was a complete rhythm section in himself. He could fill in with that left hand beautifully.

Most bass players have to watch Erroll's left hand. Just like me, he liked to play in goofy keys such as E and A and F sharp. Some guys want to strangle you when you get the keys like that. Sharp keys turned him on, so the bass player had to stand right behind him and watch his left hand like a hawk.

ALYCE BROOKS

Alyce Brooks played piano with Erroll Garner at Mercur's Music Bar in downtown Pittsburgh in mid-1943. A native of Pittsburgh, Alyce Brooks was a featured pianist at the famous Three Deuces in Chicago before returning to Mercur's.

Wherever there was a piano, I always tried to be there. There was a little after-hours club across from the Crawford Grill on Wylie Avenue called the Berryman and West. I had never heard of Erroll at the time, but when he walked in someone said, "That's Erroll Garner! He plays terrific." He sat down at the piano and started to play like he had four hands. It was unbelievable! I decided to sit down beside him on the stool and said, "Let's play a duet." I like to do this kind of thing. We played together, and that's how I met Erroll. After that I made it a point to go to this place because I knew eventually he would come in.

I was playing at different clubs here in Pittsburgh, mostly downtown, and I was booked into Chicago. It was after I came back from Chicago that I went into Mercur's Music Bar, and Erroll, I understand, had been there and had left. He went to New York and then later came back to Mercur's. So I was on the bill with Erroll. I was there for about 10 or 11 months and I left again and went back to Chicago.

Mercur's was a place that was always open. It was also open for Erroll because when we left, there was better money in a place like New York. There still is, let's face it. Everybody that played piano at Mercur's had a little of Erroll rubbed off on them. They sat there and they played. You could hear Erroll all over the place from 5 o'clock in the afternoon until closing because it was just one of those things.

Three things about Erroll: He was great, he always smoked, and he was always late. I went to work about 5 o'clock, and I worked a forty-five-minute set. Then Erroll came in and usually had a cigarette in hand and since no cigarettes were allowed on the stand, he would give me the cigarette to put out for him. I would put the cigarette out for him, and Erroll and I would play together the last fifteen minutes of my set. I would go off with "I May Be Wrong (But I Think You're Wonderful)," which I dedicated to him. Then Erroll played for a half an hour, then someone would join him. When I came back on, he would play a jazz version of "Alice Blue Gown," which he dedicated to me. It's kind of hard to remember just how the schedule went, but it was set so that everybody knew just what they were doing.

I had come to work as usual about 5 P.M., and Mr. Mercur had said to me that he was tired of Erroll coming in late. Erroll was great enough to be late, but Mr. Mercur had become very upset with him because when Erroll was late, I had to play over until he got there. So he said to me, "I'm not going to put up with it anymore," and he said, "When Erroll walks in tonight, I'm firing him; this is his last night." Of course, I had no comment because he was the boss, and he was talking to me. Erroll finally walked in, and he gets in just in time to run up on the stand. But what happened was the customers started stopping him at the door. The piano stand was at the other end of the room. They are greeting Erroll, stopping him and telling him how glad they are to see him. They are shaking his hand, and it's taking him twice as long to get up to the stand. By the time he got down to the end of the stand, Mr. Mercur just turned and walked away and never said one word to Erroll.

Erroll would take you on a trip and he loved it. He'd start out playing a tune in one key, and you played together and without any modulation he'd go right into another key, and you just went right on with him. Sometimes he would jump from an A flat to a B natural, and if the song is difficult, you just let him go. He would just sit there at the piano and laugh.

JEWEL WALTERS

Jewel Walters managed Paul's "Edgewaters" Restaurant in Wanamassa, New Jersey, near the Jersey shore resort city of Asbury Park. After owner Paul O'Brien died in October, 1943, she continued to manage Paul's until her retirement in 1970. She was partly responsible for bringing Erroll Garner in during the summers of 1942 and 1944.

It was in 1942, when Paul was still alive, that Charlie Stewart, our house organist, met Erroll Garner at an after-hours tavern on Springwood Avenue in Asbury Park. Erroll was on vacation in Asbury Park when Charlie came back to Paul and said, "I heard a piano player last night that was out of this world." Paul said to him, "Bring him over." In a couple of days, instead of going back to Pittsburgh, he stayed all summer at Paul's.

Paul ran a very strict place, and everybody had to be dressed to go in. There were a lot of shore places that were more casual, but we were back from the shore in a place called Wanamassa in Ocean Township, New Jersey. All of our help wore tuxedoes, and we had two pianos and an organ going all the time. We always had three or four piano players and an organist. They alternated since some of them didn't want to work every night.

Bob Brittingham worked opposite Erroll during the summer of 1942. All of the boys used to love to go to his home because his family had a tennis court. They were above average people, a lovely family. A couple of ladies would say to me, "I always knew where my son was after school. He'd be over at Bob Brittingham's playing tennis." He was a wonderful man.

We had two pianos and an organ on the first floor behind the bar and a separate piano at the upstairs bar for the overflow crowd. Paul had the place hooked up so that you could be upstairs and hear the music downstairs. He had speakers all over the house.

When Erroll, Bob Brittingham, and Charlie Stewart were together in 1942, one would come in at 7 o'clock and start playing piano or organ, the other would come in twenty minutes later, then the third would join in. There was constant music from 7 P.M. until our 3 o'clock closing.

Putney Dandridge and Charlie Stewart were playing during the summer of 1944 with Erroll. Putney was close with Bill "Bojangles" Robinson, who often came in to see him. Putney had been with Bill for years when they were traveling at the Palace Theater in New York. Putney was a drinker and Bill said, "He would be playing the piano, and all of a sudden his head would go down and he'd be falling asleep. I'd tap him on the shoulder, and he'd never miss a note. He kept right on going." Putney was a really great entertainer, but he had lung trouble and died in New York in 1946 after he left Paul's.

Asbury Park Press   June 17, 1944

DAVE KELNER

*Dave Kelner was born on January 28, 1914, in Philadelphia. As a pianist
and organist at Paul's "Edgewaters" in Asbury Park, New Jersey, for over
25 years, Kelner's early associations have been with Xavier Cugat, Sammy
Kaye, and Glenn Miller's Army Air Force Band.*

I came to Paul's when Charlie Stewart was playing with Erroll Garner
around September of 1944. I remember my boss saying that when Erroll
Garner was there, they were standing around the bar three or four deep.
It was a big circular bar with music in the middle of the bar and people
sitting around at tables having dinner. Charlie Stewart was there more or
less all year 'round, and Erroll came in just for the summer months.

Paul O'Brien was nuts for jazz. He was a famous character around the
Asbury Park area. He ran that place even during prohibition days and
was known for having police dogs strolling the grounds. It was fabulous
and an historical place built like a colonial southern mansion. It was
originally a home which he converted into a supper club. Paul went to
Harlem to get these pianists to come down. He had a place on the grounds
for all of them to stay.

The money was not that great, but he gave them dinners and a lot to
drink. Money was not the object in those days. Playing to be seen and
heard was important.

Paul's "Edgewaters" was a place where people from Newark and Jersey
City, cities close to New York, would gather. They used to come down
for the summer and rent homes and go to the beach.

Timme Rosenkrantz used to come in and sit at the bar to hear the talent,
looking for people to record. He took Erroll back to New York [September
1944] and this was the beginning of Erroll Garner's fortune.

Erroll had this habit of looking at someone in the audience and playing to him. If he saw somebody gettin' knocked out, he would just devote all that shit to that one person. That was his thing.

RALPH BASS

The Street—52nd Street 1944-1949

TEDDY REIG

Teddy Reig was born in Harlem on November 23, 1918. He managed Erroll Garner in the late 1940s and recorded him on Reig's own 3 Deuces label.

I met Erroll when he came out of Pittsburgh. Erroll was the one piano player that I have to say had more heart than anybody I ever knew. Erroll, when he came to New York, would come into the Three Deuces, which was Art Tatum's stronghold. Erroll was the only piano player that would go there with a trio and didn't give a damn about Tatum. From there he rolled. All of these piano fans who came in to hear Tatum fell in love with Erroll.

Erroll was looking for a job then. He was the only guy that they could get that would sit and go opposite Tatum with no fear. Everybody would get whitewashed. How could a piano player go in there against Tatum? We were in Chicago. Erroll, George Shearing, and I stopped in to see Art Tatum at the Three Deuces. Tatum had a trick that he would always use when there was a piano player in the house. Whoever the piano player was, he would call their name and do something absolutely fantastic. Most of the time they would lean over and fall off their chair. If you're gonna talk about piano, Tatum is God and Erroll is a good, old time, hustlin' piano player. He used to work the after-hour joints. He knew all the tunes, and knew them well. Nothing bothered him. He was unbelievable in that respect.

I was an A&R man for Savoy when Erroll had his famous version of "Laura." When we got to the WOR Studios at 1440 Broadway, we had to walk up to the eighteenth floor. The elevators were on strike. As hungry as we were for money, up the stairs we went. Before we started up the stairs somebody suggested about getting a jug, so we got some brandy. We would go up a few stairs and sit down and sip, and by the time we got upstairs in the building, we were crocked out of our nut. John Levy Jr. and a kid by the name of George DeHart, the drummer, were with us. But what makes it interesting is that a masterpiece like "Laura" came out of all that!

Erroll recorded for me. I'd set up the deal with the record company. We set up a record company on a label called 3 Deuces, and I brought Erroll back from California and put him in the Three Deuces [New York] with Kai Winding. These jerky people didn't pay no money. They'd give you $350 for two weeks. If you picked the option up for two more, you'd get $400, two more, you'd get $450. For eight weeks $500, and you bottom out, but you'd have an option to renew at $500 a week.

I gave him a record contract to sweeten it up, and then we started to roll. The first eight weeks were fantastic. Then another club was born on Broadway, which later became Birdland, and he didn't do quite that well on the second time around. What irked the people at the Three Deuces was that the money was a little higher because they started paying him $350, and they were upset about giving him $500 from the beginning. I said, "Well, if you're not happy, I'll give you your money back." So they said, "O.K." And at the end of these two weeks, the Birdland people were in a crack. I also had Erroll as a main attraction at the Apollo Theater. So I went over and got the Birdland people and I said, "Hey! Give me $1500 for Erroll, and I'll bring him in here," 'cause they didn't have an attraction. Nobody was selling because the big club was Bop City on 49th and Broadway.

JOHN COLLINS

Guitarist John Collins was born in Montgomery, Alabama, on September 20, 1912. As part of the Slam Stewart Quartet at the Three Deuces, Collins recalls his impressions of the Garner style. Still active today, Collins recently played in the 1983 Monterey Jazz Festival and had an extensive tour of Europe. His mother, Georgia Gorham, was a demonstration pianist for W. C. Handy.

I met Erroll in Pittsburgh around 1941 when I was with Fletcher Henderson. He was playing with a band at a club called the Ritz on the top of Webster Avenue. The one thing that fascinated me was he had this handkerchief, and while he was playing, he could stop and wipe his face and not hardly miss a bar. At the same time Jimmy Blanton was in town playing with Fate Marable on the riverboat from St. Louis to Pittsburgh.

I saw them there at the same time; this is why I remember this so vividly.

The next time I picked up with Erroll was when I got out of the Army in January of 1946. I was with Erroll, Slam Stewart, and Doc West at the Three Deuces. After a very short time, Erroll left and Billy Taylor joined us. Later Billy left, and we went to Europe and Erroll joined us again in Paris [May 1948].

Erroll had just won the Pianist of the Year Award. He was not aware of it, and when we got to Paris, they had this big reception waiting for him at the airport. We thought it was for Coleman Hawkins because it was his first time back since before the war. This was like his homecoming, but actually they were there to see Erroll. When Erroll found out it was for him, he was flabbergasted.

All these people were there: Nicole Barclay was there with her husband Eddie Barclay [Barclay Records]. They were trying to record him. Erroll and I had a suite together, and she and her husband were up there every day trying to persuade Erroll to record, but he wouldn't.

Erroll was a stylist; he could make you laugh or he could make you cry. He was something else! He had his own style; he could put you in many moods. He was entirely different which I admired. He didn't go toward be-bop or any one style; he was the way he felt.

NORMA SHEPHERD

Norma Shepherd was born in Washington, D.C., and came from a musical family. As a pianist and singer, she worked opposite Erroll Garner at Tondelayo's in late 1944.

I was working on the East Side across Fifth Avenue, at a club called La Vie Parisienne. It was one of those posh supper clubs. On my break, when the show was over, I'd go across to Tondelayo's because I knew her. I think she had been sending messages to me too, that she would like for me to come to work for her. Eventually, I got around to working at Tondelayo's.

This is where I first saw and heard Erroll. Man, I had never heard anything like that before. I was a great fan of Art Tatum. Even though Erroll was playing for a male singer, I was so carried away by his playing, his style, his energy, and everything about him that I couldn't wait for my breaks to get over so I could hear him. Then we became friendly, and I began to tell people about Erroll who were in the business and who had better connections than I. I finally persuaded Billy Moore and Roger Segure (who arranged for all the top bands in that period, like Charlie Barnet, Count Basie and Benny Goodman) to come down here and hear

THE NEW JAZZ FOUNDATION

PRESENTS

An Evening of Modern Music

STARRING

COLEMAN HAWKINS
DIZZY GILLESPIE

AND HIS QUINTET WITH

CHARLEY PARKER   MAX ROACH
CURLEY RUSSELL   AL HAIG

BIG SID CATLETT
PEARL BAILEY
BUCK CLAYTON
DON BYAS

AND INTRODUCING

ERROLL GARNER

AND HIS TRIO

AL HALL   HAROLD WEST

Friday Evening, June 22nd, 1945, 8:15 P.M.

AT

TOWN HALL

113-123 WEST 43rd STREET, NEW YORK CITY

Concert Direction: MONTE KAY, Room 3606, 16 Court Street, Brooklyn, N. Y.
Narration: SYMPHONY SID

TICKETS: $3.00 — $2.40 — $1.80 — $1.20
Advance Sale at: RAINBOW MUSIC SHOP, 102 West 125th Street, New York City
COMMODORE MUSIC SHOP, 136 East 42nd Street, New York City
G & R RECORD SHOP, 162 Prince Street, Newark, N. J.
RECORD HAVEN, 716 Rockaway Avenue, Brooklyn, N. Y.; 106-42 New York Blvd., Jamaica, N. Y.
TOWN HALL BOX OFFICE (Beginning June 15th)
Address Mail Orders to SYMPHONY SID, WHOM, 29 West 57th Street, New York 19, N. Y.

this guy Erroll Garner. I was with them when they heard Erroll. They were just carried away! Erroll was still playing for this mediocre singer; maybe he was a good singer, but I don't know because Erroll's playing overshadowed him. Anytime he finished singing, we would applaud like crazy because we wanted Erroll to play some more. It looked like most of his playing was behind the singer, which we thought was just a crime. He'd keep on singing 'cause he thought we were applauding for him, and we were really applauding for Erroll.

The guys got so interested in him that they started to speak to Bob Thiele, who is now a big producer and husband of Teresa Brewer. At that time he had a small label called Signature Records. They persuaded him to go and hear Erroll Garner, and he recorded him. As far as I know, this was one of the first recordings that Erroll made. Although I don't go around beating my chest about it, I feel I was responsible for it in a way. Maybe in Erroll's past somewhere he recorded for someone else. I don't know; I do know that he recorded for Bob Thiele.

Erroll and I had gotten in the habit of "hanging out." We used to go to the White Rose Bar on Sixth Avenue because it was the only place we could afford, plus it was the hangout for all the musicians and show people. There was nothing personal between me and Erroll—we just enjoyed hanging out. I worked opposite Erroll at Tondelayo's as a singer and pianist. I was also a standup singer on WMCA radio for two years.

I lived in a neighborhood where most of the top musicians lived, such as Oscar Pettiford, Jimmy Anderson, and Erroll. All of them lived in the same apartment house across the street from me. At times we would meet on the corner by the subway and rap. I could go on naming names of some of the biggest names who lived in that neighborhood, but I'll just say I was in such good company and proud of it.

SLAM STEWART

Leroy "Slam" Stewart was born in Englewood, New Jersey, on September 21, 1914. For over fifty years, he has distinguished himself as one of the most unique bass stylists in the world. His association with Erroll Garner started in late 1944 when Stewart discovered Garner at Tondelayo's, a small club at the east end of 52nd Street. On May 20, 1984, Stewart received an honorary Doctor of Music degree from the State University of New York at Binghamton.

I was with the Art Tatum Trio at the Three Deuces. Tiny Grimes was with us at that time, and also on guitar was John Collins. And, of course, if I remember correctly, Art Tatum became ill and he had to return home. He had to go out West to his home and left me in charge of the activities of the trio at the Three Deuces. In fact, the owners of the Three Deuces,

Sammy Kaye and Irving Alexander, approached me with the idea of
getting another piano player to take Tatum's place.

I had heard at that time about Erroll Garner. In fact, I had met him
not long before then. He was working on "The Street" not too far from
the Three Deuces at a place called Tondelayo's. We used to meet every
once in a while for a few drinks at the White Rose Bar, around the corner
on Sixth Avenue.

I immediately went down to Tondelayo's and had a talk with Erroll
and told him what was happening with us at the Three Deuces. Art Tatum
had to leave, and they left me in charge of the trio. In spite of the fact
that he had this job at Tondelayo's, I was wondering if he could try it
out anyway—play a set at Tondelayo's, and in between, if he had the
strength, run down and play with me and the trio at the Three Deuces.
We approached his boss, John Levy, about the idea, and he said it was
all right with him. So, automatically, it happened that way.

There were quite a few musicians working right next door at the Famous
Door and across the street at the Onyx Club. As far as the piano players
were concerned, I was very interested in Erroll Garner's work. He really
knocked me out with what he did on that piano. So I thought he would
be the proper one to fill in for Art Tatum. I'm very glad it happened that
way. You should have seen him, though. He would start off at Tondelayo's
where he was working—start off his first set—and after he finished, we
adjusted the time where it worked out all right. He'd run down and play
a set with us, go on back and play another set at his place. It was back
and forth, back and forth. It was wonderful! And he loved it! This lasted
about a week, and his boss let him come to the Deuces full time.

Erroll didn't stay with me too long, if I remember correctly, because
after Erroll left, I remember I did a couple of other things. I left the Three
Deuces, and Erroll went his way, and I went mine, and I came back to
the Three Deuces with Billy Taylor as pianist.

During the time Erroll was with me, I was invited to join Benny Goodman down at a theater on Sixth Avenue, not too far from the Three
Deuces. I was invited by Benny Goodman to fill in for his brother, Harry,
the bass player. He became ill, and Benny Goodman asked me to come
in and fill in on the show. They were doing a show called *Seven Lively
Arts*. Now, there's another situation where I did the show, and John
Collins or Tiny Grimes was on guitar, and Erroll was on piano. The two
of them would do the show until I finished my show, and then I ran up
to the Three Deuces and joined them again.

Erroll left the group to go out to the West Coast [January 1946]. He
had some other obligations, I think, that he had to go through. I started
looking for another pianist and wound up with Billy Taylor. Somehow,
if I'm not mistaken, Billy was working on and off near 52nd Street. I finally
gave him a call and, fortunately, I got a hold of him, and he worked with
the trio. I also had a drummer by the name of Doc West with me, so
we had a quartet.

I met Timme Rosenkrantz when I was in the Three Deuces. He used to come by, and that's about the first time that I met Timme, and I think he had an office or at least if it wasn't an office, he lived right across the street from the Three Deuces. I think he lived over the Onyx Club. That's the first time I ever met him. A lot of the musicians used to have sessions in his apartment. That's when I became acquainted with Timme.

They were paying our group fairly well at the Three Deuces. The fellas were making about $250 per week; I made $300. That was good money in those days. I had a nice apartment and a car, too. It wasn't bad.

Erroll never did grunt with me. It might be possible that before he left, he may have started grunting. He may have gotten the idea from me when I sang along with my bass fiddle.

I think Erroll was fairly versed in the notes and what have you. He had to be. No doubt he had to have a good ear, too, because he'd pick up something in seconds just by listening to the music. He'd hear a whole chorus of something and come out with it as though he were reading it. To me it didn't make any difference whether he could read or not. He was so good.

I had planned to have him join me for a concert here in Binghamton [New York]. As a matter of fact, I thought about him at times and said, "Why not get Erroll Garner to come play?" I used to do quite a few programs for this museum and even up at the State University I used to bring in a lot of the cats which included Dizzy Gillespie, Clark Terry, and a lot of musicians. So, I was thinking of bringing Erroll to do a thing at Roberson Center, and before I got around to it, he had passed away. We finally did the concert in his honor in March, 1978.

I was working with Art Tatum at the Black Hawk nightclub, which is where I first met my wife, Claire. In fact, Erroll was out there at the same time. He just came by that particular night to say "Hello." That was one of the few times out there that I had met him. Somehow Claire was doing a single in San Francisco. She happened to be on the same night. I happened to meet her. You know how it is when you get together with different musicians, especially when they come by to see you. That was the first time I met my wife, which was through Erroll.

CLAIRE STEWART

While a night club singer and pianist, Claire Stewart met Erroll Garner in upstate New York during the late 1940s. Although this association started after Garner's 52nd Street days, it is only fitting that Claire's recollections follow those of her husband, Slam. Garner introduced the two at a club in California in the early 1950s. Almost twenty years later they were married.

I met Erroll in Utica, New York. Then, after Erroll left Slam, he started touring around doing solo piano, and I went into a club in Utica, and Erroll was playing at Jerry Marsh's. Jerry Marsh's was on one street and then there was Tommy Joy's, which was a tiny little club that's infamous. If anyone's from the Utica area, they all know who Tommy Joy was, this tiny little club that had six tables with hams and cheeses hanging over the bar. If anyone came in the door, you literally had to stand in the telephone booth to let them by. You could go up the alley from Jerry Marsh's through Tommy Joy's little place, if you could get through, and up the street about four doors where I was playing. Now I've set the scene for it.

We had heard about Erroll. He always called himself "Earl" not "Erroll," so I've always pronounced it that way because that's the way he used to say it. So, one night I had a night off, and I decided I would go down to Jerry's and hear this man play, and so I went in, and here is this little man sitting at the piano in the most impossible clothes I had ever seen in my life, weaving back and forth from one end of the piano stool to the other. I remember when I went in, I'm a gal alone, probably about 1946. There's a two-chair table near the piano, so I thought that would be a good place for me to sit. As I'm walking in, I'm watching these horrible clothes and this weaving back and forth, so I sat with my back to him, because it was really bad, great big plaid, a big wide tie with daisies on it, and this weaving back and forth. I loved the sound, but I just literally could not watch this scene. So I stayed while he played the set, and then I left.

I found out that Erroll got through at 1 A.M., and I got through at midnight. So, a couple of more times, I went down after I got through and listened to him, and I liked very much what I heard. One night, he comes up through the alley to see me. He had an intermission. Then night after night, he would run up though the alley, through Tommy Joy's, up the street, and every time he came in, he would ask me to play "Clair de lune," which he immediately dubbed me because my name is Claire. He was trying so hard to learn it. So, one night he asked me, "Can I ask you a question? How come, when you come in to see me, you always sit with your back to me?" I said, "I can't stand those horrible clothes!" He said, "What's wrong with my clothes?" I said, "Number one, you're much too little to be wearing big plaids. Number two, you don't wear a daisy tie with a plaid suit. Then there is the weaving back and forth. It's like watching a tennis match. I get dizzy. I love what I hear, but I don't like what I see." He didn't say anything. He was not sitting on a telephone book either; he was playing a lot of left-hand stride piano. He was doing the late left hand bit too, but he was playing some nice left-hand piano.

A couple of weeks later, he called me on my gig. He said, "Could you come down when you get through work tonight?" I said, "Why, what's up?" "Nothing, just make sure you come down when you get through playing." So I went down, and here he sits straight as an arrow, no weaving, in a gorgeous new gray suit with a very subdued tie, and he looked wonderful. So, I went in and sat down, and for the first time I faced him. He would start to weave, and then he'd get that little elfin grin and then he'd stop and catch himself. Martha Glaser always said, "He became such a dapper dresser, and I think it must be your fault."

I worked at the Lake George Hotel, and during 1950 or '51 he was there. He would call me and I would call him, but we never did see each other because I couldn't get any time off. I didn't see him, but I did talk to him. And then, a place in Albany opened called the Jazz Casino down on Green Street, which was the worst street in the city. It was so bad that you could not walk to work. You couldn't walk down the street. It had the doorman with the gold braid, the whole smear. You had to take a cab. God help you if you drove your car and left it. It was a horrible scene. They had a lot of jazz people and about every two weeks, they changed the show. One night I went in. I was intermission pianist in this whole deal, and the boss said, "Erroll Garner's coming in next week." I said, "Fine." That Monday night when I went to work, I was sitting at the end of the bar, and Erroll came in to go work his first night. The boss just raved. "Oh, I would like you to meet Erroll Garner," he said, and Erroll just stood there grinning, you know, that elfin grin of his, and he came over and put his arms around me and kissed me and said, " 'Clair de lune,' what are you doing here?" So, we worked those two weeks together. He was marvelous. That was the first time I'd ever been on the same bill with him, that we actually worked together.

Erroll wasn't driving at that time. He didn't have a car. One day he called me and said let's go for a ride. We took my car and went out in the country and stopped at a little inn to have lunch. They had an upright piano, so after lunch he went over and he started to play, and I played, and he played. We were there about four or five hours, and we had all these farmers who were around listening to us. We were out in the country. We were laughing about this whole scene with all these farmers with the straw hats and the jeans. Let's put it where it's at. So Erroll said, "Teach me 'Lullaby in Rhythm.' " I said, "Okay." Then he said, "Teach me 'A Hundred Years from Today.' " And it's funny because in the same kind of scene prior to that, Pete Johnson had taught me "A Hundred Years from Today." Now Erroll wants to know this song.

I worked several places in Albany. I would go out on the road periodically, but I worked an awful lot of clubs in Albany, and I had my pick of anything I wanted because I was the only woman pianist there. Pianist, singer—I was the only one. I had no competition. So, I could work . . . I was like Slam at the Three Deuces. I could pick my spot and stay there as long as I wanted. I went to work at Yazzy's, and guess who walked in? Mr. Garner walked in! The boss, who was a big fan of his, just about fell over, you know, when Erroll walked in. "Get him to play! Get him to play!" So I asked Erroll, "How about playing a tune?" He said, "Yeah, if you sing one." So I get up to the piano and I gave the tune—I can't remember what it was—he's giving me this lost look and says, "Where do I start?" I said, "A flat," and he says, "Show me A flat!" So I reached over and just laid my hands on the keys without actually playing and he nodded at me. He started right in and played the whole thing in A flat. It was marvelous.

He'd come in to do his show, and he used to ask me . . . he'd say, "Do you think, if I got a simple version of 'Clair de lune,' you could teach me to read it?" I said, "Erroll, it would take you two years to learn how to read, and I couldn't stand you for two years, and you couldn't stand me for two years, so why don't you just forget it!"

In 1954 I went to California and I saw Erroll was at the Black Hawk. I thought well, I'll go down and see him. So I went down, and while I was there, Mr. Slam Stewart came in to see Erroll. He was on tour with Art Tatum and Stan Kenton, and I guess Slam had played the show, and then after the show he came in to see Erroll. So that's where we met. Erroll introduced us. Isn't that nice? That started the whole beautiful mess!

There was a pianist, Connie Berry, and her husband (I can't remember her husband's name 'cause that was her stage name). He played guitar, and they had a pretty good size apartment over in the urban development, which was then a new thing in Utica. It became a hangout for musicians. You always knew that you could go there. The musicians would pay her for food, and she was a good cook. In fact, one night, I remember being there, and half the Stan Kenton band came in. It was a place where it was an in thing to know, and you didn't tell anybody 'cause only musicians went. Well, Erroll and I would go over there, and sometimes Bobby Henderson would go with us.

Gene Rodgers was playing in Utica. In fact, Gene was at Tommy Joy's—he used to break the strings every night, so it was absolutely dangerous to stand anywhere near the piano or sit around one of those six tables 'cause the strings would fly. So the four of us would usually get together 'cause we were all around this area, you know, where we could go to each other's club. We would go over to Connie's house, and she had an upright piano, and every night she played "Clair de lune." She was driving me crazy. That's on top of the club. In fact, my boss got a little upset about Erroll's asking me to play "Clair de lune" 'cause it was hardly nightclub stuff. He was not too happy about Erroll running in asking me to do this. So Erroll kind of cooled it in the club 'cause I had told him, "Look, the boss is getting a little salty about your coming in bugging me with this tune." So then we got to go over to Connie's, and the only reason he wanted me to go over there was so I'd play "Clair de lune." In the meantime, he's listening like mad trying to pick it all up.

Well the first night, the boss wanted to introduce him to me at the Jazz Casino. And, the next thing I hear is Erroll saying, "Did you hear the record I cut for you?" I said, "Are you talking about 'Impressions'?" because it was "Clair de lune," the first part of it. His next statement was,

"I got the first part right, but I really screwed up the rest of it, didn't I?" And I said, "Well, Erroll, Debussy wishes he'd written it like that, let's put it that way." It's very nice and I like it. As a matter of fact, it was on the jukebox in the bar. There was another song on that same jukebox. It was the one that Oscar Peterson cut for him, "Tribute to Garner." When anybody would play it, he would almost fly through the ceiling. He didn't like that at all. He thought Peterson was imitating him and I said, "Not true, Erroll. As a matter of fact, he plays you better than you play you." That's the way I talked to him, always. And that really did it. He didn't say any more.

I went down one night to see Erroll and Gene Wright, who was an old friend. I had worked with him at the Jazz Casino, and they were both at Cafe Society. Erroll asked me to play, so I played a couple and then somehow or other all the musicians wound up at a long table while we were seated there. Erroll knew that I had played for Billie Holiday about three months before, and would you believe she walked in? When she saw the musicians, she came over to our table. Erroll, who was seated right by me, said to Billie, "Now, you remember Claire. She played for you three months ago in Albany at the Casino?" and Billie said, "I've never been in that city in my life!" and Erroll's kicking me under the table. I said, "Shut up. I am not going to say anything to embarrass her." I mean, I wasn't about to argue with her, but it was a matter of record that she'd been there.

After the party broke up and the guys were through playing, Erroll asked Gene and I to come up to his pad. And I think it was around 127th Street and Amsterdam, somewhere in that section, and we went into his pad. He had some records there, probably a dozen, and they were all David Rose-type straight-on things, which he told us that night that that's the type of record from which he learned all his tunes. To learn a new song, he would play these albums. And they were so straight, I mean, there was no jazz—they were straight. So he would really get the melodic line and learn the tunes and the changes. But he had never told me that before. That's the way he learned a tune because he couldn't read.

Before "Misty" was published, he taught the song to me, and I used to play it a lot. People would say, "What is that?" I knew it wasn't published and I'd say, "Well, it's a song that Erroll Garner wrote." But it didn't have the name "Misty." In fact, I don't think it had a name. It was just something that he had, but he did teach it to me, and I think that he and I were probably the only two playing it for a long time. Then when it was finally recorded, he got a name to it, and I was so proud of him. I want to tell you, that song haunts Slam and I. For instance, we stopped at a little country inn on a trip. We walk in and guess what's playing? It'll come on at times you least expect it. We'll walk in places you don't expect to hear it, and here it comes. It almost haunts us—that one song!

RALPH BASS

Ralph Bass produced and recorded Erroll Garner on his own Portrait label, which was named exclusively for Garner. Bass was born in the Bronx, New York, on May 1, 1911, and attended Colgate University. He worked for Paul Reiner at Black and White Records from 1941 to 1944 and started his own Bop label in 1944. From 1948 to 1951, he was with Herman Lubinsky of Savoy Records. Bass has also been associated with King Records and, until a few years ago, the Chicago office of Chess Records.

I had heard about Erroll because he was working over at a place called the Toddle House in Culver City [California]. It was kind of a girly thing, you know, one of them dives, and Erroll played intermission piano. It was no jazz joint. So I went to see him to make a deal on a recording session. I thought I'd put Erroll on the Bop label which was a jazz label, but then thought I'd put him on a special label, because Bop was referring to "BeBop" at the time. I made a special label for Erroll called Portrait.

I went down there, and Erroll impressed me so much, I brought him to the studio. We went into the studio, and I didn't know how to work with Erroll. I'd never worked with him before, but I found out that everything had to be one take with him. He'd go and do something—bang! I let him go, and I didn't try and tell him nothing. I let him be himself completely, and I did four sides with him.

Meanwhile, I was expecting the record to come out on my Portrait label and that Herman Lubinsky would handle it. Herman had advanced me the bread to do the session because I was going to do Garner. So, next thing I know, Jack Rosen, who was pressing for Herman Lubinsky, had a pressing plant right around the corner from Radio Recorders, which was the best studio in Los Angeles. He called me one day and said, "Ralph, regarding the Erroll Garner thing," and I said, "Did you get the master yet?" He said, "No." So later he called me up and said, "Hey! This is coming out on Savoy," and I said, "What?" I called up Herman Lubinsky and I said, "Hey now, motherfucker, what're you tryin' to do? This is supposed to be on our label called Portrait." Lubinsky said, "Well, Portrait had no money; I paid for the date." And I said, "Dirty motherfucker." So, meanwhile, the record comes out. What the hell could I do? I couldn't do anything. I had no papers. Erroll comes over to see me and he's hollerin' "Goddamn motherfucker, why didn't you tell me this was comin' out on Savoy?" I said, "Erroll, I didn't know. I swear I didn't know." He never believed me. I said, "Well, why are you so against Savoy?" So he said, "I don't wanna record for that motherfucker Lubinsky—no kinda way."

I found out later that there was an elevator strike in New York, and the studio that Lubinsky was gonna record at was on the eighteenth floor.

He made Erroll walk up those goddamned eighteen flights, and he never forgot it. He said to Lubinsky, "I'll never record for you again." I didn't know it. I was the dope, see. That's why Herman was pushing me to record it on my label called Portrait. He would agree to anything, knowing that if he said Savoy, Erroll would've never, ever recorded.

Now then almost nine months go by, and Erroll calls me. He said, "Can I see ya?" I said, "Yeah, come on over." He came up and we talked, and he said, "Hey, I want you to make another record of me." I didn't say anything because he had said to me, "No way would I ever record for Savoy." Herman, meanwhile, hired me as the A&R man. So Erroll said "Now, everybody knows about Erroll Garner playing the piano. But nobody has ever heard him sing." And I said okay—I know damned well what he was looking for. I'd heard that he had an accident and that he wrecked his car, and he needed some bread. So, I think I gave him $500, and in those days that was a lot of bread. He said, "OK." I went over to Cliff McDonald's studio. Cliff was an old friend of mine, and it was during the record ban. I think it was in '45, '46, whatever it was—'46, somewhere around there. Cliff set up the original Mutual Broadcasting System. He had a studio on Cahuenga Boulevard in Hollywood right near Santa Monica, between Santa Monica Boulevard and Hollywood Boulevard. I took Erroll over there, and he always had a great bass player, and he always had a fuck blues drummer. This time he came in with John Simmons, the bass player. Knowing Erroll now, I said to myself "I'm gonna fuck this motherfuckin' Savoy. I'm gonna pull some sides out." I told Erroll how many sides that I was gonna do. I was gonna do six sides, and I was gonna keep two for myself, you dig, and give four to Herman.

I had a fifth of booze (I forget what kind of booze) and some beer in a six-pack. Erroll liked to drink the beer; he used to drink the booze and the beer for a chaser. So Cliff said, "I'm ready to start." I said to Cliff, "Man, you go about your business. I'll call you when I need you." Knowing Erroll as a producer, I had to psyche him out like I did with other artists. I've always tried to play up their strengths and play down their weaknesses to get the most of the artist in the studio. Erroll sat down and started talkin'. He starts jivin' and shit, talkin' about bullshit, ya know, just shit! They were drinking, and then finally when I saw Erroll move over to the piano, I knew he was ready. I called Cliff and I said, "OK, Cliff, we're ready now. Now look, don't say nothing." I said, "Erroll, at 2:15 I'll give you the sign—start gettin' the fuck out." In other words, in those days we had no more than three minutes a side. Preferably 2:30 or 2:45. We didn't make any LP's or albums. We made singles. Erroll looked at my sign, and I would turn my arm in a circle, meaning get the fuck out at 2:15. Erroll had a habit of looking at someone in the audience and playing to him. If he saw somebody gettin' knocked out, he would just devote all that shit to that one person. That was his thing. So, I was the one! I just looked like I was being knocked out, but I don't normally carry on like that, nodding my head—shakin' it like I'm going crazy. But

I did it; I overdid it. At 2:15 he played his ass off. At 2:15 I kinda circled my arm and told him to get the fuck out.

The thing about Erroll was that he played songs that he played every night, things he knows. That wasn't the greatest. You had to give Erroll something he could compose. I came to the studio with a whole bunch of standard songs, and I'd say, "How about this?" and he'd say, "Okay" and I knew he'd played it. So I said, "I don't dig that." And I said, "Let's try this one." He said, "How does the channel go? Hum it to me." Then I knew he'd never played it before—that's the one I wanted. Ya dig? Both of them, "Penthouse Serenade" and "Stairway to the Stars."

Now, we get the vocal ["That's My Baby"] over with; he sounded worse than Pops [Louis Armstrong]. I knew that was just a come-on to him. We never put the vocal out. Then one day he calls me up and he says, "Hey, I want that record back, when I did the singing. Don't put it out." I said, "I can't do that. You got paid for it, man. I can't control that shit no more. Why don't you want to put it out?" He said, "Well, if that becomes a hit, then I'm going to have to sing, and I don't wanna sing, I just wanna play piano." I said, "I'll tell you what, give me one more session. You give me a session and I'll give you that side back." So I called Herman up and Herman made a deal. That's why I did the extra side. I did one of the sides on that date and the other side on the other date.

Erroll posing for his first-grade picture, Lincoln School, Pittsburgh, probably 1927. (Martha Murray)

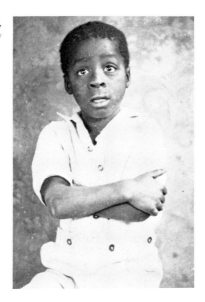

Erroll's father, Ernest, being honored on his retirement from Westinghouse, Pittsburgh, 1949. (Martha Murray)

A

Above, Erroll's mother, Estella, outside their home at 6914 Fifth Avenue, Pittsburgh, late 1940s. (Martha Murray) *Left, below,* looking down North St. Clair Street from where Erroll's birthplace previously stood. Today, the site is a small playground. (J. Doran) *Below, right,* the Garner Family moved to this house (second from left) on Rowan Avenue in September, 1925. Erroll had his first piano lesson here from Miss Madge Bowman. (J. Doran)

Leroy Brown's Orchestra, Harlem Casino, probably April 1940. From left to right: Andrew Penn (tb), Leroy Brown (as), Joe Porter (tb), Byron Garrison (ts), Dave Page (tp), Guy Hunter (as), William Mosby (tp), Joe Westray (g), James "Honey Boy" Minor (drums and vibraphone), George Howell (b), Erroll Garner (p). (Leroy Brown) *Below,* the rhythm section. Left to right: James "Honey Boy" Minor, Joe Westray, Garner, George Howell, Harlem Casino, Pittsburgh, probably April 1940. (Leroy Brown)

C

Left, at the piano, probably 1939 or 1940. (Martha Murray) *Right,* early publicity photo, probably 1941. (Martha Murray)

Bob Brittingham (left) and Erroll provide entertainment at Paul's "Edgewaters," Asbury Park, New Jersey, Summer 1942. (Martha Murray)

D

Left, sitting in with the Stuff Smith Trio, Onyx Club, New York, December 1944. (Photo by Charles Nadell, courtesy Frank Driggs Collection) *Right,* Garner on the grounds at Paul's "Edgewaters," Asbury Park, New Jersey, Summer 1944. (Martha Murray)

With friends at Mercur's Music Bar, Pittsburgh, probably 1943 or 1944. (Martha Murray)

Above, Slam Stewart Quartet. Left to right: Stewart, Mike Bryan, Doc West, and Garner, Three Deuces, New York, 1945. (Frank Driggs Collection) *Below,* looking east on New York's 52nd Street from the Three Deuces where Garner was featured, ca. 1949. (© 1982 Frank Driggs Collection)

Above, left to right: Leonard Gaskin, Garner, and Charlie Smith, Three Deuces, New York, July 20, 1949. (Leonard Gaskin) *Below,* left to right: Leonard Gaskin, Garner, and Denzil Best, Three Deuces, New York, December 26, 1949. (Leonard Gaskin)

Above, with Leonard Gaskin, Three Deuces, New York, Summer 1949. (William P. Gottlieb) *Below,* Garner with Wyatt "Bull" Ruther, Basin Street East, probably 1954. (Frank Driggs Collection)

Garner's star on Hollywood Boulevard's "Walk of Fame." (Bob Waits)

Right, Pasadena Civic Auditorium, Pasadena, California, July 22, 1956. (Ray Avery) *Below,* left to right: Teddy Wilson, Eddie Heywood, Garner, and Earl "Fatha" Hines, Embers, New York, 1959. (Stanley Dance)

Appearing on BBC-TV with Kelly Martin, London, probably 1963. (David Redfern)

Garner's bassist for 13 years, Eddie Calhoun, probably 1963. (David Redfern)

Left to right: Fats Heard, Wyatt "Bull" Ruther, Garner, Civic Auditorium, Boston, ca. 1953. (Fats Heard)

J

Above, opening night at Mr. Kelly's, Chicago, September 14, 1970. (*Chicago Tribune*) *Top right,* Garner with Leroy Brown, where Garner received an honorary membership in the Pittsburgh Press Club, March 22, 1972. (Leroy Brown) *Right,* Garner with Ernest McCarty, Jr., Brandi's Wharf, Philadelphia, March 17, 1972. (J. Doran Collection)

Below, Don Sollash welcomes Erroll to Dobell's Record Shop, London, probably 1963. (Don Sollash)

K

Relaxing at Tivoli Gardens, Copenhagen, July 31, 1970. (Politikens Pressefoto)

In concert at Tivoli Gardens, Copenhagen, early August, 1970. (Politikens Pressefoto)

Monterey Jazz Festival (California), September 18, 1971. (Ray Avery)

Above, Garner's tombstone, Homewood Cemetery, Pittsburgh. Note the incorrect birthdate of 1923 (should read 1921). (J. Doran) *Right,* the last known photo of Garner, Los Angeles, 1976. (Rosalyn Noisette)

Garner's funeral, St. James A.M.E. Church, Pittsburgh. Pall bearers, left to right: Russell Williams, James "Honey Boy" Minor, Carl Arter, Lawrence Peeler, Leroy Brown (hidden), Walter Harper. In the background is Garner's sister, Martha Murray and brother, Linton. Pittsburgh, January 7, 1977. (*Pittsburgh Post Gazette*)

M

Above, Erroll's parents, Ernest and Estella on Easter Sunday, Pittsburgh, late 1960s. (Ruth Moore) *Left,* Garner's sister, Ruth Moore with nephew, Ralph, September 1983. (James Turner)

Erroll's sister, Berniece and twin brother, Ernest, Pittsburgh, March 1983. (J. Doran)

N

Left, Erroll's sister, Martha, Pittsburgh, February 1984. (J. Doran) *Right,* Erroll's twin, Ernest, in church, Pittsburgh, April 15, 1984. (Berniece Franklin)

The Linton Garner Family. Left to right: sons, Linton, Jr., and Leslie, wife Frances, and Linton, Montreal, 1977. (Frances Garner)

O

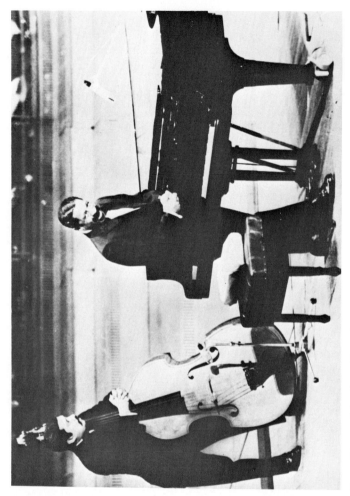

Victor Venegas joins the audience in applause as Garner takes his bow, Philharmonie Hall, Berlin, 1970. (Ullstein Bilderdienst)

*I used to kid Erroll a lot because sometimes he was just sitting at the piano
and I would say, "What are you thinking about? Looks like your dreaming
about something." He would play this little melody; it was only about four
bars. As it turned out, it was the first four bars of "Misty."*

FATS HEARD

The Rhythm Section
1947-1955

RED CALLENDER
(Bass)

*George "Red" Callender was born in Richmond, Virginia, on March 6, 1918.
He was raised in Atlantic City, New Jersey, and attended school in Borden-
town, New Jersey. Callender came to California at the age of eighteen with
Eddie Heywood, Sr., for a show called Blanche Thompson's Brown Skin
Models. He joined Louis Armstrong in November of 1937 when George
"Pops" Foster became ill. Callender is highly regarded today as a bassist
and tuba player and does extensive studio work.*

Norman Granz was raving about this young cat who played piano about
1944 or '45. I guess he saw Erroll when he went through Pittsburgh or
52nd Street in New York. I first met him in a joint off San Pedro Boulevard
called the Casablanca. I was working there with my trio of Jack LaRue
and Lucky Ennois when Erroll came in. I fell in love with his playing on
the spot. Erroll replaced Jack LaRue in our group.

Erroll, Harold West, and I used to live together in the same house on
28th Street in Los Angeles. That's how we formed the trio and became
good friends. Hal [West] cooked for us and he was top grade. We were
together for the better part of a year.

There were a whole bunch of people at different times that were involved
in the Charlie Parker recording sessions—people like Howard McGhee,
Dexter Gordon, and Wardell Gray. We recorded at the C.P. MacGregor
Studios on Western Avenue in Los Angeles [February 19, 1947]. At the
session with Garner, we recorded "Pastel" and "Trio." "Pastel" was my
song. I used to play it on the piano, and Erroll heard it and dug it, so

we recorded it. It was originally titled, "Please Let Me Forget." Ross Russell, who produced the session, suggested the title, "Pastel." A lot of people thought Erroll wrote the song, but he didn't—it's all mine.

I also wrote the bridge to "Trio" on the other side, but I didn't get any credit for that. Erroll was just fooling around with the changes, and when we got to the bridge, I filled in that part of the melody.

Erroll went back to New York, and at that time I was getting involved in studio work because that's where the money was. I remember I made a big record date with him with Leith Stevens conducting out there in Los Angeles. As a matter of fact, somewhere around 1946 or '47, we recorded "Pastel" with a double sextet-type thing with a French horn and all to be released on Capitol. Fran Kelley was the producer. It must be on the Capitol shelves somewhere because it was never released.

Erroll had almost a magical way of hearing things. He could hear something once, and he had it. We'd run it down and, you know, it was uncanny—he had magic!

J.C. HEARD
(Drums)

James Charles Heard was born on October 8, 1917, in Dayton, Ohio. He was a drummer for Teddy Wilson's Big Band during 1939–40 and with Benny Carter in 1942. He was with Cab Calloway from 1942 to 1946. His primary association with Erroll Garner started in April 1948, at the Three Deuces, with Oscar Pettiford on bass. In May, 1984 he was awarded the Michigan Council Recipient's Award for Music. Still as youthful as ever, Heard says, "Age is something you can't stop, but the mind and body don't have to go along with that. After all, I'm not afraid of dying, I just don't want to be there when it happens."

I met Erroll in Pittsburgh around 1943 or '44 when I was with Cab Calloway at the Stanley Theater. We were trying to decide where to go, and someone said, "There's a little guy who can play the hell out of the piano." So we said, "Let's go and check him out."

He was working in some joint down there in a cellar, some downstairs basement. He was playing by himself . . . . Oh man, I thought he had a bass and drummer . . . . It was just him playing his butt off. It just knocked us out because of the way he plays that left hand; he plays straight, just like a guitar player . . . bomp, bomp, bomp . . . and the right hand is improvised and all kinds of shit.

Erroll and I worked together in the spring of '48 at the Three Deuces with Oscar Pettiford. Leonard Feather just brought a guy over from England called George Shearing, who was playing intermission piano while we were off stage. At the time Shearing was playing just like Fats Waller. After about six months, Erroll had an offer to record, and he wanted to go off on his own, so we put George Shearing in the trio. George played everything just like Erroll Garner did. It was a funny thing—exactly—note for note—just like him. Next thing that happened, Leonard Feather recorded George Shearing with vibraphone, guitar, and the piano. Our group broke up, and I got another band and went on the road with Norman Granz and the Jazz at the Philharmonic, and Oscar Pettiford went his way.

Oscar was sweet as pie. He drank a lot; he had a bad whiskey habit, but other than that when he was playing, hey, listen . . . that's who Ray Brown patterned from. I'll run the bass players down, from when I was playing music, as the great soloists: Jimmy Blanton started off as far as great soloists on the bass, and Oscar Pettiford got from Blanton, Ray Brown got from Pettiford . . . Paul Chambers got from Ray, and a lot of other guys got from Paul Chambers and so on and so on.

Irving Alexander wanted to bring an all-star thing at the Three Deuces, so he approached me and got Erroll and Oscar to come down and everybody agreed. That was it! We all knew each other anyway. We'd jam with each other at the after-hours spots. Everybody would play with each other sometime, not steady, but just in jam sessions and things. We listened to guys when we went playing . . . . That's how guys knew everybody's style. That's how you could play with different people.

We had a place called Monroe's Uptown House at 133rd and Seventh Avenue. We played Minton's Playhouse on 118th Street and Seventh Avenue. That was a hell of a spot. Erroll and I used to jam up there. In fact, Thelonious Monk used to work there. The guy that ran the place, Teddy Hill, used to have a band. They had another place called Crawford's way up on St. Nicholas Avenue and 145th Street. All the musicians used to come in there in the morning like Art Tatum, Fats Waller, Teddy Wilson and everybody, and they'd have piano battles. Tonight would be a piano battle. Everybody would go up there because they know all the piano players are battling each other. At that time it was all the greatest piano players in the world. The next night we might have a tenor battle. That means all the great tenor players like Lester Young, Ben Webster, Coleman Hawkins, Don Byas . . . . Can you imagine that kind of music, man. These guys played because they didn't have to worry about sheet music; they just played like they wanted to play. Nobody would tell you that you had to be commercial. Just blow!

We used to start at the Three Deuces around 9:30 or 10 o'clock. At 4 o'clock in the morning people would be wanting some more, so that's why we'd go uptown to these after-hours spots and stay 'til 9 o'clock when the kids were going to school. Oh shit, man, you kidding, I don't have to tell you . . . . We were all young . . . everybody's young and having a good time.

LEONARD GASKIN
(Bass)

Leonard Gaskin was born August 25, 1920, in Brooklyn, New York. Gaskin recorded with Garner in 1949 and went on tour during various periods from 1949 to 1953. Today he is featured with the Sy Oliver Orchestra at the Rainbow Room in New York City.

I had been working on 52nd Street with Charlie Parker, Dizzy, Miles, Coleman Hawkins, Eddie South, and Charlie Shavers. I was a regular on 52nd Street, and that's where I met Erroll. I worked with Erroll at the Three Deuces toward the latter part of 1949. Charlie Smith was the drummer. Sometime during that period we had a record date with Johnny Hartman. I don't recall the details of the date, but I do remember two of the tunes were "Home" and "Remember." It was a very nice date. When the record came out, it was very noisy, but the music was to my liking.

Later that year [1949] we played the Apollo Theater, and I went out on the first tour with Erroll, more or less. It wasn't an extensive tour. I remember we went to Detroit, Chicago, and a couple of places. This was his entrée to traveling, having never been to these places.

In 1952 we went on a tour called *Piano Parade*. The drummer was Wesley Landers. In early 1953 I took a leave of absence from the trio, and Al Hall took my place for a while because I went to school to study television production and programming.

I rejoined Erroll when they went to Mack's Tavern in Atlantic City [July 1953]. This was the first time Erroll was ever booked at Mack's Tavern. The drummer was Fats Heard, and we're sitting there waiting for Erroll to show up. The place is jammed, and he doesn't show up 'til way after midnight. When he finally shows up, the front of his car is all smashed in, and he had a long, long story about being held up.

Erroll would rehearse something one way and play it another way when it came to a record date. He'd be in another key, so you never knew, but it always went well. It was crazy! We're supposed to make a record date so anything we had talked about, rehearsed, or preplanned went out the window. We'd eventually do the eight sides one after the other.

Many records, after they were released, they would call me in to put in the bass. I dubbed in a lot of them. By that time he was recording for almost 30 labels, so a lot of those that you hear, I personally dubbed.

JOHN SIMMONS
(Bass)

John Simmons was born June 14, 1918, in Haskell, Oklahoma, and died of emphysema in Los Angeles on September 19, 1979.
The following interview with John Simmons was conducted by Patricia Willard in January, 1977, and is reprinted courtesy of the National Endowment for the Arts, Jazz Oral History Program, Institute of Jazz Studies, Rutgers University, Newark, New Jersey.

Ms. Willard: You joined Erroll in New York or out here?
Mr. Simmons: I joined him in New York. See, he said if anything comes of the records that I had a job.
Ms. Willard: Which records were these?
Mr. Simmons: The ones we made out here for Ralph Bass, his first records that made him a hit.
Ms. Willard: And those were made—
Mr. Simmons: Here in Los Angeles.
Ms. Willard: In what year?
Mr. Simmons: '48, late '48. And Erroll—about December, '48.
Ms. Willard: Do you remember what you recorded with him?
Mr. Simmons: Oh, some of the tunes: "Cottage for Sale," "Penthouse Serenade," "I'm in the Mood for Love," you name it.
Ms. Willard: What label were these on?
Mr. Simmons: They weren't on a label. See, Ralph Bass just gave us a record date and took the masters and sold them to Savoy.
Ms. Willard: So they came out on Savoy.
Mr. Simmons: They came out on Savoy. But we didn't record for Savoy.
Ms. Willard: Uh-huh. Who played drums on these records?
Mr. Simmons: There was no drums. Yes, there was. I'm sorry. The first day Alvin Stoller played drums. He played two days, I think. And the next day or day and a half Jesse Price played 'til we finished the date. And I never thought that Jesse Price could play that soft, but he was playing with brushes, so he couldn't play too loud, you know. And Erroll was playing an old upright piano that sounded like a barroom piano, you know, but he got something out of it; that barroom sound disappeared. He was milking the piano, you know, petting it. And I was asking him, I said, "Erroll, what chord was that?" And somehow he was under the impression that the bottom note was the name of the chord. He didn't know anything about inversions, you know, like you can take the bottom note and put it on the top, and the next note, you know, might be the bass tone, but it's still the same chord. And he'd call me, and he'd say, "This is a B flat," and I'd hit the B flat, and oh, I was out of tune. I'd

hit the wrong note. B Flat. And what happened, we were playing in E-Flat and he played a B Flat chord, and he said it was E-Flat, you know. So I moved my position over to his left hand to watch his left hand. I knew the keyboard well enough to try to anticipate his movements, you know, just what section of the piano he was going to have that left hand in, you know. And I was a bundle of nerves behind this, reading this man's mind, you know. And people say, "Oh, you all sound so good. You sound like a happy marriage." I say, "Well." He took me through the wringer. And like if some celebrities would happen in the club, you'd say, oh, he's going low. Now, he's really going to play for them. He would play his worst.

Ms. Willard: Why do you suppose that was?

Mr. Simmons: I don't know. I don't know if it was stage fright or what. And then he would start to compose. He'd turn around to me and say, "You're on your own." I'd say, "I'm on my own? I've been on my own all the time." This is nothing new. Even the tunes that I knew I had to learn them all over again because he had a homemade set of charts that he played, you know, turnbacks and things. They weren't the standard changes. See, because he played by ear, and he played what he heard, you know. So I had to learn bass all over again, his style. So we eventually got it together, and we had three pieces there, and for a while it sounded like a band because Shadow Wilson and I was accentuating with him at different intervals. I knew where he was going from one time to the next. Whenever he would start an introduction, he wouldn't play an intro. He would just start hitting the bass notes, not any particular ones, just a fistful of bass notes. Blop, blop, blop, you know, real dissonant things, you know, not intended to be musical, just a sound. And I knew what tune he was going to play right away.

[Laughter]

Ms. Willard: When did Shadow join him?

Mr. Simmons: Shadow joined him in '50. This first drummer that he had when he came back from Paris didn't pan out. His name was Harold West. He was half Chinese and Negro. And we called him Chink. But he wanted to play with sticks, and by playing with Erroll Garner, he thought he was a star, you know, and he was going to be heard, and he was drowning Erroll out with sticks, you know. So at this time, Erroll asked me, he said, "Man, can't you do something with him?" I said, "No, I can't do anything with him. This is your group." You know.

Ms. Willard: Erroll went to Paris in, what, late '49?

Mr. Simmons: No, early '49, because he had been in the Three Deuces.

Ms. Willard: He played the Three Deuces in July because I was there.

Mr. Simmons: With Oscar Pettiford and J.C. Heard?

Ms. Willard: I think so. I remember the Three Deuces had not had jazz, and they were restarting—they had not had jazz for awhile, and they were starting a jazz policy again with Erroll's opening.

Mr. Simmons: Oh, really?

Ms. Willard: That's what they were announcing, and that was like about July, June or July, but I think it was July of '49.

Mr. Simmons: Well, whenever.

Ms. Willard: And I think Oscar was with him.

Mr. Simmons: Well, I didn't know anything about the Three Deuces starting a jazz policy. I had worked in the Three Deuces before I had worked with Erroll Garner.

Ms. Willard: Back to '49, you worked with Erroll part of the time. What else did you do in 1949? You weren't with Erroll all of the time, were you?

Mr. Simmons: Well, as soon as he came back from Paris, I was with Erroll from '49, the latter part of '49—I think it was the latter part of '49. In fact, I'm almost sure it was the latter part of '49. Then '49, '50, '51, '52. And then I got arrested, and he was told not to come near me. It would do something to his drawing attraction, you know.

Ms. Willard: Who told him that?

Mr. Simmons: Martha Glaser.

Ms. Willard: His manager.

Mr. Simmons: Yes. No relation to Joe Glaser.

Ms. Willard: Uh-huh. She was his manager.

Mr. Simmons: Yeah.

Ms. Willard: She's still his manager.

Mr. Simmons: Yeah.

WYATT RUTHER
(Bass)

Wyatt "Bull" Ruther played bass for Erroll Garner during various periods from 1951 to 1955. He was born on February 5, 1923, in Pittsburgh, Pennsylvania.

I lived approximately three blocks from the Garners. I knew the Garners all through school. I first met Erroll at the Lincoln School in Pittsburgh. He was a little older than I, and he played the piano and I played the xylophone in the school orchestra. At Westinghouse High School I played the trombone and Erroll played the tuba. Mr. Carl McVicker was our music teacher.

I was a trombone player in the service, and they had too many trombone players and no bass players, so I decided to take up the bass. I started with Erroll in 1951; at that time I was working with Dave Brubeck. When we were in New York I saw Erroll, and he said he needed a bass player. I was getting a little disenchanted with Dave Brubeck, so I switched over to Erroll. Some time after I started with Erroll, he lent me to Lena Horne for about eight months.

I left Erroll in May, 1955, after our gig at the Boston Harbor Club in Rochester, New York. I had paternity problems in New York, so I thought it would be easier to leave the group.

Fats Heard left when I was still with the band, and he had Kenny Dennis on drums, former husband of Nancy Wilson, replace Fats. Fats had stayed in Cleveland and Erroll picked up Kenny Dennis out of Philadelphia. I believe Kenny Dennis stayed with the group until Denzil Best joined Erroll around the summer of 1955.

Today I'm playing bass in the Vancouver area. I've been at it for awhile. I've been playing it since 1946 and haven't been out of work once the whole time.

FATS HEARD
(Drums)

Eugene "Fats" Heard worked as Erroll Garner's drummer from 1953 to 1955. He was born in Cleveland, Ohio, on October 10, 1923. Today he is a real estate salesman.

Erroll taught me one thing about music, that you can play anything and make it sound good. Jazz musicians have hangups about certain sounds, etcetera. I remember one night we walked from Birdland during intermission up to Roseland Ballroom, where Les Brown was playing. Oh, the place was packed. Les Brown was the one who played in the band for Bob Hope on his road shows. I had never heard Erroll play "You Are My Sunshine." We had never played it on the bandstand, but we listened to Les Brown's arrangement. The place was jumping and swinging, and it was crowded. We had to push our way in to get near the bandstand. We went back, and Erroll played the exact arrangement on the next set. He knew his instrument, although as a drummer I wasn't concerned with keys as far as what key he was playing in, but I do know, he would start out in one key and wind up where he wanted to hear it. So the keyboard was just an instrument to him; I don't think it mattered. He could play it in any key he wanted to.

I used to kid Erroll a lot because sometimes he was just sitting at the piano, and I would say, "What are you thinking about? Looks like you're dreaming about something." He would play this little melody; it was only about four bars. As it turned out, it was the first four bars of "Misty." I remember we were cutting that day [July 27, 1954]. As a matter of fact, I think that was the day Candido was on as our conga drummer. At any rate, we had run out of things to play and he said, "What could we play?" and I said, "Play that little tune." That's how Misty came about. As far as I can remember, that was the first time he ever played it, on that date. You may have heard parts of it in other songs because Erroll was well known for his long introductions and sort of doodling around until he went into a tune. It's a possibility that you heard it in some of the other tunes, but never competely.

I remember when Wyatt Ruther and I first joined Erroll. I went to New York and met him at his apartment, and he called me to rehearsal the next day or so; I think it was the Nola Recording Studio. He called a rehearsal that day, and we showed up, and he would always do tunes and do it the way he wanted. Ruther would write down keys. It was funny. We opened at Storyville in Boston. I think that was my first date with him. We must have rehearsed three hours or more. He knew the keyboard so well that he could play the tune where he wanted to hear it at that particular time. Bull Ruther was writing keys down at the rehearsal, and Erroll would start out in that key, and by the time he actually got into the tune, he might be anywhere. After our Storyville gig Ruther said, "Man, this cat's not playing in the keys we rehearsed in." I said, "Well, he's just playing where they sound good to him."

It was great being a drummer for him. He taught me that any tune you wanted to play you could play. People used to ask him to play ridiculous tunes, and Erroll would play them if he felt like it, and it would sound good. As a matter fact, I don't think I can ever remember him turning down a request. He could just play anything.

The way I met Erroll was I was talking to this psychologist, Jim Bard, and mentioned the fact that Erroll called. He knew Erroll from Pittsburgh. I think Erroll came into town with Shadow Wilson. Shadow was late or something and I happened to be there. The Bards are nice people. They introduced me to Erroll, and I think they were the ones that called me one morning. I was working with a pianist, George Peters, at the time. Buster Bennett was the sax player; Bill Grinage on bass in early 1953. I had worked awhile on the road with Lionel Hampton, prior to that, right after I came out of the service, which was around 1943. I worked with Lionel for a couple of years. I did a gig with Coleman Hawkins, when I was in high school, at a place they called Benny Mason's Farm. I think I joined Erroll in January 1953. I remember our first gig being the old

Storyville. I followed Shadow into the group, so it could have been a week after him. I stayed with Erroll for the next couple of years.

We were at the Comedy Club in Baltimore, and I think the narcotics squad had busted the previous drummer. I believe it was Anita O'Day's drummer. The police must have had a "hard on" for drummers. I walked off the bandstand one night, and they wanted to search me, go to my hotel, and go through my bags. It was really kind of funny but it made me so angry. I had a big ladies hat bag and shoe bag—a big fiberglass thing that would hold more than a regular piece of luggage. This bag had a combination on it. He threw my stuff around, but when he got to this little mechanical lead pencil with a lead holder, he thought he had something! He said, "Ah ha," and pulled the top off of it and turned it over in his hand, and all this lead fell out. It made me angry 'cause they were throwing stuff out of my bags, and I just didn't appreciate it. We knew a guy that worked in the district attorney's office, and I had called him and he said, "Well, they didn't mistreat you so you can't really do anything." I guess they had a thing for musicians. That didn't happen too often.

Erroll was nice to me. I can remember we went to Miami, and I think we went to open up the *Birdland on the Beach* show. I told Erroll we are going to be here during the holidays, and I'd like to bring my wife and daughter down, and he gave me a raise. I never drew any of my money out ahead of time like the rest of them did. When payday came, I liked to get all of my money , so I budgeted myself. I remember once, I believe we were in Tampa, I told Erroll, "I think I'll go on home," and he gave me $100. Now I could say some bad things, not about Erroll, but you know about the pay. Back in those days I think I was making on a regular basis, not counting extra things, I think I was making $350 [per week]. That was pretty good money back then. That didn't include the record dates or the TV shots and whatever. I don't remember what my pay was on the concerts, whether it was on a weekly basis or per show.

I had had a taste of the road with Lionel Hampton. That's one of the reasons I didn't get along with Lionel. I'm sure if you know anything about Lionel you've heard of Gladys, his wife. She sort of handled the money in his band, 'cause Lionel offered me good money and good raises, and they never came through. I didn't have any problems with Erroll. I was just as happy; he paid me and we got along great. Like I said, I don't know any bad things about Erroll; the only bad things come with the people associated with Erroll. That's all water over the damn, not even worth mentioning again.

Basically I wanted to spend more time at home with my family, which is why I left. So rather than me be unhappy, which in turn would make Erroll unhappy, I told him I was leaving. I think we were in Canada when I submitted my notice. That was just before *Concert by the Sea* [September 19, 1955].

AL HALL

(Bass)

*Al Hall played bass with Garner for various club, concert, and recording
sessions from 1945 to 1963. Born March 8, 1915, Hall is now working on
his own book. "I want to straighten out a lot of mythical things about jazz
for my grandsons. I don't expect to be Hemingway—I just want to tell David
and Alex how it really was."*

I met Erroll when he first came up on 52nd Street when Art Tatum was
working at the Three Deuces, and Erroll came in as a visitor and then
finally working as the in-between and what not. He created a sensation
that I have never seen, and it never let up. In fact, he was responsible
for George Shearing's changing his style and Lenny Tristano trying to find
it and various other pianists. That's what I think of Erroll Garner, a born
genius, God's gift to the piano keys.

We entertained so much during that time that you worked with anybody
that was playing, anytime it felt good. During the war we did V-Discs,
so there were multiple combinations of people like [Hot Lips] Page and
Slam [Stewart]. When we were working and playing together then, we
weren't involved with critics' opinions and who was great or who wasn't.
We played to enjoy ourselves. Then, we did it out of love, compassion,
and appreciation for one another's talent. We didn't put it in a box and
tie a ribbon around it just to find out what it was. You had the critics
that became Ph.D.'s from college trying to analyze what was already done.

Erroll had been in a taxicab accident, and he got a concussion [May
17, 1956]. They [Columbia] were worried that it affected his brain or his
creativity, so they hurriedly called a record session. Martha [Glaser] called
me to do the Columbia engagement, so Specs [Powell] and I were the other
components.

We played, and after the session got underway they had a list of tunes
that we played. After that, since all the tunes were one take, we used to
get in the corner and whisper what we were going to play next. We didn't
tell them in the booth because they gave us the freedom to do whatever
we wanted to do. Erroll would start an introduction, and only Specs and
I knew what he was going to play. That was *The Most Happy Piano* date
(June 7, 1956).

We did the session at the Columbia 30th Street Studio. We didn't even
know about the accident. On our break we would sneak around to our
usual corner bar to get a few drinks. He had to sneak a taste because they
were still worried and, of course, still watching him.

At the same studio I was involved with one of the *Other Voices* sessions
with Mitch Miller as the guest conductor. After *Other Voices* was on the

market, Erroll played with the Cleveland Symphony Orchestra at the
Cleveland Auditorium in front of 7,000 people. The Cleveland Symphony
played the score of *Other Voices*. Then at another portion of it the trio
performed at the same concert without the orchestra. Osie Johnson was
the drummer for this occasion. The album was promoted well and it's still
in print.

I never watched his hands. Erroll had confidence enough in me to know
the proper chords for the left hand, and unrelentlessly I used that, and
that gave him the opportunity to do whatever else he wanted to do. That
was one of the fallacies that other rhythm sections made because they'd
try to lay back with him, and he didn't want that. He needed a fortress
so that he could do whatever he wanted. That was our rapport. He started
the tune . . . whatever he wanted to play, and I played the notes that I
know belong to that tune. He could deviate in any way he wanted in
harmony with what I did, so that made another dimension. Instead of a
unison, which would make it one, he could go elsewhere.

SPECS POWELL
(Drums)

*Gordon "Specs" Powell was born in New York City on June 5, 1922. He
played with Edgar Hayes and Benny Carter, and he also worked on 52nd
Street with Teddy Wilson, Billie Holiday, and Benny Goodman. His television
credits include The Ed Sullivan Show, Candid Camera and I've Got a Secret.*

Erroll and I were both young kids in New York, and there used to be
a lot of jam sessions. They were in lofts, and many of us got together
at the after-hours clubs.

I enjoyed working with Erroll because he was a spontaneous individual.
He gave the kind of backing to the group that would sound like a brass
section in the Count Basie Orchestra, these big fat chords and not the usual
comping.

The first time I saw him was in Tondelayo's while I was with Red Norvo
at the Three Deuces. He had this down home, dirty-type of playing style.
He was just good to look at and he looked happy.

During the session with the Mitch Miller Orchestra, I think Erroll was
slightly uncomfortable because he was boxed into the arrangements. But
in those days they started to put strings behind Charlie Parker and a
number of people so they could "clean up" jazz and make it into a pop
commodity. They did the same thing to Erroll, which was great, because

you had his style plus the style of the orchestra and the arranging of Nat Pierce. What they did was really magnificent. All of those tunes that were involved in the Columbia legal battle were all one take. That's because of the talent of the man and the agility of the people working with him. If you listen to it, it sounds like we rehearsed everything, but we didn't. He would discuss it once, the tune and the tempo of the tune. He would then stop, and John Hammond would show his approval, and off he'd go, and we were right with him. His playing was a big band type of style. After a while he created his own clichés, and we just went where he was going.

I don't think anyone ever again could come close to Erroll's standard of quality with so little concern about each take. He never made a bad take; it was a question of choosing those which maintained his highest standard.

The Columbia Years

GEORGE AVAKIAN

George Avakian produced the majority of Garner's albums at Columbia Records. Avakian was born on March 15, 1919, in the town of Armavir, north of the Caucasus Mountains in the Soviet Union. Intensely proud of his Armenian heritage, Avakian declares, "The whole business of getting interested in jazz, I think, was an outgrowth of being interested in anything that was ethnic. I found elements in jazz which reminded me of Armenian music."

I first heard of Erroll when I got out of the Army. My youngest brother, Aram, who had been around the jazz scene, was raving about Erroll Garner and urged me to listen to his records. So I did, but I thought Aram was crazy because this guy couldn't keep time. "You have to keep listening," he told me, and he was right. (If Aram hadn't become such a great photographer and film maker, he would have been a natural for the record business.) Once I caught on to Erroll's personal sense of time, I became a fan, buying his records and listening to him in clubs.

Pop albums were a minor category in the business until about a year after Columbia created the 33⅓ long-playing disc. This was great for classical music, but it took a while for pop customers to get interested in buying albums. Once it got started, the demand for ten-inch pop LP's began to boom. The sales department ran a survey which showed that there were pianos in an amazing percentage of homes, but there were very few piano albums on the market. So I started recording piano albums of every possible description; I must have produced 18 or 20 of them in a month and a half.

Erroll wasn't under exclusive contract to anyone at the time, so we signed him to one of the standard one-shot *Piano Moods* contracts. That's how our association began. Erroll and I got to know each other for the first time, working on that album; you can't really get to know a musician just hanging out between sets at a club.

We hit it off fine, and although the first album didn't sell too well—it was buried in that long series—I had decided by then that he was the greatest thing to come along on the piano since Earl Hines, so we negotiated a long-term contract. I didn't look very smart when the next album didn't sell much either, but as soon as we shifted to 12-inch pop albums, Erroll's magical ability to build and sustain longer performances made him a standout. His sales picked up, I was able to get some promotional money behind him, and Martha Glaser really took off in booking him on a higher level; Erroll soon became a star for the company.

I produced every one of his sessions. Oddly enough, the only album I didn't produce was his biggest seller of all time, *Concert by the Sea.* Yet I had to work harder on that one than any of the others, by far; it couldn't have been released otherwise. Sounds strange, but it'll make sense when I explain.

It all happened because an Army radio station near Carmel wanted to tape the performance and play it on the post radio station for the soldiers who couldn't get to the concert. They assured Martha that it couldn't be heard off the post, so she gave them permission, provided they gave her the tape after the broadcast so she could do anything she wanted with it. She didn't expect to be able to use it; it would just be a 7½ speed monaural half-track tape. She was merely making a nice gesture.

But when she heard it, she called me and said, "Hey, this is a marvelous performance; the quality isn't too hot, but I'm sure you can work on it." I said, "What? A 7½ half-track from a little dinky Wollensak or something?" I couldn't believe it would be any good, but Martha was so enthusiastic about Erroll's playing I said, "OK, send it to me."

I was floored by the poor sound quality. I mean, a piano is the hardest instrument to record really well, but this was pretty awful. On the other hand, the performance was fantastic. It took about two weeks of hard labor, inventing filters and boosters as we experimented our way through the murk, but we managed to make a good-sounding master out of it. The rest, as they say, is history—still the all-time biggest selling jazz piano album of them all.

The studio dates were a ball. Each session with Erroll was as relaxed as you can imagine. He'd come in and never let me know what he intended to do. We never had a formula for a particular album; Erroll would play whatever he felt like at the time, and then we'd pick the performances that would comprise a good album; after that we'd come up with a title. Martha was really good at that; she had a quick wit, and most of the album titles were hers.

Usually, I couldn't announce the title before a take because—you know Erroll— he wouldn't even let the bassist and drummer know what he was going to do. He'd just give me a big smile or nod, and I would say, "OK, take one."

There was a streak, which I probably wrote about somewhere in the liner notes, where he made some incredible number of one-take performances. There was one take where he just stopped on his own accord; I don't think it had anything to do with the engineering. He started up again and ripped off forty or more tunes. It was unbelievable! I was afraid people would say I was exaggerating or that I was out of my mind. Some takes were better than others, and we would simply pick the best ones. I don't think anyone ever again could come close to Erroll's standard of quality with so little concern about each take. He never made a bad take; it was a question of choosing those which maintained his highest standard.

After awhile we found a particular place on the floor of the 30th Street studio where Erroll's piano sounded best. I did that with various artists. I recorded Dave Brubeck with his piano in a certain position in the room. You get to find out where a particular artist sounds best.

There was always a special microphone which sounded best. The engineer always made sure he would have that on hand. If I'm not mistaken, I think we recorded Erroll with him sitting to my right when I looked at him, so the piano was turned around or the reverse of the Brubeck setup. Brubeck sounded best when he had it positioned in such a way where the top of the piano was pointing towards us.

It wasn't all as casual as it sounds because the engineers and I were very well prepared. Through experience, trial-and-error, gradually we discovered with every artist the best way to set him up.

I used to go up to Erroll's apartment, right next to the Russian Tea Room. The building is gone now; it's just an empty parking lot. He had a long, rambling apartment on two levels. I have a feeling it was two buildings put together; they broke through a wall to make this big apartment. We would just sit, talk, and play records, and he would occasionally break out a bottle of Otard, his favorite cognac. Erroll Garner, what can you say about him? He was one of the most wonderful people I ever knew. It's as simple as that!

THE CASE OF GARNER VS. COLUMBIA

Erroll Garner is one of the most spontaneous and prolific performers in jazz. Not only does he reel off an endless stream of standards in a concert, but he also often composes on the spot. Some of his tunes—*Misty, Solitaire,* and *Dreamy*—have become hits. All were transcribed from tapes; Garner neither reads nor writes music.

Garner is just as spontaneous in the recording studio. George Avakian, who supervised many Garner dates for Columbia Records, once recorded 19 tunes (97 minutes of music) in three hours (with a half-hour out for sandwiches) with Garner. Recording supervisors usually hope to achieve four three-minute takes in three hours of recording, obtained only after innumerable retakes. A Garner date usually produces an awesome number of usable one-takes so good that they cannot be improved upon.

This prodigious output was heartwarming to Columbia not only because it kept production costs down but also because the company was able to build up a sizable backlog of tracks, which meant money in the bank with an artist as popular as Garner has become.

Thus, the relationship between Garner and Columbia was a cordial one—until recently.

But now Garner and his manager, Martha Glaser, are involved in a complicated lawsuit against Columbia over the pianist's exclusive recording contract with the label. When all the legal complications are sorted out, the case may have a bearing on countless future contracts between jazz artists and record firms.

This is what the Garner-Columbia case is about:

When Garner left EmArcy-Mercury in 1956, he signed a five-year agreement with Columbia that gave him rights of approval on all sides to be released; at the termination of the contract (it originally was scheduled to expire in June, 1961), the balance of the approved, but unused, tapes was to be turned over to him. The company also agreed to release three LPs and six single records a year.

During the year 1956-57, only one or two singles were released. Garner complained to Mitch Miller, who had become the pianist's A&R contact when Avakian left Columbia. Miller checked into the matter and agreed with Garner: Columbia had erred. But he asked Garner to sign a waiver for that year. Garner signed.

In March, 1958, Garner made a record date. It turned out to be the last date for Columbia. Three months later—at the end of the second year of the contract—no further singles had been issued.

In November, 1958, Garner took the matter to the American Federation of Musicians, accusing Columbia of breach of contract. He asked the union for its clearance to sign with another label. In June, 1959, when Miller asked Garner to do another record date, the pianist refused.

So Columbia decided that it would simply assemble a new album out of the stockpile of unused tracks. The resultant LP, *The One and Only Garner,* was released in June, 1960. Two of the tracks had been recorded in February, 1953 (prior to the signing of the exclusive contract between Garner and Columbia), while the remaining six tracks came from the June, 1956, date supervised by Avakian.

Garner's attorneys promptly obtained an injunction to restrain Columbia from selling the disc and asking the company to remove the LP from record-store shelves. The grounds for the demand? Garner said he had not approved the six sides from the Avakian date. He said they were essentially rejects.

"I can't understand," the pianist said, "how a company run by such eminent musicians as Goddard Lieberson and Mitch Miller would want to release substandard performances, despite my protests. It puts the artists in an awkward and impossible position. And, what's more, it is unfair to the consumer."

The date from which the six tracks came—the session produced the album called *The Most Happy Piano*—was not made under the best of conditions. Garner had just come out of the hospital, where he had been recovering from a concussion suffered in a taxi crash. He was eager to start work under his new contract, signed only a week before, even though his regular bassist and drummer were on vacation, and Garner did not want their vacations short.

Bassist Al Hall and drummer Specs Powell went into the studio as substitutes. Garner did 19 tunes, unrehearsed and without retakes. These facts are related in Avakian's liner notes for *The Most Happy Piano*. Garner's position is that it was physically impossible to hear playbacks of 19 numbers in the three hours.

Columbia's attorneys retorted that it had been assumed that Garner had heard the playbacks of the six tunes used in *The One and Only Garner;* it is common practice for musicians to hear a playback immediately after cutting a track. The attorneys also pointed out that Garner is one of the very few artists to have an approval clause in a contract.

Garner further complained that he has never received an inventory of the tunes he has on tape in Columbia's vaults, though, he said, he has asked for one. He said that with the contract breached, he felt he should get back all the usable material that has been approved and be given the chance to check the titles he had not okayed.

Garner's suit argued that "the issuance of the unapproved tracks could do irreparable damage to the pianist's artistic reputation. The kind of harm that cannot be cured with money . . . ." (One trade paper already has reviewed *The One and Only Garner* as subpar Garner; *down beat* was asked by Martha Glaser not to review it at all, pending the outcome of the case, and has not.)

In May of this year, the AFM advised Garner that it would sustain his contention that Columbia had breached the contract. The union gave him its blessing to sign with another record company until the controversy was resolved. Miss Glaser since has entered negotiations with another label.

Meanwhile, Columbia maintains that it was Garner who breached the contract—by refusing to record in June, 1959. It, in turn, has sued Garner for $600,000—for failure to appear for recording sessions.

Up to this point, Garner seems to be faring best in the legal struggle. In July, he won the initial round when New York Supreme Court Justice Morris Spector granted a temporary injunction against the release of the album. The restraining order also prohibited the company from pressing, selling, distributing, and advertising the LP.

The next day, Columbia appealed the injunction in the appellate division of the Supreme Court. At the same time, the company asked the court to withhold the temporary injunction until the appeal had a chance to be argued.

The appeals court was closed during August. But Judge Bernard Botein of the appellate court ruled that the injunction would remain in effect at least until the Fall appeals court considers it in September.

Judge Botein, on an action by Columbia, asked Garner's attorney, Walter Hofer, to post a bond of $40,000 in behalf of his client. If Justice Spector's decision is overturned, Garner could lose all or part of this bond.

Whatever the outcome of the case, it is an enormously significant one for recording artists. It marks the first time in the history of the record business that an artist has successfully gone to court to force a company to take a disc off the market.

A year ago, singer Lena Horne sued RCA Victor over the release of the album of *Porgy and Bess* that she made with Harry Belafonte. The New York Supreme Court rejected her case. But, unlike Garner, Miss Horne had no approval clause in her contract.

If Garner is upheld this month and wins a permanent injunction against the sale of the LP, it will be another first for him.

Even if Columbia loses the case, the firm cannot be entirely unhappy about its association with Garner. His *Concert by the Sea* LP, made early in the life of the battered contract, has sold more than 500,000 copies.

But regardless of Columbia's state of mind, this case is likely to have a permanent effect upon future contracts between artists and the labels with which they sign. If Garner wins, it follows that other strong-selling recording artists will demand equal, if not more concessions, when their contracts come up for renewal.

It is not inconceivable to envision approval rights, return of unused tapes, and guaranteed releases, as bargaining factors of the future. Such items may become the determining points upon which a record affiliation is established.

But if Garner wins, what will happen to the small independent jazz labels, which depend on having backlogs as an investment? No longer will they be able to store up sides recorded by jazz artists, when they are little known, with the hope the artist will make it big in future years, even if on another label. This has kept some of the jazz independents alive.

The final outcome of the Garner litigation will be watched closely. Artists will be hopeful, while the businessmen in the record industry will view with alarm. [In August, 1962, the Garner vs. Columbia case was settled out-of-court].

George Hoefer, "The Case of Garner Vs. Columbia," *down beat,* October 13, 1960, pp. 17-18. Reprinted by permission of *down beat* magazine.

*We played St. Mary's College across the street from Notre Dame in Indiana
... Erroll opened up with "Love for Sale," ... I said, "Man, how could
you possibly have come up with "Love for Sale," and he said, "I don't know!
It just popped up into my head and I played it." I expected them to stop
the concert with all those nuns out there.*

EDDIE CALHOUN

The Rhythm Section
1955–1966

EDDIE CALHOUN
(Bass)

*Eddie Calhoun started playing bass during the Depression. He recalls, "No-
body had any money for instruments, but everyone wanted to sing or something, so we just made our own instruments out of tin cans, string, and rope."
Born in Clarksdale, Mississippi, on November 13, 1921, Calhoun's family
came to Chicago when he was six months old. Calhoun was working at the
6312 Club in Chicago with Johnny Griffin, Junior Mance, Eddie
"Cleanhead" Vinson, and Buddy Smith when a friend, Claude Jones, asked
him if he would like to work with Erroll Garner. "It was fine with me, 'cause
I had been waiting for him all my life," Calhoun declared. "It was one of
those things where I saw him once and said, 'Now that's the guy I want to
play with.'"*

Erroll was in town for a couple of days, and he had to go to St. Louis.
When he came back from St. Louis, I got a call from him. I went to see
him at his hotel, and he asked me if I wanted to join his trio. I jumped
at the chance. He gave me money and told me to pick up a plane ticket
and meet him in California.

When I got to California, I ran into Denzil Best, who was waiting for
Erroll too. So as soon as Erroll got there, he took us to a haberdasher,
and we got our suits and tuxedos and things. I really didn't expect to stay
more than a couple of weeks until his bass player, Wyatt Ruther, got out
of jail. I figured I'd be there a couple of weeks and then that would be
it. But after we got to California, he called a rehearsal; that was one of

the few rehearsals that we had, because he never did rehearse. When we got to rehearsal, the club was full of all these California musicians who had heard about the rehearsal, so Erroll wouldn't rehearse. Then he called a rehearsal for the next day, and they were there again, and he wouldn't rehearse then either. So that was our rehearsal; when we played a gig, that was the rehearsal. We never had a rehearsal, and I played with Erroll for 13 years, starting back in 1955.

That was two weeks before *Concert by the Sea,* in Carmel, California. There is a story behind that. We were working at the Black Hawk, in San Francisco, and then they had this side concert, which was on a Monday night down at Carmel. At the time we were playing they had a thing at the Black Hawk that whoever works there, Dave Brubeck worked opposite them on the weekend if they wanted to. So they had a big sign up—Dave Brubeck and Erroll Garner. When I saw it, I called Erroll up, because we were staying right in the hotel next door to the place, and he said he didn't know anything about it. Anyway, that weekend they had the two groups there.

On the first night Erroll just didn't play well at all. He just lollygagged and got drunk. The next afternoon he got himself back together, and when he came to work, he chopped them up like mincemeat. *Concert by the Sea* was the aftermath. The next day we went down to Carmel, and we were still smokin' from that Sunday night at the Black Hawk. When we got back to San Francisco, Tuesday morning, they had a sign on the door from the night before, "Due to circumstances beyond our control the club will be closed tonight." Dave Brubeck was in the hospital. They said it shook him up so much they just put him in the hospital for a couple of days. He didn't have to play but one set, and that was it—it just destroyed Brubeck. *Concert by the Sea* was the next night after that incident.

Afterwards, Paul Desmond told me, "I told Dave not to come in here." It was up to him whether he came in the club or not. After that, Martha put it in the contract to make sure there weren't any other pianists on the bill with him. That was because he wouldn't have to have the pressure or the competition of another pianist on the job.

The way *Concert by the Sea* came about was that a guy that was putting in the PA system at the hall also had a recorder connected into the PA system that we didn't know anything about. What it was is that he was picking it up over the microphone for the hall. After the concert we all went to a party, and the guy presented the tape to Erroll, which he bought right then. I think he paid around $400 for it. I guess he took it knowing that he would give it to Columbia. The concert was such a good concert that I knew if he didn't give it to Columbia, he would put it out himself.

Erroll could hear sounds that the ordinary person couldn't hear. He could hear up into an animal range and, therefore, he could hear sounds and put the combination of sounds together that made him distinct from most people. The sounds he would put together harmonically by our standards would be wrong, but from what he heard and what he could add to it, would make it right. I learned from him that he could put together three sounds and make a fourth off of those sounds.

Erroll was an artist too. Erroll could draw very well and could have easily been an artist. He had a natural gift for drawing and would do modern art or just anything he decided to draw.

The reason I left the trio was because of money; that was the only reason. It was Martha's doings, but he had to condone it, or it couldn't have been done. I remember how much I made, but I'd really like to keep that quiet because it wasn't that much, and I don't want to deface his name.

One time we were on the Jackie Gleason Show, and Jackie Gleason had a little song that he used as an opening for his show. It was a funny little ditty. Anybody could play it, but Erroll couldn't remember the damn thing. He wanted Erroll to play this thing on the show. Every time Gleason would hum it, Erroll would play it different. What they finally had to do was to put up a screen in back of him, and then Hank Jones stood behind this screen and hummed it to him while we were on. The funniest damn thing was that Hank was out there, and he still didn't play it right. Boy, I tell you, I could have went through the floor, I was so embarrassed. But Erroll played close to it. With Erroll's talents you just could not buckle him down like that.

We played a thing with the Kalamazoo Symphony. It was a kids' symphony up there. They must have had a hundred kids in the band. We would play maybe half-an-hour, and Kelly and I went down, and all the kids went up, so we went to the back of the auditorium. The band went into their overture and shit, and when it was Erroll's turn, he just sat there. He forgot what he had to play. The conductor had the good sense to make the band, by just holding his hand up and waving his baton, hold the note until Erroll finally came down with something. Boy, you talk about a conglomeration of shit going on for about 20 to 25 seconds until he finally got together. He never did get the introduction right. They had practiced and practiced. It was so damn funny. If I had been there on the stage, maybe I could have prevented this from happening. These were the little things that happened 'cause like I said, he couldn't read. His whole thing was from the heart. He didn't have to learn how to play the piano; he knew how to play it.

Martha would always try to downplay the sidemen. That was the reason that she, instead of putting our names on the jackets like she should have done, put them all inside the jackets. That was just how low she thought about us.

He had several road managers. She kept them as long as they did what she wanted them to do, which was to report to her every action that he did and every move he made. If they did that, then they stayed awhile. If they didn't do that, she didn't keep them. She was a very smart woman, in the sense that she knew how to get things done on the road, at any level she wanted to.

We were on our way to Paris, and the plane got out on the runway, and all the way out there at the end, you know, where they turn around and rev the engines up before you take off. It was a propeller plane. Anyway, they revved the engines up and then cut back and taxied back to the terminal, and, sure enough, she came running up in a jeep with some papers or something. Kelly and I made a bet and I won. I said when that plane turned around and went back, I said, "That's Martha." Sure enough it was; she really knew how to handle men.

The weather turned sour; it was bad but it didn't turn nasty. We were waiting in the airport to take off to go, and while we were there, this plane was coming in, but it ran off the end of the runway. Now we were supposed to get on that plane, but Martha wouldn't let us get on it. She cancelled the show and called it an "act of God."

Duke Ellington was one of the few big-time pianists that knew Erroll's ability. Monk knew it. I'm talking about the piano players now that really knew the way he was. They knew that he was a genius in his own right because they played the instrument that he played, for one thing. Oscar Peterson was an admirer of Erroll's, but I always had a feeling that Oscar thought the talent should have been his. He knew that Erroll had this extra thing that he or none of the rest of them had. As much as Oscar played, Erroll could come along and play five notes that would cover all the thousands that he had played.

I'm considered one of your better bass players around Chicago. I don't read well, but I don't really have to read. Now my playing is really coming into its own, in my later years, more so than it was in my younger years. Of course, being with Erroll has done a lot for me because harmonically the things that he used to play I can still remember. Many times it will give me an advantage on a person that never was exposed to him or his way of playing. His technique has rubbed off on me to the point where I have become very dominant in my playing, and it sticks right out like a sore thumb. I find myself now adapting a lot of techniques that he used, like color and phrasing. I automatically do it and the next thing I realize, the piano player that I'm working with will be falling into the line of this type of rhythm. It would be such a dominant type of playing. He haunts me. Sometimes his presence gets so strong I can't play anything but what he did. I'm talking about now, after he is dead all these years. It's almost like I'm playing with Erroll instead of the actual guy I'm working with.

One of the nicest clubs to work in was the London House in Chicago. Erroll was well liked there, and he and the bosses there had a very good relationship. I'll never forget when we were on the bandstand playing, and this waiter came through the door out of the kitchen, and he must have come through the wrong side or something. Anyway, somebody caught him right in the middle of the door; trays full of plates went all over the floor. Before anything could be said or done (we were playing when it happened), I remember Erroll made the sound of those plates crashing—on the piano. He made the exact sound of those plates. It just cracked everybody up, the boss included. Nobody got mad. He always played well at the London House.

I remember one night in Cleveland, Erroll used to be notorious for being late. Erroll called up from Toledo, which is quite a ways from Cleveland. At the time he called, we were supposed to be on the bandstand. Later he called again and said the taxi had a flat tire and as soon as they got it fixed he'd be there. About another half-hour he called up again and asked who was there. The place closed at 2 o'clock. Erroll got to work at ten minutes after one. He did play the last few minutes. We were supposed to go on at 9 o'clock.

In Philadelphia they fined him about $1,500 for that. We were supposed to open up at a Philadelphia club. Anyway, Erroll didn't show up all night. At that time he wasn't making the big, big money. The highest that Erroll got when I was working with him was $1,000 a night, if he worked in a club. I never knew what he got on his concerts.

When we traveled, everything was first class. Sol Hurok was like the impresario, they called him. We got top-notch, A-Number-One treatment when we traveled with him. He always had our itinerary all made up and a road man out there with us to do his job. Of course, he and Martha must have gotten along fairly well. She must have respected him very highly because we never had any problems. Erroll was under Sol's concert tour for two years, somewhere in 1957–59. During that time it was a pleasure because everything was first class: traveling, hotels, etc. We were still under Sol Hurok when we went to Europe. They have their own impresarios over there like they do here, and then they hook you up to one of the offices that they are affiliated with, and then you go under them over there. When we were in Europe, we were always under the booking office of Philips. Philips usually handled our whole tour, and then they subcontracted out along the way, but it was still under Philips' tour.

I'll tell you one thing I do remember. We played St. Mary's College, across the street from Notre Dame in Indiana, and I remember this very well. Erroll opened up with "Love for Sale," and I could have died, but nobody really caught on to the tune. Can you imagine him opening up St. Mary's College with "Love for Sale?" Man, we laughed about that later. I said, "Man, how could you possibly have come up with "Love for Sale," and he said, "I don't know! It just popped up into my head, and I played it." I expected them to stop the concert with all those nuns out there.

KELLY MARTIN
(Drums)

Kelly Martin was born in Lake City, South Carolina, on September 16, 1914. When he was seventeen years old, he moved to Detroit with his aunt and attended intermediate school, which is where he started playing drums. After high school, Martin played with Erskine Hawkins from 1944 to 1946. He was with Jimmie Lunceford's big band for a short time and then worked New York's 52nd Street with Ben Webster, and later with Roy Eldridge. He also traveled with Teddy Wilson. Martin joined Erroll Garner in Pittsburgh at the Copa Club in October 1956 and left the group in Pittsburgh in 1966.

After I left Erskine Hawkins, I was free-lancing around New York, working with Ben Webster and Roy Eldridge down on 52nd Street. John Simmons and Shadow Wilson were working with Erroll at the time. Shadow and I were good friends. I met him in Detroit years ago when he was with Lionel Hampton. Shadow was always a baseball fan. It was during the days of Joe DiMaggio and all the star Yankees. If Erroll had a job around New York and a ball game was on at the time, Shadow would fake an accident. Ya know, like he got his hand hurt or his thumb; he'd put a bandage on or something. When he wanted to catch a Yankee game, he wouldn't mention anything to Erroll about it; he would just call me and say, "Can you make the gig for me?" So I'd go on the gigs with him when Shadow didn't show up. I'd show up on the job and Erroll would say, "Hey, 'K'...! 'K'...!" He was very congenial and he liked my style of playing. That was my first introduction to playing with Erroll.

Phil Moore was the cause of me being with Erroll later on [1956] because he was on his way to Chicago, and Erroll was at the London House. Denzil Best had left Erroll to come back to New York, so Erroll had a local drummer around Chicago. Phil stopped in to see Erroll, and Erroll mentioned he needed a drummer, so Phil said, "Why don't you get Kelly Martin?" Erroll called me right from the club and asked me to meet him at the Copa Club in Pittsburgh.

When I joined Erroll, I went to Pittsburgh and I stayed in the hotel, near the place downtown. He was like an act they had plus another band, so I went early and set my drums up, on the side of the floor. Erroll was supposed to go on at 9 or 10 o'clock. I got down there, and about a half-hour before we went on, I met Eddie Calhoun. I said, "I used to play with Erroll years ago with Shadow Wilson. What you all doing now?" Eddie said, "Man, I don't know." He said, "Man, I can't tell you nothing; we just get up there and play! I don't know what this cat is going to do." I said, "What?" So about five or ten minutes before the guy announced Erroll Garner, Erroll came in, we shook hands, and he said, "Hey 'K,'

Hoo-chi-coo, glad you could make it." And by this time the announcer was announcing Erroll Garner's trio. Well, I finally got a chance at the last minute. I said, "Hey man, what are we going to do?" Erroll looked at me and said, "Let's get up there and play." That's the way it happened, no rehearsal, nothing.

Shadow Wilson used to tell me, "Just keep your eyes on this guy 'cause if you take your eyes off him, he'll turn left 'cause he's thinking every minute." He'd take an intro and play it for sixteen bars, maybe twelve, depending on how he'd feel, and then he'd jump into something. Everything he does you can mostly tell by the expression on his face. He said, "Sit where you can look at his face." John Simmons, who was a good bass player, would sit on his left-hand side, and all them good bass players, that know a little about the piano, they would watch his left hand. He didn't care anything about keys, so they would follow his left hand in the bass clef. But the ones that tried to read stuff had trouble. His whole idea about playing the piano was different.

The recording sessions with Erroll were a killer. He'd like to do the recording sessions late at night or early in the morning, like around 4 o'clock, and the guy would put the tape on, and we just got to playing like we'd be playing in a joint. We'd play and we'd stop and take a break and then come back and play again. The way they did it, they played a tape over, and the one that we didn't make any mistakes on, that's the one that they would use.

Martha Glaser was all for him. I got along with her. I think it was our first trip to Europe, on TWA out of LaGuardia. It was a big plane, and Eddie and I were sitting up, and the plane got to the runway just about to take off, and suddenly he slowed down. Eddie said right off, "I bet you Hoo-chi-coo or Martha forgot something." I said, "Are you kidding? This is a transoceanic flight and on a major runway." We bet $5. So pretty soon the captain came over the intercom and stated, "Ladies and gentlemen, we have a very important gentleman on this plane, and he left some papers at the airport. He'll only be a second, and we will be on our way." We were in the first-class lounge, and everybody was talking, you know how they do, and Eddie snatched that $5 out of my hand. I wouldn't have believed it. Martha came rolling up in this jeep with his attaché case, and then we were on our way.

There were only three of us, and we played places like Berlin; we played for Princess Beatrice at the Amsterdam Sheraton Hotel. In fact, we were the only American act on the bill. It was for one of her charities—some country had a volcano disaster or something. In Zurich we played this large hall, and I noticed this peculiar look on Erroll's face. In the middle of a number, he got up and walked off the stage, and the next thing I heard was this scuffling. Here's this guy down there with a tape recorder between the curtains. That really pissed Erroll off. They do that over in Europe a lot. They invite you to a party and have the whole thing set up and suggest a jam session, get it all on tape, and then when you leave, they put a record out on you. Anyway, the situation was resolved and Erroll came back and finished the concert. That was about the only static that we ran into over there.

We did the French Lick [Indiana] thing. It was with Duke Ellington. It was great! On the day that Duke and Erroll played, it was just the two of them: Erroll would do the first half and Duke would do the second. They were terrific; it was beautiful. Duke and Erroll didn't like the idea of all those groups on there, everybody getting on and off the stage, and a whole lot of time for setting up. Duke had Jimmy Rushing, Johnny Hodges, and Harry Carney. In the first place, Erroll admired Duke, and I'm sure Duke admired Erroll too. Duke had such a classy way of presenting himself; he was strictly a class man.

Duke had a room that overlooked the tent where we were playing 'cause I saw him sitting up in his window when we were on. There is just so much that three pieces can do. It was a very appreciative crowd: there was the Erroll Garner crowd, that liked his style, and Duke had his crowd. We started right in on the first number. Duke was up in his window just listening. After we finished and had a slight intermission, the band had arrived and set up, and they started playing, and Duke was still up in his room. He didn't come on the bandstand, not 'til about five or six numbers later.

I finally understood why Duke did this. At first the opening was all piano with Erroll Garner. When the band came on, he let his band play until they got the Erroll Garner piano sound out of the people there. I thought it was so great the way he did it. He had his own style at the piano; he was a man with a lot of class and good thinking ability. I just got the willies. He was a real slick guy.

We'd go to a bar and have a taste, and as my glass got empty, I would start hitting on the empty glass with a swizzle stick. That was just the drumming in me. And you can bet your bottom dollar, that sound would get to Erroll, and the first two numbers he played in that sound, E natural, B natural, whatever. So Eddie would say to Erroll, "Hey man," after we got through, "why did you play in that key? You never play in that key." Erroll said, "I know, but it did sound pretty in that key, didn't it?" Eddie used to say he was going to break my fingers next time I went to hit on those glasses with Erroll around. Erroll would match the sound of the swizzle stick hitting the glass. It didn't make no difference to me 'cause I didn't have to change keys with the drums.

I learned to play golf while I was at the Concord in Upstate New York. Billy Eckstine got me interested in the game. I learned to play pretty well because I'd been playing since 1952, and I became very interested in the game.

Someone gave Erroll a set of golf clubs so I said, "Why don't you come out with me and see if you like the game?" I used to teach him. He'd hit the ball, and sometimes he'd miss it completely, and he laughed. He never took the game too seriously. I'd say, "Erroll, you've got to concen-

trate," and I'd get so involved in teaching him that I would forget how
to hit the ball myself. So I quit telling him, and I'd walk off and leave
him halfway down the fairway.

It was a whole different story when he got up to the putting green. He'd
be 35 to 40 feet from the hole and just casually take his putter and tap
the ball, and it would roll right into the hole. Man, here I am strugglin',
trying to get the ball in the hole and end up with a double bogey. Erroll
would take one stroke on the green and finish up before I could get there.
He'd chop up that fairway, but on the green he was terrific.

News got around the golf course that Erroll was playing golf. I think
the MacGregor people that make golf clubs sent him a brand new set of
clubs up to his apartment at Carnegie Hall. He's short, and they had to
measure the clubs. I guess they wanted to get some advertisement out of
it . . . Erroll Garner and golf . . . . They sent this guy a brand new set and
a pro up there to measure the clubs and have them cut off so he could
use them. They didn't even send me a ball. I said, "Ain't this something.
I taught this dude how to play." They were looking for a name. They
didn't even send me a ball or a tee!

I think Martha Glaser, you know how she is, was talking. She said,
"Oh, Erroll's on the golf course," ya know, something classy. Something
classy to say about Erroll, ya dig? He's out there choppin' up that golf
course, and I'm trying to help him.

Martha liked Erroll to hang out with me. He had that heavy insurance,
and they didn't want him hanging up in Harlem because it would void
his insurance; it would be a risk with the company.

I had my car, and a couple of times I drove him out to the golf course
so they told him, "Look, hire a limousine." Finally he got a contract with
the Carnegie Limousine Service. They said if he got hurt in my car, the
best he could get was $20,000. A big company like Carnegie could go a
long ways. The limousine driver would bring him up here, and we'd sit
here and have a few drinks, and he'd say, "Man, fix me some eggs or
something." The limousine driver would be out there for hours, but Erroll
was a good tipper. He'd take care of the guys. He wasn't a short coat
like a lot of performers. They want that attention and everything, but they
don't want to give up no money. Guys that are making that long dollar
can afford it, and some of them were making that long dollar and didn't
know how to tip. But Erroll, he learned a long time ago, like Charlie Parker
and them, 'cause they go to a town and couldn't get a place to stay, so
they had to use some money to get it.

I left him in Pittsburgh around 1966. It could have been December 3,
1966, at Carnegie Hall that I did my last show with Erroll. I left the group
because Erroll had wanted to make a change. After Eddie left, he and
I worked together for ten years, and we worked up all these gimmicks.
This is the way I assume it. People used to say that we sounded like one,
like the different punctuations we knew. He told me that he enjoyed the
stay, and that he should get somebody new to give him some new ideas.

I didn't mind; ten years was quite a while to play with one guy, and we did some nice things together. Later, I saw him after he got sick in Chicago, shortly before he died. I was in California on a vacation and I ran into him at the Baked Potato Club in Hollywood, where Teddy Edwards was playing. He told me that he had pneumonia in Chicago and that he was very sick. We talked and had a few drinks there, and I came back to New York, and later on I heard he died.

He used to play soft when the audience was talking too much; the louder they got, the softer we would play. There was always someone in the audience that would come to hear you, and when they don't hear anything, they would start to shush everybody. As soon as they quieted down, Erroll would go back into the song. He would just pretend he was playing, with his fingers going over the keyboard and not making any sound.

We were in Tokyo, and while having dinner we couldn't get a waitress or nothing. Erroll says, "Ebee-deebee, Hoochie-coochie-coo." He slips out a few of them fives, and the joint gets surrounded. We've got all these plates on the table, and I thought to myself, "How did he do this?" It was ridiculous! He had his own language.

NAT PIERCE

On the Road

NAT PIERCE

Nat Pierce was born on July 16, 1925, in Somerville, Massachusetts. "Piano was technically my first instrument," Pierce says. "I tried to play the clarinet for about a week, but I was horrible." His first big band job was with Shorty Sherock. Later, Pierce was associated with Larry Clinton, Ray Borden, and Woody Herman. He was Erroll Garner's road manager and also wrote the orchestral arrangements on Garner's Other Voices *album with the Mitch Miller Orchestra. Today he is co-leader with Frankie Capp of Juggernaut, a big band which mainly plays the West coast.*

Erroll only played by ear, and sometimes he didn't get the complete picture. He would listen to the radio; that's how he learned most of his music. A lot of it he learned wrong because he would turn on the radio and listen to eight bars one day, and the next day that eight bars would be gone, and the next eight bars would be coming up. When he put them both together, it wouldn't always be correct, but that's what his ear told him.

He made a record years ago, "I'll Remember April," on his *Concert by the Sea* album, and he plays the first 16 bars twice before he gets to the bridge, but that's the way he heard it. I'm not putting him down, but that's the way he thought it should have been done in the first place.

I used to teach him songs like, "The Look of Love," and some of the Beatles' songs. Martha Glaser would send me out to get the sheet music, and then we would make an appointment at the Nola Studios on 57th Street. There was a room where they used to do recitals. There were two pianos there, and I would play the tune as it was on the sheet music. Erroll

would be walking around looking out the window, smoking a cigarette
or something. Before I knew it, he's at the other piano; he would have
a symphony composed from this little silly ditty I was playing.
From what he played, if I was close enough, I could see what he was doing, but I
can do a pretty good imitation of him when the muse hits me. It's a hard
thing to pick his brain; you can't do that.
He used to drive his band nuts, particularly the bass player and the
drummer. He could play anything and everything in any key. Most players
that play by ear play in the black notes anyway, such as F sharp, B natural,
all the keys that nobody else plays in. He played them too, but not
deliberately because he would get into one of his symphonic introductions,
and then he wouldn't know what the hell he was going to do next. Finally,
he would flow into the tune, and it just wasn't like the way he played
it the night before. It was in a new key and a whole new conception. It
still came out like Erroll Garner, but the guys were always struggling away
trying to figure out which way he was going. He would laugh, giggle, and
carry on, and say, "I got you again."
Technically he had his own technique that he developed himself. A lot
of it was like this . . . with one finger. If you know anything about playing
a piano, playing like this (with one finger), instead of the actual way you
are taught . . . putting fingers underneath; it's really hard to make that
come out smooth, but he developed it to a point where he sounded like
he was doing it the correct way, but it never was. There was no technique.
It was just a home-grown adventure.
Erroll was left-handed. He could play the whole piano with his left hand
if he wanted to. He was very aware of sounds. Sometimes he would take
the whole palm of his hand and go, "Bam! Ding, ding, ding! Bam! Ding,
ding, ding! Bam!" He would always accent, just like a drummer. He was
a great stride pianist, but she [Martha Glaser] would never let him. If she
wanted him to do that, why didn't she let him do it? After he's gone, it's
too late.
He could have made a whole bunch of records like that; she didn't want
him to do anything [out of the ordinary], but by the time he got to a record
date, he had a different idea of what he wanted to do. He would always
do that medley, that beautiful closing medley [after club dates or concerts]
thing; he could have made an LP out of that, including every song known
to mankind in the middle. So he would fall back on "Lover Man" or
something like that 'cause she wouldn't let him do that; he was recording
the same song over and over again. What he really wanted to do was stretch
out. In those days when he'd play on the radio, you don't have any ten-
minute song; it has to be three minutes. It was kind of confining for him.
If he just sat down and played, he could still be playing right now. That's
how long the song would be because of his inventiveness. He could be
changing and changing and changing forever. He was very confined to
a degree but never in rehearsal or outside of the recording studio.
You can't compare a natural talent to a studied talent. Everybody has

a different style; either you like it or you don't. A lot of people didn't like Erroll. They say he was too stylized. Very few pianists have had that throughout the history of jazz—maybe five—where you hear the first two or three bars and you know exactly who's playing. Everybody else sounds like an offshoot of one of them. Naturally, nobody can play perfectly like someone else.

When I was arranging the parts for the Mitch Miller Orchestra, we didn't have cassette recorders. It was strictly dictation. A lot of those songs Erroll had never played before. Sometimes I had to stop him and ask, "How do you want the brass to sound?" He told me quite a bit, but eventually I had to use my own discretion.

Then came the record date, and he didn't remember any of this. I played his parts while he watched and listened. Then he sat down and played what he thought was right from what I had played. In the meantime, the band was playing the same thing all the time. You can hear some strange little things on those records, where he missed and then covered himself very quickly.

It was hard to control him; he didn't know what the hell was going on, so he just played through the whole thing, and the band orchestration was superfluous. It was hard to say, "Don't play yet; the band is going to play these eight bars." There was a lot of creativity going on at all times, and although it may sound like he played the same thing twice, I don't think he did. Everybody has what they call "coat hangers"—their own individual licks that they always played. But they were his licks; they weren't stolen from anyone else.

There were three sessions with Mitch Miller; 1956 was the first one. "Misty" he could always play. As for "On the Street Where You Live," he dropped a couple of bars on the turnaround, but we had to change the music to the way he wanted it. He could play a song with all the wrong chords at all the wrong times and make it sound correct. That's what he did with "The Very Thought of You" on that record. The chords were away from the chords in the original, but it sounded perfect. His mind took him to those places. We didn't have many takes on those sessions; I doubt if we went past four on some of them.

"Misty" was written before me, and it was recorded on Mercury in the early 50s [July 27, 1954]. Then there were some hits like the Johnny Mathis and Sarah Vaughan vocal versions, but all with the wrong bridge. Erroll is the only one who plays the correct bridge to make it easier for one to sing and hear. They put words to it, and they changed it just a bit, but the last four bars of the bridge are different than the way he plays it on the Mitch Miller record. That's the real melody on the bridge. We used to laugh about it. He said, "You and me are the only ones that know the right bridge on this song."

We were in New York in 1969 when he was recording "Mood Island," a new song that he had just put together. While in the middle of the song, Martha shut off the red light and screamed over the mike, "Stop, stop," and he didn't stop; he kept on playing. He finally finished, and she asked him why he didn't stop. She said, "You made a mistake and you're just wasting time." Erroll said, "I just wanted to see how it would come out." It's like he had no control. Like something was telling him he's got to figure this out. It was something higher up; it makes you want to believe in God because of this talent he had. He wanted to see how *it* would come out, not how he could make *it* come out; how *it* was going to come out by itself anyway, but he just wanted to be along with *it*.

He did a lot of rubato on his introductions. Everybody says he played behind the beat with his right hand, and many people complained that that's why they didn't like him. Not so! He just made the beat just as wide as it's supposed to be. Some piano players would play staccato, and he would play legato. His style never really changed; he got technically more proficient as the years went on. The first record you ever heard by Erroll still sounds like Erroll, right out of the wall sounding like a fully formed jazz pianist.

Erroll did not have perfect pitch. There is another pitch called relative pitch. He had 4000% of that. To a guy with perfect pitch, it hurts inside when something is out of tune, so consequently, they are always making allowances to get back in tune the way their insides tell them. Some people can play this way and others cannot, and it just drives them up a wall like a tire screeching outside, and it's a little flat. Erroll was very aware of sounds, and he could match sounds he heard around him on the piano. He chased a bumble bee around while playing "Red Top" on his *Concert by the Sea* album. Wherever the bee went, he was playing that note. You can hear some people laughing in there, too.

In Japan, he stopped the concert because a string broke on the piano. He stopped and got up in the middle of a tune. He wrapped it around something, and he continued the concert. He was struck by a string when he was younger, and it left a scar over his eye. It was close; it was a steel string, and it could have whipped his eye out. That was right before intermission. He was never in bad form. Some nights it seemed like he was just going through the motions, but even then some of the stuff was just great; I sometimes wished I had taped some of it.

Erroll liked the Baldwin piano, so he went to the Baldwin factory in Cincinnati. In the earlier days of piano making, these fellows were true craftsmen. They were real proud of what they were making, and I believe they offered him a piano because he endorsed Baldwin. He went through the factory playing all these pianos. After playing a hundred pianos, how do you tell which one is the best? This little old man came over and tapped him on the shoulder and said, "Mr. Garner, I think I have just what you want. I've never let this one out; I've been working on this for years." Erroll played it and said, "That's it," and they sent it to his house.

I was road manager for Erroll because Martha Glaser could trust me. No sense of sending anyone out on the road with any man if the people involved are not friends. Before and afterwards, I was road manager for

Woody Herman. It was easier with 16 guys because we had a bus. But when you've got one guy living over here and another guy living over there and I've got to get Erroll to the airport and I've got to worry—"Is the drummer coming from the west side? Is this guy coming from the east side? Is this guy coming at all?"—it gets very hairy and then many phone calls to the airport at the takeoff point from Martha Glaser: "Is so-and-so there? Is everything all right?" There was no panic, but by the time it was all put together, it was chaos.

Martha used to give him a hundred $5 bills. That's a lot of money. It would fit into a small wallet, and he would peel them off. When we got to an airport and there was a problem, Erroll would go, "Hoochie-coochie-coo, Ebee-deebee," he tells this guy. That was his lick, skin on the hands, the whole thing. Wherever he went, all over the world, it was "Hoochie-coochie-coo."

We were in Tokyo, and while having dinner, we couldn't get a waitress or nothing. Erroll says, "Ebee-deebee, Hoochie-coochie-coo." He slips out a few of them fives, and the joint gets surrounded. We've got all these plates on the table, and I thought to myself, "How did he do this?" It was ridiculous! He had his own language. If he knew you were married, he'd say, "Hoochie-coochie-coo. How's Mamacita?" Everyone that knew him—skycaps, bell hops, taxi drivers—it was no problem. They'd say, "Oh, Mr. Garner." You've got a fuckin' bass as big as a coffin, and he slips a few of those fives out. We went through . . . talk about first class. I wished I could have done that with Woody's band, but I didn't have the resources to do that. We had no trouble in the traveling department whatsoever, which proves the old point that money talks. A quick five here, a quick five there. He went all over the world like that, "Hoochie-coochie-coo, Ebee-deebee." He could talk to the world with those three lines. It was unbelievable!

Martha did a very good job with Erroll. She was a loyal manager. She refused anybody else, and she has stuck to that to this day, as far as I know. Maybe in his later years of traveling around, she overpriced him and didn't want him to work these little rooms because she couldn't get any money for him. Although he would go in and play free, she wouldn't know that. There was no way to control him; that's probably why one of the reasons she'd say, "No, you sit in the hotel room; I'll get you a job next week. Don't be running around disappearing." He could disappear pretty good too, just to get away from the policing activity that was going on.

It was like confining a tiger in a cage. He keeps pacing back and forth; he gets very unhappy, "Let me out." Martha used to tell him to stop smoking, which only made him run out and buy two more cartons. He was that type of guy. He was extroverted but shy in some ways. He attracted people wherever he went.

JACK BRADLEY

Jack Bradley, a noted jazz photographer, was road manager for Erroll Garner during various periods between 1972 and 1974. Born January 3, 1934, in Hyannis, Massachusetts, Bradley came to New York in 1959 as a Merchant Marine Officer but soon, he says, "My love for jazz overcame my love for the Merchant Marines." Bradley was the co-founder and managing director of the New York Jazz Museum. He was Louis Armstrong's personal photographer and has recently received a grant from the National Endowment for the Arts to do a photo history of Armstrong. Bradley was also Bobby Hackett's personal manager.

One of Erroll's fans in Philadelphia asked him how he got his name. Erroll replied, "I was named after Errol Flynn." He said it with such seriousness I thought I had just witnessed a great historical jazz fact. Later, when I started to think about it, I realized that Errol Flynn must have been a mere baby when Erroll Garner was born. He was just putting the fan, me, and everyone else on.

I really never did meet Erroll on a personal basis until I became his road manager. I believe it was Dan Morgenstern who recommended me to Martha Glaser. I was a friend of Dan's, and I had worked previously as manager for Bobby Hackett, and Martha called me and wanted me to make a trip down to Philadelphia as Erroll's road manager.

I had just finished working with Bobby Hackett, traveling with him, and Bobby was such an opposite from Erroll because Bobby was almost helpless. When he played the horn, he did it perfect, but it was other areas he just couldn't handle. I did everything for Bobby, and I worked almost 24 hours a day. With Erroll it was completely different. Erroll was completely self-sufficient in almost every way. I would arrange for the transportation, hotels and, when we got to the gig, set up the sound and lights, check out the hotel and rooms, and see what type of publicity they had. Martha would tell me if he had any interviews with any television people, what reviewers to contact, who was expected at the house, and who wasn't. I had to keep count of who was in the house, the tunes that were played, the number of people that were there, the lights, and the sound—the typical things that road managers do. It was easy with Erroll because I just have to show up as a rule, at eight that night, make sure the lights and sound are okay, do a test, and make sure the guys got on the stand and got off at the right time. At the end of the show, really my gig was over. Very often we would hang out at the club, listen to some music, have fun, whatever. Then Erroll wouldn't expect me until the next evening, unless of course there was some interview. I was always after him. "Do you want anything: clothes, laundry, food?" Whatever he wanted, I was available, but he said, "No, I can do it myself." He just wanted to do his own thing; he could take care of all that, and he'd see me on the evening of the gig. Although he wasn't always late, he was never early either. He'd worry the shit out of you, but he'd be there so cool and relaxed. He didn't appear to worry about anything, and he'd tell you not to worry; he would always be there, except for this one night.

We were out in Kansas City for a week at the Hyatt Regency out there, and it was about a half-hour before show time, and there was no Erroll. I knocked on his hotel room, and there was no answer. By coincidence Martha called up, "Is everything cool? Where's Erroll?" I told her I don't really know, but he's around here somewhere, but everything is cool. I'm looking in the restaurant, lobby, knocking on his door again. Of course, by this time Martha's calling me every five minutes. Finally it's showtime and no Erroll. The rest of the band's there, and I went and got the security guard and went to Erroll's room. I said, "Look, let me in the room. Maybe he's asleep," and we unlocked the door, and I go in and there's Erroll asleep, which he's never done before. He jumped up when we walked in the room and tried to convince us that he wasn't asleep, and he said he was just getting ready, and he'd be there in a minute, and he was down in ten minutes and did the job. It was really a moment of panic. It had never happened before or since while I was with him.

The show he did was tremendous as always, probably greater. Even listening to "Misty" every evening was always different—different beat, different tempo, different changes—and he always kept the band on their toes because they never knew what he was going to do next. The bass player always stood at the bottom of the piano so he could watch Erroll's hands and try to anticipate what he was going to do next.

Martha Glaser is a fantastic person, I really mean that: unbelievable personality, one of the strongest women I've ever met. She did a lot for Erroll to give him the recognition that he deserved. She turned many people off along the way, but she had her goals, and Erroll was treated like the consummate artist that he was. He went first class all the way. Any great artist deserves that. It was in the contract that no matter where we appeared, there would have to be a nine-foot Baldwin grand piano there. Another stipulation was that there'd have to be a piano tuner.

The afternoon that we arrived before a gig we did a run-through to make sure the piano was in tune. The tuner usually would have to be on hand the first couple of nights to touch up the tuning if it was off. Another one of my duties was to check with Erroll every night to see how the piano was and if it was a little off, I would call the tuner, and he'd be available to come down and tune it to make sure it was up to Erroll's specifications. Any great artist should have at least a good instrument that is in tune. Erroll, I believe, was one of the first ones that was fortunate enough to be treated like this. And much of that credit goes to Martha Glaser.

Erroll was really one of the most marvelous human beings I ever met. For the great artist he was, he was a most humble, self-effacing individual. You would never know he was the genius of the piano that he was. He treated everyone with respect and consideration. He never demanded anything of other people; he just wanted to do his job and play wonderful music, have a ball, and be left alone. Yet, I never saw him deny anyone an autograph. His dressing room was always open for his friends and fans. He found time for everyone: old and young, rich and poor, black and white. He just had it all covered as a human being, and I find that difficult to separate from Erroll the musician because it all came out in his music—his love, devotion, caring, his love of beautiful melodies. He just wanted to create beautiful music and make people happy and he succeeded admirably!

... Erroll would play an introduction, and we would just sit there; he'd play that intro and bang—just magically, man, it was number one!

JIMMIE SMITH

The Rhythm Section
1967–1975

JIMMIE SMITH
(Drums)

Jimmie Smith was born in Newark, New Jersey, on January 27, 1938, and studied drums with Max Kaplan and Al Jamanski. His training on cymbals was with Charlie Perry. He attended the Juilliard School for two years and has worked with Lambert, Hendricks and Ross, Lionel Hampton, Della Reese, Benny Carter, Ray Brown, Art Pepper, and organist Jimmy Smith. The two were once booked on tour as Jimmy Smith and Jimmie Smith.

I joined Erroll in 1967, and I stayed with him for seven years. It was the latter part of the year when I joined him. I was working at a club called the Pied Piper in Los Angeles, and he came in and listened to me play. I had gone to do the Monterey Jazz Festival, and when I came back in town, there was a maître d' by the name of Bill Jones who told me that Erroll was looking for me and that he wanted me to join his group. The first place I played with him was the Tropicana in Las Vegas.

I always remember when we would have a rehearsal with the symphony. Everything was written down, but as you know, Erroll never played the same thing the same way twice. The conductor would be leading the band, and Erroll would just improvise and would take it somewhere else but he would always end correctly. I told him he was a genius. He was a modest man, and he would just roll those big eyes and say, "Hoo-chi-coo." I'm a type of person who gave him his accolades while he was living. Erroll and I had a rapport that wasn't merely a relationship between leader and sideman. That's the way he was with his sidemen because everybody gave everybody space. We respected each other, and we had so much fun on the road.

I used to kid with him; I used to go up and sit with him, and he would give you his heart. I'd say, "Hooch man, give me some orange juice, some instant orange juice." He was like a father with a family. If a cat needed some money, the cat would say, "Hey Erroll, man, like I'm a little short; lend me some money." Erroll would disappear and come back with new, fresh money; he would never give you old money. He was just so pure; he had that magic, and you would just love to be around him.

The seven years I was in the group we had five bass players because that bass chair was very hard. I felt privileged to hold that drum chair down because Erroll had so many great cats like Shadow Wilson, Denzil Best, Kelly Martin, and a young cat like myself moves in because "The Man" is looking for me to join his group. Being with Erroll was an honor. I mean, he had Denzil Best, who was the greatest brush man in the world, other than ol' man Jo Jones. Here I am a young man sitting there. Erroll just taught me so much about dynamics and how to play so quietly but so effectively.

Erroll taught me how to listen. He taught me discipline because I was a young, cocky man who wanted to play fast, but Erroll played so much piano that you just had to keep time and put your little things in there, you know, get in there and get out. Erroll played so much piano and we never rehearsed. The seven years I was with Erroll, we never rehearsed, and Erroll would play an introduction, and we would just sit there; he'd play that intro and bang—just magically, man, it was number one!

I never played with him when he was with the big symphony orchestras because Martha Glaser didn't let us do that. What we would do is, Erroll would go and do the first half, and then the trio would come on for the second half. The conductor would be up there conducting, and Erroll would substitute different chords. He'd be right, but it wouldn't be written down on the conductor's sheet, and the conductor would be looking as if he was saying, "Where is he, where is he?" On the down beat he'd come on in there and do his thing because Erroll knew where he was at all times.

One time we went to England. Jon Hendricks had a gig and man, we didn't know nothing. Jon wanted us to go to Birmingham to play this gig with him. Jon got a train, and it must have been fourth class 'cause we stood up all the way. When we got back, Erroll said, "Hey cats, where've you been?" We said, "We went to Birmingham to do this gig with Jon," and Erroll said, "The union is on me because you knocked some other cats out of the way." We didn't know that; we were just doing Jon a favor because we were with the old group. When you go to England, you have to get a work permit. We got Erroll in trouble, and he had to pay the union man off. Erroll never said anything more to us.

We went to Yugoslavia and the guards met us at the plane. They were like SS Gestapo Storm Troopers. When we checked into the hotel, it was like looking back in time. They were like 20 years behind, cameras sitting on tripods. All four of us ate; I had a four-course dinner, and we spent $20 for four people. We went downstairs and asked the hotel clerk to call a cab. We wanted to go out on the town. The man said, "There ain't no town; this is Yugoslavia." They didn't have to tell us twice; we went back to our rooms.

Erroll was good to us. We never dealt with Martha. Erroll dealt with Martha; we dealt with Erroll. If we were going on tour, it was like we were working for the CIA; it was a big secret. Erroll told us in the beginning, "Man, you got any problems, don't go to Martha. Come to me; I'll straighten it out." She was taking care of all the business. She was like his Jewish mother.

When Erroll records, he doesn't really know what he's going to play. That's the secret of the thing. The band would be there, and we'd be out playing rhythm, and he'd be in the booth listening to us. We were just playing around. Those things we did on *Gemini,* Erroll would let us be in the studio for an hour before he'd come out and record. He would just listen to us mess around. When he came out, there wasn't any talk about "take two, take three." It was always one take. I imagined he was just physically or mentally getting himself together.

Today you hear people copy Count Basie, Duke Ellington, and the other masters. But you haven't ever heard anybody play over eight bars of Erroll Garner. It was a unique style. I have played with all the greats, but man, there is only one, and that's Erroll Garner. Erroll Garner was the Master!

Erroll had that spiritual thing, and you could hear it in his playing. Today you can sit back and listen to one of his albums, and it would put chills through your soul. It's just simplicity—not a whole lot of notes—it's just simplicity. I recorded an album with Oscar Peterson titled, *Macho 77.* I have never played that fast before. He was playing so fast, but it didn't have nothing to do with nothing because I've been with the Master.

Some people were a little scared of Erroll because he was such a genius. They had this attitude like, if a cat can't read music, it was a no-no. They put Erroll Garner down because he couldn't read. But sit him down at the piano, it was God's gift. But some people didn't see that; they'd say, "Well he can't read the music." Every time he would play a song it would just get better. I was talking to Ray Brown, and he said he spent all his time in the book. He said people spend all their time trying to keep time with a metronome; they just don't know how to come out of the book. It's like a mechanical thing. My teacher said, "Rhythm is like a rock in motion coming down hill: it picks up momentum. It's not how much you play, it's what you play, 'cause simplicity gets in every time."

I said, "Erroll, you know, man, I'm going to give compliments to you now while you're alive so you can hear, not after you're dead. Everybody usually gives you accolades after you're dead and gone, and you can't hear them." I used to say, "Hooch, man, you're a genius," and he would do nothing but roll those big, brown eyes and smile.

JOSÉ MANGUAL
(Conga Drums)

José Mangual was born in Juana Viaz, Puerto Rico, on March 18, 1924. Originally a bongo drummer, he worked with Machito from 1942 to 1959 and then traveled with Herbie Mann. He worked as a conga drummer with Erroll Garner from 1967 to 1975.

I first met Erroll at Birdland in the late '40s, maybe the beginning of the '50s. When Erroll was playing 52nd Street, he used to go to Birdland to listen to Machito's Band. He used to sit with us. But the first time I played with him was in '67. Johnny Pacheco was making a recording with him. One day Pacheco couldn't make it, and he sent me to finish the album, *That's My Kick.* I saw Erroll and we hadn't seen each other in a long time 'cause he was traveling, and I was traveling the other way. So we met, and he asked me if I wanted to play with him. He wanted me to go to Mexico with him. Our first date was a concert at Bellas Artes in Mexico City.

When I first went with Erroll, I didn't want to carry the bongos for a little group like that, so I used the conga drums. The sound of a bongo drum was too tinny for a little group. You need a little body, something deep. Erroll was always looking for different sounds. He wanted to use a guitar because we made an album together with a fellow by the name of Wally Richardson.

Erroll was generous to everybody. If anybody needed anything, he was there. I remember at the St. Regis Hotel [New York City], a guy came over from Harlem . . . took a cab, didn't have any money. He went inside; he sat there for the show and drank. Meanwhile, the cab driver was waiting for him, you know, the clock is running. So when we finished, the guy comes over, and the cab driver came in with a policeman to make the guy pay. Erroll said, "Here, don't worry about it," and he paid him. He didn't even know the guy! He didn't know the guy, but he just didn't want the guy to go to jail.

You know, like sometimes you travel with a leader, anybody, and you have a following. And you play some extra gigs or whatever—a radio show or a television show—and most of the leaders, they stay with the money; they take that money, and they won't give you anything extra. Erroll used to give us extra money. If we did anything extra, we got paid for it.

ERNEST McCARTY, JR.
(Bass)

Ernest McCarty, Jr., was born in Chicago, Illinois, on March 26, 1941. He attended DuSable High School and played bass in the symphony orchestra at Roosevelt University. Prior to joining Garner in 1970, McCarty collaborated with Oscar Brown, Jr., to write the original production of Jazz '66. *McCarty's other credits include* I Dream't I Dwelt at Bloomingdales, The Exchange, *and* Life After Comas. *He is the co-author of the off-Broadway production* Dinah-The Queen of the Blues.

Meeting Erroll Garner catapulted me to a level on the bass, which completely wiped out any desire I had to play with a symphony orchestra. I could let that whole situation go without carrying it for the rest of my life, on my death bed at ninety-nine years old saying, "But I never played with a symphony orchestra." That was no longer a priority goal. At that time I was dreaming that it was everything. When I met Garner and I was playing bass, that was so far above playing bass in a symphony orchestra that I didn't have to carry that hangup any more.

I worked with Dorothy Donegan before; Lou Donaldson and I worked with a lot of people, but Garner was a spiritual union. From the first day with Garner, there had been nothing like it. I got a chance to see the world—things I read about in books. I had gone to Europe and Japan with Odetta, as her bass player in 1969, but I saw the world from a different viewpoint with Erroll, I mean South America. The level of people he came in contact with were of the diplomatic level. These fans were not the traditional jazz fans that I always saw. I saw the dudes in the clubs with the shades on in the back with the chicks, but I never saw any princesses that were jazz fans; I never saw any daughters of generals like I saw in Brazil. No one ever told me that the music that was spawned in the South had something to give to all kinds of people. The entities in his music would reach them, and Erroll had so much of it. When Erroll went to Europe, people would wait for him like he was a messiah. I don't mean in an omnipotent way, but I mean people loved him. The type of people who were loving him were people of some importance. I didn't know that a jazz musician was in a world like that; I only thought they were junkies. No one ever told me that jazz was a highly political occupation as well. Some of the tours were partially government-sponsored.

When we went behind the iron curtain, there were some emotional things going on between the director of a TV show in Belgrade [Yugoslavia] and Erroll. This director wanted the piano to be positioned a certain way, and Erroll wanted it his way, so we had a standoff for a couple of hours. Erroll canceled the TV show.

The next night we had the concert. We were playing on the stage, and the hammer and sickle were behind us in one of these big halls. All of the diplomats and government officials are sittin' out in front. We were all so mad; all four of us were mad. We were going to show these communists what it's about. Erroll played a set that was so ridiculous that during the intermission two soldiers brought the director in, each holding his arm to give his apology to Erroll. Then he was off to Siberia in his suede suit with his ascot on, just like Hollywood. We don't speak the language; we don't know what they told the people that we did. The only thing that could happen was the entities in the spirit that's in the music that's in the man has got to completely set the record straight. Erroll could talk to people, no matter what their language was, through the piano.

I met Erroll at the Apartment Supper Club. I was standing in for another bass player, Victor Gaskin, who never came back. They liked me and asked me to stay, but I kept trying to find a bass player 'cause it was six shows a night, and I didn't want to do that. I couldn't find anybody. Erroll and others would come in, and one night when he came in, he called me over to his table. He asked me if I was interested, and I said, "Yeah, man," so we set up for the audition at Nola Studio on 57th Street, and I played and that was that. A couple of weeks later I was in South America.

It was [July] 1970 when I got started with Erroll. We went to Venezuela; then we went to Brazil. The first city in Brazil we went to was Rio de Janeiro. It was nice, laid back and real nice. Then we went to São Paulo, a city similar to Chicago, an industrial city, one that even looked like Pittsburgh. We were appearing in this colosseum, which was sold out. There were people outside of the gate the night of the concert trying to get in. The next night there were a few thousand out there. They had to bring in the militia to hold the crowd back from breaking down the gate. When we got back to the hotel, there were hundreds of people waiting; chicks all over the place, totally unbelievable! I cried when we left Brazil; I couldn't understand a place where people were so nice and understood the music.

Argentina was just the opposite: people came to the concert, but when it was over they just disappeared. They were cold. In Venezuela we were greeted by machine guns and soldiers. I think South America was going through some major political changes in the '70s.

Within a week of my audition with Erroll, we went to South America. The drummer that went with us was Bill English. He was fired at the end of the gig at Mr. Kelly's [Chicago]. We then opened up at the Persian Room of the Plaza Hotel [New York], and that's when Jimmie Smith joined us. I think Erroll was the first jazz artist to ever appear there, which was one of the things in Martha's favor because she did some good things for Erroll, but she also did some other things. Now I'm trying to be even-handed here.

We played the Frog and Nightgown in Raleigh, North Carolina. He had mentioned that he had some relatives there or that he lived there once. Maybe that explains why we went there. It was only a four-day gig. They were all grumbling about the money, and I said, "Hey, it's only four days. Where else do you think the money is coming from?"

Erroll and I had another kind of relationship going on. I felt being able to play with this man was payment enough, and everybody is not like that. We very seldom ever worked over the Christmas holidays. We did a couple of Thanksgivings; we did Lennie's-on-the-Turnpike in Massachusetts. We played the Workshop in Boston one time, which was a strange kind of place. Here Erroll is a jazz pianist, but the people who follow the grassroot jazz didn't think that much of him. They liked people like Herbie Hancock. The people who were in the upward class all over the world loved him.

I knew he didn't die from the emphysema. On the last trip, Erroll had a whole attaché case of medicine he was supposed to take. Too much medication! Erroll had to have some special kind of capsule. I don't care what they say, but I knew Erroll was terminally ill.

When we went to Luxembourg in 1974, following a tour that Duke Ellington made, Erroll was getting rooms that Duke had stayed in, and Erroll wouldn't sleep in them. He said, "No, Duke just died." I could tell in his music and in his eyes that he was getting weak. It's a different kind of weakness when you're sweating, getting rid of alcohol, than when you're getting weak because you have no resistance. You have a feeling and you know it isn't right. He just wasn't the same. I think that if you know that your time is coming close, you want to let it all hang out. If somebody says you got a year to live, why should you care?

Martha kept him business-wise. She controlled his artistic output. Now from the *Gemini* album, he could not even stretch out the way he wanted to, which means in his last days or years he knows that he is not going to be able to do anything. Why should I even try to be creative when I know that I can't do it? Martha wanted it a certain way. That's going to make one bored to have to keep imitating, or doing the same shit. Erroll Garner was just imitating Erroll Garner.

I felt that boredom had set in. Erroll should have had some projects to work on just like everyone else: some kind of writing, some kind of movie, some kind of theatrical piece, or even just writing material for a new album. But obviously there was nothing. He had nothing to do but smoke cigarettes, cigars, anything; he didn't care. He was supposed to be taking his medication, not smoking or drinking, and that's just what he was doing twice as much of. I don't know if he even took his medication because he never took it around anyone.

I know that from looking at Oscar Brown, Jr., mess up his career, I started recognizing the signs, being a bass player. A bass player is like the catcher on a baseball team. You can see the whole game, musically speaking. I'd see the signs of no progress. There were certain gigs that we never went back on. Why didn't he repeat a place? We repeated the Maisonette [New York], but the Frog and Nightgown was never repeated;

we never repeated the Blue Max in Chicago, probably due to Martha, because when he was touring with Andy Williams, they came to Erroll and said, "We can't have you anymore 'cause Martha is driving us crazy."

I left Erroll in 1974 after the tour in Denver. I had a big blowout with José. José didn't like me very much, for whatever reason it was. Maybe it was because I wore a hat. So he was always involved in my personal life and I told him, "You're just like a little bitch." That particular time I had just had it; my father just died, and I had a big, big, blowout with José. Martha sent me a letter telling me that she didn't think my services were going to be needed anymore. And that was that! Erroll was coming to Mr. Kelly's in 1975, and he got sick, and that was that. The letter I got was just from Martha. Erroll never signed nothing; he never signed any checks either.

When I first joined the group, I was young, much younger than everybody else. They were going to teach me to travel, although I had been around the world three times. Just because I looked young, I had to grow a beard to get some respect. Then when the people found out that I was into a lot of other things, like shows for Broadway and off-Broadway, Erroll came when we got off the plane in California and said, "I'm not going to lose you to Broadway, am I?" I told him, "No." There was the problem of envy and jealousy; I was doing one-man shows, movies, and commercials. All José was doing was running some little joint, and then Jimmie was just playing and laying back and being wonderful. So none of those things helped, and my attitude was that I didn't care about what anybody felt as long as Erroll liked what I was doing. He hired me. Martha didn't hire me.

Martha used to come to my house, and I would talk to her and set her straight in my house. I said, "You don't come to my house and tell me where the chairs should be." None of them would do that to Martha, which was another thing to hold against me. I used to do all the sound checks; Martha's errand was to make sure they're all wearing the same color ties. Okay, I'm the youngest guy in the group, and here I am doing these things. I felt that with a man as international as Erroll is, you can't have a mind that small. I tried and finally I just said, "The hell with it. I'm just going to play."

The last tour we went on was in the Spring, to Louisville, Kentucky, and Baltimore. It was just Erroll and I. José and Jimmie didn't come. Early 1974, Jimmie decided he just wasn't going to come, and José said he had bursitis. It was just Erroll and I doing a duo with the Louisville Symphony. When we went to Milwaukee that year, I got Arlington Davis, a drummer from Chicago, to play the Milwaukee set, which made everybody jealous then. I said, "Look, the man needed a drummer." I was getting tired of all of that, so I just said, "José, listen man, I'm not a child." The last time I saw Erroll, it was in a hotel room in Denver. I knew we were going to play Mr. Kelly's in Chicago next, and I was going to be there already when she wrote me. Chicago is my home, so I saved her the plane fare.

When my father died, I became the head of the family, and I had a lot of responsibilities. Then, of course, when Erroll passed away, I had to be the patriarch on the artistic side. "Why should I regress?" I thought. "Life is a perpetual upward spiral." So I said, "Okay, that's the way it fits in the cosmos." As long as I played bass with Erroll Garner, I would never go off into writing. I would never have done the things that I'm doing now.

BRIAN TORFF
(Bass)

Although Brian Torff only played ten days (February 11–20, 1975) for Erroll Garner, they were the last ten days of Garner's career. Since then, Torff has achieved international recognition as one of the world's finest bassists, playing with such greats as Mary Lou Williams, Stephane Grappelli, Marian McPartland, Tony Bennett, and almost three years as a duo with George Shearing. Born March 16, 1954, in Hinsdale, Illinois, Torff studied at the Berklee College of Music and the Manhattan School of Music.

My professional career began when I was twenty years old, and my first opportunity was with Cleo Laine. I toured with her in October of 1974, and after that I came off the road to play at a club called St. James Infirmary in the Village [New York City]. I met Nancy Bell there, who at the time was working for Erroll Garner. She liked my playing very much, and I expressed how much I admired Mr. Garner's playing.

It was the end of January, early February [1975], I got a call from Martha Glaser asking if I would be interested in working with Erroll Garner. I was stunned at first. I just couldn't believe it; I thought it was a joke because here I was still in music school and getting an incredible opportunity to play with this giant. I very shakily agreed and Miss Glaser made it very clear that if I didn't cut the mustard, that I would be on the first plane back to New York. Martha really stunned me on that first phone conversation because I was a naive kid from the Midwest, and I wasn't used to the New York style of dealing with people. It's almost like she just didn't want to hire me. It was like she called me because she couldn't find anybody else. She said to me, "I'm concerned about this because I really don't think that young white bass players swing." That kind of stunned me because how do you argue with something like that? You can't say, "Yes ma'am, I really do swing." Music should never be put on a racial level. This has nothing to do with the art, so I just sort of stammered.

Two hours later Erroll Garner called me from Los Angeles. I was very concerned about being properly prepared musically because quite frankly, I was raised on the music of the Beatles, and my jazz experience was limited; therefore, I had a limited repertoire of the tunes that Erroll Garner played. I said, "Mr. Garner, when will we rehearse?" He said, "Well, our first job is on February 11, so I think we'll rehearse on February 10!" That scared the living daylights out of me because I thought, here I have one rehearsal to learn all his music.

I went to the record store and bought as many records as I could afford and started sweating it out, learning all these songs. As it turned out, we never did have a rehearsal. We flew to Washington, D.C., and opened at a club called the Etcetera Club. I believe we played a couple of tunes before we went on that night. That was how I began with Erroll.

Fortunately, I have some piano background, so I started to become good at reading piano players' hands. I kind of looked down at his hands, and there were many tunes that he played that I didn't know that well or that I vaguely remembered hearing, but Erroll laid it down very clearly for me. He would play these long symphonic introductions, often having little to do with the piece he was about to play. I would be sweating bullets the whole time wondering what was going to come up. He was very kind to me; he knew how nervous I was and how much I wanted to make good. Ronnie Cole was the drummer, and José Mangual, the conga drummer, was wonderful also. We were all pulling together. So he would lay down the chords in a way that I could see them and hear them. He had that raspy sort of voice, and I must admit, the first week I couldn't understand a word he said most of the time because it was unlike anything I had ever heard before. He'd turn to me and rasp something, and I'd say, "Yea, yea," not having the slightest idea of what he said to me. I just figured that was cool.

I could usually tell by his left hand what key he was in, but I do remember once he called out to me, "Misty in E flat," but he would actually be playing in B natural or G flat. He didn't do this to throw me off. To him all the keys were the same. Erroll had no key preferences that I could see. He just simply played the piano.

When we were in Washington, D.C., he had a cold and was coughing. It was the kind of cough that was a raspy, smoker's cough. He seemed to be breaking out in a cold sweat a lot. We got to Chicago and opened at Mr. Kelly's on a Monday [February 17, 1975]. This was a big deal for me because Chicago is my hometown, so here I was coming home to play with this jazz giant, so I was thrilled to pieces.

As the week progressed, the cough seemed to get worse and worse. We played Thursday night [February 20, 1975] and did a couple of sets. Friday morning I got a call from his road manager (Bill Layne) telling me that all our subsequent work was canceled because Erroll was going into the hospital. He explained to me that in the middle of the night Erroll had kicked the covers off because the room got so hot, and then the heat shut off. I'm not clear on the details, but apparently he caught pneumonia. I was in shock because in the short time I was with Erroll, I became very fond of him, and what had been such a beautiful thing was suddenly ending so quickly. I went back to New York within a day or two after that, and it took me months to recover from that. I was devastated!

The very last song he played was the blues original in A flat. I really had fun with this blues tune because toward the end it was like Erroll and I were chasing each other, so instead of just playing a walking bass, I would start playing lines like a cat chasing a mouse. We really got into some interplay, and if the opportunity would have been there, I think we would have continued that kind of thing because he really enjoyed it. I don't think he had done that much before because I think he worked with more conventional bass players who laid down the beat and stayed in the background. He liked the fact that I was doing something different, and it seemed to turn him on.

The last night my mother was there, and I put a small cassette recorder on her table. I asked Erroll if it was all right if I taped the show because I was trying to learn all this music. I had no rehearsal and every night was like a new thing. Erroll said, "It's fine with me; you don't even have to ask." Subsequently, Martha Glaser insisted that I return the tape and if I didn't, she threatened to sue me. She said, "Erroll would have killed you if he found out." It makes me think sometimes, "Did Erroll really ever get to think for himself?" He certainly didn't seem to object.

What I remember most about Erroll Garner was standing in the kitchen at Mr. Kelly's. He turned to me and said, "I just try to make every night just like a party for the people." That was really his philosophy as far as I could tell. I never forgot that, and that's really what it's all about. We can get very serious and talk about the music as an art form; we can talk about it from a sociological standpoint, but basically I agree with him, that above all this music is supposed to make people feel good. There are other pianists with more technique but Erroll was a happy musician who could get a smile out of the piano, and that made his audience smile. It was just as simple as that.

*He didn't know the power and the strength of love that people had for him.
I don't think he even knew how many people just admired him for him and
not just for his music. He didn't realize what a precedent he set upon the
universe.*

The Final Years
1975–1977

ROSALYN NOISETTE

*Rosalyn Noisette was Garner's closest companion during the last six years
of his life. In this interview she discusses his personality, likes, dislikes, and
the tearful last moments of his life.*

I met Erroll at a party that was given by people in the entertainment field.
I went to the party, and I was not very happy with the situation, the people,
and what they were doing at the party. I met somebody that felt the same
way, and it was Erroll. During that time we ended up talking and being
together, and we decided to leave the party along with other folks who
also wanted to leave. It ended up that the other folks entertained us. They
left and I was with Erroll ever since.

I lived with Erroll. My relationship with him was a man to a little girl
and later a man to a woman. I grew to love him as I did because of his
natural being. He was one of those type individuals that I had never
encountered before. He understood and felt everything about our relationship, my spirit, my being, my love for him, and even my dishonesty,
which he even told to me, which made me more honest than I had ever
been. His love of nature is what I picked up on to make me be a more
natural person than I was before I met him.

Erroll could tell if you were ill by your scent, which many other people
really couldn't understand. He could tell if you were happy, or unhappy
through people's natural scents. He had a natural aura about himself.

He loved to cook. He cooked roasts especially. Whenever I was going
to cook a roast, he wanted to do it himself. He took pride in the way

he cooked, and he cooked good. He loved fresh vegetables, and he knew how to prepare them, and clean them and make nice dishes with them. He liked to cook and he loved to eat. The two go together.

He ate out quite a bit as well. Fact is, a lot of the dishes that he learned how to fix at home were some things that he had eaten out. He would get the chefs to come out and tell him how they fixed a particular meal that Erroll or I might have enjoyed. I learned how to make veal piccata that way.

He loved old movies, real old movies. Generally he loved television, but he would fuss about a lot of the actors and how they got on there. He said some of them must have got on TV because their mothers must have owned the show. He loved Burgess Meredith, Laurence Olivier. He didn't like Robert Vaughn or Richard Burton. He liked comedy, good comedy; he also liked English humor very much. He told a lot of British jokes, too. He had very good timing with jokes.

As far as musicians, I know he loved Fats Waller; he played a lot of his records. He played so many different types of music; he even listened to rock. He liked country music. He was telling me about a song he heard when he was on the road, and I never got to hear it; it was a blues song about a lady that took everything including the wallpaper on the wall. He was trying to tell me about this song, but he couldn't get all the lyrics together. I never got to hear it; I wish he had taped it or something 'cause he sure loved that song. He had some of his own records around the house; he played them sometimes. He used to listen to particular songs before he went out on tour. I don't know why he did that; he didn't rehearse before he went on tour, so that must have served as his rehearsal. All the records that he had on 78s he recorded on reel-to-reel.

He played golf, he liked to go shopping, he liked to go to the park, he liked to ride. He liked to take long rides in his car. We took long rides up and down the coast; he liked to watch the ocean. We even went as far as Encinitas [California] to see the ocean. Just on the spur of the moment, he liked to take rides. We once went up the coast north of Los Angeles up past Santa Barbara. He loved listening to his music and cruising. First, he had a gold Eldorado that got demolished. No one was in the car. Then he had a blue Eldorado after that, and later he got a black Cadillac, a rather large car, almost like a limousine. He was a good driver. He liked to cruise. Whenever he felt like going for a ride, it didn't matter what time of day or night it was. To him the time of day you sleep didn't make any difference. When you want to sleep, you sleep.

He played golf occasionally; I'd say that in four years he probably played golf about six times. But there may have been other times that I didn't know about. He had little left-handed clubs.

Erroll was an artist. He was very much into geometric shapes and colors. He did beautiful art work; he did a lot of sketches and oil paintings. He loved to doodle any time. He'd come back to his work a couple times before it was finished. Some days he did one sketch, and other days he did several; it just depended on how much extra time he had. He spent a lot of time and got the right equipment for his work. He had a big leather case to carry his supplies in. He had oils, charcoals, colored magic markers, even had something that you spray on top of the paintings or sketches so it doesn't smear. He displayed his work in the house, but he never framed them.

Very seldom did anyone come to the house. He wasn't one to talk about anything he did, including his own music. People just didn't come to his house. He would meet them someplace else. He just didn't want any company; he thought that was his own private domain, and he didn't want any other little spirits in there. Once in awhile a few members of my family would come to visit; my brother would stay there. He got along fine with my brother; the two of them were buddies. Sometimes I thought the two of them were teaming up against me. You know how fellows are. He even taught my brother how to box and use his left hand.

He took me to Sak's Fifth Avenue to get an evening dress one day. He didn't tell me why; he just said he wanted to help me pick out a dress. We got a beautiful evening gown in pastel colors of pink and green in a floral arrangement. That evening I wore it to the Parisian Room of the Beverly Hills Hotel, which is done in pink and green. I blended in very well. We were the only people in the restaurant most of the evening. We danced, and he got up and played the piano to me. He must have played four songs. All the help in the place was at the table. It was a beautiful evening; it was very romantic. It was the most romantic evening anybody could ever want. Erroll was romantic—period! He was elegant. Just the way he looked at you was romantic. For him to play music to me, I felt I was going to melt and slide under the table.

I went shopping one day down at the Farmer's Market in Los Angeles, and when I came back, I had put some money on a dog, a poodle, but this one didn't want to be picked up. Erroll went back to pick up the dog and he bit him. He had quite a few names for this little dog. We finally settled on Diablotin which in French means "little devil." He was a dark brown French poodle. The dog's full name is Monsieur Diablotin Noisette Garner. After he was full grown, he weighed five pounds. The dog thought he was a big dog. They were buddies; sometimes I thought they had a conspiracy against me because I'd say, "Come here," or something, and they would both go the other way. Erroll used to take the dog out bar-hopping with him during the day while I was home. The dog went every place with Erroll. I found out my dog liked beer and peanuts! You know, both of them would come home drunk. They were both characters. Since Erroll trained him, he had his character. Diablotin was trying to get into the garbage one time; he was too little to get in there, so what does Erroll do? He goes over and puts the dog in the garbage and says if that's what you want, that's what you get! He wouldn't go near the garbage after that. The dog's got class and he got it from Erroll. Erroll had one or two German shepherds in his lifetime, but other than that, while we were together, the only dog we had was Diablotin. Erroll always said our dog was not a dog.

We would go to the movies, but it had to be next door to a little bar or something 'cause he couldn't sit still for any period of time. He'd watch about fifteen minutes of the movie and go out for about fifteen minutes and come back in. He was into movies; he probably could have gone into cinematography or something.

The first time I ever knew he was ill was in New Orleans. When I walked into the house, I had to turn around and walk back out again. There was such an energy force in there that I could have never related to. I'm glad I was young at the time because if I had been older, I would have laughed completely. I went in there and this energy force was crazy! It was like lights shooting from here to there and there to here. I went back out the door; then I came back in because something told me that something was wrong. A few minutes later, the phone rang. It was Erroll, and he said, "I tried to reach you and I'm not well, and it's not working." I didn't understand what he was talking about, so I asked him, "What do you mean it's not working?" He said, "I can't work," and he wouldn't tell me why. The presence that I felt, I knew something was wrong. So I talked for awhile, and he said that he was going to be home soon and not to worry. That was all that I got out of the conversation at that time. Later I learned that he had cancer.

He had an operation in Los Angeles, and I believe he had part of his lung removed. He didn't even let me know about that. He never liked T-shirts, and he wouldn't take one off until I said, "No, no." When he took his shirt off, I saw all the stitches. That was in 1975. I'm not sure when in 1975 because in California you don't deal with seasons, and with Erroll you don't deal with day or night. You just deal with the situation. I wasn't one that cared, after being with Erroll, whether it was day or night.

On occasion, I suppose knowing about the cancer changed his attitude or mood. He became very hostile about some situations, which was very unusual for him. I knew when he was upset with other people or when he was upset with himself. I would not particularly talk to him about those situations because I knew he was a person that because he was in the public, he had to have some form of privacy. If he wanted to talk to me, he would.

Being on the road for so long, he wanted to come home. I think it was more his business than his public that kept him from becoming a home-body. His manager, accountants, record companies, kept him from becoming a homebody because they, in a sense, ran his life. Some of these people tried to run my life, but he didn't want to talk to or be a part of any of that. He became very frustrated at the situation, and it just left him in a position which was something that I'd never, ever seen him in. I never had seen him ill either. He was a very good actor with his public when he was ill. He was a very alive, open person, but as soon as he got home, he changed.

The second bout that I know of was not long before he passed away. He wouldn't talk about that. He let me know about the first one simply because he couldn't hide it from me that easily. When he got the second bout, I kind of felt it. He had a lot of hostile feelings that were not really directed to me or to anyone but himself. He wouldn't talk to me. I wanted to give him a little time. It was during the holidays [December 1976] and he just wouldn't communicate. He wanted me to go someplace with my family, not far away. He told me when he needed me he'd call me. He actually demanded that I go there. I went up to Oakland [California]. He liked those relatives in Oakland; they were my cousins. They were the only relatives of mine that he liked.

While he was in the hospital for the second bout of cancer, he said, "Please, during the holiday while I'm in the hospital, you go up there and if I need you, I'll let you know." I didn't really want to go without him, but I did. I bought a Christmas tree, one that was $10 a foot and the tree was seven feet. The cabs were out, and I had to carry that tree on a bus. Unfortunately, Erroll never saw the tree or the presents under the tree. He came home one day before he died.

He called me from the hospital, and he said that he was going to come out. I brought in the New Year with Erroll on the telephone. I got there the next day, January 2, and he wanted to go back to the hospital. I was home on the 2nd around 11 A.M., and I went by the "hole in the wall" [another apartment] to pick up some things for him. I went back to the apartment, and when I got there, he wanted several things. He didn't sound well at all. He had a hard time breathing. He had asthma, but he had a harder time breathing, and he wanted to go back to the hospital, which wasn't like him at all. I was in distress trying to get people to the apartment. The L.A. cabs were on strike, but I knew half the staff at the Beverly Hills Cab Company, and even though it was outside the boundaries of Beverly Hills, they would come there if I called. They asked me if I wanted an ambulance. Erroll heard that, and he immediately slammed the phone down. He said, "I don't want an ambulance. I want a cab." Then he said, "Don't get uptight." He wanted his brown socks, and I went and found them and gave them to him.

The cab came and I took him to go to the cab. He was very, very insistent on a Pepsi, and he wasn't a "pop" person (but I always kept Pepsi). He wanted brown socks, a Pepsi, and he wanted to go back to the hospital. He wore brown pants and whatever else matched. I was very nervous because he didn't sound like himself. He didn't want to go, but I talked him into going. Then after he wanted to go, I didn't know what to do. I saw that he got his brown socks and the Pepsi. I didn't think he had diabetes. He had never used any medicine before. However, after he was taken away, I found all kinds of medicines like insulin for diabetics that had never been used and stuff that I had never seen before. The way I feel about it, he might have had or been in a diabetic coma 'cause he was demanding something sweet. He demanded it right then, and he was never a demanding person until then. When he came back from the hospital, he came back with all this stuff, and I didn't find it until it was too late. We were going down to get the cab and we got into the elevator. He acted like he didn't want to get in the elevator. I said, "Come on," and he said, "Okay." That was the last thing he said. He came in the elevator and just held on to me. After that there was nothing. By the time we got down to the first floor, he collapsed. I called and screamed and hollered—he had fallen to the floor and when I called, there was nothing. I screamed for the paramedics; I believe three people called the paramedics—two people in the apartment building and one person across the street. When they finally came, they had the biggest fight in the world because they had to deal with me, and they said there was nothing they could do. Before the paramedics came, I knew he had passed away because of the way his body had doubled up. Nobody closed his eyes, so I knelt down and closed his eyes. He held on to me all the way down. He passed away at 12:32 P.M.

He wanted somebody to remember him, and he asked me if I would remember him. And I told him, of course [laughter], nobody could forget him. He should have written the song, "I'll Never Be the Same Again," for me. He didn't know the power and the strength of love that people had for him. I don't think he even knew how many people just admired him for him and not just for his music. He didn't realize what a precedent he set upon the universe. I knew he wanted to be loved and he had the greatest love to pass out all across the world, not just to you, not just to me, but to everyone. He had it. He had more love, far greater than anybody I've ever met.

EPILOGUE

During Garner's February, 1975, appearance at the Etcetera Club in Washington, D.C., he was in obvious pain. He was playing as beautifully as ever, but he was coughing profusely throughout his performances. He tried to hide his cough by keeping his mouth closed and turning his head slightly away from the audience. To those of us at the first few tables, he was apparently very uncomfortable.

On Monday morning, February 17, Garner flew to Chicago with his group, where he was met by his road manager, Bill Layne. It was opening night at Mr. Kelly's, and Ed Eberstadt, Garner's close friend, reports, "Erroll usually stayed at the Drake Hotel, which was several blocks from Mr. Kelly's. After the last show on Monday, we went to the Playboy Club for a drink. I told Erroll I would see him Friday night. I called him Thursday evening about 6 o'clock. Erroll eventually came to the phone and said he wasn't feeling well and was going to check into the hospital."

Garner performed Thursday evening, but by this time his condition had worsened. He was admitted the following evening (February 21) to Chicago's Northwestern Memorial Hospital. He had trouble breathing, a productive cough, and a temperature of almost 104°. The diagnosis was right-sided viral pneumonia. After the first week with antibiotic therapy, he showed gradual improvement, but by the time of his discharge (March 6) it became obvious from X-rays that he had lung cancer.

In April 1975, Garner was admitted to Cedars-Sinai Medical Center, Los Angeles, where he underwent an open thoracotomy (April 8). A malignant lesion in the right lung was found. An attempt was made to remove his right lung, but surgeons found it impossible because the cancer had already involved the pericardium. A full course of radiation therapy was then administered to the right chest area which gave him a remission which lasted for 19 months.

Garner's progress was fair until December 1976, when he was admitted to Cedars-Sinai Medical Center (December 14) for shortness of breath, loss of weight and appetite, and a severe cough which he was unable to control. At his own request, he was released on Wednesday, December 29, and died January 2, 1977 (see Noisette interview). The following morning the *Los Angeles Times* reported, "Erroll Louis Garner, 53 (55 was the correct age at death), one of the greats of jazz piano history, died Sunday afternoon in an ambulance en route to Cedars-Sinai Medical Center (Garner actually died in the elevator of his apartment) in Los Angeles. Garner had been released from the hospital Wednesday after almost two years of intermittent illness. Death was attributed to emphysema." Other newspapers throughout the world carried similar reports. Although Garner had a history of emphysema, death was due to his lungs being diffusely involved with cancer and also fluid around the heart having collected because of the cancerous spread. It is unclear why these facts were not made known publicly.

Illustration by Claire P. Kayser

Garner's brother, Linton, accompanied the body on a flight to Pittsburgh, where a wake was held at Spriggs-Watson Funeral Home. Over 2,000 persons paid their last respects. Flowers and condolences poured in from all over the world. Tony Bennett, Bill Cosby, and President Jimmy Carter were among the many friends and fans to send their condolences.

Friday morning, January 7, the day of the funeral, Pittsburgh was cloudy, the ground was snow covered, and temperatures were in the mid-twenties. At 9 o'clock the body was moved to St. James A.M.E. Church for viewing until the funeral service was to begin at 1 P.M. Erroll looked distinguished. He was dressed in a dark suit with a navy-blue tie, his hair was combed straight back without his characteristic "patent-leather" look.

Visibly upset, Martha Glaser waited in the vestibule of the church until the casket was closed. She couldn't bear to see Erroll laid out. She sent in two key chains—a red and green key chain—signifying the "Big Apple" (New York City), which was one of Erroll's last requests. She wanted the key chains to go into the casket. The funeral attendant tucked them under his right arm.

By now the church was full. In attendance were two of Garner's close musical friends, Teddy Wilson and Earl "Fatha" Hines. Organist George Spaulding played a medley of three of Garner's favorite tunes: "Laura," "In a Sentimental Mood" (which Garner often used as a prelude to "My Funny Valentine"), and "Penthouse Serenade." As Spaulding was completing the medley with "Penthouse Serenade," the funeral attendents carefully tucked the white satin inside and closed the casket, a few minutes after the 1 o'clock service was to begin.

Reverend Floyd Alexander, who presided over the service, accompanied the Garner family to their place, and the service began. The eulogy was delivered by Reverend John Garcia Gensel, Pastor of St. Peter's Lutheran Church, New York City. Christian Renninger, in his article "Magic Hard to Replace," recalls Gensel's remarks. "Erroll's was a flowing kind of music; he could walk from the garden, to the sea, to the forest and into the city. You didn't always know where he was going, but when he took you there, you were right with him."

After Reverend Gensel's eulogy, Garner's Mercury recording of "Misty" was played. As the congregation filed out, the cloudy, cold Pittsburgh morning gave way to a crisp, clear, sunny afternoon. The funeral proceeded to Homewood Cemetery where Garner's body was buried next to his mother and father. Today the site is marked with a magnificent Vermont marble tombstone with a piano carved at the top. The inscription reads: "He gave of himself unselfishly."

As I stood next to Martha Glaser during the graveside service, I couldn't help but think of the elegant version of "Someone to Watch Over Me" that he played for me at the Sahara Hotel in Las Vegas. His music changed my life. As I stood there I felt sad that we were burying Erroll, but happy that our lives had overlapped.

These 1971 stamps issued from the Republic of Mali, honors three jazz greats: Nat "King" Cole, Garner, and Louis Armstrong. (J. Doran Collection)

II. His Times

Courtesy of Chester Commodore

CHRONOLOGY

The Chronology which follows is an account of Erroll Garner's ancestral background, as well as personal and professional events which occurred throughout his life. The first section, The Garner Family Chronology, is accompanied by a diagram on the following pages to allow the reader to graphically trace the Garner lineage. The second section, Erroll Garner Chronology, provides a detailed account of Garner's life.

The sources for the Erroll Garner Chronology are: 1) periodicals and books which are cited after each entry; 2) clippings, which in most cases do not include page numbers, were made available from the files of the following institutions—Carnegie Library, Pittsburgh; Detroit Public Library; Hillman Library, University of Pittsburgh; Institute of Jazz Studies, Rutgers University, Newark, New Jersey; Los Angeles Public Library; Pasadena (California) Public Library; Philadelphia Public Library; Rodgers and Hammerstein Archives of Recorded Sound, Lincoln Center Library, New York; Schomberg Center for Research in Black Culture, New York; Seattle Public Library; and The Vivian G. Harsh Collection of Afro-American History and Literature, Carter G. Woodson Library, Chicago; and 3) personal notes and observations made by the author through interviews and memorabilia provided by scores of zealous Garner devotees throughout the world.

For their enormous time and personal research on my behalf, I am gratefully indebted to Carolyn Hager of the Randolph County (North Carolina) Historical Society for her assistance in the preparation of the Garner lineage and to Katherine Bushman, whose prior research of the Darcus Family made my work much easier. Garner's sister, Martha Murray, graciously submitted to my many hours of intensive questioning on the family background and also provided me with details from the Darcus Family Bible.

In no way does this Chronology purport to be complete. Until now, very little was known of Garner's activities prior to his arrival at New York's Tondelayo's Club in September, 1944. Although there is evidence that he was in New York prior to this as an accompanist with singer Ann Lewis, no substantial documentation of his whereabouts could be found. An extensive search of the local Pittsburgh newspapers was conducted, to no avail, to confirm his playing with Fate Marable's band on the Pittsburgh riverboats. Although many of these questions go unanswered, hopefully this Chronology will be enjoyed "as is" and will provide a basis to assist future Garner researchers in their continuing quest to carry on the legacy of this great man.

DARCUS FAMILY

ADAM DARCUS
b. ?
d. ?

CHARLES R. DARCUS
b. October 9, 1828
Port Republic, Va.
d. September 7, 1905
Augusta Co., Va.

NELLY
(Maiden name unknown)
b. ?
d. ?

ESTELLA DARCUS
b. August 10, 1890
New Hope, Va.
d. June 3, 1973
Pittsburgh, Pa.

m. January 30, 1890
New Hope, Va.

JOSEPH LEWIS
b. February 3, 1826
Albermarle Co., Va.
d. After 1890

MARTHA E. LEWIS
b. June 1, 1861
Louisa Courthouse, Va.
d. March 12, 1912
Augusta Co., Va.

?

MARTHA CAROLINE
b. January 2, 1914
Pittsburgh, Pa.

RUTH VIRGINIA
b. December 26, 1917
Pittsburgh, Pa.

ERNEST SKEEN
b. June 15, 1921
Pittsburgh, Pa.

m. June 2, 1913

GARNER FAMILY

ALEXANDER GARNER
b. June 1822
Randolph Co., N.C.
d. After 1900
Randolph Co., N.C.

Commence
cohabitation as slaves
September 10, 1847
Marriage registered
September 10, 1866

GEORGE A. GARNER
b. 1847
Randolph Co., N.C.
d. 1893
Randolph Co., N.C.

PENNINA
(Maiden name unknown)
b. May 1825
Randolph Co., N.C.
d. After 1900
Randolph Co., N.C.

LOUIS ERNEST GARNER
b. July 19, 1884
Thomasville, N.C.
d. May 14, 1970
Pittsburgh, Pa.

m. January 6, 1867
Randolph Co., N.C.

LINTON SYLVESTER
b. March 25, 1915
Thomasville, N.C.

MARY BERNIECE
b. July 14, 1919
Pittsburgh, Pa.

DANIEL SKEEN
b. 1826
Randolph Co., N.C.
d. January 8, 1914
Randolph Co., N.C.

CAROLINE SKEEN
b. June, 1852
Randolph Co., N.C.
d. December 10, 1924
Randolph Co., N.C.

m. ca. 1845
Randolph Co., N.C.

CARROLL LOUIS
b. June 15, 1921
Pittsburgh, Pa.
d. January 2, 1977
Los Angeles, Ca.

Pittsburgh, Pa.

SARAH
(Maiden name unknown)
b. 1820
Randolph Co., N.C.
d. ca. 1880
Randolph Co., N.C.

Abbreviations:
b. = born   Co. = County
d. = died   N.C. = North Carolina
m. = married   Pa. = Pennsylvania
Ca. = California   Va. = Virginia

GARNER FAMILY CHRONOLOGY

Although conjectural, from all information available through the Randolph County Historical Society, Erroll Garner's family name was taken from the white slave owner Frederick Garner (1806-ca.1881). Documented in the September 15, 1860 Slave Schedule, Western Division, Randolph County, Frederick Garner lists seven slaves, including a 38-year-old black male which describes Erroll Garner's great-grandfather, Alexander (born June, 1822). In all probability, this is how Erroll Garner's name originated.

1820   Sarah (Skeen) (paternal great grandmother) born, Randolph County, North Carolina. *Note:* Maiden name is unknown.

1822   **June:** Alexander Garner (paternal great grandfather) born, Randolph County, North Carolina.

1825   **May:** Pennina (Garner) (paternal great grandmother) born, Randolph County, North Carolina. *Note:* Maiden name is unknown.

1826   Daniel Skeen (paternal great grandfather) born, Randolph County, North Carolina.
   February 3: Joseph Lewis (maternal great grandfather) born Albermarle County, Virginia. *Note:* Joseph Lewis' parents: Jerry and Nellie.

1828   **October 9:** Charles R. Darcus (maternal grandfather) born, Port Republic, Virginia. *Note:* Charles Darcus' parents: Adam and Nelly.

1847   **September 10:** Alexander Garner and Pennina Garner commence cohabitation as slaves in Randolph County, North Carolina. *Note:* When emancipation took place after the Civil War the marriage of Alexander and Pennina Garner was registered on September 10, 1866.
   George A. Garner (paternal grandfather) born, Randolph County, North Carolina.

1852   **June:** Caroline (Garner) Skeen (paternal grandmother) born, Randolph County, North Carolina.

1861   **June 1:** Martha E. (Darcus) Lewis (maternal grandmother) born, Louisa Courthouse, Virginia.

1867   **January 6:** George A. Garner (paternal grandfather) and Caroline Skeen (paternal grandmother) marry, Randolph County, North Carolina.

1880   (ca.) Sarah Skeen (paternal great grandmother) dies, Randolph County, North Carolina.

1884   **July 19:** Louis Ernest Garner (father) born, Thomasville, Randolph County, North Carolina.

1890   **January 30:** Charles R. Darcus (maternal grandfather) and Martha E. Lewis (maternal grandmother) marry, New Hope, Virginia; Thomas Briley, minister.

August 10: Estella (Garner) Darcus (mother) born, New Hope, Virginia.

1893   George A. Garner (paternal grandfather) dies, Randolph County, North Carolina.

1905   **September 7:** Charles R. Darcus (maternal grandfather) dies, Augusta County, Virginia.

1912   **March 12:** Martha E. (Lewis) Darcus (maternal grandmother) dies, Augusta County, Virginia.

1913   **June 2:** Louis Ernest Garner and Estella Darcus marry at the Sheffey home, 200 Everett Street, Pittsburgh; W.J. Carter, minister.

1914   **January 2:** Martha Caroline Garner (sister) born, Pittsburgh.
January 8: Daniel Skeen (paternal great grandfather) dies, Randolph County, North Carolina.

1915   **March 25:** Linton Sylvester Garner (brother) born, Thomasville, North Carolina.

1917   **December 26:** Ruth Virginia Garner (sister) born, Pittsburgh.

1919   **July 14:** Mary Berniece Garner (sister) born, Pittsburgh.

1921   **June 15:** Erroll Louis and Ernest Skeen Garner born, Pittsburgh. (See Erroll Garner Chronology.)

1924   **December 10:** Caroline Skeen Garner (paternal grandmother) dies, Randolph County, North Carolina.

1970   **May 14:** Louis Ernest Garner (father) dies, Ivy Nursing Home, Pittsburgh.

1973   **June 3:** Estella Darcus Garner (mother) dies, West Penn Hospital, Pittsburgh.

ERROLL GARNER CHRONOLOGY

Instrument Abbreviations

as	alto saxophone	o	organ
b	bass	p	piano
cd	conga drums	tb	trombone
cl	clarinet	tp	trumpet
d	drums	ts	tenor saxophone
g	guitar	v	vocal

1921 **June 15:** Erroll Louis Garner and twin brother Ernest Skeen Garner born on the 2nd floor at 212 North St. Clair Street, East Liberty, Pittsburgh. *Birth Certificate. Note:* Ernest was born at 8:15 a.m. and Erroll at 8:25 a.m. Dr. S.O. Cherry delivered the twins.

1925 **September:** Family moves to 6605 Rowan Avenue where Erroll has first piano lesson from Miss Madge Bowman.

1926 **September 7:** Starts kindergarten at the Lincoln School, Pittsburgh.

1931 **February 4:** Erroll and Ernest transfer to the Larimer School, Pittsburgh.
December 12: Makes first radio appearance with the Kan-D-Kids on KQV Radio, Pittsburgh. Nicknamed "Gumdrop." *Pittsburgh Courier,* March 5, 1932, p. 9 sec. 2.

1932 **February 13:** With the Kan-D-Kids, 9:15–9:45 a.m. on KQV Radio, Pittsburgh. *Pittsburgh Press,* February 12, 1932, p. 20.
February 20: With the Kan-D-Kids, 9:30–10:00 a.m. on KQV Radio Pittsburgh. *Pittsburgh Sun-Telegraph,* February 19, 1932, p. 17.
March 5: With the Kan-D-Kids, 9:15–9:45 a.m. on KQV Radio, Pittsburgh. *Pittsburgh Courier,* February 27, 1932, p. 7.

1933 **January 7:** With the Kan-D-Kids, 9:30–10:00 a.m. on KQV Radio, Pittsburgh. *Pittsburgh Press,* January 6, 1933, p. 28.
May 20: With the Kan-D-Kids, 11:30–12 noon on KQV Radio, Pittsburgh. *Pittsburgh Sun-Telegraph,* May 19, 1933, p. 15.

1935 **September 3:** Enters the junior vocational class at Westinghouse High School, Pittsburgh.

1937 **December 30:** Makes first recording at George Hyde Studio, Pittsburgh.

1938 **Summer** (one year): Melody Bar, Pittsburgh. Personnel: Leroy Brown (as, cl), Erroll Garner (p), Dave Page (tp), Leroy Jones (d).

1939   February 25: Original Kan-D-Kids given a celebrity party, Savoy Ballroom, Pittsburgh. *Pittsburgh Courier,* March 4, 1939, p. 21.
April 25: Withdraws from Westinghouse High School.
August 19: With Leroy Brown's Orchestra, Club Mirador, Homestead, Pennsylvania. *Pittsburgh Courier,* August 19, 1939, p. 21.

1940   January (early): With Leroy Brown's Orchestra, Club Mirador, Homestead, Pennsylvania. *Pittsburgh Courier,* January 13, 1940, p. 20.
January (late): With Leroy Brown's Orchestra at Gus Greenlee's Harlem Casino. *Pittsburgh Courier,* January 20, 1940, p. 20.
March 19: With Leroy Brown's Orchestra. "The United Council of Clubs presents its Sadie Hawkins Dance at the Harlem Casino," Pittsburgh. *Pittsburgh Courier,* March 9, 1940, p. 21.
April: The Leroy Brown Orchestra with Erroll Garner closes the Harlem Casino. *Pittsburgh Courier,* April 27, 1940, p. 21.
April 28: With Leroy Brown's Orchestra. "Midnight Jamboree," Snowball Edmonds, MC, Triangle Theater, Pittsburgh. Ibid.
May 22: "Leroy Brown and his NBC Orchestra, 'Gigantic Battle of Swing,' Savoy Ballroom. Brown's band features Honey Boy (James Minor), Gumdrop (Erroll Garner), Ghost (George Howell), and the sensational rhythm section." *Pittsburgh Courier,* May 18, 1940, p. 21.
September 2: With Leroy Brown's Orchestra. Wheeling, West Virginia and Donora, Pennsylvania. *Pittsburgh Courier,* August 24, 1940, p. 21.
November 21 (Thanksgiving Day): Erroll Garner and His Orchestra—Sophisticated Six, Matsko Hall, Rankin, Pennsylvania. *Pittsburgh Courier,* November 30, 1940, p. 20.
December 29: With Leroy Brown's Orchestra, Russian Hall, Homestead, Pennsylvania. *Pittsburgh Courier,* December 21, 1940, p. 21.

1941   January 19: With Leroy Brown's Orchestra, Musician's Club, Pittsburgh. *Pittsburgh Courier,* January 11, 1941, p. 21.
April 13: With Leroy Brown's Orchestra, Ritz Cafe, Pittsburgh. *Pittsburgh Courier,* April 12, 1941, p. 20.
June 28: Finishes in second place to Cornelius "Neeny" Waters in the Pittsburgh Musicians and Entertainers Popularity Contest, Roosevelt Theater. *Pittsburgh Courier,* June 28, 1941, p. 21.
November 29: With Leroy Brown's Orchestra, Melody Bar, Pittsburgh. *Pittsburgh Courier,* November 29, 1941, p. 21.
December: Leaves for N.Y.C. *Pittsburgh Courier,* December 27, 1941, p. 20.

1942   January–May: Accompanies singer Ann Lewis in N.Y.C. *Note:* This entry in the chronology has been confirmed from interviews

only. Leroy Brown recalls that Garner did not stay with Ann Lewis
for very long, preferring to go out on his own as a solo artist.
July: Paul O'Brien's, Logantown Road, Wanamassa (Asbury
Park), New Jersey. Also on bill: Charles Stewart (o), and Bob
Brittingham (p, o). *Asbury Park Press,* July 3, 1942, p. 5.
September–October: Paul O'Brien's, Wanamassa (Asbury Park),
New Jersey. Also on bill: Charles Stewart (o), and Bob Brittingham
(p, o). *Spotlite Magazine,* September 12, 1942, p. 4. *Note:* In this
ad Garner was billed as "Errol Flynn Garner."

1943   **January–March:** Red Door, Pittsburgh.
March (late): Accompanies singer Anne Baker, Mercur's Music
Bar, 23 Graeme Street, Pittsburgh. *Pittsburgh Post Gazette,* March
22, 1943, p. 20.
April: Accompanies singer Anne Baker, Mercur's Music Bar, Pitts-
burgh. Also on bill: Dale Harkness (p), Sherdina Walker (p, v)
and Alice Gerber (v). Mercur's Music Bar, Pittsburgh. *Pittsburgh
Post Gazette,* April 12, 1943, p. 12.
May: Joins Dale Harkness at the twin pianos. Alyce Brooks re-
places Sherdina Walker as pianist and vocalist. Mercur's Music
Bar, Pittsburgh. *Pittsburgh Post Gazette,* May 26, 1943, p. 12.
August: With Dale Harkness on the twin pianos. Mercur's Music
Bar, Pittsburgh. *Pittsburgh Post Gazette,* August 13, 1943, p. 14.
October: "Dale Harkness and Erroll Garner, the twin pianists who
furnish the musical background for the continuous entertainment
at the Mercur's Music Bar have been at the Graeme Street spot
so long the comment now is that they go with the lease there. The
Music Bar also features in the singing department Alice Gerber,
Betty St. Clair and Betty Dayton." *Pittsburgh Post Gazette,* Octo-
ber 8, 1943, p. 26.
November: Accompanies singer Betty St. Clair. Mercur's Music
Bar, Pittsburgh. *Pittsburgh Post Gazette,* November 29, 1943, p.
26.
December: "Freddy Rose, the Hammond Organ Ace, is spotlighted
nightly along with Erroll Garner, the keyboard wizard." Mercur's
Music Bar, Pittsburgh. *Pittsburgh Post Gazette,* December 13,
1943, p. 26.

1944   **April:** With Jerry Tagress on the twin pianos. Mercur's Music Bar,
Pittsburgh. *Pittsburgh Post Gazette,* April 19, 1944, p. 24.
April 24: Opens with Reid Jaynes on the twin pianos. Mercur's
Music Bar, Pittsburgh. *Pittsburgh Post Gazette,* April 24, 1944, p.
24.
May: "Still popular with the patrons of Mercur's Music Bar is the
keyboard team of Erroll Garner and Reid Jaynes. They are heard
nightly in duets and request numbers at the twin baby grands.
Newcomer Sylvester Trent, local piano ace, is now going into his

third consecutive week here is also clicking solidly with his soloing of both classical and light opera favorites." *Pittsburgh Post Gazette,* May 27, 1944, p. 12.

June: Paul's "Edgewaters," Wanamassa (Asbury Park), New Jersey. Also on bill: Charles Stewart (o), and Putney Dandridge (p), *Asbury Park Press,* June 10, 1944, p. 4.

July: Paul's "Edgewaters," Wanamassa (Asbury Park), New Jersey. Also on bill: Charles Stewart (o), and Putney Dandridge (p). *Asbury Park Press,* July 22, 1944, p. 4.

September 15: Tondelayo's, N.Y.C. *Pittsburgh Courier,* September 23, 1944, p. 13.

October: Tondelayo's, N.Y.C. Also featured: Billy Daniels and Ann Cornell. *Metronome,* October, 1944, p. 10.

December 20: Jazz Concert, Times Hall, N.Y.C., 8:30 p.m. First in a concert series of "The New Jazz" sponsored by *View* magazine. Participants: Pearl Bailey, Barney Bigard, Don Byas, Stuff Smith, and others. *Program.*

1945   **February:** With Slam Stewart (b), Mike Bryan (g), Harold "Doc" West (d). Three Deuces, 72 W. 52nd Street, N.Y.C. Also on bill: Dorothy Donegan and Don Byas. *New York Amsterdam News,* February 10, 1945, p. 5B.

March 25: Palm Sunday Dance and Jam Session. Lincoln Square Center, N.Y.C. With Dizzy Gillespie's All Stars: Ben Webster, Cozy Cole, Tiny Grimes and Don Byas. *New York Amsterdam News,* March 24, 1945, p. 5B.

April 26–August 4: Three Deuces, N.Y.C. "Dizzy Gillespie, Don Byas and Erroll Garner in a band of their own." *New Yorker,* April 28–July 28, 1945.

May 30: Memorial Day Benefit Jam Session and Dance. Lincoln Square Center, N.Y.C. Also on bill: Dizzy Gillespie, Ben Webster, Don Byas, Slam Stewart and "Big" Sid Catlett. *New York Amsterdam News,* May 26, 1945, p. 2B.

June 22: Town Hall, N.Y.C., 8:15 p.m., "New Jazz Foundation." Trio features Al Hall (b), Harold "Doc" West (d).

August 25: "Atlantic Spotlight," NBC Radio, N.Y.C., with Slam Stewart. *V-Discs: A History and Discography,* Richard S. Sears, Greenwood Press, 1980, p. 333.

October 4–January 19, 1946: With the Slam Stewart Trio, Three Deuces, N.Y.C. *New Yorker,* October 6, 1945–January 12, 1946.

November 17: "Atlantic Spotlight," NBC Radio, N.Y.C., with Slam Stewart. *V-Discs: A History and Discography,* Richard S. Sears, Greenwood Press, 1980, p. 333.

December 9: "RCA Victor Show," N.Y.C. *V-Discs: A History and Discography,* Richard S. Sears, Greenwood Press, 1980 p. 333.

1946 **January 10:** Opens, Suzie Q, Los Angeles. *Metronome,* February, 1946, p. 49.
April 2: "Hollywood Independent Citizens Committee and Norman Granz present National Anti-Poll Tax Rally." Elks Auditorium, Los Angeles. *Los Angeles Sentinel,* March 28, 1946, pp. 10, 11.
May: Susie Q, Los Angeles. *Capitol Magazine,* May 1946, p. 4.
June 24: Fran Kelley's Swingposium, Embassy Auditorium, Los Angeles. *Metronome,* August, 1946, p. 46.
July 20: Honored by the Frogs Club "Night of Stars." Pittsburgh.
August 7: "Tribute to a Star" awarded by the Citizens of Pittsburgh. *Program.*
December 21: Lincoln Theater, Los Angeles, California. "Erroll Garner Trio plays the first annual Sentinel Christmas Basket Benefit." *Los Angeles Sentinel,* January 2, 1947, p. 15.

1947 **June 10:** Glendale Civic Auditorium, Glendale, California. "Jazz Concert: Featured will be a number of jazz stars headed by Esquire Gold Award winner Erroll Garner, and featuring drummer, Zutty Singleton." *Los Angeles Sentinel,* June 5, 1947, p. 20.

1948 **March:** Copa Club, Pittsburgh. *down beat,* March 10, 1948, p. 21.
April: Three Deuces, N.Y.C. *down beat,* April 7, 1948, p. 21. *Note:* Accompanied by Oscar Pettiford (b), J.C. Heard (d).
May: "Erroll Garner Trio have one on wax titled, *'Trio'* with the flipover *'Pastel'.*" *Los Angeles Sentinel,* May 27, 1948, p. 23.
May 7: Flies from LaGuardia Field to Paris' LeBourget. *down beat,* April 21, 1948, p. 3.
May 9: Marigny Theater, Paris. *down beat,* April 21, 1948, p. 3; *Le Monde* (Paris), May 11, 1948; *Le Monde,* May 12, 1948, p. 6.
June 30–July 22: Appears with the Esquire All Stars: Lucky Thompson (ts), Bill Harris (tb), Oscar Pettiford (b), Shelly Manne (d), Red Rodney (tp), at the Royal Roost, N.Y.C. *Program.*
September–October: The Haig, Los Angeles. *Capitol News,* November, 1948.
November 2 (one week): Million Dollar Theater, Los Angeles. *Capitol News,* November, 1948.

1949 **February 5:** "Jazz at the Elks," Elks Auditorium, Los Angeles. *Los Angeles Sentinel,* February 3, 1949, p. C4; February 10, 1949, p. C5.
March 27: Alpha Bowling Club, Los Angeles. *Los Angeles Sentinel,* March 24, 1949, pp C4, C5.
July: "Signs with Variety Artists, a new booking firm." *down beat,* July 29, 1949, p. 9.
July 21–October 5: Three Deuces, N.Y.C. *New Yorker,* July 23–Oc-

tober 1, 1949. *Note:* Accompanied by Leonard Gaskin (b), and Charlie Smith (d).

August: Century Records issues four Erroll Garner sides, cut in 1944 by Timme Rosenkrantz on a home recorder. *down beat,* August 26, 1949, p. 2.

September 6: Town Hall, N.Y.C. Also on bill: Harry Belafonte, Lenny Tristano, Charlie Parker, Bud Powell and Miles Davis. *New York American,* September 3, 1949, p. 17.

September 30 (one week): Apollo Theater, N.Y.C. Also on bill: Georgie Auld and Sarah Vaughan. *New York American,* October 1, 1949, p. 19.

October: Leaves the Three Deuces, N.Y.C., after a three-month run. *down beat,* November 18, 1949, p. 12.

October 23: Corpus Christi Auditorium, Chicago, Illinois. *down beat,* November 18, 1949, p. 5.

December (early): Flame Show Bar, Detroit, Michigan. *Los Angeles Sentinel,* December 8, 1949, p. B7.

December: Doubles in daytime at Apollo Theater and at Three Deuces at night. *Los Angeles Sentinel,* December 8, 1949, p. B7.

December 14–January 11, 1950: Three Deuces, N.Y.C. *New Yorker,* December 10, 1949–January 7, 1950.

1950   **January 12–26:** Birdland, N.Y.C. *New Yorker,* January 14–21, 1950.

January 26–February 1: Birdland, N.Y.C. "Three crack pianists—Erroll Garner, Bud Powell, and Dick Hyman—under one rooftree." *New Yorker,* January 28, 1950, p. 6.

February 17: Opens at the Blue Note, Chicago. *Chicago Daily News,* February 18, 1950.

March 19: Orchestra Hall, Chicago. *Program.*

March 27: Cleveland Music Hall, Cleveland.

June 1–7: Birdland, N.Y.C. *New Yorker,* June 3, 1950, p. 6.

June 8–14: Birdland, N.Y.C. "Erroll Garner, now equipped with a trio, plays masterly piano and Bud Powell, Fats Navarro, J.J. Johnson and others fill in." *New Yorker,* June 10, 1950, p. 6.

June 15: Celebrates birthday, Birdland, N.Y.C. *Our World,* October, 1950, p. 36; *Chicago Defender,* July 8, 1950, p. 20.

June 15–21: Birdland, N.Y.C. "Through Wednesday, June 21, the trio topped by the spellbinding Erroll Garner, Bud Powell, Fats Navarro, J.J. Johnson and others are on deck too." *New Yorker,* June 17, 1950, p. 4.

August: Two weeks at Longbar Showboat, San Francisco. *down beat,* September 22, 1950, p. 8.

September–October: Cafe Society. *Billboard,* October 28, 1950, p. 57.

November 9: Pre-Armistice Day Ball. American Legion Hall, Sewickley, Pennsylvania.

December 1–14: Birdland, N.Y.C. *New Yorker,* December 16, 1950, p. 8.

December 3: Town Hall, N.Y.C. *Metronome,* February, 1951; *New York Herald Tribune,* December 4, 1950; *Variety,* December 6, 1950, p. 43.

December 6–14: Birdland, N.Y.C., with John Simmons (b), Shadow Wilson (d). *New Yorker,* December 8, 1950, p. 8.

December (late): Three Towers Inn, Somerville, New Jersey.

1951   **January 4** (one week): Apollo Theater, N.Y.C.

February 4: With Sarah Vaughan and trio. Richmond, Virginia.

February 5: "Zeta Phi Beta Sorority presents Erroll Garner with John Simmons and Shadow Wilson in its second Blue and White Revue." Fries Memorial Auditorium, Winston-Salem Teachers College, Winston-Salem, North Carolina. *Program.*

March 15–21: Birdland, N.Y.C. *New Yorker,* March 10, 1951, p. 6.

March 22–28: Birdland, N.Y.C., with John Simmons (b) and Shadow Wilson (d). Also on bill: Slim Gaillard, Charlie Parker with strings. *New Yorker,* March 17, 1951; *New Yorker,* March 24, 1951, p. 6.

July 23–29: Sky Bar, Cleveland.

1952   **January:** Cafe Society, N.Y.C. *Time,* January 7, 1952.

February 21–March 26: The Embers, N.Y.C. *New Yorker,* February 23–March 22, 1952.

April 12: "Piano Parade." Masonic Temple, Detroit, Michigan. Also on bill: Meade Lux Lewis, Pete Johnson, and Art Tatum. *Program.*

April 19: Massey Hall, Toronto, Canada. Appears with Art Tatum in Piano Parade.

May 8–14: Birdland, N.Y.C. "A bumper piano festival, ending Wednesday, May 14, with Art Tatum's trio (including Slam Stewart and Everett Barksdale). Erroll Garner's trio and those long-lost boogie-woogie men, Meade Lux Lewis and Pete Johnson." *New Yorker,* May 10, 1952, p. 8.

June 30–July 16: The Embers, N.Y.C. *New Yorker,* June 28–July 19, 1952.

July (late): Chicago Theater, Chicago. Also appearing are Toni Arden and Bobby Wayne. *down beat,* August 27, 1952, p. 6.

1953   **February 12–April 8:** Birdland, N.Y.C. *New Yorker,* February 14–April 4, 1953.

April 25: New Show Bar, St. Louis. *down beat,* April 22, 1953, p. 46.

April 27 (one week): Yankee Inn, Akron, Ohio. *down beat,* April 22, 1953, p. 46.

May 11 (one week): Hi Hat, Boston. *down beat,* May 6, 1953, p. 22.

May 18–June 13: The Embers, N.Y.C. *New Yorker,* May 16–June 13, 1953.

June 25–July 1: Birdland, N.Y.C. *New Yorker,* June 27, 1953, p. 7.

July 17–30: Mack's Tavern, Atlantic City, New Jersey. *down beat,* July 15, 1953, p. 30.

August 14–September 6: Tiffany, Los Angeles. *down beat,* August 26, 1953, p. 22.

September 8–October 5: Blackhawk, San Francisco. *down beat,* September 9, 1953, p. 22.

October 9–15: Offbeat, Omaha, Nebraska. *down beat,* October 7, 1953, p. 26.

November 8: Modern American Jazz Festival. Also on bill: Stan Kenton Orchestra, June Christy, Slim Gaillard, Candido, Stan Getz, and Dizzy Gillespie. "Stan Kenton: Artistry in Rhythm," Dr. William F. Lee III, *Creative Press,* 1980, p. 184.

November 8: Bushnell Memorial Auditorium, Hartford Connecticut. *Rockville Connecticut Journal,* November 5, 1953.

November 22–29: Storyville, Boston. *down beat,* November 18, 1953, p. 23.

December 10–January 6, 1954: Birdland, N.Y.C. *down beat,* December 30, 1953, p. 18.

1954   **January 8–17:** Storyville, Boston. *down beat,* January 13, 1954, p. 34.

March 8–April 10: The Embers, N.Y.C. *down beat,* March 10, 1954, p. 22.

April 9: Appears at Carnegie Hall, N.Y.C., in a benefit for the New York Lighthouse for the Blind.

April 12–18: Rendezvous, Philadelphia. *down beat,* April 7, 1954, p. 18.

April 23: Basin Street, N.Y.C. *down beat,* April 21, 1954, p. 42.

May 7–16: Hi Hat, Boston. *down beat,* May 5, 1954.

June 1–6: Comedy Club, Baltimore. *down beat,* June 16, 1954, p. 18.

July 12–24: Campbell's, London, Ontario. *down beat,* July 28, 1954, p. 22.

August 6–26: Blackhawk, San Francisco. *down beat,* August 11, 1954 p. 22.

August 26–September 6: Zardi's, Hollywood, California. *down beat,* September 8, 1954, p. 26.

September 8–12: Blue Note, Chicago. *down beat,* September 8, 1954, p. 26.

September 13–26: Scaleris, Milwaukee, Wisconsin. *down beat,* September 8, 1954, p. 26.

October 28–November 10: Rouge Club, River Rouge, Michigan. *down beat,* October 20, 1954, p. 23.
November 16–28: Basin Street, N.Y.C. *down beat,* November 3, 1954, p. 23.
November 29–December 4: Blue Note, Chicago. *down beat,* November 17, 1954, p. 23.
December 6–12: Comedy, Baltimore. *down beat,* December 15, 1954, p. 18.
December 13–January 29: The Embers, N.Y.C. *New Yorker,* December 11–January 29, 1955.

1955 **February 1–6:** Blue Note, Philadelphia. *down beat,* January 26, 1955, p. 22.
March 6: 1st Annual Benefit for the Gateway Athletic Association. Syria Mosque, Pittsburgh. *Pittsburgh Courier,* March 5, 1955, p. 20.
March 15–21: Waluhaje Club, Atlanta, Georgia. *down beat,* March 23, 1955, p. 22.
March 30–April 10: Storyville, Boston. *down beat,* April 6, 1955, p. 18.
April 12: Copa Club, Pittsburgh.
April 21–May 4: Birdland, N.Y.C. *down beat,* May 4, 1955, p. 32.
April 28: County Center, White Plains, New York. Also on bill: Lionel Hampton's Orchestra, The Chet Baker Quartet, Gerry Mulligan, Stan Rubin and his Tiger Town Five. Garry Moore, MC.
May 6–15: Boston Harbor, Rochester, New York. *down beat,* May 18, 1955, p. 40. *Note:* Wyatt Ruther leaves the group after this engagement.
May 14: Courier Command Performance Concert. Detroit, Michigan.
May 16–28: Town Tavern, Toronto, Ontario, Canada. *down beat,* May 18, 1955, p. 40.
May 30–June 5: Loop, Cleveland, Ohio. *down beat,* June 15, 1955, p. 37.
June 10: Philadelphia Music Festival, Municipal Stadium, Philadelphia. *Philadelphia Inquirer,* May 8, 1955.
June 16–June 29: Basin Street, N.Y.C. *down beat,* June 19, 1955, p. 42.
July 15: Newport Jazz Festival, Newport, Rhode Island. *Program.*
July 27–August 7: Blue Note, Chicago. *down beat,* August 10, 1955, p. 36. *down beat,* August 10, p. 4.
August 11–13: Riviera, St. Louis, Missouri. *down beat,* August 24, 1955, p. 32.
August 19–September 5: Zardi's, Hollywood, California. *down beat,* August 24, 1955, p. 32.

September: Zardi's, Hollywood, California. "Erroll Garner breaks in at Zardi's with his new rhythm section of Eddie Calhoun." *Variety,* September 14, 1955, p. 56.

September 6–26: Blackhawk, San Francisco. *down beat,* September 14, 1955, p. 56.

September 19: Sunset Auditorium, Carmel, California. *Note:* It was at this concert that Erroll Garner's famous album, *Concert by the Sea* was recorded.

October 31–November 6: Colonial Tavern, Toronto, Canada. *down beat,* November 2, 1955, p. 48.

November 14–19: Blue Note, Philadelphia. *down beat,* November 30, 1955, p. 52.

November 21–27: Storyville, Boston. *down beat,* November 16, 1955, p. 32.

December 4: Celebrity, Providence, Rhode Island. *down beat,* December 14, 1955, p. 48.

December 6–17: Colonial Tavern, Toronto, Canada. *down beat,* December 14, 1955, p. 48.

December 25–January 1, 1956: Waluhaje Club, Atlanta, Georgia. *down beat,* December 28, 1955, p. 30.

1956 **February 1:** Opens at the Blue Note, Chicago. *Chicago Sun-Times,* January 29, 1956.

March: Brooklyn Academy of Music, Brooklyn, New York. *Chicago Daily News,* January 28, 1956.

April 29: Plays at annual Scholarship Fund Concert of Kappa Beta Sigma Chapter of Phi Beta Sigma Fraternity, Town Hall, N.Y.C. *New York Age,* March 31, 1956; *Amsterdam News,* April 14, 1956.

May 14: Junior Achievement Awards Luncheon, Bridgeport Brass Foundation Community Center, Bridgeport, Connecticut. *Bridgeport Post,* May 6, 1956.

May 17: Plays for Teen Council of Harlem YMCA, at the "Y" Gymnasium Annex, West 35th Street, N.Y.C. *New York Age,* May 19, 1956.

May 17: "Jazz pianist Erroll Garner suffered a brain concussion last night when he was injuried in a taxicab accident." *Newark New Jersey News,* May 18, 1956.

May (late): Recovering from auto accident at Lenox Hill Hospital, N.Y.C. *Billboard,* June 2, 1956.

July 22: Pasadena Civic Auditorium, Pasadena, California.

August 24: New York Jazz Festival, Randall's Island Stadium, *New York Herald Tribune,* August 25, 1956.

September: London House, Chicago. *Variety,* September 26, 1956, p. 49.

October 15 (one week): Copa Club, 818 Liberty, Pittsburgh. *Pittsburgh Post Gazette,* October 15, 1956, p. 18. *Note:* Kelly Martin joins trio during this engagement.

1957   **March:** Peacock Lane, Hollywood, California. *Billboard,* March
23, 1957, p. 23.
June 7: Starts European tour. *Melody Maker,* January 5, 1957.
July 5: Newport Jazz Festival, Newport, Rhode Island. *Program.*
July 31 (four weeks): London House, Chicago. *Chicago Daily
News,* July 27, 1957.
August 15: Featured with Cleveland Symphony Orchestra,
Cleveland, Ohio. *Variety,* August 21, 1957, p. 43.
October 30 (two weeks): Blue Note, Chicago. *Chicago Defender,*
November 2, 1957, p. 18.
November 22: Garry Moore Show. *Baltimore Afro American,* No-
vember 9, 1957, p. 5.
November 27: "The Big Record" (TV) Patti Page, hostess. Ibid.
December 1: Leaves for Paris. Ibid.
December: Receives "Grand Prix du Disque" in Paris. *Norfolk
(Virginia) Journal & Guide,* December 28, 1957, p. 14.
December: Receives the Down Beat Award for the most outstand-
ing intrumentalist of the year; presented at the Olympia Theater,
Paris, France. *Chicago Defender,* January 11, 1958, p. 18.
December 16–26: Olympia Theater, Paris. *Norfolk Journal and
Guide,* December 28, 1957, p. 14; *Melody Maker,* December 21,
1957.
December 28: Cafe Society, N.Y.C.

1958   **January 26:** Appears on Percy Faith Show (CBS Radio). *Billboard,*
January 27, 1958, p. 18.
January 31: Symphony Hall, Boston, Massachusetts. *Billboard,*
February 17, 1958.
February: Awarded a gold disc for becoming the first jazz artist
to sell a million copies of an LP album, *Concert by the Sea. Jet,*
February 27, 1958, p. 62.
February 2: University of Massachusetts. *Billboard,* January 27,
1958, p. 18.
March 22: Union College, Cranford, New Jersey.
April 2: Opens at the Blue Note, Chicago. *Chicago Sun-Times,*
April 2, 1958.
May: Sol Hurok announces signing of Garner for exclusive rep-
resentation in North America. *New York Amsterdam News,* May
17, 1958, p. 13; *Norfolk Journal & Guide,* May 17, 1958, p. 21.
June 29: The Surf, Nantasket, Massachusetts. *Quincy, (Massachu-
setts) Patriot-Ledger.* June 30, 1958.
July 2, 4: Ravinia Festival, Ravinia Park, Illinois. *Variety,* July
9, 1958, p. 60; *Chicago Sun-Times,* June 29, 1958.
July 21, 22: Storyville Cape Cod, Harwich, Massachusetts. *Variety,*
July 23, 1958.
August 10: Carousel Music Theater, Framingham, Massachusetts.

Variety, August 13, 1958. *Chicago Defender,* August 16, 1958, p. 15.

August 15–17: French Lick Jazz Festival, French Lick, Indiana.
September 27: Oakdale Musical Theater, Wallingford, Connecticut. *Variety,* October 1, 1958.
October 12: Concert, Orchestra Hall, Chicago. *Chicago Sun Times,* October 9, 1958.
October 17: Lisner Auditorium, Washington, D.C. *Variety,* October 22, 1958.
November 14: Massey Hall, Toronto, Ontario, Canada. *Toronto Telegram,* November 15, 1958.
November 15: Masonic Auditorium, Detroit, Michigan. *Detroit News,* November 13, 1958.
December 2: University of Vermont, Burlington, Vermont. *Billboard,* December 8, 1958; *New York Amsterdam News,* December 20, 1958, p. 28.
December 5: Practical Arts Auditorium, Manchester, New Hampshire. *Manchester Union Leader,* November 28, 1958; *Manchester News,* December 7, 1958; *New York Amsterdam News,* December 20, 1958, p. 28.
December 21: Montreal TV appearance. *New York Amsterdam News,* December 20, 1958, p. 28.

1959   **January 2** (two weeks): Black Orchid, Chicago, Illinois. *New York Amsterdam News,* December 20, 1958, p. 28; *Pittsburgh Courier,* December 27, 1958, p. 23.

January 17: Symphony Hall, Boston, Massachusetts. *down beat,* March 5, 1959. *New York Amsterdam News,* December 20, 1958, p. 23; *Variety,* January 21, 1959, p. 64.
January 30: Peristyle, Toledo, Ohio. *Program.*
February 13: Opera House of Kiel Auditorium, St. Louis, Missouri. *St. Louis Globe Democrat,* January 18, 1959.
February 21: Cleveland Music Hall, Cleveland, Ohio. *Variety,* February 25, 1959.
February 24: Navajo Civic Center, Window Rock, Arizona. *Albuquerque Journal,* February 27, 1959.
March 27: Phoenix Union High School Auditorium, Phoenix, Arizona. *Arizona Republic,* March 28, 1959.
April 10–19: Storyville, Boston. *New York Post,* April 2, 1959.
April 30: Syria Mosque, Pittsburgh. *Pittsburgh Courier,* March 28, 1959, p. 22.
May 24: Oakdale Music Theater, Wallingford, Connecticut.
July 4: Newport Jazz Festival, Newport, Rhode Island. *Program.*
July 8: Concert, Ravinia Park, Chicago. *Chicago Daily News,* July 2, 1959.

August 3: Brandywine Music Circus, Concordville, Pennsylvania. *Philadelphia Inquirer,* July 26, 1959.

August 15-September 30: European Tour.

October 16: "Erroll Garner moves into Carnegie Hall this Friday night under the auspices of impresario Sol Hurok." *New York Post,* October 13, 1959; *Billboard,* October 26, 1959, p. 16.

November 3: Berkeley Community Theater, Berkeley, California. *Oakland Tribune,* November 4, 1959.

November 11: Orpheum Theater, Seattle, Washington. *Seattle Post-Intelligencer,* November 12, 1959.

December 5: Mosque Theater, Newark, New Jersey. *New York Post,* October 30, 1959.

December 12: Eisner & Lubin Auditorium, N.Y.C. *Program.*

1960 **January 11-15:** Arthur Godfrey Show. *Minneapolis Tribune,* January 15, 1960.

January 18-23: Freddie's Cafe, Minneapolis, Minnesota. Ibid.

January 27: Perry Como Show. Ibid.

February 18: Massey Hall, Toronto, Ontario, Canada. *Toronto Telegram,* February 19, 1960.

February 26: Masonic Temple, Detroit, Michigan. *Detroit Free Press,* February 21, 1960.

March 5: White Plains County Center, White Plains, New York. *New York Post,* March 4, 1960.

March 19: Concert, Opera House, Chicago. *Chicago Daily News,* February 29, 1960; *Chicago Sun-Times,* March 16, 1960.

May: Fairmont Hotel, San Francisco. *Variety,* May 25, 1960, p. 66.

July 11: Westbury Music Fair, Westbury, New York. *New York Herald Tribune,* July 10, 1960.

July 19: "Erroll Garner won his fight for a temporary injunction against Columbia Records last week. On Tuesday, Judge Spector of the New York Supreme Court signed the Garner order prohibiting Columbia Records from pressing, selling, distributing, and advertising the Columbia album *The One and Only Erroll Garner.*" *Billboard,* July 25, 1960, p. 3.

September 6: "Erroll Garner will continue to seek relief from a runaway unauthorized album release when he forces Columbia Records in court for the fourth time." *New York Amsterdam News,* September 10, 1960, p. 13.

September 14-October 4: Basin Street East, N.Y.C. *down beat,* September 15, 1960, p. 39.

October: "Erroll Garner is suing Columbia for $100,000 and Columbia in turn, is suing Garner for $600,000 for breach of contract. The hassle started when Columbia released an album, *The One and Only Erroll Garner,* last June without his having approved the material as stipulated by his contract with the firm." *New York Courier*, October 22, 1960, p. 4.

October 23: Ed Sullivan Show, N.Y.C. *Press Release: Martha Glaser.*

November 4–November 20: Crescendo, Los Angeles. *Press Release: Martha Glaser.*

1961   January: Freddie's, Minneapolis, Minnesota. *Variety*, January 25, 1961, p. 54.

January 10: Concert tour for the spring of 1961, under the auspices of Sol Hurok begins. *Press Release: Martha Glaser.*

January 17: University Auditorium, Michigan State University, East Lansing, Michigan.

February: "Erroll Garner announced that his attorneys had placed Columbia Records on notice to the effect that the diskery had no right to issue a new album which bears the pianist's name." *The New York Courier*, February 25, 1961, p. 4.

February: "The feud between Erroll Garner and Columbia Records flared up again last week. The new hassle was sparked by Columbia's release of an LP titled, *The Provocative Erroll Garner* which the pianist claims is an unauthorized release." *Variety*, February 15, 1961, p. 53.

February 23: City Auditorium Music Hall, Omaha, Nebraska. *Omaha World Herald*, February 21, 1961.

March 4: Waikiki Shell, Honolulu, Hawaii. *down beat*, February 2, 1961, p. 48.

March 30–April 12: Basin Street East, N.Y.C. *Variety*, April 12, 1961, p. 53; *Billboard*, April 3, 1961, p. 8.

April 21: Academy of Music, Philadelphia. *Philadelphia Bulletin*, April 22, 1961; *Philadelphia Inquirer*, April 16, 1961.

May: *Dreamstreet* issued. First new recording in three years. *New York Courier*, May 27, 1961, p. 23.

May 29: "New AM-PAR contract prohibits record club handling of Garner releases." *Billboard*, June 5, 1961, p. 3; *Billboard*, June 12, 1961, pp. 1, 21, and 4; *New York Courier*, June 17, 1961, p. 21.

June 8: Opens, Crescendo, Los Angeles. *Variety*, June 21, 1961, p. 58; *down beat*, June 8, 1961, p. 50.

June: Records for own label Octave and appoints ABC Paramount as the label's releasing firm in the U.S. *Billboard*, August 18, 1962, p. 14.

July 3: Westbury Music Fair, Westbury, New York. *Detroit Courier*, July 8, 1961.

October (late): Miramar Supper Club, Columbus, Ohio. *down beat*, October 26, 1961, p. 12.

December: Appears at benefit for the Hudson Guild Neighborhood

House Christmas Fund during the holidays. *Press Release: Martha Glaser,* January 3, 1962.

1962 **February 17:** Orpheum Theater, Seattle, Washington. *Program.*
March 5: Massey Hall, Toronto, Ontario, Canada. *Toronto Daily Star,* March 5, 1962.
April 6: Berkeley Community Theater, Berkeley, California. *Program.*
April 7: Masonic Memorial Temple, San Francisco. *Program.*
May 10: Begins European Tour in Munich, West Germany. *Variety,* May 9, 1962, p. 63.
May 12: Amsterdam, The Netherlands.
May 19: Berlin, West Germany.
May 22: Zurich, Switzerland.
May 24: Berne, Switzerland.
May 26: Royal Festival Hall, London, England. *Variety,* May 9, 1962, p. 63.
May 30: Liverpool, England.
May 31: Leicester, England.
June: Tours England. *New York Courier,* June 16, 1962.
June 2: London, England.
June 3: Free Trade Hall, Manchester, England.
June 4: Colston Hall, Bristol, England.
June 6: Birmingham, England.
June 7: Colston Hall, Bristol, England.
June 8: Colston Hall, Bristol, England.
June 9: The Astoria Cinema, Finsbury Park, London, England. *Melody Maker,* June 2, 1962.
June 10: Gaumont State Theater, Kilburn, London, England. Ibid.
June 13: Salle Pleyel, Paris, France. *Variety,* June 20, 1962, p. 49.
June 17: London, England.
July: London House, Chicago. *Chicago Sun-Times,* July 8, 1962.
August: Settles long-standing dispute with Columbia Records in an out-of-court settlement. *Billboard,* August 18, 1962, pp. 5, 14; *Variety,* August 15, 1962, p. 41.
August 14: Guest soloist, San Diego Symphony Orchestra, San Diego, California.
August 20–25: World's Fair Play House, Seattle World's Fair, Seattle, Washington. *Program.*

1963 **January 30:** Kraft Music Hall with Perry Como. *Chicago Daily Defender,* January 22, 1963, p. 16.
April 7: Orchestra Hall, Chicago. *Chicago Daily Defender,* April 3, 1963.
July 5–July 28: London House, Chicago. *Chicago Defender,* June 29–July 5, 1963, p. 12; July 6–July 12, 1963, p. 11.
October 12: Royal Festival Hall, London, England.

October 13: Odeon, Hammersmith, London, England.
October 14: De Montfort Hall, Leicester, England.
October 17: City Hall, Newcastle-upon-Tyne, England.
October 19: Free Trade Hall, Manchester, England.
October 20: Royal Festival Hall, London, England.
October 21: Town Hall, Birmingham, England.
October 25: Colston Hall, Bristol, England.
October 26: Astoria, Finsbury Park, London, England.
October 27: Odeon, Hammersmith, London, England.
October 30: City Hall, Sheffield, England.
November 1: London, England.
November 2: Fairfield Hall, Croydon, Surrey, England.

1964 **January 22:** Toronto, Ontario, Canada.
September: Berkshire Music Barn, Lenox, Massachusetts.
September 4: New York World's Fair, Singer Bowl, N.Y.C.
October 10: Odeon, Hammersmith, London, England. *Program.*
October 17: Free Trade Hall, Manchester, England.
October 28: Fairfield Hall, Croydon, Surrey, England. *Program.*
October 30: The Dome, Brighton, England. *Program.*
November 7: Concertgebouw, Amsterdam, The Netherlands.
November 27–December 4: Five concerts in Basel, Geneva, Lausanne and Zurich, Switzerland. *Press Release: Martha Glaser.*

1965 **February 5:** Massey Hall, Toronto, Ontario, Canada. *Toronto Telegram,* February 6, 1965.
February 6: Lafayette College, Easton, Pennsylvania. *Announcement: Today Show,* January 26, 1965.
February 14: Music Hall, Kansas City, Missouri. *Ibid.*
February 16–28: London House, Chicago. *down beat,* January 28, 1965, p. 44.
May 20 (two weeks): Village Gate, N.Y.C. *Press Release: Ivan Black,* May 13, 1965; *Variety,* May 26, 1965, p. 61; *New York Post,* May 27, 1965.
August 24–September 5: London House, Chicago. *down beat,* August 26, 1965.
November 12: Opera House, Seattle, Washington. *Seattle Times,* November 13, 1965.
November 19: San Jose Civic Auditorium, San Jose, California. *San Francisco Chronicle.* November 14, 1965.
December 4: Appears with Lexington Symphony Orchestra, Lexington, Kentucky. *down beat,* December 30, 1965, p. 16.
December 13: Paris, France. Featured on two-hour Eurovision TV Spectacular for the benefit of underprivileged children in France. *down beat,* December 30, 1965, p. 16.

1966 **April 29:** Montreux International Television Festival, Montreux, Switzerland.
May–early June: Tours Europe and England. *Chicago Defender,* June 18–24, 1966, p. 15.
May 29: New Victoria Cinema, London, England.
June 9: Fairfield Hall, Croydon, Surrey, England. *Program.*
July 7: Greensboro Municipal Auditorium, Greensboro, North Carolina. *Chicago Defender,* June 18–24, 1966, p. 15; *Michigan Chronicle,* June 18, 1966.
July 9: Indiana University, Bloomington, Indiana. Ibid.
July 12–July 24: London House, Chicago. *Chicago Defender,* July 16–22, 1966, p. 13.
November 12: Lisner Auditorium, George Washington University, Washington, D.C. *Washington Afro-American,* November 19, 1966; *Detroit Courier,* November 19, 1966.
December 3: Carnegie Music Hall, Pittsburgh. *Press Release: Martha Glaser.*
December 4: Named Variety Club Tent No. 1's "Man of the Year in Music" at its 39th annual banquet at the Penn Sheraton Hotel, Pittsburgh. *Variety,* December 14, 1966, p. 49.

1967 **February 18:** Carnegie Hall Concert, N.Y.C. "Jazz in the Great Tradition." Personnel: Milt Hinton (b), Herbert Lovelle (d), Wally Richardson (g), José Mangual (cd). *Program: New York Amsterdam News,* February 11, 1967, p. 18; *Variety,* February 22, 1967, p. 56, *New York World Journal Tribune,* February 20, 1967.
March 16–25: Edgewater Inn, Seattle, Washington. *Seattle Times,* March 17, 1967.
March 31 (three weeks): Tropicana Blue Room, Las Vegas, Nevada. *Press Release: Martha Glaser; Variety,* April 12, 1967, p. 65.
April 26–May 6: Basin Street West, San Francisco, California. *Press Release: Martha Glaser.*
May 13: Guest soloist, Cincinnati Symphony Orchestra Music Hall, Cincinnati, Ohio. *Detroit Courier,* May 13, 1967.
May 17: Leaves U.S. for concert and television appearances in Paris and London. *Press Release: Martha Glaser.*
May 21: London Palladium (TV), London, England. *Press Release: Martha Glaser.*
May 24: Broadcast, Radio Europe No. 1, Paris, France. *Press Release: Martha Glaser.*
May 25: Salle Pleyel, Paris, France. *Press Release: Martha Glaser.*
June 15–25: Carter Barron Amphitheater, Washington, D.C. *down beat,* September 7, 1967.
June 26–July 1: Living Room, Cincinnati, Ohio. *Press Release: Martha Glaser.*
July 17–23: Greek Theater with Andy Williams, Los Angeles. *down beat,* August 10, 1967, p. 14; *Press Release: Martha Glaser.*

October 29: "Arrives in Hamburg where he will be feted by Deutsche Grammophone which will distribute his MGM recordings in Germany, including his hit album *That's My Kick.*" *Press Release: Martha Glaser.*

November 1–8: Concerts in Berlin, Munich, and Stuttgart. *Detroit Courier,* November 4, 1967.

November 6: Andy Williams Show. Ibid.

November 9–11: Milwaukee Symphony Orchestra, Milwaukee, Wisconsin. *Billboard,* September 17, 1967.

November 25: Baltimore Symphony Orchestra, Baltimore, Maryland. *Program.*

1968   **February 5** (two weeks): Al Hirt's Club, New Orleans. *down beat,* February 22, 1968, p. 13.

February 22: War Memorial Auditorium, Fort Lauderdale, Florida.

February 26 (one week): Lennie's-on-the-Turnpike, near Boston. *down beat,* February 22, 1968, p. 13.

March 4–9: Embers, Indianapolis, Indiana. *down beat,* February 22, 1968, p. 13.

April 5: University of Detroit, Town and Gown Celebrity Series, Memorial Building, Detroit, Michigan. *Michigan Chronicle,* March 30, 1968.

May 4: Kongresshalle, Vienna, Austria.

May 24 (three weeks): Tropicana Hotel, Las Vegas, Nevada. *down beat,* July 11, 1968, p. 43.

June 17–29: Byrd's Nest, Silver Springs, Maryland. *down beat,* May 30, 1968, p. 46.

July 1 (two weeks): Lennie's-on-the-Turnpike, near Boston.

August 5 (one week): Holiday House, Monroeville, Pennsylvania. *Pittsburgh Press,* August 7, 1968.

October 1–5: D.J's, Seattle, Washington. *Program.*

November 23: Cincinnati Symphony Orchestra, Cincinnati, Ohio. *Program.*

December 19 (three weeks): Venetian Room, Fairmont Hotel, San Francisco. *Michigan Chronicle,* December 21, 1968.

1969   **January:** MGM Records releases *"Up in Erroll's Room."* *Chicago Defender,* January 16, 1969, p. 15.

February 21: Roehm Junior High Auditorium, Berea, Ohio.

March 3–23: Hong Kong Bar, Century Plaza Hotel, Los Angeles. *Billboard,* March 29, 1969, p. 16.

April 21–May 1: Begins European tour in Basel, Switzerland. Will also play concerts in Zurich, Paris, Bordeaux, and Vienna. Appears on TV shows in France and Holland. *down beat,* May 15, 1969, p. 13.

May 1: Berlin, West Germany. *down beat,* May 15, 1969, p. 13.

May 2: Hamburg, West Germany. Ibid.

May 5: Munich, West Germany. Ibid.

June 9–21: Isy's Supper Club, Vancouver, British Columbia, Canada. *down beat,* June 12, 1969, p. 13.

June 22: Lakefront Festival, Outdoor Concert sponsored by Joseph P. Schlitz Brewing Company, Milwaukee War Memorial Park, Milwaukee, Wisconsin. *down beat,* June 12, 1969, p. 13; *Milwaukee Courier,* May 24, 1969.

August 26–September 3: Concord, California Festival. *down beat,* October 16, 1969, p. 41.

September 15–20: Embers, Indianapolis, Indiana. *Program.*

September 23–October 5: Mister Kelly's, Chicago. *Chicago Sun-Times,* September 29, 1969, p. 55; *Chicago Defender,* October 1, 1969, p. 14; *Variety,* October 1, 1969, p. 65; *Chicago Defender,* October 2, 1969, p. 20.

October 17: With Oklahoma Symphony Orchestra, Imperial Ballroom, Skirvin Hotel, Oklahoma City, Oklahoma. *Chicago Defender,* October 1, 1969, p. 14; *Sunday Oklahoman,* Showcase Section, October 12, 1969, p. 3.

November (early): Paul's Mall, Boston. *Billboard,* November 15, 1969, pp. 26, 57.

1970 **February:** Japan tour. *down beat,* March 19, 1970, p. 13.

February 28: Boston Globe Festival, Boston, Massachusetts. Ibid.

April 12: Carnegie Music Hall, Pittsburgh.

April–May: European tour. *down beat,* March 19, 1970, p. 13.

June: Antibes Festival, France. *Press Release: Martha Glaser.*

June 2: "Jazz pianist Erroll Garner aided local school authorities by appearing with his trio at Henninger High School (Syracuse, N.Y.) in a concert aimed at quieting the students who for the past week had been disrupting classes in all junior and senior high schools throughout the city, forcing authorities to close school for a time. The concert served to calm the rife-torn student body and reportedly conditions have returned to normal." *Variety,* June 3, 1970, p. 45.

July 8–20: South American tour: Caracas, Rio de Janeiro, São Paulo, Buenos Aires, Montevideo, Santiago. *Michigan Chronicle,* July 11, 1970. *Note:* Ernest McCarty, Jr., bassist, joins group on this tour.

July 23–24: Antibes and St. Tropez, France. *down beat,* July 23, 1970, p. 20.

August 1–15: Tivoli Gardens, Copenhagen, Denmark. *down beat,* July 23, 1970, p. 12.

September: Signs with Mercury Records. *Variety,* September 23, 1970, p. 68.

September 14–26: Mr. Kelly's, Chicago. *down beat,* September 17,

1970, p. 11; *Chicago Tribune,* September 13, 1970; *Variety,* September 23, 1970, p. 71.
October 28–November 17: Persian Room, Plaza Hotel, N.Y.C. *Village Voice,* November 5, 1970; *Billboard,* November 7, 1970, p. 23.

1971   **March:** Records "Misty" for the motion picture *Play Misty For Me. down beat,* April 1, 1971, p. 12.
April 16–24: Royal York Hotel, Toronto, Ontario, Canada. *down beat,* April 1, 1971, p. 12.
May 4: Brussels, Belgium. Ibid.
May 6: Antwerp, Belgium. Ibid.
May 7: Montbeliard, France. Ibid.
May 11: Paris, France. Ibid.
May 12: Berlin, West Germany. Ibid.
May 17: Copenhagen, Denmark. Ibid.
July 2: Meadowbrook Festival, Detroit, Michigan.
September 18: Monterey Jazz Festival, Monterey, California. *Program.*
October 18–30: Maisonette Room, St. Regis Hotel, N.Y.C. *Variety,* October 27, 1971, p. 69; *Billboard,* November 6, 1971, p. 14; *New York Times,* October 22, 1971.
November 5–7: Philadelphia.
November 12: Severance Hall, Cleveland, Ohio. *Cleveland Plain Dealer,* November 12, 1971.

1972   **February** (early): Hyatt Regency O'Hare, Chicago.
March 11: With Orlando Symphony Orchestra, Orlando, Florida. *Announcement: Mike Douglas Show,* March 16, 1972.
March 17–19: Brandi's Wharf, Philadelphia. *down beat,* March 16, 1972, p. 11.
March 22: Honored by the Pittsburgh Press Club which makes him an honorary member. *down beat,* May 25, 1972.
April–May: Tours Europe. *Press Release: Martha Glaser.*
April 22: Copenhagen, Denmark. *down beat,* May 25, 1972, p. 10.
May 6: Odeon, Hammersmith, London, England. *Program.*
May 19–20: TV Appearance, Belgrade, Yugoslavia. *down beat,* May 25, 1972, p. 10.
June 15–July 3: Far East tour includes Australia, Japan, Hong Kong, and Hawaii. *down beat,* March 16, 1972, p. 11; *down beat,* May 25, 1972, p. 10.
June 20: Tokyo, Japan.
July 31–August 6: Loser's Club, Dallas, Texas. *down beat,* September 14, 1972, p. 11; *Dallas Times Herald,* July 30, 1972, p. 2-K.
August 7–12: O.D.'s Club, Houston, Texas. *down beat,* September 14, 1972, p. 11.

September 4: Wolftrap Farm (Vienna, Virginia). *down beat,* September 14, 1972, p. 11.

October 3–16: With Johnny Mathis, Congo Room, Sahara Hotel, Las Vegas, Nevada. *Variety,* October 11, 1972; *Billboard,* October 21, 1972, p. 10; *Vegas Visitor,* October 6–12, 1972, p. 1.

October 23–November 11: Maisonette Room, St. Regis Hotel, N.Y.C. *Variety,* November 1, 1972, p. 63.

November 13–19: Paul's Mall, Boston.

November 20–21: Nazareth Arts Center, Nazareth College, Pittsford, New York.

November 24: Denver Symphony Orchestra, Auditorium Theater, Denver, Colorado. *Program.*

November 25: Colorado Springs Symphony Orchestra, City Auditorium, Colorado Springs, Colorado. *Program.*

1973   **January 14:** Cincinnati Symphony Orchestra, Cincinnati, Ohio. *Program.*

April 28: Heinz Hall, Pittsburgh. *Pittsburgh Press,* April 8, 1973.

July: Frog and Nightgown, Raleigh, North Carolina.

July 10: Temple University Music Festival, Philadelphia. *Philadelphia Evening Bulletin,* July 11, 1973.

July 18: Schaefer Music Series, Central Park, N.Y.C.

August 6: Saratoga Springs, Florida. *down beat,* August 16, 1973, p. 13.

August 8–15: Tours France, Ibid.

August 18: Central Park, N.Y.C. *down beat,* September 13, 1973, p. 11.

October 15–20: Scot's Inn, Columbus, Ohio.

October 22–23: Brown Derby, Norton, Ohio.

November 21: Concert, Masonic Auditorium, Detroit, Michigan. *Detroit News,* November 20, 1973.

November 23: Concert, Hartford, Connecticut.

November 26–December 9: Mr. Kelly's, Chicago, Illinois. *Variety,* December 5, 1973, p. 52.

December 11: With Indianapolis Symphony Orchestra, Clowes Memorial Hall, Indianapolis, Indiana. *Program.*

December 13: Concert, Sarasota, Florida.

1974   **January 21–26:** Just Jazz Club, Philadelphia. *Philadelphia Inquirer,* January 20, 1974.

April 22: Belgrade, Yugoslavia. *down beat,* March 28, 1974, p. 11.

April 26: Brussels, Belgium. *down beat,* May 9, 1974, p. 10.

April 28: Munich, West Germany.

April 29: Hamburg, West Germany.

April 30: Hannover, West Germany.

May 2: Berlin, West Germany. *down beat,* May 9, 1974, p. 11.

May 11: Düsseldorf, West Germany.

May 12: Frankfurt, West Germany.

May 15: Paris, France. *down beat,* May 23, 1974.

May 24–25: With Detroit Symphony Orchestra, Detroit Light Guard Armory, Detroit, Michigan. *Michigan Chronicle,* May 25, 1974.

May: *Magician* released: first album in 18 months. *New York Times,* May 27, 1974.

May 27–June 15: Maisonette Room, St. Regis Hotel, N.Y.C. *down beat,* May 23, 1974, p. 10; *New York Times,* May 27, 1974; *Variety,* May 29, 1974, p. 55; *Billboard,* June 20, 1974, p. 24.

July 8–20: Hyatt Regency Hotel, Atlanta, Georgia. *down beat,* August 15, 1974, p. 10.

July 23–29: Tours French Riviera. *down beat,* August 15, 1974, p. 10.

August 16: With National Symphony Orchestra, Washington, D.C. *down beat,* August 15, 1974, p. 10.

August 20: With Ray Charles, Robin Hood Dell, Philadelphia. *down beat,* August 15, 1974, p. 10.

1975   **January 17–18:** Great American Music Hall, San Francisco. *down beat,* January 30, 1975.

February 11–16: Etcetera Club, Washington, D.C.

February 17–20: Mr. Kelly's, Chicago. *down beat,* February 27, 1975. *Note:* Thursday evening, February 20, 1975, was the last public performance by Erroll Garner.

February 21 (6:05 p.m.): Admitted to Northwestern Memorial Hospital, Chicago, for viral pneumonia.

March 6 (1:00 p.m.): Discharged from Northwestern Memorial Hospital, Chicago.

April 8: Surgery reveals carcinoma (cancer) of the right lung. Cedars-Sinai Medical Center, Los Angeles.

1976   **April 16:** Signs Last Will and Testament, Los Angeles.

December 14 (5:45 p.m.): Admitted to Cedars-Sinai Medical Center, Los Angeles, for carcinoma (cancer) of the right lung with metastasis to the pericardium.

December 29 (4:30 p.m.): Discharged from Cedars-Sinai Medical Center, Los Angeles.

1977   **January 2** (12:32 p.m.): Dies, Los Angeles. Immediate cause of death is (a) cardiac arrest due to (b) metastasis, cancer to the pericardium due to (c) cancer of the lung. *Death Certificate.*

January 4 (9:00 a.m.): Linton S. Garner (brother) accompanies the body on a flight from Los Angeles to Pittsburgh.

January 5–6: Wake at Spriggs-Watson Funeral Home, Pittsburgh.

January 7 (1:00 p.m.): Funeral, St. James A.M.E. Church, Pittsburgh. Pall Bearers: Walt Harper, Leroy Brown, Carl Arter,

Eugene Peeler, Russell Williams, James "Honey Boy" Minor. Laid to rest next to his mother and father at Homewood Cemetery, Pittsburgh.
February 13: Tribute at Central Presbyterian Church, Park Avenue and 64th Street, N.Y.C. *New York Times,* February 11, 1977.
April: "Garner estate of $425,000 to be split between manager and family." *Jet,* April 14, 1977, p. 19.
June 15: "Erroll Garner Day" proclaimed by Mayor Richard Caliguiri of Pittsburgh and Milton J. Shapp, Governor of Pennsylvania. *New York Daily Challenge,* July 25, 1977, p. 5.
June 24–July 4: The 1977 Newport Jazz Festival (N.Y.C.) dedicated to the memory of Erroll Garner. *Chicago Tribune,* April 10, 1977, p. 6, sec. 6.
June 29: Solo Piano Tribute to Garner. Participants: Teddy Wilson, Adam Makowicz, George Shearing, and Earl "Fatha" Hines. Carnegie Hall, N.Y.C. *Program.*
September 28: Honored by his colleagues in the American Society of Composers, Authors and Publishers. The Society presents its highest award, "The Pied Piper," to the artist's brother, Linton Garner. *Press Release: ASCAP; Chicago Sun-Times,* September 28, 1977, p. 6.
November 10: Tribute, Fairfield Hall, Croydon, England.

1978 **January:** Erroll Garner Songbook introduced by Cherry Lane Music Co., Port Chester, N.Y. *Jet,* January 5, 1978. p. 54.
March 3–5: Tribute to Garner, Roberson Center, Binghamton, New York. Slam Stewart Trio +1: Slam Stewart (b), Dick Hyman (p), Chuck Wayne (g), Bill Reichenbach (d). *Binghamton Press,* March 4, 1978, p. 1–8; March 7, 1978, p. 11-A.
June 16: The University of Pittsburgh presents a Tribute to Garner, Westinghouse High School, Pittsburgh. *Program.*

1979 **May:** The Erroll Garner Memorial Foundation is established; scholarships of $1500 are planned. *Atlanta Daily World,* May 13, 1979, p. 9; *Jet,* May 31, 1979, p. 58.

1981 **July:** *Erroll Garner, Master of the Keyboard,* Book-of-the-Month Club Records is introduced. *Boston Globe,* July 16, 1981, p. 12.

1982 **February 19:** "Roger Woods, a junior and music major at Howard University, is the first winner of an Erroll Garner Memorial Foundation Scholarship Award. Selected in a nationwide competition, Woods will receive the award of $1500 at a program in the Recital Hall of Crampton Auditorium, on the Howard University campus in Washington, D.C." *Press Release: Martha Glaser.*

III. His Recorded Music

Appearing at the Village Gate, New York, 1965. (Ellis Feibush)

ERROLL GARNER'S RECORDED MUSIC

Erroll Garner's recorded output has been extraordinary. With so many titles and labels with which to contend, the intent of this discography is to orient the collector to Garner's commercial and unissued recordings.

This discography is based on previous works by Erik Wiedemann, Tom Sachs, Martin Rand, and Jorgen Grunnet Jepsen. The format used is based on Arnold Laubich and Ray Spencer's book, *Art Tatum: A Guide to His Recorded Music.* Their unique approach takes full advantage of modern computer technology. This work is a similar effort.

The section on Unissued Sessions, which follows the Discography, uses a comparable format. It includes all tapes believed to be in existence of Garner's performances on TV, radio, clubs, concert appearances, and studio recordings, where none of the titles were commercially issued. These tapes, although not for general distribution, are of great significance to the researcher in tracing the history of Garner's recorded music.

The Compilation of Issued Discs section provides an alphabetical listing of all known discs in which Garner appears on one or more titles. Each title on the disc is listed alphabetically and is accompanied by an index number so that information on a particular title can be easily accessed in the Discography.

The scope of Erroll Garner's Recorded Music is to include all commercially released recordings, transcriptions, and unissued tapes known to the author as of February, 1984. Naturally, errors will exist. For this I apologize, and any corrections or updated information would be sincerely appreciated. Only in this way can the work go on and the fullest appreciation of Erroll Garner's artistry be shared and enjoyed by all.

HOW TO USE THIS DISCOGRAPHY

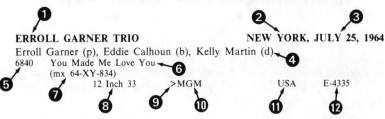

ERROLL GARNER TRIO   **NEW YORK, JULY 25, 1964**
Erroll Garner (p), Eddie Calhoun (b), Kelly Martin (d)
6840   You Made Me Love You
        (mx 64-XY-834)
                12 Inch 33   >MGM   USA   E-4335

1. Name of the group.
2. City where recording session took place.
3. Date of the session.
4. Artists participating in the session with appropriate instrument abbreviation following each name.
5. Index number. This arbitrary number is used to cross reference subsequent lists in the discography.
6. Song title.
7. Matrix number (mx). This number is usually assigned to a song title (side of a record) at the time of performance and is normally etched between the last groove and the label of the disc.
8. Record format includes diameter of the record and playing speed.
9. Arrow identifies original issue.
10. Record manufacturer.
11. Country or continent in which the record was issued.
12. Catalog number issued by the record manufacturer.

Geographic Abbreviations

Aus	Australia	Ity	Italy
Bel	Belgium	Jap	Japan
Can	Canada	Neth	The Netherlands
Cze	Czechoslovakia	Scot	Scotland
Den	Denmark	Swe	Sweden
EGer	East Germany	Swi	Switzerland
Eng	England	USA	United States of America
Eur	Europe	Urg	Uruguay
Fra	France	WGer	West Germany

Instrument Abbreviations

ar	arranger	g	guitar
as	alto saxophone	o	organ
b	bass	ob	oboe
bs	baritone saxophone	p	piano
cd	conga drums	pi	piccolo
ce	cello	sax	saxophone
cl	clarinet	tu	tuba
co	conductor	tb	trombone
d	drums	tmb	tambourine
eh	English horn	tp	trumpet
f	flute	ts	tenor saxophone
fb	fender bass	v	vocal
fh	fluegelhorn	vn	violin
frh	French horn		

Record Format Abbreviations

78	78 rpm
45	45 rpm
33	33⅓ rpm
EP	Extended play recording, normally 45 rpm
TX	Electrical transcription, normally 33⅓ rpm

DISCOGRAPHY

With the exception of the Rex session on December 18, 1944 and the Times Hall Concert of December 20, 1944, all of the recordings that follow (from October 20, 1944 through December 26, 1944) were made privately by Timme Rosenkrantz in his apartment at 7 W. 46th Street, New York City. For this period only, the unissued sessions are included. All other unissued sessions are contained in the Unissued Section of this discography.

ERROLL GARNER   **NEW YORK, OCTOBER 20, 1944**
WITH INEZ CAVANAUGH

Erroll Garner (p), Inez Cavanaugh (v)

0010	I'm in the Mood for Love	Unissued
0020	Somebody Loves Me	Unissued

ERROLL GARNER   **NEW YORK, NOVEMBER 3, 1944**

Asterisk (*) denotes Inez Cavanaugh, vocal.

Erroll Garner (p), Inez Cavanaugh (v)*

0030	I'm in the Mood for Love	Unissued
0040	Gaslight	Unissued
0050	Somebody Loves Me*	Unissued
	Note: Breakdown (20 sec.)	
0060	Somebody Loves Me*	Unissued
0070	Between the Devil and the Deep Blue Sea	Unissued

ERROLL GARNER   **NEW YORK, NOVEMBER 16, 1944**

Asterisk (*) denotes Inez Cavanaugh, vocal.

Erroll Garner (p), Inez Cavanaugh (v)*

0080	The Clock Stood Still			
	10 Inch 33	>Blue Note	USA	BLP5016
	Note: "The Clock Stood Still" was originally titled "No Time at All."			
0090	The Fighting Cocks			Unissued
0100	Memories of You*			Unissued
0110	More Than You Know*			Unissued
0120	Embraceable You* (4 min., 45 sec.)			Unissued
0130	Embraceable You* (5 min., 20 sec.)			Unissued

ERROLL GARNER   **NEW YORK, NOVEMBER 18, 1944**

Erroll Garner (p)

0140	Floating on a Cloud			
	10 Inch 33	>Blue Note	USA	BLP5008
		New York	Den	Unnumbered
	12 Inch 33	BNP	Fra	25.101
	Note: "Floating on a Cloud" was originally titled "Afterthought."			

0150   Cloudburst

10 Inch 33	Vogue	Fra	LD 064
12 Inch 33	Baronet	USA	B109
	Concert Hall	USA	J1269
	>Dial	USA	902
	Hall of Fame	USA	JG-610
	Jazztone	USA	J1269
	Premier	USA	PM9042
	Premier	USA	PS9042
	Spinorama	USA	M181
	Spinorama	USA	S181

ERROLL GARNER   NEW YORK, NOVEMBER 22, 1944
Erroll Garner (p)
0160   Autumn Mood

10 Inch 33	>Blue Note	USA	BLP5008
	New York	Den	Unnumbered
12 Inch 33	BNP	Fra	25.101

        Note: "Autumn Mood" was originally titled "Thanksgivin' Mood."

0170   Variations on a Theme (Part 1)
       (mx 9471)

10 Inch 78	>Selmer	Fra	Y7139

        Note: "Variations on a Theme (Part 1)" is Garner's arrangement of "Clair de lune."

0180   Variations on a Theme (Part 2)
       (mx 9472)

10 Inch 78	Polydor	Fra	580.066
	>Selmer	Fra	Y7139

        Note: "Variations on a Theme (Part 2)" is titled "Moonlight Moods" on Polydor 580.066. It is also an improvised version of "Clair de lune."

ERROLL GARNER   NEW YORK, NOVEMBER 24, 1944
WITH VIC DICKENSON
Erroll Garner (p), Vic Dickenson (tb)
0190   Achin' a Blues   Unissued
0200   On the Sunny Side of the Street

10 Inch 33	>Blue Note	USA	BLP5014
12 Inch 33	BNP	Fra	25.102

        Note: "On the Sunny Side of the Street" is abbreviated omitting the trombone portion.

0210   Drizzly Afternoon   Unissued

ALL STARS ORCHESTRA   NEW YORK, DECEMBER, 1944
Erroll Garner (p), Bobby Pratt (tb), Barney Bigard (cl), George Wettling (d)
0220   It Had to Be You   Unissued
0230   I Surrender, Dear

10 Inch 33	>Blue Note	USA	BLP5008
	New York	Den	Unnumbered
12 Inch 33	BNP	Fra	25.102

        Note: "I Surrender, Dear" (Erroll Garner) is abbreviated omitting the trombone and clarinet passages. It is titled "Beg Your Pardon" on New York (Denmark).

ALL STARS ORCHESTRA   NEW YORK, DECEMBER, 1944
Erroll Garner (p), Eli "Lucky" Thompson (ts), unknown (v)
0240   All the Things You Are   Unissued
       Omit unknown (v). Add Hezekiah "Stuff" Smith (vn).
0250   Toe Jam Blues   Unissued
       Add Bobby Pratt (tb)
0260   Test Pilots (Part 1)
       (mx 239-1-12a)

		10 Inch 78	Ducretet Thomson	Fra	Y8170
			>Selmer	Fra	Y7228
0270	Test Pilots (Part 2)				
	(mx 240-a-12b)				
		10 Inch 78	Ducretet Thomson	Fra	Y8170
			>Selmer	Fra	Y7228

ERROLL GARNER   **NEW YORK, DECEMBER 10–12, 1944**

Erroll Garner (p)

0280	Overture to Dawn				
		10 Inch 33	>Blue Note	USA	BLP5007
		12 Inch 33	BNP	Fra	25.101
0290	Erroll's Concerto				
		10 Inch 33	>Blue Note	USA	BLP5008
			New York	Den	Unnumbered
		12 Inch 33	BNP	Fra	25.101

Note: "Erroll's Concerto" was originally titled, "To You." On the Timme Rosenkrantz transcription log, the title of this tune was "For You," which he crossed out to make "To You."

0300	Yesterdays				
		10 Inch 33	>Blue Note	USA	BLP5014
		12 Inch 33	BNP	Fra	25.102

ERROLL GARNER   **NEW YORK, DECEMBER 14, 1944**

Erroll Garner (p)

0310	All the Things You Are (Part 1)				
	(mx EG185-A)				
		10 Inch 78	>Century	USA	1504
		10 Inch 33	Blue Note	USA	BLP5016

Note: See note below "All the Things You Are (Part 2)."

0320	All the Things You Are (Part 2)				
	(mx EG185-B)				
		10 Inch 78	>Century	USA	1504
		10 Inch 33	Blue Note	USA	BLP5016

Note: "All the Things You Are" (Parts 1 & 2) were sold to Sam Meltzer, Century Records, for USA rights only. Timme Rosenkrantz retained all European and foreign rights.

0330	I Hear a Rhapsody (Part 1)				
	(mx 215a12a)				
		10 Inch 78	Ducretet Thomson	Fra	Y8165
			New York	Den	122
			>Selmer	Fra	Y7216
		10 Inch 33	Blue Note	USA	BLP5007
		12 Inch 33	BNP	Fra	25.101
0340	I Hear a Rhapsody (Part 2)				
	(mx 216a12b)				
		10 Inch 78	Ducretet Thomson	Fra	Y8165
			New York	Den	122
			>Selmer	Fra	Y7216
		10 Inch 33	Blue Note	USA	BLP5007
		12 Inch 33	BNP	Fra	25.101
0350	Erroll's Reverie				
		10 Inch 33	>Blue Note	USA	BLP5015

Note: "Erroll's Reverie" was originally titled "In My Reverie."

0360	You Were Born to Be Kissed				
		10 Inch 33	>Blue Note	USA	BLP5007
		12 Inch 33	BNP	Fra	25.101

ERROLL GARNER TRIO   **NEW YORK, DECEMBER 18, 1944**

Erroll Garner (p), John Simmons (b), Harold "Doc" West (d)

0370	Perdido (mx RK-5)				
		10 Inch 78	>Atlantic	USA	678
		10 Inch 33	Atlantic	USA	ALR 128
			Blue Star	Fra	BLP6833
			Felsted	Eng	EDL87015
		12 Inch 33	Clarion	USA	610
			Musidisc	Fra	30JA5101
0380	Soft and Warm (mx RK-6)				
		10 Inch 78	>Rex	USA	J503
		10 Inch 33	Atlantic	USA	ALR 128
			Blue Star	Fra	BLP6833
			Felsted	Eng	EDL87015
		12 Inch 33	Clarion	USA	610
			Musidisc	Fra	30JA5101
0390	Everything Happens to Me (mx RK-7)				
		10 Inch 78	Atlantic	USA	678
			>Rex	USA	J503
		10 Inch 33	Atlantic	USA	ALR 128
			Blue Star	Fra	BLP6833
			Felsted	Eng	EDL87015
		12 Inch 33	Musidisc	Fra	30JA5101
0400	I'm in the Mood for Love (mx RK-8)				
		10 Inch 78	>Rex	USA	J502
		10 Inch 33	Atlantic	USA	ALR 128
			Blue Star	Fra	BLP6833
			Felsted	Eng	EDL87015
		12 Inch 33	Clarion	USA	610
			Musidisc	Fra	30JA5101
0410	All the Things You Are (mx RK-9)				
		10 Inch 33	>Atlantic	USA	ALR 128
			Blue Star	Fra	BLP6833
			Felsted	Eng	EDL87015
		12 Inch 33	Musidisc	Fra	30JA5101
0420	Blue Room (mx RK-10)				
		10 Inch 78	>Rex	USA	J502
		12 Inch 33	Musidisc	Fra	30JA5101
0430	I Get a Kick Out of You (mx RK-11)				
		10 Inch 33	>Atlantic	USA	ALR 128
			Blue Star	Fra	BLP6833
			Felsted	Eng	EDL87015
		12 Inch 33	Musidisc	Fra	30JA5101
0440	Blues I Can't Forget (mx RK-12)				
		10 Inch 78	Atlantic	USA	677
			>Rex	USA	J501
		10 Inch 33	Atlantic	USA	ALR 128
			Blue Star	Fra	BLP6833
			Felsted	Eng	EDL87015
		12 Inch 33	Clarion	USA	610
			Musidisc	Fra	30JA5101
0450	Boogie Woogie Boogie (mx RK-13)				
		10 Inch 78	>Rex	USA	J501
		10 Inch 33	Atlantic	USA	ALR 128

	Blue Star	Fra	BLP6833
	Felsted	Eng	EDL87015
12 Inch 33	Musidisc	Fra	30JA5101

0460   Gliss in the Dark
       (mx RK-14)

| 10 Inch 78 | >Atlantic | USA | 677 |
| 12 Inch 33 | Musidisc | Fra | 30JA5101 |

Note: "Gliss in the Dark" (Erroll Garner) is titled "Erroll's Bounce" on Musidisc 30JA5101 (see also August 30, 1945 and April 22, 1947 sessions).

ERROLL GARNER   **NEW YORK, DECEMBER 20, 1944**
       Times Hall

Some references give the location of this concert as Town Hall. It has been verified from the program that the concert took place at Times Hall, 240 W. 44th Street, New York City.

Erroll Garner (p)
0470   The Fighting Cocks
       (mx EG182-A)

10 Inch 78	>Century	USA	1503
	New York	Den	117
10 Inch 33	Blue Note	USA	BLP5015
12 Inch 33	BNP	Fra	25.102

Note: See note below "A Lick and a Promise."

0480   A Lick and a Promise
       (mx EG183-A)

10 Inch 78	>Century	USA	1503
	New York	Den	117
10 Inch 33	Blue Note	USA	BLP5015

Note: "The Fighting Cocks" and "A Lick and a Promise" were sold to Sam Meltzer, Century Records, for USA rights only. Timme Rosenkrantz retained all European and foreign rights.

0490   Opus 1

| 10 Inch 33 | >Blue Note | USA | BLP5016 |

Note: "Opus 1" was originally titled "In the Beginning" as documented by Timme Rosenkrantz. It is also the same tune as "White Rose Bounce" (see also January 10, 1945 session).

0500   Gaslight

| 10 Inch 33 | >Blue Note | USA | BLP5016 |

0510   Twistin' the Cat's Tail (with unknown guitar)
       (mx 10474)

10 Inch 78	>Selmer	Fra	Y7086
10 Inch 33	Blue Note	USA	BLP5014
12 Inch 33	BNP	Fra	25.102

Note: "Twistin' the Cat's Tail" is titled "Fast Company" on Blue Note BLP5014 and BNP 25.102. Aural evidence of an announcer and an audience is present on Selmer Y7086. This title does not appear on the original program for the Times Hall Concert.

ERROLL GARNER   **NEW YORK, DECEMBER 22, 1944**
Erroll Garner (p)
0520   Variations on a Nursery Rhyme (Mairzy Doats, Yes, We Have No Bananas, The Music
       Goes 'Round and 'Round, Everything I've Got [Belongs to You])

10 Inch 33	Vogue	Fra	LD 064
12 Inch 33	Baronet	USA	B109
	Concert Hall	USA	J1269
	>Dial	USA	902
	Hall of Fame	USA	JG-610
	Jazztone	USA	J1269

ERROLL GARNER   **NEW YORK, DECEMBER 23-25, 1944**
Asterisk (*) denotes unknown bass.
Erroll Garner (p), unknown (b)*
0530   Just You, Just Me*
       (mx 233-B20A)
              10 Inch 78   Ducretet Thomson   Fra   Y8166
                                New York   Den   118
                                >Selmer   Fra   Y7225
              Note: See note for "Yesterdays" below.
0540   Yesterdays*
       (mx 234-B20B)
              10 Inch 78   Ducretet Thomson   Fra   Y8166
                                New York   Den   118
                                >Selmer   Fra   Y7225
              Note: According to Danish discographer Erik Wiedemann, Timme Rosenkrantz
              placed "Just You, Just Me" and "Yesterdays" in the December 23-25, 1944
              period. There is evidence of an audience on both takes. It is possible that this session
              belongs to the Times Hall concert of December 20, 1944. However, it is not listed
              in the Rosenkrantz transcription log for that date.
       Omit unknown (b).
0550   You're Blasé   Unissued
0560   More Than You Know   Unissued
0570   Easy to Love
              10 Inch 33   Vogue   Fra   LD 064
              12 Inch 33   Baronet   USA   B109
                                Concert Hall   USA   J1269
                                >Dial   USA   902
                                Hall of Fame   USA   JG-610
                                Jazztone   USA   J1269
                                Premier   USA   PM9042
                                Premier   USA   PS9042
                                Spinorama   USA   M181
                                Spinorama   USA   S181
0580   Duke for Dinner
              10 Inch 33   >Blue Note   USA   BLP5015
              12 Inch 33   BNP   Fra   25.102
              Note: "Duke for Dinner" was originally titled "Duke and Swee' Pea for Dinner."
              "Duke" and "Swee' Pea" refer to Duke Ellington and Billy Strayhorn respectively.
0590   Love Is the Thing (Part 1)
       (mx 7005)
              10 Inch 78   >Futurama   USA   3006
                                Jubilee   USA   5052
              Note: "Love Is the Thing (Part 1)" was exchanged with Arthur Bangel, Futurama
              Record Company, for "Rockin' with the Bop," "Bop Beam," "Not Too Bop,"
              and "Bop Hat" by Moe Koffman's Main Stemmers. Timme Rosenkrantz retained
              all European rights.
              "Be My Love" (mx 7006) appears in the ca. 1950 session.
0600   A Lick and a Promise   Unissued
0610   Blue Grass   Unissued
0620   In the Beginning
              10 Inch 33   Vogue   Fra   LD 064
              12 Inch 33   Baronet   USA   B109
                                Concert Hall   USA   J1269
                                >Dial   USA   902
                                Hall of Fame   USA   JG-610
                                Jazztone   USA   J1269
                                Premier   USA   PM9042
                                Premier   USA   PS9042
                                77 Records   Eng   77-LA-12-6
                                Spinorama   USA   M181
                                Spinorama   USA   S181
              Note: "In the Beginning" is also titled "Opus 1" (see December 20, 1944 session).

0630   I Got Rhythm
                10 Inch 33   >Blue Note   USA   BLP5014
                12 Inch 33   BNP   Fra   25.102
                Note: Although unissued on Disc Records, the "I Got Rhythm" master was sold
                to Sam Meltzer, Disc Records, by Timme Rosenkrantz.
0640   Am I Blue/Holiday for Strings (medley)   Unissued
0650   Embraceable You   Unissued
                Note: "Embraceable You" is a vocal by Erroll Garner.
0660   It's the Talk of the Town   Unissued
                Note: "It's the Talk of the Town" is a vocal by Erroll Garner.

ERROLL GARNER   NEW YORK, DECEMBER 24, 1944
"Great Christmas" is one tune (9 min., 20 sec.) divided into the following
three parts.
This title was exchanged with Arthur Bangel, Futurama Record Company,
for "Rockin' with the Bop," "Bop Beam," "Not Too Bop" and "Bop Hat"
by Moe Koffman's Main Stemmers. Timme Rosenkrantz retained all European rights.
Erroll Garner (p)
0670   Great Christmas (Part 1)
        (mx MS-7003)
                10 Inch 78   >Futurama   USA   3005
                                  New York   Den   124
                Note: "Great Christmas (Part 1)" is a ballad version of "Silent Night" and "Jingle
                Bells." On Futurama, the time is 2 min., 18 sec. On New York the time is 4 min.,
                20 sec.; therefore the latter 2 min., 2 sec. on New York is the first part of "Great
                Christmas (Part 2)" on Futurama (see below).
0680   Great Christmas (Part 2)
        (mx MS-7004)
                10 Inch 78   >Futurama   USA   3005
                Note: "Great Christmas (Part 2)" is an uptempo and stride version of "Jingle
                Bells."
0690   Great Christmas–White Christmas (Part 2)
        (mx N.Y. 1915m)
                10 Inch 78   >New York   Den   124

ERROLL GARNER ALL STARS   NEW YORK, DECEMBER 26, 1944
Erroll Garner (p), Charlie Shavers (tp), Vic Dickenson (tb), Lem Davis (as), Leroy
"Slam" Stewart (b), Cliff Leeman (d)
0700   Gaslight
                12 Inch 33   >77 Records   Eng   77-LA-12-6
0710   Red Cross
                12 Inch 33   >77 Records   Eng   77-LA-12-6
                Note: Shavers' first chorus is omitted.
        Omit: Dickenson and Davis
0720   He Pulled a Fast One (Part 1)
        (mx 6933-D861-3)
                10 Inch 78   Baronet   Den   47.501
                                  >Disc   USA   5501
                                   Disc   Fra   5501
                                   Jazz Selection   Fra   47501
                                   Jazz Star   Den   A47501
                7 Inch 45EP   77 Records   Eng   77 EPEU-2
0730   He Pulled a Fast One (Part 2)
        (mx 6934-D862-1)
                10 Inch 78   Baronet   Den   47.501
                                  >Disc   Fra   5501
                                   Jazz Selection   Fra   A47501

		Jazz Star	Den	A7501
	7 Inch 45EP	77 Records	Eng	77 EPEU-2

Note: At the beginning of the original acetate, unidentified voices requested "Cherokee." A female voice (perhaps Inez Cavanaugh) requested, "He Pulled a Fast One." Another voice (identified as Erroll Garner) said, "This ain't Cherokee! What she say? Wanna' pull a fast one?"

Jazz Star is Timme Rosenkrantz's label, which originated in Denmark but was pressed in Sweden.

Add: Dickenson and Davis
0740   Meatless Pay Day (Part 1)
       (mx 9473)

	10 Inch 78	>Selmer	Fra	Y7137
	12 Inch 33	77 Records	Eng	77-LA-12-6

0750   Meatless Pay Day (Part 2)
       (mx 9474)

	10 Inch 78	>Selmer	Fra	Y7137
	12 Inch 33	77 Records	Eng	77-LA-12-6

Add Hank D'Amico (cl)
0760   Geronimo (Part 1)
       (mx 9475)

	10 Inch 78	>Selmer	Fra	Y7138
	7 Inch 45EP	77 Records	Eng	77 EPEU-2

0770   Geronimo (Part 2)
       (mx 9476)

	10 Inch 78	>Selmer	Fra	Y7138
	7 Inch 45EP	77 Records	Eng	77 EPEU-2

Note: The opening theme and the first two of D'Amico's twelve bar solos are omitted.

The title "Geronimo" originated from the name of the leader of the North American Apache Indians (ca. 1829-1909).

Omit: Dickenson and Davis; add unknown (v).
0780   I Don't Stand a Ghost of a Chance with You   Unissued

Omit unknown (v)
0790   Keep Happy Baby

	12 Inch 33	>77 Records	Eng	77-LA-12-6

Note: The first choruses by Garner and Shavers are omitted. D'Amico's portion is omitted completely.

Add: Dickenson and Davis
0800   Loot to Boot   Unissued
0810   7 West 46th Street   Unissued

Note: "7 West 46th Street" was originally titled "His Father Was an Old Gardener."

ERROLL GARNER TRIO   **NEW YORK, JANUARY 10, 1945**

Erroll Garner (p), Eddie Brown (b), Harold "Doc" West (d)
0820   White Rose Bounce
       (mx BW-67)

	10 Inch 78	>Black and White	USA	15
		Imperial	USA	5078
		Omega	USA	7862
	7 Inch 45EP	Imperial	USA	IMP-102
		London	Eng	RE-U 1066
	12 Inch 33	Imperial	USA	LP9246
		Prestige	USA	P-24052
	16 Inch TX	AFRS Downbeat	USA	216

Note: On the test pressing of this take in the Timme Rosenkrantz collection, the title is "In the Beginning." "White Rose Bounce" was named for the White Rose Bar on Sixth Avenue, near 52nd Street, New York City.

0830   Twistin' the Cat's Tail
       (mx BW-68)

	10 Inch 78	>Black and White	USA	16
		Imperial	USA	5078
		Omega	USA	7862
	7 Inch 45EP	Imperial	USA	IMP-102
		London	Eng	RE-U 1066
	12 Inch 33	Imperial	USA	LP9246
	16 Inch TX	AFRS Downbeat	USA	216

Note: On the test pressing of this take in the Timme Rosenkrantz collection, the title is "Erroll's Boogie."

0840   Movin' Around
(mx BW-69)

	10 Inch 78	>Black and White	USA	16
		Imperial	USA	5059
	7 Inch 45EP	Imperial	USA	IMP-102
		London	Eng	RE-U 1066

Note: On the test pressing of this take in the Timme Rosenkrantz collection, the title is "The Campbells Are Coming."

0850   Night and Day
(mx BW-70)

	10 Inch 78	>Black and White	USA	15
		Imperial	USA	5059
	7 Inch 45EP	Imperial	USA	IMP-102
		London	Eng	RE-U 1066
	12 Inch 33	Imperial	USA	LP9246
	16 Inch TX	AFRS Downbeat	USA	216

SLAM STEWART QUARTET   **NEW YORK, JANUARY 30, 1945**

Erroll Garner (p), Mike Bryan (g), Leroy "Slam" Stewart (b), Harold "Doc" West (d)

0860   Play, Fiddle, Play
(mx 5780-3)

	10 Inch 78	>Savoy	USA	537
		Savoy	Eng	537
	7 Inch 45EP	Deege	Fra	XP-80620
		Savoy	USA	XP-8062
	12 Inch 33	BYG	Fra	529161
		Savoy	USA	MG12067
		Savoy	USA	SJL1118

0870   Dark Eyesky
(mx 5781-2)

	10 Inch 78	>Savoy	USA	537
		Savoy	Eng	537
	7 Inch 45EP	Deege	Fra	XP-80620
		Savoy	USA	XP-8062
	10 Inch 33	Savoy	USA	MG15026
	12 Inch 33	BYG	Fra	529161
		Savoy	USA	MG12067
		Savoy	USA	SJL1118

0880   Laff Slam Laff
(mx 5782-2)

	10 Inch 78	>Savoy	USA	538
		Savoy	Eng	538
	7 Inch 45EP	Deege	Fra	XP-80620
		Savoy	USA	XP-8062
	12 Inch 33	Savoy	USA	SJL1118

Note: "Laff Slam Slam" was the title of the original issue on Savoy 538. "Laff Slam Laff" is the title on Savoy SJL1118. According to Bob Porter and Leroy "Slam" Stewart, "Laff Slam Laff" is the correct title.

0890   Jumpin' at the Deuces
(mx 5783-1)

10 Inch 78	>Savoy	USA	538
	Savoy	Eng	538
7 Inch 45EP	Deege	Fra	XP-80620
	Savoy	USA	XP-8062
12 Inch 33	Savoy	USA	SJL1118

GEORGIE AULD'S ORCHESTRA   NEW YORK, FEBRUARY 7, 1945

Asterisk (*) denotes Patti Powers, vocal.
Double asterisk (**) denotes Gordon Drake, vocal.

Georgie Auld (co, ts, as); Billy Butterfield, John "Dizzy" Gillespie, Al Killian, Jimmy Roma (tps); John D'Agostino, Eli Robinson, James "Trummy" Young (tbs); Mascagni "Musky" Ruffo, Gene Zanoni (as); Al Cohn, Al Young (ts); Manny Albam (bs); Erroll Garner (p); Mike Bryan (g); Greig "Chubby" Jackson (b); Rossiere "Shadow" Wilson (d); Turk Van Lake (ar); Patti Powers (v)*; Gordon Drake (v)**.

0900	Georgie Porgie			
	(mx G550-A1)			
	10 Inch 78	>Guild	USA	113
		Musicraft	USA	375
	12 Inch 33	Allegro	USA	LP4009
		Musicraft	USA	MVS 501
0910	Sweetheart of All My Dreams*			
	(mx G551-A1)			
	10 Inch 78	>Guild	USA	113
	12 Inch 33	Musicraft	USA	MVS 501
0920	I Fall in Love Too Easily**			
	(mx G552-A1)			
	10 Inch 78	>Guild	USA	116
0930	In the Middle			
	(mx G553-A1)			
	10 Inch 78	>Guild	USA	116
		Musicraft	USA	376
	12 Inch 33	Allegro	USA	LP1697
		Allegro	USA	LP3102
		Allegro	USA	LP4009
		Musicraft	USA	MVS 501
		Phoenix	USA	LP-4
		Smithsonian	USA	PZ13455

ERROLL GARNER   NEW YORK, MARCH 9, 1945

Erroll Garner (p)

0940	Sweet Lorraine			
	(mx SRC114)			
	10 Inch 78	Mello-Roll	USA	75114
		Shelton	USA	14006
		>Signature	USA	15136
	7 Inch 45EP	Brunswick	USA	EB 71001
		Vogue	Fra	EPL 7006
	12 Inch 33	Astor Maps	Aus	7570
		Brunswick	Eng	LAT8169
		Brunswick	WGer	87016LPBM
		Coral	USA	COPS1869
		Decca	USA	DFX140
		Decca	USA	DL8386
		Decca	USA	LP8401
		Doctor X Jazz	USA	FW38851
0950	Yesterdays			
	(mx SRC115)			

		10 Inch 78	Mello-Roll	USA	75114
			Shelton	USA	14006
			>Signature	USA	15135
		7 Inch 45EP	Brunswick	USA	EB 71001
			Vogue	Fra	EPL 7006
		12 Inch 33	Coral	USA	CRL57040
			Doctor X Jazz	USA	FW38851
0960	Loot to Boot				
	(mx SRC116-2A)				
		10 Inch 78	Mello-Roll	USA	75115
			Shelton	USA	14005
			>Signature	USA	15136
		7 Inch 45EP	Brunswick	USA	EB 71001
			Vogue	Fra	EPL 7006
		12 Inch 33	Coral	USA	CRL57040
			Doctor X Jazz	USA	FW38851
0970	Gaslight				
	(mx SRC117)				
		10 Inch 78	Mello-Roll	USA	75115
			Shelton	USA	14005
			>Signature	USA	15135
		7 Inch 45EP	Brunswick	USA	EB 71001
			Vogue	Fra	EPL 7006
		12 Inch 33	Coral	USA	CRL57040
			Doctor X Jazz	USA	FW38851

DON BYAS QUARTET   NEW YORK, AUGUST 30, 1945

Don Byas (ts), Erroll Garner (p), Leroy "Slam" Stewart (b), Harold "Doc" West (d)

0980	Three O'Clock in the Morning				
	(mx MF14)				
		10 Inch 78	>Super Disc	USA	1006
		7 Inch 45EP	MGM	USA	EP-579
		12 Inch 33	Alamac	USA	QSR2447
			Jazz Society	Swe	AA500
			Musidisc	Fra	30JA5106
0990	One O'Clock Jump				
	(mx MF15)				
		10 Inch 78	>Super Disc	USA	1006
		12 Inch 33	Alamac	USA	QSR2447
			Jazz Society	Swe	AA500
			Musidisc	Fra	30JA5106
1000	Harvard Blues				
	(mx MF16)				
		10 Inch 78	>Super Disc	USA	1007
		12 Inch 33	Alamac	USA	QSR2447
			Jazz Society	Swe	AA500
			Musidisc	Fra	30JA5106

Note: MF17 is "St. Louis Blues Boogie" by the Erskine Butterfield Quartet.

1010	Slammin' Around				
	(mx MF18)				
		10 Inch 78	>Super Disc	USA	1008
		7 Inch 45EP	MGM	USA	EP-579
		12 Inch 33	Alamac	USA	QSR2447
			Jazz Society	Swe	AA500
			Musidisc	Fra	30JA5106

ERROLL GARNER TRIO   NEW YORK, AUGUST 30, 1945

Erroll Garner (p), John Levy, Jr. (b), Bill DeArango (g)

| 1020 | Loot to Boot |
| | (mx ZZ-4830) |

		12 Inch 33	Festival	Fra	Album 279
			Jazz Connoisseur	Ity	JC001
		16 Inch TX	>Associated	USA	60813A
1030	White Rose Bounce (mistitled as Movin' Around) (mx ZZ-4830)				
		12 Inch 33	Festival	Fra	Album 279
			Jazz Connoisseur	Ity	JC001
		16 Inch TX	>Associated	USA	60813A
1040	Bounce with Me (mx ZZ-4830)				
		12 Inch 33	Festival	Fra	Album 279
			Jazz Connoisseur	Ity	JC001
		16 Inch TX	>Associated	USA	60813A
1050	Erroll's Bounce (piano solo) (mx ZZ-4830)				
		12 Inch 33	Festival	Fra	Album 279
			Jazz Connoisseur	Ity	JC001
		16 Inch TX	>Associated	USA	60813A
1060	You Made Me Love You (piano solo) (mx ZZ-4831)				
		12 Inch 33	Festival	Fra	Album 279
			Jazz Connoisseur	Ity	JC001
		16 Inch TX	>Associated	USA	60813B
1070	What Is This Thing Called Love? (piano solo) (mx ZZ-4831)				
		12 Inch 33	Festival	Fra	Album 279
			Jazz Connoisseur	Ity	JC001
		16 Inch TX	>Associated	USA	60813B
1080	Baby, Won't You Please Come Home (piano solo) (mx ZZ-4831)				
		12 Inch 33	Festival	Fra	Album 279
			Jazz Connoisseur	Ity	JC001
		16 Inch TX	>Associated	USA	60813B
1090	Sweet Lorraine (mx ZZ-4831)				
		12 Inch 33	Festival	Fra	Album 279
			Jazz Connoisseur	Ity	JC001
		16 Inch TX	>Associated	USA	60813B
1100	All the Things You Are (piano solo) (mx ZZ-4832)				
		12 Inch 33	Festival	Fra	Album 279
			Jazz Connoisseur	Ity	JC001
		16 Inch TX	>Associated	USA	60808A
1110	I Get a Kick Out of You (piano solo) (mx ZZ-4832)				
		12 Inch 33	Festival	Fra	Album 279
			Jazz Connoisseur	Ity	JC001
		16 Inch TX	>Associated	USA	60808A
1120	For You (piano solo) (mx ZZ-4832)				
		12 Inch 33	Festival	Fra	Album 279
			Jazz Connoisseur	Ity	JC001
		16 Inch TX	>Associated	USA	60808A
1130	Mood Indigo (piano solo) (mx ZZ-4832)				
		12 Inch 33	Festival	Fra	Album 279
			Jazz Connoisseur	Ity	JC001
		16 Inch TX	>Associated	USA	60808A
1140	Somebody Loves Me (piano solo) (mx ZZ-4836)				
		12 Inch 33	Festival	Fra	Album 279
			Jazz Connoisseur	Ity	JC001
		16 Inch TX	>Associated	USA	60808B

1150   I Cried for You (piano solo)
       (mx ZZ-4836)

	12 Inch 33	Festival	Fra	Album 279
		Jazz Connoisseur	Ity	JC001
	16 Inch TX	>Associated	USA	60808B

ERROLL GARNER TRIO   NEW YORK, SEPTEMBER 7, 1945
Erroll Garner (p), John Levy, Jr. (b), Bill DeArango (g)

1160   Sweet Georgia Brown
       (mx ZZ-4835)

	12 Inch 33	Festival	Fra	Album 279
		Jazz Connoisseur	Ity	JC001
	16 Inch TX	>Associated	USA	60810A

1170   How Deep Is the Ocean (How High Is the Sky)
       (mx ZZ-4835)

	12 Inch 33	Festival	Fra	Album 279
		Jazz Connoisseur	Ity	JC002
	16 Inch TX	>Associated	USA	60810A

1180   Blue Skies
       (mx ZZ-4835)

	12 Inch 33	Festival	Fra	Album 279
		Jazz Connoisseur	Ity	JC001
	16 Inch TX	>Associated	USA	60810A

1190   I Can't Get Started
       (mx ZZ-4835)

	12 Inch 33	Festival	Fra	Album 279
		Jazz Connoisseur	Ity	JC002
	16 Inch TX	>Associated	USA	60810A

1200   Body and Soul
       (mx ZZ-4836)

| | 12 Inch 33 | Festival | Fra | Album 279 |
| | | >Jazz Connoisseur | Ity | JC002 |

Note: "Rosetta" is mistitled "Body and Soul" on Associated 60808B. Both versions of "Rosetta" are identical (see below—"Rosetta"). "Body and Soul," therefore, is unissued on Associated.

1210   I Can't Give You Anything But Love
       (mx ZZ-4836)

	12 Inch 33	Festival	Fra	Album 279
		Jazz Connoisseur	Ity	JC002
	16 Inch TX	>Associated	USA	60808B

1220   Blue Room
       (mx ZZ-4837)

	12 Inch 33	Festival	Fra	Album 279
		Jazz Connoisseur	Ity	JC002
	16 Inch TX	>Associated	USA	60809A

1230   Oh, Lady Be Good!
       (mx ZZ-4837)

	12 Inch 33	Festival	Fra	Album 279
		Jazz Connoisseur	Ity	JC002
	16 Inch TX	>Associated	USA	60809A

1240   Liza
       (mx ZZ-4837)

	12 Inch 33	Festival	Fra	Album 279
		Jazz Connoisseur	Ity	JC002
	16 Inch TX	>Associated	USA	60809A

1250   April in Paris
       (mx ZZ-4837)

	12 Inch 33	Festival	Fra	Album 279
		Jazz Connoisseur	Ity	JC002
	16 Inch TX	>Associated	USA	60809A

1260   Night and Day
       (mx ZZ-4837)

		12 Inch 33	Festival	Fra	Album 279
			Jazz Connoisseur	Ity	JC002
		16 Inch TX	>Associated	USA	60809A
1270	Rosetta				
	(mx ZZ-4838)				
		12 Inch 33	Festival	Fra	Album 279
			Jazz Connoisseur	Ity	JC002
		16 Inch TX	>Associated	USA	60809B
1280	It Had to Be You				
	(mx ZZ-4838)				
		12 Inch 33	Festival	Fra	Album 279
			Jazz Connoisseur	Ity	JC002
		16 Inch TX	>Associated	USA	60809B
1290	St. Louis Blues				
	(mx ZZ-4838)				
		12 Inch 33	Festival	Fra	Album 279
			Jazz Connoisseur	Ity	JC002
		16 Inch TX	>Associated	USA	60809B
1300	On the Sunny Side of the Street				
	(mx ZZ-4838)				
		12 Inch 33	Festival	Fra	Album 279
			Jazz Connoisseur	Ity	JC002
		16 Inch TX	>Associated	USA	60809B
1310	I Know That You Know				
	(mx ZZ-4838)				
		12 Inch 33	Festival	Fra	Album 279
			Jazz Connoisseur	Ity	JC002
		16 Inch TX	>Associated	USA	60809B

SLAM STEWART TRIO   NEW YORK, SEPTEMBER 7, 1945

Erroll Garner (p), Leroy "Slam" Stewart (b), Harold "Doc" West (d)

1320	Hop, Skip and Jump				
	(mx S1275S)				
		10 Inch 78	Arco	USA	1224
			Blue Star	Fra	114
			>Manor	USA	1012
		12 Inch 33	Onyx	USA	ORI 203
			Polydor	Eng	2344049
			Polydor	WGer	2310326
1330	Sherry Lynn Flip				
	(mx S1276S)				
		10 Inch 78	Arco	USA	1223
			Blue Star	Fra	115
			Felsted	Eng	ED82006
			>Manor	USA	1028
		12 Inch 33	Onyx	USA	ORI 203
			Polydor	Eng	2344049
			Polydor	WGer	2310326
1340	Three Blind Micesky				
	(mx S1277S)				
		10 Inch 78	Arco	USA	1224
			Blue Star	Fra	114
			>Manor	USA	1012
		12 Inch 33	Onyx	USA	ORI 203
			Polydor	Eng	2344049
			Polydor	WGer	2310326
1350	Blue, Brown and Beige				
	(mx S1278S)				
		10 Inch 78	Arco	USA	1223
			Blue Star	Fra	115
			Felsted	Eng	ED82006
			>Manor	USA	1028

12 Inch 33	Onyx	USA	ORI 203
	Polydor	Eng	2344049
	Polydor	WGer	2310326

ERROLL GARNER TRIO   NEW YORK, SEPTEMBER 25, 1945
Erroll Garner (p), John Levy, Jr. (b), George DeHart (d)

1360   Laura
        (mx 5837-3)

10 Inch 78	Regal	USA	R104
	>Savoy	USA	571
	Savoy	Eng	571
7 Inch 45	Savoy	USA	45-571
7 Inch 45EP	Savoy	USA	XP-8007
10 Inch 33	Savoy	USA	MG15001
	Savoy	Fra	255SV152
12 Inch 33	BYG	Fra	529143
	Festival	Fra	166
	London	Eng	LTZ-C 15126
	Musidisc	Fra	CV1047
	Savoy	USA	MG12003
	Savoy	USA	SJL2207
	Savoy	Jap	WAJ-701
	Savoy-Musidisc	Fra	6005
16 Inch TX	AFRS Downbeat	USA	216

1370   Stardust
        (mx 5838-1)

10 Inch 78	Regal	USA	R127
	>Savoy	USA	577
7 Inch 45	Savoy	USA	45-577
7 Inch 45EP	Ember	Eng	EP-4529
	Savoy	USA	XP-8012
10 Inch 33	Savoy	USA	MG15001
	Savoy	Fra	255SV152
12 Inch 33	BYG	Fra	529110
	BYG	Fra	529144
	Ember	Eng	LP3329
	Festival	Fra	166
	Galaxy	USA	4815
	I Grandi del Jazz	Ity	GDJ-88
	Joker	Ity	SM3718
	Koala	USA	AW14135
	London	Eng	LTZ-C 15125
	Musidisc	Fra	CV1047
	Rondolette	USA	A15
	Savoy	USA	MG12002
	Savoy	USA	SJL2207
	Savoy-Musidisc	Fra	6004

1380   Somebody Loves Me
        (mx 5839-2)

10 Inch 78	Regal	USA	R104
	>Savoy	USA	571
	Savoy	Eng	571
7 Inch 45	Savoy	USA	45-571
7 Inch 45EP	Savoy	USA	XP-8008
10 Inch 33	Savoy	USA	MG15001
	Savoy	Fra	255SV152
12 Inch 33	BYG	Fra	529110
	Bellaphon	WGer	BJS4045
	Eros	Eng	ERL50047
	Everest	USA	FS245
	Festival	Fra	166
	I Grandi del Jazz	Ity	GDJ-88

		London	Eng	LTZ-C 15125
		Quadrifoglio	Ity	VDS208
		Realm	Eng	RM116
		Savoy	USA	MG12002
		Savoy	USA	SJL2207
		Savoy-Musidisc	Fra	6004
		Vogue	Fra	LDM 30230
	16 Inch TX	AFRS Downbeat	USA	216

Note: Titled "Somebody Loves You" on Bellaphon BJS4045.

1390 Indiana (Back Home Again in Indiana)
      (mx 5840-2)

		Regal	USA	R127
	10 Inch 78	>Savoy	USA	577
	7 Inch 45	Savoy	USA	45-577
	7 Inch 45EP	Savoy	USA	XP-8012
	10 Inch 33	Savoy	USA	MG15001
	12 Inch 33	BYG	Fra	529110
		Eros	Eng	ERL50047
		Festival	Fra	166
		I Grandi del Jazz	Ity	GDJ-88
		London	Eng	LTZ-C 15125
		Realm	Eng	RM116
		Savoy	USA	MG12002
		Savoy	USA	SJL2207
		Savoy-Musidisc	Fra	6004

ERROLL GARNER   NEW YORK, OCTOBER 14, 1945

This session was recorded at the apartment of Timme Rosenkrantz, 7 W.
46th Street, New York City and sold by Rosenkrantz to Moe Asch, Disc
Record Company.

Erroll Garner (p)

1400 Man O' Mine
      (mx D 231)

		>Disc	USA	5001
	10 Inch 78	Disc	Fra	5001
		Ducretet Thomson	Fra	Y8164
		New York	Den	119
		Selmer	Fra	Y7136

Note: "Man O' Mine" is another version of "The Man I Love." Issued as "The
Man I Love" on Ducretet Thomson Y8164, New York 119 and Selmer Y7136.

1410 Oh, Lady Be Good!
      (mx D 232)

		>Disc	USA	5002
	10 Inch 78	Disc	Fra	5002
		Holiday	USA	4003
		Melodisc	Eng	1135
	12 Inch 33	Folkways	USA	FJ 2852

Note: Some issues of Folkways FJ 2852 contain "Farewell to Riverside" by Joe
Sullivan instead of "Oh, Lady Be Good!"

1420 Don't Blame Me
      (mx D 233)

		Arco	USA	1214
	10 Inch 78	>Disc	USA	5003
		Disc	Fra	5001
		Ducretet Thomson	Fra	Y8164
		Melodisc	Eng	1135
		Selmer	Fra	Y7136

1430 How High the Moon
      (mx D 234)

		>Arco	USA	1214
	10 Inch 78	Holiday	USA	4003
		New York	Den	119

DON BYAS QUARTET   **NEW YORK, NOVEMBER 1, 1945**
Issued as Erroll Garner Quartet on Jazz Selection, Summit and Vogue.
Don Byas (ts), Erroll Garner (p), Leroy "Slam" Stewart (b), Harold "Doc" West
(d)

1440   Humoresque
        (mx WS-501)
               10 Inch 78   >Arista   USA   5000
                                 Jazz Selection   Fra   670
                                 Summit   USA   104
               12 Inch 33   Alamac   USA   QSR2447
                                 Jazz Society   Swe   AA500
                                 Musidisc   Fra   30JA5106
1450   Wrap Your Troubles in Dreams
        (mx WS-502)
               10 Inch 78   >Arista   USA   5000
                                 Jazz Selection   Fra   675
                                 Summit   USA   103
                                 Vogue   Eng   V2069
               12 Inch 33   Alamac   USA   QSR2447
                                 Jazz Society   Swe   AA500
                                 Musidisc   Fra   30JA5106
1460   Smoke Gets in Your Eyes
        (mx WS-503)
               10 Inch 78   >Arista   USA   5001
                                 Jazz Selection   Fra   670
                                 Summit   USA   104
               12 Inch 33   Alamac   USA   QSR2447
                                 Jazz Society   Swe   AA500
                                 Musidisc   Fra   30JA5106
1470   Slamboree
        (mx WS-504)
               10 Inch 78   >Arista   USA   5001
                                 Jazz Selection   Fra   675
                                 Summit   USA   103
                                 Vogue   Eng   V2069
               12 Inch 33   Alamac   USA   QSR2447
                                 Jazz Society   Swe   AA500
                                 Musidisc   Fra   30JA5106

ERROLL GARNER   **NEW YORK, DECEMBER 5, 1945**
Erroll Garner (p)
1480   All the Things You Are
        (mx 157)   Unissued
1490   Embraceable You
        (mx 158-3)
               10 Inch 78   Le Chant du Monde   Swi   29712
                                 >Mercury   USA   A-1001
                7 Inch 45   Mercury   USA   1001-X45
               10 Inch 33   Mercury   USA   MG25117
                                 Metronome   Swe   BLP-10
               12 Inch 33   Fontana Special   Eng   6430135
                                 Mercury   USA   MG20009
                                 Mercury   Eng   MPL6507
                                 Mercury   Fra   200009MG
                                 Mercury   Fra   6641688
                                 Mercury   Neth   6641589
1500   I've Got You Under My Skin
        (mx 159-2)
               10 Inch 78   Austroton-Mercury   WGer   5195V
                                 Le Chant du Monde   Swi   29701
                                 >Mercury   USA   A-1003
                                 Regina-Mercury   WGer   RM-70218

		7 Inch 45	Mercury	USA	1003-X45
		7 Inch 45EP	EmArcy	USA	EP-1-6073
			Mercury	USA	EP-1-3168
			Mercury	Fra	MEP14036
		10 Inch 33	EmArcy	USA	MG26042
			Mercury	USA	MG25157
			Mercury	Eng	MG26042
			Mercury	Fra	MLP7051
		12 Inch 33	Mercury	USA	MG20009
			Mercury	Eng	MPL6507
			Mercury	Fra	200009MG
			Mercury	Fra	6641688
1510	Always				
	(mx 160-2)				
		10 Inch 78	>Mercury	USA	A-1002
		7 Inch 45	Mercury	USA	1002-X45
		10 Inch 33	Mercury	USA	MG25117
			Metronome	Swe	BLP-10
		12 Inch 33	Fontana Special	Eng	6430135
			Mercury	USA	MG20009
			Mercury	Eng	MPL6507
			Mercury	Fra	200009MG
			Mercury	Fra	6641688
			Mercury	Neth	6641589
1520	My Heart Stood Still				
	(mx 161)				Unissued
1530	Sometimes I'm Happy				
	(mx 162-1)				
		10 Inch 78	>Mercury	USA	A-1002
		7 Inch 45	Mercury	USA	1002-X45
		10 Inch 33	Mercury	USA	MG25117
			Metronome	Swe	BLP-10
		12 Inch 33	Mercury	USA	MG20009
			Mercury	Eng	MPL6507
			Mercury	Fra	200009MG
			Mercury	Fra	6641688
1540	Lover Come Back to Me				
	(mx 163-2)				
		10 Inch 78	Le Chant du Monde	Swi	29712
			>Mercury	USA	A-1001
		7 Inch 45	Mercury	USA	1001-X45
		10 Inch 33	Mercury	USA	MG25117
		12 Inch 33	Mercury	USA	MG20009
			Mercury	Eng	MPL6507
			Mercury	Fra	200009MG
			Mercury	Fra	6641688
1550	I Can't Get Started				
	(mx 164-1)				
		10 Inch 78	Austroton-Mercury	WGer	5195V
			Le Chant du Monde	Swi	29701
			>Mercury	USA	A-1003
		7 Inch 45	Mercury	USA	1003-X45
		10 Inch 33	Mercury	USA	MG25117
			Metronome	Swe	BLP-10
		12 Inch 33	Mercury	USA	MG20009
			Mercury	Eng	MPL6507
			Mercury	Fra	200009MG
			Mercury	Fra	6641688
1560	Symphony				
	(mx 165-2)				
		10 Inch 78	>Mercury	USA	2040
1570	Bouncin' with Me				
	(mx 166-1/-2/-3)				
		10 Inch 78	>Mercury	USA	2040

	7 Inch 45EP	Mercury	USA	EP-1-3168
		Mercury	Fra	MEP14036
	10 Inch 33	EmArcy	USA	MG26042
		Mercury	USA	MG25157
		Mercury	Eng	MG26042
		Mercury	Fra	MLP7051
	12 Inch 33	Mercury	Fra	6641688
		Trip Jazz	USA	TLP5504

Note: Three pressings are extant on "Bouncin' with Me" (Mercury 2040). Matrix numbers 166-1/-2/-3 are identical (2 min., 37 sec.).

1580   High Octane
      (mx 167)

	7 Inch 45EP	EmArcy	USA	EP-1-6073
		Mercury	USA	EP-1-3168
		Mercury	Fra	MEP14036
	10 Inch 33	EmArcy	USA	MG26042
		>Mercury	USA	MG25157
		Mercury	Eng	MG26042
		Mercury	Fra	MLP7051
	12 Inch 33	Mercury	Fra	6641688

ERROLL GARNER   **NEW YORK, DECEMBER 9, 1945**
Erroll Garner (p)
1585   Laura
      (mx ASSR-12-12-3)

| | 16 Inch TX | >AFRS Music America | | |
| | | Loves Best | USA | 79 |

BOYD RAEBURN'S ORCHESTRA   **LOS ANGELES, ca. EARLY 1946**
According to Jack McKinney, the following personnel are definitely not Raeburn's, even though these performances were released under his name on Hep 22. This studio session was produced by Fran Kelley, probably in conjunction with her Swingposium concert of June 24, 1946, which was to be released on her Fran-tone label. This, of course, never happened.
Asterisk (*) denotes David Allyn, vocal.
Harry Klee (as, f), Ray Still (ob), Lenny Hartman (eh), Sammy Sachelle (bc), Hy Mandel (bs), Vince DeRosa (frh), Leonard "Lucky" Ennois (g), Alan Reuss (g), Harry Babasin (b), George "Red" Callender (b), Erroll Garner (p), Jackie Mills (d), Tommy Talbert (ar), David Allyn (v)*

1590   Black Night and Fog*

| | 12 Inch 33 | Hep | Scot | 22 |
| | 16 Inch TX | >AFRS Downbeat | USA | 263 |

1600   C Jam Blues

| | 12 Inch 33 | Hep | Scot | 22 |
| | 16 Inch TX | >AFRS Downbeat | USA | 263 |

1610   Please Let Me Forget*

| | 12 Inch 33 | Hep | Scot | 22 |
| | 16 Inch TX | >AFRS Downbeat | USA | 263 |

Note: "Please Let Me Forget" (George "Red" Callender) is also titled "Pastel" (see also February 19, 1947 session).

1620   Caravan

| | 12 Inch 33 | Hep | Scot | 22 |
| | 16 Inch TX | >AFRS Downbeat | USA | 263 |

ERROLL GARNER   **HOLLYWOOD, LATE FEBRUARY, 1946**
Erroll Garner (p)
1630   Laura
      (mx JDB204)

		12 Inch 78	>V Disc	USA	735B
		12 Inch 33	Joyce	USA	LP-5004
		16 Inch TX	AFRS Jubilee	USA	170
1640	Yesterdays				
	(mx JDB204)				
		12 Inch 78	>V Disc	USA	735B
		12 Inch 33	Joyce	USA	LP-5004
		16 Inch TX	AFRS Jubilee	USA	170

ERROLL GARNER   **HOLLYWOOD, LATE FEBRUARY, 1946**

Erroll Garner (p)

1650	Erroll's Bounce				
		16 Inch TX	>AFRS Jubilee	USA	171

ERROLL GARNER TRIO   **HOLLYWOOD, APRIL 9, 1946**

Erroll Garner (p), George "Red" Callender (b), Nick Fatool (d)

1660	Full Moon and Empty Arms				
	(mx 332-1)				
		10 Inch 78	>Mercury	USA	A-1033
		7 Inch 45	Mercury	USA	1033-X45
		7 Inch 45EP	EmArcy	USA	EP-1-6073
		10 Inch 33	EmArcy	USA	MG26042
			Mercury	USA	MG25157
			Mercury	Eng	MG26042
			Mercury	Fra	MLP7051
		12 Inch 33	Mercury	USA	MG20009
			Mercury	Eng	MPL6507
			Mercury	Fra	200009MG
			Mercury	Fra	6641688
			Trip Jazz	USA	TLP5504
		16 Inch TX	AFRS Downbeat	USA	Q39
1670	Frantonality				
	(mx 333-1/-2)				
		10 Inch 78	>Mercury	USA	5008
			Mercury-Sphinx	Bel	M6
		7 Inch 45EP	EmArcy	USA	EP-1-6073
			Mercury	Fra	126046MCE
		10 Inch 33	EmArcy	USA	MG26042
			Mercury	USA	MG25157
			Mercury	Eng	MG26042
			Mercury	Fra	MLP7051
		12 Inch 33	Mercury	USA	MG20662
			Mercury	USA	SR60662
			Mercury	Fra	135.008MCY
			Mercury	Fra	125008MCL
			Mercury	Fra	6641688
			Mercury	Neth	6336320
			Mercury	Neth	6641589

Note: Some issues are titled "Frantenality." The correct title is "Frantonality," which was derived from the name of Fran Kelley's Fran-tone Records. Matrix numbers 333-1/2 are identical (2 min., 54 sec.).

1680	If I Loved You				
	(mx 334-1)				
		10 Inch 78	>Mercury	USA	A-1034
		7 Inch 45	Mercury	USA	1034-X45
		10 Inch 33	EmArcy	USA	MG26042
			Mercury	USA	MG25157
			Mercury	Eng	MG26042
			Mercury	Fra	MLP7051
		12 Inch 33	Mercury	USA	MG20009
			Mercury	Eng	MPL6507

	Mercury	Fra	6641688
	Mercury	Fra	200009MG
	Trip Jazz	USA	TLP5504

1690 For You
(mx 335-1)

10 Inch 78	>Mercury	USA	A-1034
	Mercury-Sphinx	Bel	M6
7 Inch 45	Mercury	USA	1034-X45
10 Inch 33	Mercury	USA	MG25117
	Metronome	Swe	BLP-10
12 Inch 33	Mercury	USA	MG20009
	Mercury	Eng	MPL6507
	Mercury	Fra	200009MG
	Mercury	Fra	6641688

ERROLL GARNER   **LOS ANGELES, MAY, 1946**
Erroll Garner (p)
1700 Diane

16 Inch TX	>AFRS Jubilee	USA	181

1710 Erroll's Bounce

16 Inch TX	>AFRS Jubilee	USA	181

ERROLL GARNER TRIO   **HOLLYWOOD, JULY 14, 1946**
Erroll Garner (p), George "Red" Callender (b), Lou Singer (d)
1720 Memories of You
(mx 450-1)

10 Inch 78	>Mercury	USA	A-1033
7 Inch 45	Mercury	USA	1033-X45
10 Inch 33	Mercury	USA	MG25117
	Metronome	Swe	BLP-10
12 Inch 33	Mercury	USA	MG20009
	Mercury	Eng	MPL6507
	Mercury	Fra	200009MG
	Mercury	Fra	6641688

1730 Blue Skies
(mx 451-1)

10 Inch 78	>Mercury	USA	A-1032
	Mercury	Jap	J-52
	Regina-Mercury	WGer	RM-70218
7 Inch 45	Mercury	USA	1032-X45
10 Inch 33	Mercury	USA	MG25117
	Metronome	Swe	BLP-10
12 Inch 33	Mercury	USA	MG20009
	Mercury	Eng	MPL6507
	Mercury	Fra	200009MG
	Mercury	Fra	6641688

1740 Don't Blame Me
(mx 452-1)

10 Inch 78	>Mercury	USA	A-1032
	Mercury	Jap	J-52
7 Inch 45	Mercury	USA	1032-X45
7 Inch 45EP	Mercury	USA	EP-1-3168
	Mercury	Fra	MEP14036
10 Inch 33	EmArcy	USA	MG26042
	Mercury	USA	MG25157
	Mercury	Eng	MG26042
	Mercury	Fra	MLP7051
	Metronome	Swe	BLP-10
12 Inch 33	Mercury	USA	MG20009
	Mercury	Eng	MPL6507
	Mercury	Fra	200009MG
	Mercury	Fra	6641688

1750   Where or When
       (mx 453-1/-2)
                 10 Inch 78   >Mercury   USA   5008
                 12 Inch 33   Fontana   Jap   SFON-7049
                                  Mercury   USA   MG20662
                                  Mercury   USA   SR60662
                                  Mercury   Fra   135.008MCY
                                  Mercury   Fra   125008MCL
                                  Mercury   Fra   6641688
                                  Mercury   Neth   6336320
                                  Mercury   Neth   6641589
       *Note: Two pressings are extant on "Where or When" (Mercury 5008). Matrix
       numbers 453-1/-2 are identical (2 min., 59 sec).*

CHARLIE PARKER QUARTET   HOLLYWOOD, FEBRUARY 19, 1947
Asterisk (*) denotes Earl Coleman, vocal.

Charlie Parker (as), Erroll Garner (p), George "Red" Callender (b), Harold "Doc"
West (d), Earl Coleman (v)*

1760   This Is Always*
       (mx D 1051-C)
                 10 Inch 78   >Dial   USA   1019
                                  Metronome   Swe   B 582
                 12 Inch 33   Dial   USA   905
                                  Saga   Eng   6907AG
                                  Spotlite   Eng   102
1770   This Is Always*
       (mx D 1051-D)
                 10 Inch 33   >Dial   USA   202
                 12 Inch 33   Saga   Eng   ERO 8005
                                  Spotlite   Eng   102
1780   Dark Shadows*
       (mx D 1052-A)
                  7 Inch 45EP   Jazz Selection   Swe   JEP4537
                 10 Inch 33   >Dial   USA   202
                                  Vogue   Eng   LDE 016
                 12 Inch 33   Saga   Eng   ERO 8005
                                  Saga   Eng   6907AG
                                  Spotlite   Eng   102
                                  Vogue   Eng   LAE 12002
                                  Vogue   Fra   CLD 753
                                  Vogue   Fra   LDM 30067
1790   Dark Shadows*
       (mx D 1052-B)
                 10 Inch 33   Vogue   Fra   LD 059
                 12 Inch 33   >Dial   USA   901
                                  Spotlite   Eng   102
1800   Dark Shadows*
       (mx D 1052-C)
                 10 Inch 78   >Dial   USA   1014
                 12 Inch 33   Spotlite   Eng   102
1810   Dark Shadows*
       (mx D 1052-D)
                 12 Inch 33   >Spotlite   Eng   102
                                  Spotlite   Eng   105
1820   Bird's Nest
       (mx D 1053-A)
                 12 Inch 33   >Dial   USA   905
                                  Spotlite   Eng   102
1830   Bird's Nest
       (mx D 1053-B)
                 12 Inch 33   >Dial   USA   905
                                  Spotlite   Eng   102

1840   Bird's Nest
      (mx D 1053-C)

	10 Inch 78	Blue Star	Fra	62
		Cupol	Swe	4341
		Dial	USA	1014
		Dial	USA	1015
		Esquire	Eng	10-017
		Le Chant du Monde	Swi	29608
		Tono	Den	BZ19003
	7 Inch 45EP	Cupol	Swe	CEP38
		Esquire	Eng	EP57
	10 Inch 33	>Dial	USA	202
	12 Inch 33	Baronet	USA	B107
		Egmont	Eng	AJS-3
		Fonit	Ity	LPU8009
		Jazz Reactivation	Eng	JR116
		Jazztone	USA	J1214
		MGM	WGer	65-104
		Parker	USA	PLP407
		Rhapsody	Eng	RHAP5
		Spotlite	Eng	102
		Verve	Eng	VLP 9105

              Note: "Bird's Nest (1053-A, 1053-B, 1053-C) has the same chord sequence as "I Got Rhythm" with an altered middle eight.

1850   Blow Top Blues
      (mx D 1054-A)

	10 Inch 33	>Dial	USA	202
	12 Inch 33	Baronet	USA	B107
		Dial	USA	901
		Fonit	Ity	LPU8009
		Jazz Reactivation	Eng	JR116
		Jazztone	USA	J1214
		Quadrifoglio	Ity	VDS9437
		Saga	Eng	6911AG
		Spotlite	Eng	102
		Vogue	Fra	CLD 753
		Vogue	Fra	LDM 30067

              Note: 1054-A "Blow Top Blues" is titled "Hot Blues" on Dial 202, Jazztone J1214, Baronet B107 and Vogue CLD 753. 1054-A "Blow Top Blues" is titled "Hot Blues" on Vogue LDM 30067 and as "Cool Blues" on Spotlite, Saga and Quadrifoglio.

1860   Blow Top Blues
      (mx D 1054-B)

	10 Inch 78	Swing	Fra	406
	10 Inch 33	Vogue	Eng	LDE 004
		Vogue	Fra	LD 057
	12 Inch 33	Baronet	USA	B107
		>Dial	USA	901
		Egmont	Eng	AJS-3
		Fonit	Ity	LPU8009
		Jazz Selection	Swe	JSL702
		Jazztone	USA	J1214
		Parker	USA	PLP407
		Rhapsody	Eng	RHAP5
		Spotlite	Eng	102
		Verve	Eng	VLP 9105
		Vogue	Eng	LAE 12002
		Vogue	Fra	LDM 30067

              Note: 1054-B "Blow Top Blues" is titled "Cool Blues" on Jazztone J1214, Baronet B107 and as "Hot Blues" on Swing, Vogue and Jazz Selection.

1870   Cool Blues
      (mx D 1054-C-D)

	10 Inch 78	>Dial	USA	1015
	10 Inch 33	Dial	USA	202

	12 Inch 33	Dial	USA	901
		Saga	Eng	ERO 8005
		Saga	Eng	6907AG
		Spotlite	Eng	102
1880	Cool Blues			
	(mx D 1054-D)			
	10 Inch 78	Blue Star	Fra	62
		Cupol	Swe	4341
		Esquire	Eng	10-017
		Le Chant du Monde	Swi	29608
		Tono	Den	BZ19003
		Vogue	Eng	V2244
	7 Inch 45EP	Cupol	Swe	CEP38
		Esquire	Eng	EP57
	10 Inch 33	Vogue	Eng	LDE 004
	12 Inch 33	>Dial	USA	901
		MGM	WGer	65-104
		Quadrifoglio	Ity	VDS9437
		Saga	Eng	6911AG
		Spotlite	Eng	102
		Vogue	Eng	LAE 12002

Same session, Parker and Coleman out.

1890	Pastel			
	(mx D 1055-BB)			
	10 Inch 78	Blue Star	Fra	96
		Celson	Ity	QB7035
		>Dial	USA	1016
		Esquire	Eng	10-176
		Metronome	Swe	B 516
		Monogram	USA	119
		Music	Ity	1130
	10 Inch 33	Blue Star	Fra	BLP6814
		Concert Hall	USA	CHJ1001
		Dial	USA	205
		Guilde du Jazz	Fra	J1001
	12 Inch 33	Cie Ind. Disque	Fra	CVM42.004
		Columbia	Eng	33SX1557
		Fonit	Ity	LPU8001
		Guest Star	USA	G 1403
		Hall of Fame	USA	JG-604
		I Grandi del Jazz	Ity	GDJ-88
		Jazztone	USA	J1203
		Roulette	USA	RE-110
		Roulette	Aus	VJL2-0264
		Roulette	Jap	MJ-7069
		Royal Roost	USA	LP-2256
		Royal Roost	USA	RLP 2213
		Spotlite	Eng	SPJ 129
		Vogue	Fra	DP-28
		Vogue	Fra	LAE 12209
		Vogue	Fra	MDR 9168
		WGM (Roulette)	USA	2A

Note: The vocal version of "Pastel" (George "Red" Callender) is titled "Please Let Me Forget."

1900	Trio			
	(mx D 1056-A)			
	12 Inch 33	>Spotlite	Eng	SPJ 129
1910	Trio			
	(mx D 1056-B)			
	10 Inch 78	Blue Star	Fra	96
		Celson	Ity	QB7035
		>Dial	USA	1016
		Esquire	Eng	10-176

	Metronome	Swe	B 516
	Monogram	USA	119
	Music	Ity	1130
7 Inch 33	Jazztone	USA	J738
10 Inch 33	Club Nat. du Disque	Fra	JSP100
	Concert Hall	USA	CHJ1001
	Concert Hall	Eng	DJ-100E
	Dial	USA	205
	Guilde du Jazz	Fra	J1001
	Jazztone	USA	J-SPEC 100
12 Inch 33	Cie Ind. Disque	Fra	22000
	Cie Ind. Disque	Fra	CVM42.004
	Columbia	Eng	33SX1557
	Fonit	Ity	LPU8001
	Guest Star	USA	G 1403
	Hall of Fame	USA	JG-604
	I Grandi del Jazz	Ity	GDJ-88
	Jazztone	USA	J1203
	Roulette	USA	RE-110
	Roulette	Aus	VJL2-0264
	Roulette	Jap	MJ-7069
	Royal Roost	USA	LP-2256
	Royal Roost	USA	RLP 2213
	Spotlite	Eng	SPJ 129
	Vogue	Eng	LAE 12209
	Vogue	Fra	MDR 9168
	Vogue	Fra	DP-28
	WGM (Roulette)	USA	2A

ERROLL GARNER TRIO **LOS ANGELES, MARCH, 1947**
Erroll Garner (p), George "Red" Callender (b), Harold "Doc" West (d)
1920   Trio

16 Inch TX	>AFRS Jubilee	USA	230

ERROLL GARNER **HOLLYWOOD, APRIL 22, 1947**
Erroll Garner (p)
1930   Erroll's Bounce
(mx D7VB-0514)

10 Inch 78	>RCA Victor	USA	20-3087
7 Inch 45	RCA Victor	USA	27-0146
7 Inch 45EP	Camden	USA	CAE420
10 Inch 33	His Master's Voice	Eng	DLP-1022
	RCA Victor	USA	LEJ-4
12 Inch 33	Camden	USA	CAL-328
	Camden	USA	CAL-384
	Camden	USA	CAL-882
	Camden	USA	CAS-882
	Camden	Aus	CAM49
	Camden	Eng	CDN118
	RCA Victor	USA	FXM37143
	RCA Victor	Fra	430.278
	RCA Victor	Fra	430.633
	RCA Victor	Ity	LPM10044

1940   Erroll's Blues
(mx D7VB-0515)

10 Inch 78	>RCA Victor	USA	20-3087
7 Inch 45	RCA Victor	USA	EJB3001
7 Inch 45EP	Camden	USA	CAE420
	His Master's Voice	Eng	EP-7EG8074
10 Inch 33	RCA Victor	USA	LPT31

	12 Inch 33	Camden	USA	ACL-7015
		Camden	USA	CAL-384
		Camden	USA	CAL-882
		Camden	USA	CAS-882
		RCA Victor	USA	FXM37143
		RCA Victor	USA	LJM3001
		RCA Victor	Jap	RJL-2520

1950 I Can't Escape from You
      (mx D7VB-0516)

	10 Inch 78	Electrola	WGer	EG7897
		>RCA Victor	USA	20-4723
		RCA Victor	USA	EG7897
	7 Inch 45	RCA Victor	USA	47-4723
	7 Inch 45EP	Camden	USA	CAE420
	12 Inch 33	Camden	USA	ACL-7015
		Camden	USA	CAL-384
		Camden	USA	CAL-882
		Camden	USA	CAS-882
		RCA Victor	Jap	RJL-2520

Note: Electrola EG7897 is unissued.

1960 Stairway to the Stars
      (mx D7VB-0517)

	10 Inch 78	Electrola	WGer	EG7897
		>RCA Victor	USA	20-4723
		RCA Victor	USA	EG7897
	7 Inch 45	RCA Victor	USA	47-4723
	7 Inch 45EP	Camden	USA	CAE420
	12 Inch 33	Camden	USA	ACL-7015
		Camden	USA	CAL-384
		Camden	USA	CAL-882
		Camden	USA	CAS-882
		RCA Victor	Jap	RJL-2520

Note: Electrola EG7897 is unissued.

GENE NORMAN'S "JUST JAZZ" CONCERT   PASADENA, CA, APRIL 29, 1947

Erroll Garner (p), Wardell Gray (ts), Jackie Mills (d)

1970 Blue Lou (Rehearsal)

	12 Inch 33	>Fontana	Eng	FJL907
		Fontana	Fra	683907JCL
		Trio	Jap	PA3145

Add: Irving Ashby (g), George "Red" Callender (b)

1980 Blue Lou (Part 1)
      (mx MM 912)

	10 Inch 78	Jazz Selection	Fra	568
		>Modern	USA	20-640
		Music	Ity	JH1012
		Vogue	Den	V568
		Vogue	Eng	V2047
	7 Inch 45	Modern	USA	45-126
	7 Inch 45EP	Vogue	Eng	EPV 1002
	10 Inch 33	Modern	USA	MOD 2008
		Vogue	Fra	LD 024
	12 Inch 33	Crown	USA	CLP5003
		Crown	USA	CLP5004
		Crown	USA	CLP5056
		Crown	USA	CLP5278
		Crown	USA	CLP5424
		Crown	USA	CST278
		Modern	USA	1203
		Modern	USA	LMP1204

		United	USA	US 7722
		Vogue	Eng	LAE 12001
		Vogue	Eng	VJT 3003
		Vogue	Fra	CMDGN 766
		Vogue	Fra	LDM 30003

1990   Blue Lou (Part 2)
        (mx MM 913)

		Jazz Selection	Fra	568
10 Inch 78		>Modern	USA	20-640
		Music	Ity	JH1012
		Vogue	Den	V568
		Vogue	Eng	V2047
7 Inch 45		Modern	USA	45-126
7 Inch 45EP		Vogue	Eng	EPV 1002
10 Inch 33		Modern	USA	MOD 2008
		Vogue	Fra	LD 024
12 Inch 33		Crown	USA	CLP5003
		Crown	USA	CLP5004
		Crown	USA	CLP5056
		Crown	USA	CLP5278
		Crown	USA	CLP5424
		Crown	USA	CST278
		Modern	USA	1203
		Modern	USA	LMP1204
		United	USA	US 7722
		Vogue	Eng	LAE 12001
		Vogue	Eng	VJT 3003
		Vogue	Fra	CMDGN 766
		Vogue	Fra	LDM 30003

Note: Vogue CMDGN 766 contains an unedited version of "Blue Lou" (9 min., 18 sec.).

Add: Howard McGhee (tp), Vic Dickenson (tb), Benny Carter (as)

2000   One O'Clock Jump
        (mx MM 914)

		Gazell	Swe	2005
10 Inch 78		Jazz Selection	Fra	571
		>Modern	USA	20-641
		Music	Ity	JH1040
		Vogue	Eng	V2271
10 Inch 33		Vogue	Fra	LD 024
12 Inch 33		Crown	USA	CLP5004
		Crown	USA	CLP5293
		Crown	USA	CLP5420
		Crown	USA	CST293
		Crown	USA	CST420
		Modern	USA	1207
		Modern	USA	LMP1204
		United	USA	US 7722
		Vogue	Eng	LAE 12001
		Vogue	Eng	VJT 3003
		Vogue	Fra	CMDGN 766
		Vogue	Fra	LDM 30003
16 Inch TX		AFRS Jubilee	USA	262

Note: See note below "Four O'Clock Jump" (2030).

2010   Two O'Clock Jump
        (mx MM 915)

		Gazell	Swe	2005
10 Inch 78		Jazz Selection	Fra	571
		>Modern	USA	20-641
		Music	Ity	JH1040
		Vogue	Eng	V2271
10 Inch 33		Vogue	Fra	LD 024

		12 Inch 33	Crown	USA	CLP5004
			Crown	USA	CST293
			Crown	USA	CST420
			Modern	USA	1207
			Modern	USA	LMP1204
			United	USA	US 7722
			Vogue	Eng	LAE 12001
			Vogue	Eng	VJT 3003
			Vogue	Fra	CMDGN 766
			Vogue	Fra	LDM 30003
2020	Three O'Clock Jump (mx MM 916)				
		10 Inch 78	Gazell	Swe	2006
			Jazz Selection	Fra	572
			>Modern	USA	20-642
			Music	Ity	JH1041
			Vogue	Eng	V2272
		10 Inch 33	Vogue	Fra	LD 024
		12 Inch 33	Crown	USA	CLP5004
			Crown	USA	CST293
			Crown	USA	CST420
			Modern	USA	1207
			Modern	USA	LMP1204
			United	USA	US 7722
			Vogue	Eng	LAE 12001
			Vogue	Eng	VJT 3003
			Vogue	Fra	CMDGN 766
			Vogue	Fra	LDM 30003
2030	Four O'Clock Jump (mx MM 917)				
		10 Inch 78	Gazell	Swe	2006
			Jazz Selection	Fra	572
			>Modern	USA	20-642
			Music	Ity	JH1041
			Vogue	Eng	V2272
		10 Inch 33	Vogue	Fra	LD 024
		12 Inch 33	Crown	USA	CLP5004
			Crown	USA	CST293
			Crown	USA	CST420
			Modern	USA	1207
			Modern	USA	LMP1204
			United	USA	US 7722
			Vogue	Eng	LAE 12001
			Vogue	Eng	VJT 3003
			Vogue	Fra	CMDGN 766
			Vogue	Fra	LDM 30003

Note: Index numbers 2000-2030 are one tune, "One O'Clock Jump," but was divided into the above four titles.

Omit: Wardell Gray, Howard McGhee, Vic Dickenson and Benny Carter.

2040	Lover (Part 1) (mx MM 5A-N)				
		10 Inch 78	Jazz Selection	Fra	566
			>Modern	USA	20-650
			Vogue	Den	V566
			Vogue	Eng	V2004
		7 Inch 45	Modern	USA	45-102
		10 Inch 33	Modern	USA	MOD 2008
			Vogue	Fra	LD 024
		12 Inch 33	Crown	USA	CLP275
			Crown	USA	CLP5003
			Crown	USA	CLP5404
			Crown	USA	CST404

		USA	1203
	Modern	USA	1203
	Vogue	Eng	LAE 12001
	Vogue	Eng	VJT 3003
	Vogue	Fra	CMDGN 766

2050 Lover (Part 2)
      (mx MM 5B-N)

10 Inch 78	Jazz Selection	Fra	566
	>Modern	USA	20-650
	Vogue	Den	V566
	Vogue	Eng	V2004
7 Inch 45	Modern	USA	45-102
10 Inch 33	Modern	USA	MOD 2008
	Vogue	Fra	LD 024
12 Inch 33	Crown	USA	CLP275
	Crown	USA	CLP5003
	Crown	USA	CLP5404
	Crown	USA	CST404
	Modern	USA	1203
	Vogue	Eng	LAE 12001
	Vogue	Eng	VJT 3003
	Vogue	Fra	CMDGN 766

Omit: Mills, Ashby and Callender; Erroll Garner piano solo.

2060 Erroll's Bounce

16 Inch TX	>AFRS Jubilee	USA	262

ERROLL GARNER   **HOLLYWOOD, JUNE 10, 1947**

Erroll Garner (p)

2070 Play, Piano, Play
      (mx D 1091-C)

10 Inch 78	Blue Star	Fra	63
	Cupol	Swe	4319
	>Dial	USA	1026
	Esquire	Eng	10-026
7 Inch 45EP	Sonet	Den	SXP-2854
10 Inch 33	Blue Star	Fra	BLP6814
	Concert Hall	USA	CHJ1001
	Dial	USA	205
12 Inch 33	Celson	Ity	QB7006
	Cie Ind. Disque	Fra	22000
	Cie Ind. Disque	Fra	CVM42.004
	Columbia	Eng	33SX1557
	Fonit	Ity	LPU8001
	Hall of Fame	USA	JG-604
	I Grandi del Jazz	Ity	GDJ-88
	Jazztone	USA	J1203
	Roulette	USA	RE-110
	Roulette	Aus	VJL2-0264
	Roulette	Jap	MJ-7069
	Roulette	Jap	MJ-7072
	Royal Roost	USA	LP-2256
	Royal Roost	USA	RLP 2213
	Spotlight	Eng	SPJ 129
	Vogue	Eng	LAE 12209
	Vogue	Fra	DP-28
	Vogue	Fra	DP-64
	Vogue	Fra	MDR 9168

Note: "Play, Piano, Play" is Garner's improvised version of "Play, Fiddle, Play"
(see also "Play, Fiddle, Play," January 30, 1945).

2080 Love Is the Strangest Game
      (mx D 1092-A)

		10 Inch 33	>Dial	USA	205
			Guilde du Jazz	Fra	J1001
		12 Inch 33	Spotlite	Eng	SPJ 129
2090	Love Is the Strangest Game (mx D 1092-B)				
		10 Inch 78	>Dial	USA	1041
		12 Inch 33	Spotlite	Eng	SPJ 129
2100	Love Is the Strangest Game (mx D 1092-C)				
		10 Inch 33	>Concert Hall	USA	CHJ1001
		12 Inch 33	Fonit	Ity	LPU8001
			Hall of Fame	USA	JG-604
			Jazztone	USA	J1203
2110	Blues Garni (mx D 1093-A)				
		10 Inch 78	Blue Star	Fra	110
			Celson	Ity	QB7034
		10 Inch 33	Blue Star	Fra	BLP6814
			Concert Hall	USA	CHJ1001
			>Dial	USA	205
			Guilde du Jazz	Fra	J1001
		12 Inch 33	Fonit	Ity	LPU8009
			Hall of Fame	USA	JG-604
			Jazztone	USA	J1203
			Spotlite	Eng	SPJ 129
2120	Don't Worry 'Bout Me (mx D 1094-A)				
		10 Inch 33	>Dial	USA	205
		12 Inch 33	Spotlite	Eng	SPJ 129
2130	Don't Worry 'Bout Me (mx D 1094-B)				
		10 Inch 78	Blue Star	Fra	135
			Esquire	Eng	10-104
		7 Inch 45EP	Sonet	Den	SXP-2854
		10 Inch 33	Blue Star	Fra	BLP6814
		12 Inch 33	Cie Ind. Disque	Fra	CVM42.004
			Columbia	Eng	33SX1557
			I Grandi del Jazz	Ity	GDJ-88
			Roulette	USA	RE-110
			Roulette	Aus	VJL2-0264
			>Royal Roost	USA	RLP 2213
			Spotlite	Eng	SPJ 129
			Vogue	Eng	LAE 12209
			Vogue	Fra	DP-28
			Vogue	Fra	MDR 9168
2140	Don't Worry 'Bout Me (mx D 1094-C)				
		12 Inch 33	>Spotlite	Eng	SPJ 129
2150	Loose Nut (mx D 1095-A)				
		10 Inch 78	>Dial	USA	1041
		12 Inch 33	Coral	USA	CRL57040
			Fonit	Ity	LPU8008
			Hall of Fame	USA	JG-604
			Jazztone	USA	J1203
2160	Loose Nut (mx D 1095-B)				
		10 Inch 33	>Dial	USA	208
		12 Inch 33	Spotlite	Eng	SPJ 129
2170	Love for Sale (mx D 1096-A)				
		10 Inch 78	Blue Star	Fra	135
			Dial	USA	760

		>Dial	USA	1031
		Esquire	Eng	10-104
7 Inch 45EP		Sonet	Den	SXP-2854
10 Inch 33		Blue Star	Fra	BLP6814
		Dial	USA	205
12 Inch 33		Cie Ind. Disque	Fra	22000
		Cie Ind. Disque	Fra	CVM42.004
		Columbia	Eng	33SX1557
		CORE	USA	100
		I Grandi del Jazz	Ity	GDJ-88
		Mode	Fra	MDINT 9200
		Roulette	USA	RE-110
		Roulette	Aus	VJL2-0264
		Royal Roost	USA	RLP 2213
		Spotlite	Eng	SPJ 129
		Vogue	Eng	LAE 12209
		Vogue	Fra	DP-28
		Vogue	Fra	MDR 9168

2180 Frankie and Johnny Fantasy
      (mx D 1097-A)

	Blue Star	Fra	63
10 Inch 78	Celson	Ity	QB7006
	Cupol	Swe	4319
	>Dial	USA	1026
	Esquire	Eng	10-026
7 Inch 45EP	Sonet	Den	SXP-2854
10 Inch 33	Dial	USA	208
12 Inch 33	Cie Ind. Disque	Fra	22000
	Cie Ind. Disque	Fra	CVM42.004
	Columbia	Eng	33SX1557
	Fonit	Ity	LPU8001
	Guest Star	USA	G 1403
	Hall of Fame	USA	JG-604
	I Grandi del Jazz	Ity	GDJ-88
	Jazztone	USA	J1203
	Roulette	USA	RE-110
	Roulette	Aus	VJL2-0264
	Roulette	Jap	MJ-7069
	Royal Roost	USA	LP-2256
	Royal Roost	USA	RLP 2213
	Royal Roost	USA	OJ-1
	Smithsonian	USA	P11895
	Spotlite	Eng	SPJ 129
	Vogue	Eng	LAE 12209
	Vogue	Fra	DP-28
	Vogue	Fra	MDR 9168
	WGM (Roulette)	USA	2A

Note: D 1097-A is titled "Frankie and Garni" on Blue Star 63.

2190 Sloe Gin Fizz
      (mx D 1098-A)

	Blue Star	Fra	110
10 Inch 78	Celson	Ity	QB7034
	Dial	USA	760
	>Dial	USA	1031
10 Inch 33	Blue Star	Fra	BLP6814
	Dial	USA	205
12 Inch 33	Spotlite	Eng	SPJ 129

Note: D 1098-A is titled "Barclay Bounce" on Blue Star 110 for Eddie Barclay,
owner of Blue Star Records.

2200 Talk No Holes (In My Clothes)
      (mx D 1098-B)

7 Inch 33	Jazztone	USA	J738
10 Inch 33	>Guilde du Jazz	Fra	J1001

Note: D1098-B is titled "Take No Holes" on Jazztone J738.

ERROLL GARNER   **LOS ANGELES, ca. DEC., 1947/JAN., 1948**
Erroll Garner (p)
2210   Erroll's Blues
                16 Inch TX   AFRS Jubilee   USA   259

ERROLL GARNER TRIO   **PASADENA, CA, APRIL 1948**
Erroll Garner (p), Ulysses Livingston (g), John Simmons (b)
2220   Cherchez la Femme
        (mx JJ-6X-103)
                10 Inch 78   Jazz Selection   Fra   791
                10 Inch 33   Vogue   Fra   LD 031
                12 Inch 33   Vogue   Fra   CMDGN 9853
                                  Vogue   Fra   DP-28
                                  Vogue   Fra   LD 560-30
                16 Inch TX   >AFRS Just Jazz   USA   13
2230   Indiana (Back Home Again in Indiana)
        (mx JJ-6X-104)
                10 Inch 78   Vogue   Eng   V2230
                10 Inch 33   Vogue   Fra   LD 031
                12 Inch 33   Vogue   Fra   CMDGN 9853
                                  Vogue   Fra   DP-28
                                  Vogue   Fra   LD 560-30
                16 Inch TX   >AFRS Just Jazz   USA   13

ERROLL GARNER   **PARIS, MAY 15, 1948**
Erroll Garner (p)
2240   Lover Man (Oh, Where Can You Be?)
        (mx ST2298-1)
                10 Inch 78   >Apollo   USA   797
2250   Lover Man (Oh, Where Can You Be?)
        (mx ST2298-2)
                10 Inch 78   Gazell   Swe   3004
                                  Jazz Parade   Eng   B2
                                  Music   Ity   JH1056
                                  >Vogue   Fra   5003
                12 Inch 33   Grand Award   USA   GA 33-321
2260   What Is This Thing Called Love?
        (mx ST2299-1)
                10 Inch 78   Apollo   USA   797
                                  Gazell   Swe   3004
                                  Jazz Parade   Eng   B2
                                  Music   Ity   JH1039
                                  >Vogue   Fra   5003
                12 Inch 33   Grand Award   USA   GA 33-321
                                  Modern   USA   1203
                                  Vogue   Fra   CMDINT 9515
2270   Early in Paris
        (mx ST2300-2)
                10 Inch 78   Apollo   USA   798
                                  Exclusive Jazz   Swe   9102
                                  Music   Ity   JH1039
                                  Vogue   Eng   V2026
                                  >Vogue   Fra   5002
                10 Inch 33   Vogue   Fra   LD 031
                12 Inch 33   Grand Award   USA   GA 33-321
                Note: "Early in Paris" (Erroll Garner) is titled "Erroll Garner in Paris" on Apollo
                798.
2280   These Foolish Things (Remind Me of You)
        (mx ST2301-2)

	10 Inch 78	Apollo	USA	798
		Exclusive Jazz	Swe	9102
		Music	Ity	JH1056
		Vogue	Eng	V2026
		>Vogue	Fra	5002
	12 Inch 33	Grand Award	USA	GA 33-321

ERROLL GARNER   PARIS, MAY 16, 1948
The two sessions that follow were from the same concert broadcast over
Paris-Inter at 9 p.m., May 16, 1948 at the Marigny Theater.
Erroll Garner (p)

2290	Laura			
	12 Inch 33	Europa	Ity	EJ-1020
		>I Giganti del Jazz	Ity	GJ24
2300	Play, Piano, Play			
	12 Inch 33	Europa	Ity	EJ-1020
		>I Giganti del Jazz	Ity	GJ24
2310	Frankie and Johnny Fantasy			
	12 Inch 33	Europa	Ity	EJ-1020
		>I Giganti del Jazz	Ity	GJ24

Add: Jimmy Heath (as), Howard McGhee (tp), John Collins (g), Percy Heath
(b), Kenny Clarke (d).

2320	I Surrender, Dear			
	12 Inch 33	Europa	Ity	EJ-1020
		>I Giganti del Jazz	Ity	GJ24

COLEMAN HAWKINS QUARTET   PARIS, MAY 16, 1948
Coleman Hawkins (ts), Erroll Garner (p), Percy Heath (b), Kenny Clarke (d)

2330	Cocktails for Two			
	12 Inch 33	Europa	Ity	EJ-1020
		>I Giganti del Jazz	Ity	GJ24

GENE NORMAN'S "JUST JAZZ"   PASADENA, CA, JULY 26, 1948
CONCERT
Erroll Garner (p), possibly Oscar Moore (g), Nelson Boyd (b), Teddy Stewart (d)

2340	Just You, Just Me			
	(mx MM1002)			
	10 Inch 78	Jazz Selection	Fra	579
		>Modern	USA	20-696
		Vogue	Eng	V2274
	7 Inch 45	Modern	USA	45-127
	10 Inch 33	Modern	USA	MOD 2008
		Vogue	Fra	LD 031
	12 Inch 33	Crown	USA	CLP5003
		Crown	USA	CLP5004
		Crown	USA	CLP5424
		Crown	USA	CST278
		Modern	USA	1203
		United	USA	US 7722
		Vogue	Eng	VJT 3003
		Vogue	Fra	CMDGN 9853
		Vogue	Fra	DP-28
		Vogue	Fra	LD 560-30

ERROLL GARNER TRIO   LOS ANGELES, FEBRUARY 2, 1949
Some sources give Sunday, February 20, 1949 as the date of this session.
According to Bob Porter, the correct date is Wednesday, February 2, 1949.
Erroll Garner (p), John Simmons (b), Alvin Stoller (d)

2350	I Surrender, Dear			
	(mx BOP210-1)			Unissued
2360	I Surrender, Dear			
	(mx BOP210-2)			Unissued
2370	I Surrender, Dear			
	(mx BOP210-3)			
	10 Inch 78	>Savoy	USA	701
	7 Inch 45	Savoy	USA	45-701
	7 Inch 45EP	Savoy	USA	XP-8015
	10 Inch 33	Festival	Aus	CFR10-231
		Savoy	USA	MG15004
	12 Inch 33	BYG	Fra	529143
		Ember	Eng	EMB-3329
		Festival	Fra	166
		Galaxy	USA	4815
		Joker	Ity	SM3719
		Koala	USA	AW14135
		London	Eng	LTZ-C 15126
		Musidisc	Fra	CV1047
		Rondolette	USA	A15
		Savoy	USA	MG12003
		Savoy	USA	SJL2207
		Savoy-Musidisc	Fra	6005
		Savoy	Jap	WAJ-701
2380	I Only Have Eyes for You			
	(mx BOP211-1)			Unissued
2390	I Only Have Eyes for You			
	(mx BOP211-2)			Unissued
	Note: Breakdown (2 min., 33 sec.)			
2400	I Only Have Eyes for You			
	(mx BOP211-3)			
	10 Inch 78	>Savoy	USA	723
	7 Inch 45	Savoy	USA	45-723
	7 Inch 45EP	Savoy	USA	XP-8011
	10 Inch 33	Savoy	USA	MG15000
		Savoy	Fra	255SV152
	12 Inch 33	BYG	Fra	529144
		Joker	Ity	SM3718
		Musidisc	Fra	CV1047
		Savoy	USA	MG12008
		Savoy	USA	SJL1118
		Savoy-Musidisc	Fra	6006
2405	That's My Baby			
	(mx BOP212-1)			Unissued
2410	That's My Baby			
	(mx BOP212-2)			Unissued
	Note: "That's My Baby" (BOP212-1/-2) is a vocal by Erroll Garner.			
2420	Stompin' at the Savoy			
	(mx BOP213-1)			
	10 Inch 78	>Savoy	USA	727
	7 Inch 45	Savoy	USA	45-727
	7 Inch 45EP	Ember	Eng	EP-4529
		Savoy	USA	XP-8012
	10 Inch 33	Savoy	USA	MG15000
	12 Inch 33	BYG	Fra	529110
		BYG	Fra	529144
		Bellaphon	WGer	BJS4045
		Ember	Eng	EMB-3329
		Eros	Eng	ERL50047
		Everest	USA	FS245
		Festival	Fra	166
		Galaxy	USA	4815
		I Grandi del Jazz	Ity	GDJ-88

Koala	USA	AW14135
London	Eng	LTZ-C 15125
Quadrifoglio	Ity	VDS208
Realm	Eng	RM116
Rondolette	USA	A15
Savoy	USA	MG12002
Savoy	USA	SJL2207
Savoy-Musidisc	Fra	6004
Vogue	Fra	LDM 30230

ERROLL GARNER TRIO   LOS ANGELES, MARCH 29, 1949

Although March 29, 1949 is the only date given in previous discographies, it is unlikely that all of the tunes in this session were recorded in one day. Aural evidence indicates that some tunes were done on different pianos and under different studio conditions. John Simmons, in his January, 1977 interview with Patricia Willard, related that the sessions were two or three days, with Alvin Stoller playing the first day or two and Jesse Price finishing the date.

Erroll Garner (p), John Simmons (b), Alvin Stoller (d)

2425   I Cover the Waterfront
        (mx B4400-4)

10 Inch 78	>Savoy	USA	688
	Savoy	Eng	688
7 Inch 45	Savoy	USA	45-688
7 Inch 45EP	Savoy	USA	XP-8015
10 Inch 33	Savoy	USA	MG15026
12 Inch 33	BYG	Fra	529110
	Eros	Eng	ERL50047
	Festival	Fra	166
	I Grandi del Jazz	Ity	GDJ-88
	London	Eng	LTZ-C 15125
	Realm	Eng	RM116
	Savoy	USA	MG12002
	Savoy	USA	SJL2207
	Savoy-Musidisc	Fra	6004

2430   It's Easy to Remember
        (mx B4401-2)

10 Inch 78	>Savoy	USA	728
7 Inch 45	Savoy	USA	45-728
10 Inch 33	Savoy	USA	MG15026
12 Inch 33	BYG	Fra	529143
	Festival	Fra	166
	Joker	Ity	SM3719
	London	Eng	LTZ-C 15126
	Savoy	USA	MG12003
	Savoy	USA	SJL2207
	Savoy	Jap	WAJ-701
	Savoy-Musidisc	Fra	6005

2440   Penthouse Serenade (When We're Alone)
        (mx B4402-3)

10 Inch 78	>Savoy	USA	688
	Savoy	Eng	688
7 Inch 45	Savoy	USA	45-688
7 Inch 45EP	Savoy	USA	XP-8010
	Savoy-Musidisc	Fra	SA3011
10 Inch 33	Savoy	USA	MG15001
12 Inch 33	BYG	Fra	529110
	Eros	Eng	ERL50047
	Festival	Fra	166
	Joker	Ity	SM3718

			London	Eng	LTZ-C 15125
			Musidisc	Fra	CV1047
			Realm	Eng	RM116
			Savoy	USA	MG12002
			Savoy	USA	SJL2207
			Savoy-Musidisc	Fra	6006
2450	Love Walked In				
	(mx B4403-2)				
		10 Inch 78	>Savoy	USA	701
		7 Inch 45	Savoy	USA	45-701
		7 Inch 45EP	Savoy	USA	XP-8014
		10 Inch 33	Savoy	USA	MG15026
		12 Inch 33	BYG	Fra	529110
			Eros	Eng	ERL50047
			Festival	Fra	166
			London	Eng	LTZ-C 15125
			Realm	Eng	RM116
			Savoy	USA	MG12002
			Savoy	USA	SJL2207
			Savoy-Musidisc	Fra	6004
2460	September Song				
	(mx B4404-1)				
		10 Inch 78	>Savoy	USA	727
		7 Inch 45	Savoy	USA	45-727
		7 Inch 45EP	Savoy	USA	XP-8008
		10 Inch 33	Savoy	USA	MG15000
			Savoy	Fra	255SV152
		12 Inch 33	BYG	Fra	529144
			Festival	Fra	166
			Joker	Ity	SM3718
			Musidisc	Fra	CV1047
			Savoy	USA	MG12008
			Savoy	USA	SJL1118
			Savoy-Musidisc	Fra	6006
2470	Body and Soul				
	(mx B4405-3)				
		10 Inch 78	>Savoy	USA	728
		7 Inch 45	Savoy	USA	45-728
		7 Inch 45EP	Savoy	USA	XP-8011
		10 Inch 33	Savoy	USA	MG15001
		12 Inch 33	BYG	Fra	529110
			Festival	Fra	166
			Joker	Ity	SM3718
			London	Eng	LTZ-C 15125
			Savoy	USA	MG12002
			Savoy	USA	SJL2207
			Savoy-Musidisc	Fra	6004
2480	All the Things You Are				
	(mx B4406-2)				
		10 Inch 78	>Savoy	USA	739
			Savoy	USA	782
		7 Inch 45	Savoy	USA	45-739
			Savoy	USA	45-782
		7 Inch 45EP	Savoy	USA	XP-8012
		10 Inch 33	Savoy	USA	MG15000
			Savoy	Fra	255SV111
		12 Inch 33	BYG	Fra	529144
			Festival	Fra	166
			Joker	Ity	SM3718
			Musidisc	Fra	CV1047
			Savoy	USA	MG12008
			Savoy	USA	SJL1118
			Savoy-Musidisc	Fra	6006

2490   I Don't Stand a Ghost of a Chance with You
        (mx B4407-1)

	10 Inch 78	>Savoy	USA	724
	7 Inch 45	Savoy	USA	45-724
	7 Inch 45EP	Savoy	USA	XP-8015
	10 Inch 33	Savoy	USA	MG15026
	12 Inch 33	BYG	Fra	529110
		Eros	Eng	ERL50047
		Festival	Fra	166
		I Grandi del Jazz	Ity	GDJ-88
		London	Eng	LTZ-C 15125
		Realm	Eng	RM116
		Savoy	USA	MG12002
		Savoy	USA	SJL2207
		Savoy-Musidisc	Fra	6004

           Note: See February 2, 1949 session for matrix numbers B4408 and B4409.
2500   Yesterdays
        (mx B4410-1)

	7 Inch 45EP	Savoy	USA	XP-8008
	10 Inch 33	>Savoy	USA	MG15000
	12 Inch 33	Savoy	USA	SJL1118

           Note: It is the opinion of the author that "Yesterdays" (mx B4410-1) was not
           played by Erroll Garner. It is probably Beryl Booker.
2510   Goodbye
        (mx B4411)

	10 Inch 78	>Savoy	USA	782
	7 Inch 45	Savoy	USA	45-782
	7 Inch 45EP	Savoy	USA	XP-8014
	10 Inch 33	Savoy	USA	MG15026
	12 Inch 33	BYG	Fra	529144
		Festival	Fra	166
		London	Eng	LTZ-C 15126
		Savoy	USA	MG12003
		Savoy	USA	SJL2207
		Savoy	Jap	WJ-701
		Savoy-Musidisc	Fra	6006

           Note: Matrix number HNY 4007 has been noted on Savoy 45-782A. Aural evidence
           indicates this title does not belong to this session.
2520   A Cottage for Sale
        (mx B4412-2)

	10 Inch 78	>Savoy	USA	725
	7 Inch 45	Savoy	USA	45-725
	7 Inch 45EP	Savoy	USA	XP-8014
	10 Inch 33	Festival	Aus	CFR10-231
		Savoy	USA	MG15004
		Savoy	Fra	255SV152
	12 Inch 33	BYG	Fra	529144
		Festival	Fra	166
		Savoy	USA	MG12008
		Savoy	USA	SJL1118
		Savoy-Musidisc	Fra	6006

           Note: Matrix number B4421 has been noted on Savoy 725 and Savoy 45-725. The
           Savoy master files show the correct matrix number to be B4412.
2530   Oh, Lady Be Good!
        (mx B4413)   Unissued
2540   I'm in the Mood for Love
        (mx B4414-1)

	10 Inch 78	>Savoy	USA	725
	7 Inch 45	Savoy	USA	45-725
	7 Inch 45EP	Savoy	USA	XP-8015
	10 Inch 33	Festival	Aus	CFR10-231
		Savoy	USA	MG15004
		Savoy	Fra	255SV152

		12 Inch 33	BYG	Fra	529143
			Festival	Fra	166
			Joker	Ity	SM3719
			London	Eng	LTZ-C 15126
			Musidisc	Fra	CV1047
			Savoy	USA	MG12003
			Savoy	USA	SJL2207
			Savoy	Jap	WAJ-701
			Savoy-Musidisc	Fra	6005
2550	I Can't Believe That You're in Love with Me				
	(mx B4415-1)				
		10 Inch 78	>Savoy	USA	723
		7 Inch 45	Savoy	USA	45-723
		7 Inch 45EP	Ember	Eng	EP-4553
			Realm	Eng	REP-4006
			Savoy	USA	XP-8007
		10 Inch 33	Savoy	USA	MG15000
			Savoy	Fra	255SV152
		12 Inch 33	BYG	Fra	529110
			Bellaphon	WGer	BJS4045
			Ember	Eng	3335
			Ember	Eng	EMB-3329
			Eros	Eng	ERL50047
			Everest	USA	FS245
			Festival	Fra	166
			Galaxy	USA	4815
			Joker	Ity	SM3718
			Koala	USA	AW14135
			London	Eng	LTZ-C 15125
			Musidisc	Fra	CV1047
			Quadrifoglio	Ity	VDS208
			Realm	Eng	RM116
			Rondolette	USA	A15
			Savoy	USA	MG12002
			Savoy	USA	SJL2207
			Savoy-Musidisc	Fra	6004
			Vogue	Fra	LDM 30230
2560	More Than You Know				
	(mx B4416-2)				
		10 Inch 78	Regent	USA	1014
			>Savoy	USA	863
		7 Inch 45	Regent	USA	45-1014
		7 Inch 45EP	Savoy	USA	XP-8009
		10 Inch 33	Savoy	USA	MG15001
		12 Inch 33	BYG	Fra	529110
			Festival	Fra	166
			Joker	Ity	SM3718
			London	Eng	LTZ-C 15125
			Musidisc	Fra	CV1047
			Savoy	USA	MG12002
			Savoy	USA	SJL2207
			Savoy-Musidisc	Fra	6004
2570	Undecided				
	(mx B4417-1)				
		10 Inch 78	Regent	USA	1004
			>Savoy	USA	862
		7 Inch 45	Regent	USA	45-1004
			Savoy	USA	45-862
		7 Inch 45EP	Realm	Eng	REP-4006
			Savoy	USA	XP-8007
		10 Inch 33	Savoy	USA	MG15000
		12 Inch 33	BYG	Fra	529110
			Eros	Eng	ERL50047

		Festival	Fra	166
		I Grandi del Jazz	Ity	GDJ-88
		London	Eng	LTZ-C 15125
		Realm	Eng	RM116
		Savoy	USA	MG12002
		Savoy	USA	SJL2207
		Savoy-Musidisc	Fra	6004
2580	Red Sails in the Sunset			
	(mx B4418-1)			
	10 Inch 78	Regent	USA	1004
		>Savoy	USA	862
	7 Inch 45	Regent	USA	45-1004
		Savoy	USA	45-862
	7 Inch 45EP	Realm	Eng	REP-4006
		Savoy	USA	XP-8007
	10 Inch 33	Savoy	USA	MG15000
	12 Inch 33	BYG	Fra	529110
		Bellaphon	WGer	BJS4045
		Ember	Eng	EMB-3329
		Eros	Eng	ERL50047
		Everest	USA	FS245
		Festival	Fra	166
		Galaxy	USA	4815
		Joker	Ity	SM3718
		Koala	USA	AW14135
		London	Eng	LTZ-C 15125
		Musidisc	Fra	CV1047
		Quadrifoglio	Ity	VDS208
		Realm	Eng	RM116
		Rondolette	USA	A15
		Savoy	USA	MG12002
		Savoy	USA	SJL2207
		Savoy-Musidisc	Fra	6004
		Vogue	Fra	LDM 30230
2590	All of Me			
	(mx B4419-1)			
	10 Inch 78	>Savoy	USA	724
	7 Inch 45	Savoy	USA	45-724
	7 Inch 45EP	Savoy	USA	XP-8014
	10 Inch 33	Festival	Aus	CFR10-231
		Savoy	USA	MG15004
		Savoy	Fra	255SV111
	12 Inch 33	BYG	Fra	529144
		Festival	Fra	166
		Joker	Ity	SM3718
		London	Eng	LTZ-C 15126
		Musidisc	Fra	CV1047
		Savoy	USA	MG12003
		Savoy	USA	SJL2207
		Savoy	Jap	WAJ-701
		Savoy-Musidisc	Fra	6006
2600	Over the Rainbow			
	(mx B4420-2)			
	10 Inch 78	Regent	USA	1014
		>Savoy	USA	863
	7 Inch 45	Regent	USA	45-1014
	7 Inch 45EP	Savoy	USA	XP-8010
		Savoy-Musidisc	Fra	SA3011
	10 Inch 33	Savoy	USA	MG15001
	12 Inch 33	BYG	Fra	529110
		Festival	Fra	166
		Joker	Ity	SM3719
		London	Eng	LTZ-C 15125

		Savoy	USA	MG12002
		Savoy	USA	SJL2207
		Savoy-Musidisc	Fra	6006
2610	These Foolish Things (Remind Me of You)			
	(mx B4421)			Unissued

GENE NORMAN'S "JUST JAZZ" CONCERT   LOS ANGELES, MID-APRIL, 1949

Erroll Garner (p), John Simmons (b), Chuck Thompson (d), Teddy Edwards (ts), Dave Lambert (v)

2620	Cherokee (Part 1)			
	(mx JJ-6X-92)			
	10 Inch 78	>Jazz Selection	Fra	663
	12 Inch 33	Crown	USA	CLP5008
		Queen Disc	Ity	Q 039
		Spotlite	Eng	SPJ 145
	16 Inch TX	AFRS Just Jazz	USA	65
		AFRS Just Jazz	USA	80
2630	Cherokee (Part 2)			
	(mx JJ-6X-93)			
	10 Inch 78	>Jazz Selection	Fra	663
	12 Inch 33	Queen Disc	Ity	Q 039
		Spotlite	Eng	SPJ 145
	16 Inch TX	AFRS Just Jazz	USA	65
		AFRS Just Jazz	USA	80

GENE NORMAN'S "JUST JAZZ" CONCERT   PASADENA, CA, MAY, 1949

Pasadena Civic Auditorium

Erroll Garner (p), John Simmons (b), Chuck Thompson (d), Dave Lambert (v)

2640	All the Things You Are			
	16 Inch TX	>AFRS Just Jazz	USA	71
2650	Fine and Dandy			
	16 Inch TX	>AFRS Just Jazz	USA	71

GENE NORMAN'S "JUST JAZZ" CONCERT   LOS ANGELES, SUMMER, 1949

According to Gene Norman, "Tenderly" and "Someone to Watch Over Me" were recorded at radio station KFWB, Los Angeles.

Erroll Garner (p)

2660	Tenderly			
	(mx MM 1133)			
	10 Inch 78	Jazz Selection	Fra	576
		>Modern	USA	20-692
		Recorded in Hollywood	USA	692
	7 Inch 45	Modern	USA	45-103
	10 Inch 33	Modern	USA	MOD 2008
		Vogue	Fra	LD 031
	12 Inch 33	Crown	USA	CLP5003
		Crown	USA	CLP5004
		Crown	USA	CLP5404
		Crown	USA	CST 275
		Crown	USA	CST404
		Modern	USA	1203
		Modern	USA	LMP1204
		United	USA	US 7722
		Vogue	Fra	CMDGN 9853
		Vogue	Fra	DP-28
		Vogue	Fra	LD 560-30

2670	Someone to Watch Over Me (mx MM 1134)			
	10 Inch 78	Jazz Selection	Fra	576
		>Modern	USA	20-692
		Recorded in Hollywood	USA	692
	7 Inch 45	Modern	USA	45-103
	10 Inch 33	Modern	USA	MOD 2008
		Vogue	Fra	LD 031
	12 Inch 33	Crown	USA	CLP5003
		Modern	USA	1203
		Vogue	Fra	CMDGN 9853
		Vogue	Fra	DP-28
		Vogue	Fra	LD 560-30

GENE NORMAN'S "JUST JAZZ" CONCERT   PASADENA, CA, SUMMER, 1949

Erroll Garner (p)

2680	Take the "A" Train (mx JJ-6X-94)			
	10 Inch 78	>Jazz Selection	Fra	749
	10 Inch 33	Vogue	Fra	LD 019
	12 Inch 33	Vogue	Fra	CMDGN 9853
		Vogue	Fra	DP-28
		Vogue	Fra	LD 560-30
2690	Georgia on My Mind (mx JJ-6X-95)			
	10 Inch 78	>Jazz Selection	Fra	749
	10 Inch 33	Vogue	Fra	LD 019
	12 Inch 33	Vogue	Fra	CMDGN 9853
		Vogue	Fra	DP-28
		Vogue	Fra	LD 560-30
2700	St. Louis Blues (mx JJ-6X-96)			
	10 Inch 78	>Jazz Selection	Fra	750
	10 Inch 33	Vogue	Fra	LD 019
	12 Inch 33	Vogue	Fra	509080
		Vogue	Fra	CMDGN 9853
		Vogue	Fra	DP-28
		Vogue	Fra	LD 560-30
2710	My Old Kentucky Home (mx JJ-6X-97)			
	10 Inch 78	>Jazz Selection	Fra	750
	10 Inch 33	Vogue	Fra	LD 019
	12 Inch 33	Vogue	Fra	CMDGN 9853
		Vogue	Fra	DP-28
		Vogue	Fra	LD 560-30
2720	Erroll's Peril (mx JJ-6X-98)			
	10 Inch 78	>Jazz Selection	Fra	753
	10 Inch 33	Vogue	Fra	LD 019
	12 Inch 33	Vogue	Fra	CMDGN 9853
		Vogue	Fra	DP-28
		Vogue	Fra	LD 560-30
2730	I'm Coming Virginia (mx JJ-6X-99)			
	10 Inch 78	>Jazz Selection	Fra	753
	10 Inch 33	Vogue	Fra	LD 019
	12 Inch 33	Vogue	Fra	CMDGN 9853
		Vogue	Fra	DP-28
		Vogue	Fra	LD 560-30
2740	Erroll's a Garner (mx JJ-6X-100)			

	10 Inch 78	>Jazz Selection	Fra	754
	10 Inch 33	Vogue	Fra	LD 019
	12 Inch 33	Vogue	Fra	CMDGN 9853
		Vogue	Fra	DP-28
		Vogue	Fra	LD 560-30

Note: Some issues of this tune are titled "Erroll-A-Garner."

2750   Stars Fell on Alabama
       (mx JJ-6X-101)

	10 Inch 78	>Jazz Selection	Fra	754
	10 Inch 33	Vogue	Fra	LD 019

Add: John Simmons (b), Chuck Thompson (d)

2760   Laura
       (mx JJ-6X-102)

	10 Inch 78	>Jazz Selection	Fra	791
	10 Inch 33	Vogue	Fra	LD 031
	12 Inch 33	Vogue	Fra	CMDGN 9853
		Vogue	Fra	DP-28
		Vogue	Fra	LD 560-30

Note: See April, 1948 session for matrix numbers JJ-6X-103 and JJ-6X-104.

2770   Lavande (Little Girl)
       (mx JJ-6X-105)

	10 Inch 78	Music	Ity	JH1132
		Vogue	Eng	V2230
	10 Inch 33	>Modern	USA	MOD 2008
		Vogue	Fra	LD 031
	12 Inch 33	Crown	USA	CLP5003
		Crown	USA	CLP5293
		Crown	USA	CLP5408
		Crown	USA	CLP5420
		Crown	USA	CST293
		Crown	USA	CST420
		Vogue	Fra	CMDGN 9853
		Vogue	Fra	DP-28
		Vogue	Fra	LD 560-30

ERROLL GARNER TRIO   NEW YORK, ca. 1949
(RELEASED DECEMBER 11, 1949)

Erroll Garner (p), John Simmons (b), Harold "Doc" West (d)

2780   Blue Skies
       (mx D-48012)

	16 Inch TX	>U.S. Treasury Dept.		
		Guest Star Series	USA	142

2790   The Huckle Buck
       (mx D-48012)

	16 Inch TX	>U.S. Treasury Dept.		
		Guest Star Series	USA	142

ERROLL GARNER TRIO   LOS ANGELES, JUNE 20, 1949

Erroll Garner (p), John Simmons (b), Alvin Stoller (d)

2800   This Can't Be Love
       (mx BOP-4522)

	10 Inch 78	Acorn	USA	305
		>Savoy	USA	768
	7 Inch 45	Savoy	USA	45-768
	7 Inch 45EP	Ember	Eng	EP-4529
		Savoy	USA	XP-8010
	10 Inch 33	Savoy	USA	MG15002
		Savoy	Fra	255SV111
	12 Inch 33	BYG	Fra	529143
		Bellaphon	WGer	BJS4045
		Ember	Eng	EMB-3329

		Everest	USA	FS245
		Festival	Fra	166
		Galaxy	USA	4815
		Joker	Ity	SM3719
		London	Eng	LTZ-C 15126
		Quadrifoglio	Ity	VDS208
		Rondolette	USA	A15
		Savoy	USA	MG12003
		Savoy	USA	SJL2207
		Savoy	Jap	WAJ-701
		Savoy-Musidisc	Fra	6005
		Vogue	Fra	LDM 30230

2810 The Man I Love
(mx B4523)

	10 Inch 78	>Savoy	USA	765
	7 Inch 45	Savoy	USA	45-765
	7 Inch 45EP	Savoy	USA	XP-8010
	10 Inch 33	Savoy	USA	MG15002
		Savoy	Fra	255SV111
	12 Inch 33	BYG	Fra	529143
		Festival	Fra	166
		Joker	Ity	SM3719
		London	Eng	LTZ-C 15126
		Savoy	USA	MG12003
		Savoy	USA	SJL2207
		Savoy	Jap	WAJ-701
		Savoy-Musidisc	Fra	6005

2820 Moonglow
(mx BOP-4524)

	10 Inch 78	>Savoy	USA	767
	7 Inch 45	Savoy	USA	45-767
	7 Inch 45EP	Ember	Eng	EP-4553
		Savoy	USA	XP-8008
	10 Inch 33	Savoy	USA	MG15002
		Savoy	Fra	255SV111
	12 Inch 33	BYG	Fra	529143
		Bellaphon	WGer	BJS4045
		Ember	Eng	EMB-3329
		Everest	USA	FS245
		Festival	Fra	166
		Galaxy	USA	4815
		Joker	Ity	SM3719
		Koala	USA	AW14135
		London	Eng	LTZ-C 15126
		Quadrifoglio	Ity	VDS208
		Rondolette	USA	A15
		Savoy	USA	MG12003
		Savoy	USA	SJL2207
		Savoy	Jap	WAJ-701
		Savoy-Musidisc	Fra	6005
		Vogue	Fra	LDM 30230

2830 I Want a Little Girl
(mx BOP-4525)

	10 Inch 78	Acorn	USA	305
		>Savoy	USA	767
	7 Inch 45	Savoy	USA	45-767
	7 Inch 45EP	Savoy	USA	XP-8009
	10 Inch 33	Savoy	USA	MG15002
	12 Inch 33	BYG	Fra	529143
		Festival	Fra	166
		Joker	Ity	SM3719
		London	Eng	LTZ-C 15126
		Savoy	USA	MG12003

			Savoy	USA	SJL2207
			Savoy	Jap	WAJ-701
			Savoy-Musidisc	Fra	6005
2840	She's Funny That Way				
	(mx BOP-4526)				
		10 Inch 78	>Savoy	USA	768
		7 Inch 45	Savoy	USA	45-768
		7 Inch 45EP	Ember	Eng	EP-4529
			Savoy	USA	XP-8009
		10 Inch 33	Savoy	USA	MG15002
			Savoy	Fra	255SV111
		12 Inch 33	BYG	Fra	529143
			Bellaphon	WGer	BJS4045
			Ember	Eng	EMB-3329
			Eros	Eng	ERL50047
			Everest	USA	FS245
			Festival	Fra	166
			Galaxy	USA	4815
			Joker	Ity	SM3719
			Koala	USA	AW14135
			London	Eng	LTZ-C 15126
			Quadrifoglio	Ity	VDS208
			Realm	Eng	RM116
			Rondolette	USA	A15
			Savoy	USA	MG12003
			Savoy	USA	SJL2207
			Savoy	Jap	WAJ-701
			Savoy-Musidisc	Fra	6005
			Vogue	Fra	LDM 30230
2850	Until the Real Thing Comes Along				
	(mx B4527)				
		10 Inch 78	>Savoy	USA	765
		7 Inch 45	Savoy	USA	45-765
		7 Inch 45EP	Savoy	USA	XP-8011
		10 Inch 33	Savoy	USA	MG15002
			Savoy	Fra	255SV111
		12 Inch 33	BYG	Fra	529143
			Eros	Eng	ERL50047
			Festival	Fra	166
			Joker	Ity	SM3719
			London	Eng	LTZ-C 15126
			Realm	Eng	RM116
			Savoy	USA	MG12003
			Savoy	USA	SJL2207
			Savoy	Jap	WAJ-701
			Savoy-Musidisc	Fra	6005
2860	I'm Confessin' (That I Love You)				
	(mx BOP-4528)				
		10 Inch 78	>Savoy	USA	757
		7 Inch 45	Savoy	USA	45-757
		7 Inch 45EP	Savoy	USA	XP-8009
		10 Inch 33	Savoy	USA	MG15002
			Savoy	Fra	255SV111
		12 Inch 33	BYG	Fra	529143
			Bellaphon	WGer	BJS4045
			Ember	Eng	EMB-3329
			Eros	Eng	ERL50047
			Everest	USA	FS245
			Festival	Fra	166
			Galaxy	USA	4815
			Joker	Ity	SM3719
			Koala	USA	AW14135
			London	Eng	LTZ-C 15126

		Musidisc	Fra	CV1047
		Quadrifoglio	Ity	VDS208
		Realm	Eng	RM116
		Rondolette	USA	A15
		Savoy	USA	MG12003
		Savoy	USA	SJL2207
		Savoy	Jap	WAJ-701
		Savoy-Musidisc	Fra	6005
		Vogue	Fra	LDM 30230

Note: Titled "Confessin' Part I" and "Confessin' Part II" on Koala AW14135.
Most issues of this tune are titled "Confessin'."

2870   Stormy Weather (Keeps Rainin' All the Time)
       (mx BOP-4529)

10 Inch 78	>Savoy	USA	757
7 Inch 45	Savoy	USA	45-757
7 Inch 45EP	Ember	Eng	EP-4553
	Realm	Eng	REP-4006
	Savoy	USA	XP-8011
10 Inch 33	Savoy	USA	MG15002
	Savoy	Fra	255SV111
12 Inch 33	BYG	Fra	529143
	Bellaphon	WGer	BJS4045
	Ember	Eng	EMB-3329
	Eros	Eng	ERL50047
	Everest	USA	FS245
	Festival	Fra	166
	Galaxy	USA	4815
	Joker	Ity	SM3719
	Koala	USA	AW14135
	London	Eng	LTZ-C 15126
	Quadrifoglio	Ity	VDS208
	Realm	Eng	RM116
	Rondolette	USA	A15
	Savoy	USA	MG12003
	Savoy	USA	SJL2207
	Savoy	Jap	WAJ-701
	Savoy-Musidisc	Fra	6005
	Vogue	Fra	LDM 30230

Note: Titled "Stormy Weather Part I" and "Stormy Weather Part II" on Koala AW14135.

ERROLL GARNER TRIO   NEW YORK, JULY 20, 1949

Erroll Garner (p), Leonard Gaskin (b), Charlie Smith (d)

2880   Reverie
       (mx A240)

10 Inch 78	>Atlantic	USA	665
	Blue Star	Fra	220
	Esquire	Eng	10-256
7 Inch 45EP	Atlantic	USA	EP506
10 Inch 33	Atlantic	USA	LP 109
	Blue Star	Fra	BLP6812
12 Inch 33	Atlantic	USA	1227
	Atlantic	USA	SD1227
	Atlantic	Fra	332.052
	Atlantic	Fra	30014
	Atlantic	WGer	ATL 50243
	Clarion	USA	610

2890   Turquoise
       (mx A241)

10 Inch 78	>Atlantic	USA	663
	Blue Star	Fra	144
	Celson	Ity	QB7072
	Esquire	Eng	10-061

		7 Inch 45EP	Atlantic	Fra	EP232006
			Atlantic	Fra	EP232010
			Atlantic	WGer	EP80002
			Music	Ity	EPM20015
		10 Inch 33	Atlantic	USA	LP 109
			Blue Star	Fra	BLP6812
			Felsted	Eng	SDL86027
		12 Inch 33	Atlantic	USA	1227
			Atlantic	USA	SD1227
			Atlantic	Eng	590.002
			Atlantic	Fra	332.052
			Atlantic	Fra	30014
			Atlantic	WGer	ATL 50243
2900	Blue and Sentimental				
	(mx A242)				
		10 Inch 78	>Atlantic	USA	667
			Blue Star	Fra	164
			Esquire	Eng	10-266
			Le Chant du Monde	Swi	29637
		7 Inch 45	Atlantic	WGer	70003
		7 Inch 45EP	Atantic	USA	EP509
			Atlantic	Fra	EP232010
		10 Inch 33	Atlantic	USA	LP 109
			Blue Star	Fra	BLP6812
		12 Inch 33	Atlantic	USA	1227
			Atlantic	USA	SD1227
			Atlantic	Eng	590.002
			Atlantic	Fra	332.052
			Atlantic	Fra	30014
			Atlantic	WGer	ATL 50243
2910	Pavanne (The Lamp Is Low)				
	(mx A243)				
		10 Inch 78	>Atlantic	USA	667
			Blue Star	Fra	164
			Esquire	Eng	10-266
			Le Chant du Monde	Swi	29637
			Tono	Den	BZ19014
		7 Inch 45EP	Atlantic	USA	EP509
			Atlantic	Fra	EP232010
		10 Inch 33	Atlantic	USA	LP 109
			Blue Star	Fra	BLP6812
		12 Inch 33	Atlantic	USA	1227
			Atlantic	USA	SD1227
			Atlantic	Fra	332.052
			Atlantic	Fra	30014
			Atlantic	WGer	ATL 50243
			Clarion	USA	610

Note: Titled "Pavanne Mood" on Esquire 10-266 and Tono BZ19014.
This take is actually "The Lamp Is Low" which is based on Maurice Ravel's
"Pavane pour une Infante Défunte." The title "Pavanne" (a different tune) was
written by Morton Gould and adapted from Gould's "American Symphonette, No.
2," Second Movement.

2920	Flamingo				
	(mx A244)				
		10 Inch 78	>Atlantic	USA	662
			Blue Star	Fra	149
			Celson	Ity	QB7065
			Esquire	Eng	10-136
			Le Chant du Monde	Swi	29601
		7 Inch 45	Atlantic	WGer	70002
		7 Inch 45EP	Atlantic	USA	EP507
		10 Inch 33	Atlantic	USA	LP 109
			Blue Star	Fra	BLP6812

		12 Inch 33	Atlantic	USA	1227
			Atlantic	USA	SD1227
			Atlantic	Eng	590.002
			Atlantic	Fra	332.052
			Atlantic	Fra	30014
			Atlantic	WGer	ATL 50243

2930 Skylark
(mx A245)

		10 Inch 78	>Atlantic	USA	666
			Monogram	USA	180
		7 Inch 45EP	Atlantic	USA	EP506
		10 Inch 33	Atlantic	USA	LP 109
			Blue Star	Fra	BLP6812
		12 Inch 33	Atlantic	USA	1227
			Atlantic	USA	SD1227
			Atlantic	Eng	590.002
			Atlantic	Fra	332.052
			Atlantic	Fra	30014
			Atlantic	WGer	ATL 50243

2940 I Can't Give You Anything But Love
(mx A246)

		10 Inch 78	>Atlantic	USA	666
			Blue Star	Fra	149
			Celson	Ity	QB7065
			Esquire	Eng	10-136
			Le Chant du Monde	Swi	29601
			Monogram	USA	180
			Tono	Den	BZ19014
		7 Inch 45	Atlantic	WGer	70003
		7 Inch 45EP	Atlantic	USA	EP506
			Atlantic	Fra	EP232010
		10 Inch 33	Atlantic	USA	LP 109
			Blue Star	Fra	BLP6812
		12 Inch 33	Atlantic	USA	1227
			Atlantic	USA	SD1227
			Atlantic	Eng	590.002
			Atlantic	Fra	332.052
			Atlantic	Fra	30014
			Atlantic	WGer	ATL 50243

2950 Impressions (Clair de lune improvisation)
(mx A247)

		10 Inch 78	>Atlantic	USA	665
			Blue Star	Fra	220
			Celson	Ity	QB7084
			Esquire	Eng	10-256
		7 Inch 45EP	Atlantic	USA	EP80002
			Music	Ity	EPM20015
		10 Inch 33	Atlantic	USA	LP 109
			Blue Star	Fra	BLP6812
		12 Inch 33	Atlantic	USA	1227
			Atlantic	USA	SD1227
			Atlantic	Eng	590.002
			Atlantic	Fra	332.052
			Atlantic	Fra	30014
			Atlantic	WGer	ATL 50243

Note: Erroll Garner dedicated "Impressions" to Claire Stewart, wife of Slam Stewart.

2960 Twilight
(mx A248)

		10 Inch 78	>Atlantic	USA	662
		7 Inch 45EP	Atlantic	USA	EP509
		10 Inch 33	Atlantic	USA	LP 109
			Blue Star	Fra	BLP6812
		12 Inch 33	Clarion	USA	610

2970	The Way You Look Tonight (mx A249)			
	10 Inch 78	>Atlantic	USA	663
		Blue Star	Fra	144
		Celson	Ity	QB7072
		Esquire	Eng	10-061
	7 Inch 45EP	Atlantic	USA	EP506
		Atlantic	Fra	EP232006
		Atlantic	WGer	EP80002
	10 Inch 33	Atlantic	USA	LP 109
		Blue Star	Fra	BLP6812
	12 Inch 33	Atlantic	USA	1227
		Atlantic	USA	SD1227
		Atlantic	Eng	590.002
		Atlantic	Fra	332.052
		Atlantic	Fra	30014
		Atlantic	WGer	ATL 50243

ERROLL GARNER TRIO   LOS ANGELES, AUGUST, 1949

Ralph Bass, who produced this session, confirms it took place in Los Angeles. However, it does not appear feasible that the session took place in August of 1949 since Garner was appearing at the Three Deuces, New York City (see Chronology—section 2).

Erroll Garner (p), John Simmons (b), Alvin Stoller (d)

2980	On the Sunny Side of the Street (mx PO-250)			
	10 Inch 78	Hollywood	USA	8500
		>Portrait	USA	8500
		Regent	USA	8500
		Savoy	USA	772
	7 Inch 45	Savoy	USA	45-772
	7 Inch 45EP	Ember	Eng	EP-4553
		Savoy	USA	XP-8013
		Savoy-Musidisc	Fra	SA3011
	10 Inch 33	Festival	Aus	CFR10-231
		Savoy	USA	MG15004
		Savoy	Fra	255SV111
	12 Inch 33	BYG	Fra	529144
		Bellaphon	WGer	BJS4045
		Ember	Eng	EMB-3329
		Everest	USA	FS245
		Galaxy	USA	4815
		Joker	Ity	SM3718
		Koala	USA	AW14135
		Musidisc	Fra	CV1047
		Rondolette	USA	A15
		Savoy	USA	MG12008
		Savoy	USA	SJL1118
		Savoy-Musidisc	Fra	6006
		Vogue	Fra	LDM 30230
2988	Rosalie (mx PO-251-1)			Unissued
2989	Rosalie (mx PO-251-2)			Unissued
2990	Rosalie (mx PO-251-3)			
	10 Inch 78	Hollywood	USA	8501
		>Portrait	USA	8501
		Regent	USA	8501
		Savoy	USA	771
	7 Inch 45	Savoy	USA	45-771

		Savoy	USA	XP-8013
		Savoy-Musidisc	Fra	SA3011
	10 Inch 33	Festival	Aus	CFR10-231
		Savoy	USA	MG15004
	12 Inch 33	BYG	Fra	529144
		Joker	Ity	SM3718
		Musidisc	Fra	CV1047
		Savoy	USA	MG12008
		Savoy	USA	SJL1118
		Savoy-Musidisc	Fra	6006

3000 Everything Happens to Me
(mx PO-252-3)

	10 Inch 78	Hollywood	USA	8501
		>Portrait	USA	8501
		Regent	USA	8501
		Savoy	USA	772
	7 Inch 45	Savoy	USA	45-772
	7 Inch 45EP	Savoy	USA	XP-8013
	10 Inch 33	Festival	Aus	CFR10-231
		Savoy	USA	MG15004
	12 Inch 33	BYG	Fra	529144
		Festival	Fra	166
		Musidisc	Fra	CCV2521
		Savoy	USA	MG12008
		Savoy	USA	SJL1118
		Savoy-Musidisc	Fra	6006

3010 Stairway to the Stars
(mx PO-253)

	10 Inch 78	Hollywood	USA	8500
		>Portrait	USA	8500
		Regent	USA	8500
		Savoy	USA	771
	7 Inch 45	Savoy	USA	45-771
	7 Inch 45EP	Savoy	USA	XP-8013
	10 Inch 33	Festival	Aus	CFR10-231
		Savoy	USA	MG15004
	12 Inch 33	BYG	Fra	529144
		Savoy	USA	MG12008
		Savoy	USA	SJL1118
		Savoy-Musidisc	Fra	6006

JOHNNY HARTMAN   **NEW YORK, AUGUST 23, 1949**
WITH THE ERROLL GARNER TRIO
Johnny Hartman (v), Erroll Garner (p), Leonard Gaskin (b), Charlie Smith (d)
3020 Remember
      (mx 2950-1)
              10 Inch 78   >Mercury   USA 5378
3030 Easy to Remember
      (mx 2951-1)
              10 Inch 78   >Mercury   USA 8152
3040 September in the Rain
      (mx 2952-1)
              10 Inch 78   >Mercury   USA 5378
3050 Home (When Shadows Fall)
      (mx 2953-1)
              10 Inch 78   >Mercury   USA 8152

ERROLL GARNER TRIO   **NEW YORK, SEPTEMBER 8, 1949**
Erroll Garner (p), Leonard Gaskin (b), Charlie Smith (d)
3060 Scatter-Brain
      (mx 1009-a2)

	10 Inch 78	>3 Deuces	USA	508
		Roost	USA	609
		Vogue	Eng	V2107
		Vogue	Fra	V3063
	7 Inch 45EP	Vogue	Fra	SPO-17054
	10 Inch 33	Roost	USA	10
		Vogue	Eng	LDE 034
		Vogue	Fra	LD 065
	12 Inch 33	EmArcy	USA	MG36026
		Mercury	USA	MG20803
		Mercury	USA	MGW12134
		Mercury	USA	ML8015
		Mercury	USA	SR60803
		Mercury	USA	SRW16134
		Trip Jazz	USA	TLP5519
		Vogue	Fra	DP-28

3070 Through a Long and Sleepless Night
      (mx 1010-a1)

	10 Inch 78	>3 Deuces	USA	505
		Vogue	Eng	V2107
		Vogue	Fra	V3063
	10 Inch 33	Vogue	Eng	LDE 034
		Vogue	Fra	LD 065
	12 Inch 33	Mercury	USA	MG20662
		Mercury	USA	SR60662
		Mercury	Fra	135.008MCY
		Mercury	Fra	125008MCL
		Mercury	Fra	6641688
		Mercury	Neth	6336320
		Mercury	Neth	6641589

Note: 3 Deuces 505 bears a matrix number of 10010 on the label but has 1010
etched on the disc.

3080 Again
      (mx 1011-a4)

	10 Inch 78	Roost	USA	610
		>3 Deuces	USA	506
		Vogue	Fra	V3071
	7 Inch 45EP	Mercury	Fra	126046MCE
		Vogue	Fra	EPL 7022
	10 Inch 33	Roost	USA	10
		Vogue	Eng	LDE 034
		Vogue	Fra	LD 065
	12 Inch 33	Mercury	USA	MG20662
		Mercury	USA	SR60662
		Mercury	Fra	135.008MCY
		Mercury	Fra	125008MCL
		Mercury	Fra	6641688
		Mercury	Neth	6336320
		Mercury	Neth	6641589

Note: 3 Deuces 506 bears a matrix number of 10011 on the label but has 1011
etched on the disc.

3090 What Is This Thing Called Love?
      (mx 1012-a1)

	10 Inch 78	>3 Deuces	USA	505
		Roost	USA	606
		Vogue	Eng	V2086
		Vogue	Fra	V3066
	7 Inch 45EP	Vogue	Fra	126046MCE
	10 Inch 33	Roost	USA	10
		Vogue	Eng	LDE 034
		Vogue	Fra	LD 065
	12 Inch 33	Fontana	Eng	FJL103
		Fontana	Fra	683253JCL

		Fontana	Jap	SFON-7049
		Fontana	Neth	858011FPY
		Mercury	USA	MG20662
		Mercury	USA	SR60662
		Mercury	Fra	135.008MCY
		Mercury	Fra	125008MCL
		Mercury	Fra	6641688
		Mercury	Neth	6336320
		Mercury	Neth	6641589
		Vogue	Fra	DP-28

Note: Titled "This Funny Thing Called Love" on Vogue LDE 034 and "This Funny Thing That They Call Love" on Vogue V2086. 3 Deuces 505 bears a matrix number of 10012 on the label but has 1012 etched on the disc.

3100   I Let a Song Go Out of My Heart
(mx 1013-a2)

	10 Inch 78	>3 Deuces	USA	507
		Vogue	Fra	V3069
	7 Inch 45EP	Vogue	Fra	EPL 7022
	10 Inch 33	Vogue	Eng	LDE 034
		Vogue	Fra	LD 065
	12 Inch 33	EmArcy	USA	MG36026
		Mercury	USA	MGW12134
		Mercury	USA	SRW16134
		Pickwick	USA	SPC-3254
		Trip Jazz	USA	TLP5519
		Vogue	Fra	DP-28

3110   Goodbye
(mx 1014-a3)

	10 Inch 78	>3 Deuces	USA	506
		Vogue	Fra	V3069
	10 Inch 33	Vogue	Eng	LDE 034
		Vogue	Fra	LD 065

Note: 3 Deuces 506 bears a matrix number of 10014 on the label but has 1014 etched on the disc.

3120   Jitterbug Waltz
(mx 1015-a1)

	10 Inch 78	>3 Deuces	USA	507
		Vogue	Eng	V2086
		Vogue	Fra	V3066
	7 Inch 45EP	Vogue	Fra	EPL 7022
	10 Inch 33	Vogue	Eng	LDE 034
		Vogue	Fra	LD 065
	12 Inch 33	EmArcy	USA	MG36026
		Mercury	USA	MGW12134
		Mercury	USA	SRW16134
		Trip Jazz	USA	TLP5519
		Vogue	Fra	DP-28

3130   Deep Purple
(mx 1016-a2)

	10 Inch 78	>3 Deuces	USA	508
		Roost	USA	604
		Vogue	Fra	V3071
	7 Inch 45EP	EmArcy	USA	EP-1-6025
		Mercury	Eng	EP-1-6025
		Vogue	Fra	EPL 7022
	10 Inch 33	EmArcy	USA	MG26016
		Roost	USA	10
		Vogue	Eng	LDE 034
		Vogue	Fra	LD 065
	12 Inch 33	EmArcy	USA	MG36026
		Mercury	USA	MGW12134
		Mercury	USA	SRW16134
		Pickwick	USA	SPC-3254
		Trip Jazz	USA	TLP5519

ERROLL GARNER   **NEW YORK, ca. 1950**
Erroll Garner (p)
3140   Be My Love
        (mx MS-7006)
                10 Inch 78   >Futurama   USA   3006
                                  Jubilee   USA   5052
        Note: "Be My Love" is titled "Love Is the Thing Part 2" on Futurama. This
        title was previously listed as December 23-25, 1944. "Be My Love" was written
        in 1949 and introduced in the motion picture "The Toast of New Orleans" in 1950.
        Therefore, this session is dated ca. 1950.

ERROLL GARNER TRIO   **NEW YORK, APRIL 12, 1950**
Erroll Garner (p), John Simmons (b), Harold "Doc" West (d)
3150   Bonny Boy
        (mx 1252)
                10 Inch 78   >Roost   USA   609
                                  Vogue   Fra   V3141
                7 Inch 45EP   EmArcy   USA   EP-1-6025
                                  Mercury   Eng   EP-1-6025
                10 Inch 33   EmArcy   USA   MG26016
                                  Roost   USA   10
                                  Vogue   Fra   LD 076
                12 Inch 33   EmArcy   USA   MG36026
                                  Mercury   USA   MGW12134
                                  Mercury   USA   SRW16134
                                  Pickwick   USA   SPC-3254
                                  Trip Jazz   USA   TLP5519
                Note: "Bonny Boy" is another version of "Danny Boy."
3160   Tippin' Out with Erroll
        (mx 1253)
                10 Inch 78   >Roost   USA   614
                                  Vogue   Fra   V3141
                7 Inch 45EP   EmArcy   USA   EP-1-6025
                                  Mercury   Eng   EP-1-6025
                10 Inch 33   EmArcy   USA   MG26016
                                  Vogue   Fra   LD 076
                12 Inch 33   EmArcy   USA   MG36026
                                  Mercury   USA   MGW12134
                                  Mercury   USA   SRW16134
                                  Pickwick   USA   SPC-3254
                                  Trip Jazz   USA   TLP5519
3170   Relaxin' at Sugar Ray's
        (mx 1254)
                10 Inch 78   >Roost   USA   604
                                  Vogue   Fra   V3143
                7 Inch 45EP   EmArcy   USA   EP-1-6025
                                  Mercury   Eng   EP-1-6025
                10 Inch 33   EmArcy   USA   MG26016
                                  Roost   USA   10
                                  Vogue   Fra   LD 076
                12 Inch 33   EmArcy   USA   MG36026
                                  Mercury   USA   MG20803
                                  Mercury   USA   MGW12134
                                  Mercury   USA   ML8015
                                  Mercury   USA   SR60803
                                  Mercury   USA   SRW16134
                                  Pickwick   USA   SPC-3254
                                  Trip Jazz   USA   TLP5519
        Note: Titled for Sugar Ray's Tavern, which was located at 2074 Seventh Avenue
        and 124th Street in New York's Harlem section. This tavern was owned by former
        boxing champion Sugar Ray Robinson.

3180   The Quaker
        (mx 1255)
                10 Inch 78   >Roost   USA   400
                                Vogue   Fra   V3144
                10 Inch 33   Vogue   Fra   LD 076
                12 Inch 33   EmArcy   USA   MG36026
                                Mercury   USA   MGW12134
                                Mercury   USA   SRW16134
                                Pickwick   USA   SPC-3254
                                Trip Jazz   USA   TLP5519
                Note: The existence of Roost 400 has not been verified.
3190   Minor with the Trio
        (mx 1256)
                10 Inch 78   >Roost   USA   400
                                Vogue   Fra   V3142
                7 Inch 45EP   EmArcy   USA   EP-1-6026
                10 Inch 33   EmArcy   USA   MG26016
                                Vogue   Fra   LD 076
                12 Inch 33   EmArcy   USA   MG36026
                                Mercury   USA   MGW12134
                                Mercury   USA   SRW16134
                                Pickwick   USA   SPC-3254
                                Trip Jazz   USA   TLP5519
                Note: The existence of Roost 400 has not been verified.
3200   No Moon
        (mx 1257)
                10 Inch 78   >Roost   USA   606
                                Vogue   Fra   V3142
                7 Inch 45EP   EmArcy   USA   EP-1-6026
                10 Inch 33   EmArcy   USA   MG26016
                                Roost   USA   10
                                Vogue   Fra   LD 076
                12 Inch 33   EmArcy   USA   MG36026
                                Mercury   USA   MGW12134
                                Mercury   USA   SRW16134
                                Pickwick   USA   SPC-3254
                                Trip Jazz   USA   TLP5519
                *Note: "No Moon" is also titled "Young Love" in the songbook "Erroll Garner,
                Five Original Piano Solos." (Copyright 1950, Michael Goldsen, Inc.)*

3210   Cologne
        (mx 1258)
                10 Inch 78   Music   Ity   JH1132
                                >Roost   USA   610
                                Vogue   Fra   V3144
                7 Inch 45EP   EmArcy   USA   EP-1-6026
                10 Inch 33   EmArcy   USA   MG26016
                                Roost   USA   10
                                Vogue   Fra   LD 076
                12 Inch 33   EmArcy   USA   MG36026
                                Mercury   USA   MGW12134
                                Mercury   USA   SRW16134
                                Pickwick   USA   SPC-3254
                                Trip Jazz   USA   TLP5519
3220   Lazy River
        (mx 1259)
                10 Inch 78   >Roost   USA   614
                                Vogue   Fra   V3143
                7 Inch 45EP   EmArcy   USA   EP-1-6026
                7 Inch 33   Storia della Musica Ity   Vol. X, No. 9
                10 Inch 33   EmArcy   USA   MG26016
                                Vogue   Fra   LD 076
                12 Inch 33   EmArcy   USA   MG36026
                                Fontana   Eng   FJL103

Fontana	Fra	683253JCL
Fontana	Jap	SFON-7049
Fontana	Neth	858011FPY
Mercury	USA	MG20803
Mercury	USA	MGW12134
Mercury	USA	ML8015
Mercury	USA	SR60803
Mercury	USA	SRW16134
Trip Jazz	USA	TLP5519

ERROLL GARNER TRIO   NEW YORK, MAY 12, 1950

Erroll Garner (p), John Simmons (b), Harold "Doc" West (d)

3230   Lullaby of the Leaves
       (mx A420)

	10 Inch 78	>Atlantic	USA	672
		Blue Star	Fra	229
		Celson	Ity	QB7081
		Esquire	Eng	10-316
	7 Inch 45EP	Atlantic	USA	EP507
	10 Inch 33	Atlantic	USA	LP 112
		Blue Star	Fra	BLP6819
		Felsted	Eng	EDL87002
	12 Inch 33	Clarion	USA	610

3240   Margie
       (mx A421)

	10 Inch 78	>Atlantic	USA	672
		Blue Star	Fra	229
		Celson	Ity	QB7081
		Esquire	Eng	10-316
	7 Inch 45EP	Atlantic	USA	EP508
	10 Inch 33	Atlantic	USA	LP 112
		Blue Star	Fra	BLP6819
		Felsted	Eng	EDL87002

3250   Summertime
       (mx A422)

	7 Inch 45	Atlantic	WGer	70002
	7 Inch 45EP	Music	Ity	EPM20015
	10 Inch 33	>Atlantic	USA	ALR 135
		Blue Star	Fra	BLP6837
	12 Inch 33	Atlantic	USA	1227
		Atlantic	USA	SD1227
		Atlantic	Eng	590.002
		Atlantic	Fra	332.052
		Atlantic	Fra	30014
		Atlantic	WGer	ATL 50243

3260   Ramona
       (mx A423)

	10 Inch 33	>Atlantic	USA	ALR 135
		Blue Star	Fra	BLP6837

3270   Perpetual Emotion
       (mx A424)

	10 Inch 78	Blue Star	Fra	226
		CGD	Ity	QB7070
	10 Inch 33	>Atlantic	USA	ALR 135
		Blue Star	Fra	BLP6837

Note: "Perpetual Emotion" was originally titled "Erroll at the Philharmonic" on the Atlantic master log. It is also titled "Garnerology" on Blue Star. "Perpetual Emotion" is the same tune as "Margin for Erroll" (see also July 2, 1951 session).

3280   Poinciana
       (mx A425)

	7 Inch 45EP	Atlantic	USA	EP508
	10 Inch 33	>Atlantic	USA	ALR 135
		Blue Star	Fra	BLP6837

3290	The Sheik of Araby			
	(mx A426)			
	10 Inch 78	>Atlantic	USA	675
		Blue Star	Fra	217
		Esquire	Eng	10-296
	7 Inch 45EP	Atlantic	USA	EP507
	10 Inch 33	Atlantic	USA	LP 112
		Blue Star	Fra	BLP6819
		Felsted	Eng	EDL87002
3300	(There Is) No Greater Love			
	(mx A427)			
	10 Inch 78	>Atlantic	USA	673
	10 Inch 33	Atlantic	USA	LP 112
		Blue Star	Fra	BLP6819
		Felsted	Eng	EDL87002
3310	Serenade in Blue			
	(mx A428)			
	10 Inch 78	>Atlantic	USA	675
	7 Inch 45EP	Music	Ity	EPM20015
	10 Inch 33	Atlantic	USA	LP 112
		Blue Star	Fra	BLP6819
		Felsted	Eng	EDL87002
		Felsted	Eng	SDL86026
	12 Inch 33	Clarion	USA	610
3320	I'm Confessin' (That I Love You)			
	(mx A429)			
	7 Inch 45EP	Atlantic	Fra	EP232006
	12 Inch 33	>Atlantic	USA	1227
		Atlantic	USA	SD1227
		Atlantic	Eng	590.002
		Atlantic	Fra	332.052
		Atlantic	Fra	30014
		Atlantic	WGer	ATL 50243
		Harlem Hit Parade	USA	HHP-5011
3330	I'll Be Seeing You			
	(mx A430)			
	10 Inch 78	>Atlantic	USA	674
	7 Inch 45EP	Atlantic	USA	EP508
	10 Inch 33	Atlantic	USA	LP 112
		Blue Star	Fra	BLP6819
		Felsted	Eng	EDL87002
3340	Trees			
	(mx A431)			
	10 Inch 78	>Atlantic	USA	674
	7 Inch 45EP	Atlantic	USA	EP507
	10 Inch 33	Atlantic	USA	LP 112
		Blue Star	Fra	BLP6819
		Felsted	Eng	EDL87002
	12 Inch 33	Clarion	USA	610
3350	I May Be Wrong (But I Think You're Wonderful)			
	(mx A432)			
	10 Inch 78	>Atlantic	USA	673
	7 Inch 45EP	Atlantic	USA	EP509
		Atlantic	Fra	EP232006
		Atlantic	WGer	EP80002
	10 Inch 33	Atlantic	USA	LP 112
		Blue Star	Fra	BLP6819
		Felsted	Eng	EDL87002
	12 Inch 33	Atlantic	USA	1227
		Atlantic	USA	SD1227
		Atlantic	Eng	590.002
		Atlantic	Fra	332.052
		Atlantic	Fra	30014
		Atlantic	WGer	ATL 50243

3360	Futuramic			
	(mx A433)			
	10 Inch 78	Blue Star	Fra	217
		Celson	Ity	QB7084
		Esquire	Eng	10-296
	7 Inch 45EP	Atlantic	USA	EP508
	10 Inch 33	>Atlantic	USA	ALR 135
		Blue Star	Fra	BLP6837
3370	Reminiscing in Blue			
	(mx A434)			
	10 Inch 33	>Atlantic	USA	ALR 135
		Blue Star	Fra	BLP6837

FLORENCE WRIGHT   **NEW YORK, MAY 24, 1950**
Florence Wright was a member of the Kan-D-Kids with Garner in Pittsburgh
over radio station KQV.
Florence Wright (v), Erroll Garner (p), unknown (b), unknown (d)

3380	The Real Gone Tune			
	(mx NSC-605-2)			
	10 Inch 78	>National	USA	9118

ERROLL GARNER TRIO   **NEW YORK, JUNE 17, 1950**
This session is a "Bands For Bonds" radio broadcast from Birdland.
Erroll Garner (p), John Simmons (b), Rossiere "Shadow" Wilson (d)

3390	What Is This Thing Called Love?			
	12 Inch 33	>Alto	USA	AL 709
3400	No Moon			
	12 Inch 33	>Alto	USA	AL 709
3410	Scatter-Brain			
	12 Inch 33	>Alto	USA	AL 709
3420	Laura			
	12 Inch 33	>Alto	USA	AL 709

ERROLL GARNER TRIO   **NEW YORK, JUNE 28, 1950**
Erroll Garner (p), John Simmons (b), Rossiere "Shadow" Wilson (d)

3430	When Johnny Comes Marching Home			
	(mx CO 44021-1)			Unissued
3440	When Johnny Comes Marching Home			
	(mx CO 44021-2)			
	10 Inch 78	Columbia	USA	39038
		>Columbia	USA	39165
	7 Inch 45	Columbia	USA	4-39165
	7 Inch 33	Columbia	USA	3-39038
	10 Inch 33	Columbia	USA	CL6139
		Columbia	Eng	33S1050
		Columbia	Fra	FP1034
	12 Inch 33	Columbia	Ity	33QS6042
		Philips	Eur	B07559L
3450	It Could Happen to You			
	(mx CO 44022)			
	10 Inch 78	>Columbia	USA	39168
	7 Inch 45	Columbia	USA	4-39168
	10 Inch 33	Columbia	USA	CL6139
		Columbia	Eng	33S1050
		Columbia	Fra	FP1034
	12 Inch 33	Columbia	Ity	33QS6042
		Philips	Eur	B07559L
3460	I Don't Know Why (I Just Do)			
	(mx CO 44023)			

		10 Inch 78	Columbia	USA	39038
			>Columbia	USA	39168
		7 Inch 45	Columbia	USA	4-39168
		7 Inch 33	Columbia	USA	3-39038
		10 Inch 33	Columbia	USA	CL2540
			Columbia	USA	CL6139
			Columbia	Eng	33S1050
			Columbia	Fra	FP1034
		12 Inch 33	Columbia	Ity	33QS6042
			Philips	Eur	B07559L

3470 My Heart Stood Still
(mx CO 44024)

	10 Inch 78	>Columbia	USA	39165
		Columbia	USA	39249
		Columbia	Eng	DC555
		Columbia	Ity	CQ2263
		Columbia	Swi	DZ797
	7 Inch 45	Columbia	USA	4-39165
		Columbia	USA	4-39249
	7 Inch 33	Columbia	USA	3-39249
	10 Inch 33	Columbia	USA	CL6139
		Columbia	Eng	33S1050
		Columbia	Fra	FP1034
	12 Inch 33	CBS	Eng	88129
		Columbia	USA	PG33424
		Columbia	Ity	33QS6042
		Philips	Eur	B07559L

3480 When You're Smiling (The Whole World Smiles with You)
(mx CO 44025-1)   Unissued
Note: Breakdown (7 sec.)

3490 When You're Smiling (The Whole World Smiles with You)
(mx CO 44025-2)   Unissued
Note: Mitch Miller announces a breakdown (1 min., 9 sec.)

3500 When You're Smiling (The Whole World Smiles with You)
(mx CO 44025-3)   Unissued
Note: Third take complete (3 min., 35 sec.)

3510 When You're Smiling (The Whole World Smiles with You)
(mx CO 44025-4)

	10 Inch 78	>Columbia	USA	39167
		Columbia	Jap	M-745
	7 Inch 45	Columbia	USA	4-39167
	10 Inch 33	Columbia	USA	CL6139
		Columbia	Eng	33S1050
		Columbia	Fra	FP1034
	12 Inch 33	CBS	Fra	84267
		Columbia	Ity	33QS6042
		Encore	USA	P14386
		Philips	Eur	B07559L

3520 Long Ago (And Far Away) (piano solo)
(mx CO 44026)

	10 Inch 78	Columbia	USA	39166
	7 Inch 45	Columbia	USA	4-39166
	10 Inch 33	Columbia	USA	CL6139
		Columbia	Eng	33S1050
		Columbia	Fra	FP1034
	12 Inch 33	Columbia	Ity	33QS6042
		Philips	Eng	BBL7426
		Philips	Eur	B47011L

3530 Poor Butterfly
(mx CO 44027-1)   Unissued
Note: Breakdown (19 sec.)

3540 Poor Butterfly
(mx CO 44027-2)   Unissued
*Note: Second take complete (2 min., 59 sec.) Unidentified voice is heard saying
"Do it again."*

3550	Poor Butterfly (mx CO 44027-3)			
	10 Inch 78	Columbia	USA	39145
		>Columbia	USA	39166
		Columbia	Eng	DC615
		Columbia	Ity	CQ2658
		Columbia	WGer	DW5278
	7 Inch 45	Columbia	USA	4-39145
		Columbia	USA	4-39166
	7 Inch 45EP	Columbia	Eng	SEG7510
		Columbia	Ity	SEDQ521
	7 Inch 33	Columbia	USA	3-39145
	10 Inch 33	Columbia	USA	CL6139
		Columbia	Eng	33S1050
		Columbia	Fra	FP1034
	12 Inch 33	CBS	Eng	88129
		CBS	Fra	52566
		CBS	WGer	S66244
		Columbia	USA	PG33424
		Columbia	Ity	33QS6042
		Harmony	USA	HS11268
		Philips	Eur	B07559L
		Realistic	USA	P13230

3560   Spring Is Here
       (mx CO 44028-1)   Unissued
       Note: Take aborted because papers fell in studio (50 sec.).
3570   Spring Is Here
       (mx CO 44028-2)   Unissued
       Note: Breakdown (4 sec.).
3580   Spring Is Here
       (mx CO 44028-3)   Unissued
       Note: Breakdown (3 sec.).
3590   Spring Is Here
       (mx CO 44028-4)   Unissued
       Note: Fourth take complete (2 min., 28 sec.) A voice identified as Erroll Garner's is heard saying "Let's do it over again."
3600   Spring Is Here
       (mx CO 44028-5)   Unissued
       Note: Breakdown (3 sec.).
3610   Spring Is Here
       (mx CO 44028-6)

	10 Inch 78	>Columbia	USA	39167
	7 Inch 45	Columbia	USA	4-39167
	10 Inch 33	Columbia	USA	CL6139
		Columbia	Eng	33S1050
		Columbia	Fra	FP1034
	12 Inch 33	CBS	Fra	84267
		Columbia	Ity	33QS6042
		Encore	USA	P14386
		Philips	Eur	B07559L

Note: "Spring Is Here" (mx CO 44028-1/2/3/4/5/6) are piano solos.

ERROLL GARNER TRIO   **NEW YORK, OCTOBER 7, 1950**
Columbia files show the date of this session to be Saturday, October 7, 1950.
The original studio disc jacket bears the date of Friday, October 20, 1950
which is crossed out and replaced with October 7, 1950.
Erroll Garner (p), John Simmons (b), Rossiere "Shadow" Wilson (d)

3620   The Petite Waltz
       (mx CO 44422)

	10 Inch 78	>Columbia	USA	39043
	7 Inch 45	Columbia	USA	4-39043
	7 Inch 45EP	Columbia	USA	B-2040

		7 Inch 33	Columbia	USA	3-39043
		12 Inch 33	CBS	Fra	62221
			Columbia	USA	CL667
3630	The Petite Waltz Bounce (mx CO 44423)				
		10 Inch 78	>Columbia	USA	39043
		7 Inch 45	Columbia	USA	4-39043
		7 Inch 45EP	Columbia	USA	B-2040
			Philips	Eng	BBE12084
			Philips	Eur	429163BE
		7 Inch 33	Columbia	USA	3-39043
		10 Inch 33	Philips	Eur	P07800R
		12 Inch 33	CBS	Fra	62221
			Columbia	USA	CL667
3640	Lover (mx CO 44424)				
		10 Inch 78	>Columbia	USA	39100
			Columbia	Eng	DC630
			Columbia	Ity	CQ2731
			Columbia	WGer	DW5278
		7 Inch 45	Columbia	USA	4-39100
		7 Inch 45EP	Columbia	Eng	SEG7510
			Columbia	Ity	SEDQ521
			Philips	Eng	BBE12429
			Philips	Eur	435145BE
		7 Inch 33	Columbia	USA	3-39100
		10 Inch 33	Columbia	Fra	FP1028
		12 Inch 33	CBS	Eng	88129
			Columbia	USA	PG33424
			Philips	Eng	BBL7426
			Philips	Eur	B47011L
			Philips	Eur	B47124L
3650	How High the Moon (mx CO 44425)				
		10 Inch 78	>Columbia	USA	39145
			Columbia	Eng	DC640
			Columbia	Ity	CQ2815
			Columbia	Jap	M-745
			Columbia	WGer	DW5260
		7 Inch 45	Columbia	USA	4-39145
		7 Inch 45EP	Columbia	USA	B-2533
			Columbia	Eng	SEG7533
			Columbia	Ity	SEDQ532
			Columbia	Jap	EM-58
			Philips	Eur	429579BE
		7 Inch 33	Columbia	USA	3-39145
		10 Inch 33	Columbia	USA	CL2540
			Columbia	Fra	FP1028
		12 Inch 33	CBS	Fra	52566
			CBS	Fra	62334
			CBS	Fra	S66309
			CBS	Neth	52706
			CBS	WGer	S66244
			Columbia	USA	CL1141
			Harmony	USA	HS11268
			Philips	Eur	B07514L
3660	People Will Say We're in Love (mx CO 44426)				
		10 Inch 78	>Columbia	USA	39100
			Columbia	WGer	DW5260
		7 Inch 45	Columbia	USA	4-39100
		7 Inch 33	Columbia	USA	3-39100
		12 Inch 33	Philips	Eng	BBL7426
			Philips	Eur	B47011L

ERROLL GARNER TRIO   **NEW YORK, JANUARY 11, 1951**
Erroll Garner (p), John Simmons (b), Rossiere "Shadow" Wilson (d)
3670   Laura
        (mx CO 45100)

	10 Inch 78	>Columbia	USA	39275
		Columbia	Den	DD663
		Columbia	Eng	DC586
		Columbia	Swi	DZ854
		Okeh	USA	6898
	7 Inch 45	Columbia	USA	4-6898
		Columbia	USA	4-39275
	7 Inch 45EP	Columbia	USA	B-777
		Columbia	USA	B-2549
		Philips	Eur	429626BE
	10 Inch 33	Columbia	USA	CL6173
		Columbia	Eng	33S1059
		Columbia	Fra	FP1035
	12 Inch 33	CBS	Eng	88129
		CBS	Fra	52566
		CBS	Fra	62914
		CBS	Fra	S66309
		CBS	Neth	21062
		CBS	Neth	52706
		CBS	WGer	S66244
		CBS-Sony	Jap	20AP1807
		Columbia	USA	CL583
		Columbia	USA	CL777
		Columbia	USA	PG33424
		Columbia	USA	XLP-36148
		Columbia	Ity	33QS6054
		Harmony	USA	HS11268
		Philips	Eng	BBL7192
		Philips	Eur	B07155L

3680   I Cover the Waterfront
        (mx CO 45101)

	10 Inch 78	>Columbia	USA	39273
	7 Inch 45	Columbia	USA	4-39273
	7 Inch 45EP	Philips	Eur	429456BE
	10 Inch 33	Columbia	USA	CL6173
		Columbia	Eng	33S1059
		Columbia	Fra	FP1035
		Philips	Eur	P07839R
	12 Inch 33	CBS	Fra	62914
		CBS	Neth	21062
		CBS-Sony	Jap	20AP1807
		Columbia	USA	CL583
		Columbia	Ity	33QS6054
		Philips	Eng	BBL7192
		Philips	Eur	B07155L

3690   Penthouse Serenade (When We're Alone)
        (mx CO 45102)

	10 Inch 78	>Columbia	USA	39276
		Columbia	Eng	DC586
		Columbia	Swi	DZ854
		Okeh	USA	6898
	7 Inch 45	Columbia	USA	4-6898
		Columbia	USA	4-39276
	7 Inch 45EP	Columbia	USA	B-2586
		Philips	Eur	429626BE
	10 Inch 33	Columbia	USA	CL6173
		Columbia	Eng	33S1059
		Columbia	Fra	FP1028
		Columbia	Fra	FP1035

		Philips	Eur	P07839R
	12 Inch 33	CBS	Fra	62914
		CBS	Neth	21062
		CBS-Sony	Jap	20AP1807
		Columbia	USA	CL583
		Columbia	Ity	33QS6054
		Columbia	Jap	PL-2043
		Philips	Eng	BBL7192
		Philips	Eur	B07155L

3700 The Way You Look Tonight
   (mx CO 45103)

	10 Inch 78	>Columbia	USA	39275
	7 Inch 45	Columbia	USA	4-39275
		Philips	Eng	45JAZ103
		Philips	Eur	362005ARF
	7 Inch 45EP	Columbia	USA	B-2586
		Philips	Eur	429579BE
	10 Inch 33	Columbia	USA	CL6173
		Columbia	Eng	33S1059
		Columbia	Fra	FP1035
		Philips	Eur	P07839R
	12 Inch 33	CBS	Eng	32260
		CBS	Fra	62914
		CBS	Fra	S66309
		CBS	Neth	21062
		CBS-Sony	Jap	20AP1807
		Columbia	USA	CL583
		Columbia	Ity	33QS6054
		Columbia	Jap	PMS68
		Columbia	Jap	YL-114
		Philips	Eng	BBL7192
		Philips	Eur	B07155L

3710 Body and Soul
   (mx CO 45104)

	10 Inch 78	>Columbia	USA	39274
	7 Inch 45	Columbia	USA	4-39274
	7 Inch 45EP	Columbia	USA	B-2549
		Philips	Eur	429456BE
	10 Inch 33	Columbia	USA	CL6173
		Columbia	Eng	33S1059
		Columbia	Fra	FP1035
		Columbia	Jap	ZL-1112
		Philips	Eur	P07839R
	12 Inch 33	CBS	Fra	62914
		CBS	Fra	S66309
		CBS	Neth	21062
		Columbia	USA	CL583
		Columbia	Ity	33QS6054
		Philips	Eng	BBL7192
		Philips	Eur	B07155L

3720 Indiana (Back Home Again in Indiana)
   (mx CO 45105)

	10 Inch 78	>Columbia	USA	39273
	7 Inch 45	Columbia	USA	4-39273
	7 Inch 45EP	Columbia	USA	B-2586
		Philips	Eur	429456BE
	10 Inch 33	Columbia	USA	CL6173
		Columbia	Eng	33S1059
		Columbia	Fra	FP1035
		Columbia	Jap	ZL-1112
		Philips	Eur	P07839R
	12 Inch 33	CBS	Fra	62914
		CBS	Fra	64947

			CBS	Fra	80245
			CBS	Fra	S67257
			CBS	Neth	21062
			Columbia	USA	CL583
			Columbia	Ity	33QS6054
			Columbia	Jap	PL-2043
			Columbia	Jap	PMS68
			Columbia	Jap	YL-114
			Philips	Eng	BBL7192
			Philips	Eur	B07155L
3730	Honeysuckle Rose				
	(mx CO 45106)				
	10 Inch 78	>Columbia		USA	39249
		Columbia		Den	DD563
		Columbia		Den	DD663
		Columbia		Eng	DC555
		Columbia		Ity	CQ2263
		Columbia		Swi	DZ797
	7 Inch 45	Columbia		USA	4-39249
	7 Inch 45EP	Columbia		USA	B-8342
		Columbia		Eng	SEG7533
		Columbia		Ity	SEDQ532
		Columbia		Jap	EM-58
		Philips		Eng	BBE12423
		Philips		Eur	429747BE
	7 Inch 33	Columbia		USA	3-39249
	12 Inch 33	CBS		Eng	88129
		CBS		Fra	62668
		CBS		Fra	S66309
		Columbia		USA	PG33424
		Philips		Eng	BBL7426
		Philips		Eur	B47011L
		Philips		Eur	B47124L
3740	I'm in the Mood for Love				
	(mx CO 45107)				
	10 Inch 78	>Columbia		USA	39274
		Columbia		Den	DD563
		Columbia		Eng	DC615
		Columbia		Ity	CQ2658
	7 Inch 45	Columbia		USA	4-39274
	7 Inch 45EP	Columbia		USA	B-2586
		Philips		Eur	429529BE
		Philips		Eur	429799BE
	10 Inch 33	Columbia		USA	CL2511
		Columbia		USA	CL6173
		Columbia		Eng	33S1059
		Columbia		Fra	FP1035
		Philips		Eur	P07839R
	12 Inch 33	CBS		Eng	32260
		CBS		Fra	62914
		CBS		Fra	S66309
		CBS		Neth	21062
		Columbia		USA	CL583
		Columbia		Ity	33QS6054
		Philips		Eng	BBL7192
		Philips		Eur	B07155L
3750	I Can't Get Started				
	(mx CO 45108)				
	7 Inch 45EP	Columbia		USA	B-1970
		Philips		Eng	BBE12047
		Philips		Eur	429112BE
	12 Inch 33	CBS		Fra	63631
		CBS		Fra	S66309

		>Columbia	USA	CL617
		Philips	Eng	BBL7034
		Philips	Eur	B07046L
3760	Play, Piano, Play			
	(mx CO 45109)			
	10 Inch 78	>Columbia	USA	39276
	7 Inch 45	Columbia	USA	4-39276
		Philips	Eur	322349BF
	7 Inch 45EP	Philips	Eng	BBE12354
		Philips	Eur	429605BE
	10 Inch 33	Columbia	USA	CL6173
		Columbia	Eng	33S1059
		Columbia	Fra	FP1035
		Philips	Eur	B07913R
		Philips	Eur	P07839R
	12 Inch 33	CBS	Fra	62914
		CBS	Neth	21062
		Columbia	USA	CL583
		Columbia	Ity	33QS6054
		Philips	Eng	BBL7192
		Philips	Eur	B07155L
3770	Undecided			
	(mx CO 45110)			
	10 Inch 78	Philips	Eur	B21560H
	7 Inch 45EP	Columbia	USA	B-1972
		Philips	Eur	429260BE
	10 Inch 33	Philips	Eur	B07748R
	12 Inch 33	CBS	Fra	63631
		CBS	Fra	S66309
		>Columbia	USA	CL617
		Philips	Eng	BBL7034
		Philips	Eur	B07046L

ERROLL GARNER   **HOLLYWOOD, FEBRUARY 7, 1951**

Erroll Garner (p)

3780	Garner in Hollywood			
	(mx K9053-1)			
	10 Inch 78	King	USA	4477
		>Recorded in		
		Hollywood	USA	124
	7 Inch 45EP	King	USA	EP252
		Parlophone	Eng	GEP8591
		Parlophone-King	Ity	KLD25015
		President	Fra	PRC349
	10 Inch 33	King	USA	LP265-17
		Vogue	Fra	LD 084
	12 Inch 33	King	USA	540
3790	Lotus Blues			
	(mx K9054-2)			
	10 Inch 78	King	USA	4477
		>Recorded in		
		Hollywood	USA	110
	10 Inch 33	King	USA	LP265-17
		Vogue	Fra	LD 084
	12 Inch 33	Festival	Fra	Album 279
		Jazz Connoisseur	Ity	JC002
3800	This Is My Beloved			
	(mx K9055-1)			
	10 Inch 78	King	USA	4478
		>Recorded in		
		Hollywood	USA	128

		7 Inch 45EP	King	USA	EP252
			Parlophone	Eng	GEP8591
			Parlophone-King	Ity	KLD25015
			President	Fra	PRC349
		10 Inch 33	King	USA	LP265-17
			Vogue	Fra	LD 084
		12 Inch 33	King	USA	540
3810	Until the Real Thing Comes Along				
	(mx K9056-1)				
		10 Inch 78	King	USA	4478
			>Recorded in		
			Hollywood	USA	124
		7 Inch 45EP	King	USA	EP252
			Parlophone	Eng	GEP8591
			Parlophone-King	Ity	KLD25015
			President	Fra	PRC349
		10 Inch 33	King	USA	LP265-17
			Vogue	Fra	LD 084
		12 Inch 33	King	USA	540
3820	Six P.M.				
	(mx K9057)				
		10 Inch 78	King	USA	4479
			>Recorded in		
			Hollywood	USA	110
			Vogue	Fra	V3118
		7 Inch 45EP	King	USA	EP252
			Parlophone	Eng	GEP8591
			Parlophone-King	Ity	KLD25015
			President	Fra	PRC349
		10 Inch 33	King	USA	LP265-17
			Vogue	Fra	LD 084
		12 Inch 33	Festival	Fra	Album 279
			Jazz Connoisseur	Ity	JC002
			King	USA	540
3830	New York Concerto				
	(mx K9058)				
		10 Inch 78	King	USA	4479
			>Recorded in		
			Hollywood	USA	128
			Vogue	Fra	V3118
		10 Inch 33	King	USA	LP265-17
			Vogue	Fra	LD 084

ERROLL GARNER TRIO   **HOLLYWOOD, JULY 2, 1951**

Erroll Garner (p), John Simmons (b), Rossiere "Shadow" Wilson (d)

3840	You're Blasé				
	(mx RHCO4532)				
		12 Inch 33	CBS	Eng	88129
			>Columbia	USA	CL1587
			Columbia	USA	PG33424
			Philips	Eur	B47081L
3850	Sophisticated Lady				
	(mx RHCO4533)				
		10 Inch 78	>Columbia	USA	39615
			Columbia	Eng	DC640
			Columbia	Ity	CQ2815
			Columbia	WGer	DW5298
		7 Inch 45	Columbia	USA	4-39615
		7 Inch 45EP	Columbia	Eng	SEG7510
			Columbia	Ity	SEDQ521
			Philips	Eur	429626BE

		10 Inch 33	Columbia	USA	CL2540
			Columbia	Fra	FP1028
		12 Inch 33	CBS	Fra	62334
			Columbia	USA	CL1141
			Philips	Eur	B07514L
3860	Ain't She Sweet?				
	(mx RHCO4534)				
		10 Inch 78	>Columbia	USA	39681
			Columbia	Den	DD575
		7 Inch 45	Columbia	USA	4-39681
		7 Inch 45EP	Philips	Eng	BBE12429
			Philips	Eur	435145BE
		12 Inch 33	CBS	Eng	88129
			CBS	Fra	62668
			Columbia	USA	PG33424
			Philips	Eng	BBL7426
			Philips	Eur	B47011L
			Philips	Eur	B47124L
3870	Margin for Erroll				
	(mx RHCO4535)				
		12 Inch 33	>Columbia	USA	CL1587
			Philips	Eng	BBL7426
			Philips	Eur	B47011L
			Philips	Eur	B47081L

Note: "Margin for Erroll" (Erroll Garner) is titled "I Didn't Know" on Philips BBL7426 and "I Don't Know" on Philips B47011L.

3880	Fine and Dandy				
	(mx RHCO4536)				
		10 Inch 78	>Columbia	USA	39615
			Columbia	Eng	DC630
			Columbia	Ity	CQ2731
			Columbia	WGer	DW5298
		7 Inch 45	Columbia	USA	4-39615
		7 Inch 45EP	Columbia	USA	B-2549
			Columbia	USA	B-8342
			Columbia	Eng	SEG7510
			Columbia	Ity	SEDQ521
			Philips	Eng	BBE12429
			Philips	Eur	435145BE
		10 Inch 33	Columbia	Fra	FP1028
		12 Inch 33	CBS	Fra	62668
			Philips	Eng	BBL7426
			Philips	Eur	B47011L
			Philips	Eur	B47124L
3890	Robbins' Nest				
	(mx RHCO4537)				
		10 Inch 78	>Columbia	USA	39580
			Columbia	Den	D578
			Columbia	Eng	DC595
			Columbia	Fra	BF488
			Columbia	Swi	DZ856
			Okeh	USA	6821
		7 Inch 45	Columbia	USA	4-39580
		7 Inch 45EP	Columbia	USA	B-2533
			Philips	Eng	BBE12354
			Philips	Eur	429605BE
		7 Inch 33	Columbia	USA	3-39580
		10 Inch 33	Columbia	USA	CL2540
			Columbia	Fra	FP1034
		12 Inch 33	CBS	Fra	62334
			Columbia	USA	CL1141
			Philips	Eur	B07514L

Note: "Robbins' Nest" refers to disc jockey, Fred Robbins.

3900   Please Don't Talk About Me When I'm Gone
       (mx RHCO4538)
              10 Inch 78   >Columbia   USA   39681
                                Columbia   Den   DD575
                                Columbia   Eng   DC595
              7 Inch 45   Columbia   USA   4-39681
3910   It's the Talk of the Town
       (mx RHCO4539)
              10 Inch 78   >Columbia   USA   39580
                                Columbia   Den   DD578
                                Columbia   Eng   DC606
                                Columbia   Fra   BF488
                                Columbia   Swi   DZ856
                                Okeh   USA   6821
              7 Inch 45   Columbia   USA   4-39580
              7 Inch 45EP   Columbia   USA   B-2040
              7 Inch 33   Columbia   USA   3-39580
              10 Inch 33   Columbia   Fra   FP1028
              12 Inch 33   CBS   Fra   62221
                                CBS   WGer   S66244
                                Columbia   USA   CB-14
                                Columbia   USA   CB-18
                                Columbia   USA   CL667
                                Philips   Eur   B07559L

ERROLL GARNER TRIO   **NEW YORK, JANUARY 3, 1952**
Erroll Garner (p), John Simmons (b), Rossiere "Shadow" Wilson (d)
3920   You're Driving Me Crazy (What Did I Do?)
       (mx CO 47289)
              10 Inch 78   >Columbia   USA   40172
                                Philips   Eur   B21238H
              7 Inch 45   Columbia   USA   4-40172
              7 Inch 45EP   Columbia   USA   B-8341
                                Philips   Eng   BBE12003
                                Philips   Eur   429009BE
              12 Inch 33   CBS   Eng   88129
                                CBS   Fra   62668
                                Columbia   USA   PG33424
3930   Ja-Da
       (mx CO 47290)
              10 Inch 78   >Columbia   USA   39713
                                Columbia   Den   DD579
                                Columbia   Eng   DC606
              7 Inch 45   Columbia   USA   4-39713
              7 Inch 45EP   Philips   Eur   429799BE
              10 Inch 33   Columbia   Fra   FP1028
              12 Inch 33   CBS   Fra   62668
3940   Summertime
       (mx CO 47291)
              10 Inch 78   >Columbia   USA   39888
                                Columbia   Eng   DC654
              7 Inch 45   Columbia   USA   4-39888
              7 Inch 45EP   Columbia   Eng   SEG7533
                                Columbia   Ity   SEDQ532
                                Columbia   Jap   EM-58
                                Philips   Eng   BBE12423
                                Philips   Eur   429747BE
              12 Inch 33   CBS   Eng   32260
                                CBS   Eng   88129
                                CBS   Fra   62668
                                CBS   Fra   S66309

		Columbia	USA	CZ-1
		Columbia	USA	PG33424
		Philips	Eng	BBL7426
		Philips	Eur	B47011L
		Philips	Eur	B47124L

3950 I Never Knew
(mx CO 47292)

	10 Inch 78	Philips	Eur	B21005H
		>Columbia	USA	39918
	7 Inch 45	Columbia	USA	4-39918
	7 Inch 45EP	Columbia	USA	B-8341
		Philips	Eng	BBE12429
		Philips	Eur	435145BE
	12 Inch 33	CBS	Eng	88129
		CBS	Fra	62668
		Columbia	USA	PG33424
		Philips	Eng	BBL7426
		Philips	Eur	B47011L
		Philips	Eur	B47124L

Note: On some issues "I Never Knew" is incorrectly titled "I Never Knew I Could Love Anybody (Like I'm Loving You)."

3960 Oh, Lady Be Good!
(mx CO 47293)

	10 Inch 78	>Columbia	USA	39713
		Columbia	Den	DD579
	7 Inch 45	Columbia	USA	4-39713
	7 Inch 45EP	Columbia	USA	B-2549
		Columbia	Eng	SEG7533
		Columbia	Ity	SEDQ532
		Columbia	Jap	EM-58
		Philips	Eur	429529BE
	10 Inch 33	Columbia	Jap	ZL-1112
		Philips	Eur	P07839R
	12 Inch 33	CBS	Fra	62914
		CBS	Neth	21062
		Columbia	USA	CL583
		Columbia	Jap	PL-2043
		Philips	Eng	BBL7192
		Philips	Eur	B07155L

3970 Am I Blue?
(mx CO 47294)

	10 Inch 78	>Columbia	USA	39918
		Philips	Eur	B21005H
	7 Inch 45	Columbia	USA	4-39918
	10 Inch 33	Columbia	USA	CL2540
	12 Inch 33	CBS	Eng	88129
		Columbia	USA	PG33424

3980 Out of Nowhere
(mx CO 47295)

	10 Inch 78	>Columbia	USA	39734
		Columbia	Den	SGD 3
		Columbia	Eng	DC600
		Columbia	WGer	DW5244
	7 Inch 45	Columbia	USA	4-39734
	7 Inch 45EP	Columbia	USA	B-2040
	10 Inch 33	Columbia	Fra	FP1028
	12 Inch 33	CBS	Fra	62221
		CBS	Fra	S66309
		CBS	WGer	S66244
		Columbia	USA	CL667
		Columbia	USA	KL5136
		Philips	Eur	B07559L

3990   Music, Maestro, Please!
       (mx CO 47296)
             10 Inch 78   >Columbia   USA   39734
                           Columbia   Den   SGD 3
                           Columbia   Eng   DC600
                           Columbia   WGer   DW5244
             7 Inch 45   Columbia   USA   4-39734
             7 Inch 45EP   Philips   Eng   BBE12423
                           Philips   Eur   429747BE
             10 Inch 33   Columbia   Fra   FP1028
             12 Inch 33   CBS   Eng   88129
                           Columbia   USA   PG33424
                           Philips   Eng   BBL7426
                           Philips   Eur   B47011L
                           Philips   Eur   B47124L
4000   Once in a While
       (mx CO 47297)
             7 Inch 45EP   Columbia   USA   B-1971
                           Philips   Eur   429752BE
             12 Inch 33   CBS   Fra   63631
                           >Columbia   USA   CL617
                           Philips   Eng   BBL7034
                           Philips   Eur   B47037L
                           Philips   Neth   B07046L
4010   Bewitched
       (mx CO 47298)
             7 Inch 45EP   Columbia   USA   B-1971
                           Philips   Eur   429260BE
             12 Inch 33   CBS   Fra   63631
                           >Columbia   USA   CL617
                           Philips   Eng   BBL7034
                           Philips   Eur   B07078L
                           Philips   Eur   B07046L

ERROLL GARNER   **NEW YORK, FEBRUARY 29, 1952**
Erroll Garner (p)
4020   What's New?
       (mx CO 47354)
             10 Inch 78   >Columbia   USA   39888
                           Columbia   Eng   DC654
                           Columbia   Ity   CQ2776
             7 Inch 45   Columbia   USA   4-39888
4030   Chopin Impressions
       (mx CO 47355)
             7 Inch 45   >Columbia   USA   4-39748
             7 Inch 45EP   Columbia   USA   5-1263
             10 Inch 33   Columbia   USA   CL6209
                           Philips   Eng   BBR8045
                           Philips   Eur   B07602R
4040   Anything Goes
       (mx CO 47356)
             7 Inch 45EP   >Columbia   USA   B-1972
             12 Inch 33   CBS   Fra   63631
                           CBS   Fra   84267
                           Columbia   USA   CL617
                           Encore   USA   P14386
                           Philips   Eng   BBL7034
                           Philips   Eur   B07046L
                           Supraphon   Cze   0 15 2113
4050   With Every Breath I Take
       (mx CO 47357)

		7 Inch 45	>Columbia	USA	4-39749
		7 Inch 45EP	Columbia	USA	5-1263
		10 Inch 33	Columbia	USA	CL6209
			Philips	Eng	BBR8045
			Philips	Eur	B07602R
4060	Willow Me				
	(mx CO 47358)				
		7 Inch 45	>Columbia	USA	4-39747
		7 Inch 45EP	Columbia	USA	5-1263
		10 Inch 33	Columbia	USA	CL6209
			Philips	Eng	BBR8045
			Philips	Eur	B07602R
4070	Cocktails for Two				
	(mx CO 47359)				
		7 Inch 45	>Columbia	USA	4-39746
		10 Inch 33	Columbia	USA	CL6209
			Philips	Eng	BBR8045
			Philips	Eur	B07602R
4080	It Don't Mean a Thing (If It Ain't Got That Swing)				
	(mx CO 47360)				
		10 Inch 78	>Columbia	USA	47364
		7 Inch 45	Columbia	USA	4-39747
		7 Inch 45EP	Philips	Eur	429221BE
		10 Inch 33	Columbia	USA	CL6209
			Philips	Eng	BBR8045
			Philips	Eur	B07602R
4090	Love Me or Leave Me				
	(mx CO 47361)				
		7 Inch 45	>Columbia	USA	4-39749
		7 Inch 45EP	Philips	Eng	BBE12084
			Philips	Eur	429163BE
		10 Inch 33	Columbia	USA	CL6209
			Philips	Eng	BBR8045
			Philips	Eur	B07602R
4100	The Music Goes 'Round and 'Round				
	(mx CO 47362)				
		12 Inch 33	>Columbia	USA	CL1512
4110	Fancy				
	(mx CO 47363)				
		12 Inch 33	CBS	Fra	62334
			>Columbia	USA	CL1141
			Philips	Eur	B07514L

Note: "Fancy" contains excerpts of what later became "Misty" (see also July 27, 1954 session).

4120	How Come You Do Me Like You Do?				
	(mx CO 47364)				
		10 Inch 78	>Columbia	USA	47364
		7 Inch 45	Columbia	USA	4-39748
		7 Inch 45EP	Philips	Eur	429221BE
		10 Inch 33	Columbia	USA	CL6209
			Philips	Eng	BBR8045
			Philips	Eur	B07602R
4130	Dancing in the Dark				
	(mx CO 47365)				
		7 Inch 45	>Columbia	USA	4-39746
		7 Inch 45EP	Columbia	USA	5-1263
		10 Inch 33	Columbia	USA	CL6209
			Philips	Eng	BBR8045
			Philips	Eng	BBR8071
			Philips	Eur	B07602R
			Philips	Eur	B07664R
		12 Inch 33	CBS	Eng	88129
			Columbia	USA	PG33424

ERROLL GARNER TRIO   **NEW YORK, MAY 10, 1952**
This session is a radio broadcast from Birdland.
Erroll Garner (p), John Simmons (b), Rossiere "Shadow" Wilson (d)

4140	Robbins' Nest			
	12 Inch 33	>Alto	USA	AL 712
		Kings of Jazz	Ity	KLJ20020
4150	These Foolish Things (Remind Me of You)			
	12 Inch 33	>Alto	USA	AL 712
		Kings of Jazz	Ity	KLJ20000
		Kings of Jazz	Ity	KLJ20020
4160	Ain't She Sweet?			
	12 Inch 33	>Alto	USA	AL 712
		Kings of Jazz	Ity	KLJ20020
4170	Garner's Escape			
	12 Inch 33	>Alto	USA	AL 712
		Kings of Jazz	Ity	KLJ20020

Note: "Garner's Escape" is "Smooth Sailing" (Arnett Cobb).

4180	Indiana (Back Home Again in Indiana)			
	12 Inch 33	>Alto	USA	AL 712
		Kings of Jazz	Ity	KLJ20020

ERROLL GARNER TRIO   **NEW YORK, FEBRUARY 27, 1953**
Erroll Garner (p), Wyatt Ruther (b), Eugene "Fats" Heard (d)

4190	Dancing Tambourine			
	(mx CO 48885)			
	7 Inch 45	Philips	Eur	322217BF
	10 Inch 33	Philips	Eur	B07910R
		Philips	Eur	B13201R
	12 Inch 33	>Columbia	USA	CL1452
		Philips	Eur	B47037L
4200	Memories of You			
	(mx CO 48886)			
	7 Inch 45EP	Columbia	USA	B-1678
		Philips	Eng	BBE12047
		Philips	Eur	429112BE
	12 Inch 33	Avan-Guard	Aus	BVL040
		CBS	Fra	62311
		CBS	Neth	68219
		>Columbia	USA	CL535
		Philips	Eng	BBL7078
		Philips	Eng	BBL7448
		Philips	Eur	B07015L
		Sony	Jap	SOPU-91
4210	'S Wonderful			
	(mx CO 48887)			
	7 Inch 45EP	Columbia	USA	B-1972
		Philips	Eur	429579BE
	12 Inch 33	CBS	Eng	32260
		CBS	Fra	63631
		CBS	Fra	S66309
		>Columbia	USA	CL617
		Philips	Eng	BBL7034
		Philips	Eur	B07046L
4220	(There Is) No Greater Love			
	(mx CO 48888)			
	7 Inch 45EP	Columbia	USA	B-1656
		Philips	Eur	429792BE
	12 Inch 33	Avan-Guard	Aus	BVL040
		CBS	Fra	62311
		CBS	Neth	68219
		>Columbia	USA	CL535

			Philips	Eng	BBL7078
			Philips	Eng	BBL7448
			Philips	Eur	B07015L
			Sony	Jap	SOPU-91

4230 Look, Ma—All Hands!
      (mx CO 48889)
              12 Inch 33   >Columbia   USA   CL1587
                                Philips   Eur   B47081L

      Note: "Look, Ma—All Hands!" is the same tune as "7-11 Jump" (see also July 27, 1954 session).

4240 Can't Help Lovin' Dat Man
      (mx CO 48890)
              7 Inch 45EP   Columbia   USA   B-1741
                                Philips   Eng   BBE12065
                                Philips   Eur   429005BE
              10 Inch 33   Columbia   USA   CL6259
                                Philips   Eng   BBR8002
                                Philips   Eur   B07622R
              12 Inch 33   CBS   Eng   88129
                                CBS   Fra   62221
                                CBS   WGer S66244
                               >Columbia   USA   CL667
                                Columbia   USA   PG33424

4250 Caravan
      (mx CO 48891)
              7 Inch 45EP   CBS   Fra   EP 5864
                                Columbia   USA   B-1656
                                Philips   Eur   429792BE
              12 Inch 33   Avan-Guard   Aus   BVL040
                                CBS   Fra   62311
                                CBS   Fra   S66309
                                CBS   Neth 68219
                               >Columbia   USA   CL535
                                Philips   Eng   BBL7078
                                Philips   Eng   BBL7448
                                Philips   Eur   B07015L
                                Sony   Jap   SOPU-91

4260 Lullaby of Birdland
      (mx CO 48892)
              7 Inch 45EP   CBS   Fra   EP 5864
                                Columbia   USA   B-2533
              12 Inch 33   Avan-Guard   Aus   BVL040
                                CBS   Fra   62311
                                CBS   Fra   S66309
                                CBS   Neth 68219
                               >Columbia   USA   CL535
                                Philips   Eng   BBL7078
                                Philips   Eng   BBL7448
                                Philips   Eur   B07015L
                                Sony   Jap   SOPU-91

4270 Cheek to Cheek
      (mx CO 48893)
              7 Inch 45   Philips   Eng   45JAZ103
                                Philips   Eur   362005ARF
              7 Inch 45EP   Columbia   USA   B-1700
                                Philips   Eur   429260BE
              10 Inch 33   Columbia   USA   CL6259
                                Columbia   Jap   ZL-1112
                                Philips   Eng   BBR8002
                                Philips   Eur   B07622R
                                Philips   Eur   P07800R
              12 Inch 33   CBS   Fra   62221
                                CBS   Fra   S66309

			CBS	WGer	S66244
			>Columbia	USA	CL667
			Columbia	USA	KL5142
4280	Once in a While				
	(mx CO 48894)				
		12 Inch 33	>Columbia	USA	CL1452
4290	Will You Still Be Mine?				
	(mx CO 48895)				
		12 Inch 33	Avan-Guard	Aus	BVL040
			CBS	Fra	62311
			CBS	Fra	84267
			CBS	Neth	68219
			Encore	USA	P14386
			Philips	Eng	BBL7078
			>Columbia	USA	CL535
			Philips	Eng	BBL7448
			Philips	Eur	B07015L
			Sony	Jap	SOPU-91
4300	Blue Ecstasy				
	(mx CO 48896)				
		12 Inch 33	>Columbia	USA	CL1587
			Philips	Eur	B47081L

Note: The vocal version of "Blue Ecstasy" is titled "The I'm Not Supposed to Be Blue Blues" (Erroll Garner/Robert Russell), recorded by Teddi King with the Al Cohn Orchestra. It is also titled "The Loving Touch" on Mercury (see also November 7, 1969 session).

4310	Avalon				
	(mx CO 48897)				
		7 Inch 45EP	Philips	Eur	429221BE
		12 Inch 33	Avan-Guard	Aus	BVL040
			CBS	Eng	88129
			CBS	Fra	62311
			CBS	Fra	84267
			CBS	Neth	68219
			>Columbia	USA	CL535
			Columbia	USA	PG33424
			Encore	USA	P14386
			Philips	Eng	BBL7078
			Philips	Eng	BBL7448
			Philips	Eur	B07015L
			Sony	Jap	SOPU-91

ERROLL GARNER TRIO   **NEW YORK, MARCH 30, 1953**
Erroll Garner (p), Wyatt Ruther (b), Eugene "Fats" Heard (d)

4320	Lullaby in Rhythm				
	(mx CO 49113)				
		10 Inch 78	Philips	Eur	B21560H
		7 Inch 45EP	Columbia	USA	B-1971
			Philips	Eng	BBE12047
			Philips	Eur	429112BE
		12 Inch 33	CBS	Fra	63631
			CBS	Fra	S66309
			>Columbia	USA	CL617
			Philips	Eng	BBL7034
			Philips	Eur	B07046L
4330	St. Louis Blues				
	(mx CO 49114)				
		10 Inch 78	>Columbia	USA	40043
			Philips	Eur	B21103H
		7 Inch 45	Columbia	USA	4-40043

		7 Inch 45EP	Columbia	USA	B-8342
			Philips	Eng	BBE12084
			Philips	Eur	429163BE
		12 Inch 33	CBS	Eng	88129
			CBS	Eng	32260
			CBS	Fra	62668
			CBS	Fra	S66309
			Columbia	USA	PG33424
4340	My Ideal				
	(mx CO 49115)				
		10 Inch 78	>Columbia	USA	40043
			Philips	Eur	B21103H
		7 Inch 45	Columbia	USA	4-40043
		7 Inch 45EP	Columbia	USA	B-8341
		12 Inch 33	CBS	Fra	62668
4350	Stompin' at the Savoy				
	(mx CO 49116)				
		7 Inch 45EP	Columbia	USA	B-1700
		10 Inch 33	Columbia	USA	CL6259
			Columbia	Jap	ZL-33
			Columbia	Jap	ZL-1112
			Philips	Eng	BBR8002
			Philips	Eng	BBR8089
			Philips	Eur	B07622R
			Philips	Eur	B07718R
			Philips	Eur	B07735R
			Philips	Fra	D99556R
		12 Inch 33	CBS	Fra	62221
			CBS	Fra	S66309
			CBS	WGer	S66244
			>Columbia	USA	CL667
			Columbia	Jap	PMS68
			Columbia	Jap	YL-114
4360	Sweet Sue-Just You				
	(mx CO 49117)				
		7 Inch 45	Philips	Eur	322349BF
		7 Inch 45EP	Columbia	USA	B-1741
			Philips	Eng	BBE12065
			Philips	Eur	429005BE
		10 Inch 33	Columbia	USA	CL6259
			Columbia	Jap	ZL-1112
			Philips	Eng	BBR8002
			Philips	Eng	BBR8098
			Philips	Eur	B07622R
			Philips	Eur	B07718R
			Philips	Eur	P07800R
		12 Inch 33	CBS	Fra	52566
			CBS	Fra	62221
			CBS	Neth	52706
			CBS	WGer	S66244
			>Columbia	USA	CL667
			Harmony	USA	HS11268
4370	Easy to Love				
	(mx CO 49118)				
		10 Inch 78	>Columbia	USA	39996
			Columbia	USA	50094
			Philips	Eur	B21117H
			Philips	Eng	PB250
		7 Inch 45	Columbia	USA	4-39996
			Columbia	USA	4-50094
			Philips	Eng	45JAZ105
			Philips	Eur	362011ARF

		7 Inch 45EP	Philips	Eur	429529BE
			Philips	Eur	430504BE
		10 Inch 33	Columbia	Jap	ZL-1112
			Philips	Eur	P07839R
		12 Inch 33	CBS	Eng	32260
			CBS	Eng	88129
			CBS	Fra	62914
			CBS	Fra	S66309
			CBS	Neth	21062
			Columbia	USA	CL583
			Columbia	USA	PG33424
			Columbia	Jap	PL-2043
			Columbia	Jap	PMS68
			Columbia	Jap	YL-114
			Philips	Eng	BBL7192
			Philips	Eur	B07155L
4380	Mean to Me				
	(mx CO 49119)				
		10 Inch 78	>Columbia	USA	40074
		7 Inch 45	Columbia	USA	4-40074
		7 Inch 45EP	Philips	Eur	429456BE
		10 Inch 33	Philips	Eur	P07839R
		12 Inch 33	CBS	Eng	88129
			CBS	Fra	62914
			CBS	Neth	21062
			Columbia	USA	CL583
			Columbia	USA	PG33424
			Philips	Eng	BBL7192
			Philips	Eur	B07155L
4390	I've Got My Love to Keep Me Warm				
	(mx CO 49120)				
		7 Inch 45EP	Columbia	USA	B-1700
		10 Inch 33	Columbia	USA	CL6259
			Philips	Eng	BBR8002
			Philips	Eur	B07622R
			Philips	Eur	P07800R
		12 Inch 33	CBS	Fra	62221
			CBS	Fra	84267
			>Columbia	USA	CL667
			Columbia	Jap	PL-2043
			Encore	USA	P14386
4400	Love for Sale				
	(mx CO 49121)				
		7 Inch 45EP	Columbia	USA	B-8341
		12 Inch 33	CBS	Eng	88129
			CBS	Fra	62668
			CBS	Fra	S66309
			>Columbia	USA	CL1587
			Columbia	USA	PG33424
			Philips	Eur	B47081L
4410	Yesterdays				
	(mx CO 49122)				
		7 Inch 45EP	Columbia	USA	B-1970
			Philips	Eur	429221BE
		12 Inch 33	CBS	Fra	63631
			>Columbia	USA	CL617
			Philips	Eng	BBL7034
			Philips	Eur	B07046L
4420	Frenesi (Cancion Tropical)				
	(mx CO 49123)				
		10 Inch 78	>Columbia	USA	40074
		7 Inch 45	Columbia	USA	4-40074

	7 Inch 45EP	Philips	Eur	429529BE
	10 Inch 33	Columbia	Jap	ZL-1112
	12 Inch 33	CBS	Fra	62914
		CBS	Neth	21062
		Columbia	USA	CL583
		Columbia	Jap	PL-2043
		Philips	Eng	BBL7192
		Philips	Eur	B07155L

4430 Oh, What a Beautiful Mornin'
(mx CO 49124)

	10 Inch 78	>Columbia	USA	40172
		Philips	Eur	B21238H
	7 Inch 45	Columbia	USA	4-40172
	7 Inch 45EP	Philips	Eng	BBE12423
		Philips	Eur	429747BE
	12 Inch 33	CBS	Fra	62668
		Philips	Eng	BBL7426
		Philips	Eur	B47011L
		Philips	Eur	B47124L

4440 Groovy Day
(mx CO 49125)

	7 Inch 45EP	Columbia	USA	B-8342
		Philips	Eng	BBE12354
		Philips	Eur	429605BE
	10 Inch 33	Philips	Eur	B07910R
	12 Inch 33	CBS	Fra	62334
		CBS	Fra	62668
		>Columbia	USA	CL1141
		Philips	Eur	B07514L

Note: "Groovy Day" (Erroll Garner) is the same tune as "Left Bank Swing" (see also March 27, 1958 session).

4450 Please Don't Talk About Me When I'm Gone
(mx CO 49126)

	7 Inch 45EP	Columbia	USA	B-!741
		Philips	Eng	BBE12065
		Philips	Eur	429005BE
		Philips	Eur	430504BE
	10 Inch 33	Columbia	USA	CL6259
		Philips	Eng	BBR8002
		Philips	Eur	B07622R
	12 Inch 33	CBS	Fra	62221
		CBS	WGer	S66244
		>Columbia	USA	CL667

4460 For Heaven's Sake
(mx CO 49127)

	7 Inch 45EP	Columbia	USA	5-1795
		Columbia	USA	B-365
		Columbia	USA	B-1970
	12 Inch 33	CBS	Fra	63631
		Columbia	USA	CL543
		>Columbia	USA	CL617
		Philips	Eng	BBL7034
		Philips	Eur	B07046L

4470 Lullaby of Birdland
(mx CO 49128)

	10 Inch 78	>Columbia	USA	39996
		Columbia	USA	50094
		Philips	Eng	PB250
		Philips	Eur	B21117H
	7 Inch 45	Columbia	USA	4-39996
		Columbia	USA	4-50094
		Philips	Eng	45JAZ105
		Philips	Eur	362011ARF

		7 Inch 45EP	Columbia	USA	B-1678
			Philips	Eng	BBE12084
			Philips	Eur	429163BE
			Philips	Eur	429626BE
		10 Inch 33	Columbia	USA	CL2540
			Philips	Eng	BBR8048
			Philips	Eur	B07646R
			Philips	Eur	B07913R
4480	Holiday for Strings				
	(mx CO 49129)				
		12 Inch 33	>Columbia	USA	CL1587
			Philips	Eur	B47081L

ERROLL GARNER TRIO   **DETROIT, JULY 8, 1954**
WITH WOODY HERMAN
The first four titles of this session are played as a medley.
Erroll Garner (p), Wyatt Ruther (b), Eugene "Fats" Heard (d), Woody Herman (v)

4490	Let's Fall in Love				
	(mx ZEP35057)	12 Inch 33	>Columbia	USA	CL651
			Philips	Eng	BBL7056
			Philips	Eur	B07082L
4500	Moonglow				
	(mx ZEP35057)	12 Inch 33	>Columbia	USA	CL651
			Philips	Eng	BBL7056
			Philips	Eur	B07082L
4510	I Don't Know Why (I Just Do)				
	(mx ZEP35058)	12 Inch 33	>Columbia	USA	CL651
			Philips	Eng	BBL7056
			Philips	Eur	B07082L
4520	You've Got Me Crying Again				
	(mx ZEP35058)	12 Inch 33	>Columbia	USA	CL651
			Philips	Eng	BBL7056
			Philips	Eur	B07082L
4530	I'm Beginning to See the Light				
	(mx ZEP35058)	7 Inch 45EP	Philips	Eur	429392BE
		12 Inch 33	>Columbia	USA	CL651
			Philips	Eng	BBL7056
			Philips	Eur	B07082L
4540	My Melancholy Baby				
	(mx ZEP35059)	7 Inch 45EP	Columbia	USA	B-2012
		12 Inch 33	>Columbia	USA	CL651
			Philips	Eng	BBL7056
			Philips	Eur	B07082L
4550	I Hadn't Anyone 'Till You				
	(mx ZEP35060)	7 Inch 45EP	Columbia	USA	B-2012
		12 Inch 33	>Columbia	USA	CL651
			Philips	Eng	BBL7056
			Philips	Eur	B07082L
4560	After You've Gone				
	(mx ZEP35060)	7 Inch 45EP	Columbia	USA	B-2012
			Philips	Eur	429392BE

		12 Inch 33	>Columbia	USA	CL651
			Philips	Eng	BBL7056
			Philips	Eur	B07082L
4570	I'll See You in My Dreams				
	(mx ZEP35061)				
		12 Inch 33	CBS	Fra	52566
			CBS	Neth	52706
			CBS	WGer	S66244
			>Columbia	USA	CL651
			Harmony	USA	HS11268
			Philips	Eng	BBL7056
			Philips	Eur	B07082L

4580 If I Could Be with You (One Hour Tonight)
      (mx ZEP35061)

		7 Inch 45EP	Philips	Eur	429392BE
		12 Inch 33	>Columbia	USA	CL651
			Philips	Eng	BBL7056
			Philips	Eur	B07082L

4590 As Time Goes By
      (mx ZEP35062)

		7 Inch 45EP	Philips	Eur	429392BE
		12 Inch 33	>Columbia	USA	CL651
			Philips	Eng	BBL7056
			Philips	Eur	B07082L

ERROLL GARNER QUARTET   CHICAGO, JULY 27, 1954

Asterisk (*) denotes Candido Camero on conga drums.
Erroll Garner (p), Wyatt Ruther (b), Eugene "Fats" Heard (d), Candido Camero
(cd)*

4600 That Old Black Magic*
      (mx y 10832-3)

		10 Inch 78	>Mercury	USA	70649
		7 Inch 45	Mercury	USA	70649X45
		7 Inch 45EP	Mercury	USA	EP-1-3277
			Mercury	Fra	MEP14116
		12 Inch 33	Mercury	USA	MG20055
			Mercury	USA	MG20803
			Mercury	USA	ML8015
			Mercury	USA	SR60803
			Mercury	Eng	MPL6501
			Mercury	Eng	MVL305
			Mercury	Fra	MPL7089

4610 Russian Lullaby*
      (mx y 10833)

		7 Inch 45EP	Mercury	USA	EP-1-3277
			Mercury	Fra	MEP14116
		12 Inch 33	>Mercury	USA	MG20055
			Mercury	Eng	MPL6501
			Mercury	Eng	MVL305
			Mercury	Fra	MPL7089

4620 Begin the Beguine*
      (mx y 10834)

		7 Inch 45EP	Mercury	USA	EP-1-3278
			Mercury	Fra	MEP14117
		12 Inch 33	>Mercury	USA	MG20055
			Mercury	Eng	MPL6501
			Mercury	Eng	MVL305
			Mercury	Fra	MPL7089

4630 Night and Day*
      (mx y 10835-3)

| | | 10 Inch 78 | >Mercury | USA | 70649 |

		7 Inch 45	Mercury	USA	70649X45
		7 Inch 45EP	Mercury	USA	EP-1-3277
			Mercury	Fra	MEP14116
		12 Inch 33	Mercury	USA	MG20055
			Mercury	Eng	MPL6501
			Mercury	Eng	MVL305
			Mercury	Fra	MPL7089
4640	Mambo Blues*				
	(mx y 10836)				
		7 Inch 45EP	Mercury	USA	EP-1-3278
			Mercury	Fra	MEP14117
		12 Inch 33	>Mercury	USA	MG20055
			Mercury	Eng	MPL6501
			Mercury	Eng	MVL305
			Mercury	Fra	MPL7089
4650	Mambo Garner*				
	(mx y 10837)				
		7 Inch 45EP	Mercury	Fra	MEP14115
		12 Inch 33	>Mercury	USA	MG20055
			Mercury	Eng	MPL6501
			Mercury	Eng	MVL305
			Mercury	Fra	MPL7089
4660	Mambo Nights*				
	(mx y 10838)				
		7 Inch 45EP	Mercury	USA	EP-1-3277
			Mercury	Fra	MEP14116
		12 Inch 33	>Mercury	USA	MG20055
			Mercury	Eng	MPL6501
			Mercury	Eng	MVL305
			Mercury	Fra	MPL7089
4670	Sweet Sue-Just You*				
	(mx y 10839)				
		7 Inch 45EP	Mercury	Fra	MEP14115
		12 Inch 33	>Mercury	USA	MG20055
			Mercury	Eng	MPL6501
			Mercury	Eng	MVL305
			Mercury	Fra	MPL7089
4680	Cherokee*				
	(mx y 10840)				
		7 Inch 45EP	Mercury	USA	EP-1-3278
			Mercury	Fra	MEP14117
		12 Inch 33	>Mercury	USA	MG20055
			Mercury	Eng	MPL6501
			Mercury	Eng	MVL305
			Mercury	Fra	MPL7089
4690	Imagination*				
	(mx y 10841)				
		12 Inch 33	EmArcy	USA	MG36069
			EmArcy	Eng	MMB12010
			Fontana	Eng	FJL103
			Fontana	Fra	683253JCL
			Fontana	Jap	SFON-7049
			Fontana	Neth	858011FPY
			>Mercury	USA	MG20803
			Mercury	USA	ML8015
			Mercury	USA	SR60803
			Mercury	Fra	6641688
	Note: See note under "Sleep" (4910).				
4700	Oh, Lady Be Good!				
	(mx y 10842)				
		7 Inch 45EP	Mercury	Eng	ZEP10096
		12 Inch 33	>EmArcy	USA	MG36069
			EmArcy	Eng	MMB12010

			Fontana	Eng	FJL103
			Fontana	Fra	683253JCL
			Fontana	Jap	SFON-7049
			Fontana	Neth	858011FPY
			Fontana Special	Eng	6430135
			Mercury	USA	MG20803
			Mercury	USA	ML8015
			Mercury	USA	SR60803
			Mercury	Fra	6641688
			Mercury	Neth	6641589
			Mercury	Neth	9279113
			Philips	Eur	6338978
4710	There's a Small Hotel				
	(mx y 10843)				
		10 Inch 78	>Mercury	USA	70487
			Mercury	Eng	MB3179
		7 Inch 45	Mercury	USA	70487X45
		7 Inch 45EP	EmArcy	USA	EP-1-6085
			Mercury	Fra	MEP14127
		12 Inch 33	EmArcy	USA	MG36001
			EmArcy	Eng	MMB12010
4720	I Wanna Be a Rugcutter				
	(mx y 10844)				
		7 Inch 45EP	EmArcy	USA	EP-1-6085
			Mercury	Fra	MEP14127
		12 Inch 33	EmArcy	USA	DEM-2
			>EmArcy	USA	MG36001
			Mercury	USA	MG36087
4730	Misty				
	(mx y 10845)				
		10 Inch 78	>Mercury	USA	70442
			Mercury	Eng	MB3167
			Mercury	Fra	10512
		7 Inch 45	Mercury	USA	C-30037X45
			Mercury	USA	70442X45
		7 Inch 45EP	EmArcy	USA	EP-1-6085
			Mercury	Fra	126046MCE
			Mercury	Fra	MEP14127
		10 Inch 33	Showcase	USA	33
		12 Inch 33	EmArcy	USA	MG36001
			EmArcy	USA	MG36086
			Fontana	Eng	FJL103
			Fontana	Fra	683253JCL
			Fontana	Jap	SFON-7049
			Fontana	Neth	858011FPY
			Mercury	USA	MG20583
			Mercury	USA	MG20662
			Mercury	USA	SR60249
			Mercury	USA	SR60662
			Mercury	Fra	135.008MCY
			Mercury	Fra	6641688
			Mercury	Fra	125008MCL
			Mercury	Neth	6336320
			Mercury	Neth	6641589
			Mercury	Neth	9279113
			Philips	Eur	6338978
4740	Sweet and Lovely*				
	(mx y 10846)				
		7 Inch 45EP	Mercury	Eng	ZEP10096
		12 Inch 33	>EmArcy	USA	MG36069
			EmArcy	Eng	MMB12010
			Mercury	Fra	6641688

4750	Rosalie (mx y 10847)				
	10 Inch 78	>Mercury	USA	70487
		Mercury	Eng	MB3179
	7 Inch 45	Mercury	USA	70487X45
	7 Inch 45EP	EmArcy	USA	EP-1-6084
		Mercury	Fra	MEP14126
	12 Inch 33	EmArcy	USA	MG36001
		EmArcy	Eng	MMB12010
		Fontana	Eng	FJL103
		Fontana	Fra	683253JCL
		Fontana	Jap	SFON-7049
		Fontana	Neth	858011FPY
4760	Exactly Like You (mx y 10848)			
	10 Inch 78	>Mercury	USA	70442
		Mercury	Eng	MB3167
		Mercury	Fra	10512
	7 Inch 45	Mercury	USA	70442X45
		Mercury	USA	C-30037X45
	12 Inch 33	Fontana	Jap	SFON-7049
		Mercury	USA	MG20662
		Mercury	USA	SR60662
		Mercury	Fra	135.008MCY
		Mercury	Fra	125008MCL
		Mercury	Fra	6641688
		Mercury	Neth	6336320
		Mercury	Neth	6641589
		Mercury	Neth	9279113
		Philips	Eur	6338978
4770	Part-Time Blues (mx y 10849)			
	7 Inch 45EP	EmArcy	USA	EP-1-6084
		Mercury	Fra	MEP14126
	12 Inch 33	>EmArcy	USA	MG36001
4780	(All of a Sudden) My Heart Sings (mx y 10850)			
	7 Inch 45EP	EmArcy	USA	EP-1-6084
		Mercury	Fra	MEP14126
	7 Inch 33	EmArcy	USA	D-EM-1
	12 Inch 33	>EmArcy	USA	MG36001
		EmArcy	Eng	MMB12010
		Fontana	Eng	FJL103
		Fontana	Fra	683253JCL
		Fontana	Jap	SFON-7049
		Fontana	Neth	858011FPY
		Fontana Special	Eng	6430135
		Mercury	USA	MG20803
		Mercury	USA	ML8015
		Mercury	USA	SR60803
		Mercury	Fra	MPL7099
		Mercury	Neth	6641589
		Mercury	Neth	9279113
		Philips	Eur	6338978
4790	I've Got the World on a String (mx y 10851)			
	7 Inch 45EP	EmArcy	USA	EP-1-6083
		Mercury	Fra	MEP14125
	12 Inch 33	>EmArcy	USA	MG36001
		EmArcy	Eng	MMB12010
		Mercury	USA	MG20803
		Mercury	USA	ML8015
		Mercury	USA	SR60803

4800   You Are My Sunshine
        (mx y 10852)
                    7 Inch 45EP   EmArcy   USA   EP-1-6083
                                       Mercury   Fra   MEP14125
                    12 Inch 33   >EmArcy   USA   MG36001
                                       Fontana   Eng   FJL103
                                       Fontana   Fra   683253JCL
                                       Fontana   Jap   SFON-7049
                                       Fontana   Neth   858011FPY
                                       Mercury   USA   MG20662
                                       Mercury   USA   SR60662
                                       Mercury   Fra   135.008MCY
                                       Mercury   Fra   125008MCL
                                       Mercury   Fra   6641688
                                       Mercury   Neth   6336320
                                       Mercury   Neth   6641589
                                       Mercury   Neth   9279113
                                       Philips   Eur   6338978
4810   Don't Worry 'Bout Me
        (mx y 10853)
                    7 Inch 45EP   EmArcy   USA   EP-1-6085
                                       Mercury   Fra   MEP14127
                    12 Inch 33   >EmArcy   USA   MG36001
4820   In a Mellow Tone
        (mx y 10854)
                    7 Inch 45EP   EmArcy   USA   EP-1-6084
                                       Mercury   Fra   MEP14126
                    12 Inch 33   >EmArcy   USA   MG36001
                                       EmArcy   Eng   MMB12010
                                       Fontana   Eng   FJL103
                                       Fontana   Fra   683253JCL
                                       Fontana   Jap   SFON-7049
                                       Fontana   Neth   858011FPY
4830   7-11 Jump
        (mx y 10855)
                    7 Inch 45EP   EmArcy   USA   EPO-1-6083
                                       Mercury   Fra   MEP14125
                    12 Inch 33   >EmArcy   USA   MG36001

        Note: "7-11 Jump" (Erroll Garner) is the same tune as "Look, Ma—All Hands!"
        (see also February 27, 1953 session).

ERROLL GARNER   **NEW YORK, MARCH 14, 1955**
Erroll Garner (p)
4840   Yesterdays
        (mx y 11381)
                    7 Inch 45EP   Mercury   Eng   ZEP10096
                    12 Inch 33   >EmArcy   USA   MG36069
                                       EmArcy   Eng   MMB12010
                                       Fontana   Eng   FJL103
                                       Fontana   Fra   683253JCL
                                       Fontana   Jap   SFON-7049
                                       Fontana   Neth   858011FPY
                                       Mercury   Fra   6641688
4850   Who?
        (mx y 11382)
                    12 Inch 33   >EmArcy   USA   MG36069
                                       EmArcy   Eng   MMB12010
                                       Mercury   Fra   6641688
4860   A Cottage for Sale
        (mx y 11383)
                    7 Inch 45EP   Mercury   USA   EP-1-3316

		12 Inch 33	>Mercury	USA	MG20063
			Mercury	USA	MG20803
			Mercury	USA	SR60803
			Mercury	Eng	ML8015
			Mercury	Eng	MVL306
4870	That Old Feeling				
	(mx y 11384)				
		7 Inch 45EP	Mercury	USA	EP-1-3316
		12 Inch 33	>Mercury	USA	MG20063
			Mercury	USA	MG20662
			Mercury	USA	SR60662
			Mercury	Eng	MVL306
			Mercury	Fra	135.008MCY
			Mercury	Fra	125008MCL
			Mercury	Fra	6641688
			Mercury	Neth	6336320
			Mercury	Neth	6641589
			Mercury	Neth	9279113
			Philips	Eur	6338978
4880	Over the Rainbow				
	(mx y 11385)				
		7 Inch 45EP	Mercury	USA	EP-1-3317
		12 Inch 33	>Mercury	USA	MG20063
			Mercury	Eng	MVL306
4890	Afternoon of an Elf				
	(mx y 11386)				
		7 Inch 45EP	Mercury	USA	EP-1-3335
		12 Inch 33	>Mercury	USA	MG20090
			Mercury	Eng	MPL6539
			Mercury	Fra	7194
4900	Solitaire				
	(mx y 11387)				
		7 Inch 45EP	Mercury	USA	EP-1-3315
		12 Inch 33	>Mercury	USA	MG20063
			Mercury	Eng	MVL306
			Mercury	Neth	9279113
			Philips	Eur	6338978
4910	Sleep				
	(mx y 11388)				
		12 Inch 33	EmArcy	USA	MG36069

Note: "Sleep" features Garner on piano and celeste. "Sleep" also appeared briefly on the original issue EmArcy MG36069 but was, for an unknown reason, replaced by "Imagination" (4690) on later issues.

4920	When a Gypsy Makes His Violin Cry				
	(mx y 11389)				
		12 Inch 33	>EmArcy	USA	MG36069
			Fontana	Eng	FJL103
			Fontana	Fra	683253JCL
			Fontana	Neth	858011FPY
			Mercury	Fra	6641688
4930	A Smooth One				
	(mx y 11390)				
		12 Inch 33	Fontana Special	Eng	6430135
			>Mercury	USA	MG20090
			Mercury	USA	MG20133
			Mercury	Eng	MPL6539
			Mercury	Fra	7194
			Mercury	Jap	MC-4
			Mercury	Neth	6641589
4940	I'll Never Smile Again				
	(mx y 11391)				
		7 Inch 45EP	Mercury	USA	EP-1-3314
		12 Inch 33	>Mercury	USA	MG20063

		Mercury	Eng	MVL306
		Mercury	Neth	9279113
		Philips	Eur	6338978

4950 Is You Is or Is You Ain't My Baby?
(mx y 11392)

	12 Inch 33	Fontana Special	Eng	6430135
		>Mercury	USA	MG20090
		Mercury	Eng	MPL6539
		Mercury	Fra	7194
		Mercury	Neth	6641589

4960 Love in Bloom
(mx y 11393)

	12 Inch 33	>Mercury	USA	MG20662
		Mercury	USA	SR60662
		Mercury	Fra	135.008MCY
		Mercury	Fra	125008MCL
		Mercury	Fra	6641688
		Mercury	Neth	6336320
		Mercury	Neth	6641589
		Mercury	Neth	9279113
		Philips	Eur	6338978

4970 Fandango
(mx y 11394)

	12 Inch 33	>Mercury	USA	MG20090
		Mercury	Eng	MPL6539
		Mercury	Fra	7194

4980 It's the Talk of the Town
(mx y 11395)

	7 Inch 45EP	Mercury	USA	EP-1-3315
	12 Inch 33	>Mercury	USA	MG20063
		Mercury	Eng	MVL306

4990 Salud Segovia
(mx y 11396)

	12 Inch 33	>EmArcy	USA	MG36069
		Mercury	Fra	6641688

Note: This title is Garner's salute to Spanish guitarist Andrés Segovia.

5000 Then You've Never Been Blue
(mx y 11397)

	7 Inch 45EP	Mercury	USA	EP-1-3314
	12 Inch 33	>Mercury	USA	MG20063
		Mercury	Eng	MVL306

5010 Don't Be That Way
(mx y 11398)

	12 Inch 33	Fontana Special	Eng	6430135
		>Mercury	USA	MG20090
		Mercury	USA	MG20133
		Mercury	USA	MG20803
		Mercury	USA	ML8015
		Mercury	USA	SR60803
		Mercury	Eng	MPL6539
		Mercury	Fra	7194
		Mercury	Jap	MC-4
		Mercury	Neth	6641589

5020 All My Loves Are You
(mx y 11399)

	12 Inch 33	>Mercury	USA	MG20090
		Mercury	Eng	MPL6539
		Mercury	Fra	7194

5030 St. James Infirmary
(mx y 11400)

	7 Inch 45EP	Mercury	USA	EP-1-3335
	12 Inch 33	Fontana Special	Eng	6430135
		>Mercury	USA	MG20090

	Mercury	Eng	MPL6539
	Mercury	Fra	7194
	Mercury	Neth	6641589
	Mercury	Neth	9279113
	Philips	Eur	6338978

ERROLL GARNER TRIO   CARMEL, CA, SEPTEMBER 19, 1955
Erroll Garner (p), Eddie Calhoun (b), Denzil Best (d)

5040	I'll Remember April			
	7 Inch 45	Columbia	USA	AE-17
	7 Inch 45EP	Columbia	USA	7-9821
		Columbia	USA	B-2573
		Philips	Eur	429394BE
	12 Inch 33	CBS	Aus	SBP234108
		CBS	Fra	62310
		CBS	Fra	S66309
		CBS	Neth	68219
		CBS	WGer	S66244
		>Columbia	USA	CL883
		Columbia	USA	CS9821
		Columbia	Jap	PL-5044
		Columbia	Jap	PMS67
		Philips	Eng	BBL7106
		Philips	Eur	B07170L
5050	Teach Me Tonight			
	7 Inch 45	Columbia	USA	AE-17
		Philips	Eur	322421BF
	7 Inch 45EP	Columbia	USA	B-2573
		Philips	Eng	BBE12184
		Philips	Eur	429496BE
	12 Inch 33	CBS	Aus	SBP234108
		CBS	Fra	62310
		CBS	Neth	68219
		CBS	WGer	S66244
		>Columbia	USA	CL883
		Columbia	USA	CS9821
		Columbia	Jap	PL-5044
		Columbia	Jap	PMS67
		Philips	Eng	BBL7106
		Philips	Eur	B07170L

Note: "Teach Me Tonight" is an abbreviated version on Philips BBL7106 (2 min., 45 sec.).

5060	Mambo Carmel			
	7 Inch 45	Columbia	USA	B-2609
		Philips	Eng	BBE12264
		Philips	Eur	429496BE
		Philips	Eur	429555BE
	12 Inch 33	CBS	Aus	SBP234108
		CBS	Fra	62310
		CBS	Neth	68219
		CBS	WGer	S66244
		>Columbia	USA	CL883
		Columbia	USA	CS9821
		Columbia	Jap	PL-5044
		Columbia	Jap	PMS67
		Philips	Eng	BBL7106
		Philips	Eur	B07170L
5070	Autumn Leaves			
	7 Inch 45EP	Columbia	USA	B-2621
		Philips	Eng	BBE12184
		Philips	Eur	429394BE

	12 Inch 33	CBS	Aus	SBP234108
		CBS	Fra	62310
		CBS	Fra	S66309
		CBS	Neth	68219
		CBS	WGer	S66244
		>Columbia	USA	CL883
		Columbia	USA	CS9821
		Columbia	Jap	PL-5044
		Columbia	Jap	PMS67
		Philips	Eng	BBL7106
		Philips	Eur	B07170L
5080	It's All Right with Me			
	7 Inch 45EP	Columbia	USA	7-9821
		Columbia	USA	B-2609
		Philips	Eng	BBE12264
		Philips	Eur	429496BE
		Philips	Eur	429555BE
	12 Inch 33	CBS	Aus	SBP234108
		CBS	Fra	62310
		CBS	Neth	68219
		CBS	WGer	S66244
		>Columbia	USA	CL883
		Columbia	USA	CS9821
		Columbia	Jap	PL-5044
		Columbia	Jap	PMS67
		Philips	Eng	BBL7106
		Philips	Eur	B07170L
5090	Red Top			
	7 Inch 45EP	Columbia	USA	B-2621
		Philips	Eur	429461BE
	12 Inch 33	CBS	Aus	SBP234108
		CBS	Fra	62310
		CBS	Neth	68219
		CBS	WGer	S66244
		>Columbia	USA	CL883
		Columbia	USA	CS9821
		Columbia	Jap	PL-5044
		Columbia	Jap	PMS67
		Philips	Eng	BBL7106
		Philips	Eur	B07170L
5100	April in Paris			
	7 Inch 45EP	Columbia	USA	7-9821
		Columbia	USA	B-2621
		Philips	Eng	BBE12264
		Philips	Eur	429461BE
		Philips	Eur	429555BE
	12 Inch 33	CBS	Aus	SBP234108
		CBS	Fra	62310
		CBS	Fra	S66309
		CBS	Neth	68219
		>Columbia	USA	CL883
		Columbia	USA	CS9821
		Columbia	Jap	PL-5044
		Columbia	Jap	PMS67
		Philips	Eng	BBL7106
		Philips	Eur	B07170L

Note: "April in Paris" is an abbreviated version on Philips BBL7106 (3 min., 45 sec.).

5110	They Can't Take That Away from Me			
	7 Inch 45EP	Columbia	USA	7-9821
		Columbia	USA	B-2609
		Philips	Eng	BBE12264
		Philips	Eur	429461BE
		Philips	Eur	429555BE

	12 Inch 33	CBS	Aus	SBP234108
		CBS	Fra	62310
		CBS	Neth	68219
		>Columbia	USA	CL883
		Columbia	USA	CS9821
		Columbia	Jap	PL-5044
		Columbia	Jap	PMS67
		Philips	Eng	BBL7106
		Philips	Eur	B07170L

Note: "They Can't Take That Away from Me" is an abbreviated version on Philips BBL7106 (3 min., 18 sec.).

5120   How Could You Do a Thing Like That to Me?

	7 Inch 45	Philips	Eur	322421BF
	7 Inch 45EP	Columbia	USA	B-2609
		Philips	Eur	429496BE
	12 Inch 33	CBS	Aus	SBP234108
		CBS	Fra	62310
		CBS	Neth	68219
		>Columbia	USA	CL883
		Columbia	USA	CS9821
		Columbia	Jap	PL-5044
		Columbia	Jap	PMS67
		Philips	Eng	BBL7106
		Philips	Eur	B07170L

Note: "How Could You Do a Thing Like That to Me?" is an abbreviated version on Philips BBL7106 (3 min., 21 sec.).

5130   Where or When

	7 Inch 45EP	Columbia	USA	B-2573
		Philips	Eng	BBE12184
		Philips	Eur	429394BE
	12 Inch 33	CBS	Aus	SBP234108
		CBS	Fra	62310
		CBS	Neth	68219
		>Columbia	USA	CL883
		Columbia	USA	CS9821
		Columbia	USA	D-3
		Columbia	Jap	PL-5044
		Columbia	Jap	PMS67
		Philips	Eng	BBL7106
		Philips	Eur	B07170L

5140   Erroll's Theme

	7 Inch 45EP	Columbia	USA	B-2573
		Philips	Eur	429461BE
	12 Inch 33	CBS	Aus	SBP234108
		CBS	Fra	62310
		CBS	Neth	68219
		CBS	WGer	S66244
		>Columbia	USA	CL883
		Columbia	USA	CS9821
		Columbia	USA	D-7
		Columbia	Jap	PL-5044
		Columbia	Jap	PMS67
		Philips	Eng	BBL7106
		Philips	Eur	B07170L

5150	I Cover the Waterfront			Unissued
5160	Bernie's Tune			Unissued
5170	Laura			Unissued
5180	The Nearness of You			Unissued

ERROLL GARNER TRIO   **NEW YORK, JUNE 7, 1956**

Erroll Garner (p), Al Hall (b), Gordon "Specs" Powell (d)

5190   Rose Room
        (mx CO 56106)

12 Inch 33	>Columbia	USA	CL1452
	Philips	Eur	B47037L

5200 But Not for Me
(mx CO 56107)

7 Inch 45EP	Columbia	USA	B-9391
	Philips	Eng	BBE12271
	Philips	Eur	429564BE
	Philips	Eur	429752BE
10 Inch 33	Philips	Eur	B07803R
	Philips	Eur	B07823R
12 Inch 33	CBS	Fra	52065
	CBS	Fra	84267
	CBS	Fra	S66309
	CBS	Neth	52706
	CBS-Sony	Jap	20AP1492
	>Columbia	USA	CL939
	Columbia	Jap	PMS68
	Columbia	Jap	YL-114
	Encore	USA	P14386
	Philips	Eng	BBL7282
	Philips	Eur	B07370L

5210 My Silent Love
(mx CO 56108)

10 Inch 33	Philips	Eur	B07910R
12 Inch 33	>Columbia	USA	CL1512

5220 Full Moon and Empty Arms
(mx CO 56109)

7 Inch 45EP	Columbia	USA	B-9391
10 Inch 33	Philips	Eur	B07823R
12 Inch 33	CBS	Fra	52065
	CBS-Sony	Jap	20AP1492
	>Columbia	USA	CL939
	Philips	Eng	BBL7282
	Philips	Eur	B07370L
	Philips	Eur	B07559L

5230 Some of These Days
(mx CO 56110)

7 Inch 45	Philips	Eur	322217BF
12 Inch 33	>Columbia	USA	CL1452
	Philips	Eur	B47037L

5240 Time on My Hands
(mx CO 56111)

7 Inch 45EP	Columbia	USA	B-9391
	Philips	Eng	BBE12271
	Philips	Eur	429564BE
10 Inch 33	Philips	Eur	B07803R
	Philips	Eur	B07823R
12 Inch 33	CBS	Fra	52065
	CBS	Neth	52706
	CBS-Sony	Jap	20AP1492
	>Columbia	USA	CL939
	Philips	Eng	BBL7282
	Philips	Eur	B07370L

5250 Girl of My Dreams
(mx CO 56112)

7 Inch 45EP	Philips	Eur	429752BE
10 Inch 33	Philips	Eur	B07803R
	Philips	Eur	B07823R
12 Inch 33	CBS	Fra	52065
	CBS	Fra	52566
	CBS-Sony	Jap	20AP1492
	>Columbia	USA	CL939
	Harmony	USA	HS11268

			Philips	Eng	BBL7282
			Philips	Eur	B07370L
5260	Alexander's Ragtime Band				
	(mx CO 56113)				
		7 Inch 45EP	Philips	Eng	BBE12271
			Philips	Eur	429564BE
			Philips	Eur	429752BE
		10 Inch 33	Philips	Eur	B07823R
		12 Inch 33	CBS	Fra	52065
			CBS	Fra	S66309
			CBS	Neth	52706
			CBS	WGer	S66244
			CBS-Sony	Jap	20AP1492
			>Columbia	USA	CL939
			Columbia	Jap	PMS68
			Columbia	Jap	YL-114
			Philips	Eng	BBL7282
			Philips	Eur	B07370L
			Philips	Eur	B07559L
5270	If It's the Last Thing I Do				
	(mx CO 56114)				
		12 Inch 33	>Columbia	USA	CL1452
			Philips	Eur	B47037L
5280	(What Can I Say) After I Say I'm Sorry?				
	(mx CO 56115)				
		10 Inch 33	Philips	Eur	B07910R
		12 Inch 33	>Columbia	USA	CL1452
			Philips	Eur	B47037L
5290	I Got It Bad and That Ain't Good				
	(mx CO 56116)				
		12 Inch 33	>Columbia	USA	CL1452
			Philips	Eur	B47037L
5300	Ol' Man River				
	(mx CO 56117)				
		7 Inch 45EP	Philips	Eng	BBE12270
			Philips	Eur	429563BE
		10 Inch 33	Philips	Eur	B07803R
			Philips	Eur	B07823R
		12 Inch 33	CBS	Fra	52065
			CBS	Fra	S66309
			CBS	Neth	52706
			CBS	WGer	S66244
			>Columbia	USA	CL939
			Columbia	Jap	PMS68
			Columbia	Jap	YL-114
			Philips	Eng	BBL7282
			Philips	Eur	B07370L
5310	Them There Eyes				
	(mx CO 56118)				
		12 Inch 33	>Columbia	USA	CL1452
			Philips	Eur	B47037L
5320	The Man I Love				
	(mx CO 56119)				
		7 Inch 45EP	Columbia	USA	B-11411
			Philips	Eur	429280BE
		10 Inch 33	>Columbia	USA	CL2606
			Philips	Eur	B07800R
		12 Inch 33	CBS	Eng	88129
			CBS	Fra	62334
			CBS	Fra	S66309
			Columbia	USA	CL1141
			Columbia	USA	PG33424
			Philips	Eur	B07514L

5330   Moonglow
       (mx CO 56120)
	7 Inch 45EP	Columbia	USA	B-11411
	10 Inch 33	>Columbia	USA	CL2606
	12 Inch 33	CBS	Fra	62334
		Columbia	USA	CL1141
		Philips	Eur	B07514L

5340   All God's Chillun Got Rhythm
       (mx 56121)
	7 Inch 45EP	Philips	Eng	BBE12354
		Philips	Eur	429280BE
		Philips	Eur	429605BE
	10 Inch 33	>Columbia	USA	CL2606
	12 Inch 33	Philips	Eur	B07514L

5350   Lenox Hill Blues
       (mx CO 56122)   Unissued
5360   Creme de Menthe
       (mx CO 56123)
	10 Inch 33	>Columbia	USA	CL2606
	12 Inch 33	CBS	Eng	88129
		CBS	Fra	62334
		CBS	Fra	84267
		Columbia	USA	CL1141
		Columbia	USA	PG33424
		Encore	USA	P14386
		Philips	Eur	B07514L

Note: "Creme de Menthe" (Erroll Garner) was later retitled "Dreamy" with lyrics by Sydney Shaw (see also September 2, 1956 session).

5370   Humoresque
       (mx CO 56124)
	7 Inch 45EP	Philips	Eur	429280BE
	10 Inch 33	>Columbia	USA	CL2606
		Philips	Eur	B07800R
	12 Inch 33	CBS	Fra	62334
		Columbia	USA	CL1141
		Philips	Eur	B07514L

ERROLL GARNER   **NEW YORK, SEPTEMBER 2, 1956**
WITH ORCHESTRA
Conducted by Mitch Miller
Erroll Garner (p); Mitch Miller (co); Al Hall (b); Gordon "Specs" Powell (d); Bernie Glow, Edward Reider, Ray Copeland, Burt Collins (tps); George Monte, Eddie Bert, Jim Dahl (tbs); Sam Marowitz, Hal McKusick, Herbie Mann, John Hafer, Charles O'Kane (sax); Julius M. Held, Arnold Eidus, Julius Schachter, Daniel Guilet, Max Hollander, Seymour Miroff, Sylvan Shulman, Harvey Shapiro, Eugene Orloff, Harry Glickman (vns); Isadore Zir, Harold Coletta (viola); Maurice Brown, Milton Lomask (ce); Nat Pierce (ar).

5380   Misty
       (mx CO 56581)
	7 Inch 45	Columbia	USA	4-33180
		>Columbia	USA	4-41067
		Columbia	USA	4-41482
		Columbia	USA	13-33180
	7 Inch 45EP	CBS	Fra	EP 5986
		Columbia	USA	B-10142
	10 Inch 33	Philips	Eur	B07821R
	12 Inch 33	CBS	Eng	32260
		CBS	Fra	S66309

				Columbia	USA	CL1014
				Columbia	USA	CS9820
				Columbia	Jap	PL-5085
				Philips	Eng	BBL7204
				Philips	Eur	B07279L
		12 Inch TX		Voices of Vista	USA	2

5390   Dreamy
(mx CO 56582)

	10 Inch 78	>Columbia	USA	40766
	7 Inch 45	CBS	Neth	CA 281.130
		Columbia	USA	4-33180
		Columbia	USA	4-40766
		Columbia	USA	13-33180
	7 Inch 45EP	CBS	Fra	EP 5986
		Columbia	USA	B-10143
	10 Inch 33	Philips	Eur	B07821R
	12 Inch 33	CBS	Eng	32260
		Columbia	USA	CL1014
		Columbia	USA	CS9820
		Columbia	Jap	PL-5085
		Philips	Eng	BBL7204
		Philips	Eur	B07279L

5400   On the Street Where You Live
(mx CO 56583)

	10 Inch 78	>Columbia	USA	40766
	7 Inch 45	CBS	Neth	CA 281.130
		Columbia	USA	4-40766
		Philips	Eur	322295BF
	7 Inch 45EP	CBS	Fra	EP 5986
		Columbia	USA	B-10142
	12 inch 33	CBS	Eng	32260
		CBS	Fra	S66309
		Columbia	USA	CL1014
		Columbia	USA	CS9820
		Columbia	USA	D-8
		Columbia	Jap	PL-5085
		Columbia	Jap	YL-145
		Philips	Eng	BBL7204
		Philips	Eur	B07279L

ERROLL GARNER TRIO   NEW YORK, SEPTEMBER 11, 1956

Erroll Garner (p), Al Hall (b), Gordon "Specs" Powell (d)

5410   Untitled Original
(mx CO 56587)   Unissued

5420   My Lonely Heart
(mx CO 56588)

	12 Inch 33	>Columbia	USA	CL1020
		Philips	Eng	BBL7184
		Philips	Eur	B07260L

5430   Mambo 207
(mx CO 56589)

	12 Inch 33	CBS	Fra	52065
		CBS	Neth	52706
		CBS-Sony	Jap	20AP1492
		>Columbia	USA	CL939
		Philips	Eng	BBL7282
		Philips	Eur	B07370L
		Philips	Eur	B07559L
		Playboy	USA	PB 1959A

5440   The Way Back Blues
(mx CO 56590)

10 Inch 78	>Columbia	USA	40899
7 Inch 45	Columbia	USA	4-40899
7 Inch 45EP	Philips	Eng	BBE12270
	Philips	Eur	429563BE
10 Inch 33	Philips	Eur	B07803R
	Philips	Eur	B07823R
12 Inch 33	CBS	Fra	52065
	CBS	Neth	52706
	CBS	WGer	S66244
	CBS-Sony	Jap	20AP1492
	Columbia	USA	CL939
	Columbia	USA	PG33402
	Philips	Eng	BBL7282
	Philips	Eur	B07370L

5450   Passing Through
(mx CO 56591)

7 Inch 45EP	Columbia	USA	B-9391
	Philips	Eng	BBE12271
	Philips	Eur	429564BE
10 Inch 33	Philips	Eur	B07803R
	Philips	Eur	B07823R
12 Inch 33	CBS	Fra	52065
	CBS	Fra	84267
	CBS-Sony	Jap	20AP1492
	>Columbia	USA	CL939
	Encore	USA	P14386
	Philips	Eng	BBL7282
	Philips	Eur	B07370L

5460   Untitled Original
(mx CO 56592)   Unissued

ERROLL GARNER   **NEW YORK, FEBRUARY 6, 1957**

Erroll Garner (p)

5470   You Go to My Head
(mx CO 57314)

12 Inch 33	>Columbia	USA	CL1512

5480   The Very Thought of You
(mx CO 57315)   Unissued

5490   Please Be Kind
(mx CO 57316)   Unissued

5500   One Night of Love
(mx CO 57317)

12 Inch 33	>Columbia	USA	CL1512

5510   All for Strauss
(mx CO 57318)   Unissued

5520   Soliloquy
(mx CO 57319)

7 Inch 45EP	Columbia	USA	B-10601
12 Inch 33	CBS	Fra	S64281
	CBS-Sony	Jap	SONP 50444
	>Columbia	USA	CL1060
	Philips	Eng	BBL7226
	Philips	Eur	B07300L

5530   I Surrender, Dear
(mx CO 57320)

12 Inch 33	CBS	Fra	S64281
	CBS-Sony	Jap	SONP 50444
	>Columbia	USA	CL1060
	Philips	Eng	BBL7226
	Philips	Eur	B07300L

5540	Stumbling			
	(mx CO 57321)			
	12 Inch 33	>Columbia	USA	CL1512
5550	Don't Take Your Love from Me			
	(mx CO 57322)			
	10 Inch 33	Philips	Eur	B07910R
	12 Inch 33	CBS	Fra	S64281
		CBS-Sony	Jap	SONP 50444
		>Columbia	USA	CL1060
		Philips	Eng	BBL7226
		Philips	Eur	B07300L
5560	You'd Be So Nice to Come Home To			
	(mx CO 57323)			
	7 Inch 45EP	Columbia	USA	B-10601
	12 Inch 33	CBS	Fra	52566
		CBS	Fra	S64281
		CBS-Sony	Jap	SONP 50444
		>Columbia	USA	CL1060
		Harmony	USA	HS11268
		Philips	Eng	BBL7226
		Philips	Eur	B07300L
5570	No More Time			
	(mx CO 57324)			
	12 Inch 33	CBS	Fra	S64281
		CBS-Sony	Jap	SONP 50444
		>Columbia	USA	CL1060
		Philips	Eng	BBL7226
		Philips	Eur	B07300L
5580	Solitaire			
	(mx CO 57325)			Unissued
5590	Until the Real Thing Comes Along			
	(mx CO 57326)			
	12 Inch 33	>Columbia	USA	CL1512
5600	If I Had You			
	(mx CO 57327)			
	12 Inch 33	CBS	Fra	S64281
		CBS-Sony	Jap	SONP 50444
		>Columbia	USA	CL1060
		Philips	Eng	BBL7226
		Philips	Eur	B07300L
5610	Don't Get Around Much Anymore			
	(mx CO 55697)			
	7 Inch 45EP	Philips	Eur	429799BE
	12 Inch 33	>Columbia	USA	CL1512
		Philips	Eur	B07910R
5620	Medley (unknown titles)			
	(mx CO 55952)			Unissued

ERROLL GARNER WITH ORCHESTRA   **NEW YORK, MAY 27, 1957**
Conducted by Mitch Miller
Erroll Garner (p); Mitch Miller (co); Bernie Glow, Alvin Goldberg, Doug Mettome, Burt Collins (tps); Urbie Green, Frank Rehak, Jim Dahl (tbs); Gene Allen, Aaron Sachs, John Hafer, Anthony Ortega, Dick Meldonian (sax); Julius M. Held, Arnold Eidus, Julius Schachter, Paul Winter, Daniel Guilet, Max Hollander, Harry Urbont, Mac Ceppos, Harry Melnikoff, Seymour Miroff (vns); Isadore Zir, Harold Coletta (viola); Arthur Winograd, Maurice Brown (ce); Milt Hinton (b); James "Osie" Johnson (d); Nat Pierce (ar).

5630	Solitaire			
	(mx CO 58029)			

		7 Inch 45	Columbia	USA	4-41482
		7 Inch 45EP	Columbia	USA	B-10143
		12 Inch 33	CBS	Eng	32260
			>Columbia	USA	CL1014
			Columbia	USA	CS9820
			Columbia	Jap	PL-5085
			Philips	Eng	BBL7204
			Philips	Eur	B07279L
5640	Other Voices				
	(mx CO 58030)				
		7 Inch 45EP	Columbia	USA	B-10141
		10 Inch 33	Philips	Eur	B07821R
		12 Inch 33	CBS	Eng	32260
			>Columbia	USA	CL1014
			Columbia	USA	CS9820
			Columbia	Jap	PL-5085
			Philips	Eng	BBL7204
			Philips	Eur	B07279L
5650	Moment's Delight				
	(mx CO 58031)				
		7 Inch 45	Columbia	USA	4-41067
		7 Inch 45EP	CBS	Fra	EP 5986
			Columbia	USA	B-10143
		10 Inch 33	Philips	Eur	B07821R
		12 Inch 33	CBS	Eng	32260
			>Columbia	USA	CL1014
			Columbia	USA	CS9820
			Columbia	Jap	PL-5085
			Philips	Eng	BBL7204
			Philips	Eur	B07279L
5660	It Might As Well Be Spring				
	(mx CO 58032)				
		7 Inch 45EP	Columbia	USA	B-10142
		10 Inch 33	Philips	Eur	B07821R
		12 Inch 33	CBS	Eng	32260
			CBS	Fra	S66309
			>Columbia	USA	CL1014
			Columbia	USA	CS9820
			Columbia	Jap	PL-5085
			Philips	Eng	BBL7204
			Philips	Eur	B07279L

ERROLL GARNER WITH ORCHESTRA   **NEW YORK, MAY 31, 1957**
Conducted by Mitch Miller
Erroll Garner (p); Mitch Miller (co); Bernie Glow, Alvin Goldberg, Doug Mettome,
Philip C. Sunkel, Jr. (tps); Frank Rehak, Jim Dahl, William Elton (tbs); Gene Allen,
Paul Quinichette, John Hafer, Anthony Ortega, Dick Meldonian (sax); Julius M.
Held, Arnold Eidus, Julius Schachter, Eugene Orloff, Harry Lookofsky, Sylvan
Shulman, Raoul Poliakin, Harry Melnikoff, Harry Katzman, Mac Ceppos (vns);
Isadore Zir, Harold Coletta (viola); Abram Borodkin, Maurice Brown (ce); Al Hall
(b); James "Osie" Johnson (d); Nat Pierce (ar).

5670	I Didn't Know What Time It Was				
	(mx CO 58041)				
		7 Inch 45EP	Columbia	USA	B-10143
		10 Inch 33	Philips	Eur	B07821R
		12 Inch 33	CBS	Eng	32260
			>Columbia	USA	CL1014
			Columbia	USA	CS9820
			Columbia	Jap	PL-5085
			Philips	Eng	BBL7204
			Philips	Eur	B07279L

5680	The Very Thought of You			
	(mx CO 58042)			
	7 Inch 45	Philips	Eur	322295BF
	7 Inch 45EP	Columbia	USA	B-10141
	10 Inch 33	Philips	Eur	B07821R
	12 Inch 33	CBS	Eng	32260
		>Columbia	USA	CL1014
		Columbia	USA	CS9820
		Columbia	Jap	PL-5085
		Philips	Eng	BBL7204
		Philips	Eur	B07279L
5690	This Is Always			
	(mx CO 58043)			
	7 Inch 45EP	Columbia	USA	B-10141
	10 Inch 33	Philips	Eur	B07821R
	12 Inch 33	CBS	Eng	32260
		>Columbia	USA	CL1014
		Columbia	USA	CS9820
		Columbia	Jap	PL-5085
		Philips	Eng	BBL7204
		Philips	Eur	B07279L

ERROLL GARNER TRIO   NEW YORK, MARCH 27, 1958

Asterisk (*) denotes Erroll Garner on harpsichord only.

Erroll Garner (p, h*), Eddie Calhoun (b), Kelly Martin (d)

5700	The Song from Moulin Rouge (Where Is Your Heart)			
	(mx CO 60712)			
	7 Inch 45EP	Philips	Eng	BBE12401
		Philips	Eur	429579BE
		Philips	Eur	429735BE
	12 Inch 33	CBS	Fra	62548
		>Columbia	USA	C2L9
		Columbia	USA	CL1212
		Columbia	USA	CS8131
		Columbia	USA	JC2L9
		Columbia	Jap	PMS68
		Columbia	Jap	YL-114
		Philips	Eng	BBL7313
		Philips	Eur	B07375L
		Philips	Eur	B07506L
5710	I Love Paris			
	(mx CO 60713)			
	7 Inch 45EP	Philips	Eng	BBE12401
		Philips	Eur	429735BE
	12 Inch 33	CBS	Fra	62548
		>Columbia	USA	C2L9
		Columbia	USA	CL1212
		Columbia	USA	CS8131
		Columbia	USA	JC2L9
		Columbia	Jap	PMS68
		Columbia	Jap	YL-114
		Philips	Eng	BBL7313
		Philips	Eur	B07375L
		Philips	Eur	B07506L
5720	The Last Time I Saw Paris			
	(mx CO 60714)			
	12 Inch 33	CBS	Fra	52566
		CBS	Fra	62548
		>Columbia	USA	C2L9
		Columbia	USA	CL1213
		Columbia	USA	CS8132
		Columbia	USA	JC2L9
		Harmony	USA	HS11268

			Philips	Eng	BBL7314
			Philips	Eur	B07375L
			Philips	Eur	B07507L
5730	My Man				
	(mx CO 60715)				
		12 Inch 33	CBS	Fra	62548
			>Columbia	USA	C2L9
			Columbia	USA	CL1213
			Columbia	USA	CS8132
			Columbia	USA	JC2L9
			Philips	Eng	BBL7314
			Philips	Eur	B07507L
5740	Paris Bounce				
	(mx CO 60716)				
		7 Inch 45EP	Philips	Eng	BBE12401
			Philips	Eur	429735BE
		12 Inch 33	CBS	Fra	62548
			>Columbia	USA	C2L9
			Columbia	USA	CL1213
			Columbia	USA	CS8132
			Columbia	USA	JC2L9
			Philips	Eng	BBL7314
			Philips	Eur	B07375L
			Philips	Eur	B07507L
5750	La Vie en Rose				
	(mx CO 60717)				
		12 Inch 33	CBS	Fra	62548
			CBS	WGer	S66244
			>Columbia	USA	C2L9
			Columbia	USA	CL1213
			Columbia	USA	CS8132
			Columbia	USA	JC2L9
			Columbia	Jap	PMS68
			Columbia	Jap	YL-114
			Harmony	USA	HS11268
			Philips	Eng	BBL7314
			Philips	Eur	B07375L
			Philips	Eur	B07507L
5760	Farewell to Paris				
	(mx CO 60718)				
		12 Inch 33	>Columbia	USA	C2L9
			Columbia	USA	CL1212
			Columbia	USA	CS8131
			Columbia	USA	JC2L9
			Philips	Eng	BBL7313
			Philips	Eur	B07506L
5770	French Doll				
	(mx CO 60719)				
		12 Inch 33	CBS	Fra	62548
			>Columbia	USA	C2L9
			Columbia	USA	CL1212
			Columbia	USA	CS8131
			Columbia	USA	JC2L9
			Philips	Eng	BBL7313
			Philips	Eur	B07506L
			Philips	Eur	B47124L

Note: "French Doll" is the same tune as the harpsichord version of "Just Blues"
(see also May 11, 1958 session).

5780	Paris Midnight				
	(mx CO 60720)				
		12 Inch 33	>Columbia	USA	C2L9
			Columbia	USA	CL1213
			Columbia	USA	CS8132

			Columbia	USA	JC2L9
			Philips	Eng	BBL7314
			Philips	Eur	B07507L
5790	Left Bank Swing (mx CO 60721)				
		12 Inch 33	>Columbia	USA	C2L9
			Columbia	USA	CL1212
			Columbia	USA	CS8131
			Columbia	USA	JC2L9
			Philips	Eng	BBL7313
			Philips	Eur	B07375L
			Philips	Eur	B07506L
			Philips	Eur	B47124L

Note: "Left Bank Swing" (Erroll Garner) is the same tune as "Groovy Day" (see also March 30, 1953 session). Lyrics were later added by George David Weiss.

5800	Louise (mx CO 60722)				
		12 Inch 33	CBS	Fra	62548
			>Columbia	USA	C2L9
			Columbia	USA	CL1212
			Columbia	USA	CS8131
			Columbia	USA	JC2L9
			Philips	Eng	BBL7313
			Philips	Eur	B07375L
			Philips	Eur	B07506L
5810	La Petite Mambo (mx CO 60723)				
		12 Inch 33	CBS	Fra	62548
			>Columbia	USA	C2L9
			Columbia	USA	CL1213
			Columbia	USA	CS8132
			Columbia	USA	JC2L9
			Philips	Eng	BBL7314
			Philips	Eur	B07375L
			Philips	Eur	B07507L
			Philips	Eur	B47124L
5820	The French Touch (mx CO 60724)				
		12 Inch 33	>Columbia	USA	C2L9
			Columbia	USA	CL1213
			Columbia	USA	CS8132
			Columbia	USA	JC2L9
			Philips	Eng	BBL7314
			Philips	Eur	B07375L
			Philips	Eur	B07507L
			Philips	Eur	B47124L
5830	Too Close for Comfort (mx CO 60725)				
		12 Inch 33	>Columbia	USA	CL1587
			Philips	Eur	B47081L
5840	Moroccan Quarter (mx CO 60726)				
		12 Inch 33	>Columbia	USA	C2L9
			Columbia	USA	CL1213
			Columbia	USA	CS8132
			Columbia	USA	JC2L9
			Columbia	USA	PB11
			Columbia	Jap	SL-3009
			Philips	Eng	BBL7314
			Philips	Eur	B07507L
5850	Don't Look for Me* (mx CO 60727)				
		12 Inch 33	>Columbia	USA	C2L9

Columbia	USA	CL1212
Columbia	USA	CS8131
Columbia	USA	JC2L9
Philips	Eng	BBL7313
Philips	Eur	B07506L

5860	Untitled Original		
	(mx CO 60728)		Unissued
5870	Untitled Original		
	(mx CO 60729)		Unissued

ERROLL GARNER TRIO   NEW YORK, MAY 11, 1958

Asterisk (*) denotes Erroll Garner on harpsichord only.
Erroll Garner (p, h*), Eddie Calhoun (b), Kelly Martin (d)

5880	I Can't Get Started*			
	(mx CO 60951)			
	7 Inch 45	>Columbia	USA	4-41231
		Philips	Eur	322327BF
	7 Inch 45EP	Philips	Eur	429510BE
5890	I Can't Give You Anything But Love			
	(mx CO 60952)			Unissued
5900	Just Blues*			
	(mx CO 60953)			
	7 Inch 45	>Columbia	USA	4-41231
	7 Inch 45EP	Philips	Eur	429510BE

Note: "Just Blues" is the same tune as the piano version of "French Doll" (see also March 27, 1958 session).

5910	Untitled Original		
	(mx CO 60954)		Unissued
5920	Untitled Original		
	(mx CO 60955)		Unissued
5930	After You've Gone		
	(mx CO 60956)		Unissued
5940	Paris Blues*			
	(mx CO 60957)			
	7 Inch 45	Philips	Eur	322327BF
	7 Inch 45EP	Philips	Eur	429510BE
	12 Inch 33	>Columbia	USA	C2L9
		Columbia	USA	CL1213
		Columbia	USA	CS8132
		Columbia	USA	JC2L9
		Philips	Eng	BBL7314
		Philips	Eur	B07507L
5950	Other Voices			
	(mx CO 60958)			Unissued
5960	Untitled Original		
	(mx CO 60959)		Unissued
5970	Untitled Original		
	(mx CO 60960)		Unissued
5980	The Surrey with the Fringe on Top		
	(mx CO 60961)		Unissued
5990	How About You?		
	(mx CO 60962)		Unissued
6000	My Ideal		
	(mx CO 60963)		Unissued
6010	Cote d'Azur*			
	(mx CO 60964)			
	7 Inch 45EP	Philips	Eur	429510BE
	12 Inch 33	>Columbia	USA	C2L9
		Columbia	USA	CL1212
		Columbia	USA	CS8131
		Columbia	USA	JC2L9
		Philips	Eng	BBL7313
		Philips	Eur	B07506L

6020	Untitled Original			
	(mx CO 60965)			Unissued
6030	When Paris Cries*			
	(mx CO 60966)			
	12 Inch 33	>Columbia	USA	C2L9
		Columbia	USA	CL1213
		Columbia	USA	CS8132
		Columbia	USA	JC2L9
		Philips	Eng	BBL7314
		Philips	Eur	B07507L
6040	Untitled Original			
	(mx CO 60967)			Unissued
6050	Love for Sale			
	(mx CO 60968)			Unissued

ERROLL GARNER TRIO   NEW YORK, RELEASED OCT. 25, 1959
Erroll Garner (p), Eddie Calhoun (b), Kelly Martin (d)

6060	Will You Still Be Mine?			
	(mx FSGRC 899)			
	16 Inch TX	>Stars for Defense	USA	160
6070	Dreamy			
	(mx FSGRC 899)			
	16 Inch TX	>Stars for Defense	USA	160
6080	Where or When			
	(mx FSGRC 899)			
	16 Inch TX	>Stars for Defense	USA	160

ERROLL GARNER TRIO   NEW YORK, ca. MARCH, 1961
Erroll Garner (p), Eddie Calhoun (b), Kelly Martin (d)

6090	Just One of Those Things			
	7 Inch 45EP	Philips	Eng	434703BE
		Philips	Eur	761903BV
	7 Inch 33	ABC Paramount	USA	ABCS 365-2
	12 Inch 33	>ABC Paramount	USA	ABC 365
		ABC Paramount	USA	ABCS 365
		Philips	Can	PHM200-002
		Philips	Can	PHS600-002
		Philips	Eng	BBL7523
		Philips	Eng	SBBL677
		Philips	Eur	842911BY
		Philips	Eur	632201BL
	12 Inch TX	Stars for Defense	USA	269
6100	I'm Gettin' Sentimental Over You			
	7 Inch 33	ABC Paramount	USA	ABCS 365-2
	12 Inch 33	>ABC Paramount	USA	ABC 365
		ABC Paramount	USA	ABCS 365
		Philips	Can	PHM200-002
		Philips	Can	PHS600-002
		Philips	Eng	BBL7523
		Philips	Eng	SBBL677
		Philips	Eur	842911BY
		Philips	Eur	632201BL
6110	Blue Lou			
	7 Inch 45EP	Philips	Eng	434703BE
		Philips	Eur	761903BV
	12 Inch 33	>ABC Paramount	USA	ABC 365
		ABC Paramount	USA	ABCS 365
		Philips	Can	PHM200-002
		Philips	Can	PHS600-002
		Philips	Eng	BBL7523
		Philips	Eng	SBBL677
		Philips	Eur	842911BY
		Philips	Eur	632201BL

6120	Come Rain or Come Shine			
	12 Inch 33	>ABC Paramount	USA	ABC 365
		ABC Paramount	USA	ABCS 365
		Philips	Can	PHM200-002
		Philips	Can	PHS600-002
		Philips	Eng	BBL7523
		Philips	Eng	SBBL677
		Philips	Eur	842911BY
		Philips	Eur	632201BL
6130	The Lady Is a Tramp			
	7 Inch 45EP	Philips	Eng	434702BE
		Philips	Eur	761902BV
	12 Inch 33	>ABC Paramount	USA	ABC 365
		ABC Paramount	USA	ABCS 365
		Philips	Can	PHM200-002
		Philips	Can	PHS600-002
		Philips	Eng	BBL7523
		Philips	Eng	SBBL677
		Philips	Eur	842911BY
		Philips	Eur	632201BL
	12 Inch TX	Stars for Defense	USA	269
6140	When You're Smiling (The Whole World Smiles with You)			
	7 Inch 45	ABC Paramount	USA	45-10260
	7 Inch 45EP	Philips	Eng	434702BE
		Philips	Eur	761902BV
	12 Inch 33	>ABC Paramount	USA	ABC 365
		ABC Paramount	USA	ABCS 365
		Philips	Can	PHM200-002
		Philips	Can	PHS600-002
		Philips	Eng	BBL7523
		Philips	Eng	SBBL677
		Philips	Eur	842911BY
		Philips	Eur	632201BL
6150	Dreamstreet			
	7 Inch 45	ABC Paramount	USA	45-10260
	7 Inch 45EP	Philips	Eng	434702BE
		Philips	Eur	761902BV
	12 Inch 33	>ABC Paramount	USA	ABC 365
		ABC Paramount	USA	ABCS 365
		Philips	Can	PHM200-002
		Philips	Can	PHS600-002
		Philips	Eng	BBL7523
		Philips	Eng	SBBL677
		Philips	Eur	842911BY
		Philips	Eur	632201BL
	12 Inch TX	Stars for Defense	USA	269
6160	Sweet Lorraine			
	7 Inch 45EP	Philips	Eng	434702BE
		Philips	Eur	761902BV
	12 Inch 33	>ABC Paramount	USA	ABC 365
		ABC Paramount	USA	ABCS 365
		Philips	Can	PHM200-002
		Philips	Can	PHS600-002
		Philips	Eng	BBL7523
		Philips	Eng	SBBL677
		Philips	Eur	632201BL
		Philips	Eur	842911BY
6170	Mambo Gotham			
	7 Inch 45EP	Philips	Eng	434703BE
		Philips	Eur	761903BV
	12 Inch 33	>ABC Paramount	USA	ABC 365
		ABC Paramount	USA	ABCS 365
		Philips	Can	PHM200-002

			Philips	Can	PHS600-002
			Philips	Eng	BBL7523
			Philips	Eng	SBBL677
			Philips	Eur	842911BY
			Philips	Eur	632201BL

6180   Oklahoma! Medley:
Oh, What a Beautiful Mornin'
People Will Say We're in Love
The Surrey with the Fringe on Top

		7 Inch 45EP	Philips	Eng	BBE12567
			Philips	Eur	434706BE
		7 Inch 33	ABC Paramount	USA	ABCS 365-3
		12 Inch 33	>ABC Paramount	USA	ABC 365
			ABC Paramount	USA	ABCS 365
			Philips	Can	PHM200-002
			Philips	Can	PHS600-002
			Philips	Eng	BBL7523
			Philips	Eng	SBBL677
			Philips	Eur	842911BY
			Philips	Eur	632201BL

Note: Philips BBE12567 is an abbreviated version featuring "The Surrey with the Fringe on Top."

ERROLL GARNER TRIO   NEW YORK, JULY 7, 1961

Erroll Garner (p), Eddie Calhoun (b), Kelly Martin (d)

6190   You Do Something to Me

	7 Inch 45	ABC Paramount	USA	45-10301
		Philips	Eng	324900BF
	7 Inch 45EP	Philips	Eng	434700BE
		Philips	Eng	BBE12510
		Philips	Eur	761900BV
	12 Inch 33	>ABC Paramount	USA	ABC 395
		ABC Paramount	USA	ABCS 395
		Book of the Month	USA	81-5403
		Octave	Jap	FL-5055
		Octave	Jap	SFL-7063
		Philips	Can	PHM200-001
		Philips	Can	PHS600-001
		Philips	Eng	BBL7519
		Philips	Eng	SBBL676
		Philips	Eur	632200BL
		Philips	Eur	842910BY

6200   My Silent Love

	7 Inch 45EP	Philips	Eng	434706BE
		Philips	Eng	BBE12567
	12 Inch 33	>ABC Paramount	USA	ABC 395
		ABC Paramount	USA	ABCS 395
		Book of the Month	USA	81-5403
		Octave	Jap	FL-5055
		Octave	Jap	SFL-7063
		Philips	Can	PHM200-001
		Philips	Can	PHS600-001
		Philips	Eng	BBL7519
		Philips	Eng	SBBL676
		Philips	Eur	632200BL
		Philips	Eur	842910BY

6210   All of Me

	7 Inch 45EP	Philips	Eng	434700BE
		Philips	Eng	BBE12510
		Philips	Eur	761900BV

	12 Inch 33	>ABC Paramount	USA	ABC 395
		ABC Paramount	USA	ABCS 395
		Book of the Month	USA	81-5403
		Octave	Jap	FL-5055
		Octave	Jap	SFL-7063
		Philips	Can	PHM200-001
		Philips	Can	PHS600-001
		Philips	Eng	BBL7519
		Philips	Eng	SBBL676
		Philips	Eur	632200BL
		Philips	Eur	842910BY
6220	Shadows			
	7 Inch 45EP	Philips	Eng	BBE12510
		Philips	Eur	761901BV
	12 Inch 33	>ABC Paramount	USA	ABC 395
		ABC Paramount	USA	ABCS 395
		Octave	Jap	FL-5055
		Octave	Jap	SFL-7063
		Philips	Can	PHM200-001
		Philips	Can	PHS600-001
		Philips	Eng	BBL7519
		Philips	Eng	SBBL676
		Philips	Eur	632200BL
		Philips	Eur	842910BY

Note: "Shadows" (Erroll Garner) was later retitled "No More Shadows" with lyrics by Edward Heyman.

6230	St. Louis Blues			
	7 Inch 45EP	Philips	Eng	434701BE
		Philips	Eur	761901BV
	7 Inch 33	ABC Paramount	USA	ABCS 395-5
	12 Inch 33	>ABC Paramount	USA	ABC 395
		ABC Paramount	USA	ABCS 395
		Book of the Month	USA	81-5403
		Octave	Jap	FL-5055
		Octave	Jap	SFL-7063
		Philips	Can	PHM200-001
		Philips	Can	PHS600-001
		Philips	Eng	BBL7519
		Philips	Eng	SBBL676
		Philips	Eur	632200BL
		Philips	Eur	842910BY
6240	Some of These Days			
	7 Inch 45	ABC Paramount	USA	45-10301
		Philips	Eng	324900BF
	7 Inch 45EP	Philips	Eng	434701BE
		Philips	Eur	761901BV
	12 Inch 33	>ABC Paramount	USA	ABC 395
		ABC Paramount	USA	ABCS 395
		Book of the Month	USA	81-5403
		Octave	Jap	FL-5055
		Octave	Jap	SFL-7063
		Philips	Can	PHM200-001
		Philips	Can	PHS600-001
		Philips	Eng	BBL7519
		Philips	Eng	SBBL676
		Philips	Eur	632200BL
		Philips	Eur	842910BY
6250	I'm in the Mood for Love			
	7 Inch 45EP	Philips	Eng	434706BE
		Philips	Eng	BBE12567
	12 Inch 33	>ABC Paramount	USA	ABC 395
		ABC Paramount	USA	ABCS 395
		Book of the Month	USA	81-5403

		Octave	Jap	FL-5055
		Octave	Jap	SFL-7063
		Philips	Can	PHM200-001
		Philips	Can	PHS600-001
		Philips	Eng	BBL7519
		Philips	Eng	SBBL676
		Philips	Eur	632200BL
		Philips	Eur	842910BY
6260	El Papa Grande			
	7 Inch 45EP	Philips	Eng	434701BE
		Philips	Eur	761901BV
	12 Inch 33	>ABC Paramount	USA	ABC 395
		ABC Paramount	USA	ABCS 395
		Octave	Jap	FL-5055
		Octave	Jap	SFL-7063
		Philips	Can	PHM200-001
		Philips	Can	PHS600-001
		Philips	Eng	BBL7519
		Philips	Eng	SBBL676
		Philips	Eur	632200BL
		Philips	Eur	842910BY
6270	The Best Things in Life Are Free			
	7 Inch 45EP	Philips	Eng	434706BE
		Philips	Eng	BBE12567
	7 Inch 33	ABC Paramount	USA	ABCS 395-5
	12 Inch 33	>ABC Paramount	USA	ABC 395
		ABC Paramount	USA	ABCS 395
		Book of the Month	USA	81-5403
		Octave	Jap	FL-5055
		Octave	Jap	SFL-7063
		Philips	Can	PHM200-001
		Philips	Can	PHS600-001
		Philips	Eng	BBL7519
		Philips	Eng	SBBL676
		Philips	Eur	632200BL
		Philips	Eur	842910BY
6280	Back in Your Own Back Yard			
	7 Inch 45EP	Philips	Eng	434700BE
		Philips	Eng	BBE12510
		Philips	Eur	761900BV
	12 Inch 33	>ABC Paramount	USA	ABC 395
		ABC Paramount	USA	ABCS 395
		Octave	Jap	FL-5055
		Octave	Jap	SFL-7063
		Philips	Can	PHM200-001
		Philips	Can	PHS600-001
		Philips	Eng	BBL7519
		Philips	Eng	SBBL676
		Philips	Eur	632200BL
		Philips	Eur	842910BY

ERROLL GARNER TRIO   **LAFAYETTE, IN, MARCH 13, 1962**
Purdue University
Erroll Garner (p), Eddie Calhoun (b), Kelly Martin (d)
6290   Indiana (Back Home Again In Indiana)
       (mx 100707)

	7 Inch 45	MGM	USA	K13836
	12 Inch 33	>MGM	USA	E-4361
		MGM	USA	SE-4361
		MGM	Eng	C-8026
		MGM	Eng	CS-8026

	MGM	WGer	665062
	Polydor	Fra	2393004
	Polydor	WGer	P76295

6300 Stardust
(mx 100708)
12 Inch 33

	>MGM	USA	E-4361
	MGM	USA	SE-4361
	MGM	Eng	C-8026
	MGM	Eng	CS-8026
	MGM	WGer	665062
	Polydor	Fra	2393004
	Polydor	WGer	P76295

6310 Mambo Erroll
(mx 100709)
12 Inch 33

	>MGM	USA	E-4361
	MGM	USA	SE-4361
	MGM	Eng	C-8026
	MGM	Eng	CS-8026
	MGM	WGer	665062
	Polydor	Fra	2393004

6320 Lulu's Back in Town
(mx 100710)
12 Inch 33

	Book of the Month	USA	81-5403
	>MGM	USA	E-4361
	MGM	USA	SE-4361
	MGM	Eng	C-8026
	MGM	Eng	CS-8026
	MGM	WGer	665062
	Polydor	Fra	2393004
	Polydor	WGer	P76295

6330 Almost Like Being in Love
(mx 100711)
12 Inch 33

	>MGM	USA	E-4361
	MGM	USA	SE-4361
	MGM	Eng	C-8026
	MGM	Eng	CS-8026
	MGM	WGer	665062
	Polydor	Fra	2393004

6340 My Funny Valentine
(mx 100712)
12 Inch 33

	>MGM	USA	E-4361
	MGM	USA	SE-4361
	MGM	Eng	C-8026
	MGM	Eng	CS-8026
	MGM	WGer	665062
	Polydor	Fra	2393004

6350 These Foolish Things (Remind Me of You)
(mx 100713)
12 Inch 33

	>MGM	USA	E-4361
	MGM	USA	SE-4361
	MGM	Eng	C-8026
	MGM	Eng	CS-8026
	MGM	WGer	665062
	Polydor	Fra	2393004
	Polydor	WGer	P76295

6360 In the Still of the Night
(mx 100714)
7 Inch 45
12 Inch 33

	MGM	USA	K13836
	>MGM	USA	E-4361
	MGM	USA	SE-4361
	MGM	Eng	C-8026
	MGM	Eng	CS-8026
	MGM	WGer	665062
	Polydor	Fra	2393004
	Polydor	WGer	P76295

ERROLL GARNER TRIO   **SEATTLE, AUGUST 20-25, 1962**
Reprise R-6080 (6370, 6380, 6400, 6410, 6420, 6460) was specially prepared in a limited edition with locked bands between tracks for broadcasters' use only.

Erroll Garner (p), Eddie Calhoun (b), Kelly Martin (d)
6370   The Way You Look Tonight
       (mx 2031)

	7 Inch 45EP	Philips	Eng	434704BE
		Philips	Eng	BE12568
	12 Inch 45	Reprise	USA	R-6080
	12 Inch 33	Book of the Month	USA	81-5403
		Philips	Can	PHS600-008
		Philips	Eng	BL7580
		Philips	Eng	SBL7580
		Philips	Eur	842912BY
		Philips	Eur	632202BL
		Philips	Jap	SFL-7140
		>Reprise	USA	R9-6080

6380   Happiness Is a Thing Called Joe
       (mx 2032)

	7 Inch 45EP	Philips	Eng	BBE12568
	12 Inch 45	Reprise	USA	R-6080
	12 Inch 33	Book of the Month	USA	81-5403
		Philips	Can	PHS600-008
		Philips	Eng	BL7580
		Philips	Eng	SBL7580
		Philips	Eur	842912BY
		Philips	Eur	632202BL
		Philips	Jap	SFL-7140
		>Reprise	USA	R9-6080

6390   Sweet and Lovely
       (mx 2033)

	7 Inch 45	Philips	Eng	BF1268
		Philips	Eur	324901BF
		Philips	Eur	327365JF
		Reprise	USA	R-20179
	7 Inch 45EP	Philips	Eng	434705BE
		Philips	Eng	BE12569
	12 Inch 33	Book of the Month	USA	81-5403
		Philips	Can	PHS600-008
		Philips	Eng	BL7580
		Philips	Eng	SBL7580
		Philips	Eur	842912BY
		Philips	Eur	632202BL
		Philips	Jap	SFL-7140
		>Reprise	USA	R9-6080

6400   Mack the Knife
       (mx 2034)

	7 Inch 45	Philips	Eng	BF1268
		Philips	Eur	324901BF
		Philips	Eur	327365JF
		Reprise	USA	R-20179
	7 Inch 45EP	Philips	Eng	434705BE
		Philips	Eng	BE12569
	12 Inch 45	Reprise	USA	R-6080
	12 Inch 33	Book of the Month	USA	81-5403
		Philips	Can	PHS600-008
		Philips	Eng	BL7580
		Philips	Eng	SBL7580
		Philips	Eur	842912BY
		Philips	Eur	632202BL
		Philips	Jap	SFL-7140
		>Reprise	USA	R9-6080

6410	Lover Come Back to Me (mx 2035)			
	12 Inch 45	Reprise	USA	R-6080
	7 Inch 33	Reprise	USA	R-40051
	12 Inch 33	Book of the Month	USA	81-5403
		Philips	Can	PHS600-008
		Philips	Eng	BL7580
		Philips	Eng	SBL7580
		Philips	Eur	842912BY
		Philips	Eur	632202BL
		Philips	Jap	SFL-7140
		>Reprise	USA	R9-6080
6420	Misty (mx 2036)			
	7 Inch 45EP	Philips	Eng	434704BE
		Philips	Eng	BBE12568
		Philips	Eng	BE12568
	12 Inch 45	Reprise	USA	R-6080
	7 Inch 33	Reprise	USA	R-40051
	12 Inch 33	Book of the Month	USA	81-5403
		Philips	Can	PHS600-008
		Philips	Eng	BL7580
		Philips	Eng	SBL7580
		Philips	Eur	842912BY
		Philips	Eur	632202BL
		Philips	Jap	SFL-7140
		>Reprise	USA	R9-6080
6430	Movin' Blues (mx 2037)			
	12 Inch 33	Philips	Can	PHS600-008
		Philips	Eng	BL7580
		Philips	Eng	SBL7580
		Philips	Eur	842912BY
		Philips	Eur	632202BL
		Philips	Jap	SFL-7140
		>Reprise	USA	R9-6080
6440	Dancing Tambourine (mx 2038)			
	7 Inch 45EP	Philips	Eng	434704BE
		Philips	Eng	BBE12568
		Philips	Eng	BE12568
	12 Inch 33	Book of the Month	USA	81-5403
		Philips	Can	PHS600-008
		Philips	Eng	BL7580
		Philips	Eng	SBL7580
		Philips	Eur	842912BY
		Philips	Eur	632202BL
		Philips	Jap	SFL-7140
		>Reprise	USA	R9-6080
6450	Thanks for the Memory (mx 2039)			
	7 Inch 45EP	Philips	Eng	434705BE
		Philips	Eng	BE12569
	12 Inch 33	Philips	Can	PHS600-008
		Philips	Eng	BL7580
		Philips	Eng	SBL7580
		Philips	Eur	632202BL
		Philips	Eur	842912BY
		Philips	Jap	SFL-7140
		>Reprise	USA	R9-6080
6460	Stride Out (mx 2040)			
	12 Inch 45	>Reprise	USA	R-6080

ERROLL GARNER TRIO   NEW YORK, RELEASED MARCH 10, 1963
Erroll Garner (p), Al Hall (b), Kelly Martin (d)
6470   Back in Your Own Back Yard
              12 Inch TX   >Stars for Defense   USA   336
6480   El Papa Grande
              12 Inch TX   >Stars for Defense   USA   336
6490   Just One of Those Things
              12 Inch TX   >Stars for Defense   USA   336

ERROLL GARNER WITH ORCHESTRA   LOS ANGELES, JULY, 1963
Conducted by Leith Stevens
Erroll Garner (p); Leith Stevens (co); Carroll "Cappy" Lewis (tp); Dick Nash, Dick
Noel, George Roberts, Bob Enevoldsen (tb); Ted Hash, Gene Cipriano, Harry Klee,
Ronnie Lang, Charles Gentry, William "Buddy" Collette (reeds and woodwinds);
Barney Kessel (g); Keith "Red" Mitchell (b); Larry Bunker, Irving Cottler, Alvin
Stoller (d, percussion); unknown string section; unidentified harp.
6500   Theme from "A New Kind of Love"
              (mx 30609)
                            7 Inch 45   Mercury   USA   72192
                                               Octave   USA   45-301
                            7 Inch 45EP   Philips   Eng   434707BE
                                               Philips   Eng   434708BE
                                               Philips   Eur   761904BV
                            12 Inch 33   >Mercury   USA   MG20859
                                               Mercury   USA   SR60859
                                               Mercury   Urg   632203
                                               Philips   Eng   BL7595
                                               Philips   Eng   SBL7595
                                               Philips   Eur   842913BY
                                               Philips   Eur   B632203L
                                               Philips   Jap   SFL-7160
                            12 Inch TX   Voices of Vista USA   2
              *Note: "Theme from 'A New Kind of Love' " (Erroll Garner) was later retitled
              "All Yours." There are no known lyrics to this title.*
6510   Mimi
              (mx 30610)
                            7 Inch 45   Mercury   USA   72192
                            12 Inch 33   >Mercury   USA   MG20859
                                               Mercury   USA   SR60859
                                               Mercury   Urg   632203
                                               Philips   Eng   BL7595
                                               Philips   Eng   SBL7595
                                               Philips   Eur   842913BY
                                               Philips   Eur   B632203L
                                               Philips   Jap   SFL-7160
                            12 Inch TX   Voices of Vista USA   2
6520   Louise
              (mx 30611)
                            12 Inch 33   >Mercury   USA   MG20859
                                               Mercury   USA   SR60859
                                               Mercury   Urg   632203
                                               Philips   Eng   BL7595
                                               Philips   Eng   SBL7595
                                               Philips   Eur   842913BY
                                               Philips   Eur   B632203L
                                               Philips   Jap   SFL-7160
6530   Fashion Interlude
              (mx 30612)
                            7 Inch 45EP   Philips   Eng   434707BE
                                               Philips   Eur   761904BV

	12 Inch 33	>Mercury	USA	MG20859
		Mercury	USA	SR60859
		Mercury	Urg	632203
		Philips	Eng	BL7595
		Philips	Eng	SBL7595
		Philips	Eur	842913BY
		Philips	Eur	B632203L
		Philips	Jap	SFL-7160

Note: "Fashion Interlude" (Erroll Garner) is titled "Fashion Montage" on Philips 761904BV, Philips 434707BE and Philips SFL-7160.

6540 Steve's Song
(mx 30613)

	7 Inch 45EP	Philips	Eng	434708BE
	12 Inch 33	>Mercury	USA	MG20859
		Mercury	USA	SR60859
		Mercury	Urg	632203
		Philips	Eng	BL7595
		Philips	Eng	SBL7595
		Philips	Eur	842913BY
		Philips	Eur	B632203L
		Philips	Jap	SFL-7160

6550 Paris Mist (Bossa Nova)
(mx 30614)

	7 Inch 45	Octave	USA	45-301
	12 Inch 33	>Mercury	USA	MG20859
		Mercury	USA	SR60859
		Mercury	Urg	632203
		Philips	Eng	BL7595
		Philips	Eng	SBL7595
		Philips	Eur	842913BY
		Philips	Eur	B632203L
		Philips	Jap	SFL-7160
	12 Inch TX	Voices of Vista	USA	2

Note: See note under Paris Mist (6580).

6560 You Brought a New Kind of Love to Me
(mx 30615)

	7 Inch 45EP	Philips	Eng	434707BE
		Philips	Eng	434708BE
		Philips	Eur	761904BV
	12 Inch 33	>Mercury	USA	MG20859
		Mercury	USA	SR60859
		Mercury	Urg	632203
		Philips	Eng	BL7595
		Philips	Eng	SBL7595
		Philips	Eur	842913BY
		Philips	Eur	B632203L
		Philips	Jap	SFL-7160

6570 In the Park in Paree
(mx 30616)

	12 Inch 33	>Mercury	USA	MG20859
		Mercury	USA	SR60859
		Mercury	Urg	632203
		Philips	Eng	BL7595
		Philips	Eng	SBL7595
		Philips	Eur	842913BY
		Philips	Eur	B632203L
		Philips	Jap	SFL-7160

6580 Paris Mist (Waltz-Swing)
(mx 30617)

	12 Inch 33	>Mercury	USA	MG20859
		Mercury	USA	SR60859
		Mercury	Urg	632203
		Philips	Eng	BL7595

		Philips	Eng	SBL7595
		Philips	Eur	842913BY
		Philips	Eur	B632203L
		Philips	Jap	SFL-7160

Note: "Paris Mist" (Erroll Garner) was later retitled "Hang Some Love on Me" with lyrics by Larry Kusik and Eddie Snyder (U.S. Copyright, November 15, 1968).

6590   The Tease
       (mx 30618)

	7 Inch 45EP	Philips	Eng	434707BE
		Philips	Eng	434708BE
		Philips	Eur	761904BV
	12 Inch 33	>Mercury	USA	MG20859
		Mercury	USA	SR60859
		Mercury	Urg	632203
		Philips	Eng	BL7595
		Philips	Eng	SBL7595
		Philips	Eur	842913BY
		Philips	Eur	B632203L
		Philips	Jap	SFL-7160

Note: "The Tease" is titled "The Teaser" on Philips 761904BV, Philips 434707BE and Philips SFL-7160.

ERROLL GARNER TRIO   MANCHESTER, ENGLAND, OCTOBER 19, 1963
       Free Trade Hall
Erroll Garner (p), Eddie Calhoun (b), Kelly Martin (d)

6600	Dancing in the Dark				
	12 Inch 33	>Jazz Groove	Eng	008	
6610	Fly Me to the Moon (In Other Words)				
	12 Inch 33	>Jazz Groove	Eng	008	
6620	Moroccan Mambo				
	12 Inch 33	>Jazz Groove	Eng	008	
6630	It Might As Well Be Spring /				
	Spring Is Here				Unissued
6640	Untitled Original				Unissued
6650	I Can't Get Started				Unissued
6660	Night and Day				Unissued
6670	Stella by Starlight				Unissued
6680	(All of a Sudden) My Heart Sings				Unissued
6690	Indiana (Back Home Again in Indiana)				Unissued
6700	That's All				Unissued
6710	One Note Samba				Unissued
6720	Autumn Leaves				
	12 Inch 33	>Jazz Groove	Eng	008	
6730	Edna May				
	12 Inch 33	>Jazz Groove	Eng	008	
6740	April in Paris				Unissued
6750	I May Be Wrong				
	(But I Think You're Wonderful)				Unissued
6760	Dark Pool				
	12 Inch 33	>Jazz Groove	Eng	008	
6770	All the Things You Are				Unissued
6780	Mambo Erroll				Unissued
6790	On Green Dolphin Street				Unissued
6800	Untitled Original				Unissued
6810	Dancing Tambourine				Unissued
6820	Thanks for the Memory				Unissued
6830	God Save the Queen				Unissued

ERROLL GARNER TRIO   **NEW YORK, JULY 25, 1964**

Erroll Garner (p), Eddie Calhoun (b), Kelly Martin (d)

6840   You Made Me Love You
        (mx 64-XY-834)

12 Inch 33	Amiga	EGer	855205
	Book of the Month	USA	81-5403
	>MGM	USA	E-4335
	MGM	USA	SE-4335
	MGM	USA	ST-90600
	MGM	Eng	C-8004
	MGM	Eng	CS-8004
	MGM	Fra	65053
	MGM	Jap	SMM-1100
	MGM	WGer	665053
	Polydor	WGer	P76295

6850   As Time Goes By
        (mx 64-XY-835)

7 Inch 45	MGM	USA	K13471
	MGM	USA	K13834
12 Inch 33	Amiga	EGer	855205
	Book of the Month	USA	81-5403
	>MGM	USA	E-4335
	MGM	USA	SE-4335
	MGM	USA	ST-90600
	MGM	Eng	C-8004
	MGM	Eng	CS-8004
	MGM	Fra	65053
	MGM	Jap	SMM-1100
	MGM	WGer	665053

6860   Sonny Boy
        (mx 64-XY-836)

7 Inch 45	MGM	USA	K13835
12 Inch 33	Amiga	EGer	855205
	>MGM	USA	E-4335
	MGM	USA	SE-4335
	MGM	USA	ST-90600
	MGM	Eng	C-8004
	MGM	Eng	CS-8004
	MGM	Fra	65053
	MGM	Jap	SMM-1100
	MGM	WGer	665053
	Polydor	WGer	P76295

6870   Charmaine
        (mx 64-XY-837)

12 Inch 33	Amiga	EGer	855205
	>MGM	USA	E-4335
	MGM	USA	SE-4335
	MGM	USA	ST-90600
	MGM	Eng	C-8004
	MGM	Eng	CS-8004
	MGM	Fra	65053
	MGM	Jap	SMM-1100
	MGM	WGer	665053

6880   I Found a Million Dollar Baby (In a Five and Ten Cent Store)
        (mx 64-XY-838)

12 Inch 33	Amiga	EGer	855205
	>MGM	USA	E-4335
	MGM	USA	SE-4335
	MGM	USA	ST-90600
	MGM	Eng	C-8004
	MGM	Eng	CS-8004
	MGM	Fra	65053
	MGM	Jap	SMM-1100
	MGM	WGer	665053

6890	I'll Get By (As Long As I Have You)			
	(mx 64-XY-839)			
	12 Inch 33	Amiga	EGer	855205
		>MGM	USA	E-4335
		MGM	USA	SE-4335
		MGM	USA	ST-90600
		MGM	Eng	C-8004
		MGM	Eng	CS-8004
		MGM	Fra	65053
		MGM	Jap	SMM-1100
		MGM	WGer	665053
		Polydor	WGer	P76295
6900	Three O'Clock in the Morning			
	(mx 64-XY-840)			
	12 Inch 33	Amiga	EGer	855205
		>MGM	USA	E-4335
		MGM	USA	SE-4335
		MGM	USA	ST-90600
		MGM	Eng	C-8004
		MGM	Eng	CS-8004
		MGM	Fra	65053
		MGM	Jap	SMM-1100
		MGM	WGer	665053
		Polydor	WGer	P76295
6910	Stella by Starlight			
	(mx 64-XY-841)			
	12 Inch 33	Amiga	EGer	855205
		Book of the Month	USA	81-5403
		>MGM	USA	E-4335
		MGM	USA	SE-4335
		MGM	USA	ST-90600
		MGM	Eng	C-8004
		MGM	Eng	CS-8004
		MGM	Fra	65053
		MGM	Jap	SMM-1100
		MGM	WGer	665053
		Polydor	WGer	P76295
6920	Jeannine, I Dream of Lilac Time			
	(mx 64-XY-842)			
	12 Inch 33	Amiga	EGer	855205
		>MGM	USA	E-4335
		MGM	USA	SE-4335
		MGM	USA	ST-90600
		MGM	Eng	C-8004
		MGM	Eng	CS-8004
		MGM	Fra	65053
		MGM	Jap	SMM-1100
		MGM	WGer	665053
		Polydor	WGer	P76295
6930	Schoner Gigolo (Just a Gigolo)			
	(mx 64-XY-843)			
	7 Inch 45	MGM	USA	K13471
		MGM	USA	K13835
	12 Inch 33	Amiga	EGer	855205
		Book of the Month	USA	81-5403
		>MGM	USA	E-4335
		MGM	USA	SE-4335
		MGM	USA	ST-90600
		MGM	Eng	C-8004
		MGM	Eng	CS-8004
		MGM	Fra	65053
		MGM	Jap	SMM-1100
		MGM	WGer	665053
		Polydor	WGer	P76295

6940	How Deep Is the Ocean (How High Is the Sky) (mx 64-XY-844)			
	12 Inch 33	Amiga	EGer	855205
		>MGM	USA	E-4335
		MGM	USA	SE-4335
		MGM	USA	ST-90600
		MGM	Eng	C-8004
		MGM	Eng	CS-8004
		MGM	Fra	65053
		MGM	Jap	SMM-1100
		MGM	WGer	665053
6950	It's Only a Paper Moon (mx 64-XY-845)			
	12 Inch 33	Amiga	EGer	855205
		>MGM	USA	E-4335
		MGM	USA	SE-4335
		MGM	USA	ST-90600
		MGM	Eng	C-8004
		MGM	Eng	CS-8004
		MGM	Fra	65053
		MGM	Jap	SMM-1100
		MGM	WGer	665053
		Polydor	WGer	P76295
6960	Paramount on Parade (Newsreel Tag) (mx 64-XY-846)			
	12 Inch 33	Amiga	EGer	855205
		>MGM	USA	E-4335
		MGM	USA	SE-4335
		MGM	USA	ST-90600
		MGM	Eng	C-8004
		MGM	Eng	CS-8004
		MGM	Fra	65053
		MGM	Jap	SMM-1100
		MGM	WGer	665053

ERROLL GARNER TRIO   **NEW YORK, ca. JULY 25, 1964**

According to Thomas Schleuszner (Berlin, West Germany), who is working on an extensive musical analysis of Garner, this session, based on aural evidence, belongs with the previous session.

Erroll Garner (p), Eddie Calhoun (b), Kelly Martin (d)

6970	Strike Up the Band			
	12 Inch 33	Bull Dog	Eng	BDL4004
		MPS	Neth	5D064D-99397
		>MPS	WGer	68.126
		Polydor	Fra	2445030
6980	Love Walked In			
	12 Inch 33	Bull Dog	Eng	BDL4004
		MPS	Neth	5D064D-99397
		>MPS	WGer	68.126
		Polydor	Fra	2445030
6990	Someone to Watch Over Me			
	12 Inch 33	Bull Dog	Eng	BDL4004
		MPS	Neth	5D064D-99397
		>MPS	WGer	68.126
		Polydor	Fra	2445030
7000	A Foggy Day			
	12 Inch 33	Bull Dog	Eng	BDL4004
		MPS	Neth	5D064D-99397
		>MPS	WGer	68.126
		Polydor	Fra	2445030

7010	Lovely to Look At			
	12 Inch 33	Bull Dog	Eng	BDL4004
		MPS	Neth	5D064D-99397
		>MPS	WGer	68.126
		Polydor	Fra	2445030
7020	Can't Help Lovin' Dat Man			
	12 Inch 33	Bull Dog	Eng	BDL4004
		MPS	Neth	5D064D-99397
		>MPS	WGer	68.126
		Polydor	Fra	2445030
7030	Make Believe			
	12 Inch 33	Bull Dog	Eng	BDL4004
		MPS	Neth	5D064D-99397
		>MPS	WGer	68.126
		Polydor	Fra	2445030
7040	Ol' Man River			
	12 Inch 33	Bull Dog	Eng	BDL4004
		MPS	Neth	5D064D-99397
		>MPS	WGer	68.126
		Polydor	Fra	2445030
7050	Dearly Beloved			
	12 Inch 33	Bull Dog	Eng	BDL4004
		MPS	Neth	5D064D-99397
		>MPS	WGer	68.126
		Polydor	Fra	2445030
7060	A Fine Romance			
	12 Inch 33	Bull Dog	Eng	BDL4004
		MPS	Neth	5D064D-99397
		>MPS	WGer	68.126
		Polydor	Fra	2445030

ERROLL GARNER TRIO MANCHESTER, ENGLAND, OCTOBER 17, 1964
Free Trade Hall
Erroll Garner (p), Eddie Calhoun (b), Kelly Martin (d)

7070	Night and Day				Unissued
7080	Fly Me to the Moon (In Other Words)				Unissued
7090	Untitled Original				Unissued
7100	It Might As Well Be Spring /				
	Spring Is Here				Unissued
7110	I Get a Kick Out of You				Unissued
7120	Stella by Starlight				Unissued
7130	Almost Like Being in Love				Unissued
7140	My Funny Valentine				Unissued
7150	Mambo Erroll				Unissued
7160	Sonny Boy				Unissued
7170	That's All				Unissued
	12 Inch 33	>Jazz Groove	Eng	008	

Note: "That's All" is an original by Erroll Garner normally used to close out his performance. It is not the popular version by Alan Brandt and Bob Haymes.

7180	Moon River				Unissued
7190	Theme from "A New Kind of Love"				Unissued
7200	These Foolish Things (Remind Me of You)				Unissued
7210	Misty				Unissued
7220	Untitled Original				Unissued
7230	More				Unissued
7240	The Nearness of You				
	12 Inch 33	>Jazz Groove	Eng	008	
7250	Where or When				Unissued
7260	Dancing Tambourine /				
	Classical Medley /				
	Thanks for the Memory				
	12 Inch 33	>Jazz Groove	Eng	008	

7270	One Note Samba			
	12 Inch 33	>Jazz Groove	Eng	008
7280	God Save the Queen			Unissued

ERROLL GARNER TRIO   AMSTERDAM, NOVEMBER 7, 1964
   Concertgebouw
Erroll Garner (p), Eddie Calhoun (b), Kelly Martin (d)

7290	Easy to Love			
	12 Inch 33	Fontana	Neth	858106FPY
		>Philips	Eng	BL7717
		Philips	Eng	SBL7717
		Philips	Eur	842914BY
		Philips	Eur	632204BL
7300	Moon River			
	12 Inch 33	Fontana	Neth	858106FPY
		>Philips	Eng	BL7717
		Philips	Eng	SBL7717
		Philips	Eur	842914BY
		Philips	Eur	632204BL
7310	What Is This Thing Called Love?			
	12 Inch 33	Fontana	Neth	858106FPY
		>Philips	Eng	BL7717
		Philips	Eng	SBL7717
		Philips	Eur	842914BY
		Philips	Eur	632204BL
7320	Gypsy in My Soul			
	12 Inch 33	Fontana	Neth	858106FPY
		>Philips	Eng	BL7717
		Philips	Eng	SBL7717
		Philips	Eur	842914BY
		Philips	Eur	632204BL
7330	On Green Dolphin Street			
	12 Inch 33	Fontana	Neth	858106FPY
		>Philips	Eng	BL7717
		Philips	Eng	SBL7717
		Philips	Eur	842914BY
		Philips	Eur	632204BL
7340	More			
	12 Inch 33	Fontana	Neth	858106FPY
		>Philips	Eng	BL7717
		Philips	Eng	SBL7717
		Philips	Eur	842914BY
		Philips	Eur	632204BL
7350	Over the Rainbow			
	12 Inch 33	Fontana	Neth	858106FPY
		>Philips	Eng	BL7717
		Philips	Eng	SBL7717
		Philips	Eur	842914BY
		Philips	Eur	632204BL
7360	Cheek to Cheek			
	12 Inch 33	Fontana	Neth	858106FPY
		>Philips	Eng	BL7717
		Philips	Eng	SBL7717
		Philips	Eur	842914BY
		Philips	Eur	632204BL

ERROLL GARNER QUINTET   NEW YORK, APRIL, 1966
Erroll Garner (p), Art Ryerson (g), Milt Hinton (b), George Jenkins (d), Johnny
Pacheco (cd)
7370   Afinidad
       (mx 100613)

	7 Inch 45	MGM	USA	K13547
		>MGM	USA	K13832
		MGM	Eng	1318
	12 Inch 33	MGM	USA	E-4463
		MGM	USA	SE-4463
		MGM	Eng	C-8047
		MGM	Eng	CS-8047
		MGM	Fra	65074
		MGM	WGer	665074
		Polydor	Fra	2393005

7380   That's My Kick
       (mx 100614)

	7 Inch 45	MGM	USA	K13547
		>MGM	USA	K13832
		MGM	Eng	1318
	12 Inch 33	MGM	USA	E-4463
		MGM	USA	SE-4463
		MGM	Eng	C-8047
		MGM	Eng	CS-8047
		MGM	Fra	65074
		MGM	WGer	665074
		Polydor	Fra	2393005

Note: Lyrics to this title were later added by Hal Shaper.

ERROLL GARNER QUINTET   NEW YORK, NOVEMBER 17, 1966
Erroll Garner (p), Wally Richardson (g), Milt Hinton (b), Herbert Lovelle (d),
José Mangual (cd)

7390   More
       (mx 101886)

	7 Inch 45	MGM	USA	K13677
		MGM	USA	K13833
	12 Inch 33	Book of the Month	USA	81-5403
		>MGM	USA	E-4463
		MGM	USA	SE-4463
		MGM	Eng	C-8047
		MGM	Eng	CS-8047
		MGM	Fra	65074
		MGM	WGer	665074
		Polydor	Fra	2393005

7400   It Ain't Necessarily So
       (mx 101887)

	7 Inch 45	MGM	USA	K13677
	12 Inch 33	Book of the Month	USA	81-5403
		>MGM	USA	E-4463
		MGM	USA	SE-4463
		MGM	Eng	C-8047
		MGM	Eng	CS-8047
		MGM	Fra	65074
		MGM	WGer	665074
		Polydor	Fra	2393005

7410   The Shadow of Your Smile
       (mx 102632)

	12 Inch 33	Book of the Month	USA	81-5403
		>MGM	USA	E-4463
		MGM	USA	SE-4463
		MGM	Eng	C-8047
		MGM	Eng	CS-8047
		MGM	Fra	65074
		MGM	WGer	665074
		Polydor	Fra	2393005

7420   Like It Is
       (mx 102633)

	7 Inch 45	MGM	USA	K13870
	12 Inch 33	Book of the Month	USA	81-5403
		>MGM	USA	E-4463
		MGM	USA	SE-4463
		MGM	Eng	C-8047
		MGM	Eng	CS-8047
		MGM	Fra	65074
		MGM	WGer	665074
		Polydor	Fra	2393005

Note: "Like It Is" (Erroll Garner) was later retitled "Shake It But Don't Break It" with lyrics by Johnny Mercer.

7430 Autumn Leaves
(mx 102634)

12 Inch 33	Book of the Month	USA	81-5403
	>MGM	USA	E-4463
	MGM	USA	SE-4463
	MGM	Eng	C-8047
	MGM	Eng	CS-8047
	MGM	Fra	65074
	MGM	WGer	665074
	Polydor	Fra	2393005

7440 Blue Moon
(mx 102635)

7 Inch 45	MGM	USA	K13870
12 Inch 33	>MGM	USA	E-4463
	MGM	USA	SE-4463
	MGM	Eng	C-8047
	MGM	Eng	CS-8047
	MGM	Fra	65074
	MGM	WGer	665074
	Polydor	Fra	2393005

7450 Gaslight
(mx 102636)

7 Inch 45	MGM	USA	K13833
	MGM	USA	K13916
12 Inch 33	>MGM	USA	E-4463
	MGM	USA	SE-4463
	MGM	Eng	C-8047
	MGM	Eng	CS-8047
	MGM	Fra	65074
	MGM	WGer	665074
	Polydor	Fra	2393005

7460 Nervous Waltz
(mx 102637)

7 Inch 45	MGM	USA	K13834
12 Inch 33	Book of the Month	USA	81-5403
	>MGM	USA	E-4463
	MGM	USA	SE-4463
	MGM	Eng	C-8047
	MGM	Eng	CS-8047
	MGM	Fra	65074
	MGM	WGer	665074
	Polydor	Fra	2393005

7470 Passing Through
(mx 102638)

12 Inch 33	>MGM	USA	E-4463
	MGM	USA	SE-4463
	MGM	Eng	C-8047
	MGM	Eng	CS-8047
	MGM	Fra	65074
	MGM	WGer	665074
	Polydor	Fra	2393005

ERROLL GARNER QUARTET   **NEW YORK, MARCH 19, 1968**
Erroll Garner (p), Ike Isaacs (b), Jimmie Smith (d), José Mangual (cd)
With The Brass Bed* (track added at a later date on titles noted with an asterisk)
Bernie Glow (tp); Marvin Stamm (tp, fh); Wayne J. Andre, James Cleveland (tbs);
Don Butterfield (tu); Pepper Adams (bs); Jerome Richardson (ts, f, pi); Don Sebesky
(ar); Richard O. Spencer (co).

7480	Watermelon Man*				
		7 Inch 45	MGM	USA	K13916
		12 Inch 33	>MGM	USA	E-4520
			MGM	USA	SE-4520
			MPS	Neth	5C064D-99438
			MPS	WGer	68.056
			MPS	WGer	15252
			Polydor	Fra	2393008
			Pye	Eng	NSPL28123
7490	It's the Talk of the Town				
		7 Inch 45	MGM	USA	K14043
		12 Inch 33	>MGM	USA	E-4520
			MGM	USA	SE-4520
			MPS	Neth	5C064D-99438
			MPS	WGer	68.056
			MPS	WGer	15252
			Polydor	Fra	2393008
			Pye	Eng	NSPL28123
7500	Groovin' High				
		12 Inch 33	>MGM	USA	E-4520
			MGM	USA	SE-4520
			MPS	Neth	5C064D-99438
			MPS	WGer	68.056
			MPS	WGer	15252
			Polydor	Fra	2393008
			Pye	Eng	NSPL28123
7510	The Girl from Ipanema				
		12 Inch 33	>MGM	USA	E-4520
			MGM	USA	SE-4520
			MPS	Neth	5C064D-99438
			MPS	WGer	68.056
			MPS	WGer	15252
			Polydor	Fra	2393008
			Pye	Eng	NSPL28123
7520	The Coffee Song				
		(They've Got an Awful Lot of Coffee in Brazil)*				
		7 Inch 45	MGM	USA	K13988
		12 Inch 33	>MGM	USA	E-4520
			MGM	USA	SE-4520
			MPS	Neth	5C064D-99438
			MPS	WGer	68.056
			MPS	WGer	15252
			Polydor	Fra	2393008
			Pye	Eng	NSPL28123
7530	Cheek to Cheek*				
		7 Inch 45	MGM	USA	K14043
		12 Inch 33	>MGM	USA	E-4520
			MGM	USA	SE-4520
			MPS	Neth	5C064D-99438
			MPS	WGer	68.056
			MPS	WGer	15252
			Polydor	Fra	2393008
			Pye	Eng	NSPL28123
7540	Up in Erroll's Room				
		7 Inch 45	MGM	USA	K13988

		12 Inch 33	>MGM	USA	E-4520
			MGM	USA	SE-4520
			MPS	Neth	5C064D-99438
			MPS	WGer	68.056
			MPS	WGer	15252
			Polydor	Fra	2393008
			Pye	Eng	NSPL28123
7550	A Lot of Livin' to Do*				
		12 Inch 33	>MGM	USA	E-4520
			MGM	USA	SE-4520
			MPS	Neth	5C064D-99438
			MPS	WGer	68.056
			MPS	WGer	15252
			Polydor	Fra	2393008
			Pye	Eng	NSPL28123
7560	All the Things You Are				
		12 Inch 33	>MGM	USA	E-4520
			MGM	USA	SE-4520
			MPS	Neth	5C064D-99438
			MPS	WGer	68.056
			MPS	WGer	15252
			Polydor	Fra	2393008
			Pye	Eng	NSPL28123
7570	I Got Rhythm*				
		12 Inch 33	Bull Dog	Eng	BDL4004
			>MGM	USA	E-4520
			MGM	USA	SE-4520
			MPS	Neth	5C064D-99438
			MPS	Neth	5D064D-99397
			MPS	WGer	68.056
			MPS	WGer	68.126
			MPS	WGer	15252
			Polydor	Fra	2393008
			Polydor	Fra	2445030
			Pye	Eng	NSPL28123

ERROLL GARNER QUARTET   CHICAGO, AUGUST 7, 1969

Asterisk (*) denotes Erroll Garner on piano and organ. Although unissued,
these tunes are the first known to feature Garner on organ.

Erroll Garner (p, o*), Gerald Jemmott (fb), Jimmie Smith (d), José Mangual (cd)

7580	Untitled Original*				
	(mx 880-1)				Unissued
7590	What Now My Love				
	(mx 881-3)				Unissued
7600	Untitled Original*				
	(mx 882-2)				Unissued
7610	Untitled Original				
	(mx 883-4)				Unissued
7620	You Turned Me Around				
	(mx 884-1)				
		12 Inch 33	Astor	Aus	SPLP1471
			MPS	Neth	5C064D-99439
			MPS	WGer	68.057
			>Mercury	USA	SR61308
			Polydor	Fra	2393015
			Pye	Eng	NSPL28214

Note: The issued version of "You Turned Me Around" fades at 5 min., 45 sec.
The entire take is 8 min., 15 sec.

7630	Call Me				
	(mx 885-4)				Unissued

7640	I Can't Get Started		
	(mx 886-2)		Unissued
7650	Lover Man (Oh, Where Can You Be?)		
	(mx 887-2)		Unissued
7660	Untitled Original		Unissued
7670	Sunny		Unissued
7680	One Note Samba		Unissued

ERROLL GARNER QUARTET   **NEW YORK, NOVEMBER 7, 1969**

Erroll Garner (p), George Duvivier (b), Joe Cocuzzo (d), José Mangual (cd)

7690	Untitled Original			
	(mx 1000-2)			Unissued
7700	The Loving Touch			
	(mx 1001-3)			
	12 Inch 33	Astor	Aus	SPLP1471
		MPS	Neth	5C064D-99439
		MPS	WGer	68.057
		>Mercury	USA	SR61308
		Polydor	Fra	2393015
		Pye	Eng	NSPL28214

Note: "The Loving Touch" (Erroll Garner) was previously titled "The I'm Not Supposed to Be Blue Blues" with lyrics by Robert Russell. It was also titled "Blue Ecstasy" on Columbia CL1587 (see also February 27, 1953 session).

7710	Watch What Happens			
	(mx 1002-2)			Unissued
7720	Girl Talk			
	(mx 1003-1)			Unissued
7730	Untitled Original			
	(mx 1004-3)			Unissued
7740	Feeling Is Believing			
	(mx 1005-4)			
	12 Inch 33	Astor	Aus	SPLP1471
		MPS	Neth	5C064D-99439
		MPS	WGer	68.057
		>Mercury	USA	SR61308
		Polydor	Fra	2393015
		Pye	Eng	NSPL28214

Note: "Feeling Is Believing" (Erroll Garner) was later retitled "Something Happens" with lyrics by Sammy Cahn.

7750	Untitled Original			
	(mx 1006-1)			Unissued
7760	Strangers in the Night			
	(mx 1007-1)			
	12 Inch 33	Astor	Aus	SPLP1471
		Book of the Month	USA	81-5403
		MPS	Neth	5C064D-99439
		MPS	WGer	68.057
		>Mercury	USA	SR61308
		Polydor	Fra	2393015
		Pye	Eng	NSPL28214
7770	Untitled Original			
	(mx 1008-1)			Unissued
7780	Mood Island			
	(mx 1009-2)			
	12 Inch 33	Astor	Aus	SPLP1471
		MPS	Neth	5C064D-99439
		MPS	WGer	68.057
		>Mercury	USA	SR61308
		Polydor	Fra	2393015
		Pye	Eng	NSPL28214

ERROLL GARNER QUARTET   **NEW YORK, DECEMBER 2, 1969**
Erroll Garner (p), George Duvivier (b), Charles Persip (d), José Mangual (cd)
7790   Paisley Eyes
        (mx 1020-3)

12 Inch 33	Astor	Aus	SPLP1471
	MPS	Neth	5C064D-99439
	MPS	WGer	68.057
	>Mercury	USA	SR61308
	Polydor	Fra	2393015
	Pye	Eng	NSPL28214

7800   I Left My Heart in San Francisco
        (mx 1021-1)   Unissued
7810   For Once in My Life
        (mx 1022-1)

12 Inch 33	Astor	Aus	SPLP1471
	Book of the Month	USA	81-5403
	MPS	Neth	5C064D-99439
	MPS	WGer	68.057
	>Mercury	USA	SR61308
	Polydor	Fra	2393015
	Pye	Eng	NSPL28214

7820   Yesterday
        (mx 1023-7)

12 Inch 33	Astor	Aus	SPLP1471
	Book of the Month	USA	81-5403
	MPS	Neth	5C064D-99439
	MPS	WGer	68.057
	>Mercury	USA	SR61308
	Polydor	Fra	2393015
	Pye	Eng	NSPL28214

7830   The Look of Love
        (mx 1024-1)

12 Inch 33	Astor	Aus	SPLP1471
	Book of the Month	USA	81-5403
	MPS	Neth	5C064D-99439
	MPS	WGer	68.057
	>Mercury	USA	SR61308
	Polydor	Fra	2393015
	Pye	Eng	NSPL28214

7840   Spinning Wheel
        (mx 1025-3)

12 Inch 33	Astor	Aus	SPLP1471
	Book of the Month	USA	81-5403
	MPS	Neth	5C064D-99439
	MPS	WGer	68.057
	>Mercury	USA	SR61308
	Polydor	Fra	2393015
	Pye	Eng	NSPL28214

7850   Untitled Original
        (mx 1026-1)   Unissued

ERROLL GARNER QUARTET   **TURIN, ITALY, MAY 9, 1971**
    RAI Auditorium
    On the record jacket of Joker and U P International, credit is incorrectly
    given to Wally Richardson (b), George Jenkins (d), Johnny Pacheco (cd).
    (Richardson's correct instrument is guitar.)
Erroll Garner (p), Ernest McCarty Jr. (b), Jimmie Smith (d), José Mangual (cd)
7860   There Will Never Be Another You

12 Inch 33	Joker	Ity	SM3911
	>U P International	Ity	LPUP 5115

7870	Girl Talk			Unissued
7880	The Shadow of Your Smile			
	12 Inch 33	Joker	Ity	SM3911
		>U P International	Ity	LPUP 5115
7890	Yesterday			
	12 Inch 33	Joker	Ity	SM3911
		>U P International	Ity	LPUP 5115
7900	The Girl from Ipanema			
	12 Inch 33	Joker	Ity	SM3911
		>U P International	Ity	LPUP 5115
7910	Misty			
	12 Inch 33	Joker	Ity	SM3911
		>U P International	Ity	LPUP 5115
7920	Tell It Like It Is			
	12 Inch 33	Joker	Ity	SM3911
		>U P International	Ity	LPUP 5115

Note: "Tell It Like It Is" (Erroll Garner) is the same tune as "Like It Is" (see also November 17, 1966 session). "Like It Is" was later retitled "Shake It But Don't Break It" with lyrics by Johnny Mercer.

7930	I'll Remember April			
	12 Inch 33	Joker	Ity	SM3911
		>U P International	Ity	LPUP 5115
7940	Misty (No. 2)			
	12 Inch 33	Joker	Ity	SM3911
		>U P International	Ity	LPUP 5115
7950	Variations on Misty			
	12 Inch 33	Joker	Ity	SM3911
		>U P International	Ity	LPUP 5115

ERROLL GARNER QUARTET   NEW YORK, DECEMBER 2, 1971

Asterisk (*) denotes Erroll Garner on piano and harpsichord.
Erroll Garner (p, h*), Ernest McCarty Jr. (b), Jimmie Smith (d), José Mangual (cd)

7960	How High the Moon			
	12 Inch 33	>London	USA	XPS617
		London	Eng	SH8461
		MPS	Neth	5C064D-99441
		MPS	WGer	68.054
		MPS	WGer	2129098-0
		Polydor	Fra	2393036
7970	It Could Happen to You			
	12 Inch 33	>London	USA	XPS617
		London	Eng	SH8461
		MPS	Neth	5C064D-99441
		MPS	WGer	68.054
		MPS	WGer	2129098-0
		Polydor	Fra	2393036
7980	Gemini			
	12 Inch 33	>London	USA	XPS617
		London	Eng	SH8461
		MPS	Neth	5C064D-99441
		MPS	WGer	68.054
		MPS	WGer	2129098-0
		Polydor	Fra	2393036
7990	When a Gypsy Makes His Violin Cry*			
	12 Inch 33	>London	USA	XPS617
		London	Eng	SH8461
		MPS	Neth	5C064D-99441
		MPS	WGer	68.054
		MPS	WGer	2129098-0
		Polydor	Fra	2393036

```
8000    Tea for Two*
            12 Inch 33      >London         USA     XPS617
                            London          Eng     SH8461
                            MPS             Neth    5C064D-99441
                            MPS             WGer    68.054
                            MPS             WGer    2129098-0
                            Polydor         Fra     2393036
8010    Something
            12 Inch 33      >London         USA     XPS617
                            London          Eng     SH8461
                            MPS             Neth    5C064D-99441
                            MPS             WGer    68.054
                            MPS             WGer    2129098-0
                            Polydor         Fra     2393036
8020    Eldorado
            12 Inch 33      >London         USA     XPS617
                            London          Eng     SH8461
                            MPS             Neth    5C064D-99441
                            MPS             WGer    68.054
                            MPS             WGer    2129098-0
                            Polydor         Fra     2393036
            Note: Named after Garner's Eldorado Cadillac.
8030    These Foolish Things (Remind Me of You)
            12 Inch 33      >London         USA     XPS617
                            London          Eng     SH8461
                            MPS             Neth    5C064D-99441
                            MPS             WGer    68.054
                            MPS             WGer    2129098-0
                            Polydor         Fra     2393036
```

ERROLL GARNER QUARTET   **NEW YORK, OCTOBER 30, 1973**

Asterisk (*) denotes Norman Gold on organ and Jackie Williams on tambourine.

Erroll Garner (p), Bob Cranshaw (b), Grady Tate (d), José Mangual (cd), Norman Gold (o)*, Jackie Williams (tmb)*

```
8040    Lover Man (Oh, Where Can You Be?)
            (mx 7301)                                       Unissued
8050    Nightwind
            (mx 7302)
            12 Inch 33      >London         USA     APS640
                            MPS             WGer    68.055
                            MPS             WGer    2129195-2
                            Pye             Eng     NSPL28213
            Note: Lyrics to this title were later added by Marcel Stellman.
8060    (They Long to Be) Close to You
            (mx 7303)
            12 Inch 33      >London         USA     APS640
                            MPS             WGer    68.055
                            MPS             WGer    2129195-2
                            Pye             Eng     NSPL28213
8070    Untitled Original
            (mx 7304)                                       Unissued
8080    Untitled Original
            (mx 7305)                                       Unissued
8090    One Good Turn*
            (mx 7306)
            12 Inch 33      >London         USA     APS640
                            MPS             WGer    68.055
                            MPS             WGer    2129195-2
                            Pye             Eng     NSPL28213
```

Note: "One Good Turn" (Erroll Garner) was previously titled "Walkin' on the Water." It was later retitled "One Good Turn Deserves Another" with lyrics by Carolyn Franklin.

8100	Mucho Gusto (mx 7307)			
	12 Inch 33	>London	USA	APS640
		MPS	WGer	68.055
		MPS	WGer	2129195-2
		Pye	Eng	NSPL28213
8110	Untitled Original (mx 7308)			Unissued
8120	Untitled Original (mx 7309)			Unissued
8130	Yesterdays (mx 7310)			
	12 Inch 33	>London	USA	APS640
		MPS	WGer	68.055
		MPS	WGer	2129195-2
		Pye	Eng	NSPL28213
8140	How About You? (mx 7311)			Unissued
8150	Someone to Watch Over Me (mx 7312)			
	12 Inch 33	>London	USA	APS640
		MPS	WGer	68.055
		MPS	WGer	2129195-2
		Pye	Eng	NSPL28213
8160	It Gets Better Every Time (mx 7314)			
	12 Inch 33	>London	USA	APS640
		MPS	WGer	68.055
		MPS	WGer	2129195-2
		Pye	Eng	NSPL28213
8170	Untitled Original (mx 7315)			Unissued
8180	Watch What Happens (mx 7316)			
	12 Inch 33	>London	USA	APS640
		MPS	WGer	68.055
		MPS	WGer	2129195-2
		Pye	Eng	NSPL28213
8190	I Only Have Eyes for You (mx 7317)			
	12 Inch 33	>London	USA	APS640
		MPS	WGer	68.055
		MPS	WGer	2129195-2
		Pye	Eng	NSPL28213

UNISSUED SESSIONS

DECEMBER 30, 1937   **PITTSBURGH**
George Hyde Studios
Nick Lomakin (ts,cl), Jimmy Pupa (tp), Erroll Garner (p), Bob Catizone (g), Ray Catizone (b), Ben Nozilo (d)

T0010   Tea for Two/Honeysuckle Rose (medley)
T0020   Exactly Like You

JANUARY 2, 1946   **NEW YORK**
"1280 Club" (WOV Radio Broadcast); Alan Courtney, host
Erroll Garner (p)

T0030   I Get a Kick Out of You
T0040   Gaslight
T0050   1280 Club Blues
T0060   Loot to Boot
T0070   Spring Is Here
T0080   Take the "A" Train
T0090   The Mood (Forgotten Concerto)
T0100   I'm Beginning to See the Light
T0101   I'm Beginning to See the Light
T0110   Candy
T0120   Laura
T0130   Clair de lune
T0140   Erroll's Bounce

OCTOBER 5, 1949   **NEW YORK**
Apollo Theater (Radio Broadcast)
Erroll Garner (p), John Simmons (b), Rossiere "Shadow" Wilson (d)

T0150   Penthouse Serenade (When We're Alone)

JUNE, 1950   **NEW YORK**
Cafe Society, Sheridan Square (WOR Radio Broadcast)
Erroll Garner (p), John Simmons (b), Rossiere "Shadow" Wilson (d)

T0160   Stompin' at the Savoy
T0170   These Foolish Things (Remind Me of You)
T0180   People Will Say We're in Love
T0190   Undecided

SEPTEMBER 16, 1950   **NEW YORK**
Cafe Society, Sheridan Square (WOR Radio Broadcast)
Erroll Garner (p), John Simmons (b), Rossiere "Shadow" Wilson (d)

T0200   When You're Smiling (The Whole World Smiles with You)
T0210   Laura
T0220   Just One of Those Things
T0230   Poor Butterfly

SEPTEMBER 16, 1950   **NEW YORK**
Cafe Society, Sheridan Square (WOR Radio Broadcast)
Erroll Garner (p), John Simmons (b), Rossiere "Shadow" Wilson (d)

T0240   When Johnny Comes Marching Home
T0250   My Heart Stood Still
T0260   Penthouse Serenade (When We're Alone)
T0270   Fine and Dandy

SEPTEMBER 18, 1950   **NEW YORK**
Cafe Society, Sheridan Square (WOR Radio Broadcast)
Erroll Garner (p), John Simmons (b), Rossiere "Shadow" Wilson (d)

T0280   Stompin' at the Savoy
T0290   I Don't Know Why (I Just Do)
T0300   Deep Purple
T0310   Undecided
T0320   Untitled Original

SEPTEMBER 20, 1950   **NEW YORK**
Cafe Society, Sheridan Square (WOR Radio Broadcast)
Erroll Garner (p), John Simmons (b), Rossiere "Shadow" Wilson (d)

T0330   Again
T0340   Rosalie
T0350   Danny Boy
T0360   What Is This Thing Called Love?

SEPTEMBER 22, 1950   **NEW YORK**
Cafe Society, Sheridan Square (WOR Radio Broadcast)
Erroll Garner (p), John Simmons (b), Rossiere "Shadow" Wilson (d)

T0370   Laura
T0380   Tea for Two
T0390   No Moon
T0400   Yesterdays

SEPTEMBER 23, 1950   **NEW YORK**
Cafe Society, Sheridan Square (WOR Radio Broadcast)
Erroll Garner (p), John Simmons (b), Rossiere "Shadow" Wilson (d)

T0410   Erroll's Theme
T0420   My Heart Stood Still
T0430   Cologne
T0440   Poor Butterfly
T0450   Just One of Those Things

SEPTEMBER 25, 1950   **NEW YORK**
Cafe Society, Sheridan Square (WOR Radio Broadcast)
Erroll Garner (p), John Simmons (b), Rossiere "Shadow" Wilson (d)

T0460	Goodbye
T0470	Scatter-Brain
T0480	Deep Purple

SEPTEMBER 27, 1950   NEW YORK
Cafe Society, Sheridan Square (WOR Radio Broadcast)
Erroll Garner (p), John Simmons (b), Rossiere "Shadow" Wilson (d)

T0490	Body and Soul
T0500	It's Only a Paper Moon
T0510	Pavanne (The Lamp Is Low)
T0520	Pastel
T0530	Erroll's Theme

SEPTEMBER 29, 1950   NEW YORK
Cafe Society, Sheridan Square (WOR Radio Broadcast)
Erroll Garner (p), John Simmons (b), Rossiere "Shadow" Wilson (d)

T0540	Rosalie
T0550	I Let a Song Go Out of My Heart
T0560	When Johnny Comes Marching Home
T0570	What Is This Thing Called Love?

OCTOBER 1, 1950   NEW YORK
Cafe Society, Sheridan Square (WOR Radio Broadcast)
Erroll Garner (p), John Simmons (b), Rossiere "Shadow" Wilson (d)

T0580	Danny Boy
T0590	Sophisticated Lady
T0600	Fine and Dandy
T0610	Penthouse Serenade (When We're Alone)

OCTOBER 2, 1950   NEW YORK
Cafe Society, Sheridan Square (WOR Radio Broadcast)
Erroll Garner (p), John Simmons (b), Rossiere "Shadow" Wilson (d)

T0620	Lullaby of the Leaves
T0630	Summertime
T0640	Margie

OCTOBER 4, 1950   NEW YORK
Cafe Society, Sheridan Square (WOR Radio Broadcast)
Erroll Garner (p), John Simmons (b), Rossiere "Shadow" Wilson (d)

T0650	This Can't Be Love
T0660	I Surrender, Dear
T0670	Blue Moon
T0680	Robbins' Nest

OCTOBER 5, 1950   NEW YORK
Cafe Society, Sheridan Square (WOR Radio Broadcast)
Erroll Garner (p), John Simmons (b), Rossiere "Shadow" Wilson (d)

T0690	I'm in the Mood for Love
T0700	Trio
T0710	No Moon
T0720	Honeysuckle Rose

OCTOBER 7, 1950   NEW YORK
Cafe Society, Sheridan Square (WOR Radio Broadcast)
Erroll Garner (p), John Simmons (b), Rossiere "Shadow" Wilson (d)

T0730   Red Sails in the Sunset
T0740   I Can't Get Started
T0750   How High the Moon
T0760   Through a Long and Sleepless Night

OCTOBER 9, 1950   NEW YORK
Cafe Society, Sheridan Square (WOR Radio Broadcast)
Erroll Garner (p), John Simmons (b), Rossiere "Shadow" Wilson (d)

T0770   Stormy Weather (Keeps Rainin' All the Time)
T0780   Relaxin' at Sugar Ray's
T0790   Goodbye

OCTOBER 10, 1950   NEW YORK
Cafe Society, Sheridan Square (WOR Radio Broadcast)
Erroll Garner (p), John Simmons (b), Rossiere "Shadow" Wilson (d)

T0800   Tippin' Out with Erroll
T0810   This Can't Be Love
T0820   No Moon
T0830   Honeysuckle Rose
T0840   Penthouse Serenade (When We're Alone)
T0850   Tippin' Out with Erroll

OCTOBER 12, 1950   NEW YORK
Cafe Society, Sheridan Square (WOR Radio Broadcast)
Frank McCarthy, host
Erroll Garner (p), John Simmons (b), Rossiere "Shadow" Wilson (d)

T0860   Tippin' Out with Erroll
T0870   People Will Say We're in Love
T0880   Blue Moon
T0890   Deep Purple
T0900   Laura
T0910   Tippin' Out with Erroll

DECEMBER 30, 1950   LOS ANGELES
Radio Broadcast
Erroll Garner (p), John Simmons (b), Rossiere "Shadow" Wilson (d), Teddy Edwards (ts), Dave Lambert (v)

T0920   Cherokee
            *Note: This title was originally recorded in early April, 1947 during Gene Norman's
            "Just Jazz" concert.*

JANUARY 9, 1951   NEW YORK
Apollo Theater (Radio Broadcast)
Erroll Garner (p), John Simmons (b), Rossiere "Shadow" Wilson (d)

T0930   The Way You Look Tonight

SEPTEMBER 15, 1951   NEW YORK
Cafe Society, Sheridan Square (WOR Radio Broadcast)
Erroll Garner (p), John Simmons (b), Rossiere "Shadow" Wilson (d)

T0940   Please Don't Talk About Me When I'm Gone
T0950   Stairway to the Stars
T0960   This Can't Be Love
T0970   Summertime
T0980   Untitled Original

FEBRUARY 14, 1952   NEW YORK
Apollo Theater (Radio Broadcast)
Asterisk (*) denotes Roy Eldridge on trumpet and Buddy Rich on drums.
Erroll Garner (p), John Simmons (b), Rossiere "Shadow" Wilson (d), Roy Eldridge
(tp)*, Buddy Rich (d)*

T0990   It's the Talk of the Town
T1000   Apollo Blues*

APRIL 19, 1952   MONTREAL
CBC Radio Broadcast; Ted Miller, host

T1010   Interview

MAY 5, 1952   NEW YORK
Birdland (NBC Radio Broadcast)
Erroll Garner (p), John Simmons (b), Rossiere "Shadow" Wilson (d)

T1020   Love for Sale
        *Note: This session originated from Birdland and was done in conjunction with "Piano
        Parade" featuring Garner, Art Tatum, Meade Lux Lewis and Pete Johnson.*

FEBRUARY 14, 1953   NEW YORK
Birdland (WOR Radio Broadcast)
Erroll Garner (p), Wyatt Ruther (b), Eugene "Fats" Heard (d)

T1030   'S Wonderful
T1040   Body and Soul
T1050   Cocktails for Two
T1060   Blues Erroll
T1070   Laura
T1080   Lullaby of Birdland
        Note: Also on the bill for this presentation were Bud Powell and Slim Gaillard.

FEBRUARY 21, 1953   NEW YORK
Birdland (WOR Radio Broadcast)
Erroll Garner (p), Wyatt Ruther (b), Eugene "Fats" Heard (d)

T1090   Fine and Dandy
T1100   These Foolish Things (Remind Me of You)
T1110   'S Wonderful
T1120   Penthouse Serenade (When We're Alone)
T1130   Blues Erroll
T1140   April in Paris
T1150   Lover

FEBRUARY 28, 1953   NEW YORK
Birdland (WOR Radio Broadcast)
Erroll Garner (p), Wyatt Ruther (b), Eugene "Fats" Heard (d)

T1160   Cocktails for Two
T1170   Penthouse Serenade (When We're Alone)
T1180   I Cover the Waterfront
T1190   Robbins' Nest
T1200   Deep Purple

MARCH 7, 1953   NEW YORK
Birdland (WOR Radio Broadcast)
Erroll Garner (p), Wyatt Ruther (b), Eugene "Fats" Heard (d)

T1210   Lullaby in Rhythm
T1220   More Than You Know
T1230   This Can't Be Love
T1240   April in Paris

AUGUST, 1953   NEW YORK
Radio Broadcast (WNEW Radio); Al "Jazzbo" Collins, host
Erroll Garner (p), Wyatt Ruther (b), Eugene "Fats" Heard (d)

T1250   When You're Smiling (The Whole World Smiles with You)
T1260   Chopsticks
T1270   Bewitched
T1271   Bewitched
T1272   Bewitched
         Note: Garner plays "Bewitched" in the styles of Meade Lux Lewis (T1270), Fats
         Waller (T1271) and Art Tatum (T1272).

JANUARY 1, 1955   NEW YORK
Embers Club (Radio Broadcast)
Erroll Garner (p), Wyatt Ruther (b), Eugene "Fats" Heard (d)

T1280   Idaho
T1290   Laura
T1300   They Can't Take That Away from Me
T1310   Avalon

MAY 7, 1955   NEW YORK
TV Broadcast (CBS-TV)
Erroll Garner with The Dorsey Brothers Orchestra

T1320   Frenesi (Cancion Tropical)/
         Penthouse Serenade (When We're Alone)/
         Indiana (Back Home Again in Indiana) (medley)
T1330   Lover

JUNE 4, 1955   NEW YORK
Birdland (Radio Broadcast)
Erroll Garner (p), Wyatt Ruther (b), Eugene "Fats" Heard (d)

T1340   Love for Sale
T1350   Misty
T1360   Will You Still Be Mine?

JUNE 24, 1955   **NEW YORK**
The Tonight Show, (WRCA-TV); Steve Allen, host
Erroll Garner (p), Woody Herman (v)

T1370   Let's Fall in Love/
         Moonglow (medley)

JUNE 25, 1955   **NEW YORK**
Birdland (WOR Radio Broadcast)
Erroll Garner (p), Wyatt Ruther (b), Eugene "Fats" Heard (d)

T1380   Lullaby of Birdland
T1390   Love for Sale
T1400   Misty
T1410   Will You Still Be Mine?
T1420   Lullaby of Birdland

JUNE 26, 1955   **NEW YORK**
Birdland (WOR Radio Broadcast)
Asterisk (*) denotes Woody Herman, vocal
Erroll Garner (p), Wyatt Ruther (b), Eugene "Fats" Heard (d) Woody Herman
(v)* with his "Third Herd"

T1430   Moonglow*
T1440   Perdido

JUNE 30, 1955   **CHICAGO**
Blue Note, NBC "Monitor" (Radio Broadcast)
Erroll Garner (p), Wyatt Ruther (b), Eugene "Fats" Heard (d)

T1450   Lullaby of Birdland
T1460   Misty
T1470   Will You Still Be Mine?

AUGUST 7, 1955   **CHICAGO**
Blue Note, NBC "Monitor" (Radio Broadcast)
Erroll Garner (p), unknown (b), unknown (d)

T1480   Easy to Love
T1490   Body and Soul
T1500   I Cover the Waterfront
T1510   Cheek to Cheek

NOVEMBER, 1955   **NEW YORK**
Basin Street East (Radio Broadcast)
Erroll Garner (p), Eddie Calhoun (b), Denzil Best (d)

T1520   Erroll's Theme
T1530   The Way You Look Tonight
T1540   I Cover the Waterfront
T1550   Penthouse Serenade (When We're Alone)
T1560   It's All Right with Me
T1570   I'm in the Mood for Love
T1580   Lover
T1590   Untitled Original

NOVEMBER 1, 1955   NEW YORK
Basin Street East (Radio Broadcast)
Erroll Garner (p), Eddie Calhoun (b), Denzil Best (d)

T1600	They Can't Take That Away from Me
T1610	Avalon

DECEMBER 22, 1955   NEW YORK
The Tonight Show (WRCA-TV); Gene Rayburn, host
Erroll Garner (p), Frank Carroll (b), Don Lamond (d)

T1620	It's All Right with Me
T1630	All the Things You Are

JANUARY 29, 1956   NEW YORK
Basin Street East (March of Dimes Radio Broadcast)
Erroll Garner (p), Eddie Calhoun (b), Denzil Best (d)

T1640	Erroll's Theme
T1650	Avalon
T1660	Misty
T1670	Love Me or Leave Me
T1680	How High the Moon
T1690	Caravan
T1700	Erroll's Theme

APRIL 23, 1956   NEW YORK
Basin Street East (Radio Broadcast)
Erroll Garner (p), Eddie Calhoun (b), Denzil Best (d)

T1710	The Lady Is a Tramp
T1720	Misty
T1730	Lullaby of Birdland
T1740	Tippin' Out with Erroll

APRIL 27, 1956   NEW YORK
The Tonight Show (WRCA-TV); Steve Allen, host
Erroll Garner (p), Frank Carroll (b), Don Lamond or Bobby Rosengarden (d),
Candido Camero (cd)

T1750	Lover
T1760	La Petite Mambo
	Note: Steve Allen erroneously announces this title as "Mambo Nights." It is "La Petite Mambo."

MAY 5, 1956   NEW YORK
Basin Street East (Radio Broadcast)
Erroll Garner (p), Eddie Calhoun (b), Denzil Best (d)

T1770	Tippin' Out with Erroll
T1780	Too Marvelous for Words
T1790	Misty
T1800	7-11 Jump
T1810	Lover

MAY 12, 1956   NEW YORK
Basin Street East (Radio Broadcast)
Erroll Garner (p), Eddie Calhoun (b), Denzil Best (d)

T1820	Stompin' at the Savoy
T1830	Misty
T1840	I'll Remember April
T1850	Love Is Here to Stay
T1860	7-11 Jump
T1870	Lover
T1880	Erroll's Theme

SEPTEMBER 8, 1956   BOSTON
Storyville (Radio Broadcast)
Erroll Garner (p), Eddie Calhoun (b), Denzil Best (d)

T1890	Erroll's Theme
T1900	I'll Remember April
T1910	Untitled Original
T1920	Misty
T1930	La Petite Mambo
T1940	Solitaire
T1950	Penthouse Serenade (When We're Alone)

Note: Eddie Calhoun confirms that Denzil Best left the trio during this engagement.

SEPTEMBER 16, 1956   CHICAGO
London House (Radio Broadcast)
Erroll Garner (p), Eddie Calhoun (b), unknown (d)

T1959	Erroll's Theme
T1960	I'll Remember April
T1970	Solitaire
T1980	7-11 Jump

FEBRUARY 23, 1957   BOSTON
Storyville (Radio Broadcast)
Erroll Garner (p), Eddie Calhoun (b), Kelly Martin (d)

T1990	Erroll's Theme
T2000	Just You, Just Me
T2010	Full Moon and Empty Arms
T2020	Passing Through
T2030	Dreamy
T2040	Where or When
T2050	Mambo Erroll
T2060	Solitaire
T2070	7-11 Jump

MARCH, 1957   NEW YORK
Basin Street East (Radio Broadcast)
Erroll Garner (p), Eddie Calhoun (b), Kelly Martin (d)

T2080	I'll Remember April
T2090	Blue Ecstasy
T2100	Stompin' at the Savoy

Note: During this broadcast, Garner introduces "Blue Ecstasy" as "Number 18."

MAY 26, 1957   NEW YORK
The Tonight Show (WRCA-TV); Steven Allen, host
Erroll Garner (p), probably Frank Carroll (b), probably Bobby Rosengarden (d)

T2110   It's All Right with Me

MAY 1, 1959   NEW YORK
Garry Moore Show (CBS-TV)
Erroll Garner (p), Eddie Calhoun (b), Kelly Martin (d)

T2120   There's a Small Hotel
T2130   La Petite Mambo

MAY 16, 1960   NEW YORK
Steve Allen Show (WRCA-TV)
Erroll Garner (p), Eddie Calhoun (b), Kelly Martin (d)

T2140   It's All Right with Me
T2150   Hallelujah (with studio orchestra and chorus)

SEPTEMBER 13, 1960   NEW YORK
Arthur Godfrey Time (WCBS Radio)
Erroll Garner (p), Gene Traxler (b), probably James "Osie" Johnson (d), Arthur
Godfrey (v), Frankie Crockett (v), Dick Hyman (o), Remo Palmieri (g), Johnny
Parker (tp), Robert "Cutty" Cutshall (tb), Johnny Mince (cl)

T2160   Between the Devil and the Deep Blue Sea
T2170   Lazy River (Cutty Cutshall with organ and rhythm)
T2171   Lazy River (Remo Palmieri with organ and rhythm)
T2172   Lazy River (Dick Hyman with organ and rhythm)
T2180   Lazy River (Erroll Garner Trio)
T2190   When Your Lover Has Gone (Erroll Garner Trio)

OCTOBER 23, 1960   NEW YORK
Ed Sullivan Show (CBS-TV)
Erroll Garner (p), Eddie Calhoun (b), Kelly Martin (d)

T2200   Dreamy
T2210   I Get a Kick Out of You

FEBRUARY 5, 1961   NEW YORK
Ed Sullivan Show (CBS-TV)
Erroll Garner (p), Eddie Calhoun (b), Kelly Martin (d)

T2220   Solitaire
T2230   It's All Right with Me

MARCH 26, 1961   NEW YORK
Ed Sullivan Show (CBS-TV)
Erroll Garner (p), Eddie Calhoun (b), Kelly Martin (d)

T2240   Oklahoma! Medley
           Oh, What a Beautiful Mornin'/
           People Will Say We're in Love/
           The Surrey with the Fringe on Top (medley)
T2250   Misty

FEBRUARY 1, 1962   NEW YORK
WNEW Radio Broadcast; Big Wilson, host
Erroll Garner (p), Eddie Calhoun (b), Kelly Martin (d)

T2260	Where or When
T2270	Misty
T2280	Will You Still Be Mine?
T2290	WNEW Theme Song
T2300	La Petite Mambo
T2310	Some of These Days
T2320	WNEW Theme Song

JUNE 3, 1962   MANCHESTER, ENGLAND
Free Trade Hall
Erroll Garner (p), Eddie Calhoun (b), Kelly Martin (d)

T2330	You Do Something to Me
T2340	My Funny Valentine
T2350	Untitled Original
T2360	These Foolish Things (Remind Me of You)
T2370	Love for Sale
T2380	April in Paris
T2390	Untitled Original
T2400	Will You Still Be Mine?
T2410	La Petite Mambo
T2420	That's All
T2430	Dancing Tambourine
T2440	Something to Remember You By
T2450	The Lady Is a Tramp
T2460	Stella by Starlight
T2470	All the Things You Are
T2480	Misty
T2490	Just You, Just Me
T2500	Thanks for the Memory
T2510	Classical Medley
T2520	God Save the Queen

JUNE 10, 1962   KILBURN, NORTH LONDON, ENGLAND
Gaumont State Theater
Erroll Garner (p), Eddie Calhoun (b), Kelly Martin (d)

T2530	Untitled Original
T2540	I Cover the Waterfront
T2550	Untitled Original
T2560	Dancing in the Dark
T2570	Cherokee
T2580	In a Sentimental Mood
T2590	Sophisticated Lady
T2600	Some of These Days
T2610	Autumn Leaves
T2620	St. Louis Blues
T2630	Erroll's Theme

JUNE 12, 1962   PARIS
Maison de l' ORTF (Radio Broadcast)
Erroll Garner (p), Eddie Calhoun (b), Kelly Martin (d)

T2640	Autumn Leaves

1963   UNKNOWN LOCATION
Radio Broadcast
Erroll Garner (p), Eddie Calhoun (b), Kelly Martin (d)

T2650   They Can't Take That Away from Me
T2660   Some of These Days
T2670   La Petite Mambo
T2680   I Cover the Waterfront
T2690   Indiana (Back Home Again in Indiana)
T2700   Laura
T2710   You Do Something to Me
T2720   Erroll's Theme

JANUARY 11, 1963   NEW YORK
The Tonight Show (WRCA-TV); Johnny Carson, host
Erroll Garner (p), George Duvivier (b), Ed Shaughnessy (d)

T2730   Misty

JANUARY 30, 1963   NEW YORK
Kraft Music Hall; Perry Como, host
Erroll Garner (p), Eddie Calhoun (b), Kelly Martin (d)

T2740   Mack the Knife
T2750   Misty (vocal by Perry Como and Phyllis McGuire)
T2760   Almost Like Being in Love

APRIL 21, 1963   NEW YORK
Ed Sullivan Show (CBS-TV)
Erroll Garner (p), Eddie Calhoun (b), Kelly Martin (d)

T2770   In the Still of the Night
T2780   Erroll's Theme
          Note: This version of "Erroll's Theme" was later retitled "That's My Kick."

MAY 6, 1963   NEW YORK
The Tonight Show (NBC-TV); Johnny Carson, host
Erroll Garner (p), George Duvivier (b), Ed Shaughnessy (d)

T2790   Lover Come Back to Me
T2800   Happiness Is a Thing Called Joe

MAY 22, 1963   UNKNOWN LOCATION
Patricia Kurland Show

T2810   Interview
          *Note: Patricia Kurland interviews Erroll Garner concerning his August, 1962 appear-
          ance at the Seattle World's Fair.*

OCTOBER 12 or 20, 1963   LONDON
Royal Festival Hall
Erroll Garner (p), Eddie Calhoun (b), Kelly Martin (d)

T2820   In the Still of the Night
T2830   Everything Happens to Me
T2840   I Get a Kick Out of You

T2850	Autumn Leaves
T2860	Untitled Original
T2870	Misty
T2880	That Old Black Magic
T2890	April in Paris
T2900	Almost Like Being in Love
T2910	All the Things You Are
T2920	Untitled Original
T2930	That's All
T2940	God Save the Queen

JANUARY, 1964   LONDON
Radio Broadcast

T2950	Interview
	Note: Erroll Garner is interviewed and the song, "You Do Something to Me" from his ABC 395 album is played.

APRIL 14, 1964   NEW YORK
Garry Moore Show (CBS-TV)
Erroll Garner (p), Eddie Calhoun (b), Kelly Martin (d)

T2960	Misty
T2970	Fly Me to the Moon (In Other Words)
T2980	On Green Dolphin Street

JUNE 16, 1964   NEW YORK
Bell Telephone Hour; Ray Bolger, host
Erroll Garner (p), Eddie Calhoun (b), Kelly Martin (d)

T2990	The Way You Look Tonight
T3000	Misty
T3010	Mack the Knife
T3020	Sweet and Lovely

OCTOBER 18, 1964   LONDON
"Sunday Night at the London Palladium" (I.T.V.)
Erroll Garner (p), Eddie Calhoun (b), Kelly Martin (d)

T3030	I Get a Kick Out of You
T3040	Misty
T3050	Just One of Those Things

ca. 1965   UNKNOWN LOCATION
Erroll Garner (p), probably Eddie Calhoun (b), probably Kelly Martin (d)

T3060	Primrose
T3070	Mary O'
T3080	Taylor-Made Blues
T3090	Just Me and You
T3100	Straight Ahead
T3110	Farewell to Paris
T3120	Nightwind

JANUARY 18, 1965   LONDON
"Jazz 625" (BBC-2 TV); Steve Race, host
Erroll Garner (p), Eddie Calhoun (b), Kelly Martin (d)

T3130   Just One of Those Things
T3140   Dreamy
T3150   What Is This Thing Called Love?
T3160   Spring Is Here/
        It Might As Well Be Spring (medley)
T3170   Lover
T3180   Laura
T3190   Sonny Boy
T3200   Erroll's Theme
        Note: This telecast was pre-recorded on October 31, 1964.

JANUARY 26, 1965   NEW YORK
The Today Show (NBC-TV); Jack Lescoulie, host
Erroll Garner (p), Eddie Calhoun (b), Kelly Martin (d)

T3210   More
T3220   Misty

JANUARY 27, 1965   NEW YORK
The Tonight Show (NBC-TV); Johnny Carson, host
Erroll Garner (p), George Duvivier (b), Ed Shaughnessy (d)

T3230   Gypsy in My Soul
T3240   Fly Me to the Moon (In Other Words)

FEBRUARY 13, 1965   NEW YORK
American Musical Theater (TV broadcast); Earl Wrightson, host
Erroll Garner (p), Eddie Calhoun (b), Kelly Martin (d)

T3250   I Get a Kick Out of You
T3260   Misty
T3270   Embraceable You
T3280   The Surrey with the Fringe on Top

FEBRUARY 20, 1965   LONDON
"Jazz 625" (BBC-2 TV); Steve Race, host
Erroll Garner (p), Eddie Calhoun (b), Kelly Martin (d)

T3290   Honeysuckle Rose
T3300   No More Shadows
T3310   Mambo Erroll
T3320   Penthouse Serenade (When We're Alone)
T3330   Jeannine, I Dream of Lilac Time
T3340   On the Street Where You Live/
        I Could Have Danced All Night (medley)
T3350   Theme from "A New Kind of Love"
T3360   The Lady Is a Tramp
T3370   Untitled Original
        Note: This telecast was pre-recorded on October 22, 1964.

MARCH 6, 1965   UNKNOWN LOCATION
Erroll Garner (p), unknown (b), unknown (d)

T3380   Misty
T3390   Tea for Two

MAY 25, 1965   **NEW YORK**
Bell Telephone Hour (TV Broadcast); "The Music of Cole Porter"
Erroll Garner (p), Eddie Calhoun (b), Kelly Martin (d)

T3400	It's All Right with Me
T3410	Begin the Beguine
T3420	I've Got You Under My Skin

MAY 27, 1965   **NEW YORK**
Village Gate
Erroll Garner (p), Eddie Calhoun (b), Kelly Martin (d)

T3430	One Note Samba
T3440	Untitled Original
T3450	Sonny Boy
T3460	What Is This Thing Called Love?
T3470	Spring Is Here/
	It Might As Well Be Spring (medley)
T3480	The Nearness of You
T3490	Almost Like Being in Love
T3500	Untitled Original
T3510	Moon River
T3520	Misty
T3530	Satin Doll
T3540	Yesterdays
T3550	Where or When
T3560	Dancing Tambourine
T3570	Classical Medley
T3580	Erroll's Theme
T3590	Untitled Original

MAY 28, 1965   **NEW YORK**
Village Gate
Erroll Garner (p), Eddie Calhoun (b), Kelly Martin (d)

T3600	Easy to Love
T3610	Theme from "A New Kind of Love"
T3620	Bess You Is My Woman/
	I Got Plenty O' Nuttin'/
	It Ain't Necessarily So/
	Bess You Is My Woman (medley)
T3630	Movin' Blues
T3640	I Cover the Waterfront
T3650	Will You Still Be Mine?
T3660	How High the Moon
T3670	My Funny Valentine
T3680	The Surrey with the Fringe on Top
T3690	Untitled Original
T3700	Stella by Starlight
T3710	Love for Sale
T3720	Someone to Watch Over Me
T3730	Sonny Boy
T3740	One Note Samba
T3750	Moon River
T3760	Where or When
T3770	Dancing Tambourine
T3780	Classical Medley

MAY 29, 1965   NEW YORK
Village Gate
Erroll Garner (p), Eddie Calhoun (b), Kelly Martin (d)

T3790	Dancing in the Dark
T3800	Stella by Starlight
T3810	On Green Dolphin Street
T3820	Untitled Original
T3830	More
T3840	Misty
T3850	St. James Infirmary
T3860	Satin Doll
T3870	Dancing Tambourine
T3880	Classical Medley
T3890	Untitled Original

MAY 30, 1965   NEW YORK
Village Gate
Erroll Garner (p), Eddie Calhoun (b), Kelly Martin (d)

T3900	One Note Samba
T3910	What's New?
T3920	More
T3930	Spring Is Here/
	It Might As Well Be Spring (medley)
T3940	Satin Doll
T3950	The Nearness of You
T3960	Gypsy in My Soul
T3970	Untitled Original
T3980	Will You Still Be Mine?
T3990	Misty

JUNE 1, 1965   NEW YORK
Village Gate
Erroll Garner (p), Eddie Calhoun (b), Kelly Martin (d)

T4000	There Will Never Be Another You
T4010	Stella by Starlight
T4020	I've Grown Accustomed to Her Face/
	On the Street Where You Live/
	I Could Have Danced All Night (medley)
T4030	Love for Sale
T4040	My Funny Valentine
T4050	Almost Like Being in Love
T4060	Moon River
T4070	Misty
T4080	The Surrey with the Fringe on Top
T4090	Dancing Tambourine
T4100	Classical Medley
T4110	Untitled Original

JUNE 2, 1965   NEW YORK
Village Gate
Erroll Garner (p), Eddie Calhoun (b), Kelly Martin (d)

T4120	All the Things You Are
T4130	On Green Dolphin Street
T4140	What Is This Thing Called Love?

T4150	Dancing Tambourine/
	Classical Medley (medley)
T4160	Untitled Original
T4170	Someone to Watch Over Me
T4180	I Get a Kick Out of You
T4190	Moon River
T4200	In the Still of the Night
T4210	Satin Doll
T4220	Where or When
T4230	Untitled Original
T4240	Thanks for the Memory
T4250	Untitled Original

JUNE 3, 1965   NEW YORK
Village Gate
Erroll Garner (p), Eddie Calhoun (b), Kelly Martin (d)

T4260	Gypsy in My Soul
T4270	Untitled Original
T4280	What Is This Thing Called Love?
T4290	The Nearness of You
T4300	Untitled Original
T4310	In the Still of the Night
T4320	More
T4330	April in Paris
T4340	Untitled Original
T4350	Misty
T4360	On Green Dolphin Street
T4370	Untitled Original
T4380	Thanks for the Memory
T4390	Untitled Original

JUNE 4, 1965   NEW YORK
Village Gate
Erroll Garner (p), Eddie Calhoun (b), Kelly Martin (d)

T4400	Satin Doll
T4410	Stella by Starlight
T4420	Almost Like Being in Love
T4430	Moon River
T4440	Misty
T4450	Love for Sale
T4460	Sonny Boy
T4470	Dancing Tambourine
T4480	Classical Medley

JUNE 5, 1965   NEW YORK
Village Gate
Erroll Garner (p), Eddie Calhoun (b), Kelly Martin (d)

T4490	Yesterdays
T4500	Where or When
T4510	Erroll's Theme
T4520	All the Things You Are
T4530	On Green Dolphin Street
T4540	What Is This Thing Called Love?

JULY 17, 1965   NEW YORK
"Fanfare" (CBS-TV); Al Hirt, host
Erroll Garner (p), Eddie Calhoun (b), Kelly Martin (d)

T4550   Sonny Boy
T4560   Dancing Tambourine
T4570   Misty
T4580   Sonny Boy (brief improvisation)
T4590   Where or When

AUGUST 18, 1965   NEW YORK
The Today Show (NBC-TV); Jack Lescoulie, host
Erroll Garner (p), Eddie Calhoun (b), Kelly Martin (d)

T4600   Blue Moon
T4610   No More Shadows
T4620   Taking a Chance on Love
T4630   Lover Come Back to Me
T4640   Misty

OCTOBER 15, 1965   PHILADELPHIA
Mike Douglas Show (Westinghouse-TV)
Erroll Garner (p), Jimmy DeJulio (b), Bobby Mariniello (d)

T4650   Misty

FEBRUARY 21, 1966   PHILADELPHIA
Mike Douglas Show (Westinghouse-TV)
Erroll Garner (p), Jimmy DeJulio (b), Bobby Mariniello (d)

T4660   I've Got You Under My Skin
T4670   I Can't Get Started
T4680   Indiana (Back Home Again in Indiana)
        Note: This title is a short rehearsal playback.
T4690   It's Only a Paper Moon
T4700   Indiana (Back Home Again in Indiana)

APRIL, 1966   STOCKHOLM
Swedish TV Broadcast (No. 1)
Erroll Garner (p), Eddie Calhoun (b), Kelly Martin (d)

T4710   Erroll's Theme
T4720   When Your Lover Has Gone
T4730   Fly Me to the Moon (In Other Words)
T4740   La Petite Mambo
T4750   My Funny Valentine
T4760   One Note Samba
T4770   Where or When
T4780   Thanks for the Memory
T4790   Erroll's Theme

APRIL, 1966   STOCKHOLM
Swedish TV Broadcast (No. 2)
Erroll Garner (p), Eddie Calhoun (b), Kelly Martin (d)

T4800   Erroll's Theme
T4810   Lover Come Back to Me

T4820   My Funny Valentine
T4830   Fly Me to the Moon (In Other Words)
T4840   Where or When
T4850   Someone to Watch Over Me
T4860   Passing Through

APRIL, 1966   ROME
Roma TV
Erroll Garner (p), Eddie Calhoun (b), Kelly Martin (d)

T4870   Dancing in the Dark
T4880   Laura
T4890   Some of These Days
T4900   Misty
T4910   Indiana (Back Home Again in Indiana)
T4920   These Foolish Things (Remind Me of You)

MAY 29, 1966   LONDON
"Sunday Night at the London Palladium" (BBC-TV); Bruce Forsythe, host
Erroll Garner (p), Eddie Calhoun (b), Kelly Martin (d)

T4930   Mambo Erroll
T4940   Misty
T4950   Three O'Clock in the Morning
         Note: This telecast was pre-recorded on May 21, 1966.

MAY 29, 1966   LONDON
New Victoria Cinema
Erroll Garner (p), Eddie Calhoun (b), Kelly Martin (d)

T4960   Beautiful Love
T4970   That's All
T4980   Untitled Original
T4990   Untitled Original
T5000   All the Things You Are
T5010   Laura
T5020   It's All Right with Me
T5030   I Want a Little Girl
T5040   The Shadow of Your Smile
T5050   Dancing in the Dark
T5060   Spring Is Here/
         It Might As Well Be Spring (medley)
T5070   Love for Sale
T5080   Lil' Darlin'
T5090   More
T5100   I've Grown Accustomed to Her Face
T5110   Quiet Nights of Quiet Stars (Corcovado)
T5120   Autumn Leaves
T5130   Misty
T5140   I've Got You Under My Skin
T5150   It Ain't Necessarily So
T5160   Where or When
T5170   Thanks for the Memory
T5180   Untitled Original

DECEMBER 2, 1966   PHILADELPHIA
Mike Douglas Show (Westinghouse-TV)
Erroll Garner (p), Jimmy DeJulio (b), Bobby Mariniello (d)

T5190   Sweet and Lovely
T5200   Theme From "A New Kind of Love"
           Note: "Theme from 'A New Kind of Love' " was later retitled "All Yours."
T5210   Movin' Blues

JANUARY 8, 1967   BURBANK, CALIFORNIA
Andy Williams Show (NBC-TV)
Erroll Garner (p), unknown (b), unknown (d)

T5220   More
T5230   The Shadow of Your Smile
T5240   Misty (Andy Williams, vocal, with NBC Orchestra)

FEBRUARY 10, 1967   PHILADELPHIA
Mike Douglas Show (Westinghouse-TV); Roberta Peters, co-hostess
Erroll Garner (p), Jimmy DeJulio (b), Bobby Mariniello (d)

T5250   Lulu's Back in Town
T5260   Autumn Leaves
T5270   Dreamy

MARCH 19, 1967   LONDON
"Hear Me Talkin' "

T5280   Interview
           Note: Erroll Garner discusses how he was influenced by the big bands.

MAY 21, 1967   LONDON
"Sunday Night at the London Palladium" (BBC-TV); Bruce Forsythe, host
Erroll Garner (p), Herbert Moskowicz (b), Walter Perkins (d), José Mangual (cd)

T5290   Autumn Leaves
T5300   Misty
T5310   More

MAY 25, 1967   PARIS
Europe No. 1 Studios (Radio Broadcast)
Erroll Garner (p), Herbert Moskowicz (b), Walter Perkins (d), José Mangual (cd)

T5320   The Shadow of Your Smile
T5330   More
T5340   Thanks for the Memory

JUNE 15, 1967   PHILADELPHIA
Mike Douglas Show (Westinghouse-TV); Allen & Rossi, co-hosts
Erroll Garner (p), Jimmy DeJulio (b), Bobby Mariniello (d)

T5350   Blue Moon
T5360   Gaslight
T5370   Happy Birthday
T5380   Autumn Leaves
T5390   There Will Never Be Another You
T5400   Strike Up the Band
           Note: Part of this telecast may have been aired on June 22, 1967 and/or June 26,
           1967.

NOVEMBER 3, 1967   **WEST BERLIN**
SFB Studios
Erroll Garner (p), Ike Isaacs (b), Jimmie Smith (d), José Mangual (cd)

T5410   Autumn Leaves
T5420   These Foolish Things (Remind Me of You)
T5430   The Shadow of Your Smile

NOVEMBER 4, 1967   **WEST BERLIN**
SFB-TV
Erroll Garner (p), Ike Isaacs (b), Jimmie Smith (d), José Mangual (cd)

T5440   Misty
T5450   Blue Moon
T5460   That's All
T5470   Untitled Original
T5480   Like It Is
T5490   More
T5500   Thanks for the Memory

NOVEMBER 6, 1967   **STUTTGART, WEST GERMANY**
TV Broadcast
Erroll Garner (p), Ike Isaacs (b), Jimmie Smith (d), José Mangual (cd)

T5510   Autumn Leaves
T5520   These Foolish Things (Remind Me of You)
T5530   The Shadow of Your Smile
T5540   Like It Is
T5550   Misty
T5560   Blue Moon
T5570   Thanks for the Memory

NOVEMBER 6, 1967   **PHILADELPHIA**
Mike Douglas Show (Westinghouse-TV)
Erroll Garner (p), Jimmy DeJulio (b), Bobby Mariniello (d)

T5580   Autumn Leaves
T5590   Solitaire
T5600   I Get a Kick Out of You

NOVEMBER 6, 1967   **BURBANK, CALIFORNIA**
Andy Williams Show (NBC-TV)
Asterisk (*) denotes Andy Williams, vocal.
Erroll Garner (p), unknown (b), unknown (d), Andy Williams (v)*

T5610   Love* (with studio orchestra and chorus)
T5620   Misty
T5630   I've Got You Under My Skin*
T5640   On the Street Where You Live*
T5650   It Had to Be You*
T5660   I Can't Give You Anything But Love*
T5670   I'm Sitting on Top of the World/
         Breezin' Along with the Breeze (medley)*
T5680   Mame*
T5690   Winchester Cathedral* (no piano)
T5700   Love Makes the World Go 'Round*

DECEMBER 14, 1967   NEW YORK
Joey Bishop Show (ABC-TV)
Erroll Garner (p), unknown (b), unknown (d)

T5710   Misty
T5720   Blue Moon

JANUARY 16, 1968   LOS ANGELES
Pat Boone Show (TV Broadcast)
Erroll Garner (p), unknown (b), unknown (d)

T5730   The Shadow of Your Smile

FEBRUARY 22, 1968   FORT LAUDERDALE, FLORIDA
War Memorial Auditorium
Erroll Garner (p), Ike Isaacs (b), Jimmie Smith (d), José Mangual (cd)

T5740   What Is This Thing Called Love?
T5750   That's All
T5760   The Girl from Ipanema
T5770   I've Grown Accustomed to Her Face
T5780   All the Things You Are
T5790   The Shadow of Your Smile
T5800   On a Clear Day (You Can See Forever)
T5810   Strangers in the Night
T5820   Untitled Original
T5830   There Will Never Be Another You
T5840   Thanks for the Memory

          Intermission

T5850   Satin Doll
T5860   I'll Remember April
T5870   Misty
T5880   One Note Samba
T5890   Laura
T5900   Love
T5910   Like It Is
T5920   A Lot of Livin' to Do
T5930   These Foolish Things (Remind Me of You)
T5940   Night and Day
T5950   Thanks for the Memory
T5960   Untitled Original

MARCH 26-28, 1968   MONTREAL
"Jazz Piano" (CBC-TV)
Erroll Garner (p), Ike Isaacs (b), Jimmie Smith (d), José Mangual (cd)

T5970   Love
T5980   Stella by Starlight
T5990   A Lot of Livin' to Do
T6000   Untitled Original
          Note: Also appearing on this telecast are Marian McPartland, Brian Browne and Bill
          Evans.

APRIL 16, 1968   PHILADELPHIA
Mike Douglas Show (Westinghouse-TV)
Erroll Garner (p), Jimmy DeJulio (b), Bobby Mariniello (d)

T6010   That's My Kick
T6020   Gaslight
T6030   The Girl from Ipanema

MAY 7, 1968   PARIS
Europe No. 1 Studios (Radio Broadcast)
Erroll Garner (p), Ike Isaacs (b), Jimmie Smith (d), José Mangual (cd)

T6040   Autumn Leaves
T6050   These Foolish Things (Remind Me of You)
T6060   Blue Moon
T6070   More
T6080   I'll Remember April

MAY 27, 1968   COPENHAGEN
Danish TV Broadcast
Erroll Garner (p), Ike Isaacs (b), Jimmie Smith (d), José Mangual (cd)

T6090   Misty
T6100   On Green Dolphin Street
T6110   The Shadow of Your Smile
T6120   I Can't Get Started
T6130   Blue Moon
T6140   More
T6150   Misty
         Note: This telecast was pre-recorded on May 9, 1968.

JULY 7, 1968   COPENHAGEN
Danish Radio Broadcast; Borge Roger Henrichsen, host
Erroll Garner (p), Ike Isaacs (b), Jimmie Smith (d), José Mangual (cd)

T6160   Misty
T6170   Autumn Leaves
T6180   Stella by Starlight
T6190   That's My Kick
T6200   These Foolish Things (Remind Me of You)
T6210   Passing Through
T6220   Misty
         Note: This broadcast was pre-recorded on May 27, 1968.

JULY 22, 1968   PHILADELPHIA
Mike Douglas Show (Westinghouse-TV)
Erroll Garner (p), Jimmy DeJulio (b), Bobby Mariniello (d)

T6230   All the Things You Are
T6240   It's the Talk of the Town
T6250   I Got Rhythm

JULY 26, 1968   LONDON
BBC-TV Broadcast; Bennie Green, host
Erroll Garner (p), Ike Isaacs (b), Jimmie Smith (d), José Mangual (cd)

T6260   Misty
T6270   Autumn Leaves

T6280	The Shadow of Your Smile
T6290	Blue Moon
T6300	Misty
T6310	Passing Through
T6320	Thanks for the Memory

Note: This telecast was pre-recorded on May 12, 1968.

JULY 28, 1968   LONDON
Don Knotts Show (BBC-TV)
Erroll Garner (p), Ike Isaacs (b), Jimmie Smith (d), José Mangual (cd)

T6330	I Get a Kick Out of You
T6340	More

Note: This telecast was pre-recorded on May 17, 1968 and was aired in the USA on July 23, 1968.

SEPTEMBER 26, 1968   LONDON
BBC-TV Broadcast; Bennie Green, host
Erroll Garner (p), Ike Isaacs (b), Jimmie Smith (d), José Mangual (cd)

T6350	Misty
T6360	All the Things You Are
T6370	I Cover the Waterfront
T6380	I've Grown Accustomed to Her Face
T6390	La Petite Mambo
T6400	Strangers in the Night
T6410	Misty

Note: This telecast was pre-recorded on May 12, 1968.

OCTOBER, 1968   VANCOUVER, BRITISH COLUMBIA
CKNW Radio; Jack Cullen, host

T6420	Interview

Note: Jack Cullen interviews Erroll Garner concerning his current engagement at Isy's Supper Club.

DECEMBER 14, 1968   MIAMI, FLORIDA
John Gary Show
Erroll Garner (p), unknown (b), unknown (d)

T6430	The Shadow of Your Smile
T6440	Misty

ca. 1969   NEW YORK
Studio recordings
Erroll Garner (p)

T6450	Feeling Is Believing
T6460	Mood Island
T6470	Paisley Eyes
T6480	You Turned Me Around
T6490	Afinidad
T6500	Like It Is
T6510	Gaslight
T6520	Walkin' with Me
T6530	Feeling Is Believing
T6540	Mood Island

Note: These solo recordings (all Garner originals), are not commercially acceptable and were probably done so the tunes could be transcribed.

JANUARY 20, 1969   **NEW YORK**
Steve Allen Show (TV Broadcast)
Asterisk (*) denotes Steve Allen and Erroll Garner on piano.
Erroll Garner (p), Steve Allen (p)*, unknown (b), unknown (d)

T6550   It's the Talk of the Town
T6560   The Girl from Ipanema
T6570   The One I Love (Belongs to Somebody Else)*

FEBRUARY 20, 1969   **NEW YORK**
Merv Griffin Show (Westinghouse-TV)
Erroll Garner (p), unknown (b), unknown (d)

T6580   Untitled Original
T6590   That's All

MAY 23, 1969   **PARIS**
Europe No. 1 Studios (Radio Broadcast)
Erroll Garner (p), Ike Isaacs (b), Jimmie Smith (d), José Mangual (cd)

T6600   Love
T6610   Untitled Original
T6620   Misty
T6630   On Green Dolphin Street
T6640   Thanks for the Memory/
           Michele (medley)
T6650   Autumn Leaves
T6660   Time After Time

JUNE, 1969   **VANCOUVER, BRITISH COLUMBIA**
CBC Radio Broadcast; Bob Smith, host

T6661   Interview
           Note: Erroll Garner discusses his rememberances of 52nd Street.

APRIL 8, 1970   **NEW YORK**
The Tonight Show (NBC-TV); Johnny Carson, host
Erroll Garner (p), Bob Haggart (b), Ed Shaughnessy (d)

T6670   One Note Samba

APRIL 12, 1970   **PITTSBURGH**
Carnegie Music Hall, 75th Anniversary of the Carnegie Library
Erroll Garner (p), Victor Venegas (b), Herbert Lovelle (d), José Mangual (cd)

T6680   Untitled Original
T6690   The Loving Touch
T6700   One Note Samba
T6710   Dreamy
T6720   The Shadow of Your Smile
           *Note: At the beginning of this concert, Mayor Flaherty declared Sunday, April 12,
           1970 "Erroll Garner Day" in Pittsburgh. This tape, recorded by family members, was
           heard by Garner's father, Ernest, while in a nursing home one month prior to his death
           (May 14, 1970).*

MAY 4, 1970   PHILADELPHIA
Mike Douglas Show (Westinghouse-TV)
Erroll Garner (p), Jimmy DeJulio (b), Bobby Mariniello (d)

| T6730 | Dreamy |
| T6740 | I'll Remember April |

MAY 13, 1970   PARIS
Europe No. 1 Studios (Radio Broadcast)
Erroll Garner (p), Victor Venegas (b), Harvey Mason (d), José Mangual (cd)

T6750	Misty
T6760	Autumn Leaves
T6770	That's All
T6780	The Girl from Ipanema
T6790	Time After Time/
	There Will Never Be Another You (medley)
T6800	Quiet Nights of Quiet Stars (Corcovado)
T6810	Love
T6820	Satin Doll
T6830	Misty

JULY 17, 1970   STOCKHOLM
Swedish TV Broadcast
Erroll Garner (p), Victor Venegas (b), Harvey Mason (d), José Mangual (cd)

T6840	Misty
T6850	Autumn Leaves
T6860	That's All
T6870	Girl Talk
T6880	There Will Never Be Another You
	Note: This telecast was pre-recorded in May, 1970.

AUGUST 28, 1970   STOCKHOLM
Swedish TV Broadcast
Erroll Garner (p), Victor Venegas (b), Harvey Mason (d), José Mangual (cd)

T6890	The Girl from Ipanema
T6900	Dreamy
T6910	Watch What Happens
T6920	Love
T6930	Misty
	Note: This telecast was pre-recorded in May, 1970.

SEPTEMBER 20, 1970   CHICAGO
Mr. Kelly's
Erroll Garner (p), Ernest McCarty, Jr. (b), Bill English (d), José Mangual (cd)

T6940	Autumn Leaves
T6950	Time After Time
T6960	On Green Dolphin Street
T6970	The Shadow of Your Smile
T6980	This Guy's in Love with You
T6990	Untitled Original
T7000	Misty

OCTOBER 16, 1970   **COPENHAGEN**
Montmartre Club "Jazz Beat" (DANSK-TV)
Erroll Garner (p), Ernest McCarty, Jr. (b), Bill English (d), José Mangual (cd)

T7010   On Green Dolphin Street
T7020   The Girl from Ipanema
T7030   Misty
T7040   Strangers in the Night
           *Note: This telecast was probably pre-recorded in August, 1970, during Garner's
           European tour.*

OCTOBER 23, 1970   **NEW YORK**
The Tonight Show (NBC-TV); Johnny Carson, host
Erroll Garner (p), Bob Haggart (b), Ed Shaughnessy (d)

T7050   Strangers in the Night

JANUARY 26, 1971   **NEW YORK**
Dick Cavett Show (ABC-TV)
Erroll Garner (p), George Duvivier (b), Bobby Rosengarden (d)

T7060   Strangers in the Night
T7070   The Look of Love
T7080   Misty

MARCH 20, 1971   **LOS ANGELES**
Pearl Bailey Show (ABC-TV)
Asterisk (*) denotes Pearl Bailey, vocal.
Erroll Garner (p), unknown (b), Louis Bellson (d), Pearl Bailey (v)*

T7090   For Once in My Life
T7100   I Got It Bad and That Ain't Good*
T7110   Misty*

APRIL 10, 1971   **LOS ANGELES**
Pearl Bailey Show (ABC-TV)
Erroll Garner (p), Ray Brown (b), Louis Bellson (d), Pearl Bailey (v)

T7120   Strangers in the Night
T7130   I Love You

MAY 26, 1971   **CHICAGO**
"Just Jazz," Program 201 (WTTW-TV)
Erroll Garner (p), Ernest McCarty, Jr. (b), Bill English (d), José Mangual (cd)

T7140   The Look of Love
T7150   That's All
T7160   The Shadow of Your Smile
T7170   Mood Island
T7180   For Once in My Life
T7190   Erroll's Theme
T7200   Medley (unknown titles)

JULY 2, 1971   **LOS ANGELES**
The Name of the Game (NBC-TV)
Erroll Garner (p)

T7210   Dreamy
T7220   Quiet Nights of Quiet Stars (Corcovado)
T7230   Strangers in the Night
T7240   Dreamy
T7250   Jingle Bells
          *Note: Erroll Garner appears and plays background music in this TV drama titled "A
          Sister from Napoli" with Peter Falk, Geraldine Page, David Wayne, Tom Ewell and
          Sheppard Strudwick.*

OCTOBER 7, 1971   LOS ANGELES
Flip Wilson Show (NBC-TV)
Asterisk (*) denotes Flip Wilson, vocal.
Erroll Garner (p), unknown (b), unknown (d), Flip Wilson (v)*

T7260   For Once in My Life
T7270   Erroll Garner Blues*

OCTOBER 14, 1971   LOS ANGELES
The Tonight Show (NBC-TV); Johnny Carson, host
Erroll Garner (p), Bob Haggart (b), Ed Shaughnessy (d)

T7280   There Will Never Be Another You
T7290   Misty

DECEMBER 2, 1971   NEW YORK
Dick Cavett Show (ABC-TV); Alan King, host
Erroll Garner (p), George Duvivier (b), Bobby Rosengarden (d)

T7300   Misty
T7310   There Will Never Be Another You

FEBRUARY 5, 1972   CHICAGO
Blue Max Room, Hyatt Regency (O'Hare) Hotel
Erroll Garner (p), Ernest McCarty, Jr. (b), Jimmie Smith (d), José Mangual (cd)

T7320   The Shadow of Your Smile
T7330   On a Clear Day (You Can See Forever)
T7340   This Guy's in Love with You
T7350   Untitled Original
T7360   That's All
T7370   Caravan
T7380   One Note Samba
T7390   Misty

FEBRUARY 11, 1972   CHICAGO
Blue Max Room, Hyatt Regency (O'Hare) Hotel
Erroll Garner (p), Ernest McCarty, Jr. (b), Jimmie Smith (d), José Mangual (cd)

T7400   Autumn Leaves
T7410   That's All
T7420   Untitled Original
T7430   Misty
T7440   The Shadow of Your Smile
T7450   This Guy's in Love with You
T7460   Lover Man (Oh, Where Can You Be?)
T7470   Untitled Original
T7480   Untitled Original
T7490   Dancing Tambourine

MARCH 16, 1972   **PHILADELPHIA**
Mike Douglas Show (Westinghouse-TV); Eva Gabor, co-hostess
Erroll Garner (p), Jimmy DeJulio (b), Bobby Mariniello (d)

T7500	It Could Happen to You
T7510	Something

MAY 6, 1972   **LONDON**
Hammersmith Odeon
Erroll Garner (p), Ernest McCarty, Jr. (b), Jimmie Smith (d), José Mangual (cd)

T7520	Afternoon of an Elf
T7530	Stella by Starlight
T7540	Autumn Leaves
T7550	Girl Talk
T7560	This Guy's in Love with You
T7570	The Shadow of Your Smile
T7580	Mood Island
T7590	Nightwind
T7600	Untitled Original
T7610	(They Long to Be) Close to You
T7620	Untitled Original
	Intermission
T7630	Don't Get Around Much Anymore
T7640	Mucho Gusto
T7650	Something
T7660	Untitled Original
T7670	Lover Man (Oh, Where Can You Be?)
T7680	Misty
T7690	On a Clear Day (You Can See Forever)
T7700	Yesterday
T7710	Gemini
T7720	When a Gypsy Makes His Violin Cry
T7730	Caravan
T7740	Untitled Original

MAY 9, 1972   **PESCARA, ITALY**
Quadrifoglio Auditorium
Erroll Garner (p), Ernest McCarty, Jr. (b), Jimmie Smith (d), José Mangual (cd)

T7750	Afternoon of an Elf
T7760	I Can't Get Started
T7770	This Guy's in Love with You
T7780	The Shadow of Your Smile
T7790	Untitled Original
T7800	Laura
T7810	Untitled Original
T7820	Misty
T7830	There Will Never Be Another You
T7840	(They Long to Be) Close to You
T7850	Something
T7860	Strangers in the Night
T7870	Nightwind
T7880	Classical Medley

JUNE, 1972   **SYDNEY, AUSTRALIA**
Sydney TV Broadcast
Erroll Garner (p), Ernest McCarty, Jr. (b), Jimmie Smith (d), José Mangual (cd)

T7890	Misty
T7900	One Note Samba/
	Slightly Out of Tune (Desafinado) (medley)
T7910	That's All
T7920	Afinidad
T7930	This Guy's in Love with You
T7940	The Shadow of Your Smile
T7950	On a Clear Day (You Can See Forever)
T7960	Laura
T7970	Misty

JUNE 20, 1972   TOKYO
Concert
Erroll Garner (p), Ernest McCarty, Jr. (b), Jimmie Smith (d), José Mangual (cd)

T7980	Afternoon of an Elf
T7990	The Shadow of Your Smile
T8000	Untitled Original
T8010	(They Long to Be) Close to You
T8020	Autumn Leaves
T8030	Yesterday
T8040	Mood Island
T8050	Untitled Original
T8060	Misty
T8070	Girl Talk
T8080	That's All
T8090	Untitled Original
T8100	Laura
T8110	This Guy's in Love with You
T8120	Something
T8130	Mucho Gusto
T8140	Someone to Watch Over Me
T8150	Untitled Original
T8160	Untitled Original

SEPTEMBER 20, 1972   PHILADELPHIA
Mike Douglas Show (Westinghouse-TV); Della Reese, co-hostess
Erroll Garner (p), Jimmy DeJulio (b), Bobby Mariniello (d)

T8170	These Foolish Things (Remind Me of You)
T8180	Something
T8190	Misty (vocal by Della Reese)

OCTOBER 3, 1972   LOS ANGELES
Merv Griffin Show (Westinghouse-TV)
Erroll Garner (p), Ray Brown (b), Jake Hanna (d)

T8200	That's My Kick
T8210	The Shadow of Your Smile
	Note: This telecast was pre-recorded on September 28, 1972.

OCTOBER 19, 1972   LOS ANGELES
The Tonight Show (NBC-TV); Joey Bishop, host
Erroll Garner (p), John Williams (b), Ed Shaughnessy (d)

| T8220 | Something |
| T8230 | Tea for Two |

JANUARY 17, 1973   **NEW YORK**
The Today Show (NBC-TV); Frank McGee, host
Erroll Garner (p), unknown (b), unknown (d)

T8240	These Foolish Things (Remind Me of You)
T8250	Eldorado
T8260	Gemini
T8270	Misty

JANUARY 23, 1973   **PARIS**
ORTF TV Studios; Frank Ténot, host
Erroll Garner (p), Ernest McCarty, Jr. (b), Jimmie Smith (d), José Mangual (cd)

T8280	Misty
T8290	Afinidad
T8300	All the Things You Are
T8310	Something
T8320	That's My Kick
T8330	The Shadow of Your Smile
T8340	The Loving Touch
T8350	Misty

FEBRUARY 12, 1973   **PHILADELPHIA**
Mike Douglas Show (Westinghouse-TV); Joe Garagiola, co-host
Erroll Garner (p), Jimmy DeJulio (b), Bobby Mariniello (d)

T8360	It Could Happen to You
T8370	Gemini

MAY 29, 1973   **LOS ANGELES**
The Tonight Show (NBC-TV); Bill Cosby, host
Erroll Garner (p), John Williams (b), Ed Shaughnessy (d)

T8380	Something Happens

JULY 18, 1973   **NEW YORK**
Schaefer Music Series in Central Park
Erroll Garner (p), Ernest McCarty, Jr. (b), Jimmie Smith (d), José Mangual (cd)

T8390	Untitled Original
T8400	It Could Happen to You
T8410	Lover Man (Oh, Where Can You Be?)
T8420	Stella by Starlight
T8430	Girl Talk
T8440	Untitled Original
T8450	Misty
T8460	The Shadow of Your Smile
T8470	Something
T8480	Untitled Original

ca. OCTOBER, 1973   **NEW YORK**
Erroll Garner (p), Norman Gold (o)

T8490	Charmaine
T8500	On the Sunny Side of the Street
T8510	Perdido
T8520	There's a Small Hotel
T8530	Misty
T8540	Untitled Original
T8550	These Foolish Things (Remind Me of You)

NOVEMBER 20, 1973   LOS ANGELES
The Tonight Show (NBC-TV); Johnny Carson, host
Erroll Garner (p), John Williams (b), Ed Shaughnessy (d)

T8560   Something Happens
T8570   Watch What Happens

DECEMBER 4, 1973   CHICAGO
Mr. Kelly's
Erroll Garner (p), Ernest McCarty, Jr. (b), Jimmie Smith (d), José Mangual (cd)

T8580   There Will Never Be Another You
T8590   Stella by Starlight
T8600   Girl Talk
T8610   Mucho Gusto
T8620   Someone to Watch Over Me
T8630   (They Long to Be) Close to You
T8640   Misty
T8650   The Look of Love

FEBRUARY 6, 1974   LONDON
BBC-1 (TV Broadcast)
Erroll Garner (p), Ernest McCarty, Jr. (b), Jimmie Smith (d), José Mangual (cd)

T8660   Misty
T8670   How High the Moon
T8680   The Shadow of Your Smile
T8690   Something

APRIL 17, 1974   LOS ANGELES
Merv Griffin Show (Westinghouse-TV)
Erroll Garner (p), Ray Brown (b), Jake Hanna (d)

T8700   I Only Have Eyes for You
T8710   Misty
T8720   Passing Through
           Note: This telecast was pre-recorded on April 3, 1974.

MAY 3, 1974   WEST BERLIN
RIAS Studios (Radio Broadcast)
Erroll Garner (p), Ernest McCarty, Jr. (b), Jimmie Smith (d), José Mangual (cd)

T8730   Misty
T8740   Mood Island
T8750   Something Happens
T8760   It Could Happen to You
T8770   Something
T8780   What Are You Doing the Rest of Your Life?/
           My Funny Valentine (medley)
T8790   I'll Remember April
T8800   Misty

DECEMBER 18, 1974   LOS ANGELES
The Tonight Show (NBC-TV); Johnny Carson, host
Erroll Garner (p), John Williams (b), Louis Bellson (d)

T8810   Misty
T8820   It Could Happen to You

FEBRUARY 14, 1975   **WASHINGTON, D.C.**
Etcetera Club
Erroll Garner (p), Brian Torff (b), Ronnie Cole (d), José Mangual (cd)

8:00 p.m. Show

T8830   Untitled Original
T8840   Lover Man (Oh, Where Can You Be?)
T8850   What Are You Doing the Rest of Your Life?/
        All the Things You Are (medley)
T8860   Untitled Original
T8870   Misty
T8880   (They Long to Be) Close to You
T8890   Yesterday/The Nearness of You (medley)
T8900   Untitled Original
T8910   Untitled Original

10:00 p.m. Show

T8920   I'll Remember April
T8930   Satin Doll
T8940   Lover Man (Oh, Where Can You Be?)
T8950   Mood Island
T8960   Someone to Watch Over Me
T8970   Afinidad

12:00 Midnight Show

T8980   Untitled Original
T8990   Untitled Original
T9000   Paris Mist
T9010   What Are You Doing the Rest of Your Life?/
        Stella by Starlight (medley)
T9020   Lover Man (Oh, Where Can You Be?)

FEBRUARY 15, 1975   **WASHINGTON, D.C.**
Etcetera Club
Erroll Garner (p), Brian Torff (b), Ronnie Cole (d), José Mangual (cd)

8:00 p.m. Show

T9030   On Green Dolphin Street
T9040   Untitled Original
T9050   Lover Man (Oh, Where Can You Be?)
T9060   What Are You Doing the Rest of Your Life?/
        All the Things You Are (medley)
T9070   Misty
T9080   (They Long to Be) Close to You
T9090   Girl Talk
T9100   You Are the Sunshine of My Life

10:00 p.m. Show

T9110   On a Clear Day (You Can See Forever)
T9120   The Nearness of You
T9130   Untitled Original
T9140   Paris Mist
T9150   Stella by Starlight
T9160   Someone to Watch Over Me
T9170   Afinidad

12:00 Midnight Show

T9180   Mood Island

T9190	I Only Have Eyes for You
T9200	Misty
T9210	Satin Doll
T9220	I Cover the Waterfront/
	This Guy's in Love with You (medley)
T9230	On Green Dolphin Street
T9240	One Note Samba
T9250	What Are You Doing the Rest of Your Life?/
	Sunny (medley)
T9260	You Are the Sunshine of My Life
T9270	Untitled Original

FEBRUARY 16, 1975   **WASHINGTON, D.C.**

Etcetera Club

Erroll Garner (p), Brian Torff (b), Ronnie Cole (d), José Mangual (cd)

8:00 p.m. Show

T9280	Untitled Original
T9290	Lover Man (Oh, Where Can You Be?)
T9300	On Green Dolphin Street
T9310	What Are You Doing the Rest of Your Life?/
	All the Things You Are (medley)
T9320	(They Long To Be) Close to You
T9330	Misty
T9340	You Are the Sunshine of My Life
T9350	This Guy's in Love with You/Girl Talk (medley)
T9360	Untitled Original

10:00 p.m. Show

T9370	Afinidad
T9380	On a Clear Day (You Can See Forever)
T9390	Someone to Watch Over Me
T9400	Untitled Original
T9410	Stella by Starlight
T9420	Misty
T9430	Satin Doll
T9440	Lover Man (Oh, Where Can You Be?)
T9450	On Green Dolphin Street
T9460	Untitled Original

12:00 Midnight Show

T9470	There Will Never Be Another You
T9480	A Cottage for Sale
T9490	Mood Island
T9500	What Are You Doing the Rest of Your Life?/
	Sunny (medley)
T9510	Laura
T9520	Misty
T9530	Something

FEBRUARY 20, 1975   **CHICAGO**

Mr. Kelly's

Erroll Garner (p), Brian Torff (b), Ronnie Cole (d), José Mangual (cd)

T9540	Unknown titles
	Note: This was the last public performance by Erroll Garner. It has been verified that a tape exists of this performance.

COMPILATION OF ISSUED DISCS

| 3 Deuces | 505 | USA | 10 Inch 78 |

3070   Through a Long and Sleepless Night
3090   What Is This Thing Called Love?

| 3 Deuces | 506 | USA | 10 Inch 78 |

3080   Again
3110   Goodbye

| 3 Deuces | 507 | USA | 10 Inch 78 |

3100   I Let a Song Go Out of My Heart
3120   Jitterbug Waltz

| 3 Deuces | 508 | USA | 10 Inch 78 |

3130   Deep Purple
3060   Scatter-Brain

| 77 Records | 77-LA-12-6 | Eng | 12 Inch 33 |

0700   Gaslight
0620   In the Beginning
0790   Keep Happy Baby
0740   Meatless Pay Day (Part 1)
0750   Meatless Pay Day (Part 2)
0710   Red Cross

| 77 Records | 77 EPEU-2 | Eng | 7 Inch 45EP |

0760   Geronimo (Part 1)
0770   Geronimo (Part 2)
0720   He Pulled a Fast One (Part 1)
0730   He Pulled a Fast One (Part 2)

| ABC Paramount | 45-10260 | USA | 7 Inch 45 |

6150   Dreamstreet
6140   When You're Smiling (The Whole World Smiles with You)

| ABC Paramount | 45-10301 | USA | 7 Inch 45 |

6240   Some of These Days
6190   You Do Something to Me

| ABC Paramount | ABC 365 | USA | 12 Inch 33 |

6110   Blue Lou
6120   Come Rain or Come Shine
6150   Dreamstreet
6100   I'm Gettin' Sentimental Over You

6090	Just One of Those Things
6130	Lady Is a Tramp, The
6170	Mambo Gotham
6180	Oklahoma! Medley:
	Oh, What a Beautiful Mornin'
	People Will Say We're in Love
	Surrey with the Fringe on Top, The
6160	Sweet Lorraine
6140	When You're Smiling (The Whole World Smiles with You)

ABC Paramount   **ABC 395**   USA   **12 Inch 33**

6210	All of Me
6280	Back in Your Own Back Yard
6270	Best Things in Life Are Free, The
6260	El Papa Grande
6250	I'm in the Mood for Love
6200	My Silent Love
6230	St. Louis Blues
6220	Shadows
6240	Some of These Days
6190	You Do Something to Me

ABC Paramount   **ABCS 365**   USA   **12 Inch 33**

6110	Blue Lou
6120	Come Rain or Come Shine
6150	Dreamstreet
6100	I'm Gettin' Sentimental Over You
6090	Just One of Those Things
6130	Lady Is a Tramp, The
6170	Mambo Gotham
6180	Oklahoma! Medley:
	Oh, What a Beautiful Mornin'
	People Will Say We're in Love
	Surrey with the Fringe on Top, The
6160	Sweet Lorraine
6140	When You're Smiling (The Whole World Smiles with You)

ABC Paramount   **ABCS 365-2**   USA   **7 Inch 33**

6100	I'm Gettin' Sentimental Over You
6090	Just One of Those Things

ABC Paramount   **ABCS 365-3**   USA   **7 Inch 33**

6180	Oklahoma! Medley:
	Oh, What a Beautiful Mornin'
	People Will Say We're in Love
	Surrey with the Fringe on Top, The

ABC Paramount   **ABCS 395**   USA   **12 Inch 33**

6210	All of Me
6280	Back in Your Own Back Yard
6270	Best Things in Life Are Free, The
6260	El Papa Grande
6250	I'm in the Mood for Love
6200	My Silent Love
6230	St. Louis Blues
6220	Shadows
6240	Some of These Days
6190	You Do Something to Me

ABC Paramount	ABCS 395-5	USA	7 Inch 33
6270	Best Things in Life Are Free, The		
6230	St. Louis Blues		

AFRS Downbeat	216	USA	16 Inch TX
1360	Laura		
0850	Night and Day		
1380	Somebody Loves Me		
0830	Twistin' the Cat's Tail		
0820	White Rose Bounce		

AFRS Downbeat	263	USA	16 Inch TX
1590	Black Night and Fog		
1600	C Jam Blues		
1620	Caravan		
1610	Please Let Me Forget		

AFRS Downbeat	Q39	USA	16 Inch TX
1660	Full Moon and Empty Arms		

AFRS Jubilee	170	USA	16 Inch TX
1630	Laura		
1640	Yesterdays		

AFRS Jubilee	171	USA	16 Inch TX
1650	Erroll's Bounce		

AFRS Jubilee	181	USA	16 Inch TX
1700	Diane		
1710	Erroll's Bounce		

AFRS Jubilee	230	USA	16 Inch TX
1920	Trio		

AFRS Jubilee	259	USA	16 Inch TX
2210	Erroll's Blues		

AFRS Jubilee	262	USA	16 Inch TX
2060	Erroll's Bounce		
2000	One O'Clock Jump		

AFRS Just Jazz	13	USA	16 Inch TX
2220	Cherchez la Femme		
2230	Indiana (Back Home Again in Indiana)		

AFRS Just Jazz	65	USA	16 Inch TX
2620	Cherokee (Part 1)		
2630	Cherokee (Part 2)		

AFRS Just Jazz	71	USA	16 Inch TX
2640	All the Things You Are		
2650	Fine and Dandy		

AFRS Just Jazz	80	USA	16 Inch TX
2620	Cherokee (Part 1)		
2630	Cherokee (Part 2)		

AFRS Music America

	Loves Best	**79**	**USA**	**16 Inch TX**
1585	Laura			

Acorn		**305**	**USA**	**10 Inch 78**
2830	I Want a Little Girl			
2800	This Can't Be Love			

Alamac		**QSR2447**	**USA**	**12 Inch 33**
1000	Harvard Blues			
1440	Humoresque			
0990	One O'Clock Jump			
1010	Slammin' Around			
1470	Slamboree			
1460	Smoke Gets in Your Eyes			
0980	Three O'Clock in the Morning			
1450	Wrap Your Troubles in Dreams			

Allegro		**LP1697**	**USA**	**12 Inch 33**
0930	In the Middle			

Allegro		**LP3102**	**USA**	**12 Inch 33**
0930	In the Middle			

Allegro		**LP4009**	**USA**	**12 Inch 33**
0900	Georgie Porgie			
0930	In the Middle			

Alto		**AL 709**	**USA**	**12 Inch 33**
3420	Laura			
3400	No Moon			
3410	Scatter-Brain			
3390	What Is This Thing Called Love?			

Alto		**AL 712**	**USA**	**12 Inch 33**
4160	Ain't She Sweet?			
4170	Garner's Escape			
4180	Indiana (Back Home Again in Indiana)			
4140	Robbins' Nest			
4150	These Foolish Things (Remind Me of You)			

Amiga		**855205**	**EGer**	**12 Inch 33**
6850	As Time Goes By			
6870	Charmaine			
6940	How Deep Is the Ocean (How High Is the Sky)			
6880	I Found a Million Dollar Baby (In a Five and Ten Cent Store)			
6890	I'll Get By (As Long As I Have You)			
6950	It's Only a Paper Moon			
6920	Jeannine, I Dream of Lilac Time			
6960	Paramount on Parade (Newsreel Tag)			
6930	Schoner Gigolo (Just a Gigolo)			
6860	Sonny Boy			
6910	Stella by Starlight			
6900	Three O'Clock in the Morning			
6840	You Made Me Love You			

Apollo		**797**	**USA**	**10 Inch 78**
2240	Lover Man (Oh, Where Can You Be?)			
2260	What Is This Thing Called Love?			

Apollo   **798**   **USA**   **10 Inch 78**
2270   Erroll Garner in Paris
2280   These Foolish Things (Remind Me of You)

Arco   **1214**   **USA**   **10 Inch 78**
1420   Don't Blame Me
1430   How High the Moon

Arco   **1223**   **USA**   **10 Inch 78**
1350   Blue, Brown and Beige
1330   Sherry Lynn Flip

Arco   **1224**   **USA**   **10 Inch 78**
1320   Hop, Skip and Jump
1340   Three Blind Micesky

Arista   **5000**   **USA**   **10 Inch 78**
1440   Humoresque
1450   Wrap Your Troubles in Dreams

Arista   **5001**   **USA**   **10 Inch 78**
1470   Slamboree
1460   Smoke Gets in Your Eyes

Associated   **60808A**   **USA**   **16 Inch TX**
1100   All the Things You Are
1120   For You
1110   I Get a Kick Out of You
1130   Mood Indigo

Associated   **60808B**   **USA**   **16 Inch TX**
1210   I Can't Give You Anything But Love
1150   I Cried for You
1140   Somebody Loves Me

Associated   **60809A**   **USA**   **16 Inch TX**
1250   April in Paris
1220   Blue Room
1240   Liza
1260   Night and Day
1230   Oh, Lady Be Good!

Associated   **60809B**   **USA**   **16 Inch TX**
1310   I Know That You Know
1280   It Had to Be You
1300   On the Sunny Side of the Street
1270   Rosetta
1290   St. Louis Blues

Associated   **60810A**   **USA**   **16 Inch TX**
1180   Blue Skies
1170   How Deep Is the Ocean (How High Is the Sky)
1190   I Can't Get Started
1160   Sweet Georgia Brown

Associated   **60813A**   **USA**   **16 Inch TX**
1040   Bounce with Me
1050   Erroll's Bounce
1020   Loot to Boot
1030   White Rose Bounce (mistitled as Movin' Around)

Associated   60813B   USA   16 Inch TX
1080   Baby, Won't You Please Come Home
1090   Sweet Lorraine
1070   What Is This Thing Called Love?
1060   You Made Me Love You

Astor   SPLP1471   Aus   12 Inch 33
7740   Feeling Is Believing
7810   For Once in My Life
7830   Look of Love, The
7700   Loving Touch, The
7780   Mood Island
7790   Paisley Eyes
7840   Spinning Wheel
7760   Strangers in the Night
7820   Yesterday
7620   You Turned Me Around

Astor Maps   7570   Aus   12 Inch 33
0940   Sweet Lorraine

Atlantic   332.052   Fra   12 Inch 33
2900   Blue and Sentimental
2920   Flamingo
2940   I Can't Give You Anything But Love
3350   I May Be Wrong (But I Think You're Wonderful)
3320   I'm Confessin' (That I Love You)
2950   Impressions
2910   Pavanne (The Lamp Is Low)
2880   Reverie
2930   Skylark
3250   Summertime
2890   Turquoise
2970   Way You Look Tonight, The

Atlantic   590.002   Eng   12 Inch 33
2900   Blue and Sentimental
2920   Flamingo
2940   I Can't Give You Anything But Love
3350   I May Be Wrong (But I Think You're Wonderful)
3320   I'm Confessin' (That I Love You)
2950   Impressions
2930   Skylark
3250   Summertime
2890   Turquoise
2970   Way You Look Tonight, The

Atlantic   662   USA   10 Inch 78
2920   Flamingo
2960   Twilight

Atlantic   663   USA   10 Inch 78
2890   Turquoise
2970   Way You Look Tonight, The

Atlantic   665   USA   10 Inch 78
2950   Impressions
2880   Reverie

Atlantic   666   USA   10 Inch 78
2940   I Can't Give You Anything But Love
2930   Skylark

Atlantic   **667**   **USA**   **10 Inch 78**
2900   Blue and Sentimental
2910   Pavanne (The Lamp Is Low)

Atlantic   **672**   **USA**   **10 Inch 78**
3230   Lullaby of the Leaves
3240   Margie

Atlantic   **673**   **USA**   **10 Inch 78**
3350   I May Be Wrong (But I Think You're Wonderful)
3300   (There Is) No Greater Love

Atlantic   **674**   **USA**   **10 Inch 78**
3330   I'll Be Seeing You
3340   Trees

Atlantic   **675**   **USA**   **10 Inch 78**
3310   Serenade in Blue
3290   Sheik of Araby, The

Atlantic   **677**   **USA**   **10 Inch 78**
0440   Blues I Can't Forget
0460   Gliss in the Dark

Atlantic   **678**   **USA**   **10 Inch 78**
0390   Everything Happens to Me
0370   Perdido

Atlantic   **1227**   **USA**   **12 Inch 33**
2900   Blue and Sentimental
2920   Flamingo
2940   I Can't Give You Anything But Love
3350   I May Be Wrong (But I Think You're Wonderful)
3320   I'm Confessin' (That I Love You)
2950   Impressions
2910   Pavanne (The Lamp Is Low)
2880   Reverie
2930   Skylark
3250   Summertime
2890   Turquoise
2970   Way You Look Tonight, The

Atlantic   **30014**   **Fra**   **12 Inch 33**
2900   Blue and Sentimental
2920   Flamingo
2940   I Can't Give You Anything But Love
3350   I May Be Wrong (But I Think You're Wonderful)
3320   I'm Confessin' (That I Love You)
2950   Impressions
2910   Pavanne (The Lamp Is Low)
2880   Reverie
2930   Skylark
3250   Summertime
2890   Turquoise
2970   Way You Look Tonight, The

Atlantic   **70002**   **WGer**   **7 Inch 45**
2920   Flamingo
3250   Summertime

Atlantic	70003	WGer	7 Inch 45
2900	Blue and Sentimental		
2940	I Can't Give You Anything But Love		

Atlantic	ALR 128	USA	10 Inch 33
0410	All the Things You Are		
0440	Blues I Can't Forget		
0450	Boogie Woogie Boogie		
0390	Everything Happens to Me		
0430	I Get a Kick Out of You		
0400	I'm in the Mood for Love		
0370	Perdido		
0380	Soft and Warm		

Atlantic	ALR 135	USA	10 Inch 33
3360	Futuramic		
3270	Perpetual Emotion		
3280	Poinciana		
3260	Ramona		
3370	Reminiscing in Blue		
3250	Summertime		

Atlantic	ATL 50243	WGer	12 Inch 33
2900	Blue and Sentimental		
2920	Flamingo		
2940	I Can't Give You Anything But Love		
3350	I May Be Wrong (But I Think You're Wonderful)		
3320	I'm Confessin' (That I Love You)		
2950	Impressions		
2910	Pavanne (The Lamp Is Low)		
2880	Reverie		
2930	Skylark		
3250	Summertime		
2890	Turquoise		
2970	Way You Look Tonight, The		

Atlantic	EP506	USA	7 Inch 45EP
2940	I Can't Give You Anything But Love		
2880	Reverie		
2930	Skylark		
2970	Way You Look Tonight, The		

Atlantic	EP507	USA	7 Inch 45EP
2920	Flamingo		
3230	Lullaby of the Leaves		
3290	Sheik of Araby, The		
3340	Trees		

Atlantic	EP508	USA	7 Inch 45EP
3360	Futuramic		
3330	I'll Be Seeing You		
3240	Margie		
3280	Poinciana		

Atlantic	EP509	USA	7 Inch 45EP
2900	Blue and Sentimental		
3350	I May Be Wrong (But I Think You're Wonderful)		
2910	Pavanne (The Lamp Is Low)		
2960	Twilight		

Atlantic		EP80002	WGer	7 Inch 45EP
3350	I May Be Wrong (But I Think You're Wonderful)			
2950	Impressions			
2890	Turquoise			
2970	Way You Look Tonight, The			

Atlantic		EP232006	Fra	7 Inch 45EP
3350	I May Be Wrong (But I Think You're Wonderful)			
3320	I'm Confessin' (That I Love You)			
2890	Turquoise			
2970	Way You Look Tonight, The			

Atlantic		EP232010	Fra	7 Inch 45EP
2900	Blue and Sentimental			
2940	I Can't Give You Anything But Love			
2910	Pavanne (The Lamp Is Low)			
2890	Turquoise			

Atlantic		LP 109	USA	10 Inch 33
2900	Blue and Sentimental			
2920	Flamingo			
2940	I Can't Give You Anything But Love			
2950	Impressions			
2910	Pavanne (The Lamp Is Low)			
2880	Reverie			
2930	Skylark			
2890	Turquoise			
2960	Twilight			
2970	Way You Look Tonight, The			

Atlantic		LP 112	USA	10 Inch 33
3350	I May Be Wrong (But I Think You're Wonderful)			
3330	I'll Be Seeing You			
3230	Lullaby of the Leaves			
3240	Margie			
3310	Serenade in Blue			
3290	Sheik of Araby, The			
3300	(There Is) No Greater Love			
3340	Trees			

Atlantic		SD1227	USA	12 Inch 33
2900	Blue and Sentimental			
2920	Flamingo			
2940	I Can't Give You Anything But Love			
3350	I May Be Wrong (But I Think You're Wonderful)			
3320	I'm Confessin' (That I Love You)			
2950	Impressions			
2910	Pavanne (The Lamp Is Low)			
2880	Reverie			
2930	Skylark			
3250	Summertime			
2890	Turquoise			
2970	Way You Look Tonight, The			

Austroton-Mercury		5195V	WGer	10 Inch 78
1550	I Can't Get Started			
1500	I've Got You Under My Skin			

Avan-Guard	**BVL040**	**Aus**	**12 Inch 33**
4310	Avalon		
4250	Caravan		
4260	Lullaby of Birdland		
4200	Memories of You		
4220	(There Is) No Greater Love		
4290	Will You Still Be Mine?		

BNP	**25.101**	**Fra**	**12 Inch 33**
0160	Autumn Mood		
0290	Erroll's Concerto		
0140	Floating on a Cloud		
0330	I Hear a Rhapsody (Part 1)		
0340	I Hear a Rhapsody (Part 2)		
0280	Overture to Dawn		
0360	You Were Born to Be Kissed		

BNP	**25.102**	**Fra**	**12 Inch 33**
0580	Duke for Dinner		
0510	Fast Company		
0470	Fighting Cocks, The		
0630	I Got Rhythm		
0230	I Surrender, Dear		
0200	On the Sunny Side of the Street		
0300	Yesterdays		

BYG	**529110**	**Fra**	**12 Inch 33**
2470	Body and Soul		
2550	I Can't Believe That You're in Love with Me		
2425	I Cover the Waterfront		
2490	I Don't Stand a Ghost of a Chance with You		
1390	Indiana (Back Home Again in Indiana)		
2450	Love Walked In		
2560	More Than You Know		
2600	Over the Rainbow		
2440	Penthouse Serenade (When We're Alone)		
2580	Red Sails in the Sunset		
1380	Somebody Loves Me		
1370	Stardust		
2420	Stompin' at the Savoy		
2570	Undecided		

BYG	**529143**	**Fra**	**12 Inch 33**
2370	I Surrender, Dear		
2830	I Want a Little Girl		
2860	I'm Confessin' (That I Love You)		
2540	I'm in the Mood for Love		
2430	It's Easy to Remember		
1360	Laura		
2810	Man I Love, The		
2820	Moonglow		
2840	She's Funny That Way		
2870	Stormy Weather (Keeps Rainin' All the Time)		
2800	This Can't Be Love		
2850	Until the Real Thing Comes Along		

BYG	**529144**	**Fra**	**12 Inch 33**
2590	All of Me		
2480	All the Things You Are		
2520	Cottage for Sale, A		
3000	Everything Happens to Me		

2510	Goodbye
2400	I Only Have Eyes for You
2980	On the Sunny Side of the Street
2990	Rosalie
2460	September Song
3010	Stairway to the Stars
1370	Stardust
2420	Stompin' at the Savoy

BYG	**529161**	**Fra**	**12 Inch 33**
0870	Dark Eyesky
0860	Play, Fiddle, Play

Baronet	**47.501**	**Den**	**10 Inch 78**
0720	He Pulled a Fast One (Part 1)
0730	He Pulled a Fast One (Part 2)

Baronet	**B107**	**USA**	**12 Inch 33**
1850	Blow Top Blues
1860	Blow Top Blues
1840	Bird's Nest

Baronet	**B109**	**USA**	**12 Inch 33**
0150	Cloudburst
0570	Easy to Love
0620	In the Beginning
0520	Variations on a Nursery Rhyme (Mairzy Doats, Yes, We Have No Bananas, The Music Goes 'Round and 'Round, Everything I've Got [Belongs to You])

Bellaphon	**BJS4045**	**WGer**	**12 Inch 33**
2550	I Can't Believe That You're in Love with Me
2860	I'm Confessin' (That I Love You)
2820	Moonglow
2980	On the Sunny Side of the Street
2580	Red Sails in the Sunset
2840	She's Funny That Way
1380	Somebody Loves Me
2420	Stompin' at the Savoy
2870	Stormy Weather (Keeps Rainin' All the Time)
2800	This Can't Be Love

Black and White	**15**	**USA**	**10 Inch 78**
0850	Night and Day
0820	White Rose Bounce

Black and White	**16**	**USA**	**10 Inch 78**
0840	Movin' Around
0830	Twistin' the Cat's Tail

Blue Note	**BLP5007**	**USA**	**10 Inch 33**
0330	I Hear a Rhapsody (Part 1)
0340	I Hear a Rhapsody (Part 2)
0280	Overture to Dawn
0360	You Were Born to Be Kissed

Blue Note	**BLP5008**	**USA**	**10 Inch 33**
0160	Autumn Mood
0290	Erroll's Concerto
0140	Floating on a Cloud
0230	I Surrender, Dear

Blue Note		**BLP5014**	USA		**10 Inch 33**
0510	Fast Company				
0630	I Got Rhythm				
0200	On the Sunny Side of the Street				
0300	Yesterdays				

Blue Note		**BLP5015**	USA		**10 Inch 33**
0580	Duke for Dinner				
0350	Erroll's Reverie				
0470	Fighting Cocks, The				
0480	Lick and a Promise, A				

Blue Note		**BLP5016**	USA		**10 Inch 33**
0310	All the Things You Are (Part 1)				
0320	All the Things You Are (Part 2)				
0080	Clock Stood Still, The				
0500	Gaslight				
0490	Opus 1				

Blue Star		**62**	Fra		**10 Inch 78**
1840	Bird's Nest				
1880	Cool Blues				

Blue Star		**63**	Fra		**10 Inch 78**
2180	Frankie and Garni				
2070	Play, Piano, Play				

Blue Star		**96**	Fra		**10 Inch 78**
1890	Pastel				
1910	Trio				

Blue Star		**110**	Fra		**10 Inch 78**
2110	Blues Garni				
2190	Barclay Bounce				

Blue Star		**114**	Fra		**10 Inch 78**
1320	Hop, Skip and Jump				
1340	Three Blind Micesky				

Blue Star		**115**	Fra		**10 Inch 78**
1350	Blue, Brown and Beige				
1330	Sherry Lynn Flip				

Blue Star		**135**	Fra		**10 Inch 78**
2130	Don't Worry 'Bout Me				
2170	Love for Sale				

Blue Star		**144**	Fra		**10 Inch 78**
2890	Turquoise				
2970	Way You Look Tonight, The				

Blue Star		**149**	Fra		**10 Inch 78**
2920	Flamingo				
2940	I Can't Give You Anything But Love				

Blue Star		**164**	Fra		**10 Inch 78**
2900	Blue and Sentimental				
2910	Pavanne (The Lamp Is Low)				

Blue Star		217	Fra	10 Inch 78
3360	Futuramic			
3290	Sheik of Araby, The			

Blue Star		220	Fra	10 Inch 78
2950	Impressions			
2880	Reverie			

Blue Star		226	Fra	10 Inch 78
3270	Garnerology			

Blue Star		229	Fra	10 Inch 78
3230	Lullaby of the Leaves			
3240	Margie			

Blue Star		BLP6812	Fra	10 Inch 33
2900	Blue and Sentimental			
2920	Flamingo			
2940	I Can't Give You Anything But Love			
2950	Impressions			
2910	Pavanne (The Lamp Is Low)			
2880	Reverie			
2930	Skylark			
2890	Turquoise			
2960	Twilight			
2970	Way You Look Tonight, The			

Blue Star		BLP6814	Fra	10 Inch 33
2110	Blues Garni			
2130	Don't Worry 'Bout Me			
2170	Love for Sale			
1890	Pastel			
2070	Play, Piano, Play			
2190	Sloe Gin Fizz			

Blue Star		BLP6819	Fra	10 Inch 33
3350	I May Be Wrong (But I Think You're Wonderful)			
3330	I'll Be Seeing You			
3230	Lullaby of the Leaves			
3240	Margie			
3310	Serenade in Blue			
3290	Sheik of Araby, The			
3300	(There Is) No Greater Love			
3340	Trees			

Blue Star		BLP6833	Fra	10 Inch 33
0410	All the Things You Are			
0440	Blues I Can't Forget			
0450	Boogie Woogie Boogie			
0390	Everything Happens to Me			
0430	I Get a Kick Out of You			
0400	I'm in the Mood for Love			
0370	Perdido			
0380	Soft and Warm			

Blue Star		BLP6837	Fra	10 Inch 33
3360	Futuramic			
3270	Perpetual Emotion			
3280	Poinciana			

3260   Ramona
3370   Reminiscing in Blue
3250   Summertime

Book of the Month   **81-5403**   **USA**   **12 Inch 33**
6210   All of Me
6850   As Time Goes By
7430   Autumn Leaves
6270   Best Things in Life Are Free, The
7810   For Once in My Life
6440   Dancing Tambourine
6380   Happiness Is a Thing Called Joe
6250   I'm in the Mood for Love
7400   It Ain't Necessarily So
7420   Like It Is
7830   Look of Love, The
6410   Lover Come Back to Me
6320   Lulu's Back in Town
6400   Mack the Knife
6420   Misty
7390   More
6200   My Silent Love
7460   Nervous Waltz
6230   St. Louis Blues
6930   Schoner Gigolo (Just a Gigolo)
7410   Shadow of Your Smile, The
6240   Some of These Days
7840   Spinning Wheel
7760   Strangers in the Night
6910   Stella by Starlight
6390   Sweet and Lovely
6370   Way You Look Tonight, The
7820   Yesterday
6190   You Do Something to Me
6840   You Made Me Love You

Brunswick   **87016LPBM**   **WGer**   **12 Inch 33**
0940   Sweet Lorraine

Brunswick   **EB 71001**   **USA**   **7 Inch 45EP**
0970   Gaslight
0960   Loot to Boot
0940   Sweet Lorraine
0950   Yesterdays

Brunswick   **LAT8169**   **Eng**   **12 Inch 33**
0940   Sweet Lorraine

Bull Dog   **BDL4004**   **Eng**   **12 Inch 33**
7020   Can't Help Lovin' Dat Man
7050   Dearly Beloved
7060   Fine Romance, A
7000   Foggy Day, A
7570   I Got Rhythm
7010   Lovely to Look At
6980   Love Walked In
7030   Make Believe
7040   Ol' Man River
6990   Someone to Watch Over Me
6970   Strike Up the Band

CBS   **21062**   **Neth**   **12 Inch 33**
3710   Body and Soul
4370   Easy to Love
4420   Frenesi (Cancion Tropical)
3680   I Cover the Waterfront
3740   I'm in the Mood for Love
3720   Indiana (Back Home Again in Indiana)
3670   Laura
4380   Mean to Me
3960   Oh, Lady Be Good!
3690   Penthouse Serenade (When We're Alone)
3760   Play, Piano, Play
3700   Way You Look Tonight, The

CBS   **32260**   **Eng**   **12 Inch 33**
5390   Dreamy
4370   Easy to Love
5670   I Didn't Know What Time It Was
3740   I'm in the Mood for Love
5660   It Might As Well Be Spring
5380   Misty
5650   Moment's Delight
5400   On the Street Where You Live
5640   Other Voices
4210   'S Wonderful
4330   St. Louis Blues
5630   Solitaire
3940   Summertime
5690   This Is Always
5680   Very Thought of You, The
3700   Way You Look Tonight, The

CBS   **52065**   **Fra**   **12 Inch 33**
5260   Alexander's Ragtime Band
5200   But Not for Me
5220   Full Moon and Empty Arms
5250   Girl of My Dreams
5430   Mambo 207
5300   Ol' Man River
5450   Passing Through
5240   Time on My Hands
5440   Way Back Blues, The

CBS   **52566**   **Fra**   **12 Inch 33**
5250   Girl of My Dreams
3650   How High the Moon
4570   I'll See You in My Dreams
5720   Last Time I Saw Paris, The
3670   Laura
3550   Poor Butterfly
4360   Sweet Sue-Just You
5560   You'd Be So Nice to Come Home To

CBS   **52706**   **Neth**   **12 Inch 33**
5260   Alexander's Ragtime Band
5200   But Not for Me
3650   How High the Moon
4570   I'll See You in My Dreams
3670   Laura
5430   Mambo 207
5300   Ol' Man River

4360	Sweet Sue-Just You
5240	Time on My Hands
5440	Way Back Blues, The

CBS		62221	Fra	12 Inch 33
4240	Can't Help Lovin' Dat Man
4270	Cheek to Cheek
3910	It's the Talk of the Town
4390	I've Got My Love to Keep Me Warm
4350	Stompin' at the Savoy
4360	Sweet Sue-Just You
3980	Out of Nowhere
3620	Petite Waltz, The
3630	Petite Waltz Bounce, The
4450	Please Don't Talk About Me When I'm Gone

CBS		62310	Fra	12 Inch 33
5100	April in Paris
5070	Autumn Leaves
5140	Erroll's Theme
5120	How Could You Do a Thing Like That to Me?
5040	I'll Remember April
5080	It's All Right with Me
5060	Mambo Carmel
5090	Red Top
5050	Teach Me Tonight
5110	They Can't Take That Away from Me
5130	Where or When

CBS		62311	Fra	12 Inch 33
4310	Avalon
4250	Caravan
4260	Lullaby of Birdland
4200	Memories of You
4220	(There Is) No Greater Love
4290	Will You Still Be Mine?

CBS		62334	Fra	12 Inch 33
5360	Creme de Menthe
4110	Fancy
4440	Groovy Day
3650	How High the Moon
5370	Humoresque
5320	Man I Love, The
5330	Moonglow
3890	Robbins' Nest
3850	Sophisticated Lady

CBS		62548	Fra	12 Inch 33
5770	French Doll
5710	I Love Paris
5810	La Petite Mambo
5750	La Vie en Rose
5720	Last Time I Saw Paris, The
5800	Louise
5730	My Man
5740	Paris Bounce
5700	Song from Moulin Rouge (Where Is Your Heart), The

CBS	62668	Fra	12 Inch 33

3860   Ain't She Sweet?
3880   Fine and Dandy
4440   Groovy Day
3730   Honeysuckle Rose
3950   I Never Knew
3930   Ja-Da
4400   Love for Sale
4340   My Ideal
4430   Oh, What a Beautiful Mornin'
4330   St. Louis Blues
3940   Summertime
3920   You're Driving Me Crazy (What Did I Do?)

CBS	62914	Fra	12 Inch 33

3710   Body and Soul
4420   Frenesi (Cancion Tropical)
4370   Easy to Love
3680   I Cover the Waterfront
3720   Indiana (Back Home Again in Indiana)
3740   I'm in the Mood for Love
3670   Laura
4380   Mean to Me
3960   Oh, Lady Be Good!
3690   Penthouse Serenade (When We're Alone)
3760   Play, Piano, Play
3700   Way You Look Tonight, The

CBS	63631	Fra	12 Inch 33

4040   Anything Goes
4010   Bewitched
4460   For Heaven's Sake
3750   I Can't Get Started
4320   Lullaby in Rhythm
4000   Once in a While
4210   'S Wonderful
3770   Undecided
4410   Yesterdays

CBS	64947	Fra	12 Inch 33

3720   Indiana (Back Home Again in Indiana)

CBS	80245	Fra	12 Inch 33

3720   Indiana (Back Home Again in Indiana)

CBS	84267	Fra	12 Inch 33

4040   Anything Goes
4310   Avalon
5200   But Not for Me
5360   Dreamy
4390   I've Got My Love to Keep Me Warm
5450   Passing Through
3610   Spring Is Here
3510   When You're Smiling (The Whole World Smiles with You)
4290   Will You Still Be Mine?

CBS	88129	Eng	12 Inch 33

3860   Ain't She Sweet?
3970   Am I Blue?
4310   Avalon

4240	Can't Help Lovin' Dat Man
4130	Dancing in the Dark
5360	Dreamy
4370	Easy to Love
3730	Honeysuckle Rose
3950	I Never Knew
3670	Laura
4400	Love for Sale
3640	Lover
5320	Man I Love, The
4380	Mean to Me
3470	My Heart Stood Still
3990	Music, Maestro, Please!
3550	Poor Butterfly
4330	St. Louis Blues
3940	Summertime
3840	You're Blasé
3920	You're Driving Me Crazy (What Did I Do?)

CBS	**CA 281.130**	**Neth**	**7 Inch 45**
5390	Dreamy		
5400	On the Street Where You Live		

CBS	**EP 5864**	**Fra**	**7 Inch 45EP**
4250	Caravan		
4260	Lullaby of Birdland		

CBS	**EP 5986**	**Fra**	**7 Inch 45EP**
5390	Dreamy		
5380	Misty		
5650	Moment's Delight		
5400	On the Street Where You Live		

CBS	**S64281**	**Fra**	**12 Inch 33**
5550	Don't Take Your Love from Me		
5530	I Surrender, Dear		
5600	If I Had You		
5570	No More Time		
5520	Soliloquy		
5560	You'd Be So Nice to Come Home To		

CBS	**S66244**	**WGer**	**12 Inch 33**
5260	Alexander's Ragtime Band		
5070	Autumn Leaves		
4240	Can't Help Lovin' Dat Man		
4270	Cheek to Cheek		
5140	Erroll's Theme		
3650	How High the Moon		
5040	I'll Remember April		
4570	I'll See You in My Dreams		
5080	It's All Right with Me		
3910	It's the Talk of the Town		
5750	La Vie en Rose		
3670	Laura		
5060	Mambo Carmel		
5300	Ol' Man River		
3980	Out of Nowhere		
4450	Please Don't Talk About Me When I'm Gone		
3550	Poor Butterfly		
5090	Red Top		

4350   Stompin' at the Savoy
4360   Sweet Sue-Just You
5050   Teach Me Tonight
5440   Way Back Blues, The

CBS   **S66309**   **Fra**   **12 Inch 33**
5260   Alexander's Ragtime Band
5100   April in Paris
5070   Autumn Leaves
3710   Body and Soul
5200   But Not for Me
4250   Caravan
4270   Cheek to Cheek
4370   Easy to Love
3730   Honeysuckle Rose
3650   How High the Moon
3750   I Can't Get Started
5040   I'll Remember April
3740   I'm in the Mood for Love
5660   It Might As Well Be Spring
3670   Laura
4400   Love for Sale
4320   Lullaby in Rhythm
4260   Lullaby of Birdland
5320   Man I Love, The
5380   Misty
5300   Ol' Man River
5400   On the Street Where You Live
3980   Out of Nowhere
4210   'S Wonderful
4330   St. Louis Blues
4350   Stompin' at the Savoy
3940   Summertime
3770   Undecided
3700   Way You Look Tonight, The

CBS   **S67257**   **Fra**   **12 Inch 33**
3720   Indiana (Back Home Again in Indiana)

CBS   **S68219**   **Neth**   **12 Inch 33**
5100   April in Paris
5070   Autumn Leaves
4310   Avalon
4250   Caravan
5140   Erroll's Theme
5120   How Could You Do a Thing Like That to Me?
5080   It's All Right with Me
5040   I'll Remember April
4260   Lullaby of Birdland
5060   Mambo Carmel
4200   Memories of You
5090   Red Top
5050   Teach Me Tonight
4220   (There Is) No Greater Love
5110   They Can't Take That Away from Me
5130   Where or When
4290   Will You Still Be Mine?

CBS   **SBP234108**   **Aus**   **12 Inch 33**
5100   April in Paris
5070   Autumn Leaves

5140   Erroll's Theme
5120   How Could You Do a Thing Like That to Me?
5040   I'll Remember April
5080   It's All Right with Me
5060   Mambo Carmel
5090   Red Top
5050   Teach Me Tonight
5110   They Can't Take That Away from Me
5130   Where or When

CBS-Sony   **20AP1492**   **Jap**   **12 Inch 33**
5260   Alexander's Ragtime Band
5200   But Not for Me
5220   Full Moon and Empty Arms
5250   Girl of My Dreams
5430   Mambo 207
5450   Passing Through
5240   Time on My Hands
5440   Way Back Blues, The

CBS-Sony   **20AP1807**   **Jap**   **12 Inch 33**
3680   I Cover the Waterfront
3670   Laura
3690   Penthouse Serenade (When We're Alone)
3700   Way You Look Tonight, The

CBS-Sony   **SONP 50444**   **Jap**   **12 Inch 33**
5550   Don't Take Your Love from Me
5530   I Surrender, Dear
5600   If I Had You
5570   No More Time
5520   Soliloquy
5560   You'd Be So Nice to Come Home To

CGD   **QB7070**   **Ity**   **10 Inch 78**
3270   Perpetual Emotion

Camden   **ACL-7015**   **USA**   **12 Inch 33**
1940   Erroll's Blues
1950   I Can't Escape from You
1960   Stairway to the Stars

Camden   **CAE420**   **USA**   **7 Inch 45EP**
1940   Erroll's Blues
1930   Erroll's Bounce
1950   I Can't Escape from You
1960   Stairway to the Stars

Camden   **CAL-328**   **USA**   **12 Inch 33**
1930   Erroll's Bounce

Camden   **CAL-882**   **USA**   **12 Inch 33**
1940   Erroll's Blues
1930   Erroll's Bounce
1950   I Can't Escape from You
1960   Stairway to the Stars

Camden	CAL-384	USA	12 Inch 33

1940   Erroll's Blues
1930   Erroll's Bounce
1950   I Can't Escape from You
1960   Stairway to the Stars

Camden	CAM49	Aus	12 Inch 33

1930   Erroll's Bounce

Camden	CAS-882	USA	12 Inch 33

1940   Erroll's Blues
1930   Erroll's Bounce
1950   I Can't Escape from You
1960   Stairway to the Stars

Camden	CDN118	Eng	12 Inch 33

1930   Erroll's Bounce

Celson	QB7006	Ity	10 Inch 78

2180   Frankie and Johnny Fantasy
2070   Play, Piano, Play

Celson	QB7034	Ity	10 Inch 78

2110   Blues Garni
2190   Sloe Gin Fizz

Celson	QB7035	Ity	10 Inch 78

1890   Pastel
1910   Trio

Celson	QB7065	Ity	10 Inch 78

2920   Flamingo
2940   I Can't Give You Anything But Love

Celson	QB7072	Ity	10 Inch 78

2890   Turquoise
2970   Way You Look Tonight, The

Celson	QB7081	Ity	10 Inch 78

3230   Lullaby of the Leaves
3240   Margie

Celson	QB7084	Ity	10 Inch 78

3360   Futuramic
2950   Impressions

Century	1503	USA	10 Inch 78

0470   Fighting Cocks, The
0480   Lick and a Promise, A

Century	1504	USA	10 Inch 78

0310   All the Things You Are (Part 1)
0320   All the Things You Are (Part 2)

Cie Ind. Disque	22000	Fra	12 Inch 33
2180	Frankie and Johnny Fantasy		
2170	Love for Sale		
2070	Play, Piano, Play		
1910	Trio		

Cie Ind. Disque	CVM42.004	Fra	12 Inch 33
2130	Don't Worry 'Bout Me		
2180	Frankie and Johnny Fantasy		
2170	Love for Sale		
1890	Pastel		
2070	Play, Piano, Play		
1910	Trio		

Clarion	610	USA	12 Inch 33
0440	Blues I Can't Forget		
0400	I'm in the Mood for Love		
3230	Lullaby of the Leaves		
2910	Pavanne (The Lamp Is Low)		
0370	Perdido		
2880	Reverie		
3310	Serenade in Blue		
0380	Soft and Warm		
3340	Trees		
2960	Twilight		

Club Nat. du Disque	JSP100	Fra	10 Inch 33
1910	Trio		

Columbia	3-39038	USA	7 Inch 33
3460	I Don't Know Why (I Just Do)		
3440	When Johnny Comes Marching Home		

Columbia	3-39043	USA	7 Inch 33
3620	Petite Waltz, The		
3630	Petite Waltz Bounce, The		

Columbia	3-39100	USA	7 Inch 33
3640	Lover		
3660	People Will Say We're in Love		

Columbia	3-39145	USA	7 Inch 33
3650	How High the Moon		
3550	Poor Butterfly		

Columbia	3-39249	USA	7 Inch 33
3730	Honeysuckle Rose		
3470	My Heart Stood Still		

Columbia	3-39580	USA	7 Inch 33
3910	It's the Talk of the Town		
3890	Robbins' Nest		

Columbia	4-6898	USA	7 Inch 45
3670	Laura		
3690	Penthouse Serenade (When We're Alone)		

Columbia   **4-33180**   USA   7 Inch 45
5390   Dreamy
5380   Misty

Columbia   **4-39043**   USA   7 Inch 45
3620   Petite Waltz, The
3630   Petite Waltz Bounce, The

Columbia   **4-39100**   USA   7 Inch 45
3640   Lover
3660   People Will Say We're in Love

Columbia   **4-39145**   USA   7 Inch 45
3650   How High the Moon
3550   Poor Butterfly

Columbia   **4-39165**   USA   7 Inch 45
3470   My Heart Stood Still
3440   When Johnny Comes Marching Home

Columbia   **4-39166**   USA   7 Inch 45
3520   Long Ago (And Far Away)
3550   Poor Butterfly

Columbia   **4-39167**   USA   7 Inch 45
3610   Spring Is Here
3510   When You're Smiling (The Whole World Smiles with You)

Columbia   **4-39168**   USA   7 Inch 45
3460   I Don't Know Why (I Just Do)
3450   It Could Happen to You

Columbia   **4-39249**   USA   7 Inch 45
3730   Honeysuckle Rose
3470   My Heart Stood Still

Columbia   **4-39273**   USA   7 Inch 45
3680   I Cover the Waterfront
3720   Indiana (Back Home Again in Indiana)

Columbia   **4-39274**   USA   7 Inch 45
3710   Body and Soul
3740   I'm in the Mood for Love

Columbia   **4-39275**   USA   7 Inch 45
3670   Laura
3700   Way You Look Tonight, The

Columbia   **4-39276**   USA   7 Inch 45
3690   Penthouse Serenade (When We're Alone)
3760   Play, Piano, Play

Columbia   **4-39580**   USA   7 Inch 45
3910   It's the Talk of the Town
3890   Robbins' Nest

Columbia   **4-39615**   **USA**   **7 Inch 45**
3880   Fine and Dandy
3850   Sophisticated Lady

Columbia   **4-39681**   **USA**   **7 Inch 45**
3860   Ain't She Sweet?
3900   Please Don't Talk About Me When I'm Gone

Columbia   **4-39713**   **USA**   **7 Inch 45**
3930   Ja-Da
3960   Oh, Lady Be Good!

Columbia   **4-39734**   **USA**   **7 Inch 45**
3990   Music, Maestro, Please!
3980   Out of Nowhere

Columbia   **4-39746**   **USA**   **7 Inch 45**
4070   Cocktails for Two
4130   Dancing in the Dark

Columbia   **4-39747**   **USA**   **7 Inch 45**
4080   It Don't Mean a Thing (If It Ain't Got That Swing)
4060   Willow Me

Columbia   **4-39748**   **USA**   **7 Inch 45**
4030   Chopin Impressions
4120   How Come You Do Me Like You Do?

Columbia   **4-39749**   **USA**   **7 Inch 45**
4090   Love Me or Leave Me
4050   With Every Breath I Take

Columbia   **4-39888**   **USA**   **7 Inch 45**
3940   Summertime
4020   What's New?

Columbia   **4-39918**   **USA**   **7 Inch 45**
3970   Am I Blue?
3950   I Never Knew

Columbia   **4-39996**   **USA**   **7 Inch 45**
4370   Easy to Love
4470   Lullaby of Birdland

Columbia   **4-40043**   **USA**   **7 Inch 45**
4340   My Ideal
4330   St. Louis Blues

Columbia   **4-40074**   **USA**   **7 Inch 45**
4420   Frenesi (Cancion Tropical)
4380   Mean to Me

Columbia   **4-40172**   **USA**   **7 Inch 45**
4430   Oh, What a Beautiful Mornin'
3920   You're Driving Me Crazy (What Did I Do?)

Columbia   4-40766   USA   7 Inch 45
5390   Dreamy
5400   On the Street Where You Live

Columbia   4-40899   USA   7 Inch 45
5440   Way Back Blues, The

Columbia   4-41067   USA   7 Inch 45
5380   Misty
5650   Moment's Delight

Columbia   4-41231   USA   7 Inch 45
5880   I Can't Get Started
5900   Just Blues

Columbia   4-41482   USA   7 Inch 45
5380   Misty
5630   Solitaire

Columbia   4-50094   USA   7 Inch 45
4370   Easy to Love
4470   Lullaby of Birdland

Columbia   5-1795   USA   7 Inch 45EP
4460   For Heaven's Sake

Columbia   7-9821   USA   7 Inch 45EP
5100   April in Paris
5040   I'll Remember April
5080   It's All Right with Me
5110   They Can't Take That Away from Me

Columbia   13-33180   USA   7 Inch 45
5390   Dreamy
5380   Misty

Columbia   33QS6042   Ity   12 Inch 33
3460   I Don't Know Why (I Just Do)
3450   It Could Happen to You
3520   Long Ago (And Far Away)
3470   My Heart Stood Still
3550   Poor Butterfly
3610   Spring Is Here
3440   When Johnny Comes Marching Home
3510   When You're Smiling (The Whole World Smiles with You)

Columbia   33QS6054   Ity   12 Inch 33
3710   Body and Soul
3680   I Cover the Waterfront
3740   I'm in the Mood for Love
3720   Indiana (Back Home Again in Indiana)
3670   Laura
3690   Penthouse Serenade (When We're Alone)
3760   Play, Piano, Play
3700   Way You Look Tonight, The

Columbia   **33S1050**   **Eng**   **10 Inch 33**
3460   I Don't Know Why (I Just Do)
3450   It Could Happen to You
3520   Long Ago (And Far Away)
3470   My Heart Stood Still
3550   Poor Butterfly
3610   Spring Is Here
3440   When Johnny Comes Marching Home
3510   When You're Smiling (The Whole World Smiles with You)

Columbia   **33S1059**   **Eng**   **10 Inch 33**
3710   Body and Soul
3680   I Cover the Waterfront
3740   I'm in the Mood for Love
3720   Indiana (Back Home Again in Indiana)
3670   Laura
3690   Penthouse Serenade (When We're Alone)
3760   Play, Piano, Play
3700   Way You Look Tonight, The

Columbia   **33SX1557**   **Eng**   **12 Inch 33**
2130   Don't Worry 'Bout Me
2180   Frankie and Johnny Fantasy
2170   Love for Sale
1890   Pastel
2070   Play, Piano, Play
1910   Trio

Columbia   **39038**   **USA**   **10 Inch 78**
3460   I Don't Know Why (I Just Do)
3440   When Johnny Comes Marching Home

Columbia   **39043**   **USA**   **10 Inch 78**
3620   Petite Waltz, The
3630   Petite Waltz Bounce, The

Columbia   **39100**   **USA**   **10 Inch 78**
3640   Lover
3660   People Will Say We're in Love

Columbia   **39145**   **USA**   **10 Inch 78**
3650   How High the Moon
3550   Poor Butterfly

Columbia   **39165**   **USA**   **10 Inch 78**
3470   My Heart Stood Still
3440   When Johnny Comes Marching Home

Columbia   **39166**   **USA**   **10 Inch 78**
3520   Long Ago (And Far Away)
3550   Poor Butterfly

Columbia   **39167**   **USA**   **10 Inch 78**
3610   Spring Is Here
3510   When You're Smiling (The Whole World Smiles with You)

Columbia   **39168**   USA   **10 Inch 78**
3460   I Don't Know Why (I Just Do)
3450   It Could Happen to You

Columbia   **39249**   USA   **10 Inch 78**
3730   Honeysuckle Rose
3470   My Heart Stood Still

Columbia   **39273**   USA   **10 Inch 78**
3680   I Cover the Waterfront
3720   Indiana (Back Home Again in Indiana)

Columbia   **39274**   USA   **10 Inch 78**
3710   Body and Soul
3740   I'm in the Mood for Love

Columbia   **39275**   USA   **10 Inch 78**
3670   Laura
3700   Way You Look Tonight, The

Columbia   **39276**   USA   **10 Inch 78**
3690   Penthouse Serenade (When We're Alone)
3760   Play, Piano, Play

Columbia   **39580**   USA   **10 Inch 78**
3910   It's the Talk of the Town
3890   Robbins' Nest

Columbia   **39615**   USA   **10 Inch 78**
3880   Fine and Dandy
3850   Sophisticated Lady

Columbia   **39681**   USA   **10 Inch 78**
3860   Ain't She Sweet?
3900   Please Don't Talk About Me When I'm Gone

Columbia   **39713**   USA   **10 Inch 78**
3930   Ja-Da
3960   Oh, Lady Be Good!

Columbia   **39734**   USA   **10 Inch 78**
3990   Music, Maestro, Please!
3980   Out of Nowhere

Columbia   **39888**   USA   **10 Inch 78**
3940   Summertime
4020   What's New?

Columbia   **39918**   USA   **10 Inch 78**
3970   Am I Blue?
3950   I Never Knew

Columbia   **39996**   USA   **10 Inch 78**
4370   Easy to Love
4470   Lullaby of Birdland

Columbia   **40043**   **USA**   **10 Inch 78**
4340   My Ideal
4330   St. Louis Blues

Columbia   **40074**   **USA**   **10 Inch 78**
4420   Frenesi (Cancion Tropical)
4380   Mean to Me

Columbia   **40172**   **USA**   **10 Inch 78**
4430   Oh, What a Beautiful Mornin'
3920   You're Driving Me Crazy (What Did I Do?)

Columbia   **40766**   **USA**   **10 Inch 78**
5390   Dreamy
5400   On the Street Where You Live

Columbia   **40899**   **USA**   **10 Inch 78**
5440   Way Back Blues, The

Columbia   **47364**   **USA**   **10 Inch 78**
4120   How Come You Do Me Like You Do?
4080   It Don't Mean a Thing (If It Ain't Got That Swing)

Columbia   **50094**   **USA**   **10 Inch 78**
4370   Easy to Love
4470   Lullaby of Birdland

Columbia   **AE-17**   **USA**   **7 Inch 45**
5040   I'll Remember April
5050   Teach Me Tonight

Columbia   **B-230**   **USA**
        Box set contains 4-39165, 4-39166, 4-39167, 4-39168.

Columbia   **B-244**   **USA**
        Box set contains 4-39273, 4-39274, 4-39275, 4-39276.

Columbia   **B-303**   **USA**
        Box set contains 4-39746, 4-39747, 4-39748, 4-39749.

Columbia   **B-365**   **USA**
        2 record set contains 5-1795.

Columbia   **B-777**   **USA**   **7 Inch 45EP**
3670   Laura

Columbia   **B-1656**   **USA**   **7 Inch 45EP**
4250   Caravan
4220   (There Is) No Greater Love

Columbia   **B-1678**   **USA**   **7 Inch 45EP**
4470   Lullaby of Birdland
4200   Memories of You

Columbia	B-1700	USA	7 Inch 45EP

4270   Cheek to Cheek
4390   I've Got My Love to Keep Me Warm
4350   Stompin' at the Savoy

Columbia	B-1741	USA	7 Inch 45EP

4240   Can't Help Lovin' Dat Man
4450   Please Don't Talk About Me When I'm Gone
4360   Sweet Sue-Just You

Columbia	B-1970	USA	7 Inch 45EP

4460   For Heaven's Sake
3750   I Can't Get Started
4410   Yesterdays

Columbia	B-1971	USA	7 Inch 45EP

4010   Bewitched
4320   Lullaby in Rhythm
4000   Once in a While

Columbia	B-1972	USA	7 Inch 45EP

4040   Anything Goes
4210   'S Wonderful
3770   Undecided

Columbia	B-2012	USA	7 Inch 45EP

4560   After You've Gone
4550   I Hadn't Anyone 'Till You
4540   My Melancholy Baby

Columbia	B-2040	USA	7 Inch 45EP

3910   It's the Talk of the Town
3980   Out of Nowhere
3620   Petite Waltz, The
3630   Petite Waltz Bounce, The

Columbia	B-2533	USA	7 Inch 45EP

3650   How High the Moon
4260   Lullaby of Birdland
3890   Robbins' Nest

Columbia	B-2549	USA	7 Inch 45EP

3710   Body and Soul
3880   Fine and Dandy
3670   Laura
3960   Oh, Lady Be Good!

Columbia	B-2573	USA	7 Inch 45EP

5140   Erroll's Theme
5040   I'll Remember April
5050   Teach Me Tonight
5130   Where or When

Columbia	B-2586	USA	7 Inch 45EP

3740   I'm in the Mood for Love
3720   Indiana (Back Home Again in Indiana)
3690   Penthouse Serenade (When We're Alone)
3700   Way You Look Tonight, The

Columbia	B-2609	USA	7 Inch 45EP

5120   How Could You Do a Thing Like That to Me?
5080   It's All Right with Me
5060   Mambo Carmel
5110   They Can't Take That Away from Me

Columbia	B-2621	USA	7 Inch 45EP

5100   April in Paris
5070   Autumn Leaves
5090   Red Top

Columbia	B-8341	USA	7 Inch 45EP

3950   I Never Knew
4400   Love for Sale
4340   My Ideal
3920   You're Driving Me Crazy (What Did I Do?)

Columbia	B-8342	USA	7 Inch 45EP

3880   Fine and Dandy
4440   Groovy Day
3730   Honeysuckle Rose
4330   St. Louis Blues

Columbia	B-9391	USA	7 Inch 45EP

5200   But Not for Me
5220   Full Moon and Empty Arms
5450   Passing Through
5240   Time on My Hands

Columbia	B-10141	USA	7 Inch 45EP

5640   Other Voices
5690   This Is Always
5680   Very Thought of You, The

Columbia	B-10142	USA	7 Inch 45EP

5660   It Might As Well Be Spring
5380   Misty
5400   On the Street Where You Live

Columbia	B-10143	USA	7 Inch 45EP

5390   Dreamy
5670   I Didn't Know What Time It Was
5650   Moment's Delight
5630   Solitaire

Columbia	B-10601	USA	7 Inch 45EP

5520   Soliloquy
5560   You'd Be So Nice to Come Home To

Columbia	B-11411	USA	7 Inch 45EP

5320   Man I Love, The
5330   Moonglow

Columbia	BF488	Fra	10 Inch 78

3910   It's the Talk of the Town
3890   Robbins' Nest

Columbia	C2L9	USA	12 Inch 33

6010   Cote d'Azur
5850   Don't Look for Me
5760   Farewell to Paris
5770   French Doll
5820   French Touch, The
5710   I Love Paris
5810   La Petite Mambo
5750   La Vie en Rose
5720   Last Time I Saw Paris, The
5790   Left Bank Swing
5800   Louise
5840   Moroccan Quarter
5730   My Man
5940   Paris Blues
5740   Paris Bounce
5780   Paris Midnight
5700   Song from Moulin Rouge (Where Is Your Heart), The
6030   When Paris Cries

Columbia	C-230	USA

Set contains 39165, 39166, 39167, 39168

Columbia	C-244	USA

Set contains 39273, 39274, 39275, 39276

Columbia	CB-14	USA	12 Inch 33

3910   It's the Talk of the Town

Columbia	CB-18	USA	12 Inch 33

3910   It's the Talk of the Town

Columbia	CL535	USA	12 Inch 33

4310   Avalon
4250   Caravan
4260   Lullaby of Birdland
4200   Memories of You
4220   (There Is) No Greater Love
4290   Will You Still Be Mine?

Columbia	CL543	USA	12 Inch 33

4460   For Heaven's Sake

Columbia	CL583	USA	12 Inch 33

3710   Body and Soul
4370   Easy to Love
4420   Frenesi (Cancion Tropical)
3680   I Cover the Waterfront
3740   I'm in the Mood for Love
3720   Indiana (Back Home Again in Indiana)
3670   Laura
4380   Mean to Me
3960   Oh, Lady Be Good!
3690   Penthouse Serenade (When We're Alone)
3760   Play, Piano, Play
3700   Way You Look Tonight, The

Columbia	CL617	USA	12 Inch 33
4040	Anything Goes		
4010	Bewitched		
4460	For Heaven's Sake		
3750	I Can't Get Started		
4320	Lullaby in Rhythm		
4000	Once in a While		
4210	'S Wonderful		
3770	Undecided		
4410	Yesterdays		

Columbia	CL651	USA	12 Inch 33
4560	After You've Gone		
4590	As Time Goes By		
4510	I Don't Know Why (I Just Do)		
4550	I Hadn't Anyone 'Till You		
4580	If I Could Be with You (One Hour Tonight)		
4570	I'll See You in My Dreams		
4530	I'm Beginning to See the Light		
4490	Let's Fall in Love		
4500	Moonglow		
4540	My Melancholy Baby		
4520	You've Got Me Crying Again		

Columbia	CL667	USA	12 Inch 33
4240	Can't Help Lovin' Dat Man		
4270	Cheek to Cheek		
3910	It's the Talk of the Town		
4390	I've Got My Love to Keep Me Warm		
3980	Out of Nowhere		
3620	Petite Waltz, The		
3630	Petite Waltz Bounce, The		
4450	Please Don't Talk About Me When I'm Gone		
4350	Stompin' at the Savoy		
4360	Sweet Sue-Just You		

Columbia	CL777	USA	12 Inch 33
3670	Laura		

Columbia	CL883	USA	12 Inch 33
5100	April in Paris		
5070	Autumn Leaves		
5140	Erroll's Theme		
5120	How Could You Do a Thing Like That to Me?		
5040	I'll Remember April		
5080	It's All Right with Me		
5060	Mambo Carmel		
5090	Red Top		
5050	Teach Me Tonight		
5110	They Can't Take That Away from Me		
5130	Where or When		

Columbia	CL939	USA	12 Inch 33
5260	Alexander's Ragtime Band		
5200	But Not for Me		
5220	Full Moon and Empty Arms		
5250	Girl of My Dreams		
5430	Mambo 207		
5300	Ol' Man River		
5450	Passing Through		
5240	Time on My Hands		
5440	Way Back Blues, The		

Columbia   **CL1014**   **USA**   **12 Inch 33**
5390   Dreamy
5670   I Didn't Know What Time It Was
5660   It Might As Well Be Spring
5380   Misty
5650   Moment's Delight
5400   On the Street Where You Live
5640   Other Voices
5630   Solitaire
5690   This Is Always
5680   Very Thought of You, The

Columbia   **CL1020**   **USA**   **12 Inch 33**
5420   My Lonely Heart

Columbia   **CL1060**   **USA**   **12 Inch 33**
5550   Don't Take Your Love from Me
5530   I Surrender, Dear
5600   If I Had You
5570   No More Time
5520   Soliloquy
5560   You'd Be So Nice to Come Home To

Columbia   **CL1141**   **USA**   **12 Inch 33**
5360   Creme de Menthe
4110   Fancy
4440   Groovy Day
3650   How High the Moon
5370   Humoresque
5320   Man I Love, The
5330   Moonglow
3890   Robbins' Nest
3850   Sophisticated Lady

Columbia   **CL1212**   **USA**   **12 Inch 33**
6010   Cote d'Azur
5850   Don't Look for Me
5760   Farewell to Paris
5770   French Doll
5710   I Love Paris
5790   Left Bank Swing
5800   Louise
5700   Song from Moulin Rouge (Where Is Your Heart), The

Columbia   **CL1213**   **USA**   **12 Inch 33**
5820   French Touch, The
5810   La Petite Mambo
5750   La Vie en Rose
5720   Last Time I Saw Paris, The
5840   Moroccan Quarter
5730   My Man
5940   Paris Blues
5740   Paris Bounce
5780   Paris Midnight
6030   When Paris Cries

Columbia   **CL1452**   **USA**   **12 Inch 33**
4190   Dancing Tambourine
5290   I Got It Bad and That Ain't Good
5270   If It's the Last Thing I Do
4280   Once in a While

5190   Rose Room
5230   Some of These Days
5310   Them There Eyes
5280   (What Can I Say) After I Say I'm Sorry?

Columbia   **CL1512**   **USA**   **12 Inch 33**
5610   Don't Get Around Much Anymore
4100   Music Goes 'Round and 'Round, The
5210   My Silent Love
5500   One Night of Love
5540   Stumbling
5590   Until the Real Thing Comes Along
5470   You Go to My Head

Columbia   **CL1587**   **USA**   **12 Inch 33**
4300   Blue Ecstasy
4480   Holiday for Strings
4230   Look, Ma—All Hands!
4400   Love for Sale
3870   Margin for Erroll
5830   Too Close for Comfort
3840   You're Blasé

Columbia   **CL2511**   **USA**   **10 Inch 33**
3740   I'm in the Mood for Love

Columbia   **CL2540**   **USA**   **10 Inch 33**
3970   Am I Blue?
3650   How High the Moon
3460   I Don't Know Why (I Just Do)
4470   Lullaby of Birdland
3890   Robbins' Nest
3850   Sophisticated Lady

Columbia   **CL2606**   **USA**   **10 Inch 33**
5340   All God's Chillun Got Rhythm
5360   Creme de Menthe
5370   Humoresque
5320   Man I Love, The
5330   Moonglow

Columbia   **CL6139**   **USA**   **10 Inch 33**
3460   I Don't Know Why (I Just Do)
3450   It Could Happen to You
3520   Long Ago (And Far Away)
3470   My Heart Stood Still
3550   Poor Butterfly
3610   Spring Is Here
3440   When Johnny Comes Marching Home
3510   When You're Smiling (The Whole World Smiles with You)

Columbia   **CL6173**   **USA**   **10 Inch 33**
3710   Body and Soul
3680   I Cover the Waterfront
3740   I'm in the Mood for Love
3720   Indiana (Back Home Again in Indiana)
3670   Laura
3690   Penthouse Serenade (When We're Alone)
3760   Play, Piano, Play
3700   Way You Look Tonight, The

Columbia	CL6209	USA	10 Inch 33

4030   Chopin Impressions
4070   Cocktails for Two
4130   Dancing in the Dark
4120   How Come You Do Me Like You Do?
4080   It Don't Mean a Thing (If It Ain't Got That Swing)
4090   Love Me or Leave Me
4060   Willow Me
4050   With Every Breath I Take

Columbia	CL6259	USA	10 Inch 33

4240   Can't Help Lovin' Dat Man
4270   Cheek to Cheek
4390   I've Got My Love to Keep Me Warm
4450   Please Don't Talk About Me When I'm Gone
4350   Stompin' at the Savoy
4360   Sweet Sue-Just You

Columbia	CQ2263	Ity	10 Inch 78

3730   Honeysuckle Rose
3470   My Heart Stood Still

Columbia	CQ2658	Ity	10 Inch 78

3740   I'm in the Mood for Love
3550   Poor Butterfly

Columbia	CQ2731	Ity	10 Inch 78

3880   Fine and Dandy
3640   Lover

Columbia	CQ2776	Ity	10 Inch 78

4020   What's New?

Columbia	CQ2815	Ity	10 Inch 78

3650   How High the Moon
3850   Sophisticated Lady

Columbia	CS8131	USA	12 Inch 33

6010   Cote d'Azur
5850   Don't Look for Me
5760   Farewell to Paris
5770   French Doll
5710   I Love Paris
5790   Left Bank Swing
5800   Louise
5700   Song from Moulin Rouge (Where Is Your Heart), The

Columbia	CS8132	USA	12 Inch 33

5820   French Touch, The
5810   La Petite Mambo
5750   La Vie en Rose
5720   Last Time I Saw Paris, The
5730   My Man
5840   Moroccan Quarter
5940   Paris Blues
5740   Paris Bounce
5780   Paris Midnight
6030   When Paris Cries

Columbia	CS9820	USA	12 Inch 33
5390	Dreamy		
5670	I Didn't Know What Time It Was		
5660	It Might As Well Be Spring		
5380	Misty		
5650	Moment's Delight		
5400	On the Street Where You Live		
5640	Other Voices		
5630	Solitaire		
5690	This Is Always		
5680	Very Thought of You, The		

Columbia	CS9821	USA	12 Inch 33
5100	April in Paris		
5070	Autumn Leaves		
5140	Erroll's Theme		
5120	How Could You Do a Thing Like That to Me?		
5040	I'll Remember April		
5080	It's All Right with Me		
5060	Mambo Carmel		
5090	Red Top		
5050	Teach Me Tonight		
5110	They Can't Take That Away from Me		
5130	Where or When		

Columbia	CZ-1	USA	12 Inch 33
3940	Summertime		

Columbia	D-3	USA	12 Inch 33
5130	Where or When		

Columbia	D-7	USA	12 Inch 33
5140	Erroll's Theme		

Columbia	D-8	USA	12 Inch 33
5400	On the Street Where You Live		

Columbia	DC555	Eng	10 Inch 78
3730	Honeysuckle Rose		
3470	My Heart Stood Still		

Columbia	DC586	Eng	10 Inch 78
3670	Laura		
3690	Penthouse Serenade (When We're Alone)		

Columbia	DC595	Eng	10 Inch 78
3900	Please Don't Talk About Me When I'm Gone		
3890	Robbins' Nest		

Columbia	DC600	Eng	10 Inch 78
3990	Music, Maestro, Please!		
3980	Out of Nowhere		

Columbia	DC606	Eng	10 Inch 78
3910	It's the Talk of the Town		
3930	Ja-Da		

Columbia   **DC615**   **Eng**   **10 Inch 78**
3740   I'm in the Mood for Love
3550   Poor Butterfly

Columbia   **DC630**   **Eng**   **10 Inch 78**
3880   Fine and Dandy
3640   Lover

Columbia   **DC640**   **Eng**   **10 Inch 78**
3650   How High the Moon
3850   Sophisticated Lady

Columbia   **DC654**   **Eng**   **10 Inch 78**
3940   Summertime
4020   What's New?

Columbia   **DD563**   **Den**   **10 Inch 78**
3730   Honeysuckle Rose
3740   I'm in the Mood for Love

Columbia   **DD575**   **Den**   **10 Inch 78**
3860   Ain't She Sweet?
3900   Please Don't Talk About Me When I'm Gone

Columbia   **DD578**   **Den**   **10 Inch 78**
3910   It's the Talk of the Town
3890   Robbins' Nest

Columbia   **DD579**   **Den**   **10 Inch 78**
3930   Ja-Da
3960   Oh, Lady Be Good!

Columbia   **DD663**   **Den**   **10 Inch 78**
3730   Honeysuckle Rose
3670   Laura

Columbia   **DW5244**   **WGer**   **10 Inch 78**
3990   Music, Maestro, Please!
3980   Out of Nowhere

Columbia   **DW5260**   **WGer**   **10 Inch 78**
3650   How High the Moon
3660   People Will Say We're in Love

Columbia   **DW5278**   **WGer**   **10 Inch 78**
3640   Lover
3550   Poor Butterfly

Columbia   **DW5298**   **WGer**   **10 Inch 78**
3880   Fine and Dandy
3850   Sophisticated Lady

Columbia   **DZ797**   **Swi**   **10 Inch 78**
3730   Honeysuckle Rose
3470   My Heart Stood Still

Columbia	DZ854	Swi	10 Inch 78
3670	Laura		
3690	Penthouse Serenade (When We're Alone)		

Columbia	DZ856	Swi	10 Inch 78
3910	It's the Talk of the Town		
3890	Robbins' Nest		

Columbia	EM-58	Jap	7 Inch 45EP
3730	Honeysuckle Rose		
3650	How High the Moon		
3960	Oh, Lady Be Good!		
3940	Summertime		

Columbia	FP1028	Fra	10 Inch 33
3880	Fine and Dandy		
3650	How High the Moon		
3910	It's the Talk of the Town		
3930	Ja-Da		
3640	Lover		
3990	Music, Maestro, Please!		
3980	Out of Nowhere		
3690	Penthouse Serenade (When We're Alone)		
3850	Sophisticated Lady		

Columbia	FP1034	Fra	10 Inch 33
3460	I Don't Know Why (I Just Do)		
3450	It Could Happen to You		
3520	Long Ago (And Far Away)		
3470	My Heart Stood Still		
3550	Poor Butterfly		
3890	Robbins' Nest		
3610	Spring Is Here		
3440	When Johnny Comes Marching Home		
3510	When You're Smiling (The Whole World Smiles with You)		

Columbia	FP1035	Fra	10 Inch 33
3710	Body and Soul		
3680	I Cover the Waterfront		
3740	I'm in the Mood for Love		
3720	Indiana (Back Home Again in Indiana)		
3670	Laura		
3690	Penthouse Serenade (When We're Alone)		
3760	Play, Piano, Play		
3700	Way You Look Tonight,The		

Columbia	JC2L9	USA	12 Inch 33
6010	Cote d'Azur		
5850	Don't Look for Me		
5760	Farewell to Paris		
5770	French Doll		
5820	French Touch, The		
5710	I Love Paris		
5810	La Petite Mambo		
5750	Le Vie en Rose		
5720	Last Time I Saw Paris, The		
5790	Left Bank Swing		
5800	Louise		
5840	Moroccan Quarter		

5730   My Man
5940   Paris Blues
5740   Paris Bounce
5780   Paris Midnight
5700   Song from Moulin Rouge (Where Is Your Heart), The
6030   When Paris Cries

Columbia   **KL5136**   **USA**   **12 Inch 33**
3980   Out of Nowhere

Columbia   **KL5142**   **USA**   **12 Inch 33**
4270   Cheek to Cheek

Columbia   **M-745**   **Jap**   **10 Inch 78**
3510   When You're Smiling (The Whole World Smiles With You)
3650   How High the Moon

Columbia   **PB11**   **USA**   **12 Inch 33**
5840   Moroccan Quarter

Columbia   **PG33402**   **USA**   **12 Inch 33**
5540   Way Back Blues, The

Columbia   **PG33424**   **USA**   **12 Inch 33**
3860   Ain't She Sweet?
3970   Am I Blue?
4310   Avalon
4240   Can't Help Lovin' Dat Man
4130   Dancing in the Dark
5360   Dreamy
4370   Easy to Love
3730   Honeysuckle Rose
3950   I Never Knew
3670   Laura
4400   Love for Sale
3640   Lover
5320   Man I Love, The
4380   Mean to Me
3990   Music, Maestro, Please!
3470   My Heart Stood Still
3550   Poor Butterfly
4330   St. Louis Blues
3940   Summertime
3840   You're Blasé
3920   You're Driving Me Crazy (What Did I Do?)

Columbia   **PL-2043**   **Jap**   **12 Inch 33**
4370   Easy to Love
4420   Frenesi (Cancion Tropical)
3720   Indiana (Back Home Again in Indiana)
4390   I've Got My Love to Keep Me Warm
3960   Oh, Lady Be Good!
3690   Penthouse Serenade (When We're Alone)

Columbia   **PL-5044**   **Jap**   **12 Inch 33**
5100   April in Paris
5070   Autumn Leaves
5140   Erroll's Theme
5120   How Could You Do a Thing Like That to Me?
5040   I'll Remember April

5080   It's All Right with Me
5060   Mambo Carmel
5090   Red Top
5050   Teach Me Tonight
5110   They Can't Take That Away from Me
5130   Where or When

| **Columbia** | **PL-5085** | **Jap** | **12 Inch 33** |

5390   Dreamy
5670   I Didn't Know What Time It Was
5660   It Might As Well Be Spring
5380   Misty
5650   Moment's Delight
5400   On the Street Where You Live
5640   Other Voices
5630   Solitaire
5690   This Is Always
5680   Very Thought of You, The

| **Columbia** | **PMS67** | **Jap** | **12 Inch 33** |

5100   April in Paris
5070   Autumn Leaves
5140   Erroll's Theme
5120   How Could You Do a Thing Like That to Me?
5040   I'll Remember April
5080   It's All Right with Me
5060   Mambo Carmel
5090   Red Top
5050   Teach Me Tonight
5110   They Can't Take That Away from Me
5130   Where or When

| **Columbia** | **PMS68** | **Jap** | **12 Inch 33** |

5260   Alexander's Ragtime Band
5200   But Not for Me
4370   Easy to Love
5710   I Love Paris
3720   Indiana (Back Home Again in Indiana)
5750   La Vie en Rose
5300   Ol' Man River
5700   Song from Moulin Rouge (Where Is Your Heart), The
4350   Stompin' at the Savoy
3700   Way You Look Tonight, The

| **Columbia** | **SEDQ521** | **Ity** | **7 inch 45EP** |

3880   Fine and Dandy
3640   Lover
3550   Poor Butterfly
3850   Sophisticated Lady

| **Columbia** | **SEDQ532** | **Ity** | **7 inch 45EP** |

3730   Honeysuckle Rose
3650   How High the Moon
3960   Oh, Lady Be Good!
3940   Summertime

| **Columbia** | **SEG7510** | **Eng** | **7 inch 45EP** |

3880   Fine and Dandy
3640   Lover
3550   Poor Butterfly
3850   Sophisticated Lady

Columbia   **SEG7533**   **Eng**   **7 inch 45EP**
3730   Honeysuckle Rose
3650   How High the Moon
3960   Oh, Lady Be Good!
3940   Summertime

Columbia   **SGD 3**   **Den**   **10 Inch 78**
3990   Music, Maestro, Please!
3980   Out of Nowhere

Columbia   **SL-3009**   **Jap**   **12 Inch 33**
5840   Moroccan Quarter

Columbia   **XLP-36148**   **USA**   **12 Inch 33**
3670   Laura

Columbia   **YL-114**   **Jap**   **12 Inch 33**
5260   Alexander's Ragtime Band
5200   But Not for Me
4370   Easy to Love
3720   Indiana (Back Home Again in Indiana)
5710   I Love Paris
5750   La Vie en Rose
5300   Ol' Man River
5700   Song from Moulin Rouge (Where Is Your Heart), The
4350   Stompin' at the Savoy
3700   Way You Look Tonight, The

Columbia   **YL-145**   **Jap**   **12 Inch 33**
5400   On the Street Where You Live

Columbia   **ZL-33**   **Jap**   **10 Inch 33**
4350   Stompin' at the Savoy

Columbia   **ZL-1112**   **Jap**   **10 Inch 33**
3710   Body and Soul
4270   Cheek to Cheek
4370   Easy to Love
4420   Frenesi (Cancion Tropical)
3720   Indiana (Back Home Again in Indiana)
3960   Oh, Lady Be Good!
4350   Stompin' at the Savoy
4360   Sweet Sue-Just You

Concert Hall   **CHJ1001**   **USA**   **10 Inch 33**
2110   Blues Garni
2100   Love Is the Strangest Game
1890   Pastel
2070   Play, Piano, Play
1910   Trio

Concert Hall   **DJ-100E**   **Eng**   **10 Inch 33**
1910   Trio

Concert Hall   **J1269**   **USA**   **12 Inch 33**
0150   Cloudburst
0570   Easy to Love
0620   In the Beginning
0520   Variations on a Nursery Rhyme (Mairzy Doats, Yes, We Have No Bananas, The Music
       Goes 'Round and 'Round, Everything I've Got [Belongs to You])

Coral		COPS1869	USA	12 Inch 33
0940	Sweet Lorraine			

Coral		CRL57040	USA	12 Inch 33
0970	Gaslight			
2150	Loose Nut			
0960	Loot to Boot			
0950	Yesterdays			

CORE		100	USA	12 Inch 33
2170	Love for Sale			

Crown		CLP275	USA	12 Inch 33
2040	Lover (Part 1)			
2050	Lover (Part 2)			

Crown		CLP5003	USA	12 Inch 33
1980	Blue Lou (Part 1)			
1990	Blue Lou (Part 2)			
2340	Just You, Just Me			
2770	Lavande (Little Girl)			
2040	Lover (Part 1)			
2050	Lover (Part 2)			
2670	Someone to Watch Over Me			
2660	Tenderly			

Crown		CLP5004	USA	12 Inch 33
1980	Blue Lou (Part 1)			
1990	Blue Lou (Part 2)			
2030	Four O'Clock Jump			
2340	Just You, Just Me			
2000	One O'Clock Jump			
2660	Tenderly			
2020	Three O'Clock Jump			
2010	Two O'Clock Jump			

Crown		CLP5008	USA	12 Inch 33
2620	Cherokee (Part 1)			

Crown		CLP5056	USA	12 Inch 33
1980	Blue Lou (Part 1)			
1990	Blue Lou (Part 2)			

Crown		CLP5278	USA	12 Inch 33
1980	Blue Lou (Part 1)			
1990	Blue Lou (Part 2)			

Crown		CLP5293	USA	12 Inch 33
2770	Lavande (Little Girl)			
2000	One O'Clock Jump			

Crown		CLP5404	USA	12 Inch 33
2040	Lover (Part 1)			
2050	Lover (Part 2)			
2660	Tenderly			

Crown		CLP5408	USA	12 Inch 33
2770	Lavande (Little Girl)			

Crown		**CLP5420**	**USA**	**12 Inch 33**
2770	Lavande (Little Girl)			
2000	One O'Clock Jump			

Crown		**CLP5424**	**USA**	**12 Inch 33**
1980	Blue Lou (Part 1)			
1990	Blue Lou (Part 2)			
2340	Just You, Just Me			

Crown		**CST275**	**USA**	**12 Inch 33**
2660	Tenderly			

Crown		**CST278**	**USA**	**12 Inch 33**
1980	Blue Lou (Part 1)			
1990	Blue Lou (Part 2)			
2340	Just You, Just Me			

Crown		**CST293**	**USA**	**12 Inch 33**
2030	Four O'Clock Jump			
2770	Lavande (Little Girl)			
2000	One O'Clock Jump			
2020	Three O'Clock Jump			
2010	Two O'Clock Jump			

Crown		**CST404**	**USA**	**12 Inch 33**
2040	Lover (Part 1)			
2050	Lover (Part 2)			
2660	Tenderly			

Crown		**CST420**	**USA**	**12 Inch 33**
2030	Four O'Clock Jump			
2770	Lavande (Little Girl)			
2000	One O'Clock Jump			
2020	Three O'Clock Jump			
2010	Two O'Clock Jump			

Cupol		**4319**	**Swe**	**10 Inch 78**
2180	Frankie and Johnny Fantasy			
2070	Play, Piano, Play			

Cupol		**4341**	**Swe**	**10 Inch 78**
1840	Bird's Nest			
1880	Cool Blues			

Cupol		**CEP38**	**Swe**	**7 Inch 45EP**
1840	Bird's Nest			
1880	Cool Blues			

Decca		**DFX140**	**USA**	**12 Inch 33**
0940	Sweet Lorraine			

Decca		**DL8386**	**USA**	**12 Inch 33**
0940	Sweet Lorraine			

Decca		**LP8401**	**USA**	**12 Inch 33**
0940	Sweet Lorraine			

Deege		XP-80620	Fra	7 Inch 45EP
0870	Dark Eyesky			
0890	Jumpin' at the Deuces			
0880	Laff Slam Laff			
0860	Play, Fiddle, Play			

Dial		202	USA	10 Inch 33
1840	Bird's Nest			
1850	Blow Top Blues			
1870	Cool Blues			
1780	Dark Shadows			
1770	This Is Always			

Dial		205	USA	10 Inch 33
2110	Blues Garni			
2120	Don't Worry 'Bout Me			
2170	Love for Sale			
2080	Love Is the Strangest Game			
1890	Pastel			
2070	Play, Piano, Play			
2190	Sloe Gin Fizz			
1910	Trio			

Dial		208	USA	10 Inch 33
2180	Frankie and Johnny Fantasy			
2160	Loose Nut			

Dial		760	USA	10 Inch 78
2170	Love for Sale			
2190	Sloe Gin Fizz			

Dial		901	USA	12 Inch 33
1850	Blow Top Blues			
1860	Blow Top Blues			
1870	Cool Blues			
1880	Cool Blues			
1790	Dark Shadows			

Dial		902	USA	12 Inch 33
0150	Cloudburst			
0570	Easy to Love			
0620	In the Beginning			
0520	Variations on a Nursery Rhyme (Mairzy Doats, Yes, We Have No Bananas, The Music Goes 'Round and 'Round, Everything I've Got [Belongs to You])			

Dial		905	USA	12 Inch 33
1820	Bird's Nest			
1830	Bird's Nest			
1760	This Is Always			

Dial		1014	USA	10 Inch 78
1840	Bird's Nest			
1800	Dark Shadows			

Dial		1015	USA	10 Inch 78
1840	Bird's Nest			
1870	Cool Blues			

Note: Some issues of Dial 1015 have excluded "Bird's Nest" and substituted "Quasimado" (Charlie Parker Sextet).

Dial	1016	USA	10 Inch 78
1890	Pastel		
1910	Trio		

Dial	1019	USA	10 Inch 78
1760	This Is Always		

Dial	1026	USA	10 Inch 78
2180	Fantasy on Frankie and Johnny		
2070	Play, Piano, Play		

Dial	1031	USA	10 Inch 78
2170	Love for Sale		
2190	Sloe Gin Fizz		

Dial	1041	USA	10 Inch 78
2150	Loose Nut		
2090	Love Is the Strangest Game		

Disc	5001	USA	10 Inch 78
1400	Man O' Mine		

Disc	5001	Fra	10 Inch 78
1420	Don't Blame Me		
1400	Man O' Mine		

Disc	5002	USA	10 Inch 78
1410	Oh, Lady Be Good!		

Disc	5002	Fra	10 Inch 78
1410	Oh, Lady Be Good!		

Disc	5003	USA	10 Inch 78
1420	Don't Blame Me		

Disc	5501	USA	10 Inch 78
0720	He Pulled a Fast One (Part 1)		

Disc	5501	Fra	10 Inch 78
0720	He Pulled a Fast One (Part 1)		
0730	He Pulled a Fast One (Part 2)		

Doctor X Jazz	FW38851	USA	12 Inch 33
0970	Gaslight		
0960	Loot to Boot		
0940	Sweet Lorraine		
0950	Yesterdays		

Ducretet Thomson	Y8164	Fra	10 Inch 78
1420	Don't Blame Me		
1400	Man I Love, The		

Ducretet Thomson	Y8165	Fra	10 Inch 78
0330	I Hear a Rhapsody (Part 1)		
0340	I Hear a Rhapsody (Part 2)		

Ducretet Thomson   **Y8166**   **Fra**   **10 Inch 78**
0530   Just You, Just Me
0540   Yesterdays

Ducretet Thomson   **Y8170**   **Fra**   **10 Inch 78**
0260   Test Pilots (Part 1)
0270   Test Pilots (Part 2)

Egmont   **AJS-3**   **Eng**   **12 Inch 33**
1840   Bird's Nest
1860   Blow Top Blues

Electrola   **EG7897**   **WGer**   **10 Inch 78**
1950   I Can't Escape from You
1960   Stairway to the Stars

EmArcy   **D-EM-1**   **USA**   **7 Inch 33**
4780   (All of a Sudden) My Heart Sings

EmArcy   **DEM-2**   **USA**   **12 Inch 33**
4720   I Wanna Be a Rugcutter

EmArcy   **EP-1-6025** **USA**   **7 Inch 45EP**
3150   Bonny Boy
3130   Deep Purple
3170   Relaxin' at Sugar Ray's
3160   Tippin' Out with Erroll

EmArcy   **EP-1-6026** **USA**   **7 Inch 45EP**
3210   Cologne
3220   Lazy River
3190   Minor with the Trio
3200   No Moon

EmArcy   **EP-1-6073** **USA**   **7 Inch 45EP**
1670   Frantonality
1660   Full Moon and Empty Arms
1580   High Octane
1500   I've Got You Under My Skin

EmArcy   **EP-1-6083** **USA**   **7 Inch 45EP**
4830   7-11 Jump
4790   I've Got the World on a String
4800   You Are My Sunshine

EmArcy   **EP-1-6084** **USA**   **7 Inch 45EP**
4780   (All of a Sudden) My Heart Sings
4820   In a Mellow Tone
4770   Part-Time Blues
4750   Rosalie

EmArcy   **EP-1-6085** **USA**   **7 Inch 45EP**
4810   Don't Worry 'Bout Me
4720   I Wanna Be a Rugcutter
4730   Misty
4710   There's a Small Hotel

EmArcy	MG26016	USA	10 Inch 33

3150   Bonny Boy
3210   Cologne
3130   Deep Purple
3220   Lazy River
3190   Minor with the Trio
3200   No Moon
3170   Relaxin' at Sugar Ray's
3160   Tippin' Out with Erroll

EmArcy	MG26042	USA	10 Inch 33

1570   Bouncin' with Me
1740   Don't Blame Me
1670   Frantonality
1660   Full Moon and Empty Arms
1580   High Octane
1680   If I Loved You
1500   I've Got You Under My Skin

EmArcy	MG36001	USA	12 Inch 33

4830   7-11 Jump
4780   (All of a Sudden) My Heart Sings
4810   Don't Worry 'Bout Me
4720   I Wanna Be a Rugcutter
4820   In a Mellow Tone
4790   I've Got the World on a String
4730   Misty
4770   Part-Time Blues
4750   Rosalie
4710   There's a Small Hotel
4800   You Are My Sunshine

EmArcy	MG36026	USA	12 Inch 33

3150   Bonny Boy
3210   Cologne
3130   Deep Purple
3100   I Let a Song Go Out of My Heart
3120   Jitterbug Waltz
3220   Lazy River
3190   Minor with the Trio
3200   No Moon
3180   Quaker, The
3170   Relaxin' at Sugar Ray's
3060   Scatter-Brain
3160   Tippin' Out with Erroll

EmArcy	MG36069	USA	12 Inch 33

4690   Imagination
4700   Oh, Lady Be Good!
4990   Salud Segovia
4910   Sleep
4740   Sweet and Lovely
4920   When a Gypsy Makes His Violin Cry
4850   Who?
4840   Yesterdays
         Note: Early issues of MG36069 contain "Sleep" and later issues substituted "Imagina-
         tion"

EmArcy	MG36086	USA	12 Inch 33

4730   Misty

EmArcy	**MMB12010**	**Eng**	**12 Inch 33**

4780 (All of a Sudden) My Heart Sings
4690 Imagination
4820 In a Mellow Tone
4790 I've Got the World on a String
4700 Oh, Lady Be Good!
4750 Rosalie
4740 Sweet and Lovely
4710 There's a Small Hotel
4850 Who?
4840 Yesterdays

Ember	**3335**	**Eng**	**12 Inch 33**

2550 I Can't Believe That You're in Love with Me

Ember	**EMB-3329**	**Eng**	**12 Inch 33**

2550 I Can't Believe That You're in Love with Me
2370 I Surrender, Dear
2860 I'm Confessin' (That I Love You)
2820 Moonglow
2980 On the Sunny Side of the Street
2580 Red Sails in the Sunset
2840 She's Funny That Way
1370 Stardust
2420 Stompin' at the Savoy
2870 Stormy Weather (Keeps Rainin' All the Time)
2800 This Can't Be Love

Ember	**EP-4529**	**Eng**	**7 Inch 45EP**

2840 She's Funny That Way
1370 Stardust
2420 Stompin' at the Savoy
2800 This Can't Be Love

Ember	**EP-4553**	**Eng**	**7 Inch 45EP**

2550 I Can't Believe That You're in Love with Me
2820 Moonglow
2980 On the Sunny Side of the Street
2870 Stormy Weather (Keeps Rainin' All the Time)

Encore	**P14386**	**USA**	**12 Inch 33**

4040 Anything Goes
4310 Avalon
5200 But Not for Me
5360 Dreamy
4390 I've Got My Love to Keep Me Warm
5450 Passing Through
3610 Spring Is Here
3510 When You're Smiling (The Whole World Smiles with You)
4290 Will You Still Be Mine?

Eros	**ERL50047**	**Eng**	**12 Inch 33**

2550 I Can't Believe That You're in Love with Me
2425 I Cover the Waterfront
2490 I Don't Stand a Ghost of a Chance with You
2860 I'm Confessin' (That I Love You)
1390 Indiana (Back Home Again in Indiana)
2450 Love Walked In
2440 Penthouse Serenade (When We're Alone)

2580	Red Sails in the Sunset
2840	She's Funny That Way
1380	Somebody Loves Me
2870	Stormy Weather (Keeps Rainin' All the Time)
2420	Stompin' at the Savoy
2570	Undecided
2850	Until the Real Thing Comes Along

Esquire   **10-017**   **Eng**   **10 Inch 78**
1840   Bird's Nest
1880   Cool Blues

Esquire   **10-026**   **Eng**   **10 Inch 78**
2180   Frankie and Johnny
2070   Play, Piano, Play

Esquire   **10-061**   **Eng**   **10 Inch 78**
2890   Turquoise
2970   Way You Look Tonight, The

Esquire   **10-104**   **Eng**   **10 Inch 78**
2130   Don't Worry 'Bout Me
2170   Love for Sale

Esquire   **10-136**   **Eng**   **10 Inch 78**
2920   Flamingo
2940   I Can't Give You Anything But Love

Esquire   **10-176**   **Eng**   **10 Inch 78**
1890   Pastel
1910   Trio

Esquire   **10-256**   **Eng**   **10 Inch 78**
2950   Impressions
2880   Reverie

Esquire   **10-266**   **Eng**   **10 Inch 78**
2900   Blue and Sentimental
2910   Pavanne Mood

Esquire   **10-296**   **Eng**   **10 Inch 78**
3360   Futuramic
3290   Sheik of Araby, The

Esquire   **10-316**   **Eng**   **10 Inch 78**
3230   Lullaby of the Leaves
3240   Margie

Esquire   **EP57**   **Eng**   **7 Inch 45EP**
1840   Bird's Nest
1880   Cool Blues

Europa   **EJ-1020**   **Ity**   **12 Inch 33**
2330   Cocktails for Two
2310   Frankie and Johnny Fantasy
2320   I Surrender, Dear
2290   Laura
2300   Play, Piano, Play

Everest   **FS245**   **USA**   **12 Inch 33**
2550   I Can't Believe That You're in Love with Me
2860   I'm Confessin' (That I Love You)
2820   Moonglow
2980   On the Sunny Side of the Street
2580   Red Sails in the Sunset
2840   She's Funny That Way
1380   Somebody Loves Me
2420   Stompin' at the Savoy
2870   Stormy Weather (Keeps Rainin' All the Time)
2800   This Can't Be Love

Exclusive Jazz   **9102**   **Swe**   **10 Inch 78**
2270   Early in Paris
2280   These Foolish Things (Remind Me of You)

Felsted   **ED82006**   **Eng**   **10 Inch 78**
1350   Blue, Brown and Beige
1330   Sherry Lynn Flip

Felsted   **EDL87002**   **Eng**   **10 Inch 33**
3350   I May Be Wrong (But I Think You're Wonderful)
3330   I'll Be Seeing You
3230   Lullaby of the Leaves
3240   Margie
3310   Serenade in Blue
3290   Sheik of Araby, The
3300   (There Is) No Greater Love
3340   Trees

Felsted   **EDL87015**   **Eng**   **10 Inch 33**
0410   All the Things You Are
0440   Blues I Can't Forget
0450   Boogie Woogie Boogie
0390   Everything Happens to Me
0430   I Get a Kick Out of You
0400   I'm in the Mood for Love
0370   Perdido
0380   Soft and Warm

Felsted   **SDL86026**   **Eng**   **10 Inch 33**
3310   Serenade in Blue

Felsted   **SDL86027**   **Eng**   **10 Inch 33**
2890   Turquoise

Festival   **166**   **Fra**   **12 Inch 33**
2590   All of Me
2480   All the Things You Are
2470   Body and Soul
2520   Cottage for Sale, A
3000   Everything Happens to Me
2510   Goodbye
2550   I Can't Believe That You're in Love with Me
2425   I Cover the Waterfront
2490   I Don't Stand a Ghost of a Chance with You
2370   I Surrender, Dear
2830   I Want a Little Girl
2860   I'm Confessin' (That I Love You)
2540   I'm in the Mood for Love

1390	Indiana (Back Home Again in Indiana)
2430	It's Easy to Remember
1360	Laura
2450	Love Walked In
2810	Man I Love, The
2820	Moonglow
2560	More Than You Know
2600	Over the Rainbow
2440	Penthouse Serenade (When We're Alone)
2580	Red Sails in the Sunset
2460	September Song
2840	She's Funny That Way
1380	Somebody Loves Me
1370	Stardust
2420	Stompin' at the Savoy
2870	Stormy Weather (Keeps Rainin' All the Time)
2800	This Can't Be Love
2570	Undecided
2850	Until the Real Thing Comes Along

Festival   **Album 279**   **Fra**   **12 Inch 33**

1100	All the Things You Are
1250	April in Paris
1080	Baby, Won't You Please Come Home
1220	Blue Room
1180	Blue Skies
1200	Body and Soul
1040	Bounce with Me
1050	Erroll's Bounce
1120	For You
1170	How Deep Is the Ocean (How High Is the Sky)
1190	I Can't Get Started
1210	I Can't Give You Anything But Love
1150	I Cried for You
1110	I Get a Kick Out of You
1310	I Know That You Know
1280	It Had to Be You
1240	Liza
1020	Loot to Boot
3790	Lotus Blues
1130	Mood Indigo
1260	Night and Day
1230	Oh, Lady Be Good!
1300	On the Sunny Side of the Street
1270	Rosetta
1290	St. Louis Blues
3820	Six P.M.
1140	Somebody Loves Me
1160	Sweet Georgia Brown
1090	Sweet Lorraine
1070	What Is This Thing Called Love?
1030	White Rose Bounce (mistitled as Movin' Around)
1060	You Made Me Love You

Festival   **CFR10-231**   **Aus**   **10 Inch 33**

2590	All of Me
2520	Cottage for Sale, A
3000	Everything Happens to Me
2370	I Surrender, Dear
2540	I'm in the Mood for Love
2980	On the Sunny Side of the Street
2990	Rosalie
3010	Stairway to the Stars

Folkways   **FJ 2852**   **USA**   **12 Inch 33**
1410   Oh, Lady Be Good!
        Note: Some issues of this album list Erroll Garner playing "Farewell to Riverside."
        This is an error and is probably Joe Sullivan.

Fonit   **LPU8001**   **Ity**   **12 Inch 33**
2180   Frankie and Johnny Fantasy
2100   Love Is the Strangest Game
1890   Pastel
2070   Play, Piano, Play
1910   Trio

Fonit   **LPU8008**   **Ity**   **12 Inch 33**
2150   Loose Nut

Fonit   **LPU8009**   **Ity**   **12 Inch 33**
1840   Bird's Nest
1850   Blow Top Blues
1860   Blow Top Blues
2110   Blues Garni

Fontana   **683253JCL**   **Fra**   **12 Inch 33**
4780   (All of a Sudden) My Heart Sings
4690   Imagination
4820   In a Mellow Tone
3220   Lazy River
4730   Misty
4700   Oh, Lady Be Good!
4750   Rosalie
3090   What Is This Thing Called Love?
4920   When a Gypsy Makes His Violin Cry
4840   Yesterdays
4800   You Are My Sunshine

Fontana   **683907JCL**   **Fra**   **12 Inch 33**
1970   Blue Lou (Rehearsal)

Fontana   **858011FPY**   **Neth**   **12 Inch 33**
4780   (All of a Sudden) My Heart Sings
4690   Imagination
4820   In a Mellow Tone
3220   Lazy River
4730   Misty
4700   Oh, Lady Be Good!
4750   Rosalie
3090   What Is This Thing Called Love?
4920   When a Gypsy Makes His Violin Cry
4840   Yesterdays
4800   You Are My Sunshine

Fontana   **858106FPY**   **Neth**   **12 Inch 33**
7360   Cheek to Cheek
7290   Easy to Love
7320   Gypsy in My Soul
7300   Moon River
7340   More
7330   On Green Dolphin Street
7350   Over the Rainbow
7310   What Is This Thing Called Love?

Fontana   **FJL103**   **Eng**   **12 Inch 33**
4780   (All of a Sudden) My Heart Sings
4690   Imagination
4820   In a Mellow Tone
3220   Lazy River
4730   Misty
4700   Oh, Lady Be Good!
4750   Rosalie
3090   What Is This Thing Called Love?
4920   When a Gypsy Makes His Violin Cry
4840   Yesterdays
4800   You Are My Sunshine

Fontana   **FJL907**   **Eng**   **12 Inch 33**
1970   Blue Lou (Rehearsal)

Fontana   **SFON-7049**   **Jap**   **12 Inch 33**
4780   (All of a Sudden) My Heart Sings
4760   Exactly Like You
4690   Imagination
4820   In a Mellow Tone
3220   Lazy River
4730   Misty
4700   Oh, Lady Be Good!
4750   Rosalie
3090   What Is This Thing Called Love?
1750   Where or When
4840   Yesterdays
4800   You Are My Sunshine

Fontana Special   **6430135**   **Eng**   **12 Inch 33**
4780   (All of a Sudden) My Heart Sings
1510   Always
5010   Don't Be That Way
1490   Embraceable You
4950   Is You Is or Is You Ain't My Baby?
4700   Oh, Lady Be Good!
5030   St. James Infirmary
4930   Smooth One, A

Futurama   **3005**   **USA**   **10 Inch 78**
0670   Great Christmas (Part 1)
0680   Great Christmas (Part 2)

Futurama   **3006**   **USA**   **10 Inch 78**
0590   Love Is the Thing (Part 1)
3140   Love Is the Thing (Part 2)

Galaxy   **4815**   **USA**   **12 Inch 33**
2550   I Can't Believe That You're in Love with Me
2370   I Surrender, Dear
2860   I'm Confessin' (That I Love You)
2820   Moonglow
2980   On the Sunny Side of the Street
2580   Red Sails in the Sunset
2840   She's Funny That Way
1370   Stardust
2420   Stompin' at the Savoy
2870   Stormy Weather (Keeps Rainin' All the Time)
2800   This Can't Be Love

Gazell		2005	Swe	10 Inch 78
2000	One O'Clock Jump			
2010	Two O'Clock Jump			

Gazell		2006	Swe	10 Inch 78
2030	Four O'Clock Jump			
2020	Three O'Clock Jump			

Gazell		3004	Swe	10 Inch 78
2250	Lover Man (Oh, Where Can You Be?)			
2260	What Is This Thing Called Love?			

Grand Award		GA 33-321	USA	12 Inch 33
2270	Erroll Garner in Paris			
2250	Lover Man (Oh, Where Can You Be?)			
2280	These Foolish Things (Remind Me of You)			
2260	What Is This Thing Called Love?			

Guest Star		G 1403	USA	12 Inch 33
2180	Frankie and Johnny Fantasy			
1890	Pastel			
1910	Trio			

Guild		113	USA	10 Inch 78
0900	Georgie Porgie			
0910	Sweetheart of All My Dreams			

Guild		116	USA	10 Inch 78
0920	I Fall in Love Too Easily			
0930	In the Middle			

Guilde du Jazz		J1001	Fra	10 Inch 33
2110	Blues Garni			
2080	Love Is the Strangest Game			
1890	Pastel			
2200	Talk No Holes (In My Clothes)			
1910	Trio			

Hall of Fame		JG-604	USA	12 Inch 33
2110	Blues Garni			
2180	Frankie and Johnny Fantasy			
2150	Loose Nut			
2100	Love Is the Strangest Game			
1890	Pastel			
2070	Play, Piano, Play			
1910	Trio			

Hall of Fame		JG-610	USA	12 Inch 33
0150	Cloudburst			
0570	Easy to Love			
0620	In the Beginning			
0520	Variations on a Nursery Rhyme (Mairzy Doats, Yes, We Have No Bananas, The Music Goes 'Round and 'Round, Everything I've Got [Belongs to You])			

Harlem Hit Parade		HHP-5011	USA	12 Inch 33
3320	I'm Confessin' (That I Love You)			

Harmony   **HS11268**   **USA**   **12 Inch 33**
5250 Girl of My Dreams
3650 How High the Moon
4570 I'll See You in My Dreams
5750 La Vie en Rose
5720 Last Time I Saw Paris, The
3670 Laura
3550 Poor Butterfly
4360 Sweet Sue-Just You
5560 You'd Be So Nice to Come Home To

Hep   **22**   **Scot**   **12 Inch 33**
1590 Black Night and Fog
1600 C Jam Blues
1620 Caravan
1610 Please Let Me Forget

His Master's Voice   **DLP-1022**   **Eng**   **10 Inch 33**
1930 Erroll's Bounce

His Master's Voice   **EP-7EG8074**   **Eng**   **7 Inch 45EP**
1940 Erroll's Blues

Holiday   **4003**   **USA**   **10 Inch 78**
1430 How High the Moon
1410 Oh, Lady Be Good!

Hollywood   **8500**   **USA**   **10 Inch 78**
2980 On the Sunny Side of the Street
3010 Stairway to the Stars

Hollywood   **8501**   **USA**   **10 Inch 78**
3000 Everything Happens to Me
2990 Rosalie

I Giganti del Jazz   **GJ24**   **Ity**   **12 Inch 33**
2330 Cocktails for Two
2310 Frankie and Johnny Fantasy
2320 I Surrender, Dear
2290 Laura
2300 Play, Piano, Play

I Grandi del Jazz   **GDJ-88**   **Ity**   **12 Inch 33**
2425 I Cover the Waterfront
2490 I Don't Stand a Ghost of a Chance with You
1390 Indiana (Back Home Again in Indiana)
2130 Don't Worry 'Bout Me
2180 Frankie and Johnny Fantasy
2170 Love for Sale
1890 Pastel
2070 Play, Piano, Play
1380 Somebody Loves Me
1370 Stardust
2420 Stompin' at the Savoy
1910 Trio
2570 Undecided

Imperial	5059	USA	10 Inch 78
0840 Movin' Around			
0850 Night and Day			

Imperial	5078	USA	10 Inch 78
0830 Twistin' the Cat's Tail			
0820 White Rose Bounce			

Imperial	IMP-102	USA	7 Inch 45EP
0840 Movin' Around			
0850 Night and Day			
0830 Twistin' the Cat's Tail			
0820 White Rose Bounce			

Imperial	LP9246	USA	12 Inch 33
0850 Night and Day			
0830 Twistin' the Cat's Tail			
0820 White Rose Bounce			

Jazz Connoisseur	JC001	Ity	12 Inch 33
1100 All the Things You Are			
1080 Baby, Won't You Please Come Home			
1180 Blue Skies			
1040 Bounce with Me			
1050 Erroll's Bounce			
1120 For You			
1150 I Cried for You			
1110 I Get a Kick Out of You			
1020 Loot to Boot			
1130 Mood Indigo			
1140 Somebody Loves Me			
1160 Sweet Georgia Brown			
1090 Sweet Lorraine			
1070 What Is This Thing Called Love?			
1030 White Rose Bounce (mistitled as Movin' Around)			
1060 You Made Me Love You			

Jazz Connoisseur	JC002	Ity	12 Inch 33
1250 April in Paris			
1220 Blue Room			
1200 Body and Soul			
1170 How Deep Is the Ocean (How High Is the Sky)			
1190 I Can't Get Started			
1210 I Can't Give You Anything But Love			
1310 I Know That You Know			
1280 It Had to Be You			
1240 Liza			
3790 Lotus Blues			
1260 Night and Day			
1230 Oh, Lady Be Good!			
1300 On the Sunny Side of the Street			
1270 Rosetta			
1290 St. Louis Blues			
3820 Six P.M.			

Jazz Groove	008	Eng	12 Inch 33
6720 Autumn Leaves			
6600 Dancing in the Dark			

7260   Dancing Tambourine/
         Classical Medley/
         Thanks for the Memory
6760   Dark Pool
6730   Edna May
6610   Fly Me to the Moon (In Other Words)
6620   Moroccan Mambo
7240   Nearness of You, The
7270   One Note Samba
7170   That's All

Jazz Parade   **B2**   **Eng**   **10 Inch 78**
2250   Lover Man (Oh, Where Can You Be?)
2260   What Is This Thing Called Love?

Jazz Reactivation   **JR116**   **Eng**   **12 Inch 33**
1840   Bird's Nest
1850   Blow Top Blues

Jazz Selection   **566**   **Fra**   **10 Inch 78**
2040   Lover (Part 1)
2050   Lover (Part 2)

Jazz Selection   **568**   **Fra**   **10 Inch 78**
1980   Blue Lou (Part 1)
1990   Blue Lou (Part 2)

Jazz Selection   **571**   **Fra**   **10 Inch 78**
2000   One O'Clock Jump
2010   Two O'Clock Jump

Jazz Selection   **572**   **Fra**   **10 Inch 78**
2030   Four O'Clock Jump
2020   Three O'Clock Jump

Jazz Selection   **576**   **Fra**   **10 Inch 78**
2670   Someone to Watch Over Me
2660   Tenderly

Jazz Selection   **579**   **Fra**   **10 Inch 78**
2340   Just You, Just Me

Jazz Selection   **663**   **Fra**   **10 Inch 78**
2620   Cherokee (Part 1)
2630   Cherokee (Part 2)

Jazz Selection   **670**   **Fra**   **10 Inch 78**
1440   Humoresque
1460   Smoke Gets in Your Eyes

Jazz Selection   **675**   **Fra**   **10 Inch 78**
1470   Slamboree
1450   Wrap Your Troubles in Dreams

Jazz Selection   **749**   **Fra**   **10 Inch 78**
2690   Georgia on My Mind
2680   Take the "A" Train

Jazz Selection   **750**   **Fra**   **10 Inch 78**
2710   My Old Kentucky Home
2700   St. Louis Blues

Jazz Selection   **753**   **Fra**   **10 Inch 78**
2720   Erroll's Peril
2730   I'm Coming Virginia

Jazz Selection   **754**   **Fra**   **10 Inch 78**
2740   Erroll's a Garner
2750   Stars Fell on Alabama

Jazz Selection   **791**   **Fra**   **10 Inch 78**
2220   Cherchez la Femme
2760   Laura

Jazz Selection   **47501**   **Fra**   **10 Inch 78**
0720   He Pulled a Fast One (Part 1)
0730   He Pulled a Fast One (Part 2)

Jazz Selection   **JEP4537**   **Swe**   **7 Inch 45EP**
1780   Dark Shadows

Jazz Selection   **JSL702**   **Swe**   **12 Inch 33**
1860   Blow Top Blues

Jazz Society   **AA500**   **Swe**   **12 Inch 33**
1000   Harvard Blues
1440   Humoresque
0990   One O'Clock Jump
1470   Slamboree
1010   Slammin' Around
1460   Smoke Gets in Your Eyes
0980   Three O'Clock in the Morning
1450   Wrap Your Troubles in Dreams

Jazz Star   **A47501**   **Den**   **10 Inch 78**
0720   He Pulled a Fast One (Part 1)
0730   He Pulled a Fast One (Part 2)

Jazztone   **J1203**   **USA**   **12 Inch 33**
2110   Blues Garni
2180   Frankie and Johnny Fantasy
2150   Loose Nut
2100   Love Is the Strangest Game
1890   Pastel
2070   Play, Piano, Play
1910   Trio

Jazztone   **J1214**   **USA**   **12 Inch 33**
1840   Bird's Nest
1850   Blow Top Blues
1860   Blow Top Blues

Jazztone   **J1269**   **USA**   **12 Inch 33**
0150   Cloudburst
0570   Easy to Love

0620   In the Beginning
0520   Variations on a Nursery Rhyme (Mairzy Doats, Yes, We Have No Bananas, The Music
        Goes 'Round and 'Round, Everything I've Got [Belongs to You])

Jazztone   **J738**   USA   **7 Inch 33**
2200   Take No Holes
1910   Trio

Jazztone   **J-SPEC 100**   USA   **10 Inch 33**
1910   Trio

Joker   **SM3718**   Ity   **12 Inch 33**
2590   All of Me
2480   All the Things You Are
2470   Body and Soul
2550   I Can't Believe That You're in Love with Me
2400   I Only Have Eyes for You
2560   More Than You Know
2980   On the Sunny Side of the Street
2440   Penthouse Serenade (When We're Alone)
2580   Red Sails in the Sunset
2990   Rosalie
2460   September Song
1370   Stardust

Joker   **SM3719**   Ity   **12 Inch 33**
2370   I Surrender, Dear
2830   I Want a Little Girl
2860   I'm Confessin' (That I Love You)
2540   I'm in the Mood for Love
2430   It's Easy to Remember
2810   Man I Love, The
2820   Moonglow
2600   Over the Rainbow
2840   She's Funny That Way
2870   Stormy Weather (Keeps Rainin' All the Time)
2800   This Can't Be Love
2850   Until the Real Thing Comes Along

Joker   **SM3911**   Ity   **12 Inch 33**
7900   Girl from Ipanema, The
7930   I'll Remember April
7910   Misty
7940   Misty (No. 2)
7880   Shadow of Your Smile, The
7920   Tell It Like It Is
7860   There Will Never Be Another You
7950   Variations on Misty
7890   Yesterday

Joyce   **LP-5004**   USA   **12 Inch 33**
1630   Laura
1640   Yesterdays

Jubilee   **5052**   USA   **10 Inch 78**
3140   Be My Love
0590   Love Is the Thing

King	**540**	USA	**12 Inch 33**

3780 Garner in Hollywood
3820 Six P.M.
3800 This Is My Beloved
3810 Until the Real Things Comes Along

King   **4477**   USA   **10 Inch 78**
3780 Garner in Hollywood
3790 Lotus Blues

King   **4478**   USA   **10 Inch 78**
3800 This Is My Beloved
3810 Until the Real Thing Comes Along

King   **4479**   USA   **10 Inch 78**
3830 New York Concerto
3820 Six P.M.

King   **EP252**   USA   **7 Inch 45EP**
3780 Garner in Hollywood
3820 Six P.M.
3800 This Is My Beloved
3810 Until the Real Thing Comes Along

King   **LP265-17**   USA   **10 Inch 33**
3780 Garner in Hollywood
3790 Lotus Blues
3830 New York Concerto
3820 Six P.M.
3800 This Is My Beloved
3810 Until the Real Thing Comes Along

Kings of Jazz   **KLJ20000**   Ity   **12 Inch 33**
4150 These Foolish Things (Remind Me of You)

Kings of Jazz   **KLJ20020**   Ity   **12 Inch 33**
4160 Ain't She Sweet?
4170 Garner's Escape
4180 Indiana (Back Home Again in Indiana)
4140 Robbins' Nest
4150 These Foolish Things (Remind Me of You)

Koala   **AW14135**   USA   **12 Inch 33**
2550 I Can't Believe That You're in Love with Me
2370 I Surrender, Dear
2860 I'm Confessin' (That I Love You)
2820 Moonglow
2980 On the Sunny Side of the Street
2580 Red Sails in the Sunset
2840 She's Funny That Way
1370 Stardust
2420 Stompin' at the Savoy
2870 Stormy Weather (Keeps Rainin' All the Time)

Le Chant du Monde **29601**   Swi   **10 Inch 78**
2920 Flamingo
2940 I Can't Give You Anything But Love

Le Chant du Monde   **29608**   **Swi**   **10 Inch 78**
1840   Bird's Nest
1880   Cool Blues

Le Chant du Monde   **29637**   **Swi**   **10 Inch 78**
2900   Blue and Sentimental
2910   Pavanne (The Lamp is Low)

Le Chant du Monde   **29701**   **Swi**   **10 Inch 78**
1550   I Can't Get Started
1500   I've Got You Under My Skin

Le Chant du Monde   **29712**   **Swi**   **10 Inch 78**
1490   Embraceable You
1540   Lover Come Back to Me

London   **APS640**   **USA**   **12 Inch 33**
8190   I Only Have Eyes for You
8160   It Gets Better Every Time
8100   Mucho Gusto
8050   Nightwind
8090   One Good Turn
8150   Someone to Watch Over Me
8060   (They Long to Be) Close to You
8180   Watch What Happens
8130   Yesterdays

London   **LTZ-C 15125**   **Eng**   **12 Inch 33**
2470   Body and Soul
2550   I Can't Believe That You're in Love with Me
2425   I Cover the Waterfront
2490   I Don't Stand a Ghost of a Chance with You
1390   Indiana (Back Home Again in Indiana)
2450   Love Walked In
2560   More Than You Know
2600   Over the Rainbow
2440   Penthouse Serenade (When We're Alone)
2580   Red Sails in the Sunset
1380   Somebody Loves Me
1370   Stardust
2420   Stompin' at the Savoy
2570   Undecided

London   **LTZ-C 15126**   **Eng**   **12 Inch 33**
2590   All of Me
2510   Goodbye
2370   I Surrender, Dear
2830   I Want a Little Girl
2860   I'm Confessin' (That I Love You)
2540   I'm in the Mood for Love
2430   It's Easy to Remember
1360   Laura
2810   Man I Love, The
2820   Moonglow
2840   She's Funny That Way
2870   Stormy Weather (Keeps Rainin' All the Time)
2800   This Can't Be Love
2850   Until the Real Thing Comes Along

London	**RE-U 1066**	**Eng**	**7 Inch 45EP**
0840	Movin' Around		
0850	Night and Day		
0830	Twistin' the Cat's Tail		
0820	White Rose Bounce		

London	**SH8461**	**Eng**	**12 Inch 33**
8020	Eldorado		
7980	Gemini		
7960	How High the Moon		
7970	It Could Happen to You		
8010	Something		
8000	Tea for Two		
8030	These Foolish Things (Remind Me of You)		
7990	When a Gypsy Makes His Violin Cry		

London	**XPS617**	**USA**	**12 Inch 33**
8020	Eldorado		
7980	Gemini		
7960	How High the Moon		
7970	It Could Happen to You		
8010	Something		
8000	Tea for Two		
8030	These Foolish Things (Remind Me of You)		
7990	When a Gypsy Makes His Violin Cry		

MGM	**65-104**	**WGer**	**12 Inch 33**
1840	Bird's Nest		
1880	Cool Blues		

MGM	**1318**	**Eng**	**7 Inch 45**
7370	Afinidad		
7380	That's My Kick		

MGM	**65053**	**Fra**	**12 Inch 33**
6850	As Time Goes By		
6870	Charmaine		
6940	How Deep Is the Ocean (How High Is the Sky)		
6880	I Found a Million Dollar Baby (In a Five and Ten Cent Store)		
6890	I'll Get By (As Long As I Have You)		
6950	It's Only a Paper Moon		
6920	Jeannine, I Dream of Lilac Time		
6960	Paramount on Parade (Newsreel Tag)		
6930	Schoner Gigolo (Just a Gigolo)		
6860	Sonny Boy		
6910	Stella by Starlight		
6900	Three O'Clock in the Morning		
6840	You Made Me Love You		

MGM	**65074**	**Fra**	**12 Inch 33**
7370	Afinidad		
7430	Autumn Leaves		
7440	Blue Moon		
7450	Gaslight		
7400	It Ain't Necessarily So		
7420	Like It Is		
7390	More		
7460	Nervous Waltz		
7470	Passing Through		
7410	Shadow of Your Smile, The		
7380	That's My Kick		

MGM   **665053**   **WGer**   **12 Inch 33**
6850   As Time Goes By
6870   Charmaine
6940   How Deep Is the Ocean (How High Is the Sky)
6880   I Found a Million Dollar Baby (In a Five and Ten Cent Store)
6890   I'll Get By (As Long As I Have You)
6950   It's Only a Paper Moon
6920   Jeannine, I Dream of Lilac Time
6960   Paramount on Parade (Newsreel Tag)
6930   Schoner Gigolo (Just a Gigolo)
6860   Sonny Boy
6910   Stella by Starlight
6900   Three O'Clock in the Morning
6840   You Made Me Love You

MGM   **665062**   **WGer**   **12 Inch 33**
6330   Almost Like Being in Love
6290   Indiana (Back Home Again in Indiana)
6360   In the Still of the Night
6320   Lulu's Back in Town
6310   Mambo Erroll
6340   My Funny Valentine
6300   Stardust
6350   These Foolish Things (Remind Me of You)

MGM   **665074**   **WGer**   **12 Inch 33**
7370   Afinidad
7430   Autumn Leaves
7440   Blue Moon
7450   Gaslight
7400   It Ain't Necessarily So
7420   Like It Is
7390   More
7460   Nervous Waltz
7470   Passing Through
7410   Shadow of Your Smile, The
7380   That's My Kick

MGM   **C-8004**   **Eng**   **12 Inch 33**
6850   As Time Goes By
6870   Charmaine
6940   How Deep Is the Ocean (How High Is the Sky)
6880   I Found a Million Dollar Baby (In a Five and Ten Cent Store)
6890   I'll Get By (As Long As I Have You)
6950   It's Only a Paper Moon
6920   Jeannine, I Dream of Lilac Time
6960   Paramount on Parade (Newsreel Tag)
6930   Schoner Gigolo (Just a Gigolo)
6860   Sonny Boy
6910   Stella by Starlight
6900   Three O'Clock in the Morning
6840   You Made Me Love You

MGM   **C-8026**   **Eng**   **12 Inch 33**
6330   Almost Like Being in Love
6360   In the Still of the Night
6290   Indiana (Back Home Again in Indiana)
6320   Lulu's Back in Town
6310   Mambo Erroll
6340   My Funny Valentine
6300   Stardust
6350   These Foolish Things (Remind Me of You)

MGM	C-8047	Eng	12 Inch 33

7370   Afinidad
7430   Autumn Leaves
7440   Blue Moon
7450   Gaslight
7400   It Ain't Necessarily So
7420   Like It Is
7390   More
7460   Nervous Waltz
7470   Passing Through
7410   Shadow of Your Smile, The
7380   That's My Kick

MGM	CS-8004	Eng	12 Inch 33

6850   As Time Goes By
6870   Charmaine
6940   How Deep Is the Ocean (How High Is the Sky)
6880   I Found a Million Dollar Baby (In a Five and Ten Cent Store)
6890   I'll Get By (As Long As I Have You)
6950   It's Only a Paper Moon
6920   Jeannine, I Dream of Lilac Time
6960   Paramount on Parade (Newsreel Tag)
6930   Schoner Gigolo (Just a Gigolo)
6860   Sonny Boy
6910   Stella by Starlight
6900   Three O'Clock in the Morning
6840   You Made Me Love You

MGM	CS-8026	Eng	12 Inch 33

6330   Almost Like Being in Love
6290   Indiana (Back Home Again in Indiana)
6360   In the Still of the Night
6320   Lulu's Back in Town
6310   Mambo Erroll
6340   My Funny Valentine
6300   Stardust
6350   These Foolish Things (Remind Me of You)

MGM	CS-8047	Eng	12 Inch 33

7370   Afinidad
7430   Autumn Leaves
7440   Blue Moon
7450   Gaslight
7400   It Ain't Necessarily So
7420   Like It Is
7390   More
7460   Nervous Waltz
7470   Passing Through
7410   Shadow of Your Smile, The
7380   That's My Kick

MGM	E-4335	USA	12 Inch 33

6850   As Time Goes By
6870   Charmaine
6940   How Deep Is the Ocean (How High Is the Sky)
6880   I Found a Million Dollar Baby (In a Five and Ten Cent Store)
6890   I'll Get By (As Long As I Have You)
6950   It's Only a Paper Moon
6920   Jeannine, I Dream of Lilac Time
6960   Paramount on Parade (Newsreel Tag)
6930   Schoner Gigolo (Just a Gigolo)
6860   Sonny Boy

6910   Stella by Starlight
6900   Three O'Clock in the Morning
6840   You Made Me Love You

MGM   E-4361   USA   12 Inch 33
6330   Almost Like Being in Love
6290   Indiana (Back Home Again in Indiana)
6360   In the Still of the Night
6320   Lulu's Back in Town
6310   Mambo Erroll
6340   My Funny Valentine
6300   Stardust
6350   These Foolish Things (Remind Me of You)

MGM   E-4463   USA   12 Inch 33
7370   Afinidad
7430   Autumn Leaves
7440   Blue Moon
7450   Gaslight
7400   It Ain't Necessarily So
7420   Like It Is
7390   More
7460   Nervous Waltz
7470   Passing Through
7410   Shadow of Your Smile, The
7380   That's My Kick

MGM   E-4520   USA   12 Inch 33
7560   All the Things You Are
7530   Cheek to Cheek
7520   Coffee Song, The
        (They've Got an Awful Lot of Coffee in Brazil)
7510   Girl from Ipanema, The
7500   Groovin' High
7570   I Got Rhythm
7490   It's the Talk of the Town
7550   Lot of Livin' to Do, A
7540   Up in Erroll's Room
7480   Watermelon Man

MGM   EP-579   USA   7 Inch 45EP
1010   Slammin' Around
0980   Three O'Clock in the Morning

MGM   K13471   USA   7 Inch 45
6850   As Time Goes By
6930   Schoner Gigolo (Just a Gigolo)

MGM   K13547   USA   7 Inch 45
7370   Afinidad
7380   That's My Kick

MGM   K13677   USA   7 Inch 45
7400   It Ain't Necessarily So
7390   More

MGM   K13832   USA   7 Inch 45
7370   Afinidad
7380   That's My Kick

MGM	**K13833**	**USA**	**7 Inch 45**
7450	Gaslight		
7390	More		

MGM	**K13834**	**USA**	**7 Inch 45**
6850	As Time Goes By		
7460	Nervous Waltz		

MGM	**K13835**	**USA**	**7 Inch 45**
6930	Schoner Gigolo (Just a Gigolo)		
6860	Sonny Boy		

MGM	**K13836**	**USA**	**7 Inch 45**
6360	In the Still of the Night		
6290	Indiana (Back Home Again in Indiana)		

MGM	**K13870**	**USA**	**7 Inch 45**
7440	Blue Moon		
7420	Like It Is		

MGM	**K13916**	**USA**	**7 Inch 45**
7450	Gaslight		
7480	Watermelon Man		

MGM	**K13988**	**USA**	**7 Inch 45**
7520	Coffee Song, The		
	(They've Got an Awful Lot of Coffee in Brazil)		
7540	Up in Erroll's Room		

MGM	**K14043**	**USA**	**7 Inch 45**
7530	Cheek to Cheek		
7490	It's the Talk of the Town		

MGM	**SE-4335**	**USA**	**12 Inch 33**
6850	As Time Goes By		
6870	Charmaine		
6940	How Deep Is the Ocean (How High Is the Sky)		
6880	I Found a Million Dollar Baby (In a Five and Ten Cent Store)		
6890	I'll Get By (As Long As I Have You)		
6950	It's Only a Paper Moon		
6920	Jeannine, I Dream of Lilac Time		
6960	Paramount on Parade (Newsreel Tag)		
6930	Schoner Gigolo (Just a Gigolo)		
6860	Sonny Boy		
6910	Stella by Starlight		
6900	Three O'Clock in the Morning		
6840	You Made Me Love You		

MGM	**SE-4361**	**USA**	**12 Inch 33**
6330	Almost Like Being in Love		
6360	In the Still of the Night		
6290	Indiana (Back Home Again in Indiana)		
6320	Lulu's Back in Town		
6310	Mambo Erroll		
6340	My Funny Valentine		
6300	Stardust		
6350	These Foolish Things (Remind Me of You)		

MGM   **SE-4463**   **USA**   **12 Inch 33**
7370   Afinidad
7430   Autumn Leaves
7440   Blue Moon
7450   Gaslight
7400   It Ain't Necessarily So
7420   Like It Is
7390   More
7460   Nervous Waltz
7470   Passing Through
7410   Shadow of Your Smile, The
7380   That's My Kick

MGM   **SE-4520**   **USA**   **12 Inch 33**
7560   All the Things You Are
7530   Cheek to Cheek
7520   Coffee Song, The
        (They've Got an Awful Lot of Coffee in Brazil)
7510   Girl from Ipanema, The
7500   Groovin' High
7570   I Got Rhythm
7490   It's the Talk of the Town
7550   Lot of Livin' to Do, A
7540   Up in Erroll's Room
7480   Watermelon Man

MGM   **SMM-1100**   **Jap**   **12 Inch 33**
6850   As Time Goes By
6870   Charmaine
6940   How Deep Is the Ocean (How High Is the Sky)
6880   I Found a Million Dollar Baby (In a Five and Ten Cent Store)
6890   I'll Get By (As Long As I Have You)
6950   It's Only a Paper Moon
6920   Jeannine, I Dream of Lilac Time
6960   Paramount on Parade (Newsreel Tag)
6930   Schoner Gigolo (Just a Gigolo)
6860   Sonny Boy
6910   Stella by Starlight
6900   Three O'Clock in the Morning
6840   You Made Me Love You

MGM   **ST-90600**   **USA**   **12 Inch 33**
6850   As Time Goes By
6870   Charmaine
6940   How Deep Is the Ocean (How High Is the Sky)
6880   I Found a Million Dollar Baby (In a Five and Ten Cent Store)
6890   I'll Get By (As Long As I Have You)
6950   It's Only a Paper Moon
6920   Jeannine, I Dream of Lilac Time
6960   Paramount on Parade (Newsreel Tag)
6930   Schoner Gigolo (Just a Gigolo)
6860   Sonny Boy
6910   Stella by Starlight
6900   Three O'Clock in the Morning
6840   You Made Me Love You

MPS   **5CO64D-99438**   **Neth**   **12 Inch 33**
7560   All the Things You Are
7530   Cheek to Cheek
7520   Coffee Song, The
        (They've Got an Awful Lot of Coffee in Brazil)

7510	Girl from Ipanema, The
7500	Groovin' High
7570	I Got Rhythm
7490	It's the Talk of the Town
7550	Lot of Livin' to Do, A
7540	Up in Erroll's Room
7480	Watermelon Man

MPS   **5C064D-99439**   Neth   **12 Inch 33**
7740	Feeling Is Believing
7810	For Once in My Life
7830	Look of Love, The
7700	Loving Touch, The
7780	Mood Island
7790	Paisley Eyes
7840	Spinning Wheel
7760	Strangers in the Night
7820	Yesterday
7620	You Turned Me Around

MPS   **5C064D-99441**   Neth   **12 Inch 33**
8020	Eldorado
7980	Gemini
7960	How High the Moon
7970	It Could Happen to You
8010	Something
8000	Tea for Two
8030	These Foolish Things (Remind Me of You)
7990	When a Gypsy Makes His Violin Cry

MPS   **5D064D-99397**   Neth   **12 Inch 33**
7020	Can't Help Lovin' Dat Man
7050	Dearly Beloved
7060	Fine Romance, A
7000	Foggy Day, A
7570	I Got Rhythm
6980	Love Walked In
7010	Lovely to Look At
7030	Make Believe
7040	Ol' Man River
6970	Strike Up the Band
6990	Someone to Watch Over Me

MPS   **68.054**   WGer   **12 Inch 33**
8020	Eldorado
7980	Gemini
7960	How High the Moon
7970	It Could Happen to You
8010	Something
8000	Tea for Two
8030	These Foolish Things (Remind Me of You)
7990	When a Gypsy Makes His Violin Cry

MPS   **68.055**   WGer   **12 Inch 33**
8190	I Only Have Eyes for You
8160	It Gets Better Every Time
8100	Mucho Gusto
8050	Nightwind
8090	One Good Turn
8150	Someone to Watch Over Me

8060   (They Long to Be) Close to You
8130   Yesterdays
8180   Watch What Happens

MPS   **68.056**   **WGer**   **12 Inch 33**
7560   All the Things You Are
7530   Cheek to Cheek
7520   Coffee Song, The
        (They've Got an Awful Lot of Coffee in Brazil)
7510   Girl from Ipanema, The
7500   Groovin' High
7570   I Got Rhythm
7490   It's the Talk of the Town
7550   Lot of Livin' to Do, A
7540   Up in Erroll's Room
7480   Watermelon Man

MPS   **68.057**   **WGer**   **12 Inch 33**
7740   Feeling Is Believing
7810   For Once in My Life
7830   Look of Love, The
7700   Loving Touch, The
7780   Mood Island
7790   Paisley Eyes
7840   Spinning Wheel
7760   Strangers in the Night
7820   Yesterday
7620   You Turned Me Around

MPS   **68.126**   **WGer**   **12 Inch 33**
7020   Can't Help Lovin' Dat Man
7050   Dearly Beloved
7060   Fine Romance, A
7000   Foggy Day, A
7570   I Got Rhythm
6980   Love Walked In
7010   Lovely to Look At
7040   Ol' Man River
7030   Make Believe
6990   Someone to Watch Over Me
6970   Strike Up the Band

MPS   **15252**   **WGer**   **12 Inch 33**
7560   All the Things You Are
7530   Cheek to Cheek
7520   Coffee Song, The
        (They've Got an Awful Lot of Coffee in Brazil)
7510   Girl from Ipanema, The
7500   Groovin' High
7570   I Got Rhythm
7490   It's the Talk of the Town
7550   Lot of Livin' to Do, A
7540   Up in Erroll's Room
7480   Watermelon Man

MPS   **2129098-0**   **WGer**   **12 Inch 33**
8020   Eldorado
7980   Gemini
7960   How High the Moon
7970   It Could Happen to You
8010   Something

```
8000   Tea for Two
8030   These Foolish Things (Remind Me of You)
7990   When a Gypsy Makes His Violin Cry
```

MPS	2129195-2	WGer	12 Inch 33

```
8190   I Only Have Eyes for You
8160   It Gets Better Every Time
8100   Mucho Gusto
8050   Nightwind
8090   One Good Turn
8150   Someone to Watch Over Me
8060   (They Long to Be) Close to You
8180   Watch What Happens
8130   Yesterdays
```

Manor	1012	USA	10 Inch 78

```
1320   Hop, Skip and Jump
1340   Three Blind Micesky
```

Manor	1028	USA	10 Inch 78

```
1330   Sherry Lynn Flip
1350   Blue, Brown and Beige
```

Mello-Roll	75114	USA	10 Inch 78

```
0940   Sweet Lorraine
0950   Yesterdays
```

Mello-Roll	75115	USA	10 Inch 78

```
0970   Gaslight
0960   Loot to Boot
```

Melodisc	1135	Eng	10 Inch 78

```
1420   Don't Blame Me
1410   Oh, Lady Be Good!
```

Mercury	135.008MCY	Fra	12 Inch 33

```
3080   Again
4760   Exactly Like You
1670   Frantonality
4960   Love in Bloom
4730   Misty
4870   That Old Feeling
3070   Through a Long and Sleepless Night
3090   What Is This Thing Called Love?
1750   Where or When
4800   You Are My Sunshine
```

Mercury	1001-X45	USA	7 Inch 45

```
1490   Embraceable You
1540   Lover Come Back to Me
```

Mercury	1002-X45	USA	7 Inch 45

```
1510   Always
1530   Sometimes I'm Happy
```

Mercury	1003-X45	USA	7 Inch 45

```
1550   I Can't Get Started
1500   I've Got You Under My Skin
```

Mercury	1032-X45	USA	7 Inch 45
1730 Blue Skies			
1740 Don't Blame Me			

Mercury	1033-X45	USA	7 Inch 45
1660 Full Moon and Empty Arms			
1720 Memories of You			

Mercury	1034-X45	USA	7 Inch 45
1680 If I Loved You			
1690 For You			

Mercury	2040	USA	10 Inch 78
1570 Bouncin' with Me			
1560 Symphony			

Mercury	5008	USA	10 Inch 78
1670 Frantonality			
1750 Where or When			

Mercury	5378	USA	10 Inch 78
3020 Remember			
3040 September in the Rain			

Mercury	7194	Fra	12 Inch 33
4890 Afternoon of an Elf			
5020 All My Loves Are You			
5010 Don't Be That Way			
4970 Fandango			
4950 Is You Is or Is You Ain't My Baby?			
5030 St. James Infirmary			
4930 Smooth One, A			

Mercury	8152	USA	10 Inch 78
3030 Easy to Remember			
3050 Home (When Shadows Fall)			

Mercury	10512	Fra	10 Inch 78
4760 Exactly Like You			
4730 Misty			

Mercury	70442	USA	10 Inch 78
4760 Exactly Like You			
4730 Misty			

Mercury	70442X45	USA	7 Inch 45
4760 Exactly Like You			
4730 Misty			

Mercury	70487	USA	10 Inch 78
4750 Rosalie			
4710 There's a Small Hotel			

Mercury	70487X45	USA	7 Inch 45
4750 Rosalie			
4710 There's a Small Hotel			

Mercury   **70649**   **USA**   **10 Inch 78**
4630   Night and Day
4600   That Old Black Magic

Mercury   **70649X45**   **USA**   **7 Inch 45**
4630   Night and Day
4600   That Old Black Magic

Mercury   **72192**   **USA**   **7 Inch 45**
6510   Mimi
6500   Theme from "A New Kind of Love"

Mercury   **125008MCL**   **Fra**   **12 Inch 33**
3080   Again
4760   Exactly Like You
1670   Frantonality
4960   Love in Bloom
4730   Misty
4870   That Old Feeling
3070   Through a Long and Sleepless Night
3090   What Is This Thing Called Love?
1750   Where or When
4800   You Are My Sunshine

Mercury   **126046MCE**   **Fra**   **7 Inch 45EP**
3080   Again
1670   Frantonality
4730   Misty
3090   What Is This Thing Called Love?

Mercury   **200009MG**   **Fra**   **12 Inch 33**
1510   Always
1730   Blue Skies
1740   Don't Blame Me
1490   Embraceable You
1690   For You
1660   Full Moon and Empty Arms
1550   I Can't Get Started
1680   If I Loved You
1500   I've Got You Under My Skin
1540   Lover Come Back to Me
1720   Memories of You
1530   Sometimes I'm Happy

Mercury   **632203**   **Urg**   **12 Inch 33**
6530   Fashion Interlude
6570   In the Park in Paree
6520   Louise
6510   Mimi
6550   Paris Mist (Bossa Nova)
6580   Paris Mist (Waltz-Swing)
6540   Steve's Song
6590   Tease, The
6500   Theme from "A New Kind of Love"
6560   You Brought a New Kind of Love to Me

Mercury   **6336320**   **Neth**   **12 Inch 33**
3080   Again
4760   Exactly Like You

1670	Frantonality
4960	Love in Bloom
4730	Misty
4870	That Old Feeling
3070	Through a Long and Sleepless Night
3090	What Is This Thing Called Love?
1750	Where or When
4800	You Are My Sunshine

Mercury   **6641589**   **Neth**   **12 Inch 33**

3080	Again
4780	(All of a Sudden) My Heart Sings
1510	Always
5010	Don't Be That Way
1490	Embraceable You
4760	Exactly Like You
1670	Frantonality
4950	Is You Is or Is You Ain't My Baby?
4960	Love in Bloom
4730	Misty
4700	Oh, Lady Be Good!
5030	St. James Infirmary
4930	Smooth One, A
4870	That Old Feeling
3070	Through a Long and Sleepless Night
3090	What Is This Thing Called Love?
1750	Where or When
4800	You Are My Sunshine

Mercury   **6641688**   **Fra**   **12 Inch 33**

3080	Again
1510	Always
1730	Blue Skies
1570	Bouncin' with Me
1740	Don't Blame Me
1490	Embraceable You
4760	Exactly Like You
1690	For You
1670	Frantonality
1660	Full Moon and Empty Arms
1580	High Octane
1550	I Can't Get Started
1680	If I Loved You
4690	Imagination
1500	I've Got You Under My Skin
4960	Love in Bloom
1540	Lover Come Back to Me
1720	Memories of You
4730	Misty
4700	Oh, Lady Be Good!
4990	Salud Segovia
1530	Sometimes I'm Happy
4740	Sweet and Lovely
4870	That Old Feeling
3070	Through a Long and Sleepless Night
3090	What Is This Thing Called Love?
4920	When a Gypsy Makes His Violin Cry
1750	Where or When
4850	Who?
4840	Yesterdays
4800	You Are My Sunshine

Mercury   9279113   **Neth**   **12 Inch 33**
4780   (All of a Sudden) My Heart Sings
4760   Exactly Like You
4940   I'll Never Smile Again
4960   Love in Bloom
4730   Misty
4700   Oh, Lady Be Good!
5030   St. James Infirmary
4900   Solitaire
4870   That Old Feeling
4800   You Are My Sunshine

Mercury   **A-10**   **USA**
Set contains A-1001, A-1002, A-1003.

Mercury   **A-10-X45**   **USA**
Set contains 1001-X45, 1002-X45, 1003-X45.

Mercury   **A-24**   **USA**
Set contains A-1032, A-1033, A-1034.

Mercury   **A-24-X45**   **USA**
Set contains 1032-X45, 1033-X45, 1034-X45.

Mercury   **A-1001**   **USA**   **10 Inch 78**
1490   Embraceable You
1540   Lover Come Back to Me

Mercury   **A-1002**   **USA**   **10 Inch 78**
1510   Always
1530   Sometimes I'm Happy

Mercury   **A-1003**   **USA**   **10 Inch 78**
1550   I Can't Get Started
1500   I've Got You Under My Skin

Mercury   **A-1032**   **USA**   **10 Inch 78**
1730   Blue Skies
1740   Don't Blame Me

Mercury   **A-1033**   **USA**   **10 Inch 78**
1660   Full Moon and Empty Arms
1720   Memories of You

Mercury   **A-1034**   **USA**   **10 Inch 78**
1680   If I Loved You
1690   For You

Mercury   **C-30037X45**   **USA**   **7 Inch 45**
4760   Exactly Like You
4730   Misty

Mercury   **EP-1-3168**   **USA**   **7 Inch 45EP**
1570   Bouncin' with Me
1740   Don't Blame Me
1580   High Octane
1500   I've Got You Under My Skin

Mercury	EP-1-3277	_ USA	7 Inch 45EP
4660 Mambo Nights			
4630 Night and Day			
4610 Russian Lullaby			
4600 That Old Black Magic			

Mercury	EP-1-3278	USA	7 Inch 45EP
4620 Begin the Beguine			
4680 Cherokee			
4640 Mambo Nights			

Mercury	EP-1-3314	USA	7 Inch 45EP
4940 I'll Never Smile Again			
5000 Then You've Never Been Blue			

Mercury	EP-1-3315	USA	7 Inch 45EP
4980 It's the Talk of the Town			
4900 Solitaire			

Mercury	EP-1-3316	USA	7 Inch 45EP
4860 Cottage for Sale, A			
4870 That Old Feeling			

Mercury	EP-1-3317	USA	7 Inch 45EP
4880 Over the Rainbow			

Mercury	EP-1-3335	USA	7 Inch 45EP
4890 Afternoon of an Elf			
5030 St. James Infirmary			

Mercury	EP-1-6025	Eng	7 Inch 45EP
3150 Bonny Boy			
3130 Deep Purple			
3170 Relaxin' at Sugar Ray's			
3160 Tippin' Out with Erroll			

Mercury	J-52	Jap	10 Inch 78
1730 Blue Skies			
1740 Don't Blame Me			

Mercury	MB3167	Eng	10 Inch 78
4760 Exactly Like You			
4730 Misty			

Mercury	MB3179	Eng	10 Inch 78
4750 Rosalie			
4710 There's a Small Hotel			

Mercury	MC-4	Jap	12 Inch 33
5010 Don't Be That Way			
4930 Smooth One, A			

Mercury	MEP14036	Fra	7 Inch 45EP
1570 Bouncin' with Me			
1740 Don't Blame Me			
1580 High Octane			
1500 I've Got You Under My Skin			

Mercury		**MEP14115**	**Fra**	**7 Inch 45EP**
4650	Mambo Garner			
4670	Sweet Sue-Just You			

Mercury		**MEP14116**	**Fra**	**7 Inch 45EP**
4660	Mambo Nights			
4630	Night and Day			
4610	Russian Lullaby			
4600	That Old Black Magic			

Mercury		**MEP14117**	**Fra**	**7 Inch 45EP**
4620	Begin the Beguine			
4680	Cherokee			
4640	Mambo Blues			

Mercury		**MEP14125**	**Fra**	**7 Inch 45EP**
4830	7-11 Jump			
4790	I've Got the World on a String			
4800	You Are My Sunshine			

Mercury		**MEP14126**	**Fra**	**7 Inch 45EP**
4780	(All of a Sudden) My Heart Sings			
4820	In a Mellow Tone			
4770	Part-Time Blues			
4750	Rosalie			

Mercury		**MEP14127**	**Fra**	**7 Inch 45EP**
4810	Don't Worry 'Bout Me			
4720	I Wanna Be a Rugcutter			
4730	Misty			
4710	There's a Small Hotel			

Mercury		**MG20009**	**USA**	**12 Inch 33**
1510	Always			
1730	Blue Skies			
1740	Don't Blame Me			
1490	Embraceable You			
1690	For You			
1660	Full Moon and Empty Arms			
1550	I Can't Get Started			
1680	If I Loved You			
1500	I've Got You Under My Skin			
1540	Lover Come Back to Me			
1720	Memories of You			
1530	Sometimes I'm Happy			

Mercury		**MG20055**	**USA**	**12 Inch 33**
4620	Begin the Beguine			
4680	Cherokee			
4640	Mambo Blues			
4650	Mambo Garner			
4660	Mambo Nights			
4630	Night and Day			
4610	Russian Lullaby			
4670	Sweet Sue-Just You			
4600	That Old Black Magic			

Mercury		**MG20063**	**USA**	**12 Inch 33**
4860	Cottage for Sale, A			

```
4940   I'll Never Smile Again
4980   It's the Talk of the Town
4880   Over the Rainbow
4900   Solitaire
4870   That Old Feeling
5000   Then You've Never Been Blue
```

Mercury   **MG20090**   **USA**   **12 Inch 33**
```
4890   Afternoon of an Elf
5020   All My Loves Are You
5010   Don't Be That Way
4970   Fandango
4950   Is You Is or Is You Ain't My Baby?
5030   St. James Infirmary
4930   Smooth One, A
```

Mercury   **MG20133**   **USA**   **12 Inch 33**
```
5010   Don't Be That Way
4930   Smooth One, A
```

Mercury   **MG20583**   **USA**   **12 Inch 33**
```
4730   Misty
```

Mercury   **MG20662**   **USA**   **12 Inch 33**
```
3080   Again
4760   Exactly Like You
1670   Frantonality
4960   Love in Bloom
4730   Misty
4870   That Old Feeling
3070   Through a Long and Sleepless Night
3090   What Is This Thing Called Love?
1750   Where or When
4800   You Are My Sunshine
```

Mercury   **MG20803**   **USA**   **12 Inch 33**
```
4780   (All of a Sudden) My Heart Sings
4860   Cottage for Sale, A
5010   Don't Be That Way
4690   Imagination
4790   I've Got the World on a String
3220   Lazy River
4700   Oh, Lady Be Good!
3170   Relaxin' at Sugar Ray's
3060   Scatter-Brain
4600   That Old Black Magic
```

Mercury   **MG20859**   **USA**   **12 Inch 33**
```
6530   Fashion Interlude
6570   In the Park in Paree
6520   Louise
6510   Mimi
6550   Paris Mist (Bossa Nova)
6580   Paris Mist (Waltz-Swing)
6540   Steve's Song
6590   Tease, The
6500   Theme from "A New Kind of Love"
6560   You Brought a New Kind of Love to Me
```

Mercury   **MG25117**   **USA**   **10 Inch 33**
1510   Always
1730   Blue Skies
1490   Embraceable You
1690   For You
1550   I Can't Get Started
1540   Lover Come Back to Me
1720   Memories of You
1530   Sometimes I'm Happy

Mercury   **MG25157**   **USA**   **10 Inch 33**
1570   Bouncin' with Me
1740   Don't Blame Me
1670   Frantonality
1660   Full Moon and Empty Arms
1580   High Octane
1680   If I Loved You
1500   I've Got You Under My Skin

Mercury   **MG26042**   **Eng**   **10 Inch 33**
1570   Bouncin' with Me
1740   Don't Blame Me
1670   Frantonality
1660   Full Moon and Empty Arms
1580   High Octane
1680   If I Loved You
1500   I've Got You Under My Skin

Mercury   **MG36087**   **USA**   **12 Inch 33**
4720   I Wanna Be a Rugcutter

Mercury   **MGW12134**   **USA**   **12 Inch 33**
3150   Bonny Boy
3210   Cologne
3130   Deep Purple
3100   I Let a Song Go Out of My Heart
3120   Jitterbug Waltz
3220   Lazy River
3190   Minor with the Trio
3200   No Moon
3180   Quaker, The
3170   Relaxin' at Sugar Ray's
3060   Scatter-Brain
3160   Tippin' Out with Erroll

Mercury   **ML8015**   **USA**   **12 Inch 33**
4780   (All of a Sudden) My Heart Sings
4860   Cottage for Sale, A
5010   Don't Be That Way
4690   Imagination
4790   I've Got the World on a String
3220   Lazy River
4700   Oh, Lady Be Good!
3170   Relaxin' at Sugar Ray's
3060   Scatter-Brain
4600   That Old Black Magic

Mercury   **MLP7051**   **Fra**   **10 Inch 33**
1570   Bouncin' with Me
1740   Don't Blame Me
1670   Frantonality
1660   Full Moon and Empty Arms
1580   High Octane
1680   If I Loved You
1500   I've Got You Under My Skin

Mercury   **MPL6501**   **Eng**   **12 Inch 33**
4620   Begin the Beguine
4680   Cherokee
4640   Mambo Blues
4650   Mambo Garner
4660   Mambo Nights
4630   Night and Day
4610   Russian Lullaby
4670   Sweet Sue-Just You
4600   That Old Black Magic

Mercury   **MPL6507**   **Eng**   **12 Inch 33**
1510   Always
1730   Blue Skies
1740   Don't Blame Me
1490   Embraceable You
1690   For You
1660   Full Moon and Empty Arms
1550   I Can't Get Started
1680   If I Loved You
1500   I've Got You Under My Skin
1540   Lover Come Back to Me
1720   Memories of You
1530   Sometimes I'm Happy

Mercury   **MPL6539**   **Eng**   **12 Inch 33**
4890   Afternoon of an Elf
5020   All My Loves Are You
5010   Don't Be That Way
4970   Fandango
4950   Is You Is or Is You Ain't My Baby?
5030   St. James Infirmary
4930   Smooth One, A

Mercury   **MPL7089**   **Fra**   **12 Inch 33**
4620   Begin the Beguine
4680   Cherokee
4640   Mambo Blues
4650   Mambo Garner
4660   Mambo Nights
4630   Night and Day
4610   Russian Lullaby
4670   Sweet Sue-Just You
4600   That Old Black Magic

Mercury   **MPL7099**   **Fra**   **12 Inch 33**
4780   (All of a Sudden) My Heart Sings

Mercury   **MVL305**   **Eng**   **12 Inch 33**
4620   Begin the Beguine
4680   Cherokee

4640	Mambo Blues
4650	Mambo Garner
4660	Mambo Nights
4630	Night and Day
4610	Russian Lullaby
4670	Sweet Sue-Just You
4600	That Old Black Magic

Mercury   **MVL306**   **Eng**   **12 Inch 33**
4860	Cottage for Sale, A
4940	I'll Never Smile Again
4980	It's the Talk of the Town
4880	Over the Rainbow
4900	Solitaire
4870	That Old Feeling
5000	Then You've Never Been Blue

Mercury   **SR60249**   **USA**   **12 Inch 33**
| 4730 | Misty |

Mercury   **SR60662**   **USA**   **12 Inch 33**
3080	Again
4760	Exactly Like You
1670	Frantonality
4960	Love in Bloom
4730	Misty
4870	That Old Feeling
3070	Through a Long and Sleepless Night
3090	What Is This Thing Called Love?
1750	Where or When
4800	You Are My Sunshine

Mercury   **SR60803**   **USA**   **12 Inch 33**
4780	(All of a Sudden) My Heart Sings
4860	Cottage for Sale, A
5010	Don't Be That Way
4690	Imagination
4790	I've Got the World on a String
3220	Lazy River
4700	Oh, Lady Be Good!
3170	Relaxin' at Sugar Ray's
3060	Scatter-Brain
4600	That Old Black Magic

Mercury   **SR60859**   **USA**   **12 Inch 33**
6530	Fashion Interlude
6570	In the Park in Paree
6520	Louise
6510	Mimi
6550	Paris Mist (Bossa Nova)
6580	Paris Mist (Waltz-Swing)
6540	Steve's Song
6590	Tease, The
6500	Theme from "A New Kind of Love"
6560	You Brought a New Kind of Love to Me

Mercury   **SR61308**   **USA**   **12 Inch 33**
7740	Feeling Is Believing
7810	For Once in My Life
7830	Look of Love, The

```
7700   Loving Touch, The
7780   Mood Island
7790   Paisley Eyes
7840   Spinning Wheel
7760   Strangers in the Night
7820   Yesterday
7620   You Turned Me Around
```

Mercury	SRW16134	USA	12 Inch 33

```
3150   Bonny Boy
3210   Cologne
3130   Deep Purple
3100   I Let a Song Go Out of My Heart
3120   Jitterbug Waltz
3220   Lazy River
3190   Minor with the Trio
3200   No Moon
3180   Quaker, The
3170   Relaxin' at Sugar Ray's
3060   Scatter-Brain
3160   Tippin' Out with Erroll
```

Mercury	ZEP10096	Eng	7 Inch 45EP

```
4700   Oh, Lady Be Good!
4740   Sweet and Lovely
4840   Yesterdays
```

Mercury-Sphnix	M6	Bel	10 Inch 78

```
1690   For You
1670   Frantonality
```

Metronome	B 516	Swe	10 Inch 78

```
1890   Pastel
1910   Trio
```

Metronome	B 582	Swe	10 Inch 78

```
1760   This Is Always
```

Metronome	BLP-10	Swe	10 Inch 33

```
1510   Always
1730   Blue Skies
1740   Don't Blame Me
1490   Embraceable You
1690   For You
1550   I Can't Get Started
1720   Memories of You
1530   Sometimes I'm Happy
```

Mode	MDINT 9200	Fra	12 Inch 33

```
2170   Love for Sale
```

Modern	20-640	USA	10 Inch 78

```
1980   Blue Lou (Part 1)
1990   Blue Lou (Part 2)
```

Modern	20-641	USA	10 Inch 78

```
2000   One O'Clock Jump
2010   Two O'Clock Jump
```

Modern	**20-642**	**USA**	**10 Inch 78**
2030	Four O'Clock Jump		
2020	Three O'Clock Jump		

Modern	**20-650**	**USA**	**10 Inch 78**
2040	Lover (Part 1)		
2050	Lover (Part 2)		

Modern	**20-692**	**USA**	**10 Inch 78**
2670	Someone to Watch Over Me		
2660	Tenderly		

Modern	**20-696**	**USA**	**10 Inch 78**
2340	Just You, Just Me		

Modern	**45-102**	**USA**	**7 Inch 45**
2040	Lover (Part 1)		
2050	Lover (Part 2)		

Modern	**45-103**	**USA**	**7 Inch 45**
2670	Someone to Watch Over Me		
2660	Tenderly		

Modern	**45-126**	**USA**	**7 Inch 45**
1980	Blue Lou (Part 1)		
1990	Blue Lou (Part 2)		

Modern	**45-127**	**USA**	**7 Inch 45**
2340	Just You, Just Me		

Modern	**1203**	**USA**	**12 Inch 33**
1980	Blue Lou (Part 1)		
1990	Blue Lou (Part 2)		
2340	Just You, Just Me		
2040	Lover (Part 1)		
2050	Lover (Part 2)		
2670	Someone to Watch Over Me		
2660	Tenderly		
2260	What Is This Thing Called Love?		

Modern	**1207**	**USA**	**12 Inch 33**
2030	Four O'Clock Jump		
2000	One O'Clock Jump		
2020	Three O'Clock Jump		
2010	Two O'Clock Jump		

Modern	**LMP1204**	**USA**	**12 Inch 33**
1980	Blue Lou (Part 1)		
1990	Blue Lou (Part 2)		
2030	Four O'Clock Jump		
2000	One O'Clock Jump		
2660	Tenderly		
2020	Three O'Clock Jump		
2010	Two O'Clock Jump		

Modern   **MOD 2008**   **USA**   **10 Inch 33**
1980   Blue Lou (Part 1)
1990   Blue Lou (Part 2)
2340   Just You, Just Me
2770   Lavande (Little Girl)
2040   Lover (Part 1)
2050   Lover (Part 2)
2670   Someone to Watch Over Me
2660   Tenderly

Monogram   **119**   **USA**   **10 Inch 78**
1890   Pastel
1910   Trio

Monogram   **180**   **USA**   **10 Inch 78**
2940   I Can't Give You Anything But Love
2930   Skylark

Music   **1130**   **Ity**   **10 Inch 78**
1890   Pastel
1910   Trio

Music   **EPM20015**   **Ity**   **7 Inch 45EP**
2950   Impressions
3310   Serenade in Blue
3250   Summertime
2890   Turquoise

Music   **JH1012**   **Ity**   **10 Inch 78**
1980   Blue Lou (Part 1)
1990   Blue Lou (Part 2)

Music   **JH1039**   **Ity**   **10 Inch 78**
2270   Early in Paris
2260   What Is This Thing Called Love?

Music   **JH1040**   **Ity**   **10 Inch 78**
2000   One O'Clock Jump
2010   Two O'Clock Jump

Music   **JH1041**   **Ity**   **10 Inch 78**
2030   Four O'Clock Jump
2020   Three O'Clock Jump

Music   **JH1056**   **Ity**   **10 Inch 78**
2250   Lover Man (Oh, Where Can You Be?)
2280   These Foolish Things (Remind Me of You)

Music   **JH1132**   **Ity**   **10 Inch 78**
3210   Cologne
2770   Lavande (Little Girl)

Musicraft   **375**   **USA**   **10 Inch 78**
0900   Georgie Porgie

Musicraft   **376**   **USA**   **10 Inch 78**
0930   In the Middle

Musicraft	**MVS501**	**USA**	**12 Inch 33**

0900   Georgie Porgie
0930   In the Middle
0910   Sweetheart of All My Dreams

Musicraft	**S1**	**USA**	

3 record set contains 375 and 376.

Musidisc	**30JA5101**	**Fra**	**12 Inch 33**

0410   All the Things You Are
0420   Blue Room
0440   Blues I Can't Forget
0450   Boogie Woogie Boogie
0390   Everything Happens to Me
0460   Erroll's Bounce
0430   I Get a Kick Out of You
0400   I'm in the Mood for Love
0370   Perdido
0380   Soft and Warm

Musidisc	**30JA5106**	**Fra**	**12 Inch 33**

1000   Harvard Blues
1440   Humoresque
0990   One O'Clock Jump
1470   Slamboree
1010   Slammin' Around
1460   Smoke Gets in Your Eyes
0980   Three O'Clock in the Morning
1450   Wrap Your Troubles in Dreams

Musidisc	**CCV2521**	**Fra**	**12 Inch 33**

3000   Everything Happens to Me

Musidisc	**CV1047**	**Fra**	**12 Inch 33**

2590   All of Me
2480   All the Things You Are
2470   Body and Soul
2550   I Can't Believe That You're in Love with Me
2400   I Only Have Eyes for You
2370   I Surrender, Dear
2860   I'm Confessin' (That I Love You)
2540   I'm in the Mood for Love
1360   Laura
2560   More Than You Know
2980   On the Sunny Side of the Street
2440   Penthouse Serenade (When We're Alone)
2580   Red Sails in the Sunset
2990   Rosalie
2460   September Song
1370   Stardust

National	**9118**	**USA**	**10 Inch 78**

3380   Real Gone Tune, The

New York	**117**	**Den**	**10 Inch 78**

0470   Fighting Cocks, The
0480   Lick and a Promise, A

New York   **118**   **Den**   **10 Inch 78**
0530   Just You, Just Me
0540   Yesterdays

New York   **119**   **Den**   **10 Inch 78**
1430   How High the Moon
1400   Man I Love, The

New York   **122**   **Den**   **10 Inch 78**
0330   I Hear a Rhapsody (Part 1)
0340   I Hear a Rhapsody (Part 2)

New York   **124**   **Den**   **10 Inch 78**
0670   Great Christmas (Part 1)
0690   Great Christmas-White Christmas (Part 2)

New York   **Unnumbered**   **Den**   **10 Inch 33**
0160   Autumn Mood
0290   Erroll's Concerto
0140   Floating on a Cloud
0230   Beg Your Pardon

Octave   **45-301**   **USA**   **7 Inch 45**
6550   Paris Mist (Bossa Nova)
6500   Theme from "A New Kind of Love"

Octave   **SFL-7063**   **Jap**   **12 Inch 33**
6210   All of Me
6280   Back in Your Own Back Yard
6270   Best Things in Life Are Free, The
6260   El Papa Grande
6250   I'm in the Mood for Love
6200   My Silent Love
6230   St. Louis Blues
6220   Shadows
6240   Some of These Days
6190   You Do Something to Me

Octave   **FL-5055**   **Jap**   **12 Inch 33**
6210   All of Me
6280   Back in Your Own Back Yard
6270   Best Things in Life Are Free, The
6260   El Papa Grande
6250   I'm in the Mood for Love
6200   My Silent Love
6230   St. Louis Blues
6220   Shadows
6240   Some of These Days
6190   You Do Something to Me

Okeh   **6821**   **USA**   **10 Inch 78**
3910   It's the Talk of the Town
3890   Robbins' Nest

Okeh   **6898**   **USA**   **10 Inch 78**
3670   Laura
3690   Penthouse Serenade (When We're Alone)

Omega   **7862**   **USA**   **10 Inch 78**
0830   Twistin' the Cat's Tail
0820   White Rose Bounce

Onyx   **ORI 203**   **USA**   **12 Inch 33**
1350   Blue, Brown and Beige
1320   Hop, Skip and Jump
1330   Sherry Lynn Flip
1340   Three Blind Micesky

Parker   **PLP407**   **USA**   **12 Inch 33**
1840   Bird's Nest
1860   Blow Top Blues

Parlophone   **GEP8591**   **Eng**   **7 Inch 45EP**
3780   Garner in Hollywood
3820   Six P.M.
3800   This Is My Beloved
3810   Until the Real Thing Comes Along

Parlophone-King   **KLD25015**   **Ity**   **7 Inch 45EP**
3780   Garner in Hollywood
3820   Six P.M.
3800   This Is My Beloved
3810   Until the Real Thing Comes Along

Philips   **45JAZ103**   **Eng**   **7 Inch 45**
4270   Cheek to Cheek
3700   Way You Look Tonight, The

Philips   **45JAZ105**   **Eng**   **7 Inch 45**
4370   Easy to Love
4470   Lullaby of Birdland

Philips   **322217BF**   **Eur**   **7 Inch 45**
4190   Dancing Tambourine
5230   Some of These Days

Philips   **322295BF**   **Eur**   **7 Inch 45**
5400   On the Street Where You Live
5680   Very Thought of You, The

Philips   **322327BF**   **Eur**   **7 Inch 45**
5880   I Can't Get Started
5940   Paris Blues

Philips   **322349BF**   **Eur**   **7 Inch 45**
3760   Play, Piano, Play
4360   Sweet Sue-Just You

Philips   **322421BF**   **Eur**   **7 Inch 45**
5120   How Could You Do a Thing Like That to Me?
5050   Teach Me Tonight

Philips   **324900BF**   **Eng**   **7 Inch 45**
6240   Some of These Days
6190   You Do Something to Me

Philips		**324901BF**	**Eur**	**7 Inch 45**
6400	Mack the Knife			
6390	Sweet and Lovely			

Philips		**327365JF**	**Eur**	**7 Inch 45**
6400	Mack the Knife			
6390	Sweet and Lovely			

Philips		**362005ARF**	**Eur**	**7 Inch 45**
4270	Cheek to Cheek			
3700	Way You Look Tonight, The			

Philips		**362011ARF**	**Eur**	**7 Inch 45**
4370	Easy to Love			
4470	Lullaby of Birdland			

Philips		**429005BE**	**Eur**	**7 Inch 45EP**
4240	Can't Help Lovin' Dat Man			
4450	Please Don't Talk About Me When I'm Gone			
4360	Sweet Sue-Just You			

Philips		**429009BE**	**Eur**	**7 Inch 45EP**
3920	You're Driving Me Crazy (What Did I Do?)			

Philips		**429112BE**	**Eur**	**7 Inch 45EP**
3750	I Can't Get Started			
4320	Lullaby in Rhythm			
4200	Memories of You			

Philips		**429163BE**	**Eur**	**7 Inch 45EP**
4090	Love Me or Leave Me			
4470	Lullaby of Birdland			
3630	Petite Waltz Bounce, The			
4330	St. Louis Blues			

Philips		**429221BE**	**Eur**	**7 Inch 45EP**
4310	Avalon			
4120	How Come You Do Me Like You Do?			
4080	It Don't Mean a Thing (If It Ain't Got That Swing)			
4410	Yesterdays			

Philips		**429260BE**	**Eur**	**7 Inch 45EP**
4010	Bewitched			
4270	Cheek to Cheek			
3770	Undecided			

Philips		**429280BE**	**Eur**	**7 Inch 45EP**
5340	All God's Chillun Got Rhythm			
5370	Humoresque			
5320	Man I Love, The			

Philips		**429392BE**	**Eur**	**7 Inch 45EP**
4560	After You've Gone			
4590	As Time Goes By			
4580	If I Could Be with You (One Hour Tonight)			
4530	I'm Beginnig to See the Light			

Philips		429394BE	Eur	7 Inch 45EP
5070	Autumn Leaves			
5040	I'll Remember April			
5130	Where or When			

Philips		429456BE	Eur	7 Inch 45EP
3710	Body and Soul			
3680	I Cover the Waterfront			
3720	Indiana (Back Home Again in Indiana)			
4380	Mean to Me			

Philips		429461BE	Eur	7 Inch 45EP
5100	April in Paris			
5140	Erroll's Theme			
5090	Red Top			
5110	They Can't Take That Away from Me			

Philips		429496BE	Eur	7 Inch 45EP
5120	How Could You Do a Thing Like That to Me?			
5080	It's All Right with Me			
5060	Mambo Carmel			
5050	Teach Me Tonight			

Philips		429510BE	Eur	7 Inch 45EP
6010	Cote d'Azur			
5880	I Can't Get Started			
5900	Just Blues			
5940	Paris Blues			

Philips		429529BE	Eur	7 Inch 45EP
4370	Easy to Love			
4420	Frenesi (Cancion Tropical)			
3740	I'm in the Mood for Love			
3960	Oh, Lady Be Good!			

Philips		429555BE	Eur	7 Inch 45EP
5100	April in Paris			
5080	It's All Right with Me			
5060	Mambo Carmel			
5110	They Can't Take That Away from Me			

Philips		429563BE	Eur	7 Inch 45EP
5300	Ol' Man River			
5440	Way Back Blues, The			

Philips		429564BE	Eur	7 Inch 45EP
5260	Alexander's Ragtime Band			
5200	But Not for Me			
5450	Passing Through			
5240	Time on My Hands			

Philips		429579BE	Eur	7 Inch 45EP
3650	How High the Moon			
4210	'S Wonderful			
5700	Song from Moulin Rouge (Where Is Your Heart), The			
3700	Way You Look Tonight, The			

Philips   **429605BE**   **Eur**   **7 Inch 45EP**
5340   All God's Chillun Got Rhythm
4440   Groovy Day
3760   Play, Piano, Play
3890   Robbins' Nest

Philips   **429626BE**   **Eur**   **7 Inch 45EP**
3670   Laura
4470   Lullaby of Birdland
3690   Penthouse Serenade (When We're Alone)
3850   Sophisticated Lady

Philips   **429735BE**   **Eur**   **7 Inch 45EP**
5710   I Love Paris
5740   Paris Bounce
5700   Song from Moulin Rouge (Where Is Your Heart), The

Philips   **429747BE**   **Eur**   **7 Inch 45EP**
3730   Honeysuckle Rose
3990   Music, Maestro, Please!
4430   Oh, What a Beautiful Mornin'
3940   Summertime

Philips   **429752BE**   **Eur**   **7 Inch 45EP**
5260   Alexander's Ragtime Band
5200   But Not for Me
5250   Girl of My Dreams
4000   Once in a While

Philips   **429792BE**   **Eur**   **7 Inch 45EP**
4250   Caravan
4220   (There Is) No Greater Love

Philips   **429799BE**   **Eur**   **7 Inch 45EP**
5610   Don't Get Around Much Anymore
3740   I'm in the Mood for Love
3930   Ja-Da

Philips   **430504BE**   **Eur**   **7 Inch 45EP**
4370   Easy to Love
4450   Please Don't Talk About Me When I'm Gone

Philips   **434700BE**   **Eng**   **7 Inch 45EP**
6210   All of Me
6280   Back in Your Own Back Yard
6190   You Do Something to Me

Philips   **434701BE**   **Eng**   **7 Inch 45EP**
6260   El Papa Grande
6230   St. Louis Blues
6240   Some of These Days

Philips   **434702BE**   **Eng**   **7 Inch 45EP**
6150   Dreamstreet
6130   Lady Is a Tramp, The
6160   Sweet Lorraine
6140   When You're Smiling (The Whole World Smiles with You)

Philips 434703BE Eng 7 Inch 45EP
6110 Blue Lou
6090 Just One of Those Things
6170 Mambo Gotham

Philips 434704BE Eng 7 Inch 45EP
6440 Dancing Tambourine
6420 Misty
6370 Way You Look Tonight, The

Philips 434705BE Eng 7 Inch 45EP
6400 Mack the Knife
6390 Sweet and Lovely
6450 Thanks for the Memory

Philips 434706BE Eng 7 Inch 45EP
6270 Best Things in Life Are Free, The
6250 I'm in the Mood for Love
6200 My Silent Love
6180 Oklahoma! Medley:
Oh, What a Beautiful Mornin'
People Will Say We're in Love
Surrey with the Fringe on Top, The

Philips 434707BE Eng 7 Inch 45EP
6530 Fashion Interlude
6590 Tease, The
6500 Theme from "A New Kind of Love"
6560 You Brought a New Kind of Love to Me

Philips 434708BE Eng 7 Inch 45EP
6540 Steve's Song
6590 Tease, The
6500 Theme from "A New Kind of Love"
6560 You Brought a New Kind of Love to Me

Philips 435145BE Eur 7 Inch 45EP
3860 Ain't She Sweet?
3880 Fine and Dandy
3950 I Never Knew
3640 Lover

Philips 632200BL Eur 12 Inch 33
6210 All of Me
6280 Back in Your Own Back Yard
6270 Best Things in Life Are Free, The
6260 El Papa Grande
6250 I'm in the Mood for Love
6200 My Silent Love
6230 St. Louis Blues
6220 Shadows
6240 Some of These Days
6190 You Do Something to Me

Philips 632201BL Eur 12 Inch 33
6110 Blue Lou
6120 Come Rain or Come Shine
6150 Dreamstreet

```
6100    I'm Gettin' Sentimental Over You
6090    Just One of Those Things
6130    Lady Is a Tramp, The
6170    Mambo Gotham
6180    Oklahoma! Medley:
        Oh, What a Beautiful Mornin'
        People Will Say We're in Love
        Surrey with the Fringe on Top, The
6160    Sweet Lorraine
6140    When You're Smiling (The Whole World Smiles with You)
```

Philips   **632202BL**   **Eur**   **12 Inch 33**
```
6440    Dancing Tambourine
6380    Happiness Is a Thing Called Joe
6410    Lover Come Back to Me
6400    Mack the Knife
6420    Misty
6430    Movin' Blues
6390    Sweet and Lovely
6450    Thanks for the Memory
6370    Way You Look Tonight, The
```

Philips   **632204BL**   **Eur**   **12 Inch 33**
```
7360    Cheek to Cheek
7290    Easy to Love
7320    Gypsy in My Soul
7300    Moon River
7340    More
7330    On Green Dolphin Street
7350    Over the Rainbow
7310    What Is This Thing Called Love?
```

Philips   **761900BV**   **Eur**   **7 Inch 45EP**
```
6210    All of Me
6280    Back in Your Own Back Yard
6190    You Do Something to Me
```

Philips   **761901BV**   **Eur**   **7 Inch 45EP**
```
6260    El Papa Grande
6230    St. Louis Blues
6220    Shadows
6240    Some of These Days
```

Philips   **761902BV**   **Eur**   **7 Inch 45EP**
```
6150    Dreamstreet
6130    Lady Is a Tramp, The
6160    Sweet Lorraine
6140    When You're Smiling (The Whole World Smiles with You)
```

Philips   **761903BV**   **Eur**   **7 Inch 45EP**
```
6110    Blue Lou
6090    Just One of Those Things
6170    Mambo Gotham
```

Philips   **761904BV**   **Eur**   **7 Inch 45EP**
```
6530    Fashion Interlude
6590    Tease, The
6500    Theme from "A New Kind of Love"
6560    You Brought a New Kind of Love to Me
```

Philips	842910BY	Eur	12 Inch 33
6210	All of Me		
6280	Back in Your Own Back Yard		
6270	Best Things in Life Are Free, The		
6260	El Papa Grande		
6250	I'm in the Mood for Love		
6200	My Silent Love		
6230	St. Louis Blues		
6220	Shadows		
6240	Some of These Days		
6190	You Do Something to Me		

Philips	842911BY	Eur	12 Inch 33
6110	Blue Lou		
6120	Come Rain or Come Shine		
6150	Dreamstreet		
6100	I'm Gettin' Sentimental Over You		
6090	Just One of Those Things		
6130	Lady Is a Tramp, The		
6170	Mambo Gotham		
6180	Oklahoma! Medley:		
	Oh, What a Beautiful Mornin'		
	People Will Say We're in Love		
	Surrey with the Fringe on Top, The		
6160	Sweet Lorraine		
6140	When You're Smiling (The Whole World Smiles with You)		

Philips	842912BY	Eur	12 Inch 33
6440	Dancing Tambourine		
6380	Happiness Is a Thing Called Joe		
6410	Lover Come Back to Me		
6400	Mack the Knife		
6420	Misty		
6430	Movin' Blues		
6390	Sweet and Lovely		
6450	Thanks for the Memory		
6370	Way You Look Tonight, The		

Philips	842913BY	Eur	12 Inch 33
6530	Fashion Interlude		
6570	In the Park in Paree		
6520	Louise		
6510	Mimi		
6550	Paris Mist (Bossa Nova)		
6580	Paris Mist (Waltz-Swing)		
6540	Steve's Song		
6590	Tease, The		
6500	Theme from "A New Kind of Love"		
6560	You Brought a New Kind of Love to Me		

Philips	842914BY	Eur	12 Inch 33
7360	Cheek to Cheek		
7290	Easy to Love		
7320	Gypsy in My Soul		
7300	Moon River		
7340	More		
7330	On Green Dolphin Street		
7350	Over the Rainbow		
7310	What Is This Thing Called Love?		

Philips   **6338978**   **Eur**   **12 Inch 33**
4780   (All of a Sudden) My Heart Sings
4760   Exactly Like You
4940   I'll Never Smile Again
4960   Love in Bloom
4730   Misty
4700   Oh, Lady Be Good!
5030   St. James Infirmary
4900   Solitaire
4870   That Old Feeling
4800   You Are My Sunshine

Philips   **B07015L**   **Eur**   **12 Inch 33**
4310   Avalon
4250   Caravan
4260   Lullaby of Birdland
4200   Memories of You
4220   (There Is) No Greater Love
4290   Will You Still Be Mine?

Philips   **B07046L**   **Eur**   **12 Inch 33**
4040   Anything Goes
4010   Bewitched
4460   For Heaven's Sake
3750   I Can't Get Started
4320   Lullaby in Rhythm
4000   Once in a While
4210   'S Wonderful
3770   Undecided
4410   Yesterdays

Philips   **B07078L**   **Eur**   **12 Inch 33**
4010   Bewitched

Philips   **B07082L**   **Eur**   **12 Inch 33**
4560   After You've Gone
4590   As Time Goes By
4510   I Don't Know Why (I Just Do)
4550   I Hadn't Anyone 'Till You
4580   If I Could Be with You (One Hour Tonight)
4570   I'll See You in My Dreams
4530   I'm Beginning to See the Light
4490   Let's Fall in Love
4500   Moonglow
4540   My Melancholy Baby
4520   You've Got Me Crying Again

Philips   **B07155L**   **Eur**   **12 Inch 33**
3710   Body and Soul
4370   Easy to Love
4420   Frenesi (Cancion Tropical)
3680   I Cover the Waterfront
3740   I'm in the Mood for Love
3720   Indiana (Back Home Again in Indiana)
3670   Laura
4380   Mean to Me
3960   Oh, Lady Be Good!
3690   Penthouse Serenade (When We're Alone)
3760   Play, Piano, Play
3700   Way You Look Tonight, The

Philips   **B07170L**   **Eur**   **12 Inch 33**
5100   April in Paris
5070   Autumn Leaves
5140   Erroll's Theme
5120   How Could You Do a Thing Like That to Me?
5040   I'll Remember April
5080   It's All Right with Me
5060   Mambo Carmel
5090   Red Top
5050   Teach Me Tonight
5110   They Can't Take That Away from Me
5130   Where or When

Philips   **B07260L**   **Eur**   **12 Inch 33**
5420   My Lonely Heart

Philips   **B07279L**   **Eur**   **12 Inch 33**
5390   Dreamy
5670   I Didn't Know What Time It Was
5660   It Might As Well Be Spring
5380   Misty
5650   Moment's Delight
5400   On the Street Where You Live
5640   Other Voices
5630   Solitaire
5690   This Is Always
5680   Very Thought of You, The

Philips   **B07300L**   **Eur**   **12 Inch 33**
5550   Don't Take Your Love from Me
5530   I Surrender, Dear
5600   If I Had You
5570   No More Time
5520   Soliloquy
5560   You'd Be So Nice to Come Home To

Philips   **B07370L**   **Eur**   **12 Inch 33**
5260   Alexander's Ragtime Band
5200   But Not for Me
5220   Full Moon and Empty Arms
5250   Girl of My Dreams
5430   Mambo 207
5300   Ol' Man River
5450   Passing Through
5240   Time on My Hands
5440   Way Back Blues, The

Philips   **B07375L**   **Eur**   **12 Inch 33**
5820   French Touch, The
5710   I Love Paris
5810   La Petite Mambo
5750   La Vie en Rose
5720   Last Time I Saw Paris, The
5790   Left Bank Swing
5800   Louise
5740   Paris Bounce
5700   Song from Moulin Rouge (Where Is Your Heart), The

Philips	**B07506L**	**Eur**	**12 Inch 33**

6010   Cote d'Azur
5850   Don't Look for Me
5760   Farewell to Paris
5770   French Doll
5710   I Love Paris
5790   Left Bank Swing
5800   Louise
5700   Song from Moulin Rouge (Where Is Your Heart), The

Philips	**B07507L**	**Eur**	**12 Inch 33**

5820   French Touch, The
5810   La Petite Mambo
5750   La Vie en Rose
5720   Last Time I Saw Paris, The
5840   Moroccan Quarter
5730   My Man
5940   Paris Blues
5740   Paris Bounce
5780   Paris Midnight
6030   When Paris Cries

Philips	**B07514L**	**Eur**	**12 Inch 33**

5340   All God's Chillun Got Rhythm
5360   Creme de Menthe
4110   Fancy
4440   Groovy Day
3650   How High the Moon
5370   Humoresque
5320   Man I Love, The
5330   Moonglow
3890   Robbins' Nest
3850   Sophisticated Lady

Philips	**B07559L**	**Eur**	**12 Inch 33**

5260   Alexander's Ragtime Band
5220   Full Moon and Empty Arms
3460   I Don't Know Why (I Just Do)
3450   It Could Happen to You
3910   It's the Talk of the Town
5430   Mambo 207
3470   My Heart Stood Still
3980   Out of Nowhere
3550   Poor Butterfly
3610   Spring Is Here
3440   When Johnny Comes Marching Home
3510   When You're Smiling (The Whole World Smiles with You)

Philips	**B07602R**	**Eur**	**10 Inch 33**

4030   Chopin Impressions
4070   Cocktails for Two
4130   Dancing in the Dark
4120   How Come You Do Me Like You Do?
4080   It Don't Mean a Thing (If It Ain't Got That Swing)
4090   Love Me or Leave Me
4060   Willow Me
4050   With Every Breath I Take

Philips		B07622R	Eur	10 Inch 33
4240	Can't Help Lovin' Dat Man			
4270	Cheek to Cheek			
4390	I've Got My Love to Keep Me Warm			
4450	Please Don't Talk About Me When I'm Gone			
4350	Stompin' at the Savoy			
4360	Sweet Sue-Just You			

Philips		B07646R	Eur	10 Inch 33
4470	Lullaby of Birdland			

Philips		B07664R	Eur	10 Inch 33
4130	Dancing in the Dark			

Philips		B07718R	Eur	10 Inch 33
4350	Stompin' at the Savoy			
4360	Sweet Sue-Just You			

Philips		B07735R	Eur	10 Inch 33
4350	Stompin' at the Savoy			

Philips		B07748R	Eur	10 Inch 33
3770	Undecided			

Philips		B07800R	Eur	10 Inch 33
5370	Humoresque			
5320	Man I Love, The			

Philips		B07803R	Eur	10 Inch 33
5200	But Not for Me			
5250	Girl of My Dreams			
5300	Ol' Man River			
5450	Passing Through			
5240	Time on My Hands			
5440	Way Back Blues, The			

Philips		B07821R	Eur	10 Inch 33
5390	Dreamy			
5670	I Didn't Know What Time It Was			
5660	It Might As Well Be Spring			
5380	Misty			
5650	Moment's Delight			
5640	Other Voices			
5690	This Is Always			
5680	Very Thought of You, The			

Philips		B07823R	Eur	10 Inch 33
5260	Alexander's Ragtime Band			
5200	But Not for Me			
5220	Full Moon and Empty Arms			
5250	Girl of My Dreams			
5300	Ol' Man River			
5450	Passing Through			
5240	Time on My Hands			
5440	Way Back Blues, The			

Philips   **B07910R**   **Eur**   **10 Inch 33**
4190   Dancing Tambourine
5610   Don't Get Around Much Anymore
5550   Don't Take Your Love from Me
4440   Groovy Day
5210   My Silent Love
5280   (What Can I Say) After I Say I'm Sorry?

Philips   **B07913R**   **Eur**   **10 Inch 33**
4470   Lullaby of Birdland
3760   Play, Piano, Play

Philips   **B13201R**   **Eur**   **10 Inch 33**
4190   Dancing Tambourine

Philips   **B21005H**   **Eur**   **10 Inch 78**
3970   Am I Blue?
3950   I Never Knew

Philips   **B21103H**   **Eur**   **10 Inch 78**
4340   My Ideal
4330   St. Louis Blues

Philips   **B21117H**   **Eur**   **10 Inch 78**
4370   Easy to Love
4470   Lullaby of Birdland

Philips   **B21238H**   **Eur**   **10 Inch 78**
4430   Oh, What a Beautiful Mornin'
3920   You're Driving Me Crazy (What Did I Do?)

Philips   **B21560H**   **Eur**   **10 Inch 78**
4320   Lullaby in Rhythm
3770   Undecided

Philips   **B47011L**   **Eur**   **12 Inch 33**
3860   Ain't She Sweet?
3880   Fine and Dandy
3730   Honeysuckle Rose
3870   I Don't Know
3950   I Never Knew
3520   Long Ago (And Far Away)
3640   Lover
3990   Music, Maestro, Please!
4430   Oh, What a Beautiful Mornin'
3660   People Will Say We're in Love
3940   Summertime

Philips   **B47037L**   **Eur**   **12 Inch 33**
4190   Dancing Tambourine
5290   I Got It Bad and That Ain't Good
5270   If It's the Last Thing I Do
4000   Once in a While
5190   Rose Room
5230   Some of These Days
5310   Them There Eyes
5280   (What Can I Say) After I Say I'm Sorry?

Philips	**B47081L**	**Eur**	**12 Inch 33**
4300	Blue Ecstasy		
4480	Holiday for Strings		
4230	Look, Ma—All Hands!		
4400	Love for Sale		
3870	Margin for Erroll		
5830	Too Close for Comfort		
3840	You're Blasé		

Philips	**B47124L**	**Eur**	**12 Inch 33**
3860	Ain't She Sweet?		
5770	French Doll		
5820	French Touch, The		
3880	Fine and Dandy		
3730	Honeysuckle Rose		
3950	I Never Knew		
5810	La Petite Mambo		
5790	Left Bank Swing		
3640	Lover		
3990	Music, Maestro, Please!		
4430	Oh, What a Beautiful Mornin'		
3940	Summertime		

Philips	**B632203L**	**Eur**	**12 Inch 33**
6530	Fashion Interlude		
6570	In the Park in Paree		
6520	Louise		
6510	Mimi		
6550	Paris Mist (Bossa Nova)		
6580	Paris Mist (Waltz-Swing)		
6540	Steve's Song		
6590	Tease, The		
6500	Theme from "A New Kind of Love"		
6560	You Brought a New Kind of Love to Me		

Philips	**BBE12003**	**Eng**	**7 Inch 45EP**
3920	You're Driving Me Crazy (What Did I Do?)		

Philips	**BBE12047**	**Eng**	**7 Inch 45EP**
3750	I Can't Get Started		
4320	Lullaby in Rhythm		
4200	Memories of You		

Philips	**BBE12065**	**Eng**	**7 Inch 45EP**
4240	Can't Help Lovin' Dat Man		
4450	Please Don't Talk About Me When I'm Gone		
4360	Sweet Sue-Just You		

Philips	**BBE12084**	**Eng**	**7 Inch 45EP**
4090	Love Me or Leave Me		
4470	Lullaby of Birdland		
3630	Petite Waltz Bounce, The		
4330	St. Louis Blues		

Philips	**BBE12184**	**Eng**	**7 Inch 45EP**
5070	Autumn Leaves		
5050	Teach Me Tonight		
5130	Where or When		

| **Philips** | **BBE12264** | **Eng** | **7 Inch 45EP** |

5100   April in Paris
5080   It's All Right with Me
5060   Mambo Carmel
5110   They Can't Take That Away from Me

| **Philips** | **BBE12270** | **Eng** | **7 Inch 45EP** |

5300   Ol' Man River
5440   Way Back Blues, The

| **Philips** | **BBE12271** | **Eng** | **7 Inch 45EP** |

5260   Alexander's Ragtime Band
5200   But Not for Me
5450   Passing Through
5240   Time on My Hands

| **Philips** | **BBE12354** | **Eng** | **7 Inch 45EP** |

5340   All God's Chillun Got Rhythm
4440   Groovy Day
3760   Play, Piano, Play
3890   Robbins' Nest

| **Philips** | **BBE12401** | **Eng** | **7 Inch 45EP** |

5710   I Love Paris
5740   Paris Bounce
5700   Song from Moulin Rouge (Where Is Your Heart), The

| **Philips** | **BBE12423** | **Eng** | **7 Inch 45EP** |

3730   Honeysuckle Rose
3990   Music, Maestro, Please!
4430   Oh, What a Beautiful Mornin'
3940   Summertime

| **Philips** | **BBE12429** | **Eng** | **7 Inch 45EP** |

3860   Ain't She Sweet?
3880   Fine and Dandy
3950   I Never Knew
3640   Lover

| **Philips** | **BBE12510** | **Eng** | **7 Inch 45EP** |

6210   All of Me
6280   Back in Your Own Back Yard
6220   Shadows
6190   You Do Something to Me

| **Philips** | **BBE12567** | **Eng** | **7 Inch 45EP** |

6270   Best Things in Life Are Free, The
6250   I'm in the Mood for Love
6200   My Silent Love
6180   Oklahoma! Medley:
       Oh, What a Beautiful Mornin'
       People Will Say We're in Love
       Surrey with the Fringe on Top, The

| **Philips** | **BBE12568** | **Eng** | **7 Inch 45EP** |

6440   Dancing Tambourine
6380   Happiness Is a Thing Called Joe
6420   Misty

Philips		**BBL7034**	**Eng**	**12 Inch 33**
4040	Anything Goes			
4010	Bewitched			
4460	For Heaven's Sake			
3750	I Can't Get Started			
4320	Lullaby in Rhythm			
4000	Once in a While			
4210	'S Wonderful			
3770	Undecided			
4410	Yesterdays			

Philips		**BBL7056**	**Eng**	**12 Inch 33**
4560	After You've Gone			
4590	As Time Goes By			
4510	I Don't Know Why (I Just Do)			
4550	I Hadn't Anyone 'Till You			
4580	If I Could Be with You (One Hour Tonight)			
4570	I'll See You in My Dreams			
4530	I'm Beginning to See the Light			
4490	Let's Fall in Love			
4500	Moonglow			
4540	My Melancholy Baby			
4520	You've Got Me Crying Again			

Philips		**BBL7078**	**Eng**	**12 Inch 33**
4310	Avalon			
4250	Caravan			
4260	Lullaby of Birdland			
4200	Memories of You			
4220	(There Is) No Greater Love			
4290	Will You Still Be Mine?			

Philips		**BBL7106**	**Eng**	**12 Inch 33**
5100	April in Paris			
5070	Autumn Leaves			
5140	Erroll's Theme			
5120	How Could You Do a Thing Like That to Me?			
5040	I'll Remember April			
5080	It's All Right with Me			
5060	Mambo Carmel			
5090	Red Top			
5050	Teach Me Tonight			
5110	They Can't Take That Away from Me			
5130	Where or When			

Philips		**BBL7184**	**Eng**	**12 Inch 33**
5420	My Lonely Heart			

Philips		**BBL7192**	**Eng**	**12 Inch 33**
3710	Body and Soul			
4370	Easy to Love			
4420	Frenesi (Cancion Tropical)			
3680	I Cover the Waterfront			
3740	I'm in the Mood for Love			
3720	Indiana (Back Home Again in Indiana)			
3670	Laura			
4380	Mean to Me			
3960	Oh, Lady Be Good!			
3690	Penthouse Serenade (When We're Alone)			
3760	Play, Piano, Play			
3700	Way You Look Tonight, The			

Philips   **BBL7204**   Eng   **12 Inch 33**
5390   Dreamy
5670   I Didn't Know What Time It Was
5660   It Might As Well Be Spring
5380   Misty
5650   Moment's Delight
5400   On the Street Where You Live
5640   Other Voices
5630   Solitaire
5690   This Is Always
5680   Very Thought of You, The

Philips   **BBL7226**   Eng   **12 Inch 33**
5550   Don't Take Your Love from Me
5530   I Surrender, Dear
5600   If I Had You
5570   No More Time
5520   Soliloquy
5560   You'd Be So Nice to Come Home To

Philips   **BBL7282**   Eng   **12 Inch 33**
5260   Alexander's Ragtime Band
5200   But Not for Me
5220   Full Moon and Empty Arms
5250   Girl of My Dreams
5430   Mambo 207
5300   Ol' Man River
5450   Passing Through
5240   Time on My Hands
5440   Way Back Blues, The

Philips   **BBL7313**   Eng   **12 Inch 33**
6010   Cote d'Azur
5850   Don't Look for Me
5760   Farewell to Paris
5770   French Doll
5710   I Love Paris
5790   Left Bank Swing
5800   Louise
5700   Song from Moulin Rouge (Where Is Your Heart), The

Philips   **BBL7314**   Eng   **12 Inch 33**
5820   French Touch, The
5810   La Petite Mambo
5750   La Vie en Rose
5720   Last Time I Saw Paris, The
5840   Moroccan Quarter
5730   My Man
5940   Paris Blues
5740   Paris Bounce
5780   Paris Midnight
6030   When Paris Cries

Philips   **BBL7426**   Eng   **12 Inch 33**
3860   Ain't She Sweet?
3880   Fine and Dandy
3730   Honeysuckle Rose
3870   I Didn't Know
3950   I Never Knew
3640   Lover

3520	Long Ago (And Far Away)
3990	Music, Maestro, Please!
4430	Oh, What a Beautiful Mornin'
3660	People Will Say We're in Love
3940	Summertime

Philips   **BBL7448**   **Eng**   **12 Inch 33**

4310	Avalon
4250	Caravan
4260	Lullaby of Birdland
4200	Memories of You
4220	(There Is) No Greater Love
4290	Will You Still Be Mine?

Philips   **BBL7519**   **Eng**   **12 Inch 33**

6210	All of Me
6280	Back in Your Own Back Yard
6270	Best Things in Life Are Free, The
6260	El Papa Grande
6250	I'm in the Mood for Love
6200	My Silent Love
6230	St. Louis Blues
6220	Shadows
6240	Some of These Days
6190	You Do Something to Me

Philips   **BBL7523**   **Eng**   **12 Inch 33**

6110	Blue Lou
6120	Come Rain or Come Shine
6150	Dreamstreet
6100	I'm Gettin' Sentimental Over You
6090	Just One of Those Things
6130	Lady Is a Tramp, The
6170	Mambo Gotham
6180	Oklahoma! Medley:
	Oh, What a Beautiful Mornin'
	People Will Say We're in Love
	Surrey with the Fringe on Top, The
6160	Sweet Lorraine
6140	When You're Smiling (The Whole World Smiles with You)

Philips   **BBR8002**   **Eng**   **10 Inch 33**

4240	Can't Help Lovin' Dat Man
4270	Cheek to Cheek
4390	I've Got My Love to Keep Me Warm
4450	Please Don't Talk About Me When I'm Gone
4350	Stompin' at the Savoy
4360	Sweet Sue-Just You

Philips   **BBR8045**   **Eng**   **10 Inch 33**

4030	Chopin Impressions
4070	Cocktails for Two
4130	Dancing in the Dark
4120	How Come You Do Me Like You Do?
4080	It Don't Mean a Thing (If It Ain't Got That Swing)
4090	Love Me or Leave Me
4060	Willow Me
4050	With Every Breath I Take

| Philips | BBR8048 | Eng | 10 Inch 33 |
| 4470 | Lullaby of Birdland | | |

| Philips | BBR8071 | Eng | 10 Inch 33 |
| 4130 | Dancing in the Dark | | |

| Philips | BBR8089 | Eng | 10 Inch 33 |
| 4350 | Stompin' at the Savoy | | |

| Philips | BBR8098 | Eng | 10 Inch 33 |
| 4360 | Sweet Sue-Just You | | |

Philips **BE12568** **Eng** **7 Inch 45EP**
6440 Dancing Tambourine
6420 Misty
6370 Way You Look Tonight, The

Philips **BE12569** **Eng** **7 Inch 45EP**
6400 Mack the Knife
6390 Sweet and Lovely
6450 Thanks for the Memory

Philips **BF1268** **Eng** **7 Inch 45**
6400 Mack the Knife
6390 Sweet and Lovely

Philips **BL7580** **Eng** **12 Inch 33**
6440 Dancing Tambourine
6380 Happiness Is a Thing Called Joe
6410 Lover Come Back to Me
6400 Mack the Knife
6420 Misty
6430 Movin' Blues
6390 Sweet and Lovely
6450 Thanks for the Memory
6370 Way You Look Tonight, The

Philips **BL7595** **Eng** **12 Inch 33**
6530 Fashion Interlude
6570 In the Park in Paree
6520 Louise
6510 Mimi
6550 Paris Mist (Bossa Nova)
6580 Paris Mist (Waltz-Swing)
6540 Steve's Song
6590 Tease, The
6500 Theme from "A New Kind of Love"
6560 You Brought a New Kind of Love to Me

Philips **BL7717** **Eng** **12 Inch 33**
7360 Cheek to Cheek
7290 Easy to Love
7320 Gypsy in My Soul
7300 Moon River
7340 More
7330 On Green Dolphin Street
7350 Over the Rainbow
7310 What Is This Thing Called Love?

Philips   **D99556R**   **Fra**   **10 Inch 33**
4350   Stompin' at the Savoy

Philips   **P07800R**   **Eur**   **10 Inch 33**
4270   Cheek to Cheek
4390   I've Got My Love to Keep Me Warm
3630   Petite Waltz Bounce, The
4360   Sweet Sue-Just You

Philips   **P07839R**   **Eur**   **10 Inch 33**
3710   Body and Soul
4370   Easy to Love
3680   I Cover the Waterfront
3740   I'm in the Mood for Love
3720   Indiana (Back Home Again in Indiana)
4380   Mean to Me
3960   Oh, Lady Be Good!
3690   Penthouse Serenade (When We're Alone)
3760   Play, Piano, Play
3700   Way You Look Tonight, The

Philips   **PB250**   **Eng**   **10 Inch 78**
4370   Easy to Love
4470   Lullaby of Birdland

Philips   **PHM200-001**   **Can**   **12 Inch 33**
6210   All of Me
6280   Back in Your Own Back Yard
6270   Best Things in Life Are Free, The
6260   El Papa Grande
6250   I'm in the Mood for Love
6200   My Silent Love
6230   St. Louis Blues
6220   Shadows
6240   Some of These Days
6190   You Do Something to Me

Philips   **PHM200-002**   **Can**   **12 Inch 33**
6110   Blue Lou
6120   Come Rain or Come Shine
6150   Dreamstreet
6100   I'm Gettin' Sentimental Over You
6090   Just One of Those Things
6130   Lady Is a Tramp, The
6170   Mambo Gotham
6180   Oklahoma! Medley:
        Oh, What a Beautiful Mornin'
        People Will Say We're in Love
        Surrey with the Fringe on Top, The
6160   Sweet Lorraine
6140   When You're Smiling (The Whole World Smiles with You)

Philips   **PHS600-001**   **Can**   **12 Inch 33**
6210   All of Me
6280   Back in Your Own Back Yard
6270   Best Things in Life Are Free, The
6260   El Papa Grande
6250   I'm in the Mood for Love
6200   My Silent Love
6230   St. Louis Blues

6220   Shadows
6240   Some of These Days
6190   You Do Something to Me

Philips   **PHS600-002**   **Can**   **12 Inch 33**
6110   Blue Lou
6120   Come Rain or Come Shine
6150   Dreamstreet
6100   I'm Gettin' Sentimental Over You
6090   Just One of Those Things
6130   Lady Is a Tramp, The
6170   Mambo Gotham
6180   Oklahoma! Medley:
        Oh, What a Beautiful Mornin'
        People Will Say We're in Love
        Surrey with the Fringe on Top, The
6160   Sweet Lorraine
6140   When You're Smiling (The Whole World Smiles with You)

Philips   **PHS600-008**   **Can**   **12 Inch 33**
6440   Dancing Tambourine
6380   Happiness Is a Thing Called Joe
6410   Lover Come Back to Me
6400   Mack the Knife
6420   Misty
6430   Movin' Blues
6390   Sweet and Lovely
6450   Thanks for the Memory
6370   Way You Look Tonight, The

Philips   **SBBL676**   **Eng**   **12 Inch 33**
6210   All of Me
6280   Back in Your Own Back Yard
6270   Best Things in Life Are Free, The
6260   El Papa Grande
6250   I'm in the Mood for Love
6200   My Silent Love
6230   St. Louis Blues
6220   Shadows
6240   Some of These Days
6190   You Do Something to Me

Philips   **SBBL677**   **Eng**   **12 Inch 33**
6110   Blue Lou
6120   Come Rain or Come Shine
6150   Dreamstreet
6100   I'm Gettin' Sentimental Over You
6090   Just One of Those Things
6130   Lady Is a Tramp, The
6170   Mambo Gotham
6180   Oklahoma! Medley:
        Oh, What a Beautiful Mornin'
        People Will Say We're in Love
        Surrey with the Fringe on Top, The
6160   Sweet Lorraine
6140   When You're Smiling (The Whole World Smiles with You)

Philips   **SBL7580**   **Eng**   **12 Inch 33**
6440   Dancing Tambourine
6380   Happiness Is a Thing Called Joe

6410   Lover Come Back to Me
6400   Mack the Knife
6420   Misty
6430   Movin' Blues
6390   Sweet and Lovely
6450   Thanks for the Memory
6370   Way You Look Tonight, The

Philips   **SBL7595**   **Eng**   **12 Inch 33**
6530   Fashion Interlude
6570   In the Park in Paree
6520   Louise
6510   Mimi
6550   Paris Mist (Bossa Nova)
6580   Paris Mist (Waltz-Swing)
6540   Steve's Song
6590   Tease, The
6500   Theme from "A New Kind of Love"
6560   You Brought a New Kind of Love to Me

Philips   **SBL7717**   **Eng**   **12 Inch 33**
7360   Cheek to Cheek
7290   Easy to Love
7320   Gypsy in My Soul
7300   Moon River
7340   More
7330   On Green Dolphin Street
7350   Over the Rainbow
7310   What Is This Thing Called Love?

Philips   **SFL-7140**   **Jap**   **12 Inch 33**
6440   Dancing Tambourine
6380   Happiness Is a Thing Called Joe
6410   Lover Come Back to Me
6400   Mack the Knife
6420   Misty
6430   Movin' Blues
6390   Sweet and Lovely
6450   Thanks for the Memory
6370   Way You Look Tonight, The

Philips   **SFL-7160**   **Jap**   **12 Inch 33**
6530   Fashion Interlude
6570   In the Park in Paree
6520   Louise
6510   Mimi
6550   Paris Mist (Bossa Nova)
6580   Paris Mist (Waltz-Swing)
6540   Steve's Song
6590   Tease, The
6500   Theme from "A New Kind of Love"
6560   You Brought a New Kind of Love to Me

Phoenix   **LP-4**   **USA**   **12 Inch 33**
0930   In the Middle

Pickwick   **SPC-3254**   **USA**   **12 Inch 33**
3150   Bonny Boy
3210   Cologne
3130   Deep Purple

```
3100    I Let a Song Go Out of My Heart
3190    Minor with the Trio
3200    No Moon
3180    Quaker, The
3170    Relaxin' at Sugar Ray's
3160    Tippin' Out with Erroll
```

Playboy   **PB 1959A**   **USA**   **12 Inch 33**
5430   Mambo 207

Polydor   **580.066**   **Fra**   **10 Inch 78**
0180   Moonlight Moods

Polydor   **2310326**   **WGer**   **12 Inch 33**
1350   Blue, Brown and Beige
1320   Hop, Skip and Jump
1330   Sherry Lynn Flip
1340   Three Blind Micesky

Polydor   **2344049**   **Eng**   **12 Inch 33**
1350   Blue, Brown and Beige
1320   Hop, Skip and Jump
1330   Sherry Lynn Flip
1340   Three Blind Micesky

Polydor   **2393004**   **Fra**   **12 Inch 33**
6330   Almost Like Being in Love
6360   In the Still of the Night
6290   Indiana (Back Home Again in Indiana)
6320   Lulu's Back in Town
6310   Mambo Erroll
6340   My Funny Valentine
6300   Stardust
6350   These Foolish Things (Remind Me of You)

Polydor   **2393005**   **Fra**   **12 Inch 33**
7370   Afinidad
7430   Autumn Leaves
7440   Blue Moon
7450   Gaslight
7400   It Ain't Necessarily So
7420   Like It Is
7390   More
7460   Nervous Waltz
7470   Passing Through
7410   Shadow of Your Smile, The
7380   That's My Kick

Polydor   **2393008**   **Fra**   **12 Inch 33**
7560   All the Things You Are
7530   Cheek to Cheek
7520   Coffee Song, The
        (They've Got an Awful Lot of Coffee in Brazil)
7510   Girl from Ipanema, The
7500   Groovin' High
7570   I Got Rhythm
7490   It's the Talk of the Town
7550   Lot of Livin' to Do, A
7540   Up in Erroll's Room
7480   Watermelon Man

Polydor   2393015   **Fra**   **12 Inch 33**
7740   Feeling Is Believing
7810   For Once in My Life
7830   Look of Love, The
7700   Loving Touch, The
7780   Mood Island
7790   Paisley Eyes
7840   Spinning Wheel
7760   Strangers in the Night
7820   Yesterday
7620   You Turned Me Around

Polydor   2393036   **Fra**   **12 Inch 33**
8020   Eldorado
7980   Gemini
7960   How High the Moon
7970   It Could Happen to You
8010   Something
8000   Tea for Two
8030   These Foolish Things (Remind Me of You)
7990   When a Gypsy Makes His Violin Cry

Polydor   2445030   **Fra**   **12 Inch 33**
7020   Can't Help Lovin' Dat Man
7050   Dearly Beloved
7060   Fine Romance, A
7000   Foggy Day, A
7570   I Got Rhythm
6980   Love Walked In
7010   Lovely to Look At
7040   Ol' Man River
7030   Only Make Believe
6990   Someone to Watch Over Me
6970   Strike Up the Band

Polydor   P76295   **WGer**   **12 Inch 33**
6890   I'll Get By (As Long As I Have You)
6360   In the Still of the Night
6290   Indiana (Back Home Again in Indiana)
6950   It's Only a Paper Moon
6920   Jeannine, I Dream of Lilac Time
6320   Lulu's Back in Town
6930   Schoner Gigolo (Just a Gigolo)
6860   Sonny Boy
6300   Stardust
6910   Stella by Starlight
6350   These Foolish Things (Remind Me of You)
6900   Three O'Clock in the Morning
6840   You Made Me Love You

Portrait   8500   **USA**   **10 Inch 78**
2980   On the Sunny Side of the Street
3010   Stairway to the Stars

Portrait   8501   **USA**   **10 Inch 78**
3000   Everything Happens to Me
2990   Rosalie

Premier   **PM9042**   **USA**   **12 Inch 33**
0150   Cloudburst
0570   Easy to Love
0620   In the Beginning

Premier   **PS9042**   **USA**   **12 Inch 33**
0150   Cloudburst
· 0570   Easy to Love
0620   In the Beginning

President   **PRC349**   **Fra**   **7 Inch 45EP**
3780   Garner in Hollywood
3820   Six P.M.
3800   This Is My Beloved
3810   Until the Real Thing Comes Along

Prestige   **P-24052**   **USA**   **12 Inch 33**
0820   White Rose Bounce

Pye   **NSPL28123**   **Eng**   **12 Inch 33**
7560   All the Things You Are
7530   Cheek to Cheek
7520   Coffee Song, The
           (They've Got an Awful Lot of Coffee in Brazil)
7510   Girl from Ipanema, The
7500   Groovin' High
7570   I Got Rhythm
7490   It's the Talk of the Town
7550   Lot of Livin' to Do, A
7540   Up in Erroll's Room
7480   Watermelon Man

Pye   **NSPL28213**   **Eng**   **12 Inch 33**
8190   I Only Have Eyes for You
8160   It Gets Better Every Time
8100   Mucho Gusto
8050   Nightwind
8090   One Good Turn
8150   Someone to Watch Over Me
8060   (They Long to Be) Close to You
8180   Watch What Happens
8130   Yesterdays

Pye   **NSPL28214**   **Eng**   **12 Inch 33**
7740   Feeling Is Believing
7810   For Once in My Life
7830   Look of Love, The
7700   Loving Touch, The
7780   Mood Island
7790   Paisley Eyes
7840   Spinning Wheel
7760   Strangers in the Night
7820   Yesterday
7620   You Turned Me Around

Quadrifoglio   **VDS208**   **Ity**   **12 Inch 33**
2550   I Can't Believe That You're in Love with Me
2860   I'm Confessin' (That I Love You)
2820   Moonglow

```
2580    Red Sails in the Sunset
2840    She's Funny That Way
2420    Stompin' at the Savoy
2870    Stormy Weather (Keeps Rainin' All the Time)
2800    This Can't Be Love
1380    Somebody Loves Me
```

Quadrifoglio   **VDS9437**   **Ity**   **12 Inch 33**
```
1850    Blow Top Blues
1880    Cool Blues
```

Queen Disc   **Q 039**   **Ity**   **12 Inch 33**
```
2620    Cherokee (Part 1)
2630    Cherokee (Part 2)
```

RCA Victor   **20-3087**   **USA**   **10 Inch 78**
```
1940    Erroll's Blues
1930    Erroll's Bounce
```

RCA Victor   **20-4723**   **USA**   **10 Inch 78**
```
1950    I Can't Escape from You
1960    Stairway to the Stars
```

RCA Victor   **27-0146**   **USA**   **7 Inch 45**
```
1930    Erroll's Bounce
```

RCA Victor   **47-4723**   **USA**   **7 Inch 45**
```
1950    I Can't Escape from You
1960    Stairway to the Stars
```

RCA Victor   **430.278**   **Fra**   **12 Inch 33**
```
1930    Erroll's Bounce
```

RCA Victor   **430.633**   **Fra**   **12 Inch 33**
```
1930    Erroll's Bounce
```

RCA Victor   **EG7897**   **USA**   **10 Inch 78**
```
1950    I Can't Escape from You
1960    Stairway to the Stars
```

RCA Victor   **EJB3001**   **USA**   **7 Inch 45**
```
1940    Erroll's Blues
```

RCA Victor   **FXM37143**   **USA**   **12 Inch 33**
```
1940    Erroll's Blues
1930    Erroll's Bounce
```

RCA Victor   **LEJ-4**   **USA**   **10 Inch 33**
```
1930    Erroll's Bounce
```

RCA Victor   **LJM3001**   **USA**   **12 Inch 33**
```
1940    Erroll's Blues
```

RCA Victor   **LPM10044**   **Ity**   **12 Inch 33**
```
1930    Erroll's Bounce
```

RCA Victor   **LPT31**   **USA**   **10 Inch 33**
1940   Erroll's Blues

RCA Victor   **RJL-2520**   **Jap**   **12 Inch 33**
1940   Erroll's Blues
1950   I Can't Escape from You
1960   Stairway to the Stars

Realistic   **P13230**   **USA**   **12 Inch 33**
3550   Poor Butterfly

Realm   **REP-4006**   **Eng**   **7 Inch 45EP**
2550   I Can't Believe That You're in Love with Me
2580   Red Sails in the Sunset
2870   Stormy Weather (Keeps Rainin' All the Time)
2570   Undecided

Realm   **RM116**   **Eng**   **12 Inch 33**
2550   I Can't Believe That You're in Love with Me
2425   I Cover the Waterfront
2490   I Don't Stand a Ghost of a Chance with You
2860   I'm Confessin' (That I Love You)
1390   Indiana (Back Home Again in Indiana)
2450   Love Walked In
2440   Penthouse Serenade (When We're Alone)
2580   Red Sails in the Sunset
2840   She's Funny That Way
1380   Somebody Loves Me
2420   Stompin' at the Savoy
2870   Stormy Weather (Keeps Rainin' All the Time)
2570   Undecided
2850   Until the Real Thing Comes Along

Recorded in Hollywood   **110**   **USA**   **10 Inch 78**
3790   Lotus Blues
3820   Six P.M.

Recorded in Hollywood   **124**   **USA**   **10 Inch 78**
3780   Garner in Hollywood
3810   Until the Real Thing Comes Along

Recorded in Hollywood   **128**   **USA**   **10 Inch 78**
3830   New York Concerto
3800   This Is My Beloved

Recorded in Hollywood   **692**   **USA**   **10 Inch 78**
2670   Someone to Watch Over Me
2660   Tenderly

Regal   **R104**   **USA**   **10 Inch 78**
1360   Laura
1380   Somebody Loves Me

Regal   **R127**   **USA**   **10 Inch 78**
1390   Indiana (Back Home Again in Indiana)
1370   Stardust

Regent   **45-1004**   USA   **7 Inch 45**
2580   Red Sails in the Sunset
2570   Undecided

Regent   **45-1014**   USA   **7 Inch 45**
2560   More Than You Know
2600   Over the Rainbow

Regent   **1004**   USA   **10 Inch 78**
2580   Red Sails in the Sunset
2570   Undecided

Regent   **1014**   USA   **10 Inch 78**
2560   More Than You Know
2600   Over the Rainbow

Regent   **8500**   USA   **10 Inch 78**
2980   On the Sunny Side of the Street
3010   Stairway to the Stars

Regent   **8501**   USA   **10 Inch 78**
3000   Everything Happens to Me
2990   Rosalie

Regina-Mercury   **RM-70218**   WGer   **10 Inch 78**
1730   Blue Skies
1500   I've Got You Under My Skin

Reprise   **R-6080**   USA   **12 Inch 45**
6380   Happiness Is a Thing Called Joe
6410   Lover Come Back to Me
6400   Mack the Knife
6420   Misty
6460   Stride Out
6370   Way You Look Tonight, The

Reprise   **R-20179**   USA   **7 Inch 45**
6400   Mack the Knife
6390   Sweet and Lovely

Reprise   **R-40051**   USA   **7 Inch 33**
6410   Lover Come Back to Me
6420   Misty

Reprise   **R9-6080**   USA   **12 Inch 33**
6440   Dancing Tambourine
6380   Happiness Is a Thing Called Joe
6410   Lover Come Back to Me
6400   Mack the Knife
6420   Misty
6430   Movin' Blues
6390   Sweet and Lovely
6450   Thanks for the Memory
6370   Way You Look Tonight, The

Rex   **J501**   USA   **10 Inch 78**
0440   Blues I Can't Forget
0450   Boogie Woogie Boogie

Rex   **J502**   USA   **10 Inch 78**
0420   Blue Room
0400   I'm in the Mood for Love

Rex   **J503**   USA   **10 Inch 78**
0390   Everything Happens to Me
0380   Soft and Warm

Rhapsody   **RHAP5**   Eng   **12 Inch 33**
1840   Bird's Nest
1860   Blow Top Blues

Rondolette   **A15**   USA   **12 Inch 33**
2550   I Can't Believe That You're in Love with Me
2370   I Surrender, Dear
2860   I'm Confessin' (That I Love You)
2820   Moonglow
2980   On the Sunny Side of the Street
2580   Red Sails in the Sunset
2840   She's Funny That Way
1370   Stardust
2420   Stompin' at the Savoy
2870   Stormy Weather (Keeps Rainin' All the Time)
2800   This Can't Be Love

Roost   **10**   USA   **10 Inch 33**
3080   Again
3150   Bonny Boy
3210   Cologne
3130   Deep Purple
3200   No Moon
3170   Relaxin' at Sugar Ray's
3060   Scatter-Brain
3090   What Is This Thing Called Love?

Roost   **400**   USA   **10 Inch 78**
3190   Minor with the Trio
3180   Quaker, The

Roost   **604**   USA   **10 Inch 78**
3130   Deep Purple
3170   Relaxin' at Sugar Ray's

Roost   **606**   USA   **10 Inch 78**
3200   No Moon
3090   What Is This Thing Called Love?

Roost   **609**   USA   **10 Inch 78**
3150   Bonny Boy
3060   Scatter-Brain

Roost   **610**   USA   **10 Inch 78**
3080   Again
3210   Cologne

Roost   **614**   USA   **10 Inch 78**
3220   Lazy River
3160   Tippin' Out with Erroll

Roulette	MJ-7069	Jap	12 Inch 33
2180	Frankie and Johnny Fantasy		
1890	Pastel		
2070	Play, Piano, Play		
1910	Trio		

Roulette	MJ-7072	Jap	12 Inch 33
2070	Play, Piano, Play		

Roulette	RE-110	USA	12 Inch 33
2130	Don't Worry 'Bout Me		
2180	Frankie and Johnny Fantasy		
2170	Love for Sale		
1890	Pastel		
2070	Play, Piano, Play		
1910	Trio		

Roulette	VJL2-0264	Aus	12 Inch 33
2130	Don't Worry 'Bout Me		
2180	Frankie and Johnny Fantasy		
2170	Love for Sale		
1890	Pastel		
2070	Play, Piano, Play		
1910	Trio		

Royal Roost	LP-2256	USA	12 Inch 33
2180	Frankie and Johnny Fantasy		
1890	Pastel		
2070	Play, Piano, Play		
1910	Trio		

Royal Roost	OJ-1	USA	12 Inch 33
2180	Frankie and Johnny Fantasy		

Royal Roost	RLP 2213	USA	12 Inch 33
2130	Don't Worry 'Bout Me		
2180	Frankie and Johnny Fantasy		
2170	Love for Sale		
1890	Pastel		
2070	Play, Piano, Play		
1910	Trio		

Saga	6907AG	Eng	12 Inch 33
1870	Cool Blues		
1780	Dark Shadows		
1760	This Is Always		

Saga	6911AG	Eng	12 Inch 33
1850	Cool Blues		
1880	Cool Blues		

Saga	ERO 8005	Eng	12 Inch 33
1870	Cool Blues		
1780	Dark Shadows		
1770	This Is Always		

Savoy	45-571	USA	7 Inch 45
1360	Laura		
1380	Somebody Loves Me		

| Savoy | **45-577** | USA | **7 Inch 45** |

1390   Indiana (Back Home Again in Indiana)
1370   Stardust

| Savoy | **45-688** | USA | **7 Inch 45** |

2425   I Cover the Waterfront
2440   Penthouse Serenade (When We're Alone)

| Savoy | **45-701** | USA | **7 Inch 45** |

2370   I Surrender, Dear
2450   Love Walked In

| Savoy | **45-723** | USA | **7 Inch 45** |

2550   I Can't Believe That You're in Love with Me
2400   I Only Have Eyes for You

| Savoy | **45-724** | USA | **7 Inch 45** |

2590   All of Me
2490   I Don't Stand a Ghost of a Chance with You

| Savoy | **45-725** | USA | **7 Inch 45** |

2520   Cottage for Sale, A
2540   I'm in the Mood for Love

| Savoy | **45-727** | USA | **7 Inch 45** |

2460   September Song
2420   Stompin' at the Savoy

| Savoy | **45-728** | USA | **7 Inch 45** |

2470   Body and Soul
2430   It's Easy to Remember

| Savoy | **45-739** | USA | **7 Inch 45** |

2480   All the Things You Are

| Savoy | **45-757** | USA | **7 Inch 45** |

2860   I'm Confessin' (That I Love You)
2870   Stormy Weather (Keeps Rainin' All the Time)

| Savoy | **45-765** | USA | **7 Inch 45** |

2810   Man I Love, The
2850   Until the Real Things Comes Along

| Savoy | **45-767** | USA | **7 Inch 45** |

2830   I Want a Little Girl
2820   Moonglow

| Savoy | **45-768** | USA | **7 Inch 45** |

2840   She's Funny That Way
2800   This Can't Be Love

| Savoy | **45-771** | USA | **7 Inch 45** |

2990   Rosalie
3010   Stairway to the Stars

Savoy		**45-772**	**USA**	**7 Inch 45**
3000	Everything Happens to Me			
2980	On the Sunny Side of the Street			

Savoy		**45-782**	**USA**	**7 Inch 45**
2480	All the Things You Are			
2510	Goodbye			

Savoy		**45-862**	**USA**	**7 Inch 45**
2580	Red Sails in the Sunset			
2570	Undecided			

Savoy		**255SV111**	**Fra**	**10 Inch 33**
2590	All of Me			
2480	All the Things You Are			
2860	I'm Confessin' (That I Love You)			
2810	Man I Love, The			
2820	Moonglow			
2980	On the Sunny Side of the Street			
2840	She's Funny That Way			
2870	Stormy Weather (Keeps Rainin' All the Time)			
2800	This Can't Be Love			
2850	Until the Real Thing Comes Along			

Savoy		**255SV152**	**Fra**	**10 Inch 33**
2520	Cottage for Sale, A			
2550	I Can't Believe That You're in Love with Me			
2400	I Only Have Eyes for You			
2540	I'm in the Mood for Love			
1360	Laura			
2460	September Song			
1380	Somebody Loves Me			
1370	Stardust			

Savoy		**537**	**USA**	**10 Inch 78**
0870	Dark Eyesky			
0860	Play, Fiddle, Play			

Savoy		**537**	**Eng**	**10 Inch 78**
0870	Dark Eyesky			
0860	Play, Fiddle, Play			

Savoy		**538**	**USA**	**10 Inch 78**
0890	Jumpin' at the Deuces			
0880	Laff Slam Laff			

Savoy		**538**	**Eng**	**10 Inch 78**
0890	Jumpin' at the Deuces			
0880	Laff Slam Laff			

Savoy		**571**	**USA**	**10 Inch 78**
1360	Laura			
1380	Somebody Loves Me			

Savoy		**571**	**Eng**	**10 Inch 78**
1360	Laura			
1380	Somebody Loves Me			

Savoy	**577**	**USA**	**10 Inch 78**
1390	Indiana (Back Home Again in Indiana)		
1370	Stardust		

Savoy	**688**	**USA**	**10 Inch 78**
2425	I Cover the Waterfront		
2440	Penthouse Serenade (When We're Alone)		

Savoy	**688**	**Eng**	**10 Inch 78**
2425	I Cover the Waterfront		
2440	Penthouse Serenade (When We're Alone)		

Savoy	**701**	**USA**	**10 Inch 78**
2370	I Surrender, Dear		
2450	Love Walked In		

Savoy	**723**	**USA**	**10 Inch 78**
2550	I Can't Believe That You're in Love with Me		
2400	I Only Have Eyes for You		

Savoy	**724**	**USA**	**10 Inch 78**
2590	All of Me		
2490	I Don't Stand a Ghost of a Chance with You		

Savoy	**725**	**USA**	**10 Inch 78**
2520	Cottage for Sale, A		
2540	I'm in the Mood for Love		

Savoy	**727**	**USA**	**10 Inch 78**
2460	September Song		
2420	Stompin' at the Savoy		

Savoy	**728**	**USA**	**10 Inch 78**
2430	It's Easy to Remember		
2470	Body and Soul		

Savoy	**739**	**USA**	**10 Inch 78**
2480	All the Things You Are		

Savoy	**757**	**USA**	**10 Inch 78**
2860	I'm Confessin' (That I Love You)		
2870	Stormy Weather (Keeps Rainin' All the Time)		

Savoy	**765**	**USA**	**10 Inch 78**
2810	Man I Love, The		
2850	Until the Real Thing Comes Along		

Savoy	**767**	**USA**	**10 Inch 78**
2830	I Want a Little Girl		
2820	Moonglow		

Savoy	**768**	**USA**	**10 Inch 78**
2840	She's Funny That Way		
2800	This Can't Be Love		

Savoy   **771**   **USA**   **10 Inch 78**
2990   Rosalie
3010   Stairway to the Stars

Savoy   **772**   **USA**   **10 Inch 78**
3000   Everything Happens to Me
2980   On the Sunny Side of the Street

Savoy   **782**   **USA**   **10 Inch 78**
2480   All the Things You Are
2510   Goodbye

Savoy   **862**   **USA**   **10 Inch 78**
2580   Red Sails in the Sunset
2570   Undecided

Savoy   **863**   **USA**   **10 Inch 78**
2560   More Than You Know
2600   Over the Rainbow

Savoy   **MG12002**   **USA**   **12 Inch 33**
2470   Body and Soul
2550   I Can't Believe That You're in Love with Me
2425   I Cover the Waterfront
2490   I Don't Stand a Ghost of a Chance with You
1390   Indiana (Back Home Again in Indiana)
2450   Love Walked In
2560   More Than You Know
2600   Over the Rainbow
2440   Penthouse Serenade (When We're Alone)
2580   Red Sails in the Sunset
1370   Stardust
1380   Somebody Loves Me
2420   Stompin' at the Savoy
2570   Undecided

Savoy   **MG12003**   **USA**   **12 Inch 33**
2590   All of Me
2510   Goodbye
2370   I Surrender, Dear
2830   I Want a Little Girl
2860   I'm Confessin' (That I Love You)
2540   I'm in the Mood for Love
2430   It's Easy to Remember
1360   Laura
2810   Man I Love, The
2820   Moonglow
2840   She's Funny That Way
2870   Stormy Weather (Keeps Rainin' All the Time)
2800   This Can't Be Love
2850   Until the Real Thing Comes Along

Savoy   **MG12008**   **USA**   **12 Inch 33**
2480   All the Things You Are
2520   Cottage for Sale, A
3000   Everything Happens to Me
2400   I Only Have Eyes for You

2980   On the Sunny Side of the Street
2290   Rosalie
2460   September Song
3010   Stairway to the Stars
       Note: Some issues of Savoy MG12008 have excluded "I Only Have Eyes for You,"
       and "On the Sunny Side of the Street."

Savoy   **MG12067**   **USA**   **12 Inch 33**
0870   Dark Eyesky
0860   Play, Fiddle, Play

Savoy   **MG15000**   **USA**   **10 Inch 33**
2480   All the Things You Are
2550   I Can't Believe That You're in Love with Me
2400   I Only Have Eyes for You
2580   Red Sails in the Sunset
2460   September Song
2420   Stompin' at the Savoy
2570   Undecided
2500   Yesterdays

Savoy   **MG15001**   **USA**   **10 Inch 33**
2470   Body and Soul
1390   Indiana (Back Home Again in Indiana)
1360   Laura
2560   More Than You Know
2600   Over the Rainbow
2440   Penthouse Serenade (When We're Alone)
1380   Somebody Loves Me
1370   Stardust

Savoy   **MG15002**   **USA**   **10 Inch 33**
2830   I Want a Little Girl
2860   I'm Confessin' (That I Love You)
2810   Man I Love, The
2820   Moonglow
2840   She's Funny That Way
2870   Stormy Weather (Keeps Rainin' All the Time)
2800   This Can't Be Love
2850   Until the Real Thing Comes Along

Savoy   **MG15004**   **USA**   **10 Inch 33**
2590   All of Me
2520   Cottage for Sale, A
3000   Everything Happens to Me
2370   I Surrender, Dear
2540   I'm in the Mood for Love
2980   On the Sunny Side of the Street
2990   Rosalie
3010   Stairway to the Stars

Savoy   **MG15026**   **USA**   **10 Inch 33**
0870   Dark Eyes
2510   Goodbye
2425   I Cover the Waterfront
2490   I Don't Stand a Ghost of a Chance with You
2430   It's Easy to Remember
2450   Love Walked In

Savoy   **SJL1118**   **USA**   **12 Inch 33**
2480   All the Things You Are
2520   Cottage for Sale, A
0870   Dark Eyesky
3000   Everything Happens to Me
2400   I Only Have Eyes for You
0890   Jumpin' at the Deuces
0880   Laff Slam Laff
2980   On the Sunny Side of the Street
0860   Play, Fiddle, Play
2990   Rosalie
2460   September Song
3010   Stairway to the Stars
2500   Yesterdays

Savoy   **SJL2207**   **USA**   **12 Inch 33**
2590   All of Me
2470   Body and Soul
2510   Goodbye
2550   I Can't Believe That You're in Love with Me
2425   I Cover the Waterfront
2490   I Don't Stand a Ghost of a Chance with You
2370   I Surrender, Dear
2830   I Want a Little Girl
2860   I'm Confessin' (That I Love You)
2540   I'm in the Mood for Love
1390   Indiana (Back Home Again in Indiana)
2430   It's Easy to Remember
1360   Laura
2450   Love Walked In
2810   Man I Love, The
2820   Moonglow
2560   More Than You Know
2600   Over the Rainbow
2440   Penthouse Serenade (When We're Alone)
2580   Red Sails in the Sunset
2840   She's Funny That Way
1380   Somebody Loves Me
1370   Stardust
2420   Stompin' at the Savoy
2870   Stormy Weather (Keeps Rainin' All the Time)
2800   This Can't Be Love
2570   Undecided
2850   Until the Real Thing Comes Along

Savoy   **WAJ-701**   **Jap**   **12 Inch 33**
2590   All of Me
2510   Goodbye
2370   I Surrender, Dear
2830   I Want a Little Girl
2860   I'm Confessin' (That I Love You)
2540   I'm in the Mood for Love
2430   It's Easy to Remember
1360   Laura
2810   Man I Love, The
2820   Moonglow
2840   She's Funny That Way
2870   Stormy Weather (Keeps Rainin' All the Time)
2800   This Can't Be Love
2850   Until the Real Thing Comes Along

Savoy   **XP-8007**   **USA**   **7 Inch 45EP**
2550   I Can't Believe That You're in Love with Me
1360   Laura
2580   Red Sails in the Sunset
2570   Undecided

Savoy   **XP-8008**   **USA**   **7 Inch 45EP**
2820   Moonglow
2460   September Song
1380   Somebody Loves Me
2500   Yesterdays

Savoy   **XP-8009**   **USA**   **7 Inch 45EP**
2830   I Want a Little Girl
2860   I'm Confessin' (That I Love You)
2560   More Than You Know
2840   She's Funny That Way

Savoy   **XP-8010**   **USA**   **7 Inch 45EP**
2810   Man I Love, The
2600   Over the Rainbow
2440   Penthouse Serenade (When We're Alone)
2800   This Can't Be Love

Savoy   **XP-8011**   **USA**   **7 Inch 45EP**
2470   Body and Soul
2400   I Only Have Eyes for You
2870   Stormy Weather (Keeps Rainin' All the Time)
2850   Until the Real Thing Comes Along

Savoy   **XP-8012**   **USA**   **7 Inch 45EP**
2480   All the Things You Are
1390   Indiana (Back Home Again in Indiana)
1370   Stardust
2420   Stompin' at the Savoy

Savoy   **XP-8013**   **USA**   **7 Inch 45EP**
3000   Everything Happens to Me
2980   On the Sunny Side of the Street
2990   Rosalie
3010   Stairway to the Stars

Savoy   **XP-8014**   **USA**   **7 Inch 45EP**
2590   All of Me
2520   Cottage for Sale, A
2510   Goodbye
2450   Love Walked In

Savoy   **XP-8015**   **USA**   **7 Inch 45EP**
2425   I Cover the Waterfront
2490   I Don't Stand a Ghost of a Chance with You
2370   I Surrender, Dear
2540   I'm in the Mood for Love

Savoy   **XP-8062**   **USA**   **7 Inch 45EP**
0870   Dark Eyesky
0890   Jumpin' at the Deuces
0880   Laff Slam Laff
0860   Play, Fiddle, Play

Savoy-Musidisc   **6004**   **Fra**   **12 Inch 33**
2470   Body and Soul
2550   I Can't Believe That You're in Love with Me
2425   I Cover the Waterfront
2490   I Don't Stand a Ghost of a Chance with You
1390   Indiana (Back Home Again in Indiana)
2450   Love Walked In
2560   More Than You Know
2580   Red Sails in the Sunset
1380   Somebody Loves Me
1370   Stardust
2420   Stompin' at the Savoy
2570   Undecided

Savoy-Musidisc   **6005**   **Fra**   **12 Inch 33**
2370   I Surrender, Dear
2830   I Want a Little Girl
2860   I'm Confessin' (That I Love You)
2540   I'm in the Mood for Love
2430   It's Easy to Remember
1360   Laura
2810   Man I Love, The
2820   Moonglow
2840   She's Funny That Way
2870   Stormy Weather (Keeps Rainin' All the Time)
2800   This Can't Be Love
2850   Until the Real Thing Comes Along

Savoy-Musidisc   **6006**   **Fra**   **12 Inch 33**
2590   All of Me
2480   All the Things You Are
2520   Cottage for Sale, A
3000   Everything Happens to Me
2510   Goodbye
2400   I Only Have Eyes for You
2980   On the Sunny Side of the Street
2600   Over the Rainbow
2440   Penthouse Serenade (When We're Alone)
2990   Rosalie
2460   September Song
3010   Stairway to the Stars

Savoy-Musidisc   **SA3011**   **Fra**   **7 Inch 45EP**
2980   On the Sunny Side of the Street
2600   Over the Rainbow
2440   Penthouse Serenade (When We're Alone)
2990   Rosalie

Selmer   **Y7086**   **Fra**   **10 Inch 78**
0510   Twistin' the Cat's Tail

Selmer   **Y7136**   **Fra**   **10 Inch 78**
1420   Don't Blame Me
1400   Man I Love, The

Selmer   **Y7137**   **Fra**   **10 Inch 78**
0740   Meatless Pay Day (Part 1)
0750   Meatless Pay Day (Part 2)

Selmer	**Y7138**	**Fra**	**10 Inch 78**
0760	Geronimo (Part 1)		
0770	Geronimo (Part 2)		

Selmer	**Y7139**	**Fra**	**10 Inch 78**
0170	Variations on a Theme (Part 1)		
0180	Variations on a Theme (Part 2)		

Selmer	**Y7216**	**Fra**	**10 Inch 78**
0330	I Hear a Rhapsody (Part 1)		
0340	I Hear a Rhapsody (Part 2)		

Selmer	**Y7225**	**Fra**	**10 Inch 78**
0530	Just You, Just Me		
0540	Yesterdays		

Selmer	**Y7228**	**Fra**	**10 Inch 78**
0260	Test Pilots (Part 1)		
0270	Test Pilots (Part 2)		

Shelton	**14005**	**USA**	**10 Inch 78**
0970	Gaslight		
0960	Loot to Boot		

Shelton	**14006**	**USA**	**10 Inch 78**
0940	Sweet Lorraine		
0950	Yesterdays		

Showcase	**33**	**USA**	**10 Inch 33**
4730	Misty		

Signature	**15135**	**USA**	**10 Inch 78**
0970	Gaslight		
0950	Yesterdays		

Signature	**15136**	**USA**	**10 Inch 78**
0960	Loot to Boot		
0940	Sweet Lorraine		

Smithsonian	**P11895**	**USA**	**12 Inch 33**
2180	Frankie and Johnny Fantasy		

Smithsonian	**PZ13455**	**USA**	**12 Inch 33**
0930	In the Middle		

Sonet	**SXP-2854**	**Den**	**7 Inch 45EP**
2130	Don't Worry 'Bout Me		
2180	Frankie and Johnny Fantasy		
2170	Love for Sale		
2070	Play, Piano, Play		

Sony	**SOPU-91**	**Jap**	**12 Inch 33**
4310	Avalon		
4250	Caravan		
4260	Lullaby of Birdland		
4200	Memories of You		

4220   (There Is) No Greater Love
4290   Will You Still Be Mine?

Spinorama	M181	USA	**12 Inch 33**

0150   Cloudburst
0570   Easy to Love
0620   In the Beginning

Spinorama	S181	USA	**12 Inch 33**

0150   Cloudburst
0570   Easy to Love
0620   In the Beginning

Spotlite	102	Eng	**12 Inch 33**

1820   Bird's Nest
1830   Bird's Nest
1840   Bird's Nest
1850   Cool Blues
1860   Cool Blues
1870   Cool Blues
1880   Cool Blues
1780   Dark Shadows
1790   Dark Shadows
1800   Dark Shadows
1810   Dark Shadows
1760   This Is Always
1770   This Is Always

Spotlite	105	Eng	**12 Inch 33**

1810   Dark Shadows

Spotlite	SPJ 129	Eng	**12 Inch 33**

2110   Blues Garni
2120   Don't Worry 'Bout Me
2130   Don't Worry 'Bout Me
2140   Don't Worry 'Bout Me
2180   Frankie and Johnny Fantasy
2160   Loose Nut
2170   Love for Sale
2080   Love Is the Strangest Game
2090   Love Is the Strangest Game
1890   Pastel
2070   Play, Piano, Play
2190   Sloe Gin Fizz
1900   Trio
1910   Trio

Spotlite	SPJ 145	Eng	**12 Inch 33**

2620   Cherokee (Part 1)
2630   Cherokee (Part 2)

Stars for Defense	160	USA	**16 Inch TX**

6070   Dreamy
6080   Where or When
6060   Will You Still Be Mine?

Stars for Defense	269	USA	**12 Inch TX**

6150   Dreamstreet
6090   Just One of Those Things
6130   Lady Is a Tramp, The

Stars for Defense   336   USA   **12 Inch TX**
6470   Back in Your Own Back Yard
6480   El Papa Grande
6490   Just One of Those Things

Storia della Musica   Vol. X, No. 9   Ity   **7 Inch 33**
3220   Lazy River

Summit   103   USA   **10 Inch 78**
1470   Slamboree
1450   Wrap Your Troubles in Dreams

Summit   104   USA   **10 Inch 78**
1440   Humoresque
1460   Smoke Gets in Your Eyes

Super Disc   1006   USA   **10 Inch 78**
0990   One O'Clock Jump
0980   Three O'Clock in the Morning

Super Disc   1007   USA   **10 Inch 78**
1000   Harvard Blues

Super Disc   1008   USA   **10 Inch 78**
1010   Slammin' Around

Supraphon   0 15 2113   Cze   **12 Inch 33**
4040   Anything Goes

Swing   406   Fra   **10 Inch 78**
1860   Blow Top Blues

Tono   BZ19003   Den   **10 Inch 78**
1840   Bird's Nest
1880   Cool Blues

Tono   BZ19014   Den   **10 Inch 78**
2940   I Can't Give You Anything But Love
2910   Pavanne Mood

Trio   PA3145   Jap   **12 Inch 33**
1970   Blue Lou

Trip Jazz   TLP5504   USA   **12 Inch 33**
1570   Bouncin' with Me
1660   Full Moon and Empty Arms
1680   If I Loved You

Trip Jazz   TLP5519   USA   **12 Inch 33**

3150   Bonny Boy
3210   Cologne
3130   Deep Purple
3100   I Let a Song Go Out of My Heart
3120   Jitterbug Waltz

3220	Lazy River
3190	Minor with the Trio
3200	No Moon
3180	Quaker, The
3170	Relaxin' at Sugar Ray's
3060	Scatter-Brain
3160	Tippin' Out with Erroll

U P International   **LPUP 5115**   **Ity**   **12 Inch 33**

7900	Girl from Ipanema, The
7930	I'll Remember April
7910	Misty
7940	Misty (No. 2)
7880	Shadow of Your Smile, The
7920	Tell It Like It Is
7860	There Will Never Be Another You
7950	Variations on Misty
7890	Yesterday

U.S. Treasury Dept.   **142**   **USA**   **16 Inch TX**
Guest Star Series

| 2780 | Blue Skies |
| 2790 | Huckle Buck, The |

United   **US 7722**   **USA**   **12 Inch 33**

1980	Blue Lou (Part 1)
1990	Blue Lou (Part 2)
2030	Four O'Clock Jump
2340	Just You, Just Me
2000	One O'Clock Jump
2660	Tenderly
2020	Three O'Clock Jump
2010	Two O'Clock Jump

V Disc   **735B**   **USA**   **12 Inch 78**

| 1630 | Laura |
| 1640 | Yesterdays |

Verve   **VLP 9105**   **Eng**   **12 Inch 33**

| 1840 | Bird's Nest |
| 1860 | Blow Top Blues |

Vogue   **5002**   **Fra**   **10 Inch 78**

| 2270 | Early in Paris |
| 2280 | These Foolish Things (Remind Me of You) |

Vogue   **5003**   **Fra**   **10 Inch 78**

| 2250 | Lover Man (Oh, Where Can You Be?) |
| 2260 | What Is This Thing Called Love? |

Vogue   **509080**   **Fra**   **12 Inch 33**

| 2700 | St. Louis Blues |

Vogue   **CLD 753**   **Fra**   **12 Inch 33**

| 1780 | Dark Shadows |
| 1850 | Hot Blues |

Vogue   **CMDGN 766**   **Fra**   **12 Inch 33**
1980   Blue Lou (Part 1)
1990   Blue Lou (Part 2)
2030   Four O'Clock Jump
2040   Lover (Part 1)
2050   Lover (Part 2)
2000   One O'Clock Jump
2020   Three O'Clock Jump
2010   Two O'Clock Jump

Vogue   **CMDGN 9853**   **Fra**   **12 Inch 33**
2220   Cherchez la Femme
2690   Georgia on My Mind
2740   Erroll's a Garner
2720   Erroll's Peril
2730   I'm Coming Virginia
2230   Indiana (Back Home Again in Indiana)
2340   Just You, Just Me
2760   Laura
2770   Lavande (Little Girl)
2710   My Old Kentucky Home
2700   St. Louis Blues
2670   Someone to Watch Over Me
2680   Take the "A" Train
2660   Tenderly

Vogue   **CMDINT 9515 Fra**   **12 Inch 33**
2260   What Is This Thing Called Love?

Vogue   **DP-28**   **Fra**   **12 Inch 33**
2220   Cherchez la Femme
2740   Erroll's a Garner
2720   Erroll's Peril
2130   Don't Worry 'Bout Me
2180   Frankie and Johnny Fantasy
2690   Georgia on My Mind
3100   I Let a Song Go Out of My Heart
2730   I'm Coming Virginia
2230   Indiana (Back Home Again in Indiana)
3120   Jitterbug Waltz
2340   Just You, Just Me
2760   Laura
2770   Lavande (Little Girl)
2170   Love for Sale
2710   My Old Kentucky Home
1890   Pastel
2070   Play, Piano, Play
2700   St. Louis Blues
3060   Scatter-Brain
2670   Someone to Watch Over Me
2680   Take the "A" Train
2660   Tenderly
1910   Trio
3090   What Is This Thing Called Love?

Vogue   **DP-64**   **Fra**   **12 Inch 33**
2070   Play, Piano, Play

Vogue		**EPL 7006**	**Fra**	**7 Inch 45EP**
0970	Gaslight			
0960	Loot to Boot			
0940	Sweet Lorraine			
0950	Yesterdays			

Vogue		**EPL 7022**	**Fra**	**7 Inch 45EP**
3080	Again			
3130	Deep Purple			
3100	I Let a Song Go Out of My Heart			
3120	Jitterbug Waltz			

Vogue		**EPV 1002**	**Eng**	**7 Inch 45EP**
1980	Blue Lou (Part 1)			
1990	Blue Lou (Part 2)			

Vogue		**LAE 12001**	**Eng**	**12 Inch 33**
1980	Blue Lou (Part 1)			
1990	Blue Lou (Part 2)			
2030	Four O'Clock Jump			
2040	Lover (Part 1)			
2050	Lover (Part 2)			
2000	One O'Clock Jump			
2020	Three O'Clock Jump			
2010	Two O'Clock Jump			

Vogue		**LAE 12002**	**Eng**	**12 Inch 33**
1860	Blow Top Blues			
1880	Cool Blues			
1780	Dark Shadows			

Vogue		**LAE 12209**	**Eng**	**12 Inch 33**
2130	Don't Worry 'Bout Me			
2180	Frankie and Johnny Fantasy			
2170	Love for Sale			
1890	Pastel			
2070	Play, Piano, Play			
1910	Trio			

Vogue		**LD 019**	**Fra**	**10 Inch 33**
2740	Erroll's a Garner			
2720	Erroll's Peril			
2690	Georgia on My Mind			
2730	I'm Coming Virginia			
2710	My Old Kentucky Home			
2700	St. Louis Blues			
2750	Stars Fell on Alabama			
2680	Take the "A" Train			

Vogue		**LD 024**	**Fra**	**10 Inch 33**
1980	Blue Lou (Part 1)			
1990	Blue Lou (Part 2)			
2030	Four O'Clock Jump			
2040	Lover (Part 1)			
2050	Lover (Part 2)			
2000	One O'Clock Jump			
2020	Three O'Clock Jump			
2010	Two O'Clock Jump			

Vogue   **LD 031**   **Fra**   **10 Inch 33**
2220   Cherchez la Femme
2270   Early in Paris
2230   Indiana (Back Home Again in Indiana)
2340   Just You, Just Me
2760   Laura
2770   Lavande (Little Girl)
2670   Someone to Watch Over Me
2660   Tenderly

Vogue   **LD 057**   **Fra**   **10 Inch 33**
1860   Hot Blues

Vogue   **LD 059**   **Fra**   **10 Inch 33**
1790   Dark Shadows

Vogue   **LD 064**   **Fra**   **10 Inch 33**
0150   Cloudburst
0570   Easy to Love
0620   In the Beginning
0520   Variations on a Nursery Rhyme (Mairzy Doats, Yes, We Have No Bananas, The Music
       Goes 'Round and 'Round, Everything I've Got [Belongs to You])

Vogue   **LD 065**   **Fra**   **10 Inch 33**
3080   Again
3130   Deep Purple
3110   Goodbye
3100   I Let a Song Go Out of My Heart
3120   Jitterbug Waltz
3060   Scatter-Brain
3070   Through a Long and Sleepless Night
3090   What Is This Thing Called Love?

Vogue   **LD 076**   **Fra**   **10 Inch 33**
3150   Bonny Boy
3210   Cologne
3220   Lazy River
3190   Minor with the Trio
3200   No Moon
3180   Quaker, The
3170   Relaxin' at Sugar Ray's
3160   Tippin' Out with Erroll

Vogue   **LD 084**   **Fra**   **10 Inch 33**
3780   Garner in Hollywood
3790   Lotus Blues
3830   New York Concerto
3820   Six P.M.
3800   This Is My Beloved
3810   Until the Real Thing Comes Along

Vogue   **LD 560-30**   **Fra**   **12 Inch 33**
2220   Cherchez la Femme
2740   Erroll's a Garner
2720   Erroll's Peril
2690   Georgia on My Mind
2730   I'm Coming Virginia
2230   Indiana (Back Home Again in Indiana)
2340   Just You, Just Me

2760	Laura
2770	Lavande (Little Girl)
2710	My Old Kentucky Home
2700	St. Louis Blues
2670	Someone to Watch Over Me
2680	Take the "A" Train
2660	Tenderly

Vogue   **LDE 004**   **Eng**   **10 Inch 33**
| 1860 | Blow Top Blues |
| 1880 | Cool Blues |

Vogue   **LDE 016**   **Eng**   **10 Inch 33**
| 1780 | Dark Shadows |

Vogue   **LDE 034**   **Eng**   **10 Inch 33**
3080	Again
3130	Deep Purple
3110	Goodbye
3100	I Let a Song Go Out of My Heart
3120	Jitterbug Waltz
3060	Scatter-Brain
3070	Through a Long and Sleepless Night
3090	What Is This Thing Called Love?

Vogue   **LDM 30003**   **Fra**   **12 Inch 33**
1980	Blue Lou (Part 1)
1990	Blue Lou (Part 2)
2030	Four O'Clock Jump
2000	One O'Clock Jump
2020	Three O'Clock Jump
2010	Two O'Clock Jump

Vogue   **LDM 30067**   **Fra**   **12 Inch 33**
1850	Blow Top Blues
1860	Blow Top Blues
1780	Dark Shadows

Vogue   **LDM 30230**   **Fra**   **12 Inch 33**
2550	I Can't Believe That You're in Love with Me
2860	I'm Confessin' (That I Love You)
2820	Moonglow
2980	On the Sunny Side of the Street
2580	Red Sails in the Sunset
2840	She's Funny That Way
1380	Somebody Loves Me
2420	Stompin' at the Savoy
2870	Stormy Weather (Keeps Rainin' All the Time)
2800	This Can't Be Love

Vogue   **MDR 9168**   **Fra**   **12 Inch 33**
2130	Don't Worry 'Bout Me
2180	Frankie and Johnny Fantasy
2170	Love for Sale
1890	Pastel
2070	Play, Piano, Play
1910	Trio

Vogue	**SPO-17054**	**Fra**	**7 Inch 45EP**
3060	Scatter-Brain		

Vogue	**V566**	**Den**	**10 Inch 78**
2040	Lover (Part 1)		
2050	Lover (Part 2)		

Vogue	**V568**	**Den**	**10 Inch 78**
1980	Blue Lou (Part 1)		
1990	Blue Lou (Part 2)		

Vogue	**V2004**	**Eng**	**10 Inch 78**
2040	Lover (Part 1)		
2050	Lover (Part 2)		

Vogue	**V2026**	**Eng**	**10 Inch 78**
2270	Early in Paris		
2280	These Foolish Things (Remind Me of You)		

Vogue	**V2047**	**Eng**	**10 Inch 78**
1980	Blue Lou (Part 1)		
1990	Blue Lou (Part 2)		

Vogue	**V2069**	**Eng**	**10 Inch 78**
1470	Slamboree		
1450	Wrap Your Troubles in Dreams		

Vogue	**V2086**	**Eng**	**10 Inch 78**
3120	Jitterbug Waltz		
3090	What Is This Thing Called Love?		

Vogue	**V2107**	**Eng**	**10 Inch 78**
3060	Scatter-Brain		
3070	Through a Long and Sleepless Night		

Vogue	**V2230**	**Eng**	**10 Inch 78**
2230	Indiana (Back Home Again in Indiana)		
2770	Lavande (Little Girl)		

Vogue	**V2244**	**Eng**	**10 Inch 78**
1880	Cool Blues		

Vogue	**V2271**	**Eng**	**10 Inch 78**
2000	One O'Clock Jump		
2010	Two O'Clock Jump		

Vogue	**V2272**	**Eng**	**10 Inch 78**
2030	Four O'Clock Jump		
2020	Three O'Clock Jump		

Vogue	**V2274**	**Eng**	**10 Inch 78**
2340	Just You, Just Me		

Vogue	**V3063**	**Fra**	**10 Inch 78**
3060	Scatter-Brain		
3070	Through a Long and Sleepless Night		

Vogue		V3066	Fra	10 Inch 78
3120	Jitterbug Waltz			
3090	What Is This Thing Called Love?			

Vogue		V3069	Fra	10 Inch 78
3110	Goodbye			
3100	I Let a Song Go Out of My Heart			

Vogue		V3071	Fra	10 Inch 78
3080	Again			
3130	Deep Purple			

Vogue		V3118	Fra	10 Inch 78
3830	New York Concerto			
3820	Six P.M.			

Vogue		V3141	Fra	10 Inch 78
3150	Bonny Boy			
3160	Tippin' Out with Erroll			

Vogue		V3142	Fra	10 Inch 78
3190	Minor with the Trio			
3200	No Moon			

Vogue		V3143	Fra	10 Inch 78
3220	Lazy River			
3170	Relaxin' at Sugar Ray's			

Vogue		V3144	Fra	10 Inch 78
3210	Cologne			
3180	Quaker, The			

Vogue		VJT 3003	Eng	12 Inch 33
1980	Blue Lou (Part 1)			
1990	Blue Lou (Part 2)			
2030	Four O'Clock Jump			
2340	Just You, Just Me			
2040	Lover (Part 1)			
2050	Lover (Part 2)			
2000	One O'Clock Jump			
2020	Three O'Clock Jump			
2010	Two O'Clock Jump			

Voices of Vista		2	USA	12 Inch TX
6510	Mimi			
5380	Misty			
6550	Paris Mist (Bossa Nova)			
6500	Theme from "A New Kind of Love"			

WGM (Roulette)		2A	USA	12 Inch 33
2180	Frankie and Johnny Fantasy			
1890	Pastel			
1910	Trio			

TITLE INDEX

All titles that are part of a medley are noted with an asterisk (*). Numbers refer to index numbers, not page numbers.

Lenox Hill Blues 5350
Let's Fall in Love 4490, T1370*
Lick and a Promise, A 0480, 0600
Like It Is (see also "Tell It Like It Is") 7420,
    T5480, T5540, T5910, T6500
Lil' Darlin' T5080
Liza 1240
Long Ago (And Far Away) 3520
Look, Ma—All Hands! (see also "7-11
    Jump") 4230
Look of Love, The 7830, T7070, T7140,
    T8650
Loose Nut 2150, 2160
Loot to Boot (see also "Opus 1") 0800,
    0960, 1020, T0060
Lot of Livin' to Do, A 7550, T5920, T5990
Lotus Blues 3790
Louise 5800, 6520
Love T5610, T5900, T5970, T6600, T6810,
    T6920
Love for Sale 2170, 4400, 6050, T1020,
    T1340, T1390, T2370, T3710, T4030,
    T4450, T5070
Love in Bloom 4960
Love Is Here to Stay T1850
Love Is the Strangest Game 2080, 2090,
    2100
Love Is the Thing (Part 1) 0590
Love Is the Thing (Part 2) (see "Be My Love")
Love Makes the World Go 'Round T5700
Love Me or Leave Me 4090, T1670
Love Walked In 2450, 6980
Lovely to Look At 7010
Lover 2040, 2050, 3640, T1150, T1330,
    T1580, T1750, T1810, T1870, T3170
Lover Come Back to Me 1540, 6410, T2790,
    T4630, T4810
Lover Man (Oh, Where Can You Be?) 2240,
    2250, 7650, 8040, T7460, T7670, T8410,
    T8840, T8940, T9020, T9050, T9290,
    T9440
Loving Touch, The (see also "Blue Ec-
    stasy") 7700, T6690, T8340
Lullaby of Birdland 4260, 4470, T1080,
    T1380, T1420, T1450, T1730
Lullaby of the Leaves 3230, T0620
Lullaby in Rhythm 4320, T1210
Lulu's Back in Town 6320, T5250
Mack the Knife 6400, T2740, T3010
Make Believe 7030
Mambo 207 5430
Mambo Blues 4640
Mambo Carmel 5060
Mambo Erroll 6310, 6780, 7150, T2050,
    T3310, T4930
Mambo Garner 4650

Mambo Gotham 6170
Mambo Nights 4660
Mame T5680
Man I Love, The (see also "Man O'
    Mine") 2810, 5320
Man O' Mine (see also "The Man I
    Love") 1400
Margie 3240, T0640
Margin for Erroll (see also "Perpetual Emo-
    tion") 3870
Mary O' T3070
Mean to Me 4380
Meatless Pay Day 0740, 0750
Medley (unknown titles) 5620, T7200
Memories of You 0100, 1720, 4200
Michele T6640*
Mimi 6510
Minor with the Trio 3190
Misty (see also "Variations On
    Misty") 4730, 5380, 6420, 7210, 7910,
    T1350, T1400, T1460, T1660, T1720,
    T1790, T1830, T1920, T2250, T2270,
    T2480, T2730, T2750, T2870, T2960,
    T3000, T3040, T3220, T3260, T3380,
    T3520, T3840, T3990, T4070, T4350,
    T4440, T4570, T4640, T4650, T4900,
    T4940, T5130, T5240, T5300, T5440,
    T5550, T5620, T5710, T5870, T6090,
    T6150, T6160, T6220, T6260, T6300,
    T6350, T6410, T6440, T6620, T6750,
    T6830, T6840, T6930, T7000, T7030,
    T7080, T7110, T7290, T7300, T7390,
    T7430, T7680, T7820, T7890, T7970,
    T8060, T8190, T8270, T8280, T8350,
    T8450, T8530, T8640, T8660, T8710,
    T8730, T8800, T8810, T8870, T9070,
    T9200, T9330, T9420, T9520
Misty (No. 2) 7940
Moment's Delight 5650
Mood, The T0090
Mood Indigo 1130
Mood Island 7780, T6460, T6540, T7170,
    T7580, T8040, T8740, T8950, T9180,
    T9590
Moon River 7180, 7300, T3510, T3750,
    T4060, T4190, T4430
Moonglow 2820, 4500, 5330, T1370*, T1430
Moonlight Moods (see "Variations on a
    Theme [Part 2]")
More 7230, 7340, 7390, T3210, T3830,
    T3920, T4320, T5090, T5220, T5310,
    T5330, T5490, T6070, T6140, T6340
More Than You Know 0110, 0560, 2560,
    T1220
Moroccan Mambo 6620
Moroccan Quarter 5840

Reverie 2880
Robbins' Nest 3890, 4140, T0680, T1190
Rosalie 2988, 2989, 2990, 4750, T0340,
    T0540
Rose Room 5190
Rosetta 1270
Russian Lullaby 4610
'S Wonderful 4210, T1030, T1110
Salud Segovia 4990
St. James Infirmary 5030, T3850
St. Louis Blues 1290, 2700, 4330, 6230,
    T2620
Satin Doll T3530, T3860, T3940, T4210,
    T4400, T5850, T6820, T8930, T9210,
    T9430
Scatter-Brain 3060, 3410, T0470
Schoner Gigolo (Just a Gigolo) 6930
September in the Rain 3040
September Song 2460
Serenade in Blue 3310
Shadow of Your Smile, The 7410, 7880,
    T5040, T5230, T5320, T5430, T5530,
    T5730, T5790, T6110, T6280, T6430,
    T6720, T6970, T7160, T7320, T7440,
    T7570, T7780, T7940, T7990, T8210,
    T8330, T8460, T8680
Shadows (see also "No More
    Shadows") 6220
Shake It, But Don't Break It (see "Like It Is")
Sheik of Araby, The 3290
Sherry Lynn Flip 1330
She's Funny That Way 2840
Six P.M. 3820
Skylark 2930
Slamboree 1470
Slammin' Around 1010
Sleep 4910
Slightly Out of Tune (Desafinado) T7900*
Sloe Gin Fizz 2190
Smoke Gets in Your Eyes 1460
Smooth One, A 4930
Smooth Sailing (see "Garner's Escape")
Soft and Warm 0380
Soliloquy 5520
Solitaire 4900, 5580, 5630, T1940, T1970,
    T2060, T2220, T5590
Some of These Days 5230, 6240, T2310,
    T2600, T2660, T4890
Somebody Loves Me 0020, 0050, 0060,
    1140, 1380
Someone to Watch Over Me 2670, 6990,
    8150, T3720, T4170, T4850, T8140,
    T8620, T8960, T9160, T9390
Something 8010, T7510, T7650, T7850,
    T8120, T8180, T8220, T8310, T8470,
    T8690, T8770, T9530

Something Happens (see also "Feeling Is Be-
    lieving") T8380, T8560, T8750
Sometimes I'm Happy 1530
Something to Remember You By T2440
Song from Moulin Rouge (Where Is Your
    Heart), The 5700
Sonny Boy 6860, 7160, T3190, T3450,
    T3730, T4460, T4550, T4580
Sophisticated Lady 3850, T0590, T2590
Spinning Wheel 7840
Spring Is Here 3560, 3570, 3580, 3590, 3600,
    3610, 6630*, 7100*, T0070, T3160*,
    T3470*, T3930*, T5060*
Stairway to the Stars 1960, 3010, T0950
Stardust 1370, 6300
Stars Fell on Alabama 2750
Stella by Starlight 6670, 6910, 7120, T2460,
    T3700, T3800, T4010, T4410, T5980,
    T6180, T7530, T8420, T8590, T9010*,
    T9150, T9410
Steve's Song 6540
Stompin' at the Savoy 2420, 4350, T0160,
    T0280, T1820, T2100
Stormy Weather (Keeps Rainin' All the
    Time) 2870, T0770
Straight Ahead T3100
Strangers in the Night 7760, T5810, T6400,
    T7040, T7050, T7060, T7120, T7230,
    T7860
Stride Out 6460
Strike Up the Band 6970, T5400
Stumbling 5540
Summertime 3250, 3940, T0630, T0970
Sunny 7670, T9250*, T9500*
Surrey with the Fringe on Top, The (see also
    "Oklahoma! Medley") 5980, T3280,
    T3680, T4080
Sweet and Lovely 4740, 6390, T3020, T5190
Sweet Georgia Brown 1160
Sweet Lorraine 0940, 1090, 6160
Sweet Sue-Just You 4360, 4670
Sweetheart of All My Dreams 0910
Symphony 1560
Take No Holes (see "Talk No Holes [In My
    Clothes]")
Take the "A" Train 2680, T0080
Taking a Chance on Love T4620
Talk No Holes (In My Clothes) 2200
Taylor-Made Blues T3080
Tea for Two 8000, T0010*, T0380, T3390,
    T8230
Teach Me Tonight 5050
Tease, The 6590
Teaser, The (see "The Tease")
Tell It Like It Is (see also "Like It Is") 7920
Tenderly 2660

What's New? 4020, T3910
When a Gypsy Makes His Violin Cry 4920,
    7990, T7720
When Johnny Comes Marching
    Home 3430, 3440, T0240, T0560
When Paris Cries 6030
When Your Lover Has Gone T2190, T4720
When You're Smiling (The Whole World
    Smiles with You) 3480, 3490, 3500,
    3510, 6140, T0200, T1250
Where or When 1750, 5130, 6080, 7250,
    T2040, T2260, T3550, T3760, T4220,
    T4500, T4590, T4770, T4840, T5160
White Rose Bounce (see also "In the Begin-
    ning" and "Opus 1") 0820, 1030
Who? 4850
Will You Still Be Mine? 4290, 6060, T1360,
    T1410, T1470, T2280, T2400, T3650,
    T3980
Willow Me 4060
Winchester Cathedral T5690
With Every Breath I Take 4050
WNEW Theme Song 2290, 2320

Wrap Your Troubles in Dreams 1450
Yesterday 7820, 7890, T7700, T8030,
    T8890*
Yesterdays 0300, 0540, 0950, 1640, 2500,
    4410, 4840, 8130, T0400, T3540, T4490
You Are My Sunshine 4800
You Are the Sunshine of My Life T9100,
    T9260, T9340
You Brought a New Kind of Love to
    Me 6560
You Do Something to Me 6190, T2330,
    T2710
You Go to My Head 5470
You Made Me Love You 1060, 6840
You Turned Me Around 7620, T6480
You Were Born to Be Kissed 0360
You'd Be So Nice to Come Home To 5560
Young Love (see "No Moon")
You're Blasé 0550, 3840
You're Driving Me Crazy (What Did I
    Do?) 3920
You've Got Me Crying Again 4520

ARTIST INDEX

Edwards, Teddy 2620, 2630, T0920
Eidus, Arnold 5380-5400, 5630-5690
Eldridge, Roy T1000
Elton, William 5670-5690
Enevoldsen, Bob 6500-6590
English, Bill T6940-T7040, T7140-T7200
Ennois, Leonard "Lucky" 1590-1620

Fatool, Nick 1660-1690

Gaskin, Leonard 2880-2970, 3020-3130
Gentry, Charles 6500-6590
Gillespie, John "Dizzy" 0900-0930
Glickman, Harry 5380-5400
Glow, Bernie 5380-5400, 5630-5690, 7480,
   7520, 7530, 7570
Godfrey, Arthur T2160
Gold, Norman 8090, T8490-T8550
Goldberg, Alvin 5630-5690
Gray, Wardell 1970
Green, Urbie 5630-5660
Guilet, Daniel 5380-5400, 5630-5660

Hafer, John 5380-5400, 5630-5690
Haggart, Bob T6670, T7050, T7280, T7290
Hall, Al 5190-5460, 5670-5690, 6470-6490
Hanna, Jake T8200, T8210, T8700-T8720
Hartman, Johnny 3020-3050
Hartman, Lenny 1590-1620
Hash, Ted 6500-6590
Hawkins, Coleman 2330
Heard, Eugene "Fats" 4190-4830, T1030-
   T1310, T1340-T1360, T1380-T1470
Heath, Jimmy 2320
Heath, Percy 2320, 2330
Held, Julius M. 5380-5400, 5630-5690
Herman, Woody 4490-4590, T1370, T1430
Hinton, Milt 5630-5660, 7370-7470
Hollander, Max 5380-5400, 5630-5660
Hyman, Dick T2160-T2172

Isaacs, Ike 7480-7570, T5410-T5570, T5740-
   T6000, T6040-T6220, T6260-T6410,
   T6600-T6660

Jackson, Greig "Chubby" 0900-0930
Jemmott, Gerald 7580-7680
Jenkins, George 7370, 7380
Johnson, James "Osie" 5630-5690, T2160-
   T2190

Katzman, Harry 5670-5690
Kessel, Barney 6500-6590
Killian, Al 0900-0930
Klee, Harry 1590-1620, 6500-6590

Lambert, Dave 2620-2650, T0920
Lamond, Don T1620, T1630, T1750, T1760
Lang, Ronnie 6500-6590
Leeman, Cliff 0700-0810
Levy, John Jr. 1020-1310, 1360-1390
Lewis, Carroll "Cappy" 6500-6590
Livingston, Ulysses 2220, 2230
Lomakin, Nick T0010, T0020
Lomask, Milton 5380-5400
Lookofsky, Harry 5670-5690
Lovelle, Herbert 7390-7470, T6680-T6720

Mandel, Hy 1590-1620
Mangual, Jose 7390-8190, T5290-T5340,
   T5410-T5570, T5740-T6000, T6040-
   T6220, T6260-T6410, T6600-T6660,
   T6680-T6720, T6750-T7040, T7140-
   T7200, T7320-T7490, T7520-T8160,
   T8280-T8350, T8390-T8480, T8580-
   T8690, T8730-T8800, T8830-T9540
Mann, Herbie 5380-5400
Mariniello, Bobby T4650-T4700, T5190-
   T5210, T5250-T5270, T5350-T5400,
   T5580-T5600, T6010-T6030, T6230-
   T6250, T6730, T6740, T7500, T7510,
   T8170-T8190, T8360, T8370
Marowitz, Sam 5380-5400
Martin, Kelly 5700-6490, 6600-7360, T1990-
   T2100, T2120-T2150, T2200-T2720,
   T2740-T2780, T2820-T2940, T2960-
   T3220, T3250-T3370, T3400-T4640,
   T4710-T5180
Mason, Harvey T6750-T6930
McCarty, Ernest Jr. 7860-8030, T6940-
   T7040, T7140-T7200, T7320-T7490,
   T7520-T8160, T8280-T8350, T8390-
   T8480, T8580-T8690, T8730-T8800
McGhee, Howard 2000-2030, 2320
McKusick, Hal 5380-5400
Meldonian, Dick 5630-5690
Melnikoff, Harry 5630-5690
Mettome, Doug 5630-5690
Miller, Mitch 5380-5400, 5630-5690
Mills, Jackie 1590-1620, 1970-2050
Mince, Johnny T2160
Miroff, Seymour 5380-5400, 5630-5660
Mitchell, Keith "Red" 6500-6590
Moore, Oscar 2340
Monte, George 5380-5400
Moskowicz, Herbert T5290-T5340

Nash, Dick 6500-6590
Noel, Dick 6500-6590
Nozilo, Ben T0010-T0020
O'Kane, Charles 5380-5400
Orloff, Eugene 5380-5400, 5670-5690
Ortega, Anthony 5630-5690

Pacheco, Johnny 7370, 7380
Palmieri, Remo T2160, T2171
Parker, Charlie 1760-1880
Parker, Johnny T2160
Perkins, Walter T5290-T5340
Persip, Charles 7790-7850
Pierce, Nat 5380-5400, 5630-5690
Poliakin, Raoul 5670-5690
Powell, Gordon "Specs" 5190-5460
Powers, Patti 0910
Pratt, Bobby 0220, 0230, 0260, 0270
Pupa, Jimmy T0010, T0020

Quinichette, Paul 5670-5690

Reese, Della T8190
Rehak, Frank 5630-5690
Reider, Edward 5380-5400
Reuss, Alan 1590-1620
Rich, Buddy T1000
Richardson, Jerome 7480, 7520, 7530, 7570
Richardson, Wally 7390-7470
Roberts, George 6500-6590
Robinson, Eli 0900-0930
Roma, Jimmy 0900-0930
Rosengarden, Bobby T1750, T1760, T2110, T7060-T7080, T7300, T7310
Ruffo, Mascagni "Musky" 0900-0930
Ruther, Wyatt 4190-4830, T1030-T1310, T1340-T1360, T1380-T1470
Ryerson, Art 7370, 7380

Sachelle, Sammy 1590-1620
Sachs, Aaron 5630-5660
Schachter, Julius 5380-5400, 5630-5690
Sebesky, Don 7480, 7520, 7530, 7570
Shapiro, Harvey 5380-5400
Shaughnessy, Ed T2730, T2790, T2800, T3230, T3240, T6670, T7050, T7280, T7290, T8220, T8230, T8380, T8560, T8570
Shavers, Charlie 0700-0810
Shulman, Sylvan 5380-5400, 5670-5690
Simmons, John 0370-0460, 2220, 2230, 2350-2650, 2760-2870, 2980-3010, 3150-3370, 3390-3770, 3840-4010, 4140-4180, T0150-T1000, T1020
Singer, Lou 1720-1750
Smith, Charlie 2880-2970, 3020-3130
Smith, Jimmie 7480-7680, 7860-8030, T5410-T5570, T5740-T6000, T6040-

T6220, T6260-T6410, T6600-T6660, T7320-T7490, T7520-T8160, T8280-T8350, T8390-T8480, T8580-T8690, T8730-T8800
Smith, Hezekiah "Stuff" 0250-0270
Spencer, Richard O. 7480, 7520, 7530, 7570
Stamm, Marvin 7480, 7520, 7530, 7570
Stevens, Leith 6500-6590
Stewart, Leroy "Slam" 0700, 0710, 0860-0890, 0980-1010, 1320-1350, 1440-1470
Stewart, Teddy 2340
Still, Ray 1590-1620
Stoller, Alvin 2350-2610, 2800-2870, 2980-3010, 6500-6590
Sunkel, Philip C. Jr. 5670-5690

Talbert, Tommy 1590-1620
Tate, Grady 8040-8190
Thompson, Chuck 2620-2650, 2760, 2770
Thompson, Eli "Lucky" 0240-0270
Torff, Brian T8830-T9540
Traxler, Gene T2160-T2190

Urbont, Harry 5630-5660

Van Lake, Turk 0900-0930
Venegas, Victor T6680-T6720, T6750-T6930

West, Harold "Doc" 0370-0460, 0820-0890, 0980-1010, 1320-1350, 1440-1470, 1760-1920, 2780, 2790, 3150-3370
Wettling, George 0220, 0230
Williams, Andy T5240, T5610, T5630-T5680
Williams, Jackie 8090
Williams, John T8220, T8230, T8380, T8560, T8570, T8810, T8820
Wilson, Flip T7270
Wilson, Rossiere "Shadow" 0900-0930, 3390-3770, 3840-4010, 4140-4180, T0150-T1000, T1020
Winograd, Arthur 5630-5660
Winter, Paul 5630-5660
Wright, Florence 3380

Young, Al 0900-0930
Young, James "Trummy" 0900-0930

Zanoni, Gene 0900-0930
Zir, Isadore 5380-5400, 5630-5690

FILMOGRAPHY

The following is a list of Garner on film or video tape. Unquestionably more exists because of the vast television exposure Garner received during his lifetime. The dates given are the actual date the performance took place, if known; otherwise an approximate date is supplied. In some instances the performance and the telecast date are the same.

October 23, 1960   Ed Sullivan Show (New York)
Erroll Garner (p), Eddie Calhoun (b), Kelly Martin (d)
    Dreamy, I Get a Kick Out of You

February 5, 1961   Ed Sullivan Show (New York)
Erroll Garner (p), Eddie Calhoun (b), Kelly Martin (d)
    Solitaire, It's All Right with Me

March 26, 1961   Ed Sullivan Show (New York)
Erroll Garner (p), Eddie Calhoun (b), Kelly Martin (d)
    Oklahoma Medley: Oh, What a Beautiful Mornin'/People Will Say We're in Love/ The Surrey with the Fringe on Top, Misty

January 30, 1963   Kraft Music Hall (New York); Perry Como, host
Erroll Garner (p), Eddie Calhoun (b), Kelly Martin (d)
    Mack the Knife, Misty (vocal by Perry Como and Phyllis McGuire backed by Garner and studio orchestra), Almost Like Being in Love

April 21, 1963   Ed Sullivan Show (New York)
Erroll Garner (p), Eddie Calhoun (b), Kelly Martin (d)
    In the Still of the Night, Erroll's Theme (retitled: That's My Kick)

May 6, 1963   Tonight Show (New York); Johnny Carson, host
Erroll Garner (p), George Duvivier (b), Ed Shaughnessy (d)
    Lover Come Back to Me, Happiness Is a Thing Called Joe

October, 1963
    Silent film footage taken with an 8mm movie camera of Garner in England. In these film clips Garner is walking the streets of London; assisting with a flat tire by the car he was riding in; boarding a plane in London

April 14, 1964   Garry Moore Show (New York)
Erroll Garner (p), Eddie Calhoun (b), Kelly Martin (d)
    Misty, Fly Me to the Moon (In Other Words), On Green Dolphin Street

June 16, 1964   Bell Telephone Hour (New York); Ray Bolger, host
Erroll Garner (p), Eddie Calhoun (b), Kelly Martin (d)
    The Way You Look Tonight, Misty, Mack the Knife, Sweet and Lovely

October 22, 1964   BBC-2TV (London); Steve Race, host
Erroll Garner (p), Eddie Calhoun (b), Kelly Martin (d)
    Honeysuckle Rose, No More Shadows, Mambo Erroll, Penthouse Serenade
    (When We're Alone), Jeannine, I Dream of Lilac Time, On the Street Where
    You Live/I Could Have Danced All Night (medley), Theme from "A New
    Kind of Love," The Lady Is a Tramp, Untitled Original

February 13, 1964   American Musical Theater (New York);
                                                        Earl Wrightson, host
Erroll Garner (p), Eddie Calhoun (b), Kelly Martin (d)
    I Get a Kick Out of You, Misty, Embraceable You, Surrey with the Fringe
    on Top
    Note: In this film clip Garner also answers questions from the audience

May 25, 1965   Bell Telephone Hour (New York)
Erroll Garner (p), Eddie Calhoun (b), Kelly Martin (d)
    It's All Right with Me, Begin the Beguine, I've Got You Under My Skin

Feburary 10, 1967   Mike Douglas Show (Philadephia)
Erroll Garner (p), Jimmy DeJulio (b), Bobby Mariniello (d)
    Lulu's Back in Town, Autumn Leaves, Dreamy

June 15, 1967   Mike Douglas Show (Philadelphia)
Erroll Garner (p), Jimmy DeJulio (b), Bobby Mariniello (d)
    Blue Moon, Gaslight, Happy Birthday, Autumn Leaves, There Will Never
    Be Another You, Strike Up the Band

May 9, 1968   Danish Telecast (Copenhagen)
Erroll Garner (p), Ike Isaacs (b), Jimmie Smith (d), José Mangual (cd)
    Misty, On Green Dolphin Street, The Shadow of Your Smile, I Can't Get
    Started, Blue Moon, More, Misty

April 8, 1970   Tonight Show (New York); Johnny Carson, host
Erroll Garner (p), Bob Haggart (b), Ed Shaughnessy (d)
    One Note Samba

May, 1970   Swedish Telecast (Stockholm)
Erroll Garner (p), Victor Venegas (b), Harvey Mason (d), José Mangual (cd)
    Misty, Autumn Leaves, That's All, Girl Talk, There Will Never Be Another
    You, The Girl from Ipanema, Dreamy, Watch What Happens, Love, Misty

August, 1970   "Jazz Beat" Montmartre Club (Copenhagen)
Erroll Garner (p), Ernest McCarty, Jr. (b), Bill English (d), José Mangual (cd)
  On Green Dolphin Street, The Girl from Ipanema, Misty, Strangers in the
  Night
  Note: At the beginning of this film clip Garner tells the interviewer that the
  only time he saw Fats Waller was at a theater in Pittsburgh. Garner said
  that he climbed through a window to get in. Garner recalled, "The piano
  was no good, so he [Fats] played organ. He played organ with an 18 piece
  band, and it sounded like 44 pieces."

October 23, 1970   Tonight Show (New York); Johnny Carson, host
Erroll Garner (p), Bob Haggart (b), Ed Shaughnessy (d)
  Strangers in the Night

May 26, 1971   "Just Jazz" (Chicago)
Erroll Garner (p), Ernest McCarty, Jr. (b), Bill English (d), José Mangual (cd)
  The Look of Love, That's All, The Shadow of Your Smile, Mood Island,
  For Once in My Life, Erroll's Theme, Medley (unknown titles)

July 2, 1971   The Name of the Game (Los Angeles)
  Garner appears as a soloist in a night club setting and plays background
  music for this TV drama titled "A Sister from Napoli." The medley of tunes
  include: Dreamy, Quiet Nights of Quiet Stars (Corcovado), Strangers in the
  Night, Dreamy, Jingle Bells

October 7, 1971   Flip Wilson Show (Los Angeles)
Erroll Garner (p), unknown (b), unknown (d), Flip Wilson (v)*
  For Once in My Life, Erroll Garner Blues*

October 14, 1971   Tonight Show (New York); Johnny Carson, host
Erroll Garner (p), Bob Haggart (b), Ed Shaughnessy (d)
  There Will Never Be Another You, Misty

September 20, 1972   Mike Douglas Show (Philadephia);
                                                    Della Reese, co-hostess
Erroll Garner (p), Jimmy DeJulio (b), Bobby Mariniello (d)
  These Foolish Things (Remind Me of You), Something, Misty (vocal by
  Della Reese)

October 19, 1972   Tonight Show (Los Angeles); Joey Bishop, host
Erroll Garner (p), John Williams (b), Ed Shaughnessy (d)
  Something, Tea for Two

January 23, 1973   ORTF TV Studios (Paris); Frank Ténot, host
Erroll Garner (p), Ernest McCarty, Jr. (b), Jimmie Smith (d), José Mangual (cd)
  Misty, Afinidad, All the Things You Are, Something, That's My Kick, The
  Shadow of Your Smile, The Loving Touch, Misty

February 12, 1973   Mike Douglas Show (Philadelphia)
Erroll Garner (p), Jimmy DeJulio (b), Bobby Mariniello (d)
  It Could Happen to You, Gemini

May 29, 1973   Tonight Show (Los Angeles); Bill Cosby, host
Erroll Garner (p), John Williams (b), Ed Shaughnessy (d)
    Something Happens

November 20, 1973   Tonight Show (Los Angeles); Johnny Carson, host
Erroll Garner (p), John Williams (b), Ed Shaughnessy (d)
    Something Happens, Watch What Happens

December 18, 1974   Tonight Show (Los Angeles); Johnny Carson, host
Erroll Garner (p), John Williams (b), Louis Bellson (d)
    Misty, It Could Happen to You

SELECTED BIBLIOGRAPHY

Allen, Walter C. *Hendersonia: The Music of Fletcher Henderson and His Musicians, a Bio-Discography.* Highland Park, New Jersey: The Author, 1973.

Balliett, Whitney. "Being a Genius." *New Yorker,* February 2, 1982, pp. 59, 60, 64, 69, 70, and 72.

_____. *New York Notes.* Boston: Houghton Mifflin, 1976.

Barr, Steven C. *The Almost Complete 78-RPM Record Dating Guide.* Privately published, 1979.

Berger, Morroe, Berger, Edward, and Patrick, James. *Benny Carter: A Life in American Music.* Metuchen, New Jersey and London: Scarecrow, 1982.

Carey, Dave, and McCarthy, Albert J., eds. *Jazz Directory, Vol. 3.* Fordingbridge, Hampshire, England: Delphic Press, 1951.

Clar, Mimi. "Erroll Garner." *The Jazz Review,* Vol. 2, No. 1, January 1959, pp. 6–10.

Craig, Warren. *Sweet and Lowdown: America's Popular Song Writers.* Metuchen, New Jersey and London: Scarecrow, 1978.

Delaunay, Charles. *New Hot Discography.* New York: Criterion Music Corporation, 1948.

Doran, James M. "Erroll Garner: A Discography Update." *Journal of Jazz Studies,* Vol. 6, No. 1 (Fall/Winter 1979), pp. 64–88.

Feather, Leonard. *The Encyclopedia of Jazz.* New York: Bonanza, 1960.

Gitler, Ira. *Jazz Masters of the 40's.* New York: Macmillan, 1966.

Grendysa, Peter A. *Atlantic Master Book Number 1.* Milwaukee, Wisconsin: The Author, 1975.

Hentoff, Nat, and McCarthy, Albert J., eds. *Jazz.* London: Jazz Book Club, 1962.

Jepsen, Jorgen Grunnet. *Jazz Records 1942-1967, Vol. 4a.* Holte, Denmark: Knudsen, 1968.

Lascelles, Gerald. "Garnering." *Jazz Journal,* Vol. 15, No. 6, June 1962, pp. 2, 40.

Laubich, Arnold and Spencer, Ray. *Art Tatum: A Guide to His Recorded Music.* Metuchen, New Jersey and London: Scarecrow, 1982.

Miner, Bill. "Sub Rosa Stuff." *Jazz Digest,* Vol. 2, No. 11/12 November/December 1973, pp. 13-18.

Ramsey Jr., Frederic. *A Guide to Longplay Jazz Records.* New York: Long Player Publications, 1954.

Rand, Martin G. *Erroll Garner Discography.* Summit, New Jersey: The Author, 1965.

Reisner, Robert. *Bird: The Legend of Charlie Parker.* New York: Da Capo Press, 1962.

Roddan, James. "Erroll Garner Records." *Jazz Monthly,* Vol. 4, No. 9, November 1958, pp. 4-7.

_____. "Erroll Garner—An Appreciation." *Jazz Monthly,* Vol. 4, No. 8, October 1958, pp. 2-6.

Ruppli, Michel. *Atlantic Records: A Discography, Volume 1.* Westport, Connecticut and London: Greenwood Press, 1979.

Ruppli, Michel with Bob Porter. *The Savoy Label: A Discography.* Westport, Connecticut and London: Greenwood Press, 1980.

Russell, Ross. *Bird Lives.* New York: Charterhouse, 1973.

Rust, Brian. *Brian Rust's Guide to Discography.* Westport, Connecticut and London: Greenwood Press, 1980.

Sachs, Tom. "Erroll Garner Discography." *Jazz Monthly,"* Vol. 4, No. 9, November 1958, pp. 7-9.*

_____. *"Erroll Garner Discography—II."* Jazz Monthly, Vol. 4, No. 10, December 1958, pp. 29–32.

_____. "Erroll Garner Discography—III." *Jazz Monthly,* Vol. 4, No. 11, January, 1959, pp. 24, 25.

Sears, Richard S. *V-Discs: A History and Discography.* Westport, Connecticut and London: Greenwood Press, 1980.

Shapiro, Nat, ed. *Popular Music.* 6 vol., New York: Adrian Press, 1964–73.

Shapiro, Nat and Hentoff, Nat. *Hear Me Talkin' to Ya.* New York: Dover Publications, 1966.

Shaw, Arnold. *Honkers and Shouters.* New York: Macmillan, 1978.

_____. *The Street That Never Slept.* New York: Coward, McCann and Geoghegan, 1971.

Taylor, Arthur. *Notes and Tones.* Leige, Belgium: The Author, 1977.

Tirro, Frank. *Jazz: A History.* New York: Norton, 1977.

Townley, Eric. *Tell Your Story.* Chigwell, England: Storyville, 1976.

Wiedemann, Erik. *Erroll Garner on Records.* Copenhagen: The Author. Date unknown.

GENERAL INDEX

This index includes all names, places and song titles in Parts 1 and 2. Also included are selected names and song titles in Part 3 which are not included in the discographical index of songs and artists. Numbers refer to page numbers. Letters refer to the photo insert section.

ADDENDUM
Unissued Sessions

1955   Chicago
Blue Note, NBC "Monitor" (Radio Broadcast); Tom Mercein, host
Erroll Garner (p), probably Wyatt Ruther (b), probably Eugene "Fats" Heard (d)
Undecided, I Only Have Eyes for You, Misty

1956   New York
Basin Street East, NBC "Monitor" (Radio Broadcast); Fred Collins, host
Erroll Garner (p), Eddie Calhoun (b), Denzil Best (d)
The Lady Is a Tramp, Erroll's Theme

September/October, 1956   Chicago
London House, NBC "Monitor" (Radio Broadcast); Tom Mercein, host
Erroll Garner (p), Eddie Calhoun (b), unknown (d)
Erroll's Theme, Undecided, Dreamy, Mambo Carmel

September/October, 1956   Chicago
London House, NBC "Monitor" (Radio Broadcast); Tom Mercein, host
Erroll Garner (p), Eddie Calhoun (b), unknown (d)
Erroll's Theme, 7-11 Jump, Dreamy, Erroll's Theme

June 15, 1957   Pennsauken, New Jersey
Red Hill Inn, Bandstand, U.S.A. (Radio Broadcast); Guy Wallace, host with Harvey
Houston announcing from the Red Hill Inn
Erroll Garner (p), Eddie Calhoun (b), Kelly Martin (d)
Erroll's Theme, Passing Through, Misty, Mambo Garner, Penthouse Sere-
nade, Dreamy, Erroll's Theme

Late October, 1957   Boston
Storyville, Bandstand U.S.A. (Radio Broadcast); Guy Wallace, host, with Dom
Cerulli, East Coast Editor of *down beat* magazine
Erroll's Theme, La Petite Mambo, Girl of My Dreams, Passing Through,
Erroll's Theme

January 26, 1958   Probably New York
Percy Faith Show (CBS Radio Broadcast)
Erroll Garner (p), probably Eddie Calhoun (b), probably Kelly Martin (d)
I'll Remember April, Dreamy (with the Woolworth Orchestra)

ca. 1959   Unknown Location
Best in Music (Radio Broadcast); Ralph (?), host
Erroll Garner (p), Eddie Calhoun (b), Kelly Martin (d)
    Erroll's Theme, Penthouse Serenade

ca. 1959   Unknown Location
Best in Music (Radio Broadcast); Ralph (?), host
Erroll Garner (p), Eddie Calhoun (b), Kelly Martin (d)
    Erroll's Theme, Mambo 207

ca. 1959   Unknown Location
Best in Music (Radio Broadcast); Ralph (?), host
Erroll Garner (p), Eddie Calhoun (b), Kelly Martin (d)
    Erroll's Theme, Other Voices

April 11 or 18, 1959   Boston
Storyville, Bandstand U.S.A. (Radio Broadcast); Guy Wallace, host, with David Allyn
Erroll Garner (p), Eddie Calhoun (b), Kelly Martin (d)
    The Man I Love, My Funny Valentine, Blue Moon, The Nearness of You, Love for Sale

April 6, 1969   Unknown Location
Art Linkletter, host
Erroll Garner (p), unknown (b), unknown (d)
    Cheek to Cheek

March 6, 1970   Unknown Location
David Frost, host
Erroll Garner (p), unknown (b), unknown (d)
    Misty

June 5, 1970   Unknown Location
Della Reese, hostess
Erroll Garner (p), unknown (b), unknown (d)
    What Now My Love

October 26, 1970   New York
Today Show
Erroll Garner (p), unknown (b), unknown (d)
    Mood Island, Yesterday, The Shadow of Your Smile

September 12, 1971   Unknown Location
Sickle-Cell Anemia Telethon
Erroll Garner (p), unknown (b), unknown (d)
    Misty, The Shadow of Your Smile

Unknown Date   Boston
Storyville, Bandstand U.S.A. (Radio Broadcast); Guy Wallace, host, with George
Avakian
Erroll Garner (p), Eddie Calhoun (b), Kelly Martin (d)
    Erroll's Theme, I'll Remember April, Dreamy, Erroll's Theme, It's All Right
    with Me, Misty, Girl of My Dreams

Unknown Date   Boston
Storyville, Bandstand U.S.A. (Radio Broadcast); Guy Wallace, host
Erroll Garner (p), Eddie Calhoun (b), Kelly Martin (d)
    Erroll's Theme, Passing Through, Misty, LaPetite Mambo, Moment's De-
    light, Where or When, Erroll's Theme

Unknown Date   Boston
Storyville, Bandstand U.S.A. (Radio Broadcast); Guy Wallace, host, with Leonard
Feather
Erroll Garner (p), Eddie Calhoun (b), Kelly Martin (d)
    I'm Confessin' (That I Love You), The Nearness of You, How Could You
    Do a Thing Like That to Me, April in Paris, Will You Will Be Mine, Erroll's
    Theme (retitled: That's My Kick)

Unknown Date   Unknown Location
Probably Bandstand U.S.A.
Erroll Garner (p), probably Eddie Calhoun (b), probably Kelly Martin (d)
    Erroll's Theme, Passing Through